fluency with Information Technology

Skills, Concepts, & Capabilities

LAWRENCE SNYDER

University of Washington

PEARSON

Addison Wesley

Boston San Francisco New York
London Toronto Sydney Tokyo Singapore Madrid
Mexico City Munich Paris Cape Town Hong Kong Montreal

Executive Editor: Susan Hartman Sullivan
Development Editor: Pat Mahtani
Assistant Editor: Galia Shokry
Marketing Manager: Nathan Schultz
Senior Production Supervisor: Jeffrey Holcomb
Project Management: Argosy Publishing
Copyeditor: William McManus
Proofreader: Eve Minkoff
Indexer: Larry Sweazy
Composition: Gillian Hall, The Aardvark Group
Text Designer: Joyce Cosentino Wells
Cover Designer: Regina Hagen Kolenda
Text and Cover Image: © 2003 Vince Cavataio/Index Stock Imagery
Prepress and Manufacturing: Caroline Fell

Access the latest information about Addison-Wesley titles from our World Wide Web site: http://www.aw.com/cs

Many of the designations used by manufacturers and sellers to distinguish their products are claimed as trademarks. Where those designations appear in this book, and Addison-Wesley was aware of a trademark claim, the designations have been printed in initial caps or all caps.

The programs and applications presented in this book have been included for their instructional value. They have been tested with care, but are not guaranteed for any particular purpose. The publisher does not offer any warranties or representations, nor does it accept any liabilities with respect to the programs or applications.

Library of Congress Cataloging-in-Publication Data

Snyder, Lawrence.
Fluency with information technology : skills, concepts, and capabilities / Lawrence Snyder.
p. cm.
"In which the secrets of computers and networks are revealed, in English, with no math, and starting at the very beginning".
Includes index.
ISBN 0-201-75491-6
1. Information technology. I. Title.

T58.5.S645 2004
004--dc22 2003057758

ISBN 0-201-75491-6

1 2 3 4 5 6 7 8 9 10-DOW-06 05 04 03

For Julie Ann, Dan, and Dave

Preface

WELCOME to *Fluency with Information Technology: Skills, Concepts, and Capabilities*. I am delighted to introduce to you a book that moves beyond the click-here-click-there form of technology instruction to one firmly founded on ideas. The time is right for a new introduction to IT because today the majority of college and post-secondary students are already familiar with computers, the Internet, and the World Wide Web. They do not need rudimentary instruction in double-clicking and resizing windows. Rather, they need to be taught to be confident, in-control users of IT. They need to know how to navigate independently in the ever-changing worlds of information and technology, to solve their problems on their own, and to be capable of fully applying the power of IT tools in the service of their personal and career goals. They must be more than literate; they must be fluent with IT.

What's Fluency with Information Technology?

The inspiration for writing this book comes from a report by the National Research Council (NRC), *Being Fluent with Information Technology*. In that study, commissioned by the National Science Foundation, the committee asserted that traditional computer literacy does not have the "staying power" students need to keep pace with the rapid changes in IT. The study concluded that the educational "bar needs to be raised" if students' knowledge is to evolve and adapt to that change. The recommended alternative, dubbed *fluency with information technology*, or *FIT*, was a package of skills, concepts, and capabilities wrapped in a project-oriented learning approach that ensures that the content is fully integrated. The goal is to help people become effective users immediately, and to prepare them for lifelong learning.

The Vision

Because fluency with information technology—I usually shorten it to *Fluency*—is a new concept that largely implements the vision of the NRC committee, I'll introduce the main components: the three-part content, the integration mechanism of projects, and the role of programming.

Three-part Content

To make students immediately effective and launch them on the path of lifelong learning, they need to be taught three types of knowledge: Skills, Concepts, and Capabilities.

> *Skills* refers to proficiency with contemporary computer applications such as email, word processing, Web searching, etc. Skills make the technology immediately useful to students and give them practical experience on which to base other learning. The Skills component approximates traditional computer literacy content; that is, Fluency *includes* literacy.

> *Concepts* refers to the fundamental knowledge underpinning IT, such as how a computer works, digital representation of information, assessing information authenticity, etc. Concepts provide the principles on which students will build new understanding as IT evolves.

> *Capabilities* refers to higher-level thinking processes such as problem solving, reasoning, complexity management, troubleshooting, etc. Capabilities embody modes of thinking that are essential to exploiting IT, but they apply broadly. Reasoning, problem solving, etc. are standard components of education, their heavy use in IT makes them topics of emphasis in the Fluency approach.

For each component, the NRC report lists ten recommended items. These are shown in the accompanying table.

Projects

The Skills, Concepts, and Capabilities represent different kinds of knowledge that are co-equal in their contribution to IT fluency. They span separate dimensions of understanding. The overall strategy is to focus on the Skills instruction in the lab, the Concepts instruction in lecture/reading material, and the Capabilities instruction in lecture/lab demonstrations. The projects are the opportunity to use the three kinds of knowledge for a specific purpose. They illustrate IT as it is often applied in practice—to solve information processing tasks of a substantial nature.

A project is a multiweek assignment to achieve a specific IT goal. An example of a project is to create a database to track medical patients in a walk-in clinic, and to give a presentation to convince an audience that patient privacy has been preserved. Students apply a variety of Skills such as using database design software, Web searching, and presentation facilities. They rely on their understanding of Concepts such as database keys, table structure, and the Join query operator. And they use Capabilities such as reasoning, debugging, complexity management, testing, and others. The components are applied together to produce the final result, leading students to an integrated understanding of IT and preparing them for significant "real life" applications of IT. The labs can be found on the book's Web site.

The NRC's List of Top Ten Skills, Concepts, and Capabilities

Fluency with Information Technology
Skills
1. Set-up a personal computer
2. Use basic operating system facilities
3. Use a word processor to create a document
4. Use a graphics or artwork package to manipulate an image
5. Connect a computer to the Internet
6. Use the Internet to locate information
7. Use a computer to communicate with others
8. Use a spreadsheet to model a simple process
9. Use a database to access information
10. Use on-line help and instructional materials
Concepts
1. Fundamentals of computers
2. Organization of information systems
3. Fundamentals of networks
4. Digital representation of information
5. Structuring information
6. Modeling and abstraction
7. Algorithmic thinking and programming
8. Universality
9. Limitations of Information Technology
10. Social impact of computers and technology
Capabilities
1. Engage in sustained reasoning
2. Manage complexity
3. Test a solution
4. Find problems in a faulty use of IT
5. Navigate a collection and assess quality of the information
6. Collaborate using IT
7. Communicate using IT about IT
8. Expect the unexpected
9. Anticipate technological change
10. Think abstractly about Information Technology

The Programming Debate

Since the advent of computer literacy nearly three decades ago, there has been ongoing debate as to whether nonspecialists should be taught programming. Rational arguments have been offered on both sides, and thoughtful, well-intentioned adherents espouse each point of view. This book does *not* claim that one must be a professional programmer to be fluent. It sees programming's significance for the general population to be much more limited: to support algorithmic thinking, reasoning, debugging, and other components of fluency. And learning the NRC committee's modest set of basic programming ideas—variable, conditional, iteration, etc.—won't make anyone a programmer. In the discussion following the publication of the report, the committee's "some, but not much" compromise on the programming question seems to have been widely accepted.

Fluency with Information Technology treats only the recommended handful of basic programming concepts. Nevertheless, the perception that programming is a difficult topic suitable only for mathematically strong "techies" raises the question of whether even this small set of concepts can be taught to a general student population. The answer is that it can and the students find it rewarding!

The programming can be found in Chapters 18, 20, and 21 (with case studies in Chapters 19 and 22), and is optional for those who do not wish to cover it.

Audience

This book is designed for (second semester) freshmen "non-techies," students who will not be majoring in science, engineering, or math. ("Techies" benefit, too, but because "hot shots" can intimidate others, they should be discouraged from taking the class, or better, encouraged to join an accelerated track or honors section.) Except for one short paragraph about encryption, which can be skipped, no mathematical skills are required beyond arithmetic. There are no prerequisites.

Most students who take Fluency will have used email, surfed the Web, and perhaps word processed, and this is more than enough preparation to be successful. Students with no experience are advised to spend a few hours acquiring some exposure to IT prior to starting Fluency.

Chapter Dependencies

I have written *Fluency with Information Technology* so it can be taught in a variety of ways. In addition to the preliminary material in Chapters 1 and 2 and the wrap-up in Chapter 24, the overall structure of the book includes standalone chapters with few dependencies, as well as small chapter sequences devoted to a sustained topic. The sequences are:

- 3, 4, 5 networking, HTML, and information
- 8, 9, 10, 11 data representations, computers, and algorithms
- 13, 14, 15 database principles and design
- 18, 19, 20, 21 programming in JavaScript

One effective way to use this design is to present one of the chapter sequences as the basis for a project assignment. Then, while the students are working on the project—projects may span two or more weeks—material from standalone chapters is covered.

Though there are many sequences, three stand out to me as especially good ways to present the material:

> *Networking cycle.* The linear sequence of chapters is designed to begin with information and networking and progressively advance through computation and databases to JavaScript, where it returns to the networking theme. This is the basic Chapter 1 to Chapter 24 sequence, adjusted by local reordering to accommodate the timing of projects as needed.

> *Internet forward.* I teach Fluency in the 1–10, 18–22, 11–17, 23–24 order. This approach begins with information and HTML, progresses through to algorithms, then jumps to JavaScript to continue the Web page building theme, and finally wraps up with databases. The strategy is dictated to a large degree by the logistics of teaching the class in a quarter (10 weeks), and is recommended for that situation.

> *Traditional.* In this approach, the material is taught to parallel the time sequence of its creation. So, information representation and computers come well before networking. In this case, the order is 1–2, (23), 8–15, 3–7, 16–24. Chapter 23, which contains more philosophical content like the Turing test and Kasparov/Deep Blue chess tournament, might optionally be presented early for its foundational content.

Each of these strategies has a compelling pedagogical justification. Which is chosen depends more on instructor taste and class logistics than on any need to present material in a specific order.

Pedagogical Features

Learning Objectives: Each chapter opens with a list of the key concepts that readers should master after reading the chapter.

There are several boxed features that appear throughout the text to aid in your understanding of the material. These are:

FITtip: Practical hints and suggestions for every day computer use.
FITbyte: Interesting facts and statistics.
FITcaution: Warnings and explanations of common mistakes.
Try It: Short, in chapter exercises with solutions provided.
Checklists: A useful list of steps for completing a specific task.

Throughout the text, we also distinguish notable material by the following features:

FITlink: Here the author shows students a practical application of some of the abstract concepts presented in the text.
Great Moments: A historical look at some of the major milestones in computing.
Great Minds: This feature takes a closer look at some of the influential pioneers in technology.

Reference material includes the following:

Glossary: Important words and phrases appear in boldface type throughout the text. A glossary of these terms is included at the end of the book.
Answers: Solutions are provided to the odd numbered exercises for the multiple choice and short answer questions.
Appendix A: HTML reference including a chart of web safe colors.
Appendix B: JavaScript programming rules.
Appendix C: Bean Counter Program: A complete JavaScript & HTML example.
Appendix D: Memory Bank Program: A complete JavaScript & HTML example.

Supplements to Instruction

The companion Web site for *Fluency with Information Technology* is at **`www.aw.com/snyder/`**, where you can find the various HTML sources, database designs, and JavaScript programs used in the textbook examples. Students are encouraged to retrieve these files to explore along with the text.

Laboratory materials. Learning Fluency is a hands-on activity, and so 14 complete laboratory exercises are available at the Web site.

PowerPoint slides. A convenient resource for teaching Fluency is the collection of PowerPoint slides available at the site.

Fluency instructor bulletin board. Share tips and ask questions of other instructors involved in teaching Fluency with Information Technology.

Note to Students

Fluency is a somewhat unusual topic, making this a somewhat unusual book. There are two things that I think you should know about using this book.

> *Learn Skills in the lab.* Of the three kinds of knowledge that define Fluency—Skills, Concepts, and Capabilities—very little of the Skills material is included in this book. The Skills content, which is mostly about how to use contemporary computer applications, changes very rapidly, making it difficult to keep up to date. But the main reason few skills are included is that they are best learned in the lab, seated in front of a computer. The lab exercises, which are online and are up to date, provide an excellent introduction to contemporary applications. They provide great coverage of the Skills.

> *Study Fluency steadily.* If this book is successful, it will change the way you think, making you a better problem solver, better at reasoning, better at debugging, etc. These Capabilities are useful in IT and elsewhere in life, so they make learning Fluency really worthwhile. But changing how you think won't happen by just putting the book under your pillow. It'll take some studying. To learn Fluency you must apply good study habits: read the book, do the end of chapter exercises (answers to odd-number exercises are printed at the back of the book), start on your

assignments early, ask questions, etc. I think it's best if you spend some time in the lab studying Fluency (not reading email) *every day*, because it takes some time for the ideas to sink in. Students with good study habits tend to do well in Fluency class, and because it improves their problem-solving abilities, etc., they become even better students! It takes some discipline but it pays.

Finally, some sections of the book are best read with a computer handy so that you can try things out. While most chapters have several sections like this, Chapters 2, 4–7, 11, 15, 16 and 18–22 are specially valuable when you "try as you go." Good luck! Writing this book has truly been a pleasure. I hope reading it is equally enjoyable.

Acknowledgments

Many people have contributed to this work. First to be thanked are my collaborators in the creation of the Fluency concept, the NRC Committee on Computer Literacy—Al Aho, Marcia Linn, Arnie Packer, Allen Tucker, Jeff Ullman, and Andy van Dam. Special thanks go to Herb Lin of the NRC staff who assisted throughout the Fluency effort, tirelessly and in his usual great good humor. Two enthusiastic supporters of Fluency— Bill Wulf of the National Academy of Engineering and John Cherniavski of the National Science Foundation—have continually supported this effort in more ways than I am aware. It has been a pleasure to know and work with this team.

As the material was developed for this book, many have contributed: Ken Yasuhara and Brian Bannon, teaching assistants on the first offering of CSE100, contributed in innumerable ways and injected a needed dose of practicality into my ideas. Grace Whiteaker, Alan Borning, and Batya Friedman have been generous with their ideas regarding Fluency. Martin Dickey of CSE and Mark Donovan of UWired have been constant sources of support. The original offerings of CSE100 benefited greatly from contributions by Nana Lowell, Anne Zald, Mike Eisenberg, and Fred Videon. Colleagues who have contributed include Frank Tompa, Martin Tompa, Carl Ebeling, Brian Kerninghan, Dotty Smith, Calvin Lin and David Mizell.

I am particularly grateful for the keen insights and valuable feedback from the reviewers of this project: Nazih Abdallah, University of Central Florida; Robert M. Aiken, Temple University; Diane M. Cassidy, University of North Carolina at Charlotte; Anne Condon, University of British Columbia; Lee D. Cornell, Minnesota State University, Mankato; Nicholas Cravotta, University of California, Berkeley; Gordon Davies, Open University; Peter J. Denning, George Mason University; Rory J. DeSimone, University of Florida; Richard C. Detmer, Middle Tennessee State University; David L. Doss, Illinois State University; John P. Dougherty, Haverford College; Philip East, University of Northern Iowa; Michael B. Eisenberg, University of Washington; Robert S. Fenchel, University of Wisconsin, Madison; Michael Gildersleeve, University of New Hampshire; Jennifer Golbeck; Michael H. Goldner; Esther Grassian, UCLA College Library; Raymond Greenlaw, Armstrong Atlantic State University; A. J. Hurst, Monash University, Australia; Malcolm G. Lane, James Madison University; Doris K. Lidtke, Towson

University; Wen Liu, ITT Technical Institute; Daniela Marghitu, Auburn University; C. Dianne Martin, George Washington University; Peter B. Miller, University of Virginia; Namdar Mogharreban, Southern Illinois University, Carbondale; Paul M. Mullins, Slippery Rock University; David R. Musicant, Carleton College; Alexander Nakhimovsky, Colgate University; Brenda C. Parker, Middle Tennessee State University; Dee Parks, Appalachian State University; Laurie J. Patterson, University of North Carolina, Wilmington; Roger Priebe, University of Texas at Austin; Paul Quan, Albuquerque Technical Vocational Institute; John Rosenberg, Monash University, Australia; Robert T. Ross, California Polytechnic State University; Zhizhang Shen, Plymouth State College; Robert J. Shive, Jr., Millsaps College; Patrick Tantalo, University of California, Santa Cruz; and Mark Urban-Lurain, Michigan State University.

Thank you to Jim McKeown and Sandra Macke for contributing to the end of chapter exercises.

The Fluency material has been a topic of discussion with many international colleagues. Discussions with Hans Hinterberger, John Rosenberg, and John Hirsch have been especially valuable in critiquing the material from an overseas perspective. Other helpful international commentary came from Anne Condon, Hannes Jonsson, Jerg Nievergelt, Clark Thomberson, Barbara Thomberson, Ewan Tempero, and Kazuo Iwama.

Among the many thoughtful computer users who have either generously described their misunderstandings about IT or patiently listened to my explanations about IT, I wish to thank Esther Snyder, Helene Fowler, Judy Watson, Brendan Healey, Victory Grund, Shelley Burr, Ken Burr, and Noelle Lamb.

It is my great pleasure to thank my editors, Susan Hartman Sulllivan, Pat Mahtani, and Mary Clare McEwing. Their enthusiasm for the project and their devotion to perfection have been inspirational. And working with them is fun. Joyce Wells has done a fantastic job with the design. Others of the Addison-Wesley team to whom I owe thanks are Michael Hirsch, Regina Kolenda, Jeff Holcomb, Galia Shokry, and Lesly Hershman. Thanks especially to Bobbie Lewis and Daniel Rausch.

Finally, my wife Julie, and sons, Dan and Dave, have been patient, encouraging, and, most important, a continual source of good humor throughout this effort. It is with my deepest appreciation that I thank them for everything.

Contents

The Master said: "To learn something and then put it into practice at the right time. Is this not a joy?

—THE ANALECTS OF CONFUCIUS

part 1

BECOMING SKILLED AT INFORMATION TECHNOLOGY

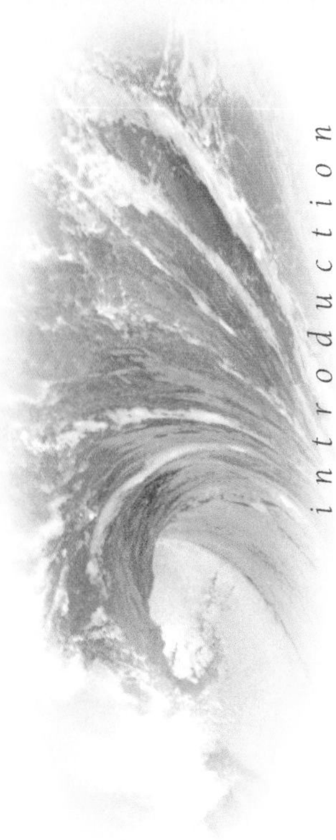

introduction

Our study of information technology begins with an introduction to both information and technology. If your contact with computers has been limited, an introduction is essential. If you are like most readers, you've used computers enough to be familiar with email, Web surfing, and perhaps word processing; but, you think, there must be many other cool and interesting ways to use information technology. You're right! And getting a firm foundation is the fastest way forward.

In this first part of our study we focus on becoming skilled at using an Internet-connected personal computer. You will learn new applications—in fact, you will learn how to learn new applications—and you will find out about the Internet and World Wide Web. By the end of this part you will be able to apply information technology to your studies, work, and recreation.

The goal is for you to become a confident, skilled user. You can achieve this goal by combining the information in Part I with daily use of computers and the Internet. We present practical, useful information that requires practice and use, making Fluency a subject in which you can immediately apply what you learn.

chapter

1 TERMS OF ENDEARMENT

Defining Information Technology

learning objectives

- Explain why it's important to know the right word in information technology
- Define some basic hardware and software terms
- Describe how the mouse clicks a button
- Define and give examples of "idea" terms
- Develop the ability to think more analytically
  - Compare speed records
  - Express an improvement in speed as a factor
- Explain the benefits of analytical thinking

It would appear that we have [as a society] reached the limits of what it is possible to achieve with computer technology, although one should be careful with such statements as they tend to sound pretty silly in 5 years.

—JOHN VON NEUMANN,
COMPUTER PIONEER 1947

TO BECOME Fluent, we need to learn the language of information technology. The people who created information technology (IT) are notorious for using acronyms, jargon, and everyday words in unusual ways. Acronyms like WYSIWYG (pronounced *WHIZ·zee·wig*), "what you see is what you get," are often meaningless even after you find out what the letters stand for. (We'll come back to the WYSIWYG story later.) Jargon like "clicking around" for navigating through an application or a series of Web pages is meaningful only after you have actually done it. And an everyday term like **window**, originally chosen to give the idea of a portal to the computer, may no longer be a good metaphor for the sophisticated computer concept. It is not surprising that people coming across these terms for the first time are confused. But is such techno-speak any more weird than, say, medical or musical terms? (For example, the terms *bilirubin* in medicine and *hemidemisemiquaver* in music seem very odd to us, too.) Technology, like medicine and music, makes better sense with a little explanation.

Our first goal in this chapter is to understand why learning the right term is essential to any new endeavor. Next, we ask some simple questions about computers (like "Where's the Start button?") as a way of reviewing terms you may already know. But, for almost every familiar term, there is a new word or idea to learn. We also introduce some new words for the physical or computational aspects of the computer. These are mostly terms you have probably already heard, so finding out exactly what they mean will help you make them part of your everyday vocabulary. Along the way, we explain basic ideas like how buttons are created and how they are clicked. This starts to demystify how the computer's virtual world works and it introduces the ideas of process and algorithm. Then we introduce the "idea" terms of IT, words like *abstraction* and *generalization*. These terms refer to deep concepts, and devoting a few minutes to understanding them will pay off throughout the rest of our Fluency study. Finally, we close with interesting stories about how people and computers have advanced, as we become more analytical thinkers.

WHY KNOW JUST THE RIGHT WORD IN IT

Why has information technology adopted so many strange terms? Because an enormous number of new ideas, concepts, and devices have been invented for IT. These phenomena had to be named so that their creators could describe them and explain them to others. Acronyms are common, because as engineers and scientists develop ideas, they often abbreviate them with the letters of the concept's description. The abbreviation sticks, and if the concept is important, its use extends beyond the laboratory. For example, when engineers invented the "small computer system interface," they abbreviated it SCSI. People began to pronounce it "skuzzy" rather than saying S-C-S-I. Naming-by-abbreviation makes a terminology full of acronyms. Critics call it "alphabet soup." But we can understand it once we understand what all those letters stand for. For example, ROM is short for "read-only memory." Even without knowing much about computers, you can guess that it is a special type of memory that cannot be written to.

Using exactly the right word at the right time is one characteristic of an educated person. Perhaps the best term to learn to use well is the French (now also English) term *le mot juste* (*luh mo·joost*), which means the right word or exact phrasing.

There are two important reasons for knowing and using le mot juste. First, understanding the terminology is basic to learning any new subject. In learning what these new words mean, we learn the ideas and concepts that they stand for. Our brains seem to be organized so that when we give a thing or idea a name, we remember it more easily. For example, in ice hockey, *icing* is the term for hitting the puck across the blue lines and across the opponent's goal line. We might not even notice this amid all the passing and slap shots. By knowing this new definition for the familiar word *icing*, we start watching for it, increasing our understanding and enjoyment of the game. Precision in using the term means precision in understanding the idea. Eventually the word stops sounding weird and becomes a part of our normal vocabulary. At that point, we use the right word without even thinking about it.

The second reason for knowing and using the right word is to communicate with others. If we use the terms properly, they'll understand us. We'll be able to ask questions and get help—something everyone starting out in a field needs to do. In information technology, using the right word to get help is especially important, because we must often get help by email, on the telephone, or through an online help facility. We have to be precise and articulate because no one will be by our side to help us describe it. If we cannot say what's wrong, we won't get the help we need. Indeed, a goal of Fluency is to be able to get help from such resources. The ability to use *le mot juste* allows us to communicate, get help, and ultimately to be self-reliant.

You could learn vocabulary by reading a computer dictionary, of course, but that's *waaay* too boring. Rather, we introduce the basic terminology by answering some of the nagging questions about IT that have unexpected answers.

WHERE'S THE START BUTTON?

Most computers are on all the time, which is why screen savers were invented. Screen savers—animations such as a kitten prancing around the screen or a changing geometric design—are programs that sleep when the computer is in use but wake up when the computer is idle for a while. They "save the screen" because a single, unchanging image could be "burned into the screen"; that is, it could permanently change the phosphorous surface of the screen, creating a "ghost" of the image that interferes with viewing. The ever-changing image keeps this from happening. (Recent technological advances have made burn-in less of a problem, but screen savers remain; also, many computers simply turn off the screen.) You can reactivate a computer by moving or clicking the mouse, or by pressing any key.

If computers are usually on, why bother to learn where the Start button is? Because sometimes they are off, and as we will see later, we might need to **cycle power**—turn the computer off and then back on. To know where to look for the power button, we need to know the different organizations of a computer.

Two Basic Organizations: Monolithic or Component

Some computers are sold as **components** with a separate monitor, computer and hard drive, speakers, and other devices. (We'll discuss the individual devices later.) Many desktop PCs are organized this way. The **monolithic** package, like an iMac or a laptop, has all the devices bundled together, as shown in Figure 1.1(a). The component approach lets you mix and match parts to fit your needs, as shown in Figure 1.1b. The all-in-one monolithic design is simpler because manufacturers decide for you which components will form a balanced, effective system. Laptops are monolithic, of course, because it is inconvenient to carry around multiple parts. Expect to use both.

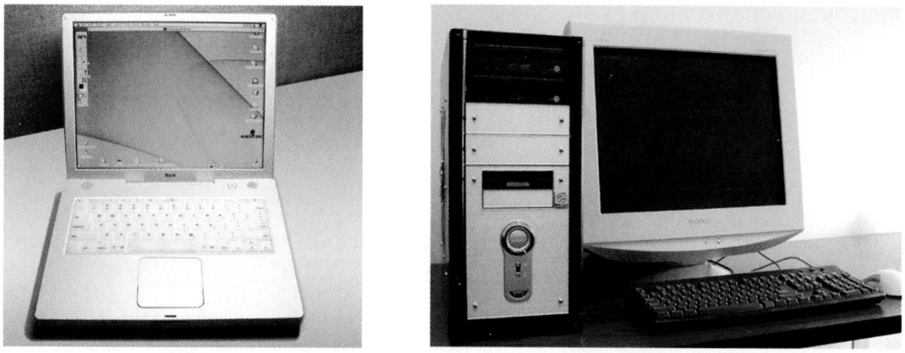

(a) (b)

Figure 1.1. *Examples of the monolithic (a) and component (b) systems.*

In the monolithic design, the **power switch** (⏻) is on the chassis or, often for Macs, on the keyboard. For component systems, the power switch is usually on a separate box near the display containing the CD and/or floppy disk drives. Most component monitors also have their own power switch, but it turns off only the monitor, not the whole computer.

The Monitor

The **monitor** is a video screen like a TV, of course. But there are many differences. Unlike passive TVs, computers are interactive, so the monitor becomes more like a blackboard showing the information created by both the computer and the user as they communicate. Modern monitors are **bit-mapped**, meaning that they display information stored in (the bits of) the computer's memory, as illustrated in Figure 1.2. TVs generally display images live or from recorded tape, captured with a camera. The big, bulky monitors are **cathode ray tubes**, abbreviated CRTs, whereas the slim, flat displays are **liquid crystal displays** (LCDs).

To emphasize the contrast between TVs and computers, notice that television can only show "reality," the images *recorded* through the camera's lens. But a computer creates the images it displays in its memory; they don't have to exist in physical reality. When a computer creates its own world, it's called **virtual reality**.

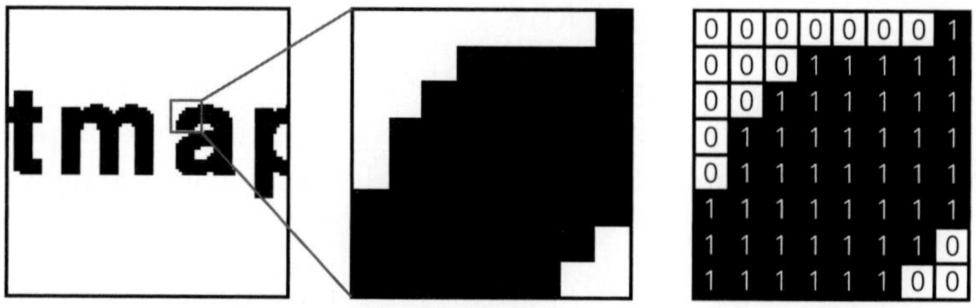

Figure 1.2. *An enlargement of a monitor's display of the word bitmap and the corresponding bits for each pixel.*

Cables

The components and the computer must be connected to each other, of course, and they must be connected to an electrical power source. For power-hungry devices like monitors, separate **power cables** are usually used, which is why there is a separate power switch. For simple devices like the keyboard or mouse, the **signal** and power wires are combined into a single cable. To help us plug in the cables correctly, the computer's sockets and the cable's plugs are often labeled with icons, as shown in Figure 1.3. So, we simply match icons.

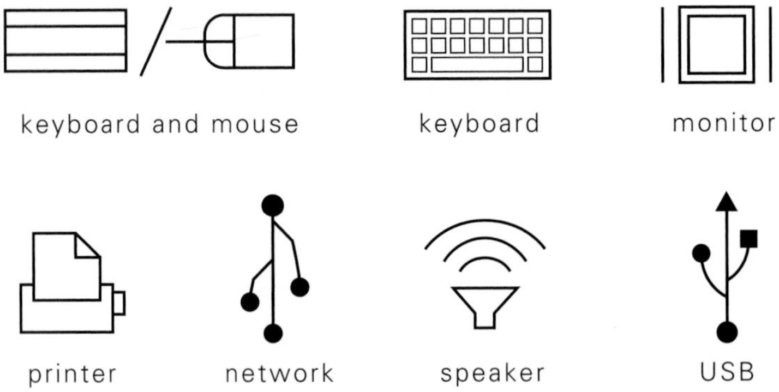

Figure 1.3. *Examples of icons and their component parts.*

FITCAUTION

Damage Control. When connecting computer components (or other electronic devices), plug in the power connection last. When disconnecting, remove the power connection first. Briefly, PILPOF—plug in last, pull out first.

Computer component plugs fit into their sockets in only one way. After you figure out which way around the plug goes in, insert it into the socket gently at first to make sure that the pins—the stiff wires making the connections—align and do not become bent. Once the plug is inserted, **seat** it by pushing it in firmly.

Notice that connectors like the red, green, blue (RGB) cable  on a monitor are usually held in place by screws or a clasp, which you should tighten after seating the cable.

Colors: RGB

Combining different amounts of the primary colors of light—red, green, and blue (RGB)—produces the colors you see on your computer monitor, as shown in Figure 1.4. The computer tells the monitor the right proportions of light to display with signals sent through the RGB cable. Any color can be created with some combination of intensities of these three colors. In computer applications, when we select a color from a "palette"—to change the color of text, for example—we are really telling the computer how much of these three colors of light to use.

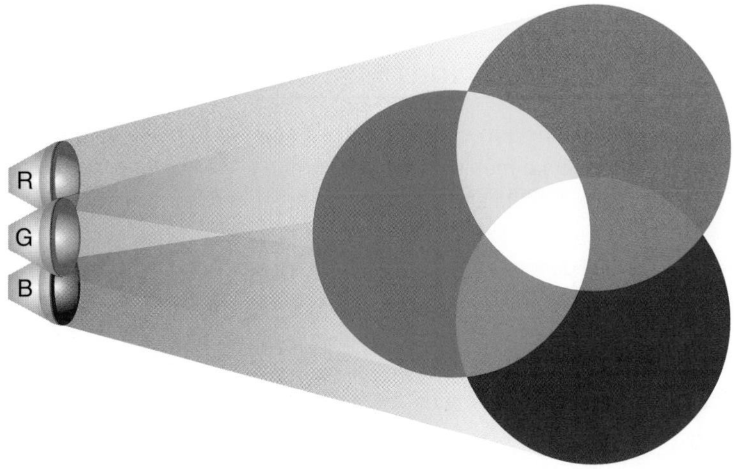

Figure 1.4. *The RGB color scheme.*

Pixels

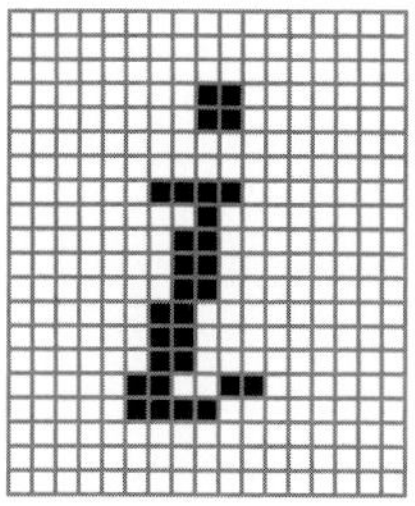

The monitor's screen is divided into a grid of small units called **picture elements**, or **pixels**. A pixel is about the size of the dot on an *i* in 10-point type. (Check this out on your monitor.) The computer displays information on the screen by drawing each pixel the color needed for the intended figure or image. For example, the pixels forming an *i* are colored black and the surrounding pixels are colored white when showing text. The size of the grid in pixels—1024 × 768 is typical for a laptop—is important when choosing a monitor because the more pixels in each row and column, the higher the resolution of the image on the screen; that is, the smoother and crisper it can be.

The computer must first create in its memory everything displayed on the screen, pixel by pixel. For computer-animated movies like *Toy Story*, creating images of dancing toys is extremely difficult. But the appearance of reality that we see on the screen when we use a computer is much easier to generate, as we demonstrate in the FITLINK beginning on page 9.

FITTIP

Image Change. The size of the pixel grid displayed on the screen can be increased or decreased using the Control Panel for the Display (Windows) or Monitor (Mac).

WHERE IS THE COMPUTER?

This may seem like an odd question to ask, but it's not. In casual conversation, most of us call the monitor sitting on a desk "the computer." Technically speaking, we're usually wrong. For the monolithic organization such as a laptop or iMac, the part that actually does the computing *is* inside the same unit as the monitor, of course. So for those cases we're right. But for component systems, the computer is

{ FITLINK }

A Virtual Button >>

It is simple to color the screen's pixels to make a figure that looks like a believable button. On a medium-gray background, the designer colors the top and left sides of a rectangle white and the bottom and right sides black. This makes the interior of the rectangle appear to project out from the surface, because the white seems to be highlights and the dark seems to be shadows from a light source at the upper left. (If the figure doesn't look much like a button, look at it from a distance.) There is nothing special about the medium-gray/white/black combination except that it gives the lighted/shadowed effect. Other colors work, too. And, by using colors with less contrast, it is possible to give the button a different "feel"; for example, less metallic, as shown in Figure 1.5.

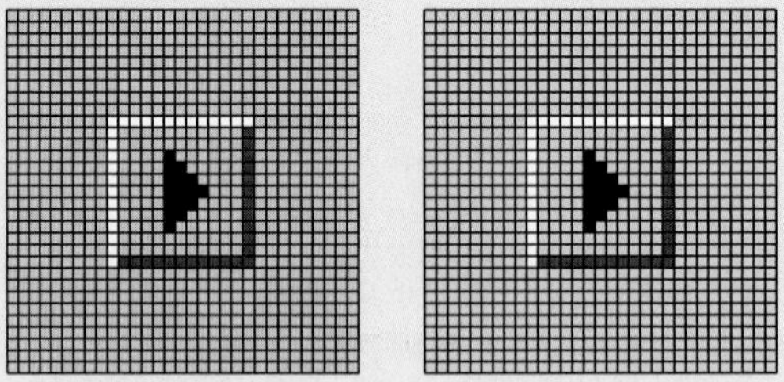

Figure 1.5. *Two virtual buttons with different "feels."*

THE ILLUSION OF BUTTON MOTION

To show that the button has been pressed reverse the black and white colors and translate the icon one position down and to the right. To **translate** a figure means to move it, unchanged, to a new position. Because our brains assume that the light source's position stays the same, the reversal of the colors changes the highlights and shadows to make the inside of the rectangle appear to be pushed in. The translation of the icon creates motion that our eyes notice, completing the illusion that the button is depressed, as shown in Figure 1.6. Notice, however, that the translation of the icon down and to the right is not really a correct motion for a button "pushed into the screen." But accuracy is less important than is the cue to our brains that there is motion.

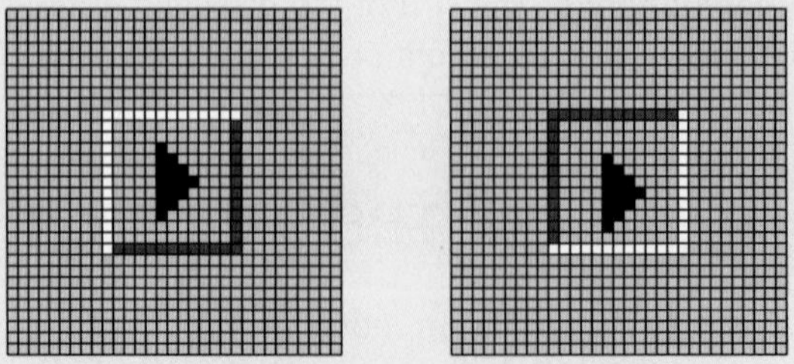

Figure 1.6. *The translation of a button icon.*

We must emphasize that there is no button anywhere inside the computer. The bits of the computer's memory have been set so that when they are displayed on the screen, the pixels appear to be a picture of a button. The computer can change the bits when necessary so that the next time they are displayed, the button looks as if it has been pushed in. Adding a "click" sound makes the illusion even more real. But there is still no button.

PRESSING A VIRTUAL BUTTON

If there is only a picture of a button, how can we "click" it with the mouse? That's a good question, which we can answer without becoming too technical.

Of course, the place to begin is with the mouse pointer. The mouse pointer is a white arrow point with a black border and, like the button, must be created by the computer. When the mouse is moved, the computer finds out in which direction it is moving and redraws the pointer translated a short distance in that direction. By repeatedly redrawing the pointer in new positions that are redisplayed rapidly, the computer produces the illusion that the pointer moves smoothly across the screen. It's the same idea as cartoon flipbooks or motion pictures: A series of still pictures, progressively different and rapidly displayed, creates motion. The frequency of display changes is called the **refresh rate** and, like motion-picture frames, is typically 30 times per second. At that rate, the human eye sees the sequence of still frames as smooth motion.

As the mouse pointer moves across the screen, the computer keeps track of which pixel is at the point of the arrow. In Figure 1.7, the computer records the position by the row and column coordinates, because the pixel grid is like graph paper. So (141, 1003) in Figure 1.7(a) means that the point pixel is in the 141st pixel row from the top of the screen and at the 1003rd pixel column from the left side of the screen. With each new position, the coordinates are updated. When the mouse is clicked, as shown in Figure 1.7(d), the computer determines which button the mouse pointer is over, and then redraws the button to look pushed in.

COORDINATING THE BUTTON AND THE MOUSE

How does the computer know which button the mouse pointer is over? It keeps a list of every button drawn on the screen, recording the coordinates of the button's upper-left and lower-right corners. So, in Figure 1.7, the button would have its upper-left corner at pixel (132, 1010) and its lower-right corner at pixel (145, 1022) (see Figure 1.8). The two corners, call them (x_1, y_1) and (x_2, y_2), determine the position of the rectangle that defines the button: the top row of white pixels is in row x_1, the left-side column of white pixels is in column y_1, the bottom row of black pixels is in row x_2, and the right-side column of black pixels is in column y_2.

Now, if the mouse pointer's point has a row coordinate between x_1 and x_2, the pointer is somewhere between the top and bottom of the button, though it may be to the left or right of the button rather than on it. But if the pointer's point also has a column coordinate between y_1 and y_2, the pointer is between the left and right sides of the button; that is, it is somewhere on the button. So, for each button with coordinates (x_1, y_1) and (x_2, y_2), the computer tests whether

$$x_1 < \text{row coordinate of mouse pointer point} < x_2$$

and

$$y_1 < \text{column coordinate of mouse pointer point} < y_2$$

are *both* true. If so, the mouse pointer's point is over that button, and the button is redrawn in the "clicked configuration." Also, other software is told that the user just clicked on the button, so it can do whatever action the button commands.

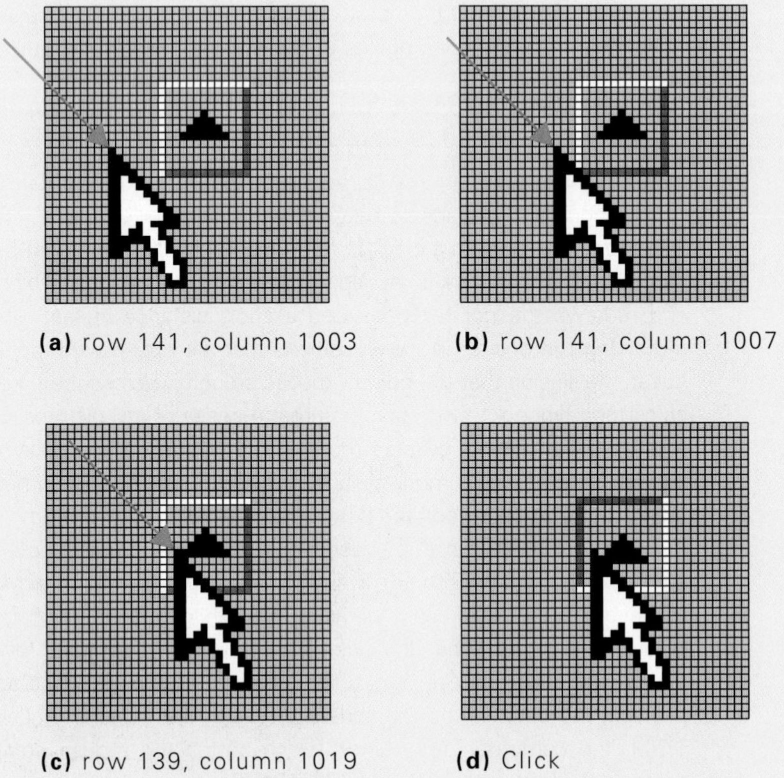

Figure 1.7. *Mouse pointer moving toward, and then clicking, a button; the coordinates of the point of the pointer are given by their row, column positions.*

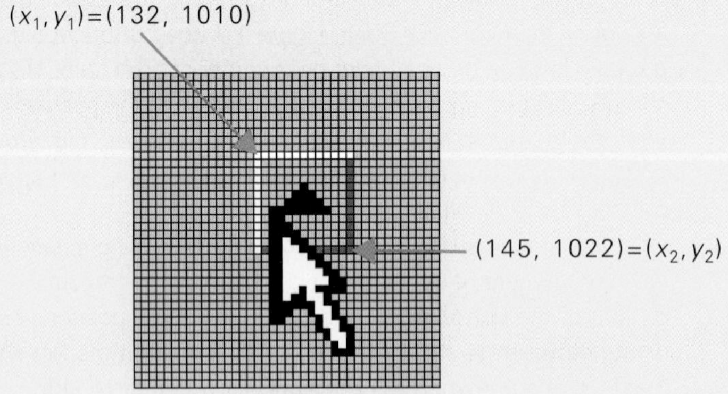

Figure 1.8. *A button's location is completely determined by the positions of its upper-left and lower-right corners.*

Creating a button and keeping track of the positions of the button and the mouse pointer may seem like a lot of work, but it makes using a computer easier (and more fun) for us. The metaphor of pressing a button to cause an action is so natural that going to the trouble of making buttons greatly simplifies our work.

not in the monitor unit, but rather in a separate box that is often on the floor below the desk or somewhere else nearby. Calling the monitor the computer is not so much a mistake as an acknowledgment that the monitor is our interface to the computer, wherever it may be physically.

In the component approach, the computer and many of its components (for example, hard disk, floppy disk drive, and CD drive) are packaged together in a box that is called the **processor box**, though it often has a fancy marketing name (for example, minitower) that has no technical meaning; see Figure 1.9. For the monolithic approach, of course, the associated disks and drives are in the same package as the monitor. It's as if the monitor were attached to the processor box, so everything in this section applies.

Motherboard

Inside the processor box is the **motherboard**, a printed circuit board containing most of the circuitry of a personal computer system, as shown in Figure 1.10. The name comes from the fact that smaller printed circuit boards, sometimes called **daughter boards**, but more often called **cards**, are plugged into the motherboard for added functionality. A motherboard is impressive to look at with all of its fine wire patterns, colorful resistors, economy of space, and so forth. (Ask your computer dealer to show you one—it's safer than looking at the one in your computer and risking harm to it.) The motherboard is a **printed circuit** or PC board. (This use of "PC" predates "PC" used for "personal computer" by decades.) Of the many parts on this PC board, only the microprocessor chip and the memory are of interest to us at the moment.

Microprocessor

The **microprocessor**, found on the motherboard, is the part of a personal computer system that computes. The microprocessor is involved in every activity of the system, everything from making the mouse pointer appear to move around the screen to locating information stored on the hard disk. The microprocessor is the "smart" part of the system, so engineers often describe the other parts of a computer as "dumb." It is surprisingly easy for a computer to be "smart," as we will see. Eventually, we will even ask, "Can a computer think?"

The "micro" part of microprocessor is archaic and no longer accurate. The term "microprocessor" was adopted around 1980 when all of the circuitry for a computer first fit onto a single silicon chip. These were technically computer processors, but they were small and primitive compared to the mainframes and the "minicomputers" of the day, so they were called *micro*processors. But improvements came so quickly that in a few years microprocessors were more powerful than the largest computers of 1980. Today's microprocessors are fast, highly optimized, loaded with features, and very sophisticated. In fact, microprocessors spend most of their time doing nothing, just waiting for us. Because there is nothing "micro" about today's microprocessors, we will simply use the proper term **processor** for the rest of this book.

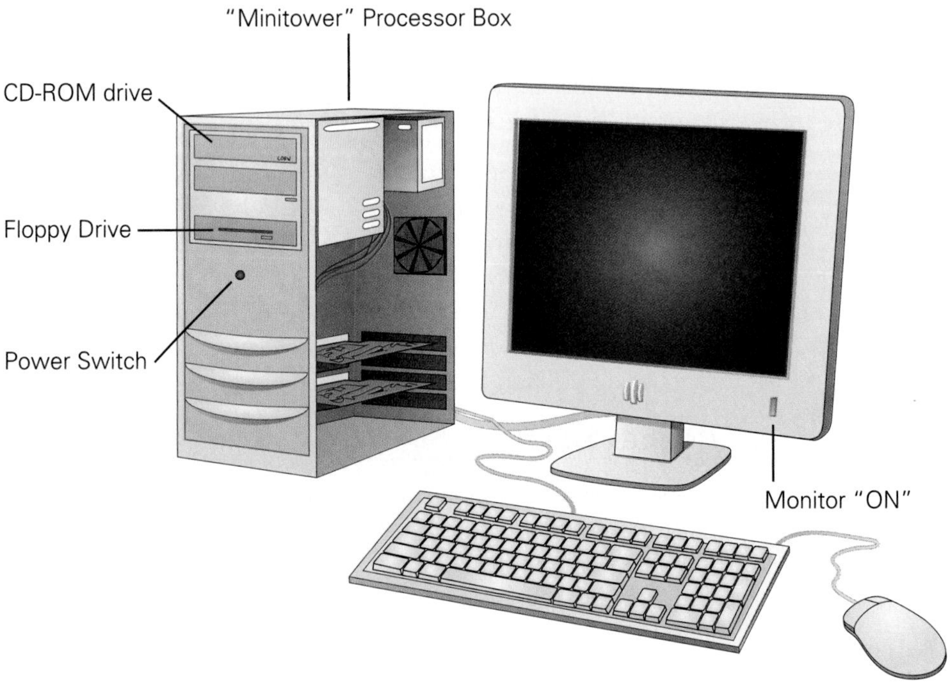

Figure 1.9. *A component-approach computer.*

Figure 1.10. *A motherboard.*

Memory

The **memory** of a computer is where a program and its data are located while the program is running. For example, when you are using a word processor, the word processing program and the document being edited are stored in the memory. (When they're not in memory, programs and data are stored on the hard disk; see the next section.) Computer memory is also called **RAM**, short for **random access memory**. The basic unit of memory is a **byte**, which will be described in Chapter 8. Today's personal computers have millions of bytes of RAM memory, or **megabytes**, from the Greek prefix **mega-** for million. (See Figure 9.9 in Chapter 9 for a list of prefixes.)

There are two basic ways to locate and retrieve, or *access*, information: sequential and random. Information stored sequentially is arranged in a line, so that when you want to get a specific item, you have to skip everything else stored before it, as shown in Figure 1.11. Cassette tapes, VCR tapes, and so on are examples of **sequential access**. **Random access** means that any item can be retrieved directly. Finding dictionary entries, library books, and numbers in a phonebook are examples of random access. Random access is faster than sequential access, as anyone wanting to watch the last scene on a VCR tape well knows.

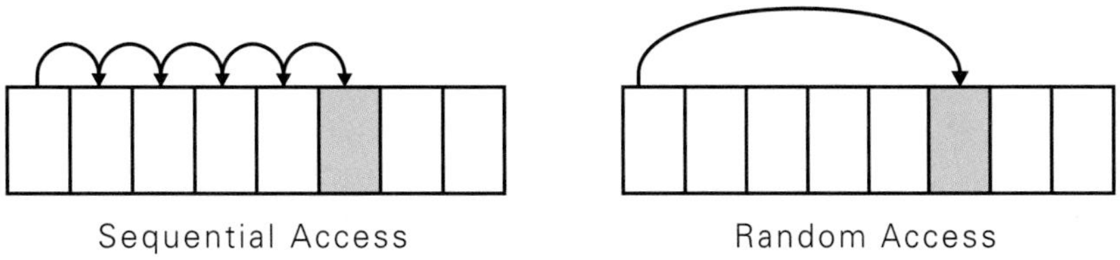

Figure 1.11. *Sequential versus random access.*

Hard Disk

The **hard disk** is not really part of a computer—it is technically a high-capacity, persistent peripheral storage device. But it is so fundamental to personal computer systems that it's helpful to think of it as a basic part. The hard disk is also referred to as the **hard drive**, and was once simply known as a **disk** before floppy disks were invented. The hard disk stores programs and data when they are not in immediate use by a computer. Disks are made from an iron compound that can be magnetized. Because the magnetism remains even when the power is off, the encoded information is still there when the power comes back on. So a disk is said to be *permanent* or *persistent* storage. A hard disk is usually located in the same box as the processor, because without access to permanent storage, the processor is crippled.

The hard disk looks like a small stack of bright metal washers with an arm that can sweep across them, as shown in Figure 1.12. The "popping" or "clicking" sound we sometimes hear is the arm moving back and forth as it accesses information on various tracks of the disk.

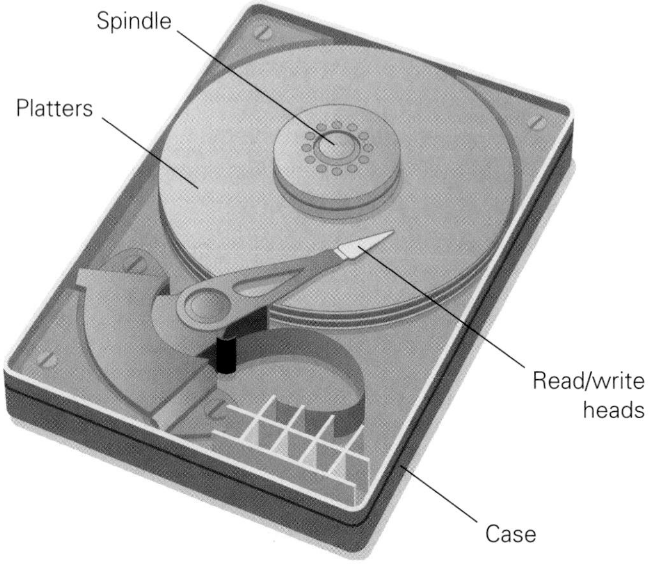

Figure 1.12. *A hard disk.*

Hard-disk Memory vs. RAM. A successful computer user must understand an important difference between the RAM memory and the hard disk memory. Today's RAM is made from integrated circuit (IC) technology, informally called **microchips**. One property of IC memory is that it is **volatile**, meaning that the information is lost when the power is turned off. So all of the information that must be permanently saved must be on the hard disk. *The point is to save your work often, which copies it from the RAM to the disk.* This limits the amount of work that will be lost if the computer crashes for some reason. If your computer crashes, you have to restart it, which may mean cycling power (turning the power off and on). When the power goes off, the information in the volatile RAM is lost, but the information saved on the nonvolatile disk will be reloaded when the computer restarts.

HOW SOFT IS SOFTWARE?

The term hardware predates computers by centuries. Originally it meant metal items like hinges and nails, used in construction. There was no need for the word software until computers were invented.

Software

Software is a collective term for programs. The name contrasts with hardware, of course, but what does it mean for software to be "soft"? When a computer function is implemented in software, the computer does the operation by following instructions. A program that figures out income taxes is an example. If the function is implemented in **hardware**, the computer does the operations directly with wires and transistors. (We say it is **hard-wired**.) The multiplication operation is an example.

The difference between "hard" and "soft" is like the difference between an innate ability, such as coughing, and a learned ability, such as reading. Innate abilities are "built in" biologically, and they're impossible to change, like hardware. Learned abilities can be easily changed and expanded. We can change from reading English to reading French, *n'est-ce pas*? A computer cannot change how it multiplies, but one minute a computer can be following the instructions to figure U.S. income tax, and the next moment it can be following instructions to compute Canadian income tax. (Computers don't *learn* to perform soft operations, of course, the way we learn to read. Rather, they are simply given the instructions and told to follow them.)

FITBYTE

The Hard Reality. The difference between hardware and software was dramatically illustrated in 1994 when a bug was discovered in the hard-wired divide operation of Intel's Pentium processor, an approximately $200 chip. Though the wrong answers were rare and tiny, the error had to be fixed. If divide had been implemented in software, as had been the usual approach in computing's early years, Intel could have sent everyone a simple patch for $1 or $2. But hardware cannot be changed, so the Pentium chips had to be recalled at a total cost of about $500 million.

Algorithms and Programs

An **algorithm** is a precise and systematic method for solving a problem. Another term for a systematic method is a **process**. Some familiar algorithms are the arithmetic operations like addition, subtraction, multiplication, and division; the process for sending a greeting card to a parent; and the method for finding a number in the telephone book. The method for determining when a mouse pointer is over a button is an algorithm. Because an algorithm's instructions are written down for some other agent (a person or a computer) to follow, precision is important.

Though we are sometimes taught algorithms, like the arithmetic algorithms, we figure out many algorithms on our own, like finding phone numbers. In Chapter 10, we introduce **algorithmic thinking**, the act of thinking up algorithms. Writing out the steps of an algorithm is **programming**, and **programs** are simply algorithms written in a specific programming language for a specific set of conditions.

When we ask a computer to do something for us, we ask it to **run** a program. This is literally what we are asking when we click on the icon for an application like Netscape. We are saying, "Run the program from the Netscape company to browse the Internet." *Run* is a correct term that has been used since the invention of computers. But a slightly better term is *execute*, because it emphasizes an important property of computing.

Execute

A computer **executes** a program when it performs instructions. The word **execute** means following a set of orders exactly as they are written. Indeed, computer pioneers used the word *orders* for what we now call instructions. The orders tell the computer to act in a specific way and in no other. When orders are given, the faithful agent is *not* supposed to think. There is no possibility for optional or independent behavior. "Following instructions literally" is what computers do when they run programs, and it is that aspect that makes "execute" a slightly better term than "run."

In addition to run and execute, **interpret** is also a correct term for following a program's instructions, as explained in Chapter 9.

Boot

Finally, the term **booting** means to start a computer and **rebooting** means to restart it. Because booting most often happens after a catastrophic error or a crash, you might guess that the term is motivated by frustration—we want to kick the computer like a football. But *booting* comes from *bootstrap*. Computers were originally started by an operator who entered a few instructions into the computer's empty memory using console push buttons. Those instructions told the computer to read in a few more instructions—a very simple operating system—from punch cards. This operating system could then read in the instructions of the real operating system from magnetic tape, similar to a VCR tape. Finally, the computer was able to start doing useful work. This incremental process was called **bootstrapping**, from the phrase "pulling yourself up by your bootstraps," because the computer basically started itself. Today this process is in the boot ROM.

THE WORDS FOR IDEAS

Though understanding the physical parts of IT—monitors, motherboards, and memory—seems very important to our success with IT, we will not be so concerned with them. Rather, we will mostly use **concept** words such as those in this section.

"Abstract"

One of the most important "idea" words used in this book is the verb *to abstract*. It has several meanings. In British mysteries, *to abstract* means *to remove*, as in to steal: "The thief abstracted the pearl necklace while the jeweler looked at the diamond ring." The meanings of *to abstract* in information technology share the idea of removal, but the thing being removed is not physical. The thing being removed is an idea or a process, and it is extracted from some form of information.

To **abstract** is to remove the basic concept, idea, or process from a situation. The removed concept is usually expressed in another, more succinct and usually more general form, called an **abstraction**.

We are familiar with abstraction in this sense. For example, parables and fables, which teach lessons in the form of stories, require us to abstract the essential point of the story. When we are told about a fox who can't reach a bunch of grapes and so calls them sour, we abstract an idea from the story: When people try but fail to reach a goal, they often change their view of the desirability of the goal.

Notice two key points here. First, many but not all of the details of the story are irrelevant to the concept. In the process of abstracting, we must decide which details of the story are relevant and which are irrelevant. The "grapes" and the "fox" are unimportant, but "failure" is important to the point. Being able to tell the difference between important and unimportant details is essential to understanding the point of a story, and to abstraction generally. Second, the idea—the abstraction—has meaning beyond the story. The point of repeating the parable, of course, is to convey an idea that applies to many situations.

"Generalize"

A process similar to abstraction is to recognize the common idea in two or more situations. Recognizing how different situations have something basic in common is why we create parables, rules, and so on.

To **generalize** is to express an idea, concept, or process that applies in many situations. The statement summing up that idea is called a **generalization**.

For example, most of us notice that twisting a faucet handle left turns water on and twisting it right turns it off. Not always—some water taps have only a single "joy stick" handle, and others have horizontal bars that pull forward—but it is true most of the time. We generalize that "on" is to the left; "off" is to the right. Perhaps we also notice that twisting lids, caps, screws, and nuts to the left usually loosens them, and right usually tightens them. Again, we generalize that left means loosen, right means tighten. We probably also generalize that both situations are really examples the same thing! A generalization of generalizations.

Noticing patterns and generalizing about them is a very valuable habit. Though generalizations do not always apply, recognizing them gives us a way to begin in a new but similar situation.

"Operationally Attuned"

Another term related to extracting concepts and processes refers to being aware of how a gadget works. To be **operationally attuned** is to apply what we know about how a device or system works as an aid to simplifying its use.

For example, we previously generalized that with few exceptions all caps, lids, screws, and nuts tighten by turning right, and loosen by turning left. We might know this intuitively, but knowing it *explicitly* makes us operationally attuned. That is, knowing this fact as a rule—some kids learn "righty-tighty, lefty loosey"—means that when a lid or nut is stuck, we can twist it very hard in the correct direction, making sure we are loosening rather than tightening it.

The term operationally attuned has been introduced here to emphasize that thinking about how information technology works makes it simpler to use. We don't expect to be experts on all of IT—no one can be. But by asking ourselves, "How does this work?" and using what we learn by thinking about the answer, we are likely to be more successful at applying IT. Our Fluency study will focus on learning enough to answer many of the "How does this work?" questions.

{FITLINK}

Tuning In >>

In our daily lives, we use hundreds of devices, systems, and processes. For some, like the ignition on the car, we quickly learn which way to turn the key because it only turns in one direction. We don't think about how it works. Using it becomes a habit. Other gadgets, however, have more leeway, and for them it helps to be attuned to their operation. One example is a deadbolt lock, which moves a metal bar from the door to the doorframe to lock the door. Thinking about how the lock works can tell us whether the door is locked or not. Referring to Figure 1.13(a), notice which way the knob is turned. By visualizing the internal works of the lock, we can imagine that the top of the knob is attached to the bar. When the knob is pointing left, the bar must be pulled back—that is, unlocked. When the knob is positioned to the right, the bar is extended, so the door is locked. (Not all deadbolt locks are this simple, nor are they all installed right side up.) We may not know how the lock really works, but explaining its operation in our own terms means that we can see at a distance whether the door is locked or unlocked. It's not a big deal, but it might save us from getting up off the sofa and trying the door to see if it's locked.

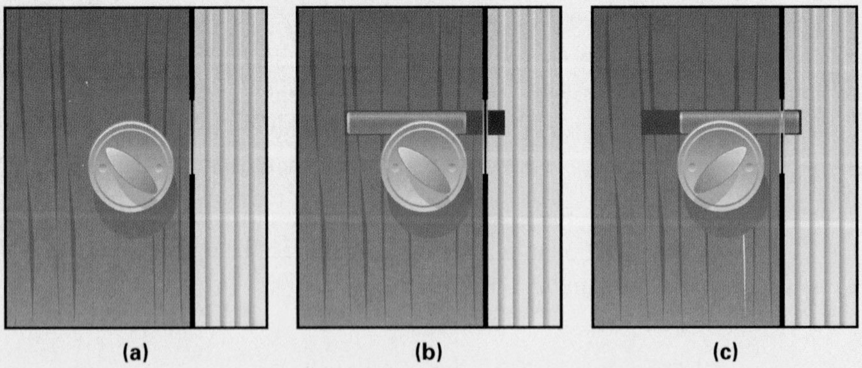

Figure 1.13. *Deadbolt lock. (a) The external view. (b) Internal components, unlocked. (c) Internal components, locked. Thinking about how the deadbolt works allows us to see at a glance whether the door is locked or not.*

"Mnemonic"

Finally, **mnemonic** is a rather unusual term that we use in IT, and in other fields as well. The silent *m* implies it's a word with an unusual past.

A mnemonic (*ni-´mä-nik*) is an aid to remembering something. The reminder can take many forms, such as pronounceable words or phrases. North Americans remember the five Great Lakes with HOMES—Huron, Ontario, Michigan, Erie, and Superior. Earlier in this chapter, we mentioned PILPOF—plug in last, pull out first—for remembering when to connect and disconnect the power cable.

There are many details about IT that we need to know only occasionally, like when to connect power. They're not worth memorizing, but they're inconvenient to look up. So, if we can think of a mnemonic that helps us remember the details when we need them, we make using technology simpler.

ANALYTICAL THINKING

Using the right terms makes learning IT simpler, but an equally valuable habit to acquire is becoming more analytical. When we say that the world record in the mile run has been improving or computer performance has been improving, we are making only very weak statements. They simply assert that things have changed over time for the better. But has the change been infinitesimally small, or has it been gigantic? How does the change compare to other changes? Since we can easily find information—that's one of the benefits, for example, of the World Wide Web—we can know an earlier measure of performance and a recent measure. Then we can compare them. Thinking analytically is essential to becoming Fluent in IT, but it is also useful in our other studies, our careers, and throughout life.

Consider the mile run as an illustration.

Mile Runs

When Moroccan miler Hicham El Guerrouj broke the world record on July 7, 1999, the news reports trumpeted that he "smashed," "eclipsed," and "shattered" the world's record set six years earlier by Noureddine Moreceli of Algeria (see Figure 1.14). El Guerrouj had run a mile in an astonishing 3 minutes, 43.13 seconds, an impressive 1.26 seconds faster than Moreceli. The descriptions were not hyperbole. People around the world truly marveled at El Guerrouj's accomplishment, even though 1.26 seconds seems like a small amount of time.

To put El Guerrouj's run into perspective, notice that 45 years had passed since Englishman Roger Bannister attracted world attention as the first man in recorded history to run a mile in less than 4 minutes (see Figure 1.14). His time was 3:59.4. In 45 years, the world's best runners improved the time for the mile by an astonishing 16.27 seconds. (Notice that El Guerrouj's 1.26 seconds was a large part of that.) As a rate, 16.27 seconds represents an improvement from 15.038 miles per hour to 16.134 miles per hour, or just over 7 percent. Given that Bannister's world-class time was the starting point, an improvement in human performance of that size is truly something to be admired.

Comparing to 20-year-olds

How do these world champions compare to average people? Most healthy people in their early 20s—the age group of the world record setters—can run a mile in 7.5 minutes. This number was chosen because it covers the ability of a majority of the people in the age range, and is approximately twice the time El Guerrouj needed. To say El Guerrouj is twice as fast as an average person is to say he is faster by a factor of 2. (The factor is found by dividing the new rate by the old.)

This factor-of-2 difference is a rough rule for the performance gap between an average person and a world champion for most physical strength activities such as running, swimming, jumping, and pole vaulting. The factor-of-2 rule tells us that no matter how hard most people try at physical activities, their performance can improve by at most twice. Of course, most of us can only dream of achieving even part of that factor-of-2 potential. Nevertheless, the factor-of-2 rule is an important benchmark.

Figure 1.14. *The runners Hicham El Guerrouj (left) and Roger Bannister (right).*

Factor of Improvememt

When we compared world champions, we said there was a 7 percent improvement and that El Guerrouj's speed was about a factor-of-2 times faster than the speed of an average person. There is a difference between expressing improvement as a **percentage** and expressing improvement as a factor. We find a **factor of improvement** by dividing the new rate by the old rate. So, to find El Guerrouj's improvement over Bannister's, we divide their rates (16.134/15.038) to get 1.07. Percentages are a closely related computation found by dividing the *amount of change* by the old rate (16.134 – 15.038) / 15.038 = 0.07 and multiplying the result by 100. The added complexity of percentage is potentially confusing, so we use the simpler factor-of-improvement method. El Guerrouj was a factor-of-1.07 times faster than Bannister and about a factor-of-2 times faster than an average person.

TRY IT

Computing the Factor of Improvement. Flyer 1, the aircraft Orville and Wilbur Wright flew at Kitty Hawk, North Carolina, went so slowly (10 mph) that the brother who wasn't piloting could run alongside as it flew just off the ground. The SR-71 Blackbird, probably the world's fastest plane, flies at 2200 mph, three times the speed of sound.

What is the factor of improvement between Blackbird and Flyer 1?

Speed of Blackbird = 2200 mph

Speed of Flyer 1 = 10 mph

Factor of improvement = 2200/10 = 220

The Blackbird is a factor-of-220 faster than Flyer 1.

Super Computers

As another example of analytical thinking, let's compare computer speeds. The UNIVAC I, the first commercial computer, unveiled in 1951 (and current when Bannister set his record), operated at a rate of nearly 100,000 addition operations (adds) per second. By comparison, a typical PC today—say, the portable IBM ThinkPad—can perform a billion additions per second or so. This factor-of-10,000 improvement over UNIVAC I (1,000,000,000/100,000) is truly remarkable. But, consider this—the ThinkPad is no record setter. It's the sort of computer a college student can afford to buy. Engineering workstations can easily do several billion adds per second, boosting the factor even higher. And an Intel computer called ASCI Red, built for Sandia National Laboratory, held the world record for computer speed in 1999, when El Guerrouj set his record. ASCI Red ran at an astonishing 2.1 trillion floating-point adds per second. (Floating-point adds are decimal arithmetic operations that are more complex than the additions used to measure the speed of the UNIVAC I.) Compared to the UNIVAC I, ASCI Red is a factor of 21 million times faster!

Perhaps nothing else in human experience has improved so dramatically. In roughly the same time period that human performance improved by a factor of 1.07 as measured by the mile run, computer performance improved by a factor of 21,000,000. Can we comprehend such a huge factor of improvement, or even the raw speed of ASCI Red?

FITTIP

Faster Still. ASCI Red was the fastest of its day, but its day has passed. Several computers have eclipsed its performance, and better designs continue to emerge. For the latest speed tests, see `www.netlib.org/benchmark/top500.html`.

FITBYTE

Think About It. Most of us can appreciate the 7 percent improvement of El Guerrouj's run over Bannister's, and probably the factor-of-2 improvement in average versus world champion performance. Those we can imagine. But factors of improvement in the thousands or millions are beyond comprehension. Notice that if El Guerrouj had improved on Bannister by a factor of 21,000,000, he'd have run the mile in 11.4 microseconds. That's 11.4 millionths of a second. What does that mean?

> Human visual perception is so slow that El Guerrouj could run 3000 miles at that rate before anyone could even notice he had moved.

> The sound would still be "inside" the starting gun 11.4 microseconds after the trigger was pulled.

> Light travels only twice as fast.

Both the raw power of today's computers and their improvement over the last half-century are almost beyond comprehension.

Benefits of Analytical Thinking

To summarize, we have made our understanding of recent speed improvements crisper by applying simple analysis. Rather than accepting the statement that the mile run and computers have improved, we found out the facts given as two measurements of performance. But once we had the data, we did not leave it as two separate observations: 100,000 additions in 1951 versus 2.1 trillion additions in 1999. Instead, we analyzed their relationship by figuring the factor of improvement: 2,100,000,000,000/100,000. ASCI Red is faster by a factor of 21 million.

This analysis let us compare the improvement to other advancements, and to put them all into perspective. The mile run, though improving by an apparently small factor of 1.07 times in 45 years, is still very impressive when we recall that champions are only about a factor-of-2 better than average people. Computer performance has improved by unimaginable amounts. Though our original statement, "the mile run and computers have improved," is correct, our analysis helps us to be much more expressive and precise. Analytical thinking helps us understand more deeply the world of information technology and the physical world in which we live.

The Story Behind WYSIWYG

The only remaining task is to define the first acronym mentioned in the chapter, **WYSIWYG**. Remember that it stands for "what you see is what you get." To understand the term, recall that the computer creates the virtual world we see on our screens. The representation the computer uses to keep track of the things on the screen is very different from the picture it shows us. For example, the text you are reading was stored in the computer as one very long line of letters, numbers, punctuation, and other characters, but it is displayed to me as a nicely formatted page like the one you are reading. The computer processes its representation—the long sequence of characters—to create the nicely formatted page. The original text editors couldn't do that, so users had to work with the long string. If you wanted to change anything, you had to imagine what it would look like printed out.

Eventually text editing systems were programmed to show the user the page as it would appear when printed. Changing the text became much easier. This property was described as "what you see [when editing] is what you get [when its printed]" or WYSIWYG. Text editors with the WYSIWYG property became known as **word processors**.

SUMMARY

In this chapter we have focused on learning IT terms in context. We started by recognizing that knowing and using *le mot juste* is important in IT for two reasons. Our brains seem to organize knowledge around words, so as we learn the words, we learn the ideas. Also, knowing the right terms helps us communicate with others in the field. Then we learned some basic terminology using questions like "Where is the Start button?" and "How soft is software?" These questions helped us review basic terms that were probably already familiar—monitor, screen saver, RAM, software, and so on. Mixed in with these discussions were new words that perhaps you didn't know—sequential access, volatile, motherboard, and so on. You will use some of these terms, like *software*, daily. Others, like *volatile*, you may never use. But the idea that it names—information is lost when the power is switched off—is very important to your everyday use of IT, making the term a secure site to anchor practical advice, "Save your work regularly." We also considered a brief list of "idea" words, such as *abstract*. These words and ideas will be used throughout our study of IT. Finally, we illustrated analytical thinking by looking at improvements in the mile run and computer speed.

We're not done, however. All of the chapters of this book introduce new terms when new ideas are introduced. Learning and remembering the terms can help you learn and remember the ideas. All of the new terms have been collected in the glossary at the end of the book. Check the glossary when a term slips your mind. In addition to the glossary in this book, there are several good online glossaries, and it's probably a good idea to find one with your Web browser and bookmark it—that is, save its URL. (Whoops, have we defined **URL** yet? No, but we will in Chapter 3. Meanwhile, check the glossary to find out what it stands for.)

EXERCISES

Multiple Choice

1. Computer monitors are different from TVs because:
   A. monitors are bit-mapped whereas TVs are not
   B. TVs are interactive whereas monitors are not
   C. monitors are CRTs whereas TVs are not
   D. more than one of the above
2. Screen savers:
   A. are useful because they prevent burn-in
   B. save energy
   C. can be turned off with a key press or a mouse click
   D. all of the above
3. The display for a laptop is most likely a:
   A. TV
   B. RGB display
   C. LCD
   D. CRT display
4. Mice and keyboards do not have power cords because:
   A. they are not electrical
   B. the power and the signal wires are in one cable
   C. they run on batteries
   D. none of the above
5. The last cable you plug in should be the:
   A. monitor cable
   B. keyboard cable
   C. printer cable
   D. power cable
6. RGB stands for:
   A. red, green, black
   B. red, gray, blue
   C. rust, black, brown
   D. red, green, blue
7. A typical monitor:
   A. has over a million pixels
   B. has a 1024 × 768 pixel grid
   C. displays pixels that are generated on the hard drive
   D. all of the above
8. How many pixels make up the button in Figure 1.8 (page 12)?
   A. 19 × 19
   B. 304
   C. 1024 × 768
   D. none of the above

9. If the computer redraws every pixel on the screen of a laptop 30 times a second, how many pixels get redrawn in a minute?
   A. 23,592,960
   B. $1024 \times 768 \times 30$
   C. $1024 \times 768 \times 60$
   D. more than one of the above

10. How is the process for clicking a check box similar to clicking a button?
   A. The tip of the arrow must be inside the *x*, *y* coordinates that make up the check box.
   B. The user must click the mouse button.
   C. The configuration of the check box must change from unchecked to checked or vice versa.
   D. all of the above

Short Answer

1. People who are knowledgeable about digital technology are called ______.
2. Knowing ______ is important to understanding technology and being understood when talking about it.
3. A ______ saves energy by shutting off the monitor when it is not in use.
4. The last cable you should plug in should be the ______.
5. How many pixels are on a typical laptop?
6. The number of times a second that images on the screen are redrawn is called the ______.
7. The ______ is the active point of the mouse pointer.
8. A specified result sought through the use of a precise and systematic method is a(n) ______.
9. ______ is the proper term used when a computer performs the instructions in a program.
10. The process of starting a computer is called ______.
11. Gleaning the central idea or concept from a situation is called ______.
12. A device that helps you remember a fact or concept is a ______.
13. A WYSIWYG text editor is called a ______.
14. On the computer, programs and information are stored on the ______.
15. The formulation of an idea, concept, or process that can be applied in many situations is called a ______.

Exercises

1. Here are some of the acronyms found in this chapter. Next to each, write its name and its meaning.

   SCSI
   IT
   CRT
   LCD
   RGB
   CD
   RAM
   ROM
   PC
   IC

2. Create a list of mnemonics that you know and their meanings.
3. Find the details of the computer system you are using. If you do not have the manual, use an ad from a newspaper, flyer, or a Web site. Write down the specifications for your system, paying close attention to the terms and specs that are unfamiliar. Make a note to learn more about these in further chapters.
4. It took Magellan's expedition three years to circumnavigate the globe. The space shuttle makes an orbit in about 90 minutes. Calculate the factor of improvement.
5. Ellery Clark of the United States won the long jump in the 1896 Olympiad in Athens, Greece with a jump of 20 feet 9 3/4 inches. The current world record is held by Mike Powell of the United States, who jumped a distance of 8.95 meters. What is the factor of improvement? Be sure to convert between feet and meters.
6. Ray Harroun won the first Indianapolis 500 in 1911 with a speed of 74.59 miles per hour. The 2002 race was won by Helio Castroneves with a speed of 166.499 mph. What is the factor of improvement?
7. In 2003, Svetlana Feofanova set the world pole vault record at 4.76 meters. William Hoyt set the record in 1896 with a vault of 3.30 meters. What is the factor of improvement that she made over the men's record of 1896? What is the percentage increase?

chapter

2 WHAT THE DIGERATI KNOW

Exploring the Human-Computer Interface

learning objectives

> Explain key ideas to experienced users (the digerati):
    - The advantages of having common features in information technology
    - The benefits of using feedback of "clicking around" and "blazing away" in exploring new applications
    - The basic principle of IT: Form follows function
> Explain how a basic search is done
> Use common methods to search and edit text:
    - Find (words, characters, spaces)
    - Shift-select
    - The placeholder technique
    - Search-and-replace (substitution)
> Demonstrate an ability to think abstactly about techology by using the basic rules of IT to learn about information technology new to you

PERHAPS the most uncomfortable part of being an inexperienced computer user is the suspicion that everyone but you is born knowing how to use technology. They seem to know automatically what to do in any situation. Maybe, you think, they have all come from the same alien planet that computers have come from.

Of course, experienced users don't really have a technology gene. Through experience, however, they have learned a certain kind of knowledge that lets them figure out what to do in most situations. Most people do not "know" this information explicitly—it is not usually taught in class. They just learn it through experience. But, you can avoid long hours of stumbling around gaining experience. In this chapter, we reveal some secrets of the digerati so that you, too, can "join the club." (Digerati is a new word for people who understand digital technology, from the word *literati*.)

The major goal for this chapter is to show you how to think about technology abstractly. We do this by asking how people learn technical skills and by considering what the creators of technology expect from us as users. This chapter will also help you understand that:

- Computer systems use consistent interfaces, standard metaphors, and common operations.
- Computer systems always give feedback while they are working.
- Making mistakes will not break the computer.
- The best way to learn to use new computer software is to try it out, expecting to make mistakes.
- Asking questions of other computer users is not evidence of being a dummy, but proof of an inquiring mind.

These ideas can help you learn new software quickly. A key abstract idea about software is that it obeys fundamental laws. This deep idea can help you in your everyday software usage, as we illustrate when we explain the principle "form follows function." We show how this principle applies to basic text searching, which helps you learn the subject without using any specific vendor's software. Such knowledge applies to every system and makes us versatile users. You, too, can become one of the digerati.

LEARNING ABOUT TECHNOLOGY

Human beings are born knowing how to chew, cough, stand, blink, smile, and so forth. They are not born knowing how to ride a bicycle, drive a car, use a food processor, or start a lawnmower. For any tool more complicated than a stick, we need some explanation about how it works and possibly some training in its use. Parents teach their children how to ride bicycles, driver's training classes explain to teenagers how to drive safely, and most products come with an owner's manual.

Some tools such as portable CD players are so intuitive that most people living in our technological society find their use "obvious." We don't need to look at the owner's manual. We can guess what the controls do because we know what operations are needed to play recordings. (Without this knowledge, the icons on the buttons would probably be meaningless.) And we can usually recover from mistakes. For example, if you were to insert a CD upside-down, it wouldn't work, so you'd turn it over and try again.

But the fact that we live in a technological society and can figure out how a CD works doesn't mean that we have any innate technological abilities. Instead, it emphasizes two facts about technology:

- Our experience using (related) devices guides us in what to expect.
- The designers who create these devices know we have that experience and design their products to match what we already know.

These two facts are key to success with information technology.

A Perfect Interface

On certain Apple Macintosh computers, when a user loads an audio CD into the computer's CD drive, the **graphical user interface** (**GUI**) shown in Figure 2.1 appears on the screen. A GUI, pronounced "*GOO-ey*," is the medium by which users interact with programs running on a personal computer. This GUI appears on the screen because the Macintosh's operating system, noting that a CD has just been inserted into the drive and recognizing that it is an audio CD, assumes the user wants to listen to it. So, it starts the software that plays audio CDs, shows the user the GUI to find out what he or she wants to play, and waits for a response.

Figure 2.1. *Graphical user interface for one version of an Apple Macintosh audio CD player.*

Using Analogy

As first-time users of this software, we look at the GUI wondering what the software does and how to use it. There is an online user's manual, but we will not need it. The GUI tells the whole story. This GUI shows us a familiar picture of a CD player, complete with digital readout in green LCD numerals, "metallic" buttons with the standard icons, and so on. No physical CD player looks exactly like this one—for example, the CD slot is the wrong size—but it is so much like a real CD player that anyone who has seen one recognizes this image immediately. So we guess that pressing the button with the Play icon () will cause the computer to play the CD. But, because this is a GUI, we can't really press a button. The action analogous to "pressing" for a computer is "clicking" with the mouse. We know this from experience. Clicking on the button with the icon for Play starts the CD playing. Because it worked, we know that the analogy of the GUI to a physical CD player is correct, and from then on we have a basic idea of how to operate the software. We didn't need lessons; no one had to help us.

Understanding the Designer's Intent

The use of the physical analogy to guide the user in learning to operate the CD player software may seem obvious, but it demonstrates a basic idea of consumer software. Like anyone who invents a new tool, software designers have to teach users how to operate their inventions. They can and do write manuals explaining all of the software's slick features, but it's much better if users can figure out the software without studying the manual. So, software designers, like physical CD player designers, try to pick easy-to-understand user interfaces. Instead of creating a GUI that requires explanation, the designers guessed that an analogy with the familiar physical CD player would be intuitive. They put a lot of time and effort into making their GUI look real by using LCD numerals, "metallic" buttons, the standard button icons, a "slot" for the CD (which plays no role but to make the metaphor more believable), a slider volume control, and so forth. And they guessed right. Anyone who has used a CD player will know how this software works, at least its basics. (The Microsoft Windows operating system audio CD player for the same software generation also uses some of these features of the physical analogy, as shown in Figure 2.2.)

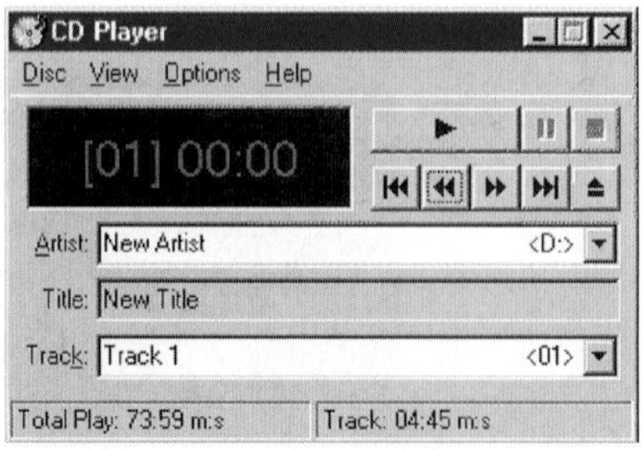

Figure 2.2. *Audio CD player GUI for the Windows operating system.*

To summarize, it is in a software designer's interest to make the GUI intuitive enough for us to figure out on our own. Though they do not always succeed as brilliantly as the designer(s) of the Macintosh audio CD GUI, we should expect as users that the software has been well crafted and that we can "brain out" how it works. We use this idea every time we need to use new software.

BASIC METAPHORS OF SOFTWARE

In software, a metaphor is an object or idea used as an analogy for a computation.

It is clear from a physical analogy how to play a CD with the audio CD player GUIs, but there is more to this software than just the seven standard buttons: Play, Stop, Eject, Last Track, Next Track, Forward, and Backward. How are we supposed to know about those other features? We can guess what some of them do, like Shuffle, because physical CD players have this feature. But we can figure out other parts of this software based on standard metaphors used in almost all consumer software GUIs. Most have suggestive graphic forms, and we see them in the audio CD player. Once we become familiar with these metaphors, we can easily guess how to interact with the software.

The following basic metaphors are used by almost all computer systems. They generally have a consistent meaning, though sometimes slightly different graphic forms.

Command Buttons

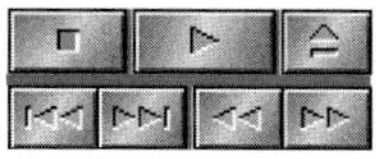

As shown in Figures 2.1 and 2.2, a command button usually looks like a 3D rectangle, highlighted and with an icon or text centered on the button, as explained in Chapter 1. This text label says what the command does. To invoke the command—that is, to tell the software to perform the operation shown on the label—we are expected to "press" the button by clicking on it with the mouse. We then get feedback telling us that the button has clicked, usually a change of color, shadow, or highlight; a text/icon change; or other indicator, such as an audible "click." (Some people think such indicators are obsessive attempts at realism, but some form of feedback is essential to effective computer use, as explained below.)

FITTIP

A Click Is Enough. When clicking on a button, it is not a good idea to press down on the mouse button for a long time, because the computer may interpret a too-long click as another action.

Slider Control

The volume control, in Figure 2.3(a), is a slider control. A **slider control** sets a value from a "continuous" range, such as volume. To move the slider, place the mouse pointer on the slider, hold down the (left) mouse button, and move in the direction of change. The most common examples of sliders are the scroll bars in a window display, usually shown at the right and bottom of the window, as shown in Figure 2.3(b). When the window is not large enough to display all of the information in the horizontal or vertical direction, a scroll bar is shown for each direction in which information has been clipped. For example, for a word processor document that doesn't all fit in a window, a scroll bar lets you move up and down or side to side to read all the text. The range is the length—the number of lines in the document—and the width—the length of the (maximum) line. Often the size of the slider of the scroll bar is scaled to show what proportion of information is displayed. Thus, if the slider takes up half of the length of the "slot," about half of the information is displayed. There are usually directional triangles ( ) at one or both ends of the scroll bar; clicking on them moves the slider one "unit" in the chosen direction.

(a) **(b)**

Figure 2.3. *Slider controls. (a) A volume control. (b) A scroll bar.*

Triangle Pointers

To reduce clutter, GUIs hide information until the user needs or wants to see it. A triangle pointer indicates the presence of hidden information. Clicking on the triangle reveals the information. You can see triangles in Figure 2.1 (below the Normal button) and in Figure 2.2 (at the ends of the Artist and Track text boxes). Clicking on the triangle pointer in Figure 2.1, for example, would result in Figure 2.4. Notice that now the direction of the pointer is reversed. Clicking on that triangle again hides the information.

Figure 2.4. *Audio CD GUI displaying the hidden titles and track information.*

Close

Any open window can be closed, and most GUIs give the user a way to do it with a click. On the Macintosh (see Figure 2.1), clicking on the empty box ( ) in the upper-left corner closes the window. On Windows systems (see Figure 2.2), clicking on the X button in the upper-right corner closes the window. A Windows application ends when its main (or only) window is closed, but if just subwindows are closed, the application generally keeps running.

These are just a few of the metaphors to illustrate the concept. There are many others, and beginning users should get to know them quickly. The point here is to emphasize that computer applications have many operations in common, and software designers purposely use these **consistent interfaces** so that they can take advantage of the user's knowledge and experience. Experienced users look for familiar metaphors, and when they recognize a new metaphor, they add it to their repertoire.

FITBYTE

Mac or PC? Is the Macintosh better than the PC, or vice versa? The question usually sets off a pointless argument. Listening to the battle, many wrongly decide that the other system must be very different and hard to use. In fact, the two systems are much more alike than they are different, sharing the concepts of this chapter and much, much more. Any competent user of one can quickly and easily learn to use the other. And *every* Fluent user should.

Menus

The primary way users interface with software is through menu choices. A **menu** lists the operations that the software can perform. A menu groups operations that are similar. A menu is either listed across the top of a window, in which case it is called a **pull-down** or **drop-down** menu, or it appears wherever the mouse is pointing when a mouse button is clicked, in which case it is called a **pop-up** menu. Both menu types work the same way.

Pulling down or popping up a menu reveals a list of operations. Sliding the mouse down the list causes the items to be highlighted as it passes over them, and clicking or releasing the mouse button selects a menu item. If the software has enough information, it does the operation immediately and the window closes. If not, it asks for more information by opening a new window. Answering these questions may mean more information is needed. Eventually the command will be fully specified and can be performed. You can stop the dialog at any time by simply moving your mouse pointer away from the menu or clicking on **Cancel**. That is, clicking on **Cancel** is the same as never having looked at the menu in the first place, no matter how much information has been entered.

Menus in most consumer software give more information that just the item list. They tell you which operations are available, say when more input is needed, and sometimes give you shortcuts. Refer to Figure 2.5 as you read these descriptions.

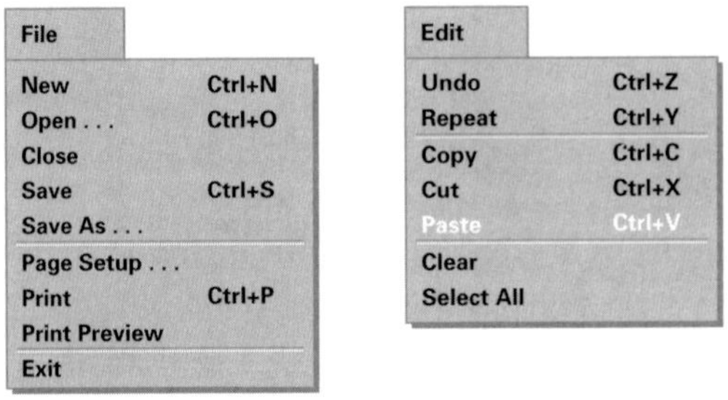

Figure 2.5. *Generic File and Edit menus.*

`Which Operations Are Available?` Unlike restaurant menus that are printed once and reused, occasionally requiring the server to explain that certain items are not available, GUI menus are created each time they are opened. So they specify exactly which operations are available. An operation may not apply in every context. For example, **Paste** is not available if nothing has been cut or copied using the **Cut** or **Copy** commands. Operations that are available are usually shown in solid color, and operations that are not available are shown in a lighter color or "gray," as shown for the **Paste** operation in Figure 2.5. Unavailable items are not highlighted as the cursor passes over them, and, of course, they cannot be selected.

`Is More Input Needed?` Some operations need further specification or more input from the user. Menu items that need further specification have a triangle pointer (▸) at the right end of the entry (see Figure 2.6). Selecting such an item pops up a menu with the additional choices. Making the selection causes the operation to be performed unless it needs still more specification. Menu items show that they need more input with an ellipsis (...) after their name. Selecting the item opens a dialog box for specifying the input. For example, in Figure 2.6, the operation **Symbol** has an ellipsis because it needs the user to specify which symbol should be inserted.

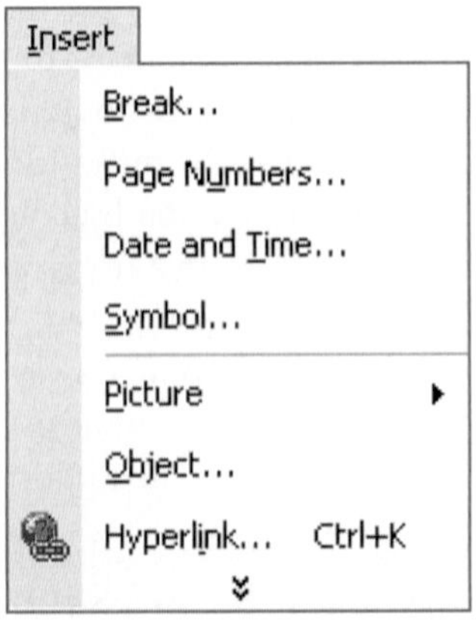

Figure 2.6. *An insert menu showing ellipses and triangle pointer.*

Is There a Shortcut? Sometimes it is more convenient to type a keyboard character than to pull down a window with the mouse. So some menu items have shortcuts. A **shortcut** is a combination of keyboard characters, shown next to the menu item, which has the same effect. For example, in Microsoft Windows, the menu choice **Copy** has the shortcut **Ctrl-C**, and **Paste** has the shortcut **Ctrl-V**. (Like the Shift key, the Control key [Ctrl] is held down while typing the associated character. Though the character is shown as a capital, you should not press the Shift key.) A **Ctrl**-plus-character combination is required so that the operating system can distinguish between the menu choice and a plain character. The Macintosh uses **Command-C** and **Command-V** for these operations—that is, the same letters. (The Command key is labeled with the "clover" symbol, [⌘].) Notice the consistency between different operating systems.

Shortcuts are not very important for a casual user, but they are extremely handy for people who use a single application intensively. The shortcut key combination can be set or changed in some systems.

Menu entries can give even more information about shortcuts. For example, Windows includes an icon as a visual cue for some operations (such as a floppy disk for **Save** and a printer for **Print**). See the Hyperlink icon in Figure 2.6.

FITBYTE

A Win for Users. The Microsoft Windows operating system includes most of the GUI metaphors developed for the Apple Macintosh, so in 1988 Apple sued Microsoft for patent infringement. Apple claimed Microsoft illegally used the "look and feel" of its Mac. The legal issues were complex, but the judge ruled that Microsoft could freely use the metaphors Apple had developed. This might not seem fair to Apple, but it was a great win for users, because it meant that GUIs could work pretty much the same on the Mac and the PC.

STANDARD GUI FUNCTIONALITY

There are some operations that almost all personal computer applications should be expected to do simply because they process information. That is, whether the information is text or spreadsheets or circuit diagrams or digitized photographs, the fact that it is information stored in a computer means that certain operations will be available in the software. We call these operations the **standard functionality**. For example, it should be possible to save the information to a file, open a file containing the saved information, create a new instance, print the file, and so on. You should expect to find these functions in almost every software application.

File Operations

To help users, the standard operations are grouped—usually with other operations specific to the application—into two menus labeled **File** and **Edit**. Generally, the operations under the **File** menu apply to whole instances of the information being processed by an application. An **instance** is one of whatever kind of information the application processes. For example, for word processors, an instance is a document; for MP3 players, an instance is a song; for photo editors, an instance is an image. So, the **File** menu items treat a whole document. The operations you can expect to see under the **File** menu and their meanings are as follows:

- **New** Create a "blank" instance of the information.
- **Open** Locate a file on the disk containing an instance of the information and read it in.
- **Close** Stop processing the current instance of the information, but keep the program available to process other instances.
- **Save** Write the current instance to the hard disk or a floppy disk, using the previous name and location.
- **Save As** Write the current instance to the hard disk or a floppy disk with a new name or location.
- **Page Setup** Specify how the printing should appear on paper; changes to the setup are rare.
- **Print** Print a copy of the current instance of the information.
- **Print Preview** Show the information as it will appear on the printout.
- **Exit** or **Quit** End the entire application.

Notice in Figure 2.5 that lines group the operations.

Edit Operations

The **Edit** operations let you make changes within an instance. They often involve selection and cursor placement. The operations are performed in a standard sequence: Select-Cut/Copy-Indicate-Paste-Revise. Selection identifies the information to be moved or copied. Selection is usually done by moving the cursor to a particular position in the instance and, while holding down either the mouse button or keyboard keys, moving the cursor to a new position. All information between the two positions is selected. Highlighting, usually color reversal, identifies the selection. If the information is to be recorded and deleted from its current position, the **Cut** command is used. The **Copy** command records but does not delete the information. Next, the new location for the information is indicated in preparation for pasting it into position, although in many applications the Indicate step is skipped and the selected information is placed in a standard position. The **Paste** command copies the information recorded in memory into the indicated position. Because a copy is made in memory, the information can be pasted again and again. Often, revisions or repositioning are required to complete the editing operation.

The operations under the **Edit** menu and their meanings are as follows:

> **Undo** Cancel the most recent editing change, returning the instance to its previous form.

> **Repeat** Apply the most recent editing change again.

> **Copy** Store a copy of the selected information in temporary storage, ready for pasting.

> **Cut** Remove the selected information and save it in temporary storage, ready for pasting.

> **Paste** Insert into the instance the information saved in the temporary storage by **Cut** or **Copy**; the information is placed either at the cursor position or at a standard position, depending on the application.

> **Clear** Delete the selected information.

> **Select All** Make the selection be the entire instance.

Notice that **Undo** is not always available because not all operations are reversible.

Because these operations are standard—available for most applications and consistent across operating systems—it is a good idea to learn their shortcuts, given in Table 2.1. (**Clear** often does not have a shortcut, to prevent accidents.) In addition, "double-click"—two (rapid) clicks with the (left) mouse button—often means **Open**.

Table 2.1 *Standard Shortcuts. These common shortcut letters for standard software operations combine with "Command" [⌘] for Mac OS or "Control" [Ctrl] for Windows.*

File Functions		**Edit Functions**	
New	N	Cut	X
Open	O	Copy	C
Save	S	Paste	V
Print	P	Select All	A
Quit	Q	Undo	Z
Redo	Y	Find	F

FITTIP

Be Selective. New users can get confused when an operation they want to use is not available (that is, it is shown in gray). Often this is because the operation needs the user to select something and nothing is selected. For example, the computer cannot perform **Copy** until you have specified what you want copied.

New Instance. Finally, notice that **New** under the **File** menu creates a "blank" **instance**. What is "blank information"? To understand this fundamental idea, notice that all information is grouped into **types**, based on its properties. So, photographs—digital images—are a type of information, and among the properties of every image is its length and width in pixels. Monthly calendars are a type of information with properties such as the number of days, year, and day of the week on which the first day falls. Text documents are another type, and the length of a document in characters is one property. Any specific piece of information—an image, month, or document—is an instance of its type. Your term paper is an instance of the document type of information; June 2003 is an instance of calendar type information. To store or process information of a given type, the computer sets up a structure to record all of the properties and store its content. A "new" or "blank" instance is simply the structure without any properties or content filled in. As an example, imagine a blank monthly calendar—seven columns of squares headed with the days of the week, a place to enter the month name, and so on. That's a **New** month, ready to receive its content. See Figure 2.7.

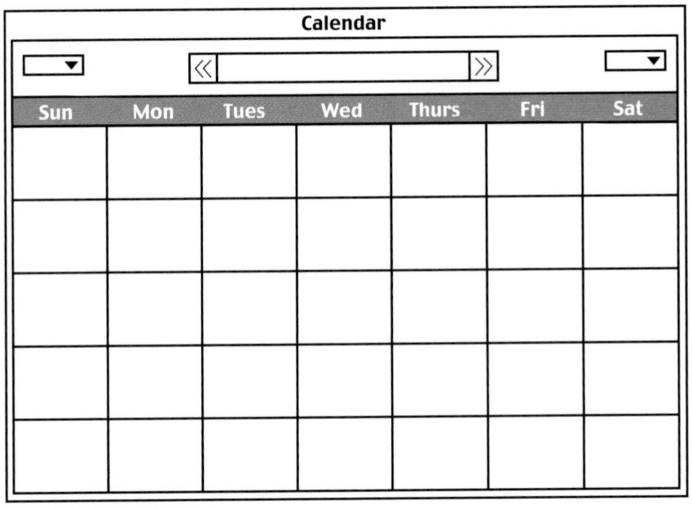

Figure 2.7. A ***New*** *monthly calendar showing one month, i.e., a "blank instance."*

Expecting Feedback

A computer is the user's assistant, ready to do whatever it is told to do. It is natural that when any assistant performs an operation, he, she, or it should report back to the person who made the request, describing the progress. This is especially true when the assistant is a computer (and therefore not very clever), because the person needs to know that the task was done and when to give the next command. So a user interface will always give the user feedback about "what's happenin'."

Feedback takes many forms, depending on what operation a user has commanded. If the operation can be performed instantaneously—that is, so fast that a person would not have to wait for it to complete—the user interface will simply indicate that the operation is complete. When the operation is an editing change, the proof that it is done is that the user can see the revision. When the effect of the command is not obvious—say, when one clicks on a button—then there is some other indication provided; for example, highlighting, shading, graying, or some other color change, or underlining.

The most common form of feedback is the indication that the computer is continuing to perform a time-consuming operation. As the operation is being carried out, the cursor is replaced with an icon such as an hourglass on Windows systems, or a wristwatch or rainbow spinner on Macintosh systems. Applications can also give the user custom feedback. A common indicator is the busy spinner, a circle divided into quarters, two white and two black, that "revolves." The file transfer application Fetch turns the cursor into a running dog. When the completion time can be predicted, applications show a meter that is "filled" as the operation progresses. Often these displays give a time estimate for when 100 percent will be reached. Finally, when an operation is processing a series of inputs, the "completion count" gives the tally of the completed instances.

FITTIP

Following Protocol. Our normal interactive use of computers alternates between our commanding the computer to do something and the computer doing it. If the computer can't finish immediately, it gives feedback showing the operation is in progress. If the computer is finished, we can see the effects of the command. Be attuned to this protocol. If nothing seems to be happening, the computer is waiting for you to give a command.

"CLICKING AROUND"

When the digerati encounter new software, they expect a consistent interface. They expect to see the basic metaphors, find standard operations, and get feedback while the application is working. Digerati automatically look for these features of the interface and begin exploring. The purpose of the exploration is to learn what the software can do.

We call the act of exploring a user interface **clicking around**. It involves noting the basic features presented by the GUI and checking each menu to see what operations are available. So, for example, on seeing a slider bar, the experienced user's response is to slide it to see what happens. On the Mac audio CD GUI shown in Figure 2.1, when we slide the bar up and down, the speaker icon above it shows—following the feedback principle—more-and-larger or fewer-and-smaller white arcs to its right. We might guess these arcs indicate more or less sound coming from the speaker. If the CD is playing, we'll also notice that the volume increases or decreases. Either way, we know that this is the volume control.

FITTIP

A Fast Start. When you're using software for the first time, practice "clicking around":

> Take a minute to study the graphics of the GUI.

> Open each window to see what operations are available.

> Determine the purpose of icons and controls.

> Have "balloon help" or "what's this?" turned on for a short explanation of icons and controls when the cursor hovers over them.

"Clicking around" can help you figure out what operations are available with the software without having to be taught or read the manual. Software manuals are notoriously dull reading and hard to use. But "clicking around" does not make them obsolete. Manuals—they're mostly online and called **Help**—are still necessary and useful. "Clicking around" works because (a) we come to the new software with technological experience, and (b) software designers try to build on what we know by using metaphors, consistent interfaces, and so forth. When the new software works like the last software did, we already "know" how to use it. The manual is usually needed only to understand advanced features or subtleties of operation. Ironically, then, the manual is most useful for experienced users, not beginners.

Returning to the audio CD GUI of Figure 2.1, when we click on the down triangle, we reveal the track list shown in Figure 2.8. As new users of this software, we may not immediately understand what the list is for, especially if the physical CD players we are familiar with do not have a play list. But, by "clicking around," we notice either that "Track 1" can be selected like text or that the cursor when moved across the text changes into the "I-beam" text editing cursor. Both indicate that we can add text. Or, perhaps, we just guess that listing off the tracks wouldn't require a large text box reading "Track 1," etc., so there must be some other purpose for it. No matter how "clicking around" cues us, we discover that we can edit the entries. We can customize the title and songs on each track to get the results shown in Figure 2.8.

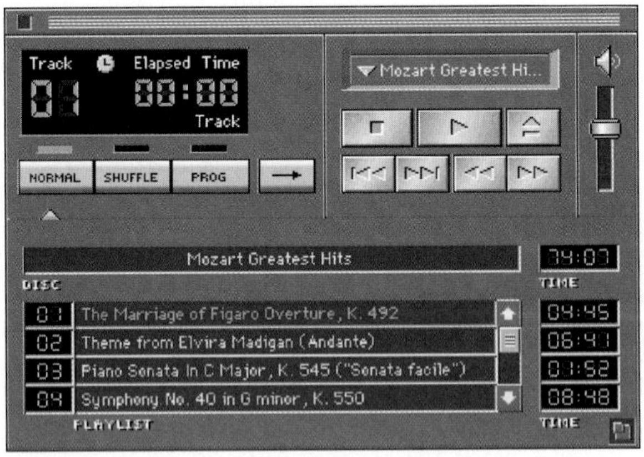

Figure 2.8. *Customized Audio CD player GUI.*

"Clicking around" is exploration and as such it may not tell us all the features of the software. We may need to experiment and test repeatedly, or give up and try again later. But the technique will usually give results. And if it doesn't, the software product designer has undoubtedly failed to some extent.

"BLAZING AWAY"

After getting to know a software application by "clicking around," the next step is to try it out. We will call this **blazing away**. The term suggests a user trying out an application assertively—exploring features even without a clear idea of what they will do. "Blazing away" can be difficult for beginning users, because they're afraid something will break if they make a mistake. A basic rule of information processing is: *Nothing will break!* If you make a mistake, the software is not going to screech and grind to a halt and then plop onto the floor with a clunk. When you make a mistake, the software may "crash" or "hang," but nothing will actually break. Most of the time, nothing happens. The software catches the mistake before doing something wrong and displays an error message. By paying attention to these messages, you can quickly learn what's legal and what isn't. Therefore, "blazing away" can be an effective way to learn about the application even if you make mistakes.

Of course, saying that nothing will break is not the same as saying that it's impossible to get into a terrible mess by "blazing away." Creating a mess is often very easy. Beginners and experts do it all the time. The difference between the two is that the experts know another basic rule of information technology: *When stuck, start over.* That may mean exiting the software. It may mean rebooting the computer. It may simply mean "undoing" a series of edits and repeating them. The simple point is that the mess has no value. It does not have to be straightened out, because it didn't cost anything to create in the first place, except for your time. Because that time will be chalked up to "experience" or "user training," there is no harm in throwing the mess out. Thus, an experienced user who is "blazing away" on a new software system will probably exit the software and restart the application over and over, without saving anything.

FITBYTE

Getting Out and Getting Back In. Starting over is so common for computer users—it's called, *getting out and getting back in*—that it's become the subject of some geek humor. A mechanical engineer, an electrical engineer, and a computer engineer are camped at Mt. Rainier. In the morning, they pack up to leave and get into their car, but it doesn't start. The ME says, "The starter motor is broken, but I can fix it," and he gets out of the car. The EE says, "No way. It's the battery, but I know what to do," and she gets out of the car. The CE says while getting out of the car, "Now, let's get back in."

Usually, we are working with new software because we have something specific we want to do, so it pays to focus on getting that task done. This means that we should "blaze away" on those operations that will contribute to completing the task. We don't have to become experts, only complete the task. Indeed, it is common for Fluent users to know only the most basic functions of the software systems they use infrequently. And, because they are not regular users, they usually forget how the applications work and have to "click around" and "blaze away" all over again.

Obviously, when you are "blazing away" and throwing away your efforts when you get into trouble, you shouldn't spend too much time creating complicated inputs. For example, if the software asks for text input and gives you space for several paragraphs, just enter "`Test text`" and go on exploring. Once you understand the system, you can focus on using the software productively.

"WATCHING OTHERS"

"Clicking around" and "blazing away" are the first steps when learning new software because we are likely to be successful using only our own observation and reasoning skills. And, if we need to know something very specific about the software, we can always read the manual or online help. However, these two extremes may not cover all of the possibilities. Complicated software systems usually have some features that are not obvious, too advanced or too specialized to the particular application to learn on our own. They are GUI features that most of us would not think to look for, and they provide capabilities that we may not even know we need.

The Shift-Select Operation

An example of such a not-so-obvious feature is the use of the Shift key in selection operations. Suppose we want to select the red and green circles of the stoplight in Figure 2.9(a) so that we can change their color, but not the yellow circle. Clicking on the red circle selects it (Figure 2.9(b)), as shown by the small boxes around the circle. Clicking on the green circle selects it and deselects the red circle (Figure 2.9(c)). Dragging the cursor across the red to the green selects all the circles (Figure 2.9(d)). So how do we select just red and green without the yellow? The problem is that when we select something (e.g., the green circle), anything that is already selected (e.g., the red circle) becomes deselected automatically. We need some way to bypass that automatic protocol.

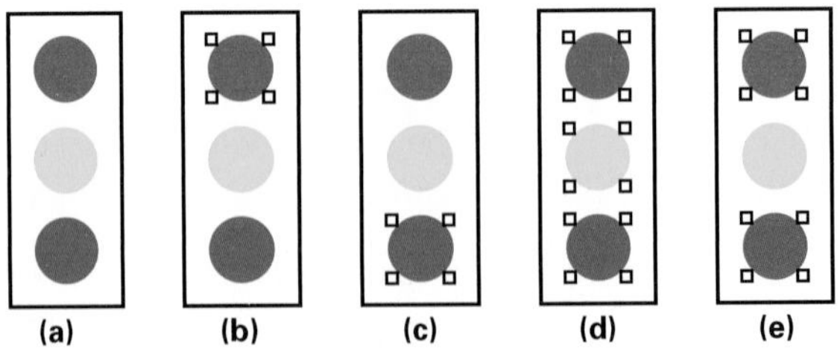

Figure 2.9. *Examples of selection.*

The solution is to select the first item (e.g., the red circle) and then hold down the Shift key while selecting the second item (e.g., the green circle). Using the Shift key during a selection has come to mean "continue selecting everything that is already selected." Because the red circle is already selected when the green circle is Shift-clicked, both become selected, completing the task.

Learning from Others

The **Shift-select** operation, meaning "continue to select the item(s) already selected," is a common feature in commercial software. Without knowing about Shift-select, however, we probably wouldn't discover it by "clicking around" or "blazing away." We would not think to try it. We might not even know that we need the feature in the first place. So how do we learn about this kind of feature?

FITTIP

Toggling Shift-select. Generally when you use Shift-select, one or more additional items will be selected, because you usually click on an unselected item. But what happens when you use Shift-select on an item that is already selected? It deselects that item only, leaving all other items selected. This property of changing to the opposite state—selecting if not selected, deselecting if selected—is called **toggling**. It is a handy feature in many situations.

We could take a course on the specific software or read the user's manual. But an alternative is to get in the habit of watching others when they use a system we are familiar with. As we watch, we should be able to follow what they are doing, though it might seem very fast. If we see an operation that we do not understand, we ask what the person did. Instead of thinking we're dummies, most people are eager to show off their know-how. Many an obscure feature, trick, or shortcut is learned while looking over the shoulder of an experienced user, so it pays to pay attention.

FITTIP

One Text Selection. Notice that for text, Shift-select usually results in the selection of all the text between the cursor's previous position and its new position; it is not usually possible to select disconnected sequences of text.

A BASIC PRINCIPLE: FORM FOLLOWS FUNCTION

A theme of this chapter is that computer systems are very much the same because software designers want users to be able to figure out how to use their systems on their own. To help this self-instruction process, designers use consistent interfaces and suggestive metaphors. Designers could be extremely creative, thinking up wild new interfaces and unusual operations. Such GUIs might be quite interesting and very cool, rather like video games with a practical purpose, but it might take years to learn and be effective with such tools. Few of us can take that much time to be productive. So instead, designers make use of the fact that consistency and familiarity help users learn quickly.

But a much deeper principle is also at work here. Designers are not just using good sense. There are limits on what information can be recorded or what operations can be computed. Many of the principles governing information and computation are too complicated for us to cover in this textbook, but these principles tell us an important fact about information technology: The task—*not* the specific software implementation—dictates the behavior of a solution. We should expect different software implementations for a task to be similar, not only because designers want them to be easy to learn, but also because they perform the same basic functions. We describe this property by the rule **form follows function**.

When we say "form follows function" in software, we do not mean that the systems look alike. Applications software from different vendors can look and feel very different even though it is for the same task. The form we are talking about is the way the basic operations of the software work.

Similar Applications Have Similar Features

So, for example, word processors all do the same sorts of things in similar ways, no matter which software company created them. The differences (and there are always differences, often big differences) are limited to the look, feel, and convenience of the software; the core functions are still the same. Word Perfect, Word, NotePad, Apple Works, Simple Text, BBText, and a dozen other systems give you a basic set of operations on text characters. They let you move a cursor around the text, select text characters, and create, copy, insert, and delete characters. They let you create an "empty" file of text—systems use the term *new*—as well as save it, name it, display it, and print it. All of those features are fundamental to text processing—they were not invented by the software companies. These features share a common functionality that determines the way all word processors work.

The same thing applies to browser programs, spreadsheet programs, drawing programs, and so on. When we learn to use an application from one software maker, we learn the core operations for that task and the features and quirks of that vendor's product. When we use software from a different vendor, we should look for and expect to recognize immediately the same basic operations. They may have a different look and feel in the second vendor's software, but they will still be there.

Take Advantage of Similarities

What's the advantage of having similarities in features and applications? Knowing that common, basic operations in programs do the same task frees us in at least three ways:

- When a new version of software is released, we should expect to learn it very quickly because it will share the core functions and many of the quirks of the earlier version.
- When we get another vendor's software for an application we know well, we should expect to use its basic features immediately.
- When we are frustrated by one vendor's software, we should try another vendor's software. Using our experience with the first system, we will learn the new system quickly. (And "voting" by buying better software should help improve overall software quality.)

In summary, because the function controls how a system works, different software implementations must share basic characteristics. You don't need to feel tied to a particular software system that you learned years ago. You should experiment with new systems; you already know the basic functional behavior.

SEARCHING TEXT USING FIND

The concept that form follows function has another advantage: It lets us learn how certain computations work without referring to any specific software system. Of course, we must focus only on the basic processing behavior rather than on the "bells and whistles" of the GUI, but learning in this way lets us apply our knowledge to any implementation. We illustrate this idea with text searching.

Many applications let us search text. Text searching, often called **Find**, is used by word processors, browsers (to look through the text of the current page), email readers, operating systems, and so on. **Find** is typically available under the **Edit** menu, because locating text is often the first step in editing it. In cases where editing doesn't make sense—say, when looking through a file structure in an operating system—**Find** may be listed under the File menu or as a "top level" application. The shortcut for Find—Command-F for Mac OS and Ctrl-F for Windows—is standard with most applications.

The things to be searched are called **tokens**. Most often, the tokens are simply the letters, numbers, and special symbols like `@` and `&` from the keyboard, which are called **characters**. However, sometimes we search for composite items, such as dates, that we want to treat as a whole. In such cases, the date would be the token, not its letters and digits. For the purposes of searching, tokens form a sequence, called the **search text**, and the tokens to be found are called the **search string**. One property of the search string is that it can be made of any tokens that could be in the text. That is, if the text can contain unprintable characters like tabs, the search string is allowed to have those characters.

How to Search

To illustrate searching, suppose the search string is "**`content`**" and the text is a sentence from Martin Luther King's "I Have a Dream" speech:

```
I have a dream that my four little children will one day
live in a nation where they will not be judged by the color
of their skin, but by the content of their character.
```

Searching begins at the beginning, or at the current cursor position if there is a cursor. Though computers use many clever ways to search text, the easiest one to understand is to think of "sliding" the search string along the text. At each position, compare to see if there is a token match. This simply means looking at corresponding token pairs to see if they are the same:

`I have a dream ...`

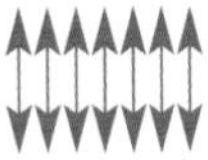

`content`

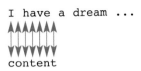

(Notice that spaces are characters, too.) If there is a match, then the process stops and you are shown the found instance. But if there is no match, slide the search string one position along and repeat:

`... by the content of ...`

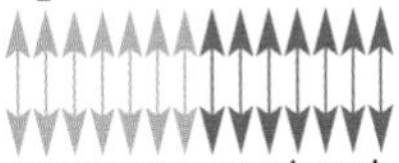

`... cccccccontent`

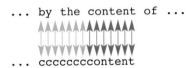

If the search string is not found when the end of the text is reached, the search stops and is unsuccessful. (Search facilities typically give you the option to continue searching from the beginning of the text if the search did not start there.) The search ends where it began when the search string is not found.

Search Complications

Character searching is easy, but to be completely successful, you should be operationally attuned. There are four things to keep in mind when you are searching: case sensitivity, hidden text, substrings, and multiword strings.

Case Sensitivity. One complication is that the characters stored in a computer are case sensitive, meaning that the uppercase letters, such as **`R`**, and lowercase letters, such as **`r`**, are different. So a match occurs only when the letters *and* the case are identical. A case-sensitive search for **`unalienable rights`** fails on Jefferson's most famous sentence from the *Declaration of Independence*:

`We hold these truths to be self-evident, that all men are created equal, that they are endowed by their Creator with certain unalienable Rights, that among these are Life, Liberty and the pursuit of Happiness.`

To find **`unalienable rights`** in a text that uses the original capitalization, we would have to ignore the case. Search tools will be case sensitive if case is important to the application. For example, word processors are usually case sensitive, but operating systems may not be. If the search can be case sensitive, the user will have the option to ignore case.

Hidden Text. Characters are stored in the computer as one continuous sequence. The characters are of two types: the keyboard characters that we type, and formatting information added by the software application. Because every system uses a different method for the formatting information and because it is usually not important to the search anyhow, we will show the formatting information here using our own invented tags.

Tags are abbreviations in paired angle brackets, such as `<Ital>`, that describe additional information about the characters (in this case, that they should be printed in italics). Tags generally come in pairs so that they can enclose text like parentheses. The second of the pair is like the first, except with a slash(/) or backslash(\) in it. (Tags will be needed often in our study, so backslash (\) will be used here for the tags of our generic application to distinguish them from later uses of slash in HTML, the OED digitization, and XML.) For example, to show that the word "Enter" should be printed in italics, a software application might represent it as `<Ital>Enter<\Ital>`. The application won't show these formatting tags to the user, but they are there.

For example, the balcony scene from *Romeo and Juliet* appears in a book of Shakespeare's plays as

> SCENE II. *Capulet's orchard.*
>
> *Enter* Romeo.
>
> *Romeo.* He jests at scars that never felt a wound.
> [*Juliet appears above at a window.*
> But, soft ! what light through yonder window breaks?
> It is the east, and Juliet is the sun.

But, this scene might be stored in the computer as follows:

```
SCENE·II.·➧<Ital>Capulet's·orchard.<\Ital>↵↵<Center><Ital>
Enter<\Ital>Romeo.<\Center>↵↵<Ital>Romeo.<\Ital>➧He·jests·
at·scars·that·never·felt·a·wound.↵<Right>[<Ital>Juliet·app
ears·above·at·a·window.<\Ital><\Right>↵But,··soft·!·what·l
ight·through·yonder·window·breaks?·↵It·is·the·east,·and·Ju
liet·is·the·sun.↵
```

The word processor's tags surround the italic text (`<Ital>`, `<\Ital>`), and the text to be centered (`<Center>`, `<\Center>`) or right-justified (`<Right>`, `<\Right>`). The user typed the other characters, and they are the ones we are interested in now. These characters include the text we see as well as formatting characters we can't see: **spaces** (·), **tabs** (➧), and **new-lines** (↵). Because these characters control formatting and have no printable form, there is no standard for how they are displayed; for example, the new-line character is the **paragraph symbol** (¶) in some systems. Users can ask that all the characters they type be displayed:

```
SCENE·II.·➧ Capulet's·orchard.↵
↵
                              Enter·Romeo.↵
↵
Romeo.➧      He·jests·at·scars·that·never·felt·a·wound.↵
                              [Juliet·appears·above·at·a·window.
↵
But,··soft·!·what·light·through·yonder·window·breaks?↵
It·is·the·east,·and·Juliet·is·the·sun.↵
```

Because the effects of the formatting are shown, it is easy to see where the non-printed formatting characters are. During a search, the software's formatting tags are generally ignored, but all of the characters typed by the user are considered. Some systems do allow tags to be searched by giving you a way to search for formatted text such as, for example, italic.

Substrings. It gets more complicated when we think of search strings as having a meaning more complex than tokens. For example, we often look for words, though the tokens are characters. The problem is that the software searches for token sequences, not the more complicated objects that we may have in mind. So searches for the search string `you` in President John Kennedy's inaugural address turn up five hits:

```
And so, my fellow Americans: ask not what
your country can do for you-ask what you
can do for your country.
My fellow citizens of the world: ask not
what America will do for you, but what
together we can do for the freedom of man.
```

Of the five hits, only three are the actual word we're looking for; the other two hits *contain* the search string. To avoid finding `your`, we could search for `·you·` because words in text are usually surrounded by spaces. However, that search discovers *no* hits in this quote because `you` doesn't appear with spaces on both sides. The five hits for `you` are followed by `r`, a dash, a new-line, an `r`, and a comma, respectively. The `you` at the end of the second line probably should have had a space between it and the new-line, but the typist left it out. Because looking only for the word `you` and avoiding `your` would mean checking for all of the possible starting and ending punctuation characters as well as blank, it is probably better to give up on finding the exact word matches and simply ignore the cases where the search string is part of another word. If the search is part of the system, such as a word processor, where words are a basic element, the ability to search for words will be available. Such cases are the same as changing the tokens from characters to words.

`Multiword Strings.` A similar problem happens with multiword search strings. The words of a multiword string are separated by spaces, but if the number of spaces in the search string is different from the number in the text being searched, no match will be found. For example, the search string

```
That's·one·small·step·for·man
```

Neil Armstrong's words on first stepping on the moon, will not be found in the quote

```
That's·one·small·step·for··man,·one·giant·leap·for·mankind.
```

because there are two spaces between **`for`** and **`man`** in the text. We could be careful about separating words by only one space when we type, but everyone makes mistakes. And more to the point, we may not have typed the text we're searching.

FITTIP

One Small Step. It is a good idea to look for single words in your search instead of longer phrases. For example, looking for **`leap`** or **`mankind`** might work because they were probably not used again in the transcript from the moon walk.

In summary, searching is the process of locating a sequence of tokens, the search string, in a longer sequence of tokens, the text. Character searches are usually limited to the characters the user has typed, though other characters may be present. User-typed characters can include nonprintable formatting characters like new-line characters. Searches look for token sequences, and the tokens (for example, characters) are often more basic than what we can build from them (for example, words). To be successful, we must think up search strings so that we find all the matches we're interested in.

EDITING TEXT USING SUBSTITUTION

Search-and-replace, also known as **substitution**, is a combination of searching and editing to make corrections in documents. The string replacing the search string is called the **replacement string**. Though substitution can apply to only one occurrence of the search string in the text, there is little advantage to using search-and-replace facility over simply searching and editing the occurrence directly. The real power of substitution comes from applying it to all occurrences of the search string. For example, if you typed "west coast" in your term paper but forgot that regions are usually capitalized, it is a simple matter to search for all occurrences of `west coast` and replace them with `West Coast`.

Because substitution can be a powerful tool that we want to study closely, we will express it in this book using a left-pointing arrow (←) between the search string and the replacement string. The capitalization example is shown as

```
west coast ← West Coast
```

Such an expression can be read, "`west coast` *is replaced by* `West Coast`" or "`West Coast` *substitutes for* `west coast`." Another example is

`Norma Jeane Mortensen` ← `Marilyn Monroe`

describing her 1946 name change when she signed her first movie contract.

We emphasize that the arrow is only a **notation** that helps us discuss substitutions in this book; it doesn't appear within the application. When using an application, a GUI is used to specify the replacement. For example, in Figure 2.7, the two text windows of the GUI correspond to the information on each side of the arrow. **Find** is the left side of the arrow, and **Replace** is the right side. We don't type the arrow in applications. It is only for our use here.

Unwanted Spaces

In the last section, we noted that multiple spaces separating words in a text complicates searching for multiword strings. Substitution can fix the "multiple spaces in a document" problem: Simply collapse double spaces to single spaces. That is, if the search string is •• and the replacement string is •, a search-and-replace over the whole document results in all pairs of spaces becoming single spaces. Expressed using the arrow notation, the "two spaces are replaced by one" substitution is

•• ← •

Of course, in some places, such as at the end of sentences, we might want double spaces. Such cases can be fixed with substitutions of the form

.• ← .••

?• ← ?••

!• ← !••

which will restore the sentence-ending double blanks after the three punctuation characters. Performing multiple changes on text is a valuable technique.

Formatting Text

One situation where substitution is particularly handy is when text is imported into a document from another source and the formatting becomes messed up. For example, suppose you find the Articles from the UN's Universal Declaration of Human Rights on the Web:

Article 1 All human beings are born free and equal in dignity and rights. They are endowed with reason and conscience and should act towards one another in a spirit of brotherhood.

Article 2 Everyone is entitled to all the rights and freedoms set forth in this Declaration, without distinction of any kind, such as race, color, sex, language, religion, political, or other opinion, national or social origin, property, birth or other status.

Furthermore, no distinction shall be made on the basis of political, jurisdictional or international status of the country or territory to which a person belongs, whether it be independent, trust, non-self-governing, or under any other limitation of sovereignty.

Article 3 Everyone has the right to life, liberty and security of person.

But when you copy the first three articles and paste them into your document, they come out looking this way:

```
        Article 1 All human beings are born free and equal in dignity and
rights. They are endowed with reason and
        conscience and should act towards one another in a spirit
of brotherhood.

        Article 2  Everyone is entitled to all the rights and freedoms set forth
 in this Declaration, without distinction of any
         kind, such as race, color, sex, language, religion, political
or other opinion, national or social origin,
        property, birth or other status.

        Furthermore, no distinction shall be made on the basis of
political, jurisdictional or international status of
        the country or territory to which a person belongs, whether
it be independent, trust, non-self-governing,
        or under any other limitation of sovereignty.

        Article 3  Everyone has the right to life, liberty and security of person.
```

The formatting is a mess. Displaying the text with the formatting characters reveals:

```
········Article·1··All·human·beings·are·born·free·and·equal·in·dignity·and·↵
rights.·They·are·endowed·with·reason·and·↵
········conscience·and·should·act·towards·one·another·in·a·spirit·↵
of·brotherhood.·↵
↵
········Article·2··Everyone·is·entitled·to·all·the·rights·and·freedoms·set·forth↵
·in·this·Declaration,·without·distinction·of·any↵
········kind,·such·as·race,·color,·sex,·language,·religion,·political·↵
or·other·opinion,·national·or·social·origin,·↵
········property,·birth·or·other·status.··↵
↵
········Furthermore,·no·distinction·shall·be·made·on·the·basis·of·↵
political,·jurisdictional·or·international·status·of·↵
········the·country·or·territory·to·which·a·person·belongs,·whether·↵
it·be·independent,·trust,·non-self-governing,·↵
········or·under·any·other·limitation·of·sovereignty.·↵
↵
········Article·3··Everyone·has·the·right·to·life,·liberty·and·security·of·person.·↵
```

We see that extra spaces and new-line characters have been inserted when we imported the text into the document.

Clearly, removing the groups of eight leading blanks is simple: replace them with nothing. When writing the substitution expression, we express "nothing" with the Greek letter epsilon, which is called the empty string; that is, the string with no letters. (Notice that epsilon is used only for writing out substitution expressions for ourselves. In the Find-and-Replace facility of an application, simply leave the replacement string empty.)

········ ← ε

Removing the leading blanks was easy because they are only at the beginning of the lines and nowhere else. Correcting the new-line characters is more of a problem.

We want to get rid of the new-lines that have been inserted within a paragraph and keep the paired new-lines that separate the paragraphs. But getting rid of single new-lines

↵ ← ε

will also get rid of *all* the new-lines! How can we keep the paired new-lines but remove the singles?

The Placeholder Technique

An easy strategy, called the **placeholder technique**, solves such problems. It begins by substituting a placeholder character for the strings we want to keep; that is, the new-line pairs. We pick # as the placeholder because it doesn't appear anywhere else in the document, but any unused character or character string will work. The substitution expression is

↵↵ ← #

Our text without the leading blanks and double new-lines now looks like this:

```
Article·1··All·human·beings·are·born·free·and·equal·in·dignity·and·↵
rights.·They·are·endowed·with·reason·and·↵
conscience·and·should·act·towards·one·another·in·a·spirit·↵
of·brotherhood.#Article·2··Everyone·is·entitled·to·all·the·rights·and·freedoms·set·forth·↵
in·this·Declaration,·without·distinction·of·any↵
kind,·such·as·race,·color,·sex,·language,·religion,·political·↵
or·other·opinion,·national·or·social·origin,·↵
property,·birth·or·other·status.#Furthermore,·no·distinction·shall·be·made·on·the·basis·of·↵
political,·jurisdictional·or·international·status·of·↵
the·country·or·territory·to·which·a·person·belongs,·whether·↵
it·be·independent,·trust,·non-self-governing,·↵
or·under·any·other·limitation·of·sovereignty.#Article·3··Everyone·has·the·right·to·life,·liberty·and·security·of·person.
```

The new-lines that remain are the ones to be removed, so we need to replace them by nothing

↵ ← ε

The resulting text has no new-line characters left:

> Article·1··All·human·beings·are·born·free·and·equal·in·dignity·and·rights.·They·are·endowed·with·reason·and·conscience·and·should·act·towards·one·another·in·a·spirit·of·brotherhood.#Article·2··Everyone·is·entitled·to·all·the·rights·and·freedoms·set·forth·in·this·Declaration,·without·distinction·of·any·kind,·such·as·race,·color,·sex,·language,·religion,·political·or·other·opinion,·national·or·social·origin,·property,·birth·or·other·status.#Furthermore,·no·distinction·shall·be·made·on·the·basis·of·political,·jurisdictional·or·international·status·of·the·country·or·territory·to·which·a·person·belongs,·whether·it·be·independent,·trust,·non-self-governing,·or·under·any·other·limitation·of·sovereignty.#Article·3··Everyone·has·the·right·to·life,·liberty·and·security·of·person.

Finally, replace the placeholder with the desired character string

← ↵↵

which gives us

> Article·1··All·human·beings·are·born·free·and·equal·in·dignity·and·rights.·They·are·endowed·with·reason·and·conscience·and·should·act·towards·one·another·in·a·spirit·of·brotherhood.·
>
> Article·2··Everyone·is·entitled·to·all·the·rights·and·freedoms·set·forth·in·this·Declaration,·without·distinction·of·any·kind,·such·as·race,·color,·sex,·language,·religion,·political·or·other·opinion,·national·or·social·origin,·property,·birth·or·other·status.··
>
> Furthermore,·no·distinction·shall·be·made·on·the·basis·of·political,·jurisdictional·or·international·status·of·the·country·or·territory·to·which·a·person·belongs,·whether·it·be·independent,·trust,·non-self-governing,·or·under·any·other·limitation·of·sovereignty.
>
> Article·3··Everyone·has·the·right·to·life,·liberty·and·security·of·person.

Except for the bold form of **Article** and its accompanying number, the result looks like the original document with only new-line pairs and no new-line singletons. The final replacements

Article 1 ← **Article 1**

Article 2 ← **Article 2**

Article 3 ← **Article 3**

completes the task.

To summarize, the placeholder technique is used to remove short search strings that are part of longer strings that we want to keep. If we were to remove the short strings directly, we'd trash the longer strings. The idea is to convert the longer strings into the placeholder temporarily. Of course, a single placeholder character can replace the long strings because all we're keeping track of is the position of the longer string. With the longer strings replaced by the placeholder, it is safe to remove the short strings. Once they are gone, the longer string can replace the placeholder. The substitution expressions

LongStringsContainingInstance(s)OfAShortString ← *Placeholder*

ShortString ← ε

Placeholder ← *LongStringsContainingInstance(s)OfAShortString*

summarize the idea.

THINKING ABOUT INFORMATION TECHNOLOGY ABSTRACTLY

We began this chapter promising to reveal some secrets known to expert computer users. And we have. Now, it is not so miraculous that the digerati appear to know how to use software they have never seen before.

We observed that application software systems must behave in ways governed by the functions they provide. Form follows function was our description of it. So, creating and editing keyboard input requires a small set of basic operations that all editing and word processing systems must have. The same applies to browsers, to spreadsheets, and so forth. This means that when we learn specific software for a specific task, we are learning both its core operations, common to all software for that task, as well as the "bells and whistles" of its GUI. So, once we've learned one vendor's software for an application, we should expect to be able to use another company's application without much difficulty. Our introduction to the core ideas of searching and substitution illustrated the point: We learned the basics without needing to look at any specific software. In addition, we learned some useful skills, such as the placeholder technique.

But the chapter's topic really concerns information technology more abstractly. We considered how people learn technology generally, and information technology in particular. Because no one is born knowing how to use technology, users must learn each new tool. The best case is when the training is simply a user's previous experience with technology. In such cases, the technology operates exactly the way users expect. Software designers try for this by using familiar features when they design computer–human interfaces and applications. They use consistent interfaces, recognizable metaphors, standard operations, and so on. So one way to explore new software is to "click around," learning it by applying what we already know, and by not being afraid to make mistakes. Thinking from the abstract to the specific guided us to using technology well. The larger lesson of this chapter, then, is to think about information technology abstractly, which is key to becoming a member of the digerati.

CHECKLIST>>

As you become a member of the digerati, you can think about technology abstractly, and be more likely to ask questions such as

- *"What do I have to learn about this software to do my task?"*
- *"What does the designer of this software expect me to know?"*

- *"What does the designer expect me to do?"*
- *"What metaphor is the software showing me?"*
- *"What additional information does this software need to do its task?"*
- *"Have I seen these operations in other software?"*

CHECKLIST>>

When you think about information technology in terms of your personal or workplace needs, you may ask questions such as

- *"Is there information technology that I am not now using that could help me with my task?"*
- *"Am I more or less productive using this technological solution for my task?"*
- *"Can I customize the technology I'm using to make myself more productive?"*
- *"Have I assessed my uses of information technology recently?"*

These and similar questions can help you use technology more effectively. Information technology, being a means rather than an end, should be continually assessed to ensure that it is fulfilling your needs as the technology changes and evolves.

SUMMARY

This chapter began by exploring how people learn to use technology. The conclusion was that people must either be taught technology or figure it out on their own. We can figure out software because designers use consistent interfaces, suggestive metaphors, standard functionality, and so on. We applied our previous experience to learn new applications, just like the digerati. We admired how the "perfect GUI" was perfectly intuitive. We learned that in computer software, nothing will break when we make mistakes, so we should explore a new application by "clicking around." We should also try it out by "blazing away," knowing that we will mess up; when we do we will throw away our work by exiting and starting over—getting out and getting back in.

Exploration is not the only way to learn, however. Some functions of a new application, like Shift-select, are not obvious, so we should watch other users and ask questions. You're not a dummy if you ask, only if you don't. We also learned that *form follows function*, so although software systems for a given task might have different icons and colors, there are basic operations that they must have in common. Thus, if we look past the "flash" of the GUI to these core operations, we can easily learn to use another manufacturer's software for the task. To demonstrate this commonality, we studied searching and substitution, which are available with many applications. As part of our discussion on editing text, we used the placeholder technique. Finally, we discussed thinking abstractly about technology. We applied general principles and ideas so that we would come to know what the digerati know and become more expert users.

EXERCISES

Multiple Choice

1. Experienced computer users are known as:
   A. digerati
   B. literati
   C. mazzerati
   D. culturati
2. What is a GUI?
   A. graphical update identification
   B. general user identification
   C. graphical user interface
   D. general update interface
3. Software designers use analogies to help a user understand software because doing so:
   A. makes it easier for the user to learn and use the software
   B. makes the software more popular
   C. is required by law
   D. more than one of the above
4. An example of a metaphor is:
   A. The player played with the heart of a lion.
   B. The silence was deafening.
   C. The computer played chess as well as the best humans.
   D. all of the above
5. Which of the following is not a common computer metaphor?
   A. buttons
   B. door handles
   C. menus
   D. sliders
6. A slider control is used for selecting:
   A. one of several options
   B. one or more of several options
   C. within a continuous range of options
   D. one or more items from a list
7. In Windows, closing a subwindow:
   A. is not allowed
   B. leaves the application running
   C. quits the application
   D. automatically saves your file

8. A dialog will open when a menu has a(n) ______ in it.
   A. shortcut
   B. ellipsis
   C. check mark
   D. separator
9. Which of the menu options in Figure 2.5 will always open a dialog?
   A. Open and Print
   B. File and Edit
   C. Clear and Exit
   D. Paste
10. Menu options that are unavailable:
   A. have a check mark by them
   B. are gray
   C. have a line through them
   D. are hidden

Short Answer

1. ______ is the word used to describe people who understand digital technology.
2. GUI stands for ______.
3. Software designers help users understand their software through the use of ______.
4. A ______ is a figure of speech where one object is likened to another.
5. ______ are used to indicate there is information available that is usually hidden.
6. Open, New, Close, and Save can usually be found in the ______ menu.
7. To avoid cluttering the screen with commands, software designers put most of their commands in ______.
8. Undo, Cut, Copy, and Paste can usually be found in the ______ menu.
9. The online manual can usually be found in the ______ menu.
10. Menus that can show up anywhere on the screen are called ______.
11. Another name for a pull-down menu is a ______.
12. When the computer needs more information from the user before it completes an action, it gets the information via a ______.
13. Menus that are unavailable are generally colored ______.
14. Menu options that will open a dialog display can be identified because they contain a(n) ______.
15. The clover-shaped shortcut key on a Macintosh is called the ______ key.

Exercises

1. Discuss the advantages of a consistent interface. Look at it from the consumer's view and from the developer's view.
2. List the technology tools you can typically use without reading the owner's manual.
3. What are the two keys to success with information technology?
4. Match the buttons on the two CD interfaces in Figures 2.1 and 2.2. Label the commands. Speculate on how the features found on only one are implemented on the other.
5. What happens when we apply the ** ← * replacement to *****? Try this out with your text editor. How many times did it find and replace? How many were left? Explain how this process worked.
6. Describe the similarities and differences between the Windows CD Player and the Windows Media Player. If you have a Mac, use the CD Player and the QuickTime Player.
7. Using Lincoln's Gettysburg Address, what appears more often, "that" or "here"?
8. How many times does the word "the" appear in Lincoln's Gettysburg Address? How many times do the letters "the" appear together in it?

chapter

3 MAKING THE CONNECTION

The Basics of Networking

learning objectives

- > Describe changes that networked computers have brought to society
- > Tell whether a communication technology (Internet, radio, LAN, etc.) is synchronous or asynchronous, broadcast or point-to-point
- > Explain the roles of Internet addresses, domain names, and DNS servers in networking
- > Distinguish between types of protocols (TCP/IP and Ethernet)
- > Describe how computers are interconnected by an ISP; by a LAN
- > Distinguish between the Internet and the World Wide Web

The presence of humans in a system containing high-speed electronic and high-speed accurate communications is quite inhibiting.

—STUART LUMAN SEATON, 1958

COMPUTERS alone are useful. Computers connected together are even more useful. Proof of this came dramatically in the mid-1990s when the Internet, long available to researchers, became generally available to the public. The **Internet** is the totality of all the wires, fibers, switches, routers, satellite links, and other hardware for transporting information between addressed computers, as shown in Figure 3.1. For the first time, people could conveniently and inexpensively connect their computers to the Internet and thereby connect to all other computers attached to the Internet. They could send email and surf the Web from home. This convenient access to volumes of information, eCommerce, chatrooms, and other capabilities greatly expanded the benefits people derived from computers.

This chapter begins by considering how connecting computers together with the Internet has changed the world. We identify five of the most significant effects of the Internet—not all of them clearly good. After we've looked at the impact of the Internet, we define some communication terms. These will help you compare the Internet with other forms of communication. Some topics are designed to give you a sense of how the Internet works without the technical details: naming computers, packets, the TCP/IP and Ethernet protocols, and connecting your computer to the Internet. Next, the World Wide Web and file structures are explained in preparation for Chapter 4 on HTML.

NETWORKED COMPUTERS CHANGE OUR LIVES

A skeptic might wonder whether all of the excitement and frenzy surrounding the Internet is anything more than hype. After all, for a hundred years, average citizens in developed countries have had access to great repositories of information in libraries, have been able to communicate with each other via telephones or the post, and have enjoyed the benefits of retail commerce. Wire services brought the news from distant locales, and broadcast media such as newspapers, radio, and television conveyed that news widely. Has anything actually changed? Very definitely.

The interconnection of computers—networking—has brought us the Information Age and with it profound changes. Now:

> Nowhere is remote.

> People are more interconnected.

> Social relationships are changing.

> English is becoming a universal language.

> Freedom of speech and of assembly have expanded.

Consider each change in detail.

Nowhere Is Remote

In the past, centers of commerce, learning, and government justly claimed a difference from more remote places in the world based on the ready access to information. But today, because of information technology, nowhere is remote any longer. For instance, comparing a person's access to information in New York, New York to Unalakleet, Alaska, we see few differences. In the past, to find a Prague subway map for vacation planning, a New Yorker might have gone to the New York City Public Library, whereas someone from Unalakleet may have been out of luck. But now, both places have the same access to information, because the best, up-to-date map is available online from the Prague subway system. Similarly, to get a share price from the NASDAQ stock exchange, both places are equal. And to find out what people think "about them Mets," it's possible either to listen to NYC radio online or join a sports chatroom of other fans.

Differences remain, of course. For example, the entire holdings of the New York City Public Library will not soon be online, so scholars and others will continue to visit the library in person. But the vast amount of new information people want or need is available electronically from the nearest Internet connection. It's as easy to read the *Sydney Morning Herald* in Sydney, Nova Scotia, as it is in Sydney, New South Wales, and unlike distributing a physical copy of the paper, readers can peruse it electronically at the same time on both sides of the world.

It may be that the claim "nowhere is remote" looks at the question backwards. Perhaps everywhere is remote in the sense of being the same distance from most information sources. For example, in many companies, information workers can choose to telecommute. Though they may be at home, physically remote from their employer, they are electronically at the same distance as if sitting in the office. Telecommuting is obviously attractive to the employee, but the employer may see advantages, too. A worker may be more productive at home in a bathrobe and fuzzy slippers than at the office choked by a power tie and fuming from a terrible commute. One result of telecommuting may be that people will choose to live in remote, picturesque places. That might ease the population burden on already congested cities, but raise the burden in places like Port Douglas, Australia; Banff, Canada; or Hania, Greece.

People Are More Interconnected

Though there may be no studies to prove it, the anecdotal evidence is that people keep in closer, more frequent contact with friends and family across the country or in foreign lands via the Internet than by telephone or mail. The advantages are that email generally costs less than the telephone and is faster than the postal mail. You can email friends or family to find out what they are having for dinner, if you're interested. Such a simple question might not be worth a phone call, especially because time differences complicate long-distance telephone communication—both parties must be connected simultaneously. The Internet gives everyone the choice of treating email as a message by reading it later or as a conversation by being online and answering it immediately.

The Web also provides the opportunity for people to meet passively. By creating a Web page describing our interests, hobbies, free-time activities, and other descriptive information, we are publishing an "advertisement" for ourselves that can be read from anywhere in the world. Most important, the Web page can be seen by "Web search engines"—programs that cruise the Internet, locating the pages on which various descriptive terms appear. Suppose you create a Web page about growing bonsai trees from *Sequoia sempervirens*. If someone else also interested in Sequoia bonsai asks a Web search engine to look for pages containing information about that topic, your page may be found. The searcher can contact you, and a friendship or collaboration based on this shared interest may blossom. In this way, people can become acquainted with others sharing similar interests without ever meeting face-to-face. The benefit of passive meeting is that it can be based on extremely narrow interests or specialties that would not support an organization or society. And associations of this form can form rapidly—a whole interest group could form around an event that is unfolding, such as a typhoon or election.

Social Interactions Are Changing

Not all aspects of information technology can be considered good. A possible dark side is that time spent in using a computer displaces other activities—the displacement effect. If people spend time with a computer surfing the Web, playing games, or engaging in other activities that displace in-person social interaction, the outcome may be less desirable. Recent studies from Carnegie-Mellon and Stanford Universities seem to show a decline in social interactions after people become intensive computer users. Claims were even made for an "increase in depression." The topic is complicated and further study is needed, but the displacement effect of using computers is certainly a potential risk.

As an example of how the problem can quickly become complicated, consider that a person's time online might be spent participating in chatrooms or sending email to friends and family. Isn't this simply a modern form of in-person social interaction? Possibly, but possibly not. Maybe we know our electronic acquaintances only superficially compared to our in-the-flesh friends. On the other hand, maybe we "open up" and speak more candidly to someone we only know anonymously. Also, the possibility of keeping in close electronic contact with family or meeting others passively who have similar interests may be more rewarding than meeting with our face-to-face acquaintances, which are limited to people who are physically nearby. The Internet is changing people's social interactions, but the long-term effects are still to be seen.

English Is Becoming a Universal Language

Since the end of World War II, there have been growing indications that English may become the universal language. Many reasons exist for this shift, including the huge influence of U.S. movies and pop culture, and the dominance of science and technology in English-speaking countries since that war. English is not yet the universal language, of course, but it is the leading candidate. IT is giving it a huge push.

Though Microsoft Windows is available in German and Japanese editions, much software is available only in English; and the non-English options are limited to only a few major languages. Still, the driving force behind people's desire to read and understand English is not software, but the World Wide Web. Most Web pages are in English, and when they are multilingual, English is usually among the choices. English is also widely used for eCommerce. The bias toward English encourages Web pages in English, reinforcing English's status as a universal language. People fluent in English have greater access to IT's benefits. Of course, computer translation can convert from English to another language, but so far these translations have not been very faithful, and they are available for only a few widely spoken languages. There will likely be no computer translators for most of the world's languages.

Interestingly, it seems that adopting English as a universal language for IT could have little effect on other languages. In non-English-speaking countries, English would be taught as a second language and the population would be bilingual. This is already the case in many countries. There is no real threat to the native language because it is used in most other aspects of daily life.

Freedom of Speech and of Assembly Have Expanded

Creating a Web page is a means of identifying ourselves. We can state who we are (or think we are) and what we believe in. The Web page can be viewed from anywhere and located by a Web search engine. Most important, it is not subject to any editorial oversight or significant restrictions. Such an unfettered, worldwide communication medium presents an unprecedented degree of freedom of speech, previously available only to those who owned broadcast channels or printing presses. It allows political and artistic expression (within the limits of the medium), and any form of self-promotion (including shameless). As with freedoms generally, free speech on the World Wide Web can be abused, leading to hate propaganda or instructions on building bombs. The opportunity for *unmediated* expression to such a large audience, however, would seem to be a new benefit of information technology and the Internet.

Along with free speech, the Internet also promotes freer association. Like-minded people can find each other by searching the Web. Once connected, they can communicate by email or form chatrooms and newsgroups. They are electronically close regardless of how far apart they are in physical space. Unlike ham radio, which relies on broadcast to connect a group, email can be private. Electronic assembly is unique in overcoming the problems of place and time for bringing people together.

There are other benefits—sensitive information on topics like contraception or religion can be accessed privately—but the five changes just described surely establish that the wonders of the Internet are not simply hype.

FITBYTE

Internet. The present-day Internet is the commercial descendant of the ARPANET, developed for the U.S. Department of Defense Advanced Research Projects Agency (DARPA). The ARPANET sent its first messages in 1969.

COMMUNICATION TYPES: SOME COMPARISONS

To understand the Internet, it is necessary to explain some basic vocabulary of communication.

Communication between two entities, be they people or computers, can be separated into two broad classes: synchronous and asynchronous. **Synchronous communication** requires that both the sender and the receiver are active at the same time. A telephone conversation is an example of synchronous communication. Both people in the conversation must perform one of the two parts of the communication—sending (talking) or receiving (listening)—at the same time. In **asynchronous communication**, the sending and the receiving occur at different times. A postcard is an example of asynchronous communication because it is written at one time and read sometime later. An answering machine or voice mail make telephones asynchronous in the sense that the caller leaves a message that the receiver listens to later. Email is also asynchronous.

FITBYTE

Spamming. Spam is unsolicited email. Spam is often sent by people promoting get-rich-quick schemes. Spam email once had subject lines like "Earn Big $$$," but spammers have become more subtle, choosing innocent subject lines to snare readers. The term is widely believed to derive from a *Monty Python* skit in which the word "spam" was chanted by Vikings to drown out restaurant conversation; that is, unwanted input harms legitimate communication. State legislatures have attempted to outlaw spam.

Another property of communication concerns the number of receivers. A single sender and many receivers is **broadcast communication**. Radio and television are examples of broadcast communication, of course. The term **multicast** is also used when there are many receivers, but the intended recipients are not the whole population. Magazines, often specialized to a topic, are an example of multicast communication. The opposite of broadcasting and multicasting is **point-to-point communication**. Telephone communication is point-to-point. The property of broadcast *versus* point-to-point communication is separate from the property of synchronous *versus* asynchronous communication.

A fundamental feature of the Internet is that it provides a general communication "fabric" linking all computers connected to it. (See Figure 3.1.) That is, the computers and the network become a single medium that can be applied in many ways to produce alternatives to established forms of communication The Internet's point-to-point asynchronous communication is like the postal system, for example, but at electronic speeds. In fact, the Internet is fast enough to mimic synchronous communication. Two or more people can have a conversation by the rapid exchange of asynchronous messages. Instant messaging is an example. So the Internet can be used like a phone. (With special software, an Internet-connected computer can *be* a phone, too.) Also, multicasting is possible, enabling small to modest-size groups to communicate via chatrooms. Finally, because it is possible to post a Web page that can be accessed by anyone, the Internet offers a form of broadcasting that compares with radio or television. The Internet is truly a universal communications medium.

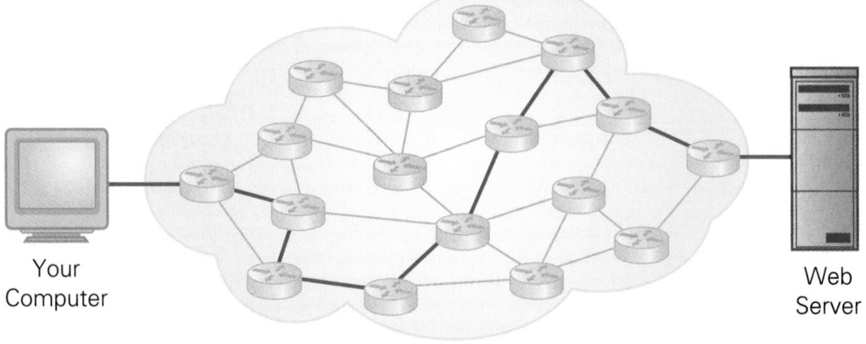

Figure 3.1. *A diagram of the Internet.*

The Internet also becomes more effective with each additional computer added to it. That is, if *x* computers are already attached to the Internet, adding one more computer results in *x* potential new connections—that computer with each of the original machines.

THE MEDIUM OF THE MESSAGE

How does the Internet transmit information such as email messages and Web pages? Complex and sophisticated technologies are used to make today's Internet work, but the basic idea is extremely simple.

The Name Game of Computer Addresses

To begin, remember that the Internet uses point-to-point communication. When anything is sent point-to-point—a phone conversation, a letter, or furniture—the destination address is required.

IP Addresses. Each computer connected to the Internet is given a unique address called its **IP address**, short for **Internet Protocol Address**. An IP address is a series of four numbers separated by dots, as shown in Figure 3.2. For example, the IP address of the computer on which I am typing this sentence is `128.95.1.207`, and the machine to which my email is usually sent is `128.95.1.4`. Although the range of each of these numbers (0–255) allows for billions of Internet addresses, IP addresses are actually in short supply.

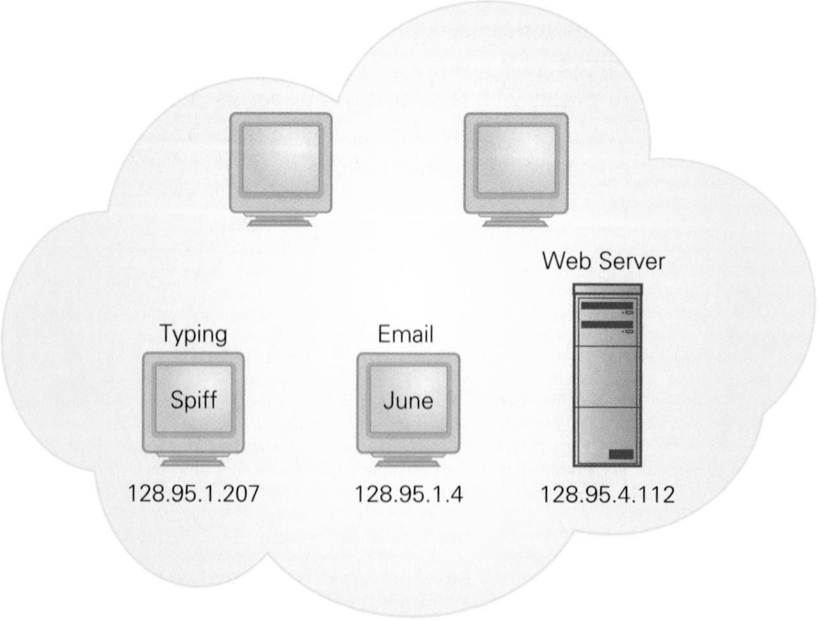

Figure 3.2. *Computers connected to the Internet are given IP addresses.*

FITBYTE

Change of Address. Since the 1970s we've used Internet Protocol Version 4 (IPv4). IPv4 specifies 4-byte IP-addresses, plenty for the days when only about 200 computers were networked. Now about 200 million computers are networked, motivating development of Internet Protocol Version 6 (IPv6). IPv6 specifies 16 byte IP-addresses, solving the IP-address problem for good.

Domain Names. Suppose we needed to know the four-number IP addresses of our friends' computers in order to send them email; the process would be very annoying and uncivilized. Instead, the Internet uses human-readable symbolic names for computers that are based on a hierarchy of *domains*. A **domain** is a related group of networked computers. For example, the name of my computer is `spiff.cs.washington.edu`, which reveals its domain membership by its structure. Pulling apart the name, my computer (`spiff`) is a member of the Computer Science and Engineering Department domain (`cs`), which is part of the University of Washington domain (`washington`), which is part of the educational domain (`edu`), as shown in Figure 3.3(a) and (b). This is a hierarchy of domains because each is a member of the next larger domain. Another of my computers, `tracer.cs.washington.edu`, has a name with a similar structure, so it is apparently a member of the same domain. Other departments at the University of Washington, such as Astronomy (`astro.washington.edu`), have names that are peers of `cs` (on the same level) within the `washington` domain, and other schools (for example, `princeton.edu`) have names that are peers with `washington` within the `edu` domain. These names are symbolic and meaningful, making them easier to read than numbers, and being arranged in a hierarchy makes them easier to remember.

FITBYTE

Where It's @. Email addresses, like domain names, have a structure. For example: `president@whitehouse.gov`. The portion to the right of the `@` sign is the **destination address**, and it has domain structure. It is processed by the sending computer(s). The information to the left of the `@` sign is the **user ID**, and it is processed by the receiving computer.

DNS Servers. How do the convenient domain names like `spiff.cs.washington.edu` get converted into the IP addresses (for example, `128.95.1.207`) that computers need? The **Domain Name System** (**DNS**) translates the hierarchical, human-readable names into the four-number IP addresses, as shown in Figure 3.4. This allows both people and computers to use their preferred scheme. Every Internet host (a computer connected to the Internet) knows the IP address of its nearest **Domain Name System server**, a computer that keeps a list of the symbolic names and the corresponding IP addresses. Whenever you use the hierarchical symbolic name to send information to some destination, your computer asks the DNS server to look up the corresponding IP address. It then uses that IP address to send the information. The DNS servers keep their information up to date dynamically (that is, on-the-fly), making the existence of IP addresses almost invisible to users.

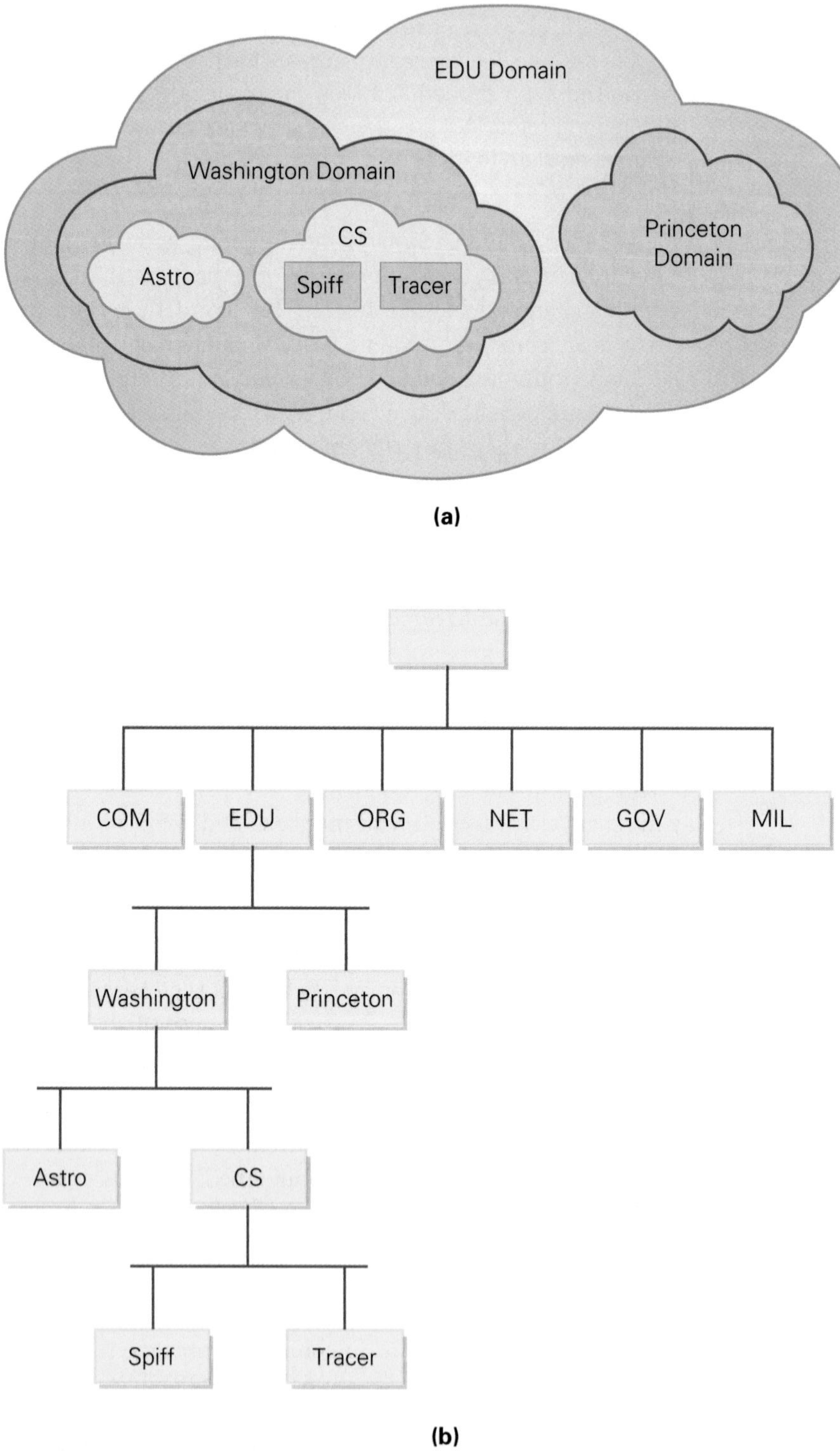

Figure 3.3. *Two diagrams of domain heirarchy.*

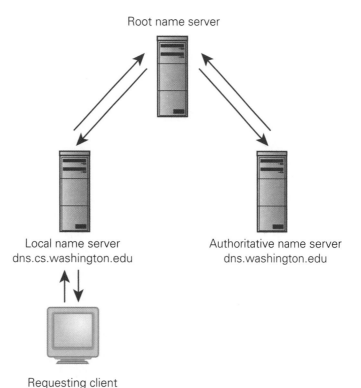

Figure 3.4. *Hosts like Spiff make requests to a local DNS server. If it knows the IP-address it replies, but if not, it asks one of 13 Root name servers. They usually know, but if not they ask the Authoritative name server. When the answer returns, all servers update their records.*

`Top-level Domains.` The `.edu` domain for educational institutions is one of several **top-level domain** names. With `.edu` the following is the original set:

- `.com` for commercial enterprises
- `.org` for organizations
- `.net` for networks
- `.mil` for the military
- `.gov` for government agencies

This set of top-level domains has recently been expanded. The original domains all apply to organizations in the United States. There is also a set of mnemonic two-letter country designators, such as `.ca` (Canada), `.uk` (United Kingdom), `.fr` (France), `.de` (Germany, as in Deutschland), `.es` (Spain, as in España), `.us` (United States), and so on. (See Table 3.1 for a complete list.) These allow domain names to be grouped by their country of origin. The period, always pronounced *dot*, simply separates the levels of the domains, and was chosen to be easy to type and say.

Table 3.1. *Top-level Country Domain Abbreviations*

AF	Afghanistan
AL	Albania
DZ	Algeria
AS	American Samoa
AD	Andorra
AO	Angola
AI	Anguilla
AQ	Antarctica
AG	Antigua & Barbuda
AR	Argentina
AM	Armenia
AW	Aruba
AU	Australia
AT	Austria
AZ	Azerbaijan
BS	Bahamas
BH	Bahrain
BD	Bangladesh
BB	Barbados
BY	Belarus
BE	Belgium
BZ	Belize
BJ	Benin
BM	Bermuda
BT	Bhutan
BO	Bolivia
BA	Bosnia & Herzegovina
BW	Botswana
BV	Bouvet Island
BR	Brazil
IO	British Indian Ocean Territory
BN	Brunei Darussalam
BG	Bulgaria
BF	Burkina Faso
BI	Burundi
KH	Cambodia
CM	Cameroon
CA	Canada
CV	Cape Verde
KY	Cayman Islands
CF	Central African Republic
TD	Chad
CL	Chile
CN	China
CX	Christmas Island
CC	Cocos (Keeling) Islands
CO	Colombia
KM	Comoros
CG	Congo
CK	Cook Islands
CR	Costa Rica
CI	Cote d'Ivoire
HR	Croatia (local name: Hrvatska)
CU	Cuba
CY	Cyprus
CZ	Czech Republic
DK	Denmark
DJ	Djibouti
DM	Dominica
DO	Dominican Republic
TP	East Timor
EC	Ecuador
EG	Egypt
SV	El Salvador
GQ	Equatorial Guinea
ER	Eritrea
EE	Estonia
ET	Ethiopia
FK	Falkland Islands (Malvinas)
FO	Faroe Islands
FJ	Fiji
FI	Finland
FR	France
FX	France, Metropolitan
GF	French Guiana
PF	French Polynesia
TF	French Southern Territories
GA	Gabon
GM	Gambia
GE	Georgia
DE	Germany
GH	Ghana
GI	Gibraltar
GR	Greece
GL	Greenland
GD	Grenada
GP	Guadeloupe
GU	Guam
GT	Guatemala
GN	Guinea
GW	Guinea-Bissau
GY	Guyana
HT	Haiti
HM	Heard & McDonald Islands
HN	Honduras
HK	Hong Kong
HU	Hungary
IS	Iceland
IN	India
ID	Indonesia
IR	Iran (Islamic Republic of)
IQ	Iraq
IE	Ireland
IL	Israel
IT	Italy
JM	Jamaica
JP	Japan
JO	Jordan
KZ	Kazakhstan
KE	Kenya
KI	Kiribati
KP	Korea, Democratic People's Republic of
KR	Korea, Republic of
KW	Kuwait
KG	Kyrgyzstan
LA	Lao People's Democratic Republic
LV	Latvia
LB	Lebanon
LS	Lesotho
LR	Liberia
LY	Libyan Arab Jamahiriya
LI	Liechtenstein
LT	Lithuania
LU	Luxembourg
MO	Macau
MK	Macedonia, the former Yugoslav Republic of
MG	Madagascar
MW	Malawi
MY	Malaysia
MV	Maldives
ML	Mali
MT	Malta
MH	Marshall Islands
MQ	Martinique
MR	Mauritania
MU	Mauritius
YT	Mayotte
MX	Mexico
FM	Micronesia
MD	Moldova, Republic of
MC	Monaco
MN	Mongolia
MS	Montserrat
MA	Morocco
MZ	Mozambique
MM	Myanmar
NA	Namibia
NR	Nauru
NP	Nepal
NL	Netherlands
NC	New Caledonia
NZ	New Zealand
NI	Nicaragua
NE	Niger
NG	Nigeria
NU	Niue
NF	Norfolk Island
MP	Northern Mariana Islands
NO	Norway
OM	Oman
PK	Pakistan
PW	Palau
PA	Panama
PG	Papua New Guinea
PY	Paraguay
PE	Peru
PH	Philippines
PN	Pitcairn
PL	Poland
PT	Portugal
PR	Puerto Rico
QA	Qatar
RE	Reunion
RO	Romania
RU	Russian Federation
RW	Rwanda
KN	Saint Kitts & Nevis
LC	Saint Lucia
VC	Saint Vincent & the Grenadines
WS	Samoa
SM	San Marino
ST	Sao Tome & Principe
SA	Saudi Arabia
SN	Senegal
SC	Seychelles
SL	Sierra Leone
SG	Singapore
SK	Slovakia (Slovak Republic)
SI	Slovenia
SB	Solomon Islands
SO	Somalia
ZA	South Africa
GS	South Georgia & South Sandwiches
ES	Spain
LK	Sri Lanka
SH	St. Helena
PM	St. Pierre & Miquelon
SD	Sudan
SR	Suriname
SJ	Svalbard & Jan Mayen Islands
SZ	Swaziland
SE	Sweden
CH	Switzerland
SY	Syrian Arab Republic
TW	Taiwan, Province of China
TJ	Tajikistan
TZ	Tanzania, United Republic of
TH	Thailand
TG	Togo
TK	Tokelau
TO	Tonga
TT	Trinidad & Tobago
TN	Tunisia
TR	Turkey
TM	Turkmenistan
TC	Turks & Caicos Islands
TV	Tuvalu
UG	Uganda
UA	Ukraine
AE	United Arab Emirates
GB	United Kingdom
US	United States
UM	United States Minor Outlying Islands
UY	Uruguay
UZ	Uzbekistan
VU	Vanuatu
VA	Vatican City State
VE	Venezuela
VN	Vietnam
VG	Virgin Islands
VI	Virgin Islands (U.S.)
WF	Wallis & Futuna Islands
EH	Western Sahara
YE	Yemen
YU	Yugoslavia
ZR	Zaire
ZM	Zambia
ZW	Zimbabwe

Following Protocol

Having figured out how a computer addresses other computers to send them information, we still need to describe how the information is actually sent. The sending process uses **Transmission Control Protocol/Internet Protocol** or **TCP/IP**. It sounds technical, and is. But the concept is easy to understand.

TCP/IP Postcard Analogy. To explain how TCP/IP works, we repeat an analogy used by Vincent Cerf, one of the pioneers of IP: Sending a message, say, an email message, is like sending your novel from Tahiti to your publisher in New York City using only postcards. How could you do that? Begin by breaking up the novel into small units, only a few sentences long, so that each unit fits on a postcard. Number each postcard to indicate where in the sequence of the novel the sentences belong, and write the publisher's address on each. As you complete the postcards, drop them into a mailbox. The postal service in Tahiti will send them to the publisher (eventually), but the cards will not be kept together, nor will they all take the same route to the publisher. Some postcards may go west, via Hong Kong, when an airplane that can carry mail is headed in that direction. Others may go east, via Los Angeles, when there is an aircraft headed in that direction. From Hong Kong and Los Angeles, there are multiple routes to New York City. Eventually the postcards arrive at the publisher, who uses the numbers to put the postcards in order and reconstruct the novel, as shown in Figure 3.5.

#1
Chapter 1:
It was a dark
and stormy night.
Rain pelted the
glass as Sir
Bulwer-Lytton
dozed
Great Books
1830 1st Ave
New York, NY
USA

1
2
3
4
5
Where's
#17?

Figure 3.5. The TCP/IP postcard analogy.

Cerf's postcard analogy makes the concept of TCP/IP clear. Sending any amount of information, including a whole novel, can be done by breaking it into a sequence of small fixed-size units. An **IP packet**, like the postcard, has space for the unit, a destination IP address, and a sequence number. IP packets are filled in order and assigned sequence numbers. The packets are sent over the Internet one at a time using whatever route is available, as shown in Figure 3.6. At the destination, they are reordered by sequence number to assemble the information.

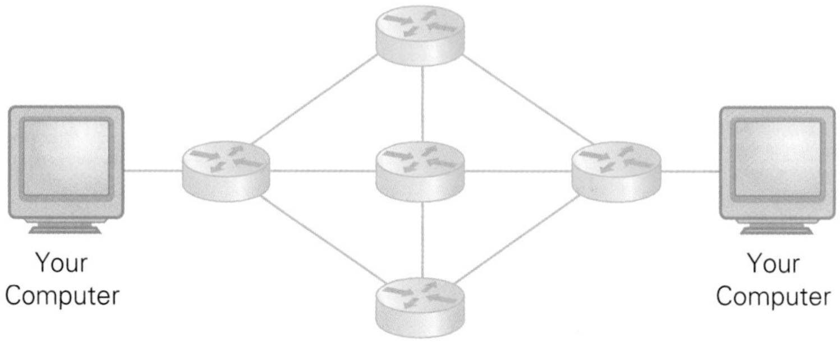

Figure 3.6. *The Internet makes use of whatever routes are available to deliver packets.*

Packets Are Independent. Consider the advantages of TCP/IP. For example, it is natural to assume that IP packets would take a single path to their destinations, like conventional telephone calls, but they do not. Because each packet can take a different route, congestion and service interruptions do not delay transmissions. If sending the first postcard via Hong Kong meant that all following postcards had to be sent via Hong Kong, then a typhoon preventing aircraft from flying between Tahiti and Hong Kong would delay transmission of the novel. But if the postcards can take any available route, the transmission can continue via Los Angeles. As a result, all of the novel might be delivered via LA before airline service is restored between Tahiti and Hong Kong. This idea motivated engineers to decide to make TCP/IP packets independent.

Moving Packets: Wires and More. Although Cerf's analogy uses postcards and airplanes, the Internet uses electrical, electronic, and optical means for communication. The original ARPAnet used long-distance telephone lines, and the Internet continues to rely on telephone carriers for long-distance connections. However, as the Internet has grown and as new technologies such as fiber optics have matured, the Internet now uses separate dedicated lines as well. Because the TCP/IP protocol describes exactly how IP packets are structured and how they are to be handled, the technology used to move the packets only concerns the carrier. The computers at each end of the communication do not know or care what medium is used because they simply send and receive IP packets. Indeed, transmissions often rely on multiple technologies as the packets move through the Internet.

Ironically, with the growth of Internet capacity, telephone companies are also sending telephone conversations over the Internet. The speech is digitized, stuffed into IP packets at the speaker's end, sent over the Internet, unpacked at the listener's end, and converted back to the analog form acceptable to a phone set. This suggests that the Internet is fast becoming the universal information carrier.

Far and Near: WAN and LAN

The Internet is a collection of **wide area networks** (**WAN**), meaning networks designed to send information between two locations widely separated and not directly connected. In our postcard analogy, Tahiti and New York City are not directly connected; that is, there is no single airline flight that goes between Tahiti and the Big Apple. So each postcard takes a sequence of airline flights to reach New York City. In the same way, the Internet is a collection of point-to-point channels, and packets must visit a sequence of computers to reach their destination. In networking terms, packets take several **hops** to be delivered. The trace in Figure 3.7 shows that a ping—a "please reply" message—from my machine `spiff` to `eth.ch`, the Swiss Federal Technical University, takes 18 hops on its route from Seattle to Zürich.

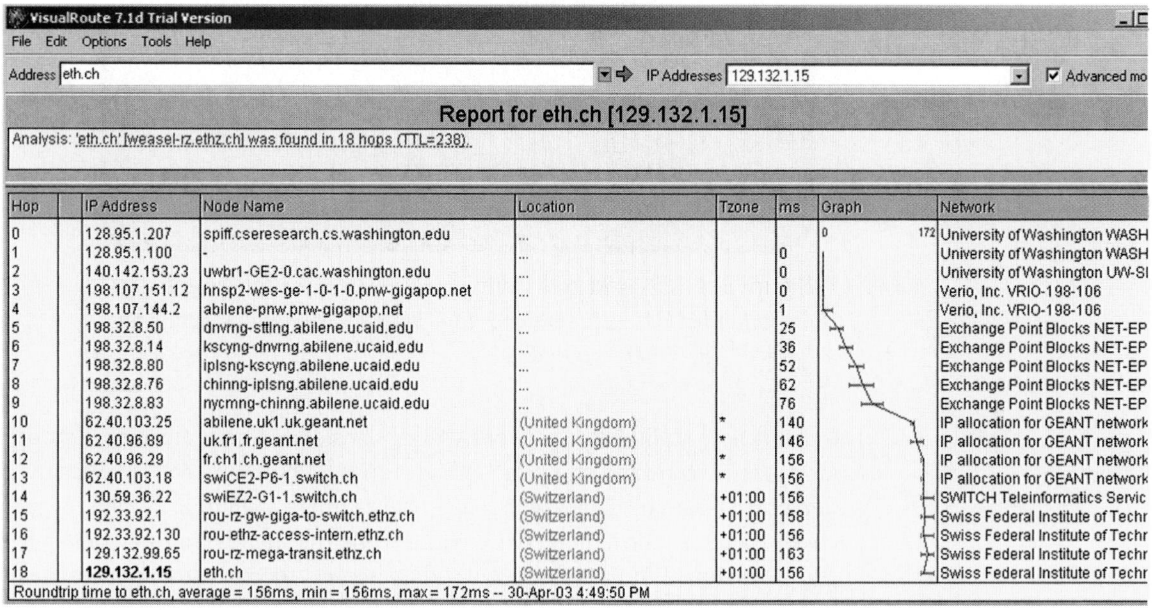

Figure 3.7. *A ping from the author's machine to eth.ch.*

When computers are close enough to be linked by a single cable or pair of wires, the interconnection is referred to as a **local area network** (**LAN**). Ethernet is the main technology for local area networks, and is appropriate for connecting all the computers in a lab or building. An Ethernet network uses a radically different approach than the Internet, but it is equally easy to understand.

Ethernet Party Analogy. Depending on the technology, the physical setup for an Ethernet network is a wire, wire pair, or optical fiber, called the **channel**, that winds past a set of computers. (Robert Metcalfe, the inventor described the channel as the "The Ether," giving the technology its name; see Figure 3.8) Engineers "tap" the channel to connect a computer, allowing it to send a signal (that is, drive an electronic pulse or light flash onto the channel). All computers connected to the channel can detect the signal, including the sender. Thus the channel supports broadcast communication.

FITBYTE

Getting Ether. Robert Metcalfe described the Ethernet (1973) as a "multipoint data communication channel with collision detection." Though *ether* refers to the medium the ancients believed held the stars and planets, Metcalfe used a co-axial cable in his first implementation, the 100-node *Alto Aloha Network* at Xerox's Palo Alto Research Center.

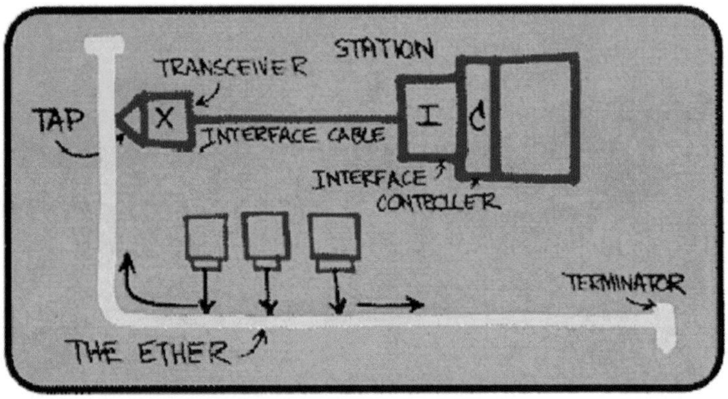

Figure 3.8. *Robert Metalfe's original drawing of the Ethernet design; the unlabeled boxes, computers, "tap" onto the wire that Metcalfe has labeled "The Ether."*

To understand how an Ethernet network works, consider another analogy. A group of friends is standing around at a party telling stories. While someone is telling a story, everyone is listening. The speaker is broadcasting to the group. When the story is over, there may be a momentary pause while the friends wait for someone to start the next story. But how do they decide who tells the next story? There is no plan or agreement as to who should speak next. Typically someone just begins talking, "I remember the time. . . ." If no one else begins talking, that speaker continues telling the story to completion. At the end of the story, there may be a pause, and then someone else will start talking. If two or more people begin talking after the pause, they will notice that others are speaking and immediately stop. There is a pause while everyone waits for someone to go ahead. Assuming speakers tend to wait a random length of time, someone will begin talking. It is possible that two or more speakers will again start at the same time, notice the situation, stop, and wait a random length of time. Eventually one person will begin telling another story.

In this analogy we have assumed all the friends are equal; that is, there is no difference in status, nor does anyone have an especially loud or soft voice. Even so, the system isn't fair, because it favors the person who waits the shortest length of time at the end of a story. Of course, we all know such people!

Ethernet communication works like the party protocol. When the channel is in use, as when someone is telling a story, all of the computers listen to it. Unlike storytelling, however, only one computer typically keeps the transmitted information; that is, this broadcast medium is being used for point-to-point communication. A pause indicates the end of the transmission when no computer is sending signals and the channel is quiet. A computer wanting to transmit starts to send signals and, at the same time, starts to listen to the channel to detect what is being transmitted on the channel. If it is exactly the information the computer sent, the computer must be the only one sending, and it completes its transmission. If not, its signals are being mixed in with signals from one or more other computers. It notices that the data is garbled, and so it stops sending immediately. The other computer(s) will stop, too. Each machine pauses for a random length of time. The computer that waits the shortest length of time begins sending, and if there are no conflicting computers, it continues. If not, the colliders repeat the process.

FITBYTE

Many Versus One. There is an important difference between the way the Internet works and the way an Ethernet works. The Internet uses a point-to-point network to implement point-to-point communication. An Ethernet uses a broadcast network for point-to-point communication. The difference is that with the Internet multiple communications can take place at once over different wires, but with the Ethernet only one communication can take place at a time. This limitation is usually not a problem, because Ethernets usually carry much less traffic.

Connecting a Computer to the Internet

How are computers actually connected to the Internet? Today there are two basic methods:

- By an Internet service provider (ISP)
- By a campus or enterprise network

Most of us use both kinds of connections in one day, depending on where we study or work. Let's look at each approach.

Connections by ISP. As the name implies, Internet service providers sell connections to the Internet. Examples of ISPs are `AOL.com` and `Earthlink.net`, but there are thousands of providers. Most home users connect to the Internet by ISPs. Here's how an ISP connection usually works:

> Users plug their computer into the telephone system just as they would connect an extension telephone. (The plug, called an RJ-11, is universal in North America, but an adapter may be needed in some foreign countries.) Then the computer's modem, which is generally built into modern personal computers, can dial up the ISP and establish a connection. This operation is similar to a fax machine dialing another fax machine. (An alternative to a dial-up line is a dedicated connection to the ISP, such as a digital subscriber line or DSL.) The modems—one at each end of the telephone connection—enable the home computer to talk to the ISP's computer so that they can send and receive information. The ISP's computer is connected to the Internet, so it relays information for its customers. For example, when you surf around the Web and click on a remote link (that is, a page stored on a distant computer), the request for the page is sent from your computer to the

ISP's computer, across the Internet to the remote computer, which then sends the Web page back across the Internet to the computer at the ISP. From there, the page is sent over the phone line to your computer and displayed on your screen.

Enterprise Network Connections (LAN). The other way to connect to the Internet is as a user of a larger networked organization such as a school, business, or governmental unit. In this case, the organization's system administrators have connected the computers in a local area network. The Ethernet technology mentioned earlier is an example of a local area network. These local networks, known as **intranets**, support communication within the organization, but they also connect to the Internet by a gateway. Information from a distant Web computer is sent across the Internet, through the gateway to the organization's intranet, and across the LAN to the user's computer.

With either method, ISP or LAN, you usually send and receive information across the Internet transparently—that is, without knowing or caring which method is used.

FITBYTE

Should I know my computer's IP address? No. If you are dialing into the Internet via an ISP, your computer is assigned a temporary IP address for use until you log out. If you access the Internet via an intranet, one of two cases applies. Your network administrator could have assigned your computer an IP address when it was set up. Alternatively, no permanent address was assigned, and your computer gets one each time it is turned on, using the Dynamic Host Computer Protocol (DHCP). In any case, the IP address is nothing you have to worry about.

THE WORLD WIDE WEB

Some of the computers connected to the Internet are **Web servers**. That is, they are computers programmed to send files to browsers running on other computers connected to the Internet. Together these Web servers and their files are the **World Wide Web** (**WWW**). The files are Web pages, but Web servers store and send many other kinds of files, too. These files are often used to create the Web page (for example, images or animations) or to help with other Web services (for example, software to play audio).

When described in these terms, the Web doesn't seem like much. And technically, it's not. What makes the World Wide Web so significant is the information contained in the files and the ability of the client and server computers to process it.

FITBYTE

No Confusion. The World Wide Web and the Internet are different: The Internet is all of the wires and routers connecting named computers. The World Wide Web is a subset of those computers (Web servers) and their files.

Requesting a Web Page

When you request a Web page, such as my university Web page (`http://www.cs.washington.edu/homes/snyder/index.html`), your browser asks for the file from a Web server computer. The Web page address, called a **Universal Resource Locator**, or **URL**, has three main parts:

Protocol. The `http://` part, which stands for Hypertext Transfer Protocol, tells the computers how to handle the file. There are other ways to send files, such as `ftp`, the File Transfer Protocol.

Server computer's name. The name is the server's IP address given by the domain, `www.cs.washington.edu`. Your computer uses the name to send a request to the server computer for the page.

Page's pathname. The pathname is the sequence following the IP address, `/homes/snyder/index.html`. The pathname tells the server which file (page) is requested and where to find it. Its structure is explained below.

All URLs have this structure, although you may not think so, because in some cases you can leave parts out and the software will fill in the missing part. (However, it is never a mistake to use the full form.)

The World Wide Web is built on a client/server relationship between computers. When you request a page, your browser is a client of the Web server. The idea is that the client is asking for some service that the server is handing out. The client/server relationship is a brief relationship that usually involves only two communications. Your computer sends the request for the page, and the server computer sends it back. That's it. In the next moment the server will answer the request of some other client, and your computer may make a request of a different server when you type in a different URL. As we learn in Chapter 16, the client/server structure is very powerful.

FITBYTE

Punctuating the Internet. Notice the structure of email addresses and URLs, and their punctuation:

Email: `receiver@domain.address`

URLs: `http://domain.address/pathname`

The `domain.address` has one or more dots, no `@`, and no slashes. Email has an `@`, but URLs do not. The `receiver` can have dots, dashes (-), and underscores (_). Spaces are not allowed in either email or URLs.

Describing a Web Page

As you know, servers do not store Web pages in the form seen on our screens. Instead, the pages are stored as a *description* of how they should appear on the screen. When the Web browser receives the description file, known as the **source** file, it creates the Web page image that we see. There are two advantages to storing and sending the source rather than the image itself:

> A description file usually requires less information.

> The browser can adapt the source image to your computer more easily than a literal pixel-by-pixel description.

For example, it is easier to shrink or expand the page from its description than by using the image itself. Though browsers show the image, they always give you the option of seeing the description, too. Next time you are online, look under **View** and find **Source** or **Page Source** in your browser. Figure 3.9 shows a simple Web page and its source.

Hypertext

To describe how a Web page should look, we usually use the **Hypertext Markup Language (HTML)**. Markup languages, long a staple of publishing and graphic design, describe the layout of a document, such as margin width, font, whether text is left justified or centered, whether text is italic or bold, where images go, and so on. Hypertext began as an experiment to break away from the straight sequence of normal text: first paragraph, second paragraph, etc. With hypertext, it is possible to jump from a point in the text to somewhere else in the text or to some other document, and then return. This feature, which breaks a document's linear sequence, gives it a more complex structure. The (usually blue) highlighted words of Web pages are *hyperlinks*, the points from which we can (optionally) jump and return. Hypertext got its name in the late 1960s from Theodore Nelson, though in his *Literary Machines* Nelson credits the original idea to computer pioneer Vannevar Bush. Combining the two ideas—markup languages and hypertext—lets us build nonlinear documents, ideal for the dynamic and highly interconnected Internet. The World Wide Web was born.

FITBYTE

Accelerating Ideas. Tim Berners-Lee invented HTML, a markup language that includes hypertext, in 1990 while he was working at CERN, the European Laboratory for Particle Physics.

In Chapter 4 we study HTML to learn how Web pages are created and processed. In Chapters 5 and 6, we explore the content of the WWW, and in Chapter 16 we consider more sophisticated Web applications.

FILE STRUCTURE

To use networks well, we need to understand file structures, though the topic is not technically part of networking. Recall from your experience using a personal computer that a **directory**—also known as a **folder**—is a named collection of files or other directories.

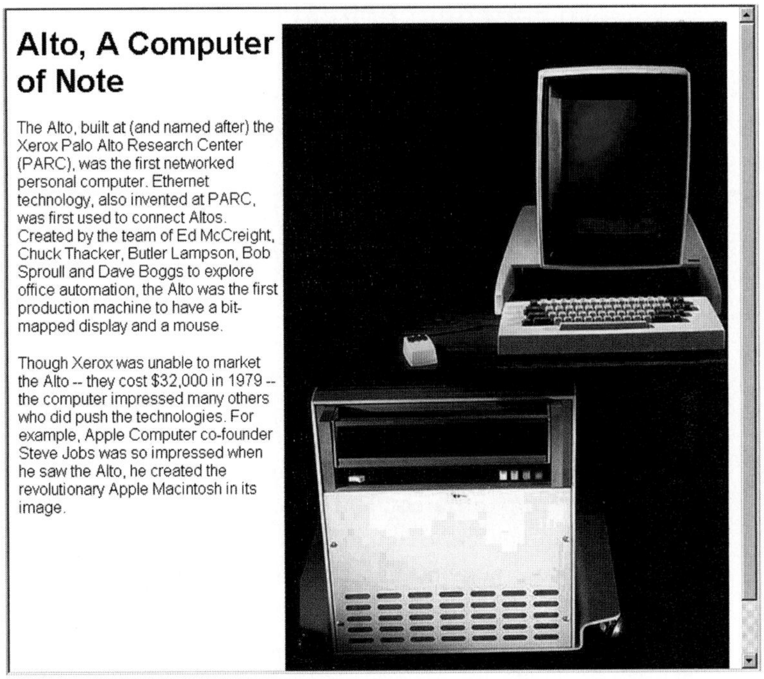


```
<html>
  <head> <title> Alto Computer </title>
  <body bgcolor="white"><font face="Helvetica">
    <img align="right" src="alto.jpg">
    <h1>Alto, A Computer of Note</h1>

    <p>The Alto, built at (and named after) the Xerox Palo
      Alto Research Center (PARC), was the first networked
      personal computer.  Ethernet technology, also invented
      at PARC, was first used to connect Altos. Created by
      the team of Ed McCreight, Chuck Thacker, Butler
      Lampson, Bob Sproull and Dave Boggs to explore office
      automation, the Alto was the first production machine
      to have a bit-mapped display and a mouse.</p>

     <p>Though Xerox was unable to market the Alto
      – they cost $32,000 in 1979 – the computer impressed
      many others who did push the technologies. For
      example, Apple Computer co-founder Steve Jobs was so
      impressed when he saw the Alto, he created the
      revolutionary Apple Macintosh in its image.</p>

  </body>
</html>
```

Figure 3.9. *A Web page and the HTML source that produced it. Notice that an additional image file,* **`alto.jpg`**, *is also required to display the page.*

Directory Hierarchy

Because directories can contain directories, which can contain files and other directories, and on and on, the whole scheme—called the **file structure** of the computer—forms the **directory hierarchy**. Think of any hierarchy as a tree, and in the case of the file structures, directories are the branch points and files are the leaves. Hierarchy trees are often drawn in odd ways, such as sideways or upside down, but in all cases two terms are standard:

> *Down or deeper* in the hierarchy means into subdirectories; that is, toward the leaves.

> *Up or higher* in the hierarchy means into enclosing directories; that is, toward the root.

Figure 3.10 shows the path between the a file, **`xerox-alto.jpg`**, a leaf in the directory hierarchy, and the **`desktop`**, a directory and the root in the directory hierarchy. For example, from **`NextLevelDown`**, "deeper" is towards **`xerox-alto.jpg`** and "higher" is towards **`Desktop`**.

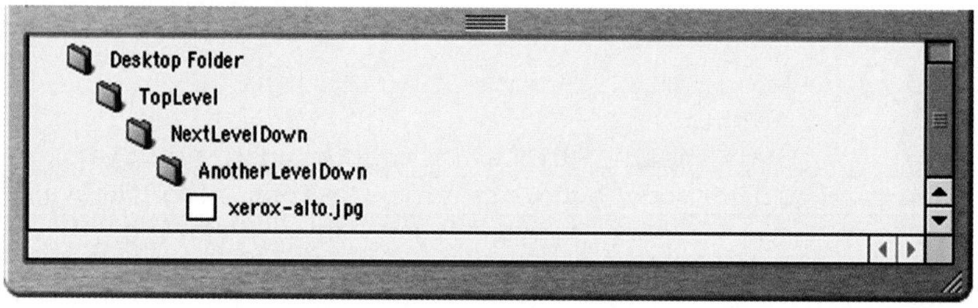

Figure 3.10. *A heirarchy diagram showing the path between* **`xerox-alto.jpg`** *and the* **`desktop`**.

Learning the "directionality" of hierarchical references makes navigating the Web simpler.

Part of the directory hierarchy is shown in the pathnames of URLs. For example, the National Air and Space Museum's URL for a brief description of Pioneer 10, the first man-made object to leave the solar system, is **`http://www.nasm.si.edu/galleries/gal100/pioneer.html`**. The page is given by a pathname, **`/galleries/ gal100/pioneer.html`**, that tells the computer how to navigate through the Air and Space Museum's directory hierarchy to the file, as shown in Figure 3.11. Each time we pass a slash (**`/`**), reading the pathname from left to right, we move into a subdirectory. That is, we go deeper into the hierarchy. We start at a top-level directory called **`galleries`**. (The NASM has 23 exhibit rooms called galleries, and we might assume that this directory contains information about each of them.) Within the **`galleries`** directory, there is a subdirectory called **`gal100`**, which we might assume refers to Gallery 100, the room containing famous "firsts" in air and space exploration. And in the **`gal100`** directory, there is a file called **`pioneer.html`**, the Web page we want.

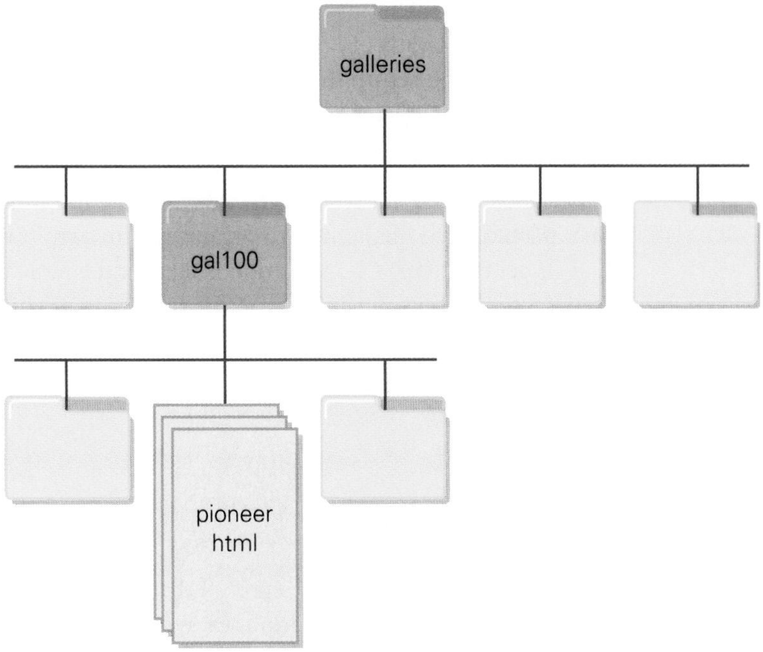

Figure 3.11. The pathname hierarchy ending in **`pioneer.html`**.

FITTIP

Case In Point. Remember that case sensitivity means computers treat upper- and lowercase letters as different. In URLs domains are not case sensitive, because they are standardized for DNS lookup. Pathnames can be case sensitive, because they tell how to navigate through the Web server's file structure, which may be case sensitive. Be careful when typing pathnames, and when in doubt, try lowercase first.

In general, the path in a URL tells the server computer where to find the requested file in the server's file structure. The server computer follows the hierarchical structure just as we did in the NASM example.

Organizing the Directory

A common way to organize the information in a directory is to list or index the files that are in the directory. The information about NASM's Gallery 100 is organized this way. There is a file in the **`gal100`** directory, **`gal100.html`**, that lists the links to Web pages about exhibits in the gallery. Because an index linking to the files in a directory is common, browsers know to look for such a file. When a URL ends in a slash (which means the last item on the path is a directory rather than a filename), the browser automatically looks for a file called **`index.html`** in that directory. So, a request for the URL

`http://www.cs.washington.edu/homes/snyder/index.html`

to my university Web page is the same as

`http://www.cs.washington.edu/homes/snyder/`

because a browser that finds the directory named **snyder** will automatically look for a file called **index.html** in it. Of course, the **index.html** file will exist only if the person who set up the Web pages and built the file hierarchy decided to organize them that way and provided the index pages. Some people do and some people don't, but the browser will try **index.html** when necessary.

Why build a hierarchy at all? Why not lump all the files into one huge directory? Most people build hierarchies to organize their own thinking and work. For example, the gallery-exhibit organization is clear and simple. Because directories cost nothing, there is no reason not to use them, and it is highly recommended. (In this book, when we create a Web page, for example, we will always use a subdirectory for organizing the pictures on the page.)

THE INTERNET AND THE WEB

Some Web servers have **www** as part of their domain name, some don't. Some Web servers, like **www.cs.washingon.edu**, seem to add on the **www** if you leave it out, and some, like New York City's Museum of Modern Art (MoMA), work either way; both **www.moma.org** and **moma.org** give the same Web page. When is the **www** required and when is it optional?

First remember that names like **www.cs.washington.edu** are simply names. That is, like **spiff**, **www** is the name of a computer, the Web server, in the **cs.washington.edu** domain. And, like all computers connected to the Internet, Web servers have IP addresses. To refer to a Web server, you *must* give its name exactly, because your computer will ask the DNS server for the Web server's IP address using that name. If the name is wrong, either you get back the IP address for the wrong computer or, more typically, the DNS lookup will fail. Your browser will give you an error message saying it could not locate the server and directing you to check the address. So, there is no option: You must give the name exactly.

But no organization taking the trouble to put a Web server on the Internet wants visitors to fail, so their Web administrators try to save users from mistakes. For example, if you try to access my Web page but forget the **www**, your request to **cs.washington.edu** will reach the wrong computer. However, that computer has been programmed to notice "**http://**" requests and to return to your browser a reply, "You probably meant **www.cs.washington.edu**." This is called a **redirection**.

Browsers are designed to try again with the recommended address. So, if when you type **http://cs.washington.edu/homes/snyder**, your location window quickly changes to **http://www.cs.washington.edu/homes/snyder**, making it seem that the **www** has been added. But all you are seeing is your browser trying the redirection address. The redirection could have been `http://www.aw.com/snyder/`, the URL for this book. In that case, the redirection looks like a replacement, which is what it really is. Redirection is used extensively at Web sites to avoid telling users that they made a mistake and to get them to where they want to be.

Rather than using redirection, some organizations, like the Museum of Modern Art simply make several names work. That is, MoMA has registered both `moma.org` and `www.moma.org` to the IP address `4.43.114.168`, saving us from making a mistake no matter which choice we make and avoiding redirection. Both names produce the same result because they connect to the same computer.

Web servers don't have to be named **www**. It's just what people usually name their Web servers. The reason that so many Web servers are named **www** is because as the Web got started, many domains added another computer to be their Web server. The server needed a name that people could remember, because redirection was not yet in wide use. Because the first groups named their servers **www**, it helped everyone's memory if later groups did, too. Now it seems like a requirement, but it is only tradition.

SUMMARY

The chapter opened with a discussion of five fundamental ways networked computers have changed the world and our lives. Next, basic types of communication were presented: point-to-point, multicast, broadcast, synchronous, and asynchronous. Most forms of communication apply a combination of these types. For example, telephones are synchronous and point-to-point. An overview of networking included IP addresses, domains, IP packets, the IP-protocol, wide area versus local area networks, Ethernet protocol, ISPs, and enterprise networks. From there we explained the difference between the Internet and the World Wide Web, terms that are commonly confused. Finally, we explained where HTML came from and reviewed file hierarchies in preparation for our study of HTML in Chapter 4.

EXERCISES

Multiple Choice

1. Passive interaction via the Internet allows interaction of individuals:
   A. separated by distance
   B. separated by time
   C. with a shared interest
   D. all of the above
2. English is becoming the universal language as a result of all of the following except:
   A. American pop culture
   B. the dominance of science and technology in English-speaking countries
   C. information technology's predominant use of English
   D. the Alto Project
3. Overall, the ability of individuals to create and publish Web pages:
   A. presents an enormous security risk
   B. extends human expression
   C. has led to a proliferation of hate pages and pornographic sites
   D. has unduly diverted huge sums from other IT projects
4. Spamming is like:
   A. telemarketing
   B. junk mail
   C. advertising inserts
   D. all of the above
5. If the Internet consisted of four computers, there would be six possible connections. If it consisted of five computers, there would be ten possible connections. How many connections are possible with ten computers?
   A. 10
   B. 30
   C. 45
   D. infinite
6. What is the potential number of IP address available?
   A. 65,536
   B. 16,777,216
   C. 4,294,967,296
   D. limitless
7. The part of an email address to the right of the @ is most like a:
   A. mailbox
   B. post office
   C. letter
   D. return address

8. DNS stands for:
   A. Determined Name of Sender
   B. Determined Not Spam
   C. Domain Name System
   D. Domain Number Sequence
9. The origins of the Internet can be traced to:
   A. news services sending wire stories to local newspapers
   B. phone companies creating the long distance system
   C. government, big business, and educational institutions conducting Cold War research
   D. the United States and USSR creating a hotline
10. As an aspiring TV exec, the ideal country to locate the top-level domain for your new quiz show "What's My IP?" would be:
    A. Papua New Guinea
    B. Cocos Islands
    C. Tuvalu
    D. Nauru

Short Answer

1. eCommerce is the shortened term for ______.
2. The interconnection of computers has led to an era called the ______.
3. A communication that goes out to many people within a specific target audience is called a ______.
4. A hierarchy of related computers on a network is called a ______.
5. Computers on the same level of a domain are known as ______.
6. A "please reply" message sent over the Internet is called a ______.
7. Computers on an Ethernet network "tap" into a cable called a ______.
8. A company that supplies connections to the Internet is called a(n) ______.
9. Intranets connect to the Internet via ______.
10. Local networks that support communications wholly within an organization are called ______.
11. Special computers that send files to Web browsers elsewhere on the Internet are known as ______.
12. The http:// in a Web address is the ______.
13. Files are often sent over the Internet via a process known by the acronym ______.
14. The source file for a Web page contains the ______ of the page, not the actual image of the page.
15. HTML stands for ______.

Exercises

1. How have networked computers made your life different from the life of your parents?
2. Discuss five changes the Information Age has brought.
3. There's an adage, "Guns don't kill people. People kill people." How does this relate to human nature and the Internet?
4. Label the following with either an S to indicate synchronous communication or an A to indicate asynchronous communication.

______	movie	______	book
______	chat session	______	concert
______	email	______	text messaging
______	video conference	______	Web board
______	Web page		

5. Go to `www.mids.org/mapsale/world/index.html` and check out the Internet maps of the world. Where is most of the traffic? Plot the course of a packet from Tahiti to New York. What routes are available and where are the bottlenecks?
6. Try the Web address above without the file name. What do you get?
7. Describe how the Internet is like a bus route, a subway route, UPS or Federal Express. How is it different from these? Go to `www.mta.nyc.ny.us/nyct/maps/submap.htm` to see a map of the NYC subway system. How does it compare? Compare the Internet to the Prague subway map by going to `www.odyssey.on.ca/~europrail/prague.htm`.
8. What industries have prospered and which ones might have suffered because of the growth of the Internet? Why?

chapter

4 MARKING UP WITH HTML

A Hypertext Markup Language Primer

learning objectives

- Know the meaning of and use hypertext terms
- Use HTML tags to structure a document
- Use the basics of HTML tag attributes
- Use HTML tags to link to other files
- Explain the differences between absolute and relative path names
- Use HTML to encode lists and tables

Most of the fundamental ideas of science are essentially simple and may as a rule be expressed in a language comprehensible to everyone.

—ALBERT EINSTEIN

WEB PAGES are created, stored, and sent in encoded form; a browser converts them into the image we see on the screen. The Hypertext Markup Language (HTML) is the main language for defining how a Web page should look. Features like background color, font, and layout are all specified in HTML. Learning to "speak" HTML is easy. So easy, in fact, that most Web pages are not created by writing HTML directly, but by using Web authoring software; that is, programs that write the HTML automatically. We will still learn HTML because it helps us understand the World Wide Web, gives us experience directing a computer to do tasks for us, and prepares us for other topics in our Fluency study. When we are finished, we will speak a new "foreign" language!

This chapter begins by reviewing the concept of tags, which we learned about in Chapter 2, and we introduce the dozen most basic HTML tags. Next comes document structuring, including details such as headings and alignment. After discussing special characters, we create an example of a text-only Web page. We decide that the page should have an image and hyperlinks, so we learn about placing images and links and how to connect them. With this knowledge we improve our example page. Finally, we introduce the basics of lists, tables, and colors, which give us more control over the "look and feel" of our Web pages.

MARKING UP WITH HTML

HTML is straightforward. The words that will appear on the Web page are simply surrounded by formatting tags describing how they should look.

Formatting with Tags

Remember from Chapter 2 that tags are words or abbreviations enclosed in angle brackets, `<` and `>`, like `<title>`, and that tags come in pairs, the second with a slash (`/`), like `</title>`. The tag pair surrounds the text to be formatted like parentheses. So the title, which every HTML Web page has, would be written as

```
<title>Tiger Woods, Masters Champion</title>
```

These two tags can be read as "beginning of title text" and "end of title text." The title is shown on the title bar of the browser when the page is being displayed (the very top of the window where the close button is). In HTML, the tags are not case sensitive, but the actual text is. So, in this example, we could have used `<TITLE>`, `<Title>`, `<tITle>`, or any other mix of lower- and uppercase letters. We will follow tradition and use only lowercase letters in tags.

Tags for Bold and Italic

HTML has tags for bold text, `<b>` and `</b>`, for italic text, `<i>` and `</i>`, and for paragraphs, `<p>` and `</p>`. You can use more than one kind of formatting at a time, such as italic bold text, by "nesting" the tags, as in

```
<p><b><i>Veni, Vidi, Vici!</i></b></p>
```

which produces

Veni, Vidi, Vici!

It doesn't matter in which order you put the tags. You get the same result if you put the bold before the italic:

```
<p><i><b>Veni, Vidi, Vici!</b></i></p>
```

The key is to make sure the tags are nested correctly. All the tags between a starting tag and its ending tag should be matched. So, in the *Veni, Vidi, Vici* example, between the starting `<p>` tag and its ending tag `</p>` all the tags match in both cases.

FITTIP

HTML is relaxed about some of these rules, but when and how is often complicated. So in this book we ignore any relaxed rules to avoid complication, because they don't make a difference in the pages you can create.

A few tags are not paired and so do not have a / ending form. One example is the horizontal rule tag, `<hr>`, which displays a horizontal line. Another example is break, `<br>`, which continues the text on the next line and is useful for ending each line of an address. These tags do not apply to multiple characters, so they don't need to surround anything.

An HTML Web page file begins with the `<html>` tag, ends with the `</html>` tag, and has the following structure:

```
<html>
  <head>
      preliminary material goes here
  </head>
  <body>
      the main content of the page goes here
  </body>
</html>
```

The section surrounded by `<head>` and `</head>` contains the beginning material like the title, and the section surrounded by `<body>` and `</body>` contains the content of the page. *This form must always be followed, and all of these tags are required.*

> FITCAUTION
>
> **Use Simple Text Editors.** While we are giving ignore-at-your-own-peril rules about a Web page's form, we should offer a caution about text editors. HTML must be written using basic ASCII characters. We discuss these in Chapter 8, but for now, think of them as the characters from the keyboard. As we learned in Chapter 2, standard word processors (e.g., WordPerfect, Word, and Claris Works) produce files of such characters, but they also include special formatting information that browsers do not like. For that reason, you *must* write HTML using a basic text editor such as NotePad (Windows), Simple Text (Mac), BBText (UNIX), or the like. And always make sure that you save the file using Text format. This way the HTML file will make sense to Web browsers. Also, always make sure that the file name ends with the `.html` extension, so that the browser knows that it is reading an HTML document.

There's not very much to HTML. By the end of the next section, we will have created a respectable Web page—our first!

STRUCTURING DOCUMENTS

The point of a markup language is to describe how a document's parts fit together. Because those parts are mostly paragraphs, headings, and text styles like italic and bold, the tags of this section are the most common and most useful.

Headings in HTML

Because documents have headings, subheadings, and so on, HTML gives us several levels of heading tags to choose from, from level one (the highest) headings, `<h1>`

and `</h1>`, to level two, `<h2>` and `</h2>`, all the way to level eight, `<h8>` and `</h8>`. The headings display the material in large font on a new line. For example,

```
<h1>Pope</h1> <h2>Cardinal</h2> <h3>Archbishop</h3>
```

would print as

> # Pope
> ## Cardinal
> ### Archbishop

You should use the heading levels in numerical order without skipping a level, although you don't have to start at 1. Notice that the headings are bold and get less "strong" (smaller and perhaps less bold) as the level number increases.

HTML Format vs. Display Format

Notice as well that although the HTML text was run together on one line, it was displayed formatted on separate lines. This illustrates the important point that the HTML source tells the browser to produce the formatted image based on the *meanings* of the tags, not on how the source instructions look. Though the source's form is unimportant, we usually write HTML in a structured way to make it easier for people to understand. There is no agreed-upon form, but the example might have been written with indenting to emphasize the levels:

```
<h1>Pope</h1>
   <h2>Cardinal</h2>
      <h3>Archbishop</h3>
```

White Space

The two forms give us the same result. Computer experts call space that has been inserted for readability **white space**. We create white space with spaces, tabs, and new lines. HTML ignores white space. The browser turns any sequence of white space characters into a single space before it begins processing the HTML. The only exception is **preformatted** information contained within `<pre>` and `</pre>` tags, which is displayed as it appears.

The fact that white space is ignored is important when the browser formats paragraphs. All text within paragraph tags, `<p>` and `</p>`, is treated as a paragraph, and any sequence of white space characters turn into a single space. So

```
<p> <b>Xeno's Paradox: </b>
Achilles and a turtle were to run a race. Achilles could
run twice as fast as the turtle. The turtle,
being a slower runner,
```

```
got a 10 meter head start, whereupon
Achilles started and ran the 10 meter distance. At that
moment the turtle was 5 meters farther. When Achilles had run
that distance the turtle had gone another 2.5 meters,
and so forth. Paradoxically, the turtle always remained
ahead. </p>
```

would appear as

> **Xeno's Paradox:** Achilles and a turtle were to run a race. Achilles could run twice as fast as the turtle. The turtle, being a slower runner, got a 10 meter head start, whereupon Achilles started and ran the 10 meter distance. At that moment the turtle was 5 meters farther. When Achilles had run that distance the turtle had gone another 2.5 meters, and so forth. Paradoxically, the turtle always remained ahead.

The width of the line is determined by the width of the browser window. Of course, a narrower or wider browser window makes the lines break in different places, which is why HTML ignores white space and changes the paragraph's formatting to fit the space available. Table 4.1 summarizes the basic HTML tags.

Table 4.1. *Basic HTML Tags*

Start Tag	End Tag	Meaning	Required
`<html>`	`</html>`	HTML document; first and last tags in an HTML file	✔
`<title>`	`</title>`	Title bar text; describes page	✔
`<head>`	`</head>`	Preliminary material; e.g., title, at start of page	✔
`<body>`	`</body>`	The main part of the page	✔
`<p>`	`</p>`	Paragraph, can use `align` attribute	
`<hr>`		Line (horiz. rule), can use `width` and `size` attributes	
`<h1> . . . <h8>`	`</h1> . . . </h8>`	Headings, eight levels, use in order, can use `align` attribute	
`<b>`	`</b>`	Bold	
`<i>`	`</i>`	Italic	
`<a href="fn">`	`</a>`	Anchor reference, *fn* must be a pathname to an HTML file	
`<img src="fn">`		Image source reference, *fn* must be pathname to `.jpg` or `.gif` file	
` `		Break, continue text on a new line	

Brackets in HTML: The Escape Symbol

Notice that there would be a problem if our Web page had to show a math relationship such as $0 < p > r$, because the browser would misinterpret $< p >$ as a paragraph tag and not display it. To show angle brackets, we use an *escape* symbol—the ampersand (`&`)—followed by an abbreviation, followed by a semicolon. For example:

> `<` displays as $<$
>
> `>` displays as $>$
>
> `&` displays as `&`

Notice that the escape symbol, the ampersand, needs an escape, too! So, our math problem would be solved in HTML by

```
<i>0 &lt; p &gt; r</i>
```

Accent Marks in HTML

Letters with accent marks also use the escape symbol. The general form is an ampersand followed by the letter—and whether it is upper- or lowercase makes a difference—followed by the name of the accent mark. So, for example, `&eacute` displays as é, `&Egrave` displays as È, `&ntilde` displays as ñ, and `&ouml` displays as ö. Table 4.2 lists a few useful special symbols for some Western European languages. You can find a complete list at

`www.w3.org/MarkUp/html13/latin1.html`

Table 4.2. *Special Symbols for Western European Language Accent Marks*

à	`à`	á	`á`	â	`â`	ã	`ã`	ä	`ä`
å	`å`	ç	`ç`	è	`è`	é	`é`	ê	`ê`
ë	`ë`	ì	`ì`	í	`í`	î	`î`	ï	`ï`
ñ	`ñ`	ò	`ò`	ó	`ó`	ô	`ô`	õ	`õ`
ö	`ö`	ø	`ø`	ù	`ù`	ú	`ú`	û	`û`
ü	`ü`								

Note: For an accent mark on a uppercase letter, make the letter following the & uppercase.

Attributes in HTML

Though most text properties are a single key term or abbreviation, some properties, such as how to align text, need more information. For example, we can't just say we want text justified; we have to say that we want it left justified, centered, or right justified. We do this by using the tag's attributes. Attributes, which are generally optional, appear inside the angle brackets.

Align, Justify. For example, paragraphs and headings have an align attribute specifying whether the text should be left justified, centered, or right justified. The attribute follows the tag word, separated by a space, and is separated from its value (in double quotes) by an equal sign. So

```
<p align = "center"> <b>Winston Churchill once observed:</b>
</p>
<p> If at 20 you are not liberal, you have no heart. </p>
<p align = "right"> If at 40 you are not conservative, you
have no mind.</p>
```

would display as

> **Winston Churchill once observed:**
>
> If at 20 you are not liberal, you have no heart.
>
> If at 40 you are not conservative, you have no mind.

Notice that when we don't specify the alignment attribute, as in the second line, the default is left justified.

Horizontal Rule Attribute. The horizontal rule tag, `<hr>`, mentioned earlier, also has attributes. One attribute, width, specifies how wide the line should be as a percentage of the browser window's width; another attribute, `size`, says how thick the line should be. So `<hr width="50%" size=1>` displays a horizontal line that takes up half of the horizontal width and is the minimum thickness, as in

---

The default size is 2. Experiment to find the size that works best for your application. Notice that the width, `50%`, is enclosed in quotation marks, but the size specification, 1, is not. This has been done for illustration purposes. HTML does not need the quotes *if a browser can figure out what is intended*. But don't take chances—put quotes around anything that follows the equal sign.

FITCAUTION

Misquotes. Quotation marks are the cause of many HTML errors. Of course, quotes must match, and it is easy to forget one of the pair. But, there are also different kinds of quotes: The simple quotes (`"` and `'`) are the kind HTML likes; the fancy, curving quotes, called "smart quotes," (as shown) are the kind HTML doesn't like. Check *carefully* for messed-up quotes when the HTML produces the wrong Web page.

Though we have introduced only a few HTML tags so far, we can already create Web pages, as shown in Figure 4.1. Study the HTML and notice the following points:

> The title is shown on the title bar of the browser window.

> The alignment attribute has been used in the level 1 heading to center the heading.

> The level 2 headings are left justified because that is the default.

> The statement of Russell's Paradox is in bold.

> The HTML source paragraphs are indented more than the `<h2>` heading lines to make them more readable.

> The line between the two paragraphs is three quarters the width of the browser window.

> Acute accents are used in Magritte's first name.

> The French phrase from the painting is in italics.

> The word *picture* is in italics for emphasis.

It's a simple page, and it was simple to produce.

FITBYTE

Compose and Check. It's a good idea always to write the text first and then format it in HTML. A productive way to work is with two windows open, your editor and your browser. After writing a few HTML formatting tags in the editor, *save* them and then check the result with the browser by *reloading* the source.

MARKING LINKS WITH ANCHOR TAGS

The example shown in Figure 4.1 may be an interesting Web page, but it doesn't use hypertext at all. It would be more informative, perhaps, if it linked to biographies of Russell and Magritte. Also, it would be easier to understand if it showed Magritte's painting or linked to it.

Two Sides of a Link

In this section we learn how to make hyperlinks. When a user clicks on a hyperlink, the browser loads a new Web page. This means there must be two parts to a hyperlink: the text in the current document that is highlighted, called the **anchor text**, and the address of the other Web page, called the **hyperlink reference**.

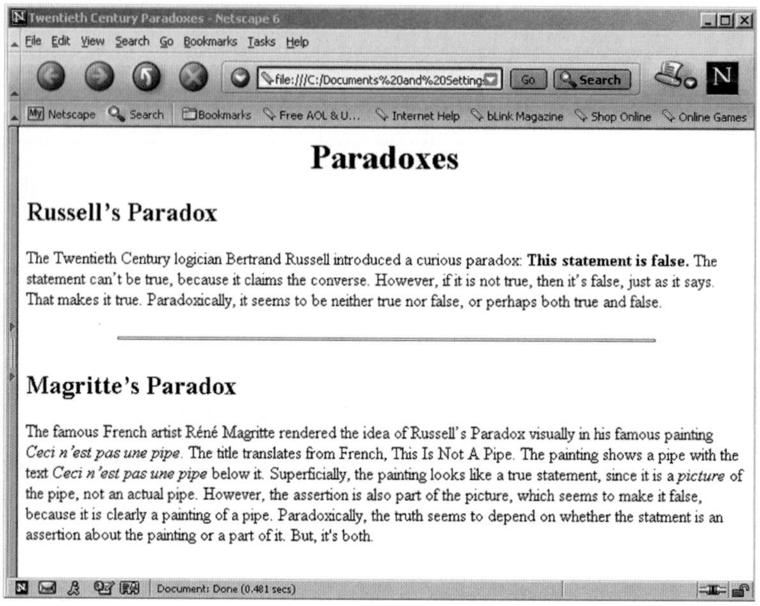


```
<html>
<head>
  <title>Twentieth Century Paradoxes</title>
</head>
<body>
<h1 align="center">Paradoxes</h1>
 <h2>Russell's Paradox</h2>
  <p> The Twentieth Century logician Bertrand Russell
  introduced a curious paradox: <b>This statement is
  false.</b> The statement can't be true, because it
  claims the converse. However, if it is not true, then
  it's false, just as it says. That makes it true.
  Paradoxically, it seems to be neither true nor false,
  or perhaps both true and false.</p>
  <hr width="75%">
 <h2> Magritte's Paradox</h2>
  <p> The famous French artist R&eacute;n&eacute; Magritte
  rendered the idea of Russell's Paradox visually in
  his famous painting <i>Ceci n'est pas une pipe</i>. The
  title translates from French, This Is Not A Pipe. The
  painting shows a pipe with the text <i>Ceci n'est pas une
  pipe</i> below it. Superficially, the painting looks like
  a true statement, since it is a <i>picture</i> of the pipe,
  not an actual pipe. However, the assertion is also part of
  the picture, which seems to make it false, because it is
  clearly a painting of a pipe. Paradoxically, the truth
  seems to depend on whether the statement is an assertion
  about the painting or a part of it. But, it's both.</p>
</body>
</html>
```

Figure 4.1. *HTML source of* `paradoxes.html` *and corresponding Web page resulting from its interpretation by a browser.*

CHECKLIST>>

Both parts of the hyperlink are specified in the **anchor tag**, constructed as follows:

- *Begin with* <a *making sure there's a space after the* a. *The* a *is for anchor.*
- *Give the hyperlink reference using* href="*filename*", *making sure to include the double quotes.*
- *Close the anchor tag with the > symbol.*
- *Specify the anchor text, which will be highlighted when it is displayed by the browser.*
- *End the hyperlink with the* </a> *tag.*

For example, suppose **http://www.bios.com/bios/sci/russell.html** were the URL for a Web biography of Bertrand Russell; we would anchor it to his last name on our Web page with the anchor tag

```
Bertrand <a href="http://www.bios.com/bios/sci/russell.html">Russell</a>
```

normal text (Bertrand) — hyperlink reference (<a href="http://www.bios.com/bios/sci/russell.html">) — anchor (Russell</a>)

This hyperlink would be displayed with Russell's last name highlighted as

Bertrand <u>Russell</u>

When the browser displays the page and the user clicks on Russell, the browser downloads the bio page given in the href. As another example, if Magritte's biography were at the same site, the text

```
<a href="http://www.bios.com/bios/art/magritte.html">Magritte</a>
```

would give the reference and anchor for his hyperlink.

Absolute Pathnames (URLs)

In these anchor tag examples, the hyperlink reference is an entire URL because the Web browser needs to know how to find the page. Remember from Chapter 3 that the URL is made from a protocol specification, **http://**, a domain or IP address, **www.bios.com**, and a path to the file, **/bios/sci/russell.html**. The files are two levels down in the directory (folder) hierarchy of the site.

From the Russell and Magritte examples, we guess that at the Bios Company site, the biographies have been grouped together in a top-level directory (see Chapter 3) called **bios**. Probably the scientists, like Russell, are grouped together in the subdirectory called **sci**, and the artists are grouped together under the subdirectory called **art**. Within these directories are the individual biography files, **russell.html** and **magritte.html**. The slash (/) separates levels in the directory hierarchy, and "crossing a slash" moves us lower in the hierarchy into a subfolder. Such complete URLs are called **absolute pathnames**, and they are the right way to reference pages at other Web sites.

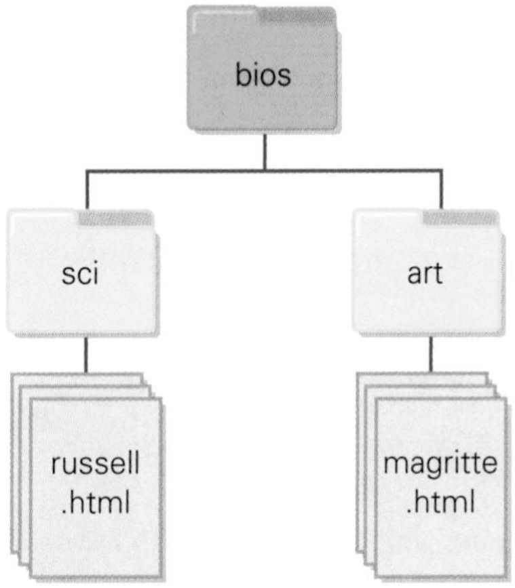

Relative Pathnames

Often a link refers to other Web pages on the same site. Because these pages will all be stored in the same or nearby directories, their anchor tags use **relative pathnames**. A relative pathname describes how to find the referenced file *relative* to the file in which the anchor tag appears. So, for example, if the anchor tag is in an HTML file in directory X, and the anchor references another file also in directory X, only the name of the file is given, not the whole path.

Suppose that we have written our own biographies for Russell and Magritte for our `paradoxes.html` page. If the files are named `russellbio.html` and `magrittebio.html`, and they are in the same directory as the `paradoxes.html`, the anchor tags of the Paradoxes page can use relative references:

```
<a href="russellbio.html">Russell</a>
```

and

```
<a href="magrittebio.html">Magritte</a>
```

This saves us typing the protocol part, the domain part, and the path to the folder part, but that's not why we like relative pathnames. Relative pathnames are more flexible, because they let us move Web files around as a group without having to change the references. This flexibility will become important when you begin managing your own Web page.

Going "Deeper" in a Directory.

Relative pathnames are very simple when the file containing the anchor and the referenced file are in the same directory—we just give the file name. When the referenced file is "deeper" in the directory hierarchy, perhaps in a folder or in a folder in a folder, we simply give the path from the current directory down to the file. For example, in the directory containing `paradoxes.html` we create a subdirectory, `biographies`, which contains the two profiles. Then the anchor for the Russell bio becomes

```
<a href="biographies/russellbio.html">Russell</a>
```

because we must say how to navigate to the file from the Paradoxes page's location. Of course, using relative pathnames means that the files for the pages must be kept together in a fixed structure, but that's the easiest solution anyway.

Going "Higher" in a Hierarchy. The only problem left is how to refer to directories higher up in the hierarchy. The technique for doing this (which comes from the UNIX operating system) is to refer to the next outer level of the hierarchy—that is, the containing directory—as `..` (pronounced "*dot dot*"). So if we imagine that the directory structure has the form

```
mypages
  biographies
    russellbio.html
    magrittebio.html
  coolstuff
    paradoxes.html
```

then, in **`paradoxes.html`**, the Russell biography anchor would be

```
<a href="../biographies/russellbio.html">Russell</a>
```

because the biography can't be reached by going down from the directory (**`coolstuff`**) containing **`paradoxes.html`**. Instead we have to go up to the next higher level to **`mypages`**. From there, we can navigate down to the bios through the **`biographies`** directory. We can use a sequence of dots and slashes (`../../`), so that each pair of dots moves the browser up higher in the hierarchy. For example, the reference

```
<a href="../../humorpages/dumbjokes/knockknock4.html">
```

would move up to the directory containing the directory containing the page, then down through the **`humorpages`** and **`dumbjokes`** directories to the actual HTML page.

Summarizing, hyperlinks are specified using anchor tags. The path to the file is given as the **`href`** attribute of the anchor tag, and the text to be highlighted, the anchor, is given between the anchor tag and its closing `</a>`. Paths can be absolute paths—that is, standard URLs—for offsite pages. Relative pathnames should be used for all onsite pages. The relative path can be just a name if the referenced file is in the same directory as the page that links to it, or it can specify a path deeper, through descendant directories, or it can use the `..` notation to move higher in the directory structure. These path rules apply to images as well as hyperlinks.

INCLUDING PICTURES WITH IMAGE TAGS

Pictures are worth a thousand words, as the saying goes, so including them in an HTML document adds to a page's content. To include pictures, we use a tag, but not an anchor tag because we don't want to *refer* to the picture. We want to display it directly on the page. (If you would rather just refer to it, use anchor tags.)

Image Tag Format

An image tag, which is analogous to an anchor tag, specifies a file containing an image. The image tag format is

```
<img src="filename">
```

where **`src`** stands for "source" and the *filename* uses the same rules for absolute and relative pathnames as anchor tags. So, for example, if the image of Magritte's painting is stored in a file **`pipe.jpg`**, in the same directory as the Paradoxes page, we can include the image with a relative pathname

```
<img src="pipe.jpg">
```

which finds the image and places it in the document.

GIF and JPEG Images

Images can come in several formats, but two of them are important for Web pages: **GIF** (pronounced either with a hard or soft *g*) and **JPEG** (pronounced *JAY-peg.*) GIF, Graphics Interchange Format, is best for cartoons and simple drawings. JPEG, named for the Joint Photographic Experts Group, is best for high-resolution photographs and complex artwork. To tell the browser which format the image is in, the file name should have the extension **`.gif`**, **`.jpg`**, or **`.jpeg`**.

Positioning the Image in the Document

The big question is, "Where does the image go on the Web page?" To understand how images are placed, notice that HTML lays out text in the browser window from *left to right*, and from *top to bottom*, the same way English is written. If the image is the same size or smaller than the letters, it is placed in line just like a letter at the point where the image tag occurs in the HTML. For example, when we insert a small image  in the text, it is simply drawn in place. This is convenient for icons or smiley faces in the text. If the image is larger than the letters  it is dropped in the text in the same way, but the line spacing is increased to separate it from the neighboring lines. The HTML default rule is: *Images are inserted in the page at the point where the tag is specified in the HTML, and the text lines up with the bottom of the image.*

We can use the **`align`** attribute in the image tag to line up the top of the image with the top of the text (**`align="top"`**) or to center the text on the image (**`align="middle"`**) in the image. In all cases, the **`bottom`** (default), **`middle`**, and **`top`** alignments apply only to the line of text in which the image has been inserted.

Another common and visually pleasing way to place images in text is to flow the text around them, either by having the image right justified with the text along the left, or vice versa. To make the text flow around the image, use the align attribute in the image tag with the value **`"right"`** or **`"left"`**. This forces the image to the right or left of the browser window. The text will continue from left to right, and from top to bottom, in the remaining space, flowing around the image.

Finally, to display an image by itself without any text around it, simply enclose the image tag within paragraph tags. That will separate it from the paragraphs above and below it. You can even center the paragraph to center the image:

> FITTIP
> **Clearer Directions.** Notice that there are two sets of tags for alignment attributes. For horizontal alignment, such as paragraph justification, use `left`, `center`, `right`. For vertical alignment, such as for placing images relative to a line of text, use `top`, `middle`, `bottom`.

So how do we put the image of Magritte's painting in the Paradoxes page? Perhaps the most pleasing solution is to right-justify it and let the paragraph flow around it. We can do this by writing

```
<img src="pipe.jpg" align="right">
```

as long as the picture doesn't take up all or most of the window, which would prevent the text from flowing naturally. To specify how large the picture should be, use the **`height`** and **`width`** attributes in the image tag. Give the size in pixels. Thus,

```
<img src="pipe.jpg" align="right" height="130" width="192">
```

specifies an image that will be about one eighth of the width of a thousand-pixel screen. If the natural size of the image is different from the **`height/width`** specifications, the browser shrinks or stretches it to fit in the allotted space. (The natural size of an image is the best size to use, if possible. However, in our example the natural size is too large, so we divide the dimensions by 3 and round to the nearest whole number.)

> FITTIP
> **Image Size.** You can find out the size of an image by checking **File > Properties** (Windows) or **File > Get Info** (Mac) of the image file.

We can also use images to fill in a background by **tiling**, copying a small image over and over to make a background pattern. Use bland, low-contrast, evenly colored images for tiling, so they are not distracting as background. Collections of pictures and graphics just for backgrounds are widely available, such as one that makes the page look like linen paper. The image is specified as the background attribute of the body tag, as in

```
<body background="filename">
```

where the *filename* has the same path properties as hyperlink references for anchor tags.

HANDLING COLOR

Color can improve a Web page dramatically, and can be used for both the background and text. The **bgcolor** attribute of the body tag will give you a solid color for the background. You can specify the color either by number, as explained later, or by using a small set of predefined color terms, as in

```
<body bgcolor="silver">
```

The color choices are shown in Table 4.3. The body tag attribute **text** can be used to give the entire document's text a specific color. The example

```
<body text="aqua" link="fuchsia">
```

illustrates controlling the link colors, too. You can change the text in specific places by using the font tag with the color attribute. So, to make Russell's Paradox red, write

```
<b><font color="red">This statement is false.</font></b>
```

Though the predefined colors are handy, you may want more than just 16 colors, and that's where the numeric colors come in.

Table 4.3. *Predefined HTML Colors*

black	silver	white	gray
red	fuchsia	maroon	purple
blue	navy	aqua	teal
lime	green	yellow	olive

Color by Number

As we mentioned briefly in Chapter 1, computer colors are often described by their amounts of red, green, and blue light. The intensity of each color is specified by a number from 0 through 255. So, for example, a zero amount of all three colors (0,0,0) produces the color black. Though it makes no difference for black, the order is always red, green, blue—so we call it **RGB color specification**. If all three colors are at full intensity (255, 255, 255), the color is white because white is a mix of the three colors of light. And, if there is full intensity of one color and none of the other two, as in

`(255, 0, 0)` Intense Red

`(0, 255, 0)` Intense Green

`(0, 0, 255)` Intense Blue

we get the three pure colors.

FITBYTE

Eye Color. The original choice of red, green, and blue comes from the color receptors in the human eye.

You can select custom colors for backgrounds and fonts in HTML by giving the three RGB intensity values. The only catch is that you do not specify them as whole numbers between 0 and 255, but as pairs of hex digits between 00 and FF. A **hexadeximal (hex) digit** is one of the symbols {0, 1, 2, 3, 4, 5, 6, 7, 8, 9, A, B, C, D, E, F} from the base-16 or hexadecimal numbering system, which we will discuss in Chapter 11. But we can use them right now without understanding hex. Because the smallest value is 00, which is the same as a normal 0, and the largest value is FF, which is the same to a normal 255, the three pure colors are expressed in HTML as

`#FF0000` Intense Red

`#00FF00` Intense Green

`#0000FF` Intense Blue

The number sign (#) means that what follows is a hexadecimal number. The easiest way to find the values for a custom color, say (255, 142, 42), which is the color of a carrot, is to look up the numbers in Table 4.4 to find their two hex digits. First find the intensity for each color in the table, and then read off the first hex digit from the left end of the row and the second hex digit from the top of the column. Thus the carrot color is

`#FF8E2A` Carrot Orange

because **`FF`** is 255, **`8E`** is 142, and **`2A`** is 42.

Though numeric colors need two levels of translation—first the translation of the color into the three RGB intensities, and then the translation of those values into hex digit pairs—they give us much more flexibility in Web page design. And they work with all browsers. For these reasons, HTML programmers tend to prefer them.

There is one other way to find the numeric specification for a color, and it is the easiest. In Appendix A, Table A.1 shows a standard set of HTML colors and their hex specification. (These colors give best results on most monitors.) Find the color in the table, and read off the hex digits.

With the information learned in the last three sections, it is possible to enhance the Web page of Figure 4.1. The result is shown in Figure 4.2. Notice the local pathnames to our own biographical profiles of Russell and Magritte, the background and text colors, the change of color for the font and for the headings, and, of course, the added image.

Table 4.4. *Hexadecimal Digit Equivalents*

Hex	0	1	2	3	4	5	6	7	8	9	A	B	C	D	E	F
0	0	1	2	3	4	5	6	7	8	9	10	11	12	13	14	15
1	16	17	18	19	20	21	22	23	24	25	26	27	28	29	30	31
2	32	33	34	35	36	37	38	39	40	41	42	43	44	45	46	47
3	48	49	50	51	52	53	54	55	56	57	58	59	60	61	62	63
4	64	65	66	67	68	69	70	71	72	73	74	75	76	77	78	79
5	80	81	82	83	84	85	86	87	88	89	90	91	92	93	94	95
6	96	97	98	99	100	101	102	103	104	105	106	107	108	109	110	111
7	112	113	114	115	116	117	118	119	120	121	122	123	124	125	126	127
8	128	129	130	131	132	133	134	135	136	137	138	139	140	141	142	143
9	144	145	146	147	148	149	150	151	152	153	154	155	156	157	158	159
A	160	161	162	163	164	165	166	167	168	169	170	171	172	173	174	175
B	176	177	178	179	180	181	182	183	184	185	186	187	188	189	190	191
C	192	193	194	195	196	197	198	199	200	201	202	203	204	205	206	207
D	208	209	210	211	212	213	214	215	216	217	218	219	220	221	222	223
E	224	225	226	227	228	229	230	231	232	233	234	235	236	237	238	239
F	240	241	242	243	244	245	246	247	248	249	250	251	252	253	254	255

Note: Find the decimal number in the table, and then combine the entries in the left column and the top row symbols to form the hexadecimal equivalent. Thus decimal 180 is hexadecimal B4.

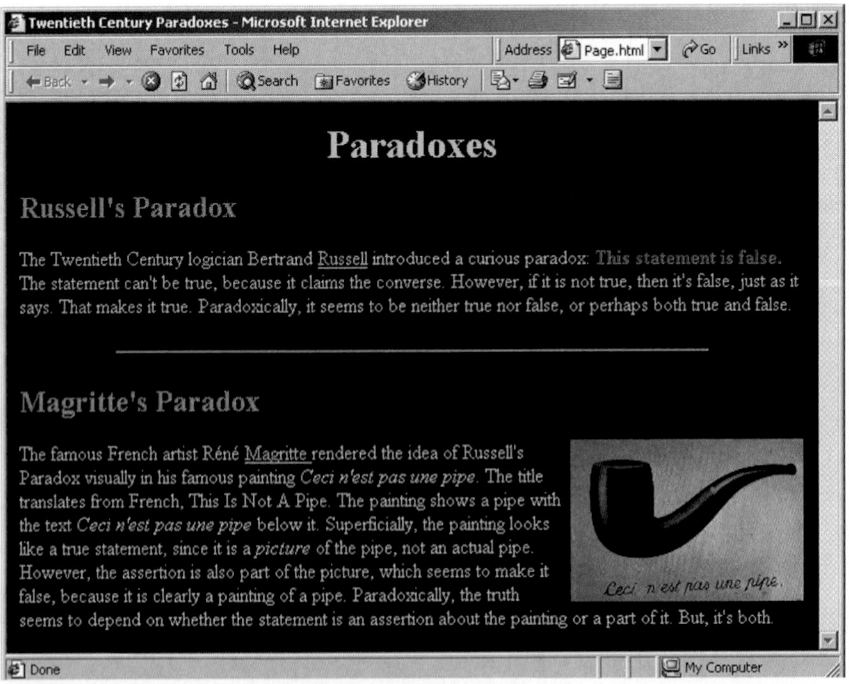

Figure 4.2. *Completed Web page and the HTML source (continued next page).*

```
<html>
  <head>
    <title>Twentieth Century Paradoxes</title>
  </head>
  <body bgcolor="#000000" text="#DDDDDD" link="#FFCC66">
    <h1 align="center"><font COLOR="yellow">Paradoxes</FONT></h1>
      <h2><font color="#FF8E2A">Russell's Paradox</font></h2>
        <p>The Twentieth Century logician Bertrand
        <a href="Russellbio.html">Russell</a> introduced a
        curious paradox: <b><font color="red">This statement
        is false.</font></b> The statement
        can't be true, because it claims the converse.
        However, if it is not true, then it's false, just as
        it says. That makes it true. Paradoxically, it seems
        to be neither true nor false, or perhaps both
        true and false.</p>

  <hr width="75%">

    <h2><font color="#FF8E2A">Magritte's Paradox</font></h2>
      <p> <img src="pipe.jpg" height="130" width="192"
      align="right"> The famous French artist
      R&eacute;n&eacute;
      <a href="Magrittebio.html">Magritte</a>
      rendered the idea of Russell's Paradox visually
      in his famous painting <i>Ceci n'est pas une pipe</i>.
      The title translates from French, This Is Not A Pipe.
      The painting shows a pipe with the text <i>Ceci n'est
      pas une pipe</i> below it. Superficially, the painting
      looks like a true statement, since it is a <i>picture</i>
      of the pipe, not an actual pipe. However, the assertion
      is also part of the picture, which seems to make it
      false, because it is clearly a painting of a pipe.
      Paradoxically, the truth seems to depend on whether the
      statement is an assertion about the painting or a part of
      it. But, it's both. </p>
  </body>
</html>
```

Figure 4.2. *Completed Web page and the HTML source (continued).*

HANDLING LISTS

There are many kinds of lists in HTML, the easiest being an unnumbered list. The unnumbered list tags `<ul>` and `</ul>` surround the items of the list, which are themselves enclosed in list item tags, `<li>` and `</li>`. The browser formats the list with each item bulleted, indented, and starting on its own line. As usual, though the form of the HTML doesn't matter to the browser, we write the HTML list instructions in list form. So, for example, the HTML for a movie list would be

```
<ul>
  <li>Luxo Jr.</li>
  <li>Toy Story</li>
  <li>Monsters Inc.</li>
</ul>
```

which would look like

- Luxo Jr.
- Toy Story
- Monsters Inc.

Another kind of list is an ordered list, which uses the tags `<ol>` and `</ol>` and replaces the bullets with numbers. Otherwise, the ordered list behaves just like an unnumbered list. Thus the HTML for the start of the list of chemical elements is

```
<ol>
  <li> Hydrogen, H, 1.008, 1 </li>
  <li> Helium, He, 4.003, 2</li>
  <li> Lithium, Li, 6.941, 2 1 </li>
  <li> Beryllium, Be, 9.012, 2 2 </li>
</ol>
```

which would look like

1. Hydrogen, H, 1.008, 1
2. Helium, He, 4.003, 2
3. Lithium, Li, 6.941, 2 1
4. Beryllium, Be, 9.012, 2 2

We can also have a list within a list, simply by making the sublists items of the main list. Applying this idea in HTML

```
<ul>
  <li>Pear</li>
  <li>Apple</li>
    <ul>
    <li>Granny Smith</li>
    <li>Fuji </li>
    </ul>
  <li>Cherry</li>
</ul>
```

would look like

- Pear
- Apple
  - Granny Smith
  - Fuji
- Cherry

Finally, there is a handy list form called the **definitional list**, indicated by the tags `<dl>` and `</dl>`. A definitional list is usually made up of a sequence of definitional terms, surrounded by the tags `<dt>` and `</dt>`, and definitional data, surrounded by the tags `<dd>` and `</dd>`. So, for example, a definitional list would be expressed in HTML as

```
<dl>
  <dt> Man </dt>
  <dd> <i>Homo sapiens</i>, the greatest achievement
   of evolution. </dd>
  <dt> Woman </dt>
  <dd> <i>Homo sapiens</i>, a greater achievement of
   evolution, and clever enough not to mention it to man.
</dd>
</dl>
```

and would be formatted by browsers as

Man
: *Homo sapiens*, the greatest achievement of evolution.

Woman
: *Homo sapiens*, a greater achievement of evolution, and clever enough not to mention it to man.

For especially short terms, a more compact form of the definitional list gives the definition on the same line as the term. Include the `compact` attribute in the `<dl>` tag for this type of list. For example, a definitional list of molecular biology abbreviations would be

```
<dl compact>
  <dt>A</dt>
  <dd>Adenine </dd>
  <dt>C</dt>
  <dd>Cytosine </dd>
  <dt>G</dt>
  <dd>Guanine </dd>
  <dt>T</dt>
  <dd>Thymine </dd>
</dl>
```

which is displayed by browsers as

A Adenine
C Cytosine
G Guanine
T Thymine

Of course, other formatting commands such as italics and bold can be used within any line items.

HANDLING TABLES

A table is a good way to present certain types of information. Creating a table in HTML is straightforward. It is like defining a list of lists, where each of the main list items, called *rows*, has one or more items, called *cells*. The browser aligns cells to form columns.

The table is enclosed in table tags, **<table>** and **</table>**. If you want the table to have a border around it, use the attribute **border** inside the table tag. Each row is enclosed in table row tags, **<tr>** and **</tr>**. The cells of each row are surrounded by table data tags, **<td>** and **</td>**. So a table with two rows, each with three cells of the form

Canada	Ottawa	English/French
Iceland	Reykjavik	Icelandic

would be defined by

```
<table border>
  <tr>
    <td>Canada</td>
    <td>Ottawa</td>
    <td>English/French</td>
  </tr>
  <tr>
    <td>Iceland</td>
    <td>Reykjavik</td>
    <td>Icelandic</td>
  </tr>
</table>
```

You can give tables captions and column headings. The caption tags are **<caption>** and **</caption>**. You place them within the table tags around the table's caption. The caption is shown centered at the top of the table in bold. You place the column headings as the first row of the table. In the heading row, you replace the table data tags with table heading tags, `<th>` and `</th>`, which also display in bold. The table row tags are `<tr>` and `</tr>` as usual. Thus we can change our example table to give it a caption and column headings:

```
<table border>
  <caption>Country Data</caption>
  <tr>
    <th>Country</th>
    <th>Capital</th>
    <th>Language(s)</th>
  </tr>
  <tr>
    <td>Canada</td>
    <td>Ottawa</td>
    <td>English/French</td>
  </tr>
  <tr>
    <td>Iceland</td>
    <td>Reykjavik</td>
    <td>Icelandic</td>
  </tr>
  <tr>
    <td>Norway</td>
    <td>Oslo</td>
    <td>Norwegian</td>
  </tr>
</table>
```

which will look like this

Country Data

Country	**Capital**	**Language(s)**
Canada	Ottawa	English/French
Iceland	Reykjavik	Icelandic
Norway	Oslo	Norwegian

Notice that the first row uses the `<th>` tag rather than the `<td>` tag to specify the headings.

Tables are a handy way to control the arrangement of information on the page. An example where this control might be desirable is when we have a series of links listed across the top of a page. The links only form a one-row table, but the table helps keep the links together. Figures 4.3 and 4.4 show two different HTML sources, one simply listing the links in sequence and the other placing the links into a table. When there is enough window space, the two solutions look the same.

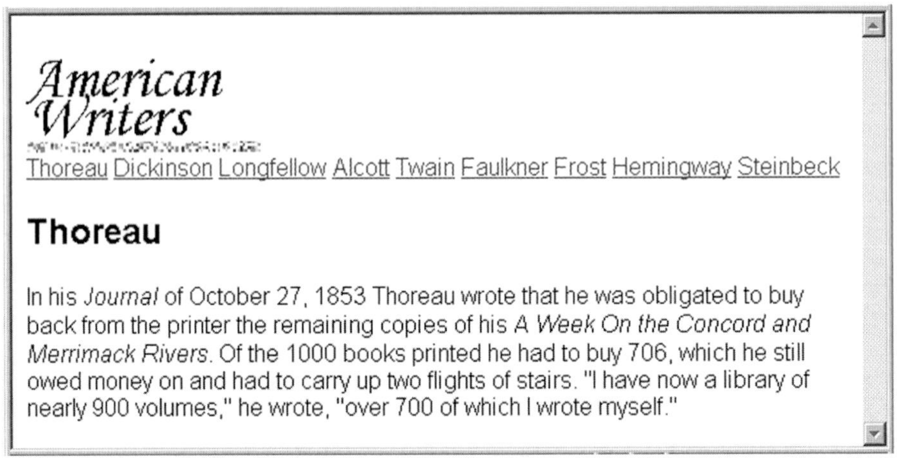


```
<html>
 <head><title>Writer's Anecdotes</title></head>
  <body bgcolor="white" text="black"><font
   face="Helvetica">
     <img src="AWA.gif"v><br>
      <a href="hdt.html">Thoreau</a>
      <a href="ed.html">Dickinson</a>
      <a href="hwl.html">Longfellow</a>
      <a href="lma.html">Alcott</a>
      <a href="sc.html">Twain</a>
      <a href="wf.html">Faulkner</a>
      <a href="rf.html">Frost</a>
      <a href="eh.html">Hemingway</a>
      <a href="js.html">Steinbeck</a>
   <h2>Thoreau</h2>
        <p>In his <i>Journal</i> of October 27, 1853 Thoreau
        wrote that he was obligated to buy back from the
        printer the remaining copies of his <i>A Week On
        the Concord and Merrimack Rivers</i>. Of the 1000
        books printed he had to buy 706, which he still
        owed money on and had to carry up two flights of
        stairs. "I have now a library of nearly 900
        volumes," he wrote, "over 700 of which I wrote
        myself."</p>
 </body>
</html>
```

Figure 4.3. *A page and its HTML for a simple listing of links.*

```
<html>
 <head><title>Writer's Anecdotes</title></head>
  <body bgcolor="white" text="black"><fontface="Helvetica">
   <img src="AWA.gif"v>
     <table>
      <tr>
       <td><a href="hdt.html">Thoreau</a></td>
       <td><a href="ed.html">Dickinson</a></td>
       <td><a href="hwl.html">Longfellow</a></td>
       <td><a href="lma.html">Alcott</a></td>
       <td><a href="sc.html">Twain</a></td>
       <td><a href="wf.html">Faulkner</a></td>
       <td><a href="rf.html">Frost</a></td>
       <td><a href="eh.html">Hemingway</a></td>
       <td><a href="js.html">Steinbeck</a></td>
      </tr>
     </table>
 <h2>Steinbeck</h2>
   <p>Steinbeck traveled to Russia several times, but
   never mastered the language. Traveling with
   photographer Robert Capa in 1947 he wrote, "...I
   admit our Russian is limited, but we can say hello,
   come in, you are beautiful, oh no you don't, and one
   which charms us but seems to have an application
   rarely needed, ‘The thumb is second cousin to the
   left foot.' We don't use that one much."</p>
 </body>
</html>
```

Figure 4.4. *A page and its HTML for listing links in a table.*

The difference comes when there is only a small amount of window space. See Figure 4.5. When there is not enough space for the full sequence of links, the browser will **wrap** (continue on the next line) the links just as it wraps normal paragraph text. But the table will keep the links together in a row; scroll bars are added and the links are hidden. Some people prefer the row to the wrap. Keeping the links in a row is an example of why tables are used even when the situation might not necessarily require a table.

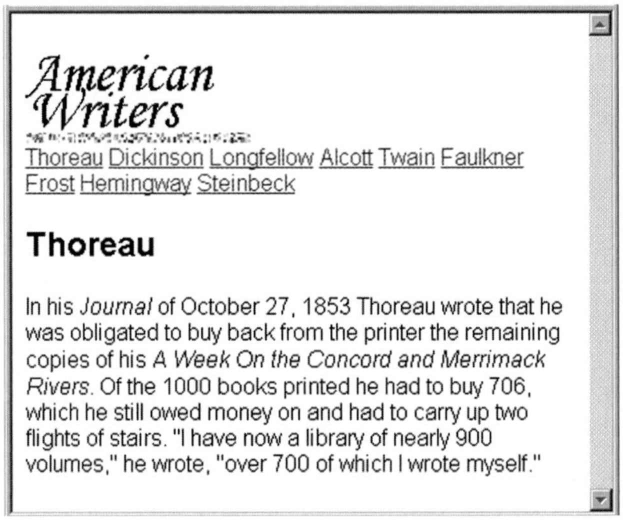

(a)

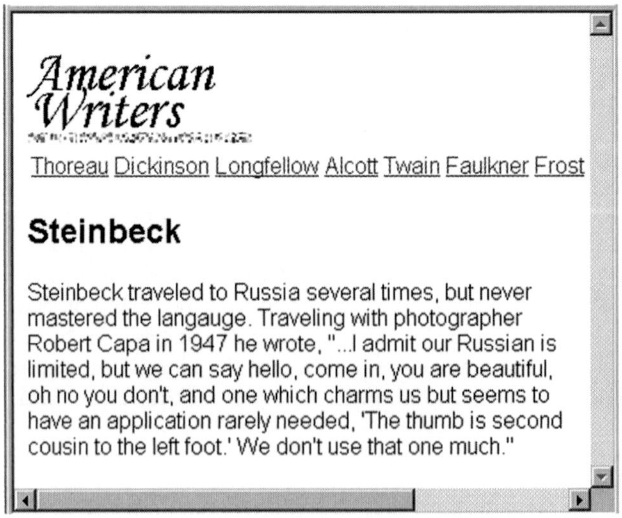

(b)

Figure 4.5. *The display of the two pages from Figures 4.3 and 4.4 in a small window showing that the table (Steinbeck page) keeps the links in a single row rather than wrapping them.*

FITBYTE

Being Perfectly Correct. Because computers do only what they are told, the browser follows the HTML commands exactly. So, the page will not look right until every HTML tag is perfectly correct. Perhaps the best advice is to be as careful and accurate as you can be when writing HTML. You have to be exact, and you will make mistakes, but it is also fun!

HTML WRAP-UP

In learning HTML, we have seen how a Web page is encoded. Though HTML has a few more exotic features than those presented here, and the other Web languages have even more powerful features, they are all variations on the same theme: Tags surround all objects that appear on the page, the context is set by specifying global properties of the page (e.g., `<body bgcolor="white">`), and each feature of the format is specified in detail, `<i>isn't it?!</i>`. It's so easy, even a computer could do it!

Indeed, that's what happens most of the time. Web authors usually don't write HTML directly; they use Web authoring tools, such as Macromedia Dreamweaver, or standard text editors like Microsoft Word, or the Composer feature of Netscape. They build the page as it should look on the screen using a WYSIWYG Web authoring program, and then the computer generates the HTML to implement it.

FITBYTE

Uploading. Pages are created and tested on a personal computer. To be accessed from other computers on the Internet, the HTML files, the image files, and the directory structure created for them must be uploaded (transmitted) to a Web server, a process often called **publishing**.

SUMMARY

Web pages are stored and transmitted in an encoded form before a browser turns them into the image we see on the screen. HTML is the most widely used form of encoding. The chapter opened by recalling the idea of using tags for formatting. A working set of about a dozen HTML tags was introduced, followed by an explanation of how links are marked with anchor tags. A key point was the use of absolute and relative pathnames. Relative pathnames refer to files deeper and higher in the directory hierarchy. Then we discussed images and their two most popular formatting schemes—JPG and GIF—and how images are placed in a page. The topics of numeric colors, lists, and tables added power to our basic understanding. A full example illustrated the ideas of the chapter. Finally, we noted that although HTML is straightforward, Web pages are usually built with WYSIWYG Web authoring tools, programs that then automatically create the HTML when the page design is complete. You can expect to use both approaches.

EXERCISES

Multiple Choice

1. HTML commands are called:
   A. hops
   B. brackets
   C. tags
   D. tokens
2. HTML tags are words enclosed in:
   A. `( )`
   B. `// \\`
   C. `{ }`
   D. `< >`
3. Which of the following would put "Sheryl Crow — In Concert" in the title bar of a Web page?
   A. `<title>Sheryl Crow – In Concert</title>`
   B. `</title> Sheryl Crow – In Concert<title>`
   C. `<title> Sheryl Crow – In Concert<title/>`
   D. `<TITLE/> Sheryl Crow – In Concert</TITLE>`
4. Which of the following tags is not paired?
   A. `<hr>`
   B. `<i>`
   C. `<p>`
   D. `<html>`
5. The `<p> </p>` tags indicate the beginning and end of a:
   A. table
   B. picture
   C. paragraph
   D. preformatted text section
6. The `<a. . .>` tag is called an:
   A. anchor
   B. address
   C. add
   D. append
7. Moving lower in a directory hierarchy is called:
   A. dropping a level
   B. crossing a slash
   C. burrowing
   D. drilling through

8. The **..** notation in a relative path of hypertext reference means to:
   A. open a folder and go down a directory
   B. close a folder and open the parent folder
   C. search a folder
   D. create a folder

9. To get an image to sit on the right side of the window with the text filling the area to the left of the image, your tag would need to look like:
   A. <img src = "mountains.jpg" align = "right">
   B. <img src align = "mountains.jpg" "right">
   C. <img = "mountains.jpg" src align = "right">
   D. <img "mountains.jpg" align src = "right">

10. The dimensions for an image on a Web page:
    A. are set using the **x** and **y** attributes
    B. are set using the **width** and **height** attributes
    C. must be set to the actual size of the image
    D. are automatically adjusted by the browser to fit in the space allotted

Short Answer

1. Today most Web pages are created using _____.
2. To improve readability of HTML text, the computer experts suggest adding ______ to the source instructions.
3. The ______ tag is a way to get more than one consecutive space in a line of a Web page.
4. ______ tags are tags inside other tags.
5. Special commands inside a tag are called ______.
6. ______ are usually used to link to pages on the same site.
7. A **..** in a hypertext reference indicates a ____ path.
8. The src in an image tag stands for _____.
9. GIF stands for ______.
10. JPEG stands for ______.
11. To get the RGB color black using hexadecimal numbers, you would write ______.
12. To put the ten greatest inventions of all time, in order, on a Web page, you should use a(n) ______.

Exercises

1. Why learn HTML at all if authoring tools will do the work for you? Give other examples of where you are expected to learn something when there are tools available that will do the work.
2. Use HTML to properly display the following.

   # General
   ## Colonel
   ### Major
   #### Captain
   ##### Lieutenant
   ###### Sergeant
   Corporal
   Private

3. Explain why a page needs to be reloaded in a browser to see the results of editing changes made in the text editor of an HTML document.
4. Indicate the hyperlink reference and the anchor text in this anchor tag. Then break down the hyperlink reference into the protocol, domain, path, and file name.

   ```
   <a href="http://www.nasm.si.edu/nasm/museum/museum.htm">
   National Air and Space Museum</a>
   ```

5. Convert your birthday (mm/dd/yy) to hexadecimal and then determine what color it is.
6. Experiment with hexadecimal colors until you find the seven combinations that will give you the colors of the rainbow.
7. Create a calendar for the current month using a table. Put the month in a caption at the top. Change the color of the text for Sunday and holidays. Make note of any special days during the month. Add an appropriate graphic to one of the blank cells at the end of the calendar.
8. Create a page with your links to your favorite friends on it. Use one column for their names, another for their homepages, and a third column for their email addresses. Link to their homepages. You can link to their email by using a mailto command. It looks like this:

   ```
   <a href="mailto:snyder@cs.washington.edu">Larry
   Snyder</a>
   ```

9. View and then print the source for the author's homepage. It's at www.cs.washington.edu/homes/snyder/index.html.

   What is the title of the page? Indicate the heading and the body for the page. Find the table. Find the list. Find the email links. Find the absolute hyperlinks and the relative hyperlinks. How many graphics are on this page?

chapter

5

SEARCHING FOR TRUTH

Locating Information on the WWW

learning objectives

- > Explain the benefits of searching in obvious places and in libraries
- > Analyze how Web site information is organized
- > Explain how a Web search engine works
- > Find information by using a search engine
- > Decide whether Web information is truth or fiction

Know not by hearsay, not tradition, . . ., nor by indulgence in speculation, . . . but know for yourselves.

—BUDDHA

A WELL-KNOWN JOKE tells of a man out for an evening walk. He meets a drunk who is under a streetlight on his hands and knees. "What are you doing?" asks the man. "Looking for my car key," replies the drunk. "You lost it here?" asks the man in conversation as he begins to help look. "No, I dropped it by the tavern." "Then why are you looking over here?" "The light's better," the drunk replies. The joke lampoons a principle—the best place to look for something is where it's likely to be found—that is key to finding information.

In this chapter we discuss searching for information and evaluating its accuracy. To find anything, we have to look where it will be found. Historically, libraries have housed well-organized archives, collections, and other information resources that are good places to look. Now many of those resources are available online, so we can update the "visit the library" advice: Log in to the library. To find what we're looking for we must also understand the hierarchical organization of information. Hierarchy speeds searching, and recognizing hierarchies when we see them helps us find information faster. Of course, using a computer to search greatly extends our reach, so we also need to understand how search engines work, how they organize the information they store, and how to interpret the results of a search. If we are going to use search engines effectively, we need to ask the right questions, which is as important as looking in the right place. But finding information and finding truthful, accurate, insightful information are two different things. So we must be aware that deceptive information lurks on the Internet, and learn to recognize accurate sources. Finally, we test our understanding by deciding whether information on a Web page is true or false.

SEARCHING IN ALL THE RIGHT PLACES

Ask a reference librarian where to find a *Scientific American*–type article on black holes and the reply will always be "*Scientific American*." Yet many of us ask questions like that because we don't think about where to look for the information we want. Reference librarians do think about it, and we can learn from them, becoming better information gatherers. That's important, because on the Web we don't have a librarian's help. The key to finding information is to think logically and creatively.

The Obvious and Familiar

If we're going to "look in the right place," we need to know where the information we want can be found. Like *Scientific American*, many sources are obvious and familiar if we think about it:

> To find tax information, ask the federal (IRS) or state tax office.

> To find the direction to Dover from London, look at a map of the United Kingdom.

> To find out how many shares of stock IBM has outstanding, check the company's annual report.

Many of the answers we want to find have an obvious source, so we can simply guess the online address: `www.irs.gov`, `www.mapquest.com`, and `www.ibm.com`, respectively.

Libraries Online

One advantage that research librarians have over most of us is that they know about many more information sources than we do. Their advantage can be our advantage if we use libraries. Libraries remain substantial information resources despite the growth of the Internet. Most college libraries and many large public libraries let you access not only the online catalog of their own collections, but also many other information resources. These libraries are just a "click away" from us all.

For example, the University of Washington's Libraries, `www.lib.washington.edu`, links to the "Top 20 Databases,"—as well as the catalogs for its and the Library of Congress's collection. See Figures 5.1(a) and (b). Many of these resources are commercial databases that UW subscribes to, so only UW students and faculty can use them. However, your library probably gives you access to similar collections. A quick glance at the resources in that list shows that plenty of specialized information is accessible and searchable online. Checking these sources is a quick and easy way to get information.

UW Libraries Catalog
ABI/INFORM global: business and management periodicals
Agricola: articles and book chapters from the National Agriculture Library
Aquatic sciences & fisheries abstracts ASFA: marine/brackish/freshwater biology, commerce, engineering, etc., literature
BIOSIS previews: life sciences literature
Books in print: books from North American publishers
Britannica online: searchable encyclopedia
Current Contents: search ® citations and tables of contents from science, social science, arts, and humanities
Electronic Journals list: http://www.lib.washington.edu/types/ejournals/
Engineering village 2: Compendex, CRC Press, Patent Office, Techstreet abstracts
ERIC: education citations covering over 750 professional journals
Expanded academic index: indexing and abstracting of 1500 scholarly journals
GeoRef: geology literature, including North America (back to 1785) and elsewhere (back to 1933)
INSPEC: indexes and abstracts, conference proceedings in physical sciences, EE and CS
LEXIS-NEXIS: full-text newspaper and other popular literature archive
MEDLINE: citations and indexes from 3900 journals in biomedicine
MLA: modern language literature bibliographic information
OCLC WorldCat: world library holdings
PsycINFO: scholarly literature for medicine, psychiatry, nursing, sociology, education, etc.
Research libraries complete: general interest literature from humanities, social science, and science periodicals
Web of science citations database: science citations, and social science citation index, 1980–present

(a)

UW Libraries List of Links	
Biographical Info	Financial Aid & Grants
Bookstores	Geographic Info
Calculators	Libraries
Career Info	News
Consumer Info	Seattle Info
Dictionaries	Statistical Info
Directories	Telephone Directories
Dissertations	Universities Elsewhere
Educational Info	UW Info
Electronic Journals	Web Tools
Encyclopedias	Writing Guides
A-Z List of Reference Tools	

(b)

Figure 5.1. *UW libraries Top 20 Databases (a), and links (b) reference.*

In addition to catalogs and databases, the UW Libraries homepage offers links to reference tools. These links are classified into various groups, shown in Figure 5.1(b).

The last entry, the A-Z List of Reference Tools—the entire list of tools—lists 223 research resources, including a list of Nobel Prize winners. There are links to the *Canadian Yellow Pages*, the *Oxford English Dictionary*, the *Catholic Encyclopedia* (1917 edition), the *Blue Book of Car Prices*, a *Middle English Dictionary*, and the *World Flag Database*. You can find the answers to many questions of burning interest by locating the right link on the list and following it.

The point is not that UW's librarians have done an especially nice job, but that libraries in general provide many online facilities that are well organized and trustworthy. For example, the Chicago Public Library, `www.chipublib.org`, lists similar resources on its Virtual Libraries page, and the Library of Congress, `www.loc.gov/library/`, has huge online collections and services for researchers. These resources are free and open to everyone. So, to find out information, go (electronically) to the library.

Pre-Digital Information

The online digital library is not yet a substitute for going to the physical library and checking out paper books and journals. Despite the billions of Web pages and digital documents, most of the *valuable information typically found in a library is not online*. Most of humankind's pre-1985 knowledge is not yet digitized. And in some cases where paper documents have been digitized, the online version is missing footnotes, references, and appendices, has unreadable equations, or is in other ways incomplete. So, the best place to begin tracking down information is to look at the online library, but don't be surprised if the information you need is not yet digital.

HOW IS INFORMATION ORGANIZED?

To help us find information, librarians, archivists, Web-page designers, and others who organize collections of information give the collections a structure to make them easier to search. The process is simple: All of the information is grouped into a small number of categories, each of which is easily described. This is the top-level *classification*. Then, the information in each category is also divided into a few subcategories, each with a simple description. These are the second-level classifications. See Figure 5.2 Those subcategories are divided, too, into still smaller categories with brief descriptions, the third-level classifications. And on and on. Eventually, the classifications become small enough that it is possible to look through the whole category to find the desired information.

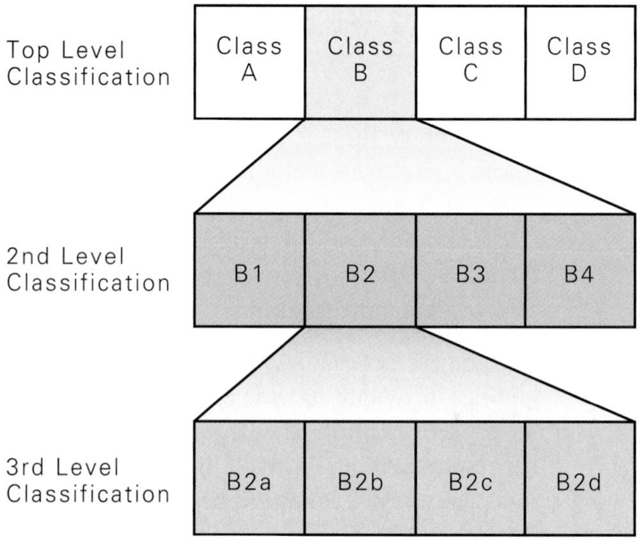

Figure 5.2. *Top level, second level and third level classifications of a collection.*

For example, a source of information about radio stations in the U.S. that carry National Public Radio might use their *geographical region* as its top-level classification, making the top-level categories:

> Northeast, Mid Atlantic, Southeast, North Central, South Central, Mountain, Pacific

Within each region, the second-level classification might use the state, making the Pacific category's subcategories:

> Alaska, California, Hawaii, Oregon, Washington

The third-level categories could be cities for states like California and Texas with several large cities having multiple public radio stations. When the final classification is small enough—Hawaii has only four NPR stations—no finer classification is needed.

There are several important properties to classifications.

- The descriptive terms must cover all of the information in the category and be easy for a searcher to apply. Region of the country, state, city, etc., have this property.
- The subcategories do not all have to use the same classification. So, the Pacific category could categorize by states, but the Northeast might categorize by cities.
- The information in the category defines how best to classify it.

There is no single way to classify information.

This structure is called a *hierarchy*, and as we discussed in Chapter 3 in connection with the directory hierarchy, it is a natural way to organize information. Remember that hierarchies are often drawn as trees. One very famous hierarchy is the "tree of life," the biological taxonomy of organisms. It is too large to display as a tree, but Table 5.1 shows the layers of classification for human beings, from the top level (highest) classification—kingdom—to the last (lowest)—species. Because hierarchies are a logical way to organize information, we find them everywhere. And because they are so intuitive, we don't often consciously notice them. Our goal for the rest of this section is to recognize hierarchies when we see them, because being aware of them speeds up our discovery of information.

FITBYTE

Choose to Exclude. Hierarchies work well not because of what we choose, but what we don't choose. For example, suppose a collection has a million items divided into ten (roughly) equal-size categories. Picking a category eliminates from consideration the 900,000 items in the other categories. If the chosen category is also classified into ten categories, the next choice eliminates another 90,000 items. With two choices we eliminated 990,000 items!

Table 5.1. *The Biological Classification of Human Beings,* Homo sapiens

Taxonomic Level	Name of Classification
Kingdom	Animalia
Phylum	Chordata
Subphylum	Vertebrata
Class	Mammalia
Order	Primates
Family	Hominoidea
Genus	*Homo*
Species	*sapiens*

For example, consider the National Public Radio Web site, `www.npr.org`, shown in Figure 5.3. We might visit this site to find audio information about current news. The site uses hierarchical organization in ways that are sometimes obvious, and sometimes not.

Recognizing a Hierarchy

Looking at the **NPR Programming** pull-down menu (Figure 5.4), we find a list of all of NPR's programs. From the scroll bar on the right, we realize that we are not seeing all of the entries. From the size of the slider, we can guess that we're looking at only about a third of the whole list. The first item (highlighted) is the entire (alphabetized) list of NPR programs, but after that we notice category terms—**Most Requested, NPR News**—separated by lines. Below these are the NPR programs in that category. What we are looking at is a one-level hierarchy of NPR's programming. They have divided all of their programs into five categories:

> Most Requested

> NPR News

> Talk

> Music

> Additional Programming

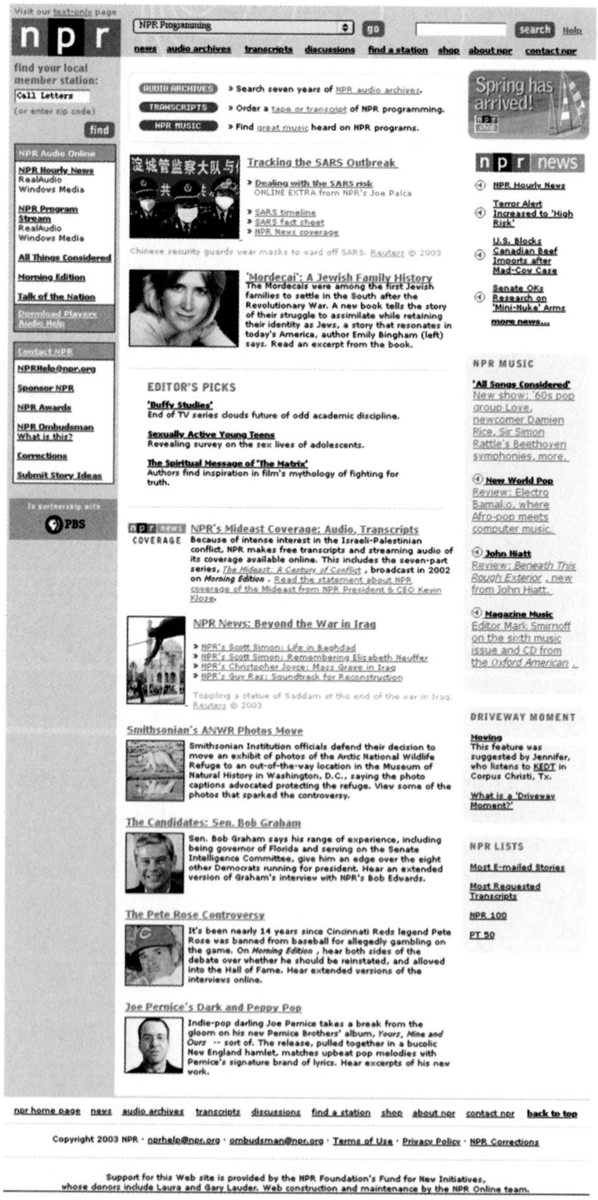

Figure 5.3. *The National Public Radio (NPR) home page www.npr.org.*

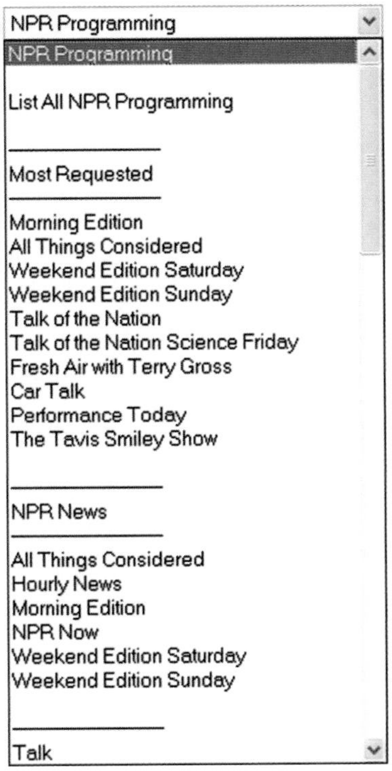

Figure 5.4. *The NPR Programming pull-down menu.*

Figure 5.5 shows the hierarchy drawn as a **tree**. The tree is drawn on its side with the **root** to the left and the **leaves** to the right. Hierarchy trees are often drawn sideways because it's more convenient to write (English) text that way. It is also common to draw them upside down, with the root at the top. Either way, the important part is not the orientation, but the branching metaphor.

Design of Hierarchies

Hierarchies are common and there are general rules for their design and terminology:

- Because hierarchy trees are often drawn with the root at the top, we say "going up in the hierarchy" and "down in the hierarchy." (Similar language—higher and deeper—was used with directory hierarchies in Chapter 3.) The terms are relative to the root being drawn at the top. So "going up" means the classifications become more inclusive. They are moving closer to the root. "Going down" means the classifications become more specific. They are farther from the root.
- The greater-than symbol (>) is a common way to show going down in a hierarchy through levels of classification:

  Classification 1 > Classification 2 > . . . > Classification *n*

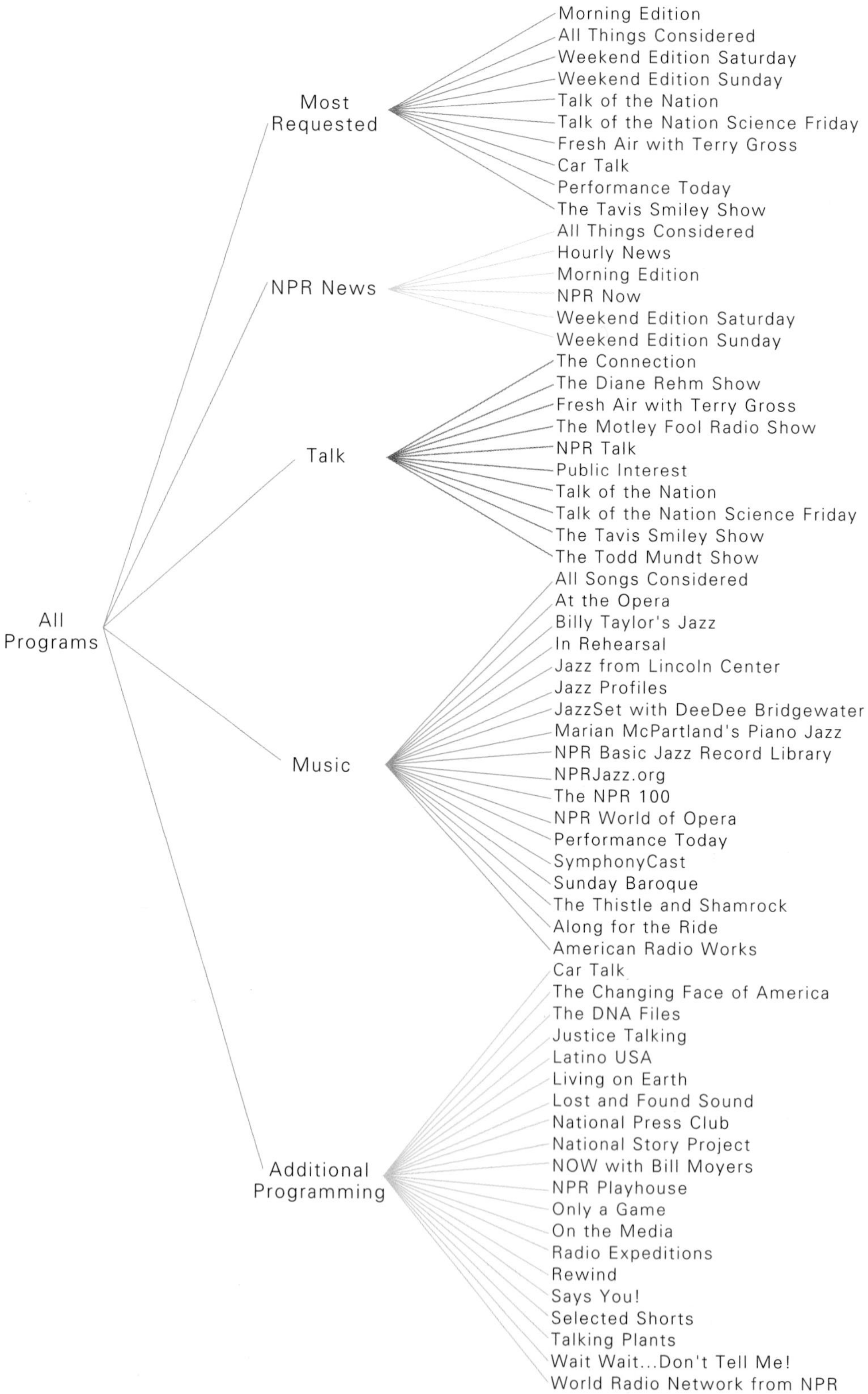

Figure 5.5. *The NPR programming hierarchy tree.*

A One-Level Hierarchy. We call NPR's Programming menu a **one-level hierarchy** because there is only one level of "branching." Counting levels of a hierarchy can be a little confusing sometimes because of all of the connecting lines, but it is easy if we keep two points in mind. First, the tree always has a root—the collection's name. Second, all trees have leaves—the things themselves. Because they exist without any hierarchy, the root and leaves must not count as levels of the hierarchy. When we ignore the root and leaves from Figure 5.5, we see one level of classification.

Partitioning of Levels. Notice that in the NPR menu example, the individual programs can be listed more than once. They can be mentioned both in the **Most Requested** category and in their own category such as **News**. For example, see *All Things Considered*. When every leaf appears once in the hierarchy, the groupings are called **partitionings**. The tree of life is a partitioning because every species is listed once. When the leaves are repeated, groupings "overlap," meaning that an item can be in more than one category. There is no best way to classify information.

Number of Levels May Differ. Finally, the number of classifications of a hierarchy need not be the same for all items. That is, the number of levels of classification between a leaf and root need not be the same for every leaf. Some groupings might require more levels of classification to get the group to a manageable size. For example, if there were many more music programs, we could imagine dividing the **Music** category of Figure 5.5 into three groups: **Jazz**, **Classical**, and **Other**. Then music programs would be reached by two levels of classification, whereas other programs would be reached by only one. A program like Performance Today would be reached by two different paths—a single level through **Most Requested**, or a double level through **Music > Classical**.

HOW IS WEB SITE INFORMATION ORGANIZED?

The NPR Web page designers have used hierarchy to help us find our favorite programs. But they and other Web designers use hierarchy in more basic ways, too.

The NPR homepage itself is the top-level classification for the whole NPR Web site. That is, all of the information on the NPR site must be organized, not just the Web pages for the programs. When we look at the NPR page, we should notice how the information is organized. The page has three basic kinds of information:

> *Classifications* are the roots of hierarchies that organize large volumes of similar types of information. Examples include the row of links listing **news**, **audio archives**, **transcripts**, **discussions**, **find a station**, **shop**, and **about NPR**. **contact us** is in this list of classifications, but it is really a single link. Notice that these classifications are also listed at the bottom of the page, and some are available from other places; for example, **more news >** links to **news**.

> *Topic clusters* are sets of related links. Examples include **Editor's Picks**, which shows three of about twenty items listed on another page (**News**), and **Special Features**, which highlights features from other NPR programming. They are not there to help us navigate the site, but to be read immediately. They are available elsewhere at the site, but have been placed on the homepage to make it interesting and immediately useful.

> *Single links* connect to very specialized pages, such as downloads of audio player software, order forms, and the hourly news stream. Single links take us to pages that either are unusual for the site (software downloads) or are popular (the news stream).

This kind of structure is common because many sites offer items of immediate interest as well as access to the rest of the site.

SEARCHING THE WEB FOR INFORMATION

A **search engine** is a collection of computer programs that helps us find information on the World Wide Web. Though programs for text searching existed long before the Web, the explosion of Web-based digital information and its distribution across the planet made the invention of search engines necessary. No one organizes the information posted on the Web, so these programs look around to find out what's out there and organize what they find. It's a big task. How do search engines do it?

How a Search Engine Works

A search engine has two basic parts: a **crawler** and a **query processor**. The crawler visits sites on the Internet, discovering Web pages and building an **index** to the Web's content. The query processor looks up user-submitted keywords in the index and reports back which Web pages the crawler has found containing those words. Popular search engines include Alta Vista, Excite, InfoSeek, Google, and Yahoo!. We will use the Google search engine as our example here (Figure 5.6).

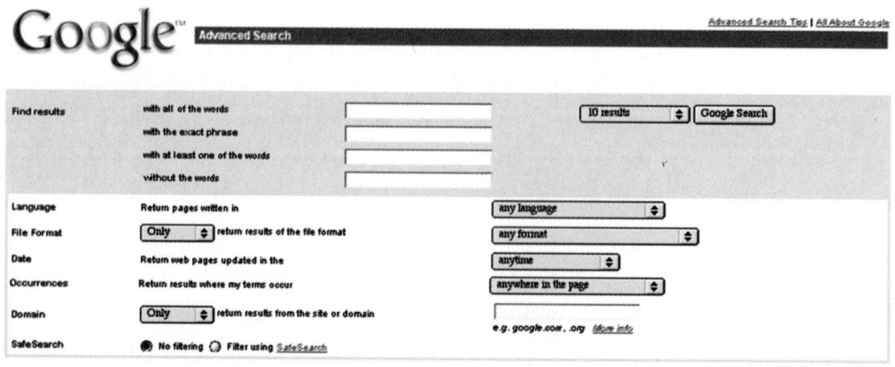

Figure 5.6. *The Google search engine's advanced search view.*

FITBYTE

A Big Name in Searching. "Google" is a variant spelling of googol, a term coined by American mathematician Edward Kasner's nine-year-old nephew Milton Sirotta for the number 10^{100}; that is, 1 followed by one hundred zeros.

Crawlers. When the crawler visits a Web page, it first identifies all the links to other Web pages on that page. It checks in its records to see if it has visited those other pages recently. If not, it adds them to its "To Do" list of pages that must be crawled. Thus crawlers find the pages to look at by saving links to pages not yet visited from pages they've already seen. (Google also lets Web page authors submit their pages to be crawled.)

The crawler also records in an index the keywords used on a page. The words can appear in either the title or the body of the page. For example, the HTML homepage for the Hot Dang! Thai restaurant (**www.hotdang.com**) might have the title block

```
<title> Hot Dang! Restaurant, Cuisine of Siam </title>
```

so, in the index, the crawler would associate the keywords "hot," "dang," "restaurant," "cuisine," and "siam" with the **www.hotdang.com** URL. Small, unspecific words like "of" are ignored. Crawlers also ignore case.

FITBYTE

Shortsightedness. Search engines crawl only a fraction (substantially less than half) of the Web. Because it is growing so fast, there are always new pages not yet visited. Librarians call the pages not crawled, the "Invisible Web." There are other reasons that crawlers miss pages:

> No page points to it, so it never gets on the To Do list
> The page is synthetic—that is, created on-the-fly for each user by software
> The page has no text (images)
> The format is one the crawler does not recognize

Google pioneered the idea of including keywords from the *anchor* (that highlighted text associated with a link) in the index. That is, the words of the highlighted text of a link *to a page* are included among the descriptive terms for that page. For example, if your Web page referenced the Hot Dang! restaurant with the text

```
. . . my favorite <a href="http://www.hotdang.com">
Thai restaurants </a> . . .
```

Thai restaurants would be the highlighted anchor and the terms "Thai" and "restaurants" would be included by Google as keywords associated with **www.hotdang.com**. Anchors help a search engine find relevant pages because the anchors often describe the page better than the page's own content. For example, the Hot Dang! restaurant's motto is "Cuisine of Siam," so the page may not actually say anywhere that it is a Thai restaurant. But your anchor does.

Query Processors. The query processor of a search engine gets keywords from a user and looks them up in the index to find the URLs of pages associated with those keywords. So, for example, when a user asks for "Thai restaurants," all of the URLs associated with those words will be reported back. If Google had crawled your page, the query processor will return `www.hotdang.com` among its responses to the "Thai restaurants" query because your anchor connected "Thai" and "restaurants" with the Hot Dang! site. Notice that in this case the Google crawler might not have crawled the Hot Dang! restaurant's site yet; that site might still be on the To Do list. But it will still know that the site is connected with the terms "Thai" and "restaurants" because of the anchor on your page. If Google had crawled the Hot Dang! site, the query processor would also return `www.hotdang.com` among the responses to the "Thai cuisine" query because "Thai" is in your anchor and "cuisine" is in the restaurant's title.

It is important to give the query processor the right terms to look up. In the next sections, we explain how to create good queries. But even when you choose exactly the right terms, you could get hundreds or thousands of relevant URLs, or **hits**. For example, suppose someone in your hometown of Dallas queries "Thai restaurants in Dallas Texas." There could be a huge list of hits, including (presumably) the homepages for all Thai restaurants, but also your homepage because it uses those words, too. But your page has nothing to do with Thai restaurants, except for your comment about liking Hot Dang!. If the search engine just returns an unordered list of all hits, the user would have to click through the whole list, looking at pages that could be completely irrelevant (see Figure 5.7). We need more help from the search engine!

Figure 5.7. *Restricting the Thai restauraunts "hits" by eliminating any page containing the word* review.

Page Ranking. Google pioneered another idea called **PageRank** that it uses to order the hits by their importance to the user. (Of course, it cannot have any clue, really, as to what you are looking for.) PageRank is Google's guess about how important a page is. It computes the PageRank by counting how many pages link to a page. The more links there are *to* a page, the more important it must be. As the Google inventors describe it, if page A links to page B, consider the link as a vote by A for B. So, for example, because your page links to `www.hotdang.com`, it "votes" for the restaurant. If many sites vote, it must be of greater interest, so the search engine lists the pages with higher PageRank first. Google also looks at whether the page doing the "voting" is itself highly ranked.

Page Ranking's Limitations. In the previous example, if a restaurant reviewer has a page that many people link to, and the reviewer's page links to Hot Dang!, Google treats that link as a more significant vote than yours, assuming fewer pages link to your homepage. Thus Google would probably list `www.hotdang.com` before your page in the list of hits resulting from the query. Page ranking is highly successful in identifying the pages of greater interest, but, of course, fame isn't everything.

PageRank's idea of one page voting for another exactly captures your purpose of citing Hot Dang! as one of your favorite Thai restaurants. But, if your link had been part of a complaint about food poisoning with the purpose of discouraging others from going to Hot Dang!, Google would still count it as a vote for the restaurant's page. Yea or nay, it's still a vote.

Asking the Right Question

After "Look where the information is to be found," the best advice to someone looking for information is "Ask the right question." The question or **query** we are asking a search engine is, "What pages are associated with the following terms . . . ?" To get the right answer back means not only choosing the right terms but also knowing how the search engine will use them. In this section, we learn how to make effective queries. (All searching facilities have slight syntactic variations.)

> FITTIP
>
> **Search Engine Rules.** Most search engines explain their specific rules in a link (located near the search window) called "Advanced" or "Hints" or some similar term. If the query rules you learn in this section don't get you the results you want, check for differences.

Words or Phrases? The first point to understand is that text-searching facilities, including search engines, generally consider each word separately. Though most English speakers think of "Thai restaurants" as a single noun phrase, most search engines treat it as two words. We can ask the search facility to look for the exact phrase by placing quotation marks around it, as in

```
"Thai restaurants"
```

which has the effect of binding the words together.

But the problem with using the exact-phrase quotes is that the match must be perfect, ignoring spaces and case. Exact matching means information in other forms will be missed. For example, these phrases:

```
Thai restaurant
restaurants featuring Thai cuisine
Thai and Asian restaurants
```

would *not* match the quoted string. For this reason search facilities treat the words as separate and allow them to occur anywhere. It is best to limit the use of exact-match quotes to phrases like titles,

```
"Crime and Punishment"
```

where the form is always the same. Notice that quoting part of a phrase, say **`"Tale of Two Cities"`**, is a safe solution when we cannot remember whether it's *The Tale of Two Cities* or *A Tale of Two Cities*.

If the words are treated independently, should the search pick pages with both of the words "Thai" and "restaurants" or pages with just one of them? If it's just one of the words, pages referring to "Thai vacations" and pages referring to "steak restaurants" would also be hits. If we want both, but ask for either, we'll get an enormous number of useless hits.

Logical Operators. So we need to spell out how the words should be processed. We do this by using **logical operators**. The three logical operators are AND, OR, and NOT. They are written using all capital letters to distinguish them from the keywords. Remember that search facilities usually ignore case, so we don't need to capitalize keywords. Capitalizing the logical operators makes them stand out for us. AND and OR are the most commonly used logical operators in queries, and they are **infix operators**, meaning that they are placed between keywords. AND means *both*. OR means *either* or *both*. So, for example, the phrase

```
Thai AND restaurants
```

finds pages with both words appearing in any position; that is, they may not be together in the given order. The query

```
Thai OR Siam
```

finds pages with either word, including pages where they both appear. Of course, we could write queries that include both operators, but we must be careful. For example, does

```
Thai OR Siam AND restaurants
```

mean either a page containing the words *Thai* and *restaurants* or *Siam* and *restaurants* or a page containing either the word *Thai* or the two words *Siam* and *restaurants*? We meant the first. The latter would hit on pages about Thai vacations. Because the query is *ambiguous* (it has more than one interpretation), there is no way of guessing how the search engine will interpret it. So, to be unambiguous, we include parentheses the way we do when we write algebra formulas:

```
(Thai OR Siam) AND restaurants
```

Now the search engine will look for pages that have *restaurants* and also either *Thai* or *Siam*.

We can use NOT to exclude pages with the given word. NOT is a prefix operator, meaning that it comes before the word to be excluded. So, to exclude restaurant review pages from the Thai restaurant search, we might write

```
Thai AND restaurants AND NOT review
```

Notice that we need the AND to show that three conditions must be met: matching *Thai*, matching *restaurants*, not matching *review*. Most often, NOT is used when we recognize a pattern of unintended interpretations.

So far, we have assumed the simplest case, where the search facility offers only a single window for giving the query. The Google Advanced Search page (recommended) gives us several windows to simplify creating queries with the logical operators. Figure 5.6 shows the GUI of the Advanced Search and each of its windows. There are separate windows for AND words, exact phrases, OR words, and NOT words. In this case, Google saves us from having to type the logical operators. (Though most of the searches illustrated in this book use Google, queries will always be written using the logical operators.) All we need to do is list the search words, separated by blanks, in the correct window. Notice that if more than one window is filled in, the search must fulfill the requirements of all windows together.

FITCAUTION

Misspellings. Correct spelling is obviously essential to effective searching. Search engines can recognize misspelled words, and ask if you meant to type another word. But it cannot guess that you've made a mistake if you mistype, for example, `trail` for `trial`. It pays to be careful.

Getting Close

We have seen that to be effective at searching, you should pick meaningful and specific keywords. Choosing the right words is sometimes easy, as when you're looking for data on ibuprofen, because the term is unique. At other times, choosing the right words is very difficult, as when you're looking for information on the fuel economy of new cars, because the obvious terms—gas mileage, cars—are extremely common. In any event, thinking for a few moments about a search strategy will really pay off.

Five Tips for an Efficient Search

Here's a recommended process for creating a search:

1. *Be clear about what sort of page you seek.* Ask yourself whether you want a source page from a company or organization (for example, the Hot Dang! restaurant), or a reference page that points to a collection of similar pages (for example, the restaurant reviewer's page), or perhaps a resource page that puts together information on the topic (for example, a guide to Thai cooking). Thinking clearly about the kind of page you want helps to direct the search toward that page.

2. *Think about what type of organization might publish the page you want.* Is the information likely to come from a company, a government agency, a university, some special organization, or another country? You might be able to guess a Web address for the site, and avoid a search altogether. If you can guess a likely URL, for example, **`www.hotdang.com`**, then try it! Even if you can't guess the URL, you can limit the search by the domain suffix—that is, the "dot com" part of a domain name. (See Figure 5.6.)

3. *List terms that are likely to appear on the pages you are looking for.* You want to find a combination of words that will appear on the the page you want and the fewest number of unwanted pages. You must include words that describe the category (for example, *Thai* and *restaurant),* and then use AND in limiting words:
   > Location-specific words such as *Dallas* AND *Texas*
   > Time-specific words such as *Monday* because businesses often give the times they're open
   > Activity-specific words such as *entrées*
   > Specialty terms such as *phad* because every Thai restaurant probably serves phad Thai

   The pages we seek have many specific properties, each with their characteristic terms. With some thought, we can come up with those terms.

4. *Assess the results.* Before looking at each returned page, check the results to see how effective the search was. Look for the two errors of including too much and not including enough. One way to include too much is to get a type of match you didn't expect. For example, all the pages about vacationing in Thailand probably describe the restaurants where tourists will eat. You can do another search with a NOT keyword (for example, `NOT vacation`) to eliminate these. The other error, not including enough, is possibly harder to recognize. For example, if we include "Monday" in our search, we eliminate all of the restaurants that are open Tuesday to Sunday. So, we must be alert to what we are not finding and consider whether we should drop some of our keywords.

5. *Consider a two-pass strategy.* Because it's hard to get the search terms just right, it is probably a good idea when using the Google search engine to use a "two-pass" strategy. First do a broad topic search, then do one or more searches within your results. Google lets you narrow your search with additional keywords. (See Figure 5.7.) Searching "within results" lets us capture the pages within the category and then try different ways of limiting the search until we find what we are looking for. If we limit the search too much, we can simply back up to the point where the hits are inclusive enough. Notice that the terms in the search-within-results window are more AND terms; that is, they are required on the page. We can force the absence of a term, say, vacation, by writing a minus sign before it like this: **–vacation**.

FITTIP

Finding the Needle. Narrowing the search to the right page is the first task, but finding the information can mean more searching on the page itself. Remember that browsers have a word-search facility, **Find**, under the **Edit** menu. To search on a page, use **Find**.

Using the principles just outlined, imagine that you plan to go windsurfing and need a sailboard. You are thinking of going to Hood River, Oregon, where the

Hood joins the Columbia, a famous windsurfing area. You're flying, so you will need to rent equipment when you arrive. Your queries yield:

sailboards	9180 hits
sailboards AND oregon	342 hits
sailboards AND oregon AND "hood river"	151 hits
sailboards AND oregon AND "hood river" AND rental	23 hits

which includes the shops and tourist facilities pages you want.

In summary, successful searches result from well-thought-out queries based on specific terms. It is wiser to spend time thinking up exact queries, possibly querying several times or searching through results to pinpoint the few pages of interest, than it is to read through many worthless pages from unspecific searches.

WEB INFORMATION: TRUTH OR FICTION?

In Chapter 3 we noted that an increased exercise of freedom of speech is a fundamental change brought about by the World Wide Web. It is possible in many countries of the world to publish anything on the Web, uncensored by companies or governments. This is a benefit, but, like all freedoms, this one carries with it some important responsibilities—not so much for the speaker, but for the reader or listener. Because anyone can publish anything on the World Wide Web, some of what gets published is false, misleading, deceptive, self-serving, slanderous, or simply disgusting. We have to be alert for this and always ask, "*Is this page legitimate, true, and correct?*" In this section we consider whether the pages we've found in our search are giving us reliable information.

Do Not Assume Too Much

The first thing to look for is who or what organization publishes the page. For example, health information from the Centers for Disease Control, the World Health Organization, or the American Medical Association is about the best that can be found. These respected organizations try to publish current and correct information, so we can trust their Web pages. Of course, they publish information based on science, and over time new discoveries might occasionally invalidate something, meaning it wasn't true. But we're not worried about such philosophical aspects of the *nature of truth*. We can assume that respected organizations publish the best information available. We're unlikely to find better.

Checking the organization that publishes the information seems like overkill. After all, if the Web site's domain name is `ama-assn.org`, it claims to be the AMA page, and it's giving out medical information, it must be the American Medical

Association, right? In fact, it is. But, just because a page seems to be from a certain organization and the domain name *seems* plausible, it isn't necessarily true. Domain names are not checked. Anyone could have reserved the domain name **ama-assn.org** and published bogus health information. You must be wary.

To illustrate that sites are not always what they appear to be, consider the hoax perpetrated from the site **www.gatt.org**. The domain name looks like it is related to the General Agreement on Tariffs and Trade, or GATT as it's known, the free-trade agreement of the 1990s. The site looks like the official publication of the World Trade Organization (WTO), the free-trade group that followed on from the GATT treaty. The page shows photographs of Michael Moore, WTO President, quotes him, and posts WTO-related free-trade news. However, the site is actually run by an *anti*-free-trade organization known as the Yes Men.

According to the January 7, 2001, *New York Times*, organizers of a meeting of international trade lawyers in Salzburg, Austria, sent mail to **www.gatt.org** inviting WTO President Moore to speak at their meeting. From **www.gatt.org** came an email reply declining on behalf of Mr. Moore, but offering (a fictitious) speaker, Dr. Andreas Bichlbauer, as a substitute. The meeting organizers accepted Dr. Bichlbauer who came to their October 2000 meeting and gave a very offensive speech critical of Italians and Americans. The perpetrators of the hoax even claimed that a WTO protestor threw a crème pie at Dr. Bichlbauer. They claimed that the pie had contained a *bacillus*, that Bichlbauer had been taken ill and hospitalized, and that he had died. The whole hoax, which caused much embarrassment, began when someone assumed that **www.gatt.org** was a legitimate WTO site.

A Two-Step Check for the Site's Publisher

How can you find out if a site is for real? A two-step process can help:

1. The InterNIC site **www.internic.net/whois.html** lists the company that assigned an IP address (i.e., domain). Type in the domain name, such as **company.com**. Included in the returned InterNIC information about the domain is a site called a **WhoIs Server** maintained by the company that assigned the address. That site will tell you who the domain's owner is.

2. Go to the **WhoIs Server** site and type in the domain name or IP address again. The information returned is the owner's name and physical address.

When checking a Web site, remember to pull out the domain name from the URL.

Elaborate hoaxes like **gatt.org** are rare, though there have been others. A more likely situation is that information is unintentionally wrong or simply fictional. In the first category is information such as "urban legends"—stories like alligators living in the New York City sewer system—that people pass along as true, although they don't have primary evidence or an authoritative basis for believing it. They heard it through a friend of a friend. Urban myths are usually harmless, but not always. In the second category, fiction and humor are meant to entertain us. April Fools' pages, alien spaceships visiting Seattle's Space Needle, and reports of one-ton squirrels fall into this category. They are fun. Every April, National Public Radio, for example, broadcasts a fictitious news story on the program *All Things Considered*. It is best to approach Web pages with some skepticism.

Characteristics of Legitimate Sites

What cues can alert a reader to misinformation? In a recent survey, Internet users thought that a site was more believable if it had these features:

> **Physical existence.** The site provided a street address, telephone number, and legal email address.

> **Expertise.** The site's authors listed references, citations, or credentials, and there were links to related sites.

> **Clarity.** The site was well organized, easy to use, and provided site-searching facilities.

> **Currency.** The site had been recently updated.

> **Professionalism.** The site's grammar, spelling, punctuation, and so forth, were correct; all links worked.

Of course, a site can have these characteristics and still not be legitimate. A site trying to fool people can take care to appear to be legitimate. If you have doubts, check it out. The name and address should be in `www.whitepages.com`. If they are not listed, maybe you should be suspicious. If it's a business, can you find the business in the yellow pages? If the author gives credentials, citations, or other links, check them out, too. By checking, you can feel confident that the information you are getting is reliable.

Check Other Sources

Finally, if the information is important to you, check it on more than one source. After all, it is very easy to use the Internet to find information, so it's equally easy to use it to confirm information. Ask yourself, "If this information were true, what other source could directly or indirectly confirm it?" Of course, we must be equally skeptical about the supporting information. For example, we cannot count the number of sites referencing information as proof that it's true, because by that reasoning the alligators in the sewer urban legend would seem to be supported by the 2050 hits on `alligator AND sewer`. A better approach is to find sites that speak directly to the topic, such as `www.snopes.com`.

THE BURMESE MOUNTAIN DOG PAGE

To test our ability to assess a site, suppose we have found `lme.mnsu.edu/akcj3/bmd.html`, a site describing the Burmese Mountain Dog. (See Figure 5.8.) The page is authoritative looking. It has been posted by someone claiming DVM credentials, probably meaning doctor of veterinary medicine. There are photographs, links to the American Kennel Club, and so on. The page seems completely legitimate and meets most of the criteria the Internet users have listed as indicating authenticity. If we ask Google to find `Burmese AND mountain AND dog`, we get 2350 hits. Many people would probably accept the page as truthful.

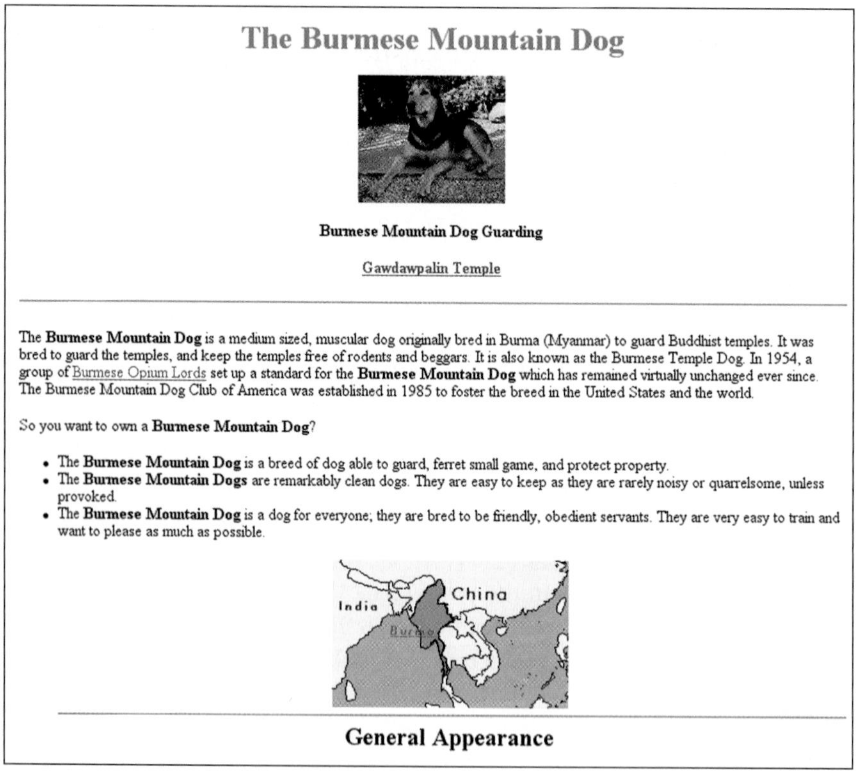
The Burmese Mountain Dog

Burmese Mountain Dog Guarding

Gawdawpalin Temple

The **Burmese Mountain Dog** is a medium sized, muscular dog originally bred in Burma (Myanmar) to guard Buddhist temples. It was bred to guard the temples, and keep the temples free of rodents and beggars. It is also known as the Burmese Temple Dog. In 1954, a group of Burmese Opium Lords set up a standard for the **Burmese Mountain Dog** which has remained virtually unchanged ever since. The Burmese Mountain Dog Club of America was established in 1985 to foster the breed in the United States and the world.

So you want to own a **Burmese Mountain Dog**?

- The **Burmese Mountain Dog** is a breed of dog able to guard, ferret small game, and protect property.
- The **Burmese Mountain Dogs** are remarkably clean dogs. They are easy to keep as they are rarely noisy or quarrelsome, unless provoked.
- The **Burmese Mountain Dog** is a dog for everyone; they are bred to be friendly, obedient servants. They are very easy to train and want to please as much as possible.

General Appearance

Figure 5.8. *The Burmese mountain dog page.*

Because the page has a link to the American Kennel Club, `akc.org`, which lists all breeds the Club recognizes, it's possible to check out the Burmese Mountain Dog. In the AKC's list of breeds, we find that there is no Burmese Mountain Dog, though there is a Bernese Mountain Dog, named for Berne, Switzerland. What gives? First, we ask if `akc.org` is legitimate by using the `InterNIC WhoIs` service, and find that it is. Next, we check `lme.mnsu.edu` and find it is the Library Media Education department of Mankato State University in Minnesota. This is a surprise. A university is usually a reliable place to get information, but we would expect it to come from the Department of Veterinary Medicine. Accepting that the AKC is giving correct information about the Bernese Mountain Dog, we conclude that either the Burmese page is a fake or the Burmese Mountain Dog is not yet a recognized breed.

It is interesting that there are so many hits on Burmese Mountain Dog, but when we ask Google to look up `bernese AND mountain AND dog` we get 17,800 hits, so the Burmese page gets fewer hits. When we look at photos of the two dogs, we notice that they look very similar. The main difference is that the Bernese has a white chest, while the Burmese has a dark chest with a brown V. Such a striking similarity suggests that someone has made a comparison, so we check for pages citing both. Checking `bernese AND burmese AND mountain AND dog` yields only 175 hits.

A phrase displayed by Google,

It's Bernese, Burmese is a cat

suggests two points: Many of these pages must be listing both cats and dogs, and there is a Burmese cat. (Removing cat (`-cat`) yields only 35 hits.) The other possibility is that people may be mispronouncing or misspelling Bernese as Burmese. A quick look at several of the pages tells us we've guessed right. Some personal pages show a photo of what the AKC calls a Bernese Mountain Dog, but they call it a Burmese Mountain Dog. Another page makes a point of saying it's from Berne rather than Burma. So, we guess that the original page is fiction, and return to it to admire how skillful a hoax it is.

SUMMARY

The secret to finding the information we're looking for is to look in the right place. The first place to look for many types of information is not the Web, but the library. The online resources at large public and university libraries are huge. Libraries not only can give us the needed information in digital form, they can also connect us with the archives of "pre-digital" information—the millions of books, journals, and manuscripts that still exist only in paper form. In many cases the best information only exists in these paper documents. We can expect to use traditional documents for years to come.

Unlike a library, where we can get the help of a reference librarian, we need software and our own intelligence to search the Internet effectively. We create queries using the logical operators of AND, OR, and NOT, and specific terms to pinpoint the information we seek. Once we've found the information, we must judge whether it is correct, to avoid being duped or misled. One way to do this is to check out the organization that publishes the page, including checking the credentials of the people who have written the information. Finally, we need to cross-check the information with other sources, especially when the information is important.

EXERCISES

Multiple Choice

1. One of the downsides of unmediated expression on the Web is:
A. a need for verification of the accuracy of the content
B. duplication of information
C. that very little information is available
D. all of the above

2. LEXIS-NEXIS would be used to locate:
A. used-car information
B. full-text newspapers
C. personal health information
D. ancient Egyptian customs

3. Searching through ERIC you would find:
A. children's names
B. government Web sites
C. professional journals
D. computer information

4. A hierarchy resembles a:
A. subway map
B. tree
C. spoked wheel
D. list

5. Someone searching with a search engine would use the:
A. crawler
B. query processor
C. index
D. anchor

6. Most Web pages are not indexed because:
A. search engines have not crawled them
B. pages are created on demand and those cannot be indexed
C. other pages do not point to it
D. all of the above

7. Google was the first search engine to get its keywords from:
A. InterNIC
B. page titles
C. anchors tags
D. user submissions

8. The results from a search using AND will be ______ than a search using OR.
A. larger
B. the same
C. smaller
D. overlapping

9. To omit a word from a search, you would:
   A. put the word MINUS in front of the word
   B. put the word in parentheses
   C. put a minus sign in front of the word
   D. put the word inside quotation marks
10. Which of the following is not a method for testing the believability of a Web site?
    A. professionalism
    B. WWW Consortium approval
    C. expertise
    D. physical existence provided by the site

Short Answer

1. Historically, the _____ has been the repository of information.
2. On the computer, you would look for information using a(n) ______.
3. ______ provide connections to specialized pages.
4. ______ are computer programs that help people find information on the Web.
5. ______ uses the keywords in the anchor link of Web pages to index its pages.
6. Counting the number of pages linked to a page helps to determine that page's ______.
7. AND, OR, and NOT are called ______.
8. Operators placed between words in a query are called ______.
9. A(n) ______ is a method of organizing information by groups.
10. If a word or phrase is enclosed in quotes in a search, the search engine will search for a(n) ______.
11. Web pages found using a search engine are called ______.
12. The ______ operator is used to exclude a word or phrase from a search.
13. In a search, the plus (+) sign is the same as using the word ______.
14. In a search, the minus (–) sign is the same as using the word ______.
15. ______ is a company that tracks information on who owns a Web site.

Exercises

1. Write down the organization chart used by Yahoo! (www.yahoo.com) for its home page. What type of classification is it?
2. Go to InterNIC (`www.internic.net/whois.html`). Type in the name of a Web site and check its information. Do the same for other companies.

3. How would you find a search engine that specializes in European Web sites? Find one and use it. What do you find?
4. Create a classification scheme for clothing items. In your list, what items could be classified in more than one group?
5. Use Switchboard.com (**`www.switchboard.com`**) to look up your phone number.
6. Use MapQuest (**`www.mapquest.com`**) to look up your address. Print the map for it.
7. What is the Web address for the New York Public Library?
8. Pick an issue. Find sites on both sides of the issue and analyze their content.

chapter

6

SEARCHING FOR GUINEA PIG B

Case Study in Online Research

learning objectives

- Explain the advantages and disadvantages of online research
- Explain the advantages and disadvantages of primary and secondary sources in research
- Apply the case study example (R. Buckminster Fuller)
  - Expand and narrow an online search, as needed
  - Use bookmarking
  - Locate primary and secondary sources
  - Assess the authority of sources
  - Use online photos, video clips, and audio clips to enhance the search
  - Resolve controversial questions online
  - Follow up on interesting side questions
- Use the skills above to be able to do a curiosity-driven online research project

Sometimes I think we are alone [in the universe]. Sometimes I think we are not. In either case, the thought is quite staggering.

—R. BUCKMINSTER FULLER

WE'RE ALL CURIOUS, and the IT knowledge we have developed so far is enough to help us track down the answers to questions we wonder about. Usually these questions are simple: "Is the Colorado ski area Telluride named after the chemical element Tellurium?" With a few clicks we find the answer, perhaps mention it to a friend, and that's that. The World Wide Web has helped us answer the question without visiting the library. Now, with the speed and convenience of the Web, we can easily add to our store of useless facts and amaze our friends.

But information technology offers us more than a simple chance to answer a single question. It lets us find out about substantial topics that interest us and probe deeply wherever our curiosity leads us. This is called **curiosity-driven research**. For centuries now, educated people who were curious about a topic would consult books, but now on-line research expands our opportunities.

Books do have certain advantages: They are generally authoritative, having been carefully researched, usually well written, and permanent. Their disadvantages are that they contain only the information the author selects, so they give us only one point of view; they can take years to produce, so the information they offer may be dated; they are static; and despite so many titles, they cover only a limited number of topics. Books remain excellent sources of information. But the fact is, a book exists because someone else was curious about a topic, researched it, and interpreted the findings. With the World Wide Web, we can pick the topic, we can do our own research, and we can make our own interpretation of what we find. That is, our own curiosity drives the research.

In this chapter we learn to do curiosity-driven research using the WWW. This gives us a chance to use the ideas introduced in earlier chapters. One goal is to explore the limits of the research that can be done on the WWW, because not everything is in digital form yet, and not everything in digital form is worth reading. Another goal is to enjoy a tour through the life and mind of an amazing man, R. Buckminster Fuller, who described himself as both an engineer and a poet. The topic requires using different kinds of information resources. Finally, we learn to fill in the gaps in our knowledge. Though the case study runs to many pages, it represents the search/research activity of a single interesting and enjoyable evening. The conclusion is that curiosity-driven research can be fun, and more interesting and rewarding than watching another rerun of *Friends*.

FITTIP

Student Aid. Curiosity-driven research can be a random process, as different discoveries grab our interest. It appears even more aimless when it's someone else's curiosity doing the driving. Though I explain why we choose the path we take, it is still possible for you to lose track of where we are. If that happens, you may want to check the summary provided at the end of the chapter in Figure 6.19, which gives an overview of the research path followed.

GETTING STARTED WITH ONLINE RESEARCH

Curiosity-driven research usually begins with a name or word we've heard or read. We wonder about it, but often we have too little information at first to begin an informed search with a search engine. In the present case, we wonder about R. Buckminster Fuller, who is a man with a unique name. Even so, performing a Google search on

```
Buckminster AND Fuller
```

produces at least 26,800 hits, way too many to consider. Limiting the search to biographies

```
Buckminster AND Fuller AND biography
```

reduces the hit count to 1600, which is still too many. So, we must gather some identifying information from another source to guide an effective search-engine search. For this case, we make use of the fact that short biographies of famous people are online. Other topics will require different resources.

Narrowing the Search

After going electronically to a convenient library, we find among its research links a list of sources for biographies, including

Biography.com	`www.biography.com/search/`
Biographical Dictionary	`www.s9.com/biography/`
Britannica Lives	`www.eb.com/people/`
Lives, the Biography Resource	`amillionlives.com`

and we try the first one. We have no reason for selecting one resource over another, but if we were to use biographies repeatedly, it would be wise to shop around. The completeness and quality of the entries vary. The response to the `Buckminster Fuller` search request is successful and is shown in Figure 6.1.

Fuller, R(ichard) Buckminster 1895–1983
Inventor, designer, poet, futurist; born in Milton, Massachusetts (great-nephew of Margaret Fuller). Leaving Harvard early, he largely educated himself while working at industrial jobs and serving in the U.S. Navy during World War I. One of the century's most original minds, he free-lanced his talents, solving problems of human shelter, nutrition, transportation, environmental pollution, and decreasing world resources, developing over 2,000 patents in the process. He developed the Dymaxion ("dynamic and maximum efficiency") House in 1927, and the Dymaxion streamlined, omnidirectional car in 1932.

Fuller wrote some 25 books, notably *Nine Chains to the Moon* (1938), *Utopia or Oblivion* (1969), *Operating Manual for Spaceship Earth* (1969), and *Critical Path* (1981). An enthusiastic educationist, he held a chair at Southern Illinois University (1959–75), and in 1962 became professor of poetry at Harvard. In his later decades he was a popular public lecturer, promoting a global strategy of seeking to do more with less through technology. His inventions include the 1927 Dymaxion House, the 1933 Dymaxion Car and, foremost, the 1947 geodesic dome. He has the distinction of having both his names used for a scientific entity, the "fullerene" (also known as a "buckyball"), a form of carbon whose molecule resembles his geodesic dome.

Figure 6.1. *Biography.com's biography of Buckminster Fuller.*

Expanding the View

Reading Fuller's biography, we learn his name is actually Richard Buckminster Fuller (RFB). The first line mentions that he is the great-nephew of Margaret Fuller. Who's she? Because we are at a biography site, we can look her up. A portion of her Biography.com entry is shown in Figure 6.2. Reading her biography, we note that they both preferred to go by their middle names. More significant parallels in their lives also exist: They were both largely self-taught, they were both intellectually gifted, and they were both concerned about making the world a better place—she through her feminist writings and he through his inventions. Her tragic shipwreck death with her new husband and young child reminds us that Buckminster Fuller's profile doesn't mention if he was married or had children. So, we seek more biographical information. We could check the other three biography sites, but since we've already found the identifying information we need to guide a Google search, we do that.

In the first biography, the term *Dymaxion,* perhaps a term Fuller thought up, is mentioned as a name of both a house and a car that he invented. Surely any biography will mention these inventions, so we search on

```
Buckminster AND Fuller AND biography AND Dymaxion
```

which reduces the number of hits from more than 1600, when only "biography" is included, to a manageable 149. Interestingly, "Buckminster" and "Dymaxion" are so unusual and so descriptive of this one person that his last name is unnecessary! Searching on `Buckminster AND Dymaxion AND biography` hits 149 times.

Fuller, (Sarah) Margaret 1810–1850
Feminist, literary critic; born in Cambridgeport, Mass. Her father, Timothy Fuller, was a prominent Massachusetts lawyer-politician who, disappointed that his child was not a boy, educated her rigorously in the classical curriculum of the day. Not until age 14 did she get to attend a school for two years (1824–26) and then she returned to Cambridge and her course of reading. Her intellectual precociousness gained her the acquaintance of various Cambridge intellectuals but her assertive and intense manner put many people off. . . . From 1836 to 1837, after visiting Ralph Waldo Emerson in Concord, she taught for Bronson Alcott in Boston, and then at a school in Providence, R.I. All the while she continued to enlarge both her intellectual accomplishments and personal acquaintances. Moving to Jamaica Plain, a suburb of Boston, in 1840, she conducted her famous "Conversations" (1840–44), discussion groups that attracted many prominent people from all around Boston. In 1840, she also joined Emerson and others to found the *Dial*, a journal devoted to the transcendentalist views; she became a contributor from the first issue and its editor (1840–42). . . . She went on to Italy in 1847 where she met Giovanni Angelo, the Marchese d'Ossoli, ten years younger and of liberal principles; they became lovers and married in 1849, but their son was born in 1848. Involved in the Roman revolution of 1848, she and her husband fled to Florence in 1849. They sailed for the U.S.A. in 1850 but the ship ran aground in a storm off Fire Island, N.Y., and Margaret's and her husband's bodies were never found.

Figure 6.2. *Biography.com excerpt for Margaret Fuller, RBF's great aunt.*

Early in the list of hits is another biography from About.com shown in Figure 6.3. Reading this biography reveals something researchers encounter all the time: Different sources differ. Whereas the first biography had described his departure from Harvard as "leaving," this one says he was "expelled." Though we could track down whether he left or was expelled, we will leave it unresolved for now. Despite so many honorary degrees, he obviously didn't take himself too seriously, based on his self-description, *Guinea Pig B*.

The second paragraph emphasizes how he overcame his despair at the death of his daughter, turned his thoughts away from suicide—"his life was not his to throw away"—and went on to see what he could do "on behalf of humanity." He actually worked on the problem of world hunger, a problem most people dismiss as not solvable. His philosophy of treating life as an experiment in "what the little, penniless, unknown individual might be able to do effectively on behalf of all humanity" is inspiring! We need to know more.

Place of Birth: Milton, Massachusetts

Education: Expelled from Harvard University during freshman year

Awards: 44 honorary doctoral degrees, Gold Medal of the American Institute of Architects, Gold Medal of the Royal Institute of British Architects and dozens of other honors. Nominated for Nobel Peace Prize.

Selected Works:

1932: The portable Dymaxion house manufactured
1934: The Dymaxion car
1938: Nine Chains to the Moon
1949: Developed the Geodesic Dome
1967: US Pavilion at Expo '67, Montreal, Canada
1969: Operating Manual for Spaceship Earth
1970: Approaching the Benign Environment

Standing only 5'2" tall, Buckminster Fuller loomed over the twentieth century. Admirers affectionately call him *Bucky*, but the name he gave himself was *Guinea Pig B*. His life, he said, was an experiment.

When he was 32, Buckminster Fuller's life seemed hopeless. He was bankrupt and without a job. He was grief stricken over the death of his first child and he had a wife and a newborn to support. Drinking heavily, he contemplated suicide. Instead, he decided that his life was not his to throw away: It belonged to the universe. He embarked on "an experiment to discover what the little, penniless, unknown individual might be able to do effectively on behalf of all humanity."

To this end, Buckminster Fuller spent the next half-century searching for "ways of doing more with less" so that all people could be fed and sheltered. Although he never obtained a degree in architecture, he was an architect and engineer who designed revolutionary structures. His famous Dymaxion House was a pre-fabricated, pole-supported dwelling. His Dymaxion car was a streamlined, three-wheeled vehicle with the engine in the rear. His Dymaxion Air-Ocean Map projected a spherical world as a flat surface with no visible distortion.

But Fuller is perhaps most famous for his creation of the geodesic dome—a remarkable, sphere-like structure based on theories of "energetic-synergetic geometry," which he developed during WWII. Efficient and economical, the geodesic dome was widely hailed as a possible solution to world housing shortages.

During his lifetime, Buckminster Fuller wrote 28 books and was awarded 25 United States patents. Although his Dymaxion car never caught on and his design for geodesic domes is rarely used for residential dwellings, Fuller made his mark in areas of architecture, mathematics, philosophy, religion, urban development, and design.

Figure 6.3. *About.com's biography of Buckminster Fuller.*

Searching for Images

Perhaps before going any further we should find out what Fuller looks like. To locate some photographs, we use Google's image search, **`www.google.com/advanced_image_search`**. Entering **`Buckminster Fuller`** yields nearly 500

`.jpg` and `.gif` images. They're not all of RBF—some people have named their cats Buckminster Fuller—but there is a wide range of interesting images of Fuller. Three images from later in life, shown in Figure 6.4, show us an intense man who also seems grandfatherly, the sort of guy who might give you the keys to the Dymaxion car for the weekend.

Figure 6.4. *Three pictures of R. Buckminster Fuller.*

Bookmarking Links

We won't take the time to look through all of these images, nor will we follow all of the links (see Figure 6.5) from the About.com biography site now. But we might want to check these out later. And we have no idea how we will use the information we will discover so we just bookmark the site. (For pictures it's easiest to *save* a copy on our computer rather than book marking the URL.)

Buckminster Fuller: Biography Fast facts about the life and works of Buckminster Fuller, affectionately known as "Bucky."

Buckminster Fuller: Quotes A compendium of quotes and excerpts from Fuller's most famous writings.

What is a Geodesic Dome? From our architecture glossary, illustration and definition of the geodesic dome, conceived by Buckminster Fuller.

Build A Geodesic Dome Model Step-by-step instructions, with diagrams, from Trevor Blake.

Spaceship Earth Facts and photo for the famous dome at Disney Epcot, which is built according to Buckminster Fuller's principles.

Buckminster Fuller: Inventions An extensive collection of resources, illustrations and links, from your Guide to Inventors.

Buckminster Fuller: Net Links Best Buckminster Fuller sites on the Web, selected by your Guide.

Geodesic Domes: Net Links Best Geodesic Dome sites on the Web, selected by your Guide.

Figure 6.5. *Additional links from About.com's biography of R. Buckminster Fuller.*

> **FITTIP**
>
> **Online Research Methodology.** When using the WWW for research, bookmark every site visited (deleting bookmarks later is trivial) and record the keywords of all searches—both search engine and site searches—in a notebook file. With this information you can revisit the sites and reconstruct the search.

PRIMARY SOURCES

To find out more about Fuller's philosophy and personal life, we decide to do another search on the exact phrase **`"Guinea Pig B"`**—a name so distinctive there cannot be any others. Recall that Google lets us search for an exact phrase; in this case the search gives 200 hits. When we change the search to **`Buckminster AND "Guinea Pig B"`** the count drops to 99. This list is a goldmine of specific information about Fuller, and we will return to it.

The first hit for the **`Buckminster AND "Guinea Pig B"`** search is a page from WNET, New York City's public television station, for a documentary they produced on Fuller's life titled "Buckminster Fuller: Thinking Out Loud." The Guinea Pig B page from this site is shown in Figure 6.6.

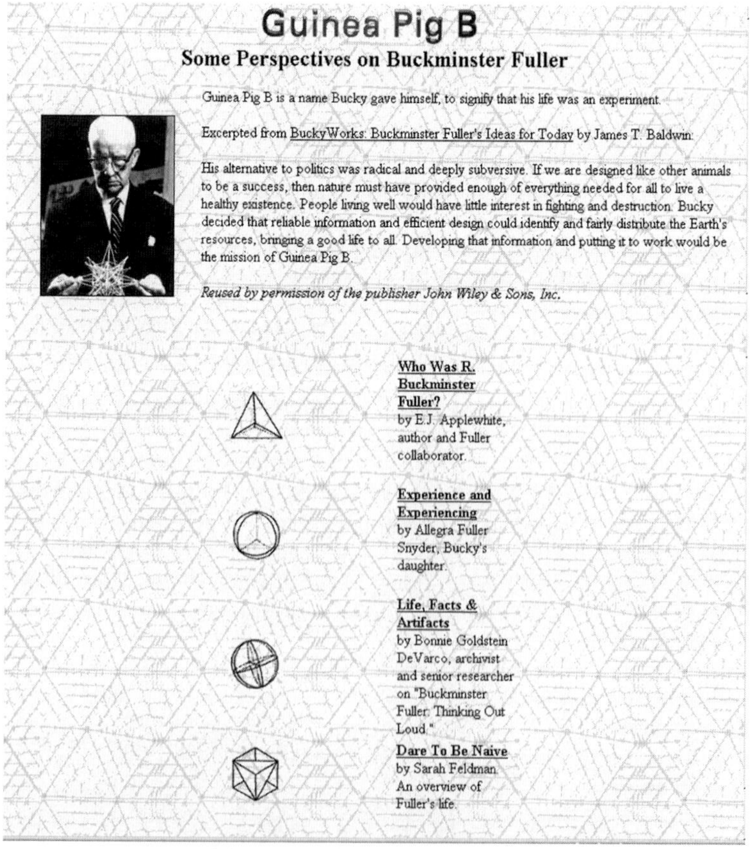

Figure 6.6. *Excerpt from WNET's Guinea Pig B page.*

The WNET page shows us a new photograph of RBF, cites a recent book about him, and quotes a small excerpt. This is all useful, but the links at the bottom of the page, to four essays, are perhaps more valuable:

Who Was R. Buckminster Fuller? by E. J. Applewhite, author and Fuller collaborator.

Experience and Experiencing by Allegra Fuller Snyder, Bucky's daughter.

Life, Facts and Artifacts by Bonnie Goldstein DeVarco, archivist and senior researcher on "Buckminster Fuller: Thinking Out Loud."

Dare To Be Naïve by Sarah Feldman. An overview of Fuller's life.

From the list we note that Fuller had a daughter, Allegra, who apparently married someone named Snyder. (No relation to the author of this text.)

Assessing the Authenticity of Sources

The importance of these essays is that they are extremely reliable sources of information. Applewhite as a collaborator and Snyder as Fuller's daughter write from direct personal experience. They are known as *primary sources*. Such information is to be preferred for several reasons. First, the information is actual experience and personal impressions. Thus the information is unbiased, except to the degree that anything a person gathers from experience is subject to that person's ability to perceive it, motivation to be objective, and expressiveness. Primary sources are not subject to the distortion or omission that can come when someone else reports information from a primary source. Such a "second-hand" report is considered a **secondary source**. If someone reports from a secondary source, creating a tertiary source, more distortion and omission are possible. Using primary sources helps us get our own impression and point of view on the subject.

Source 1 - An RBF Collaborator.

E. J. Applewhite, a collaborator, is considered a primary source (see Figure 6.7).

Who Was R. Buckminster Fuller?

by E. J. Applewhite

Buckminster Fuller had one of the most fascinating and original minds of his century. Born in 1895 in Milton, Massachusetts, he was the latest—if not the last—of the New England Transcendentalists. Like the transcendentalists, Fuller rejected the established religious and political notions of the past and adhered to an idealistic system of thought based on the essential unity of the natural world and the use of experiment and intuition as a means of understanding it. But, departing from the pattern of his New England predecessors, he proposed that only an understanding of technology in the deepest sense would afford humans a proper guide to individual conduct and the eventual salvation of society. Industrial and scientific technology, despite their disruption of established habits and values, was not a blight on the landscape, but in fact for Fuller they have a redeeming humanitarian role.

Fuller rejected the conventional disciplines of the universities by ignoring them. In their place he imposed his own self-discipline and his own novel way of thinking in a deliberate attempt—as poets and artists do—to change his generation's perception of the world. To this end he created the term Spaceship Earth to convince all his fellow passengers that they would have to work together as the crew of a ship. His was an earnest, even compulsive, program to convince his listeners that humans had a function in universe. Humans have a destiny to serve as "local problem solvers" converting their experience to the highest advantage of others.

. . .

Fuller was an architect, though he never got a degree and in fact didn't even get a license until he was awarded one as an honor when he was in his late 60s. This did not prevent him from designing the geodesic dome: the only kind of building that can be set on the ground as a complete structure—and with no limiting dimension. The strength of the frame actually increases in ratio to its size, enclosing the largest volume of space with the least area of surface. This was his virtuoso invention, and he said it illustrated his strategy of "starting with wholes" rather than parts.

He was also a poet, philosopher, inventor and mathematician, as documented amply in many other web sites on the net.

America has been in the middle of a love-hate affair with technology—and Fuller is right in the middle of it. He introduced not only a unique rationale for technology, but an esthetic of it. Likewise his synergetic geometry bears for Fuller an imperative with an ethical content for humans to reappraise their relationship to the physical universe. Manifest together as design science, they offer the prospect of a kind of secular salvation.

Figure 6.7. *Excerpt from the Applewhite essay at the WNET "Guinea Pig B" site.*

`Source 2 - RFB's Daughter.` Buckminster Fuller's daughter Allegra Fuller Snyder is clearly a primary source (see Figure 6.8).

Experience and Experiencing

by Allegra Fuller Snyder

. . .

My father was a warm, concerned and sharing father. As focused as he was on his own work he nevertheless included me in his experiences and experiencing. I remember with great clarity when I was about four years old. I was sick in bed and he was taking care of me. He sat down on the bed beside me, with his pencil in hand, and told me, through wonderful free-hand drawings, a Goldilocks story. I was Goldilocks and with his pencil he transported me, not to the Bear's house, but to universe, to help me understand something of Einstein's Theory of Relativity. What he was telling me was neither remote nor abstract. I was in a newly perceived universe. I was experiencing my father's thoughts and he was experiencing his own thinking as he communicated with me. It was exciting. We were sharing something together and I felt very warm and close to him in that experience. Something of this episode was later remembered in a book called Tetrascroll.

> . . .
>
> He loved our island in Maine because it was a physically involving place. We have no fresh water, except cistern-caught rain and well water, which has to be drawn or pumped and then hauled; kerosene and candles for light, a fire in the hearth for heat. Each of these basic requirements involves physical action to produce the needed results. . . . And then, of course, there was sailing, which he loved, where the dialog between nature and human action is so dynamic.
>
> At the heart of each one of these actions, was the sense of the "special case" that would lead to a generalized principle. Any experience would become a "special case," the doorway to larger comprehensivity. When you were around him you were aware how sensitive he was to the smallest experience. His focus could zero in on a pebble on the beach, a twig or flower along a path. Each became the stepping stone to the largest whole.
>
> "The human brain apprehends and stores each sense reported bit of information regarding each special case experience. Only special case experiences are recallable from the memory bank."
>
> . . .
>
> Intuition, imagination, all relate to and are a part of experience. Let me turn for a moment to Bucky's own words on these matters. (What follows are drawn from E.J. Applewhite's wonderful Synergetics Dictionary.)
>
> Intuition is practically physical, the kind of supersensitivity that a child has. Imagination. Image-ination involves rearranging the "furniture" of remembered experience as retrieved from the brain bank.
>
> Speaking with an audience he would say, "All that I can really give you I must always identify by experience." One of his great gifts as a speaker was the fact that he made you experience his ideas and carried you along with the connection between your experience and his experience. "Information is experience. Experience is information."
>
> . . .
>
> Where or how does experience continue to be a part of the picture when, as Bucky pointed out,
>
> "At the dawning of the twentieth century, without warning to humanity, the physical technology of Earthians' affairs was shifted over from a brain-sensed reality into a reality apprehended only by instruments."
>
> His response is that invisibility can be "understood and coped with only by experience-educated mind.
>
> . . .

Figure 6.8. *Excerpt from the Allegra Fuller Snyder essay at the WNET "Guinea Pig B" site.*

`Source 3 – An RFB Archivist.` Bonnie Goldstein DeVarco presents a fascinating account of Fuller's archive—he saved everything! Much of the content concerns specifics of the archive that are somewhat tangential to our interest. But two paragraphs stand out in her section on Ephemeralization, quoted here (see Figure 6.9).

Life, Facts and Artifacts

by Bonnie Goldstein DeVarco

EPHEMERALIZATION

Although the tactile pleasures of sorting through the physical artifacts of Bucky's life brings a dimension all its own to the discovery of who he was and who he shared his life with, almost the same could be done with the same body of materials available on a computer screen—from drawings, letters and manuscripts to "ephemerabilia," at the touch of a fingertip. In hundreds of letters spanning well over half a century, the love story of Bucky and Anne is told. Anne's letters carry a lilting youthful quality that punctuates even the most fatuous groupings of correspondence to be found in the Chronfile* boxes. Her handwriting is like a beautiful victorian stenciled wallpaper and her ardent and boundless devotion gives life to the saying that behind every great man is a great woman. It is no wonder he personally deemed his most famous geodesic dome, at the 1967 Montreal Exposition, his "Taj Majal to Anne" in honor of their 50th anniversary.

The letters of sculptor Isamu Noguchi, Bucky's lifelong friend, span decades and flavor the correspondence files with Asian subtlety, each page an artwork in and of itself, all on sheer white rice paper written with a brown fountain pen, always poignant, always aesthetically disarming. And how affecting it is to see in a letter to his mother bound into the 1928 Chronfile volume, Fuller's youthful discovery of his Great Aunt Margaret Fuller's thought and its parallels to his own as he writes, "I have been reading much by Margaret Fuller lately. I was astonished to find that some things I have been writing myself are about identical to things I find in her writings. I am terribly interested and am astounded fully that I should have grown to this age and never have read anything of her or grandfather Fuller's."

*RBF kept his correspondence and other documents in a bound file in time order called the Chronfile.

Figure 6.9. *Excerpt from the DeVarco essay at the WNET "Guinea Pig B" site.*

DeVarco's essay is based on information from the archive of Fuller's papers and artifacts, which DeVarco described as "approximately 90,000 pounds of personal history." Fuller produced this information, so it is a primary source. As an archivist and researcher, DeVarco can be presumed to be accurate and reliable. Though her essay is not technically a primary source, we can trust it.

Source 4 – An Institute Developer and Writer. Sara Feldman's essay has relied on the Fuller archive for its information, so it may be an excellent resource. As researchers, however, we wonder who she is. Her title or relationship to Fuller is not stated with the essay. For example, is she a scholar with academic credentials who we can assume tried to be accurate, or does she write advertising copy for used car companies and perhaps often embellishes the facts? We look her up in Biography.com, but she's not there. We go to the WNET Web site and search their site for her name. We get a link to her bio, which reads

Sarah Feldman

Sarah Feldman is the National Project Director for the National Teacher Training Institute (NTTI) at Thirteen/WNET New York. She is also a content developer and writer for Thirteen's wNetStation and wNetSchool, and other online venues. She taught second grade in the South Bronx and Harlem.

As a director at a national teacher-training institute, content developer, and writer with access to the Fuller archive, Feldman sounds very reliable and so we are confident that her essay is, also. See Figure 6.10 for an excerpt of her essay.

Dare to Be Naïve

by Sarah Feldman

Jobless, without savings or prospects, with a wife and newborn daughter to support, suicidal and drinking heavily, in 1927 Richard Buckminster Fuller had little reason to be optimistic about the future. R. Buckminster Fuller—or "Bucky," as he's affectionately known—transformed that low point in his life into a catalyst for transforming our planet's future as well as his own. A mathematical genius, environmentalist, architect, cartographer, poet, and an engineer of rare foresight and a philosopher of unique insight, Fuller was born in 1895 but can be truly considered a 21st century man.

Renouncing personal success and financial gain, at age 32 Fuller set out to "search for the principles governing the universe and help advance the evolution of humanity in accordance with them." Central to his mission were the ideas that 1) he had to divest himself of false ideas and "unlearn" everything he could not verify through his own experience, and 2) human nature—and nature itself—could not be reformed and therefore it was the environment—and our response to it—that must be changed. Fuller entered into a two-year period of total seclusion, and began working on design solutions to what he inferred to be mankind's central problems.

With his goal of "finding ways of doing more with less to the end that all people—everywhere—can have more and more," Fuller began designing a series of revolutionary structures. The most famous of these was the pre-fabricated, pole-suspended single-unit dwelling Dymaxion House. (The term Dymaxion was derived from the words "dynamic," "maximum," and "ion.") . . . Fuller's designs tended to be based [on] a geometry that used triangles, circles and tetrahedrons more than the traditional planes and rectangles. His Dymaxion Air-Ocean Map, which projected a spherical world as a flat surface with no visible distortion, brought him to the attention of the scientific community in 1943, and his map was the first cartographic projection of the world to ever be granted a U.S. patent.

In 1947 and 1948, Fuller's study of geodesics, "the most economical momentary relationship among a plurality of points and events," led him to his most famous invention, the geodesic dome. A hemispherical structure composed of flat, triangular panels, the domes were inexpensive to produce, lightweight yet strong space-efficient buildings. . . . Today, Fuller's geodesic domes can be found in varying sizes in countries all over the world, from Casablanca to Baton Rouge. Recognized as a landmark achievement in design and architecture, Fuller's dome was described in 1964 by Time magazine as "a kind of benchmark of the universe, what seventeenth century mystic Jakob Boehme might call 'a signature of God.'" In 1959 he joined the faculty of Southern Illinois University in Carbondale and used that as a base of operations for what Fuller called his "toings and froings." For the next two decades, Fuller globe-trotted and lectured and consulted on a variety of projects. During this period of upheaval and great change, Fuller's ideas and work in such areas as ecology, conservation, education and environmental design found an enthusiastic audience among young people all over the world. After a stint at the University Science Center in Philadelphia, in 1972 the non-profit Design Science Institute was formed in Washington, DC to perpetuate Fuller's ideas and designs.

A self-proclaimed "apolitical," Fuller maintained there was "no difference between [the] left and the right." Nevertheless, he admitted he struggled to "dare to be naïve," and retained an optimistic faith that "an omni-integrated, freely intercirculating, omni-literate world society" was within our grasp. A prolific writer, Fuller's magnum opus is undoubtedly "Synergetics: Explorations in the Geometry of Thinking," on which he collaborated with E.J. Applewhite in 1975. The work is considered a major intellectual achievement in its examinations of language, thought and the universe.

Though he only stood 5'2" tall, R. Buckminster Fuller looms large over the 20th century. Though a man of incredible intellect and vision, many of "Bucky's" fans remain most impressed by the man's awe-inspiring humility—and his abiding love for his planet and his fellow human beings. "Above all," said Fuller, "I was motivated in 1927 and ever since by the most mysterious drive we ever experience—that of love. I don't think there's any influence upon my life that compares with . . . love."

R. Buckminster Fuller

July 12, 1895–July 1, 1983

Figure 6.10. *Excerpt from the Feldman essay at the WNET "Guinea Pig B" site.*

Assessing Our Progress

So far, we have found four essays (Figures 6.7 through 6.10) about RBF and assessed the quality of their information. We have found them to be either from primary sources or from researchers who used the Fuller archive. This is excellent information, and we will take the time to read it. Notice that we do not mean that secondary or tertiary sources should not be used—we just used two from Biography.com and an About.com profile. They were unsigned biographical sketches that probably relied on generally available information about Fuller. We assumed they are accurate, though we noted a difference—one says Fuller left Harvard and the other says he was expelled. The point is that the two biographies met our need for a quick introduction. Now, because we want to find the most accurate information about Fuller's life and philosophy, we go to the source(s) ourselves.

Reading the essays gives us extraordinary insight into Buckminster Fuller and we can describe him in our own words. He believed, according to Applewhite, that technology is not the "problem" but rather the "solution," and that understanding technology deeply is the key to individual behavior as well as to "saving" society. Snyder's essay emphasized how he only trusted his direct experience as he tried to overcome the bias of conventional wisdom that he believed prevented effective thinking. He tried to do more with less. Feldman quotes Fuller as saying that he turned his life around in 1927, motivated by love, the greatest influence on his life, and DeVarco quotes his description of the Montreal geodesic dome as the "Taj Majal to Anne." It is a personal story of a deep thinker. The geodesic dome was his "virtuoso invention" [Applewhite] and *Synergetics*, a "major intellectual achievement," was his greatest work [Feldman].

And our search also allows us to resolve conflicting information. Snyder describes her father's leaving Harvard as "dismissed," another word for "expelled"—settling that question. Feldman says that Dymaxion stands for "dynamic," "maximum," and "ion," which makes more sense than the "dynamic with maximum efficiency" that we learned in the first biography.

Finding Video Clips

While thinking about this complex man, we cruise the WNET site and discover a page with two short video clips of Fuller. This is also primary information. Though downloading them takes a few moments, they show Fuller describing in his own words some of his most radical ideas. In one he says,

> This is the *real* news of the last century. It is highly feasible to take care of all of humanity at a higher standard of living than anybody has ever experienced or dreamt of, to do so without having anybody profit at the expense of another . . . so that everybody can enjoy the whole earth . . . and it can all be done by 1985.

In the video clip we not only hear what he has to say, but we see the emphasis of his gestures and hear the conviction in his voice. His tone seems to say "not only *can* we raise humanity's standard of living, we *should*." In this way the spoken word is more powerful than the written word. This digitized information has given us valuable insight.

CHRONFILE AND EVERYTHING I KNOW

Recall that the WNET page was the first item in a Google search with the terms `Buckminster AND "Guinea Pig B"`. Having gotten just about everything we could out of that page, we go to the next item, which is a link to the Buckminster Fuller Institute (BFI). See Figure 6.11.

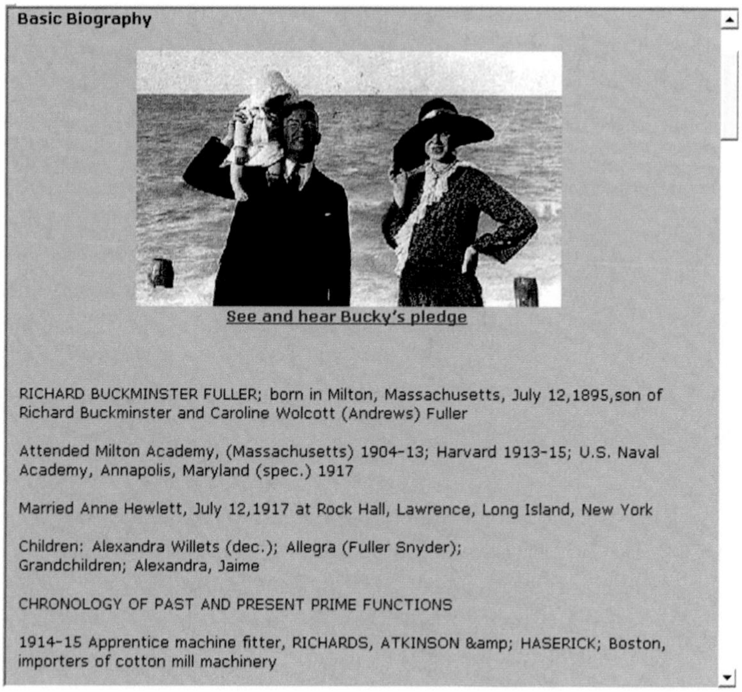

Figure 6.11. *Buckminster Fuller Institute chronology of RBF's life.*

The BFI timeline of Fuller's life is very interesting, ending with this amazing fact (not shown in the figure): *Anne* [his wife] *and Bucky died within 36 hours of one another one week before their sixty-seventh wedding anniversary!* If this page is what it seems to be—a site associated with the Fuller estate—the information is surely authoritative. Keeping in mind that some sites are hoaxes, we check to see who owns the **`bfi.org`** domain. Remember that the process of finding out who owns a domain, which takes less than a minute, was explained in Chapter 5. After a few clicks, we learn that the site is owned by the Buckminster Fuller Institute of Santa Barbara, California.

Audio Clips: Everything I Know

Clicking around the site, we find a huge amount of authoritative information, including Chronfile information, copies of whole books by Fuller, and 42 hours' worth of Fuller recordings from 1975 titled *Everything I Know*. This huge archive of online information is divided into 12 parts, each of which is subdivided into paragraph-size units called clips. We listen to a few minutes to get an idea of what *Everything I Know* is like. It's interesting, of course, and we notice from its description that it includes deep, abstract ideas as well as personal stories. Though we're interested in the deep ideas, the personal details are interesting, too. What, we wonder, does he say about Allegra?

If the archive only had the 42 hours of audio clips, we would probably have to listen to most of them to find out. However, JoAnne Ishimine has transcribed them all. This means they can be searched. So we can make a site search for **`Allegra`**. Among the hits is one where Fuller mentions how Allegra loves to dance and then describes a conversation they had.

> And, when she was twelve, she said "Daddy," we were living in New York at that time, she said "Daddy, you were brought up in Boston with the custom that it is ill mannered for men to make gestures that the man who is properly cultivated is well in possession of his movements, and he just doesn't even move his head, he just talks and sits very motionless, beautifully disciplined to do that." And she said, "I'll tell you, I don't know if I really am a dancer, but whatever I am, my body wants to talk all the time." And she said, "Daddy, I like your ideas very, very much and I want them to prevail, but I think you are frustrating your ideas by your disciplining yourself to sit motionless. I think if you'd just let yourself go things would happen way better for you." She was used to my having a lot of hard luck, nobody was paying any attention to me in those days. And so she seemed so wise that I think I did everything I could to free myself up. . . . But she did make it perfectly clear, a child does move comfortably and uses his body, so I began to let myself do [*sic*] I am utterly unaware of the motions, I assure you, but I have had moving pictures taken of me I've seen myself when I've been giving a lecture and I'm practically going all over the stage like a ballet dancer.

We can see that he *is* an animated speaker in the lectures we watched from the WNET "Buckminster Fuller: Thinking Out Loud" program.

We bookmark the *Everything I Know* archive because it is a rich resource of Fuller information, in his own words. When his ideas pique our interest, we can return to the archives.

Surfing the BFI Site

Looking around the site, we quickly come across Fuller's Dymaxion Map—the surface of the globe projected onto an icosahedron that produces a minimal-distortion flat map. Thinking of an icosahedron inside the earth and imagining the earth's curved surface shrinking down onto the icosahedron's faces gives the idea of the projection. Unfolding the icosahedron, as shown in Figure 6.12, produces the flat map (**`www.bfi.org/map_animation.html`**). There is an animation by Chris Rywalt (**`www.westnet.com/%7Ecrywalt/unfold.html`**), and watching the earth unfold a few times gives a good idea of how it works. This minimal-distortion map shows the continents in realistic proportion to one another. The specific unfolding shows the continents as one essentially contiguous island in a single sea. It's Fuller's schematic diagram for Spaceship Earth.

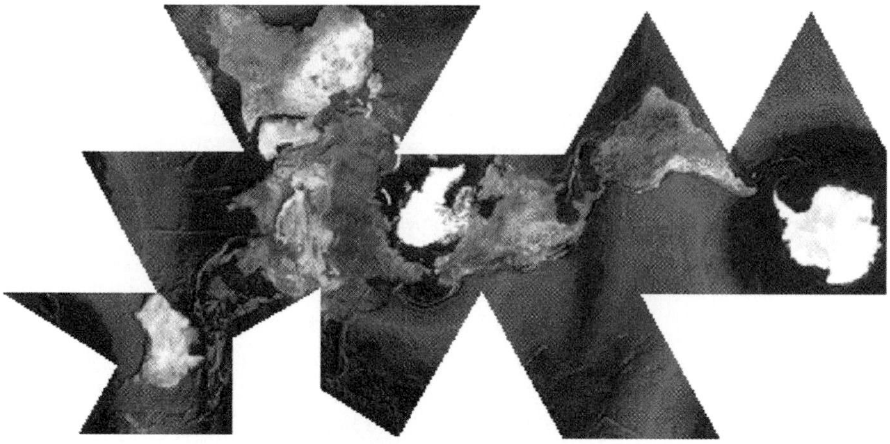

Figure 6.12. *Dymaxion Map—an unfolding of a projection of Earth onto an icosahedron.*

RESOLVING QUESTIONS

There is something confusing here. Fuller invented the geodesic dome (Figure 6.13), as we knew before we started. It's his "virtuoso invention." And he invented the Dymaxion Map (Figure 6.12). The map page tells us that the map projects the globe onto an icosahedron. But we remember the geodesic dome of the Montreal Expo '67 as smoother than an icosahedron. What's the difference? Are they the same idea? If not, how is a geodesic dome related to an icosahedron?

Figure 6.13. *Geodesic Dome—from the U.S. Pavilion at the Montreal Expo '67.*

The local BFI site may be the best place to find information about geodesics and the map's projection. Or maybe we should try a Google search on `difference AND icosahedron AND geodesic`. But, if we think about the question before starting to search, we notice that answering it could be as easy as finding out the two definitions. The best place to find definitions is in a dictionary, so we click up an online dictionary. (Again, if we forget the site name for an online dictionary, we can go to our favorite library's research or reference page to find a link to one.) The two principles at work here are (1) think about what kind of information will answer the question, and (2) look where that type of information may be found. We might be able to answer the question simply by learning the meaning of the two words.

The online dictionaries give the following definitions and drawing (see Figure 6.14):

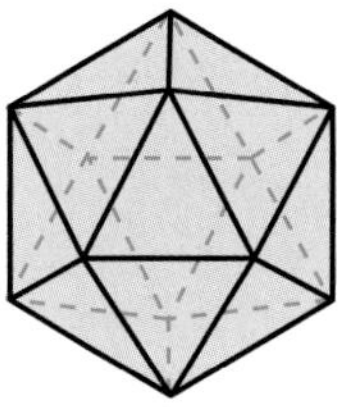

geodesic, *n*: The shortest line between two points on any mathematically defined surface.

icosahedron, *n*: A 20-sided polyhedron.

Figure 6.14. *Icosahedron.*

Obviously these are not the same. The icosahedron is a solid, and a geodesic is a line. But, this doesn't really explain how a geodesic dome differs from an icosahedron, because the definition we found is for "geodesic," a noun form, and when we refer to the "geodesic dome," we use it as an adjective. Looking further in the dictionary we find

geodesic, *adj:* Made of light straight structural elements mostly in tension <a *geodesic* dome>.

geodesic dome, *n:* A domed or vaulted structure of lightweight straight elements that form interlocking polygons.

These definitions help. The icosahedron has just 20 sides, which are triangles, and no matter how large it is—even the size of the earth—it must still have 20 sides or faces. The geodesic dome has any number of faces. From the picture of the Expo dome we can see, first, that the sides are also triangles and, second, that they are interlocking hexagons. That is, the triangles that form one hexagon can be grouped to be parts of other adjacent hexagons. Looking at the icosahedron, we see the triangles forming interlocking pentagons, and because the geodesic definition requires only "straight elements that form interlocking *polygons*," we conclude that an icosahedron is a geodesic solid. It's no surprise that Fuller came up with both the map idea and the dome idea.

We could pursue more detailed questions on structures—it's possible to build a geodesic dome from straws and pipecleaners—but we're more interested in the man than the engineering, so we continue checking the information from the `"Guinea Pig B"` search.

SECONDARY SOURCES

Our search so far has been very successful. It has shown us a complex and productive man, "one of the most original thinkers of the twentieth century." He was rational, sensitive, and used "both sides of his brain." The primary sources have been extensive and rich, including text, photographs, audio clips, video clips, and an animation. Indeed, the information is so extensive it overwhelms us—we've studied only a tiny fraction of it.

Now we have two problems. First, we need to know what is missing in our understanding of Fuller. Second, there seems to be no organization in our thinking. At the moment it is just a collection of facts. One way to solve both problems is to check some secondary sources.

Completing the Picture

Though it's always best to gather information from primary sources, secondary sources are also valuable. Secondary sources can

- Give us a more thorough investigation of the topic—certainly more thorough than ours to this point—and help us fill in gaps.
- Help us organize the information.
- Provide other authors' interpretations, including insights we have not thought of.

As always, we need to check out the sources for authenticity.

From the results of the `Buckminster AND "Guinea Pig B"` search, we find a 3000-word biography by Kirby Urner, who maintains the Synergetics Web page. (From his homepage we find that Urner is a writer and curriculum developer from Portland, Oregon.) The part of the biography shown in Figure 6.15 organizes some of the information that we've found and tells us more about Fuller's navy days. It discusses controversies regarding the independence of Fuller's ideas from those of Ken Snelson, Alexander Graham Bell, and Walter Bauersfield. These controversies are new to us.

A 20th Century Philosopher

by Kirby Urner

Originally posted: May 11, 1998; Last updated: June 19, 2000

. . .

Although the family had a four-generation tradition of sending its sons to Harvard, Fuller was too much the wild romantic to settle in and was expelled for treating an entire New York dance troupe to champagne on his own tab. The family sentenced him to hard labor in a Canadian cotton mill, where he sobered up quite a bit, but he still didn't like Harvard upon giving it a second try and was again expelled. He later returned to Harvard as the Charles Eliot Norton Professor of Poetry (1962).

Given his nautical background as a boy messing about with boats around Bear Island, Fuller was attracted to the navy, and managed to achieve a command with family assistance (1917). His marriage to Anne Hewlett was in grand military style. His native genius as an inventive soul was recognized (he developed a winch for rescuing pilots downed over water) and this led to an appointment at the Annapolis Naval Academy (1918).

At Annapolis, under the tutelage of retired admirals, Fuller felt very much at home, and began to germinate his "Great Pirates" narrative, wherein the big picture thinking then offered to young officers was a culmination of a long tradition of "thinking globally, acting locally" on the part of high seas figures, many of them pirates, and many of them lost to history because operating invisibly, over the horizon from those who kept the historical accounts (mostly landlubbers).

A few years after his honorable discharge, Fuller attempted to make money using his father-in-law's invention, a morterless brick building system, but failed in this enterprise (1926). This failure, which led to joblessness in Chicago, coupled with the trauma of losing his first child Alexandra to prolonged illness in 1922, pushed Fuller to the brink in 1927. He considered suicide but, as he put it, resolved to commit "egocide" instead, and turn the rest of his life into an experiment about what kind of positive difference the "little individual" could make on the world stage. He called himself "Guinea Pig B" (B for Bucky) and resolved to do his own thinking, starting over from scratch. Hugh Kenner likens this to Descartes' resolve to shut himself in a room until he'd discerned God's truth—a kind of archetypal commitment to a solitary journey.

. . .

It was over this concept of "tensegrity" that early divisions over the issue of Fuller's character and integrity came to the foreground. Ken Snelson, a star pupil at Black Mountain College (1948), at first enchanted by Bucky's spell, became highly disillusioned when it appeared that Fuller planned to abscond with the "tensegrity" idea without properly crediting his student.

Fuller's reputation for egomania and improperly seizing upon others' ideas as his own may be traced to this Fuller-Snelson split, and led many to question whether the geodesic dome, widely credited to Fuller (who took out a number of patents around the idea) was another case in point. . . . Alexander Graham Bell had also made extensive use of the octet truss circa 1907, another one of Fuller's key concepts (also patented).

Fuller's own archives, maintained since his death in 1983 by the Buckminster Fuller Institute (BFI) and his estate (EBF), details his side of the story and he seems to have died with a clear conscience regarding these matters—realizing they would remain bones of contention. . . .

Figure 6.15. *Excerpt from Kirby Urner's biography of R. Buckminster Fuller,* `www.grunch.net/synergetics/bio.html`.

Investigating Controversial Questions

The Snelson controversy concerns discoveries that Fuller called tensegrity, for *tension integrity*. Ken Snelson, a sculptor (`www.grunch.net/snelson/`), gives his version of its history in an email to the *International Journal of Space Structures* in answer to their request for information for a planned special publication on tensegrity (**www.grunch.net/snelson/rmoto.html**). The events happened at Black Mountain College in North Carolina in the summer of 1949. Snelson, who had met Fuller at Black Mountain the previous summer, had spent an aimless year building models or artworks (he couldn't decide whether he was an engineer or an artist) that used geometrical ideas he learned from Fuller.

Snelson's email, which we were not permitted to reprint, tells of his first morning at Black Mountain when he showed Fuller his plywood X-Piece (shown in Figure 6.16). Snelson had sent Fuller photos of the sculpture, but based on Fuller's reaction, he concluded that Fuller had not understood the design. Fuller turned it over and over, studying it carefully. Finally, Fuller asked if he could keep it. Relieved that Fuller was not annoyed with him for having used Bucky geometry for an artwork, Snelson agreed, though he hadn't planned to give it away. Later, according to Snelson, Bucky said that the sculpture had "disappeared" from his apartment.

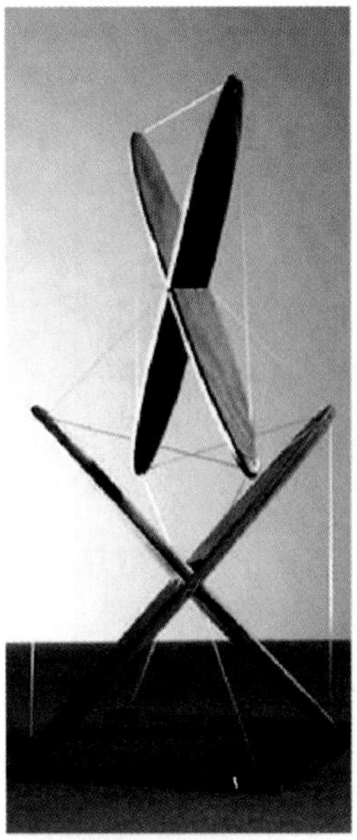

Figure 6.16. *Ken Snelson's structure at the heart of his controversy with RBF.*

At the core of Snelson's belief that he contributed to ideas Fuller took credit for is Fuller's apparently slow comprehension of the X-Piece. Snelson offers a second example of Fuller's not fully comprehending the implications of tensegrity. He says that on the next day, Fuller told him that the idea was clever, but that the configuration was wrong. Rather than using compression members in an X structure, they should be arranged in a tetrahedron. Snelson says he'd already used the tetrahedron in a mobile. He'd decided that the X structure was better than the tetrahedron because the X could grow along all three axes rather than the single axis of the tetrahedron. But he was reluctant to challenge Fuller—students just didn't do such things in those days. Again, Snelson believes Bucky didn't fully comprehend the idea, and therefore didn't think of it first.

Snelson says that the next day he built Bucky a model of the tetrahedral structure using adjustable metal curtain rods. He described himself as "wistful" watching Bucky have his picture taken with the model, but he didn't suspect Fuller's motives.

Fuller said in a letter to Snelson that he mentioned Snelson's role in speeches. But, according to Snelson, he never got credit in print. When in 1959 Fuller's tensegrity ideas were displayed at the Museum of Modern Art in New York City, Snelson, knowing the curator, forced Fuller to admit publicly that Snelson had contributed.

Searching at the Buckminster Fuller Institute for **Snelson**, we quickly find Fuller's version of the incident in *Everything I Know*, Vol. 8, though he incorrectly places it in 1958–1959:

> Then in the second summer at Black Mountain, Ken showed me a sculpture that he had made, and, in an abstract world of sculpture, and what he had made was a-a tensegrity structure. And he had a structural member out here two structural members out here, that were not touching the base, and they were being held together held they were in tension. And I explained to Ken that this was a tensegrity. Man, I

> had found, had only developed tensegrity structure in wire wheels and in universal joints. . . . When Ken Snelson showed me this little extension thing he did it was really just an arbitrary form, he saw that you could do it [tension integrity], but he was just, as I say, an artistic form or something startling to look at. And I said, "Ken, that really is the tensegrity and it's what I'm looking for because what you've done I can see relates to the octahedron and this gives me a clue of how this goes together in all the energetic geometry.
>
> So Ken opened up my eyes to the way to go into the geometry.

Fuller clearly sees Snelson as having contributed in the form of an artwork one more instance of tensegrity to the two that Fuller already knew. He seems not to be very defensive in his version.

He is also at peace with the fact that Alexander Graham Bell independently invented the octet truss—a key tensegrity structure. Fuller explains as he answers questions in an interview (`www.grunch.net/synergetics/docs/bellnote.html`):

> **Q.** It seems to me that Bell's tetrahedron, which he developed while working on kites, is very like your geodesic structure?
>
> **A.** Exactly the same.
>
> **Q.** When you developed your structures, did you know about the work of Alexander Graham Bell?
>
> **A.** I did not. I was astonished to learn about it later. It is the way nature behaves, so we both discovered nature. It isn't something you invent. You discover.

The Bell case seems to be a case of independent discovery. According to archivist DeVarco, on two different occasions Bell's descendants gave Fuller octet truss models that Bell had made. So, they apparently harbor no disagreement with this view.

Overall, Snelson's criticism of Fuller mutes the rah-rah enthusiasm of the many sites we have found. RBF has a rock-solid reputation still, but even the finest diamonds have tiny imperfections.

EXPLORING SIDE QUESTIONS

Finally, in terms of filling out our profile of Fuller, there is the repeated mention of buckminsterfullerenes. What are they? The first biography (*Biography.com*) we read ends with the statement:

> He has the distinction of having both his names used for a scientific entity, the "fullerene" (also known as a "buckyball"), a form of carbon whose molecule resembles his geodesic dome.

It's a carbon molecule. To find more, we ask Google to search on **`buckminster-fullerene`** and we find many useful links. From a *Scientific American* link we find a page from the State University of New York at Stony Brook, **`sbchem.sunysb.edu/msl/fullerene.html`**, showing images of the molecule, and we see that the structure fulfills the "interlocking polygons" requirement of the geodesic dome definition (see Figure 6.17). The next link, **`www.msu.edu/~hungerf9/bucky1.html`**, is to Michigan State University's Nanotechnology Laboratory, which gives us a definition:

> **Buckminsterfullerene**, C_{60}, the third allotrope of Carbon, was discovered in 1985 by Robert Curl, Harold Kroto, and Richard Smalley. Using laser evaporation of graphite they found C_n clusters (where n>20 and even) of which the most common were found to be C_{60} and C_{70}. For this discovery they were awarded the 1996 Nobel Prize in Chemistry.

Checking the online dictionary to find that *allotrope* means "structural form of" (making buckyballs different from graphite and diamond forms of carbon), we've answered the question: A fullerene is a stable molecule of carbon composed of 60 or 70 atoms in the shape of a geodesic sphere (see Figure 6.17). However, the discovery of fullerenes piques our curiosity, and we decide to go to the Nobel Prize site to learn more about the discovery.

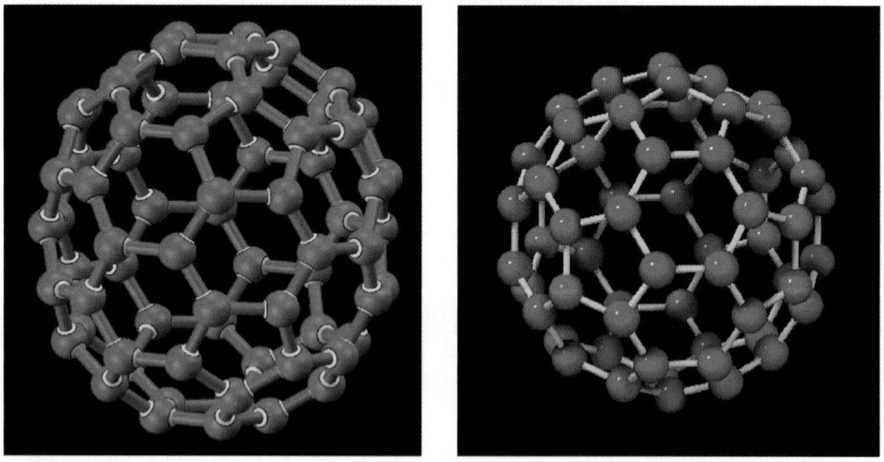

Figure 6.17. *Drawings of buckminster fullerene, C_{60} and C_{70} (also known as fullerenes or buckyballs).*

Recalling that all countries have a country extension, and that Sweden is the home of the Nobel Prize, we correctly guess at the site **`www.nobel.se`**. There we click **`chemistry`** > **`laureates`** >**`1996`** to find the page shown in Figure 6.18. From there we can read the "illustrated presentation" explaining the equipment and experiment that Curl, Kroto, and Smalley used to produce buckyballs and win the Nobel Prize. As it happens, C_{60} has the same structure as a soccer ball: 12 pentagons and 20 hexagons.

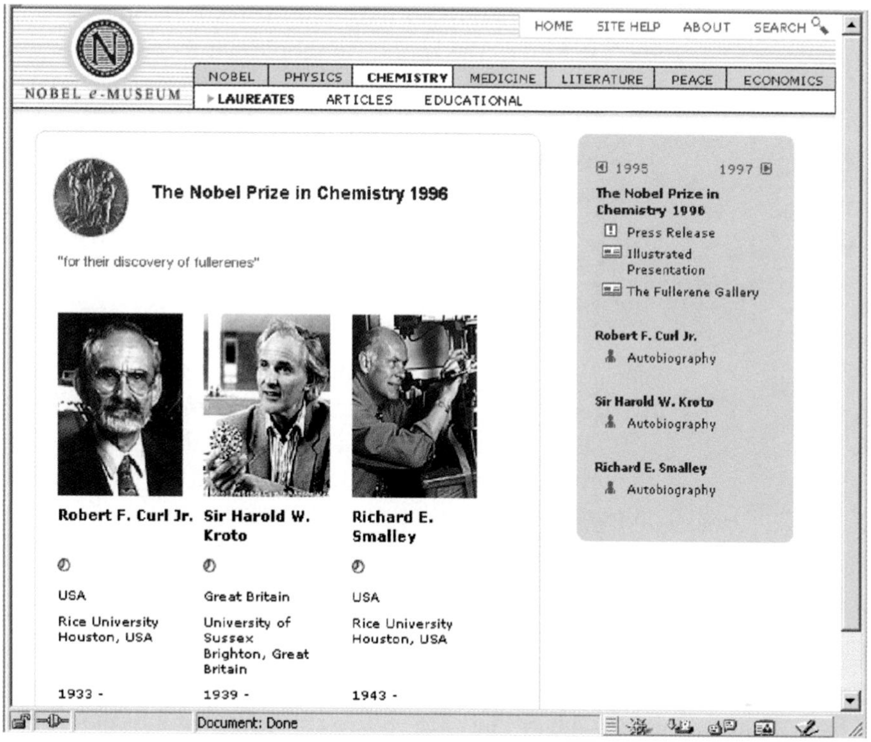

Figure 6.18. *The Nobel Prize site for the discovery of the buckminsterfullerene.*

Of course, the mention of soccer gets us to wondering how the A. C. Milan team is doing, so we click up. . . .

CASE STUDY WRAP-UP

We explored Buckminster Fuller's life only because he was an interesting person. We're finished, at least for the moment, so we can put the computer to sleep and get some sleep ourselves. But often the next step is to use the information for some other purpose, say, to write a report. In that case, before turning off the computer we should create a summary file containing:

> Bookmarks from the sites visited—they can be copied from the browser as a group

> Notebook entries of the search terms used with the search engines

> Brief notes on our impressions from the information we found—interesting discoveries, most useful sites, why we followed up on some topics and skipped others, and so forth

This information is our record of the research process, which we can use for writing the report. The reason we should write down our impressions right away is that they won't last. The amazement of new discoveries wears off, we forget things, and time changes our feelings about the content. Though it is important to have time to digest what we've learned and to organize it in our minds, the excitement of learning something new gives a fresh quality that will not be available later.

SUMMARY

The goal of this chapter has been to illustrate curiosity-driven research using the Web, and we have been quite successful (see a summary of our efforts in Figure 6.19). The two main features of this tour through Buckminster Fuller's life were the process of finding the information and the methods of deciding whether the information was authoritative. We tried to use the "right" source for the type of information we wanted.

Searching for Guinea Pig B: The Buckminster Fuller Research Path

The listing below describes the research path followed in this chapter. Most lines represent an access to a WWW document, image, audio or film clip, and so on. Indenting indicates subsidiary actions.

- Begin with a Google search because "Buckminster" is a distinctive name; fail—too many hits
- Restart by checking online biography sites to find some characterizing term; succeed—find "Dymaxion"
    - Learn basic facts about RBF's life, including that he is related to Margaret Fuller
        - Check online biography of Margaret Fuller—19th C feminist thinker, died in shipwreck
- Check Google for further biographical material using "Dymaxion"; select a highly ranked biography
    - Find that he called himself "Guinea Pig B," a characterizing, personal term
    - Discover his "little, penniless, and unknown individual" quote and his dream of helping humanity
- Check Google for photos to find out what he looks like
- Check Google using "Guinea Pig B"
    - Find WNET site and four essays: Applewhite, Snyder, DeVarco, Feldman
        - Assess sources—Applewhite and Snyder are primary, DeVarco is archivist
        - Check on Feldman, first at biography site, then WNET personnel; writer with access to papers
            - Read Applewhite's essay for professional assessment—great intellect, creative, influential
            - Read Snyder's essay for RBF as father—warm, loving, deeply believed in primary experience
            - Read Feldman's essay—threads RFB facts with personal aspects of success, tragedy, family
            - Read DeVarco's essay—the "ephemera" of RBF's life; he called Expo dome Taj Majal to Anne
        - Summarize our impressions of essays
        - View video clip; Fuller passionately argues world hunger/housing woes can be eliminated by 1985
- Visit Buckminster Fuller Institute site
    - Check BFI's authenticity

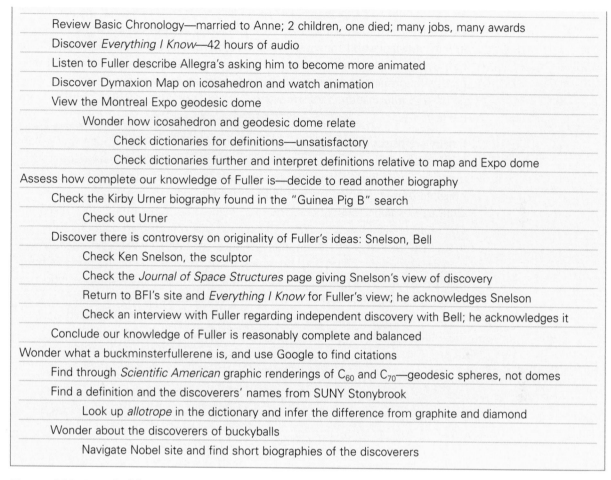

    - Review Basic Chronology—married to Anne; 2 children, one died; many jobs, many awards
    - Discover *Everything I Know*—42 hours of audio
    - Listen to Fuller describe Allegra's asking him to become more animated
    - Discover Dymaxion Map on icosahedron and watch animation
    - View the Montreal Expo geodesic dome
        - Wonder how icosahedron and geodesic dome relate
            - Check dictionaries for definitions—unsatisfactory
            - Check dictionaries further and interpret definitions relative to map and Expo dome
- Assess how complete our knowledge of Fuller is—decide to read another biography
    - Check the Kirby Urner biography found in the "Guinea Pig B" search
        - Check out Urner
    - Discover there is controversy on originality of Fuller's ideas: Snelson, Bell
        - Check Ken Snelson, the sculptor
        - Check the *Journal of Space Structures* page giving Snelson's view of discovery
        - Return to BFI's site and *Everything I Know* for Fuller's view; he acknowledges Snelson
        - Check an interview with Fuller regarding independent discovery with Bell; he acknowledges it
    - Conclude our knowledge of Fuller is reasonably complete and balanced
- Wonder what a buckminsterfullerene is, and use Google to find citations
    - Find through *Scientific American* graphic renderings of C_{60} and C_{70}—geodesic spheres, not domes
    - Find a definition and the discoverers' names from SUNY Stonybrook
        - Look up *allotrope* in the dictionary and infer the difference from graphite and diamond
    - Wonder about the discoverers of buckyballs
        - Navigate Nobel site and find short biographies of the discoverers

Figure 6.19. *Record of the case study search.*

To make the search effective, we wanted to learn enough to ask the right questions. So, we started by checking a brief biography, learned that Fuller had invented something called a Dymaxion house and car, and decided to search for biographical information containing *Dymaxion*. This greatly reduced the hits. In the same way, searching on `"Guinea Pig B"` led to a rich set of links mostly of primary sources. Later on, "buckminsterfullerene" with its narrow technical meaning led us to that information quickly. We didn't do a Web search each time we wanted information; instead we went directly to a likely source based on the type of information we wanted—dictionary, biography database, WNET personnel, the RFB Institute, the Nobel Prize page. This saved us from "aimless wandering" around the Web.

When we found information, we were always concerned with its authoritativeness. In some cases, it didn't matter much, such as when we checked the short biography to find words like *Dymaxion*. In other cases, we looked for primary sources, knowing that they are the purest forms of information about a topic because they are based on direct experience. For secondary sources, we checked the author's credentials. Secondary sources were valuable because they could both fill in gaps in our knowledge and show us how others interpreted the same information. Our goal was to learn as much as possible from primary sources so that we could interpret the information ourselves, and then to read secondary sources for more viewpoints and information. This strategy helps us to tell other people's opinions from the facts.

Finally, we began the chapter by noting that the Web is better in many ways than reading a book on a particular topic, and it is. In a short time we have found primary data from Fuller, his colleagues, and his family. We have read short biographies, looked at photographs and film clips, heard audio clips, consulted the dictionary, watched animations, and used many other types of reference material. The multimedia resources gave us the chance to form our own opinions based on more than printed words. Computer searches, including global searches with Google, site searches, and page searching, have speeded up our discovery of information. We have read parts of several authors' essays on Fuller. And the links provided by people who found the material before us have connected us to information we might not have known existed. Truly we have discovered Buckminster Fuller based on our own curiosity.

EXERCISES

True/False and Multiple Choice

1. A tertiary source draws directly from personal experience.
2. Each step away from a primary source increases the likelihood of error and omissions.
3. Books have limited research value because they:
   A. take a long time to produce
   B. contain only information the author selects
   C. contain only a single point of view
   D. all of the above
4. Advantages of the Web over a book include:
   A. the Web can be easily updated
   B. easier access
   C. dissemination of information is faster and cheaper
   D. all of the above
5. A primary source is:
   A. the only source on a topic
   B. a source with personal experience
   C. a source that has been verified
   D. all of the above
6. Secondary sources are valuable for all of the following reasons except:
   A. refuting primary sources
   B. organizing information
   C. providing interpretation
   D. filling in gaps

Short Answer

1. ______ is research for the sake of learning.
2. To look for pictures on the Web, you could do a Google search for ______.
3. The ______ folder contains a list of all the Web sites you have visited.
4. ______ are used to save the name and address of a Web site for future reference.
5. Information that comes directly from the source is called a(n) ______.
6. A ______ is someone who reports information from a primary source.

Exercises

1. Find Buckminster Fuller's birthday. Who does he share it with?
2. Do a search for Thomas Jefferson. Find a list of his inventions. Narrow the search to sites on Jefferson and one of those inventions.
3. Play "Six Degrees of Kevin Bacon" and pick two starts to see how many related hits you can find for both of them. Limit the search by ignoring topics such as reviews and books.
4. Perform a search for "Buckminster" and "Dymaxion" to see how many hits there are.
5. Do a search for Ernest Hemmingway. Locate a primary source, a secondary source, and two tertiary sources. Do the sites agree or are there inconsistencies?
6. Do a search for Richard Nixon and his dog, Checkers. Then limit the search until there are less than 100 hits.
7. Do a search for Alaska and coffee plantation. Then limit the search until there are less than 100 hits.
8. Organize the Favorites folder on your computer. Arrange the Favorites into classifications. Create additional folders as needed to organize the files. Copy the Favorites, if needed, so that they can be listed in more than one place.
9. Do a search for Grace Murray Hopper. Find a picture of the first computer bug. Read the stories behind it.

VINTON G. CERF is widely known as the co-designer of the TCP/IP protocols and the architecture of the Internet. As vice president of MCI Digital Information Services from 1982 to 1986, he led the engineering of MCI Mail, the first commercial e-mail service to be connected to the Internet. During his tenure (1976–1982) with the U.S. Department of Defense's Advanced Research Projects Agency (DARPA), he played a key role leading the development of Internet and Internet-related data packet and security technologies. Vinton holds a B.S. in Mathematics from Stanford University and a Ph.D. in Computer Science from UCLA.

How did you get started in all of this?

I was working as a programmer at UCLA in the late 1960s. My job was supported by the U.S. Defense Advanced Research Projects Agency (called ARPA then, called DARPA now). I was working in the laboratory of Prof. Leonard Kleinrock on the Network Measurement Center of the newly-created ARPANET. I was responsible for programming a computer that was used to capture performance information about the ARPANET and to report this information back for comparison with mathematical models and predictions of the performance of the network.

Several of the other graduate students and I were responsible for working on the "host level protocols" of the ARPANET—the procedures that would allow different kinds of computers on the network to interact with each other. It was a fascinating exploration into a new world (for me) of distributed computing and communication.

Did you imagine that the Internet protocol would become as pervasive as it is today when you first designed the protocol?

When Bob Kahn and I first worked on this in 1973, I think we were mostly focused on the central question: how can we make heterogeneous packet networks interoperate with one another, assuming we cannot actually change the networks themselves. We hoped that we could find a way to permit an arbitrary collection of packet-switched networks to be interconnected in a transparent fashion, so that host computers could communicate end-to-end without having to do any translations in between. I think we knew that we were dealing with powerful and expandable technology but I doubt we had a clear image of what the world would be like with 100,000,000's of computers all interlinked on the Internet.

And what do you now envision for the future of the Internet?

I believe the Internet and networks in general will continue to proliferate. There is convincing evidence that there will be billions of Internet-enabled devices on the Internet, including appliances like cell phones, refrigerators, home servers, televisions, as well as the usual array of laptops, servers, and so on.

What are the challenges you are facing?

Big challenges include support for mobility, battery life, capacity of the access links to the network, and ability to scale the optical core of the network in an unlimited fashion. Designing an interplanetary extension of the Internet is a project in which I am deeply engaged at the Jet Propulsion Laboratory. The list is long!

An interplanetary Internet?

It is an effort to standardize communication protocols used in space exploration so that each new mission can make use of earlier mission communication resources. Eventually a kind of interplanetary backbone network would arise from the accumulation of these standardized communication capabilities. This will allow investigators to have direct access to their instruments and robotic vehicles, to control sensor systems, and capture information for further analysis. I am excited by the thought that we might have nearly continuous communication with sensor systems on other planets and their satellites. It will transform space science.

You founded the Internet Society whose motto is "the Internet is for Everyone." What is it doing to achieve that objective?

The Internet Society Task Force was created to analyze and make recommendations on efforts to deal with a range of social issues linked to the Internet's fundamental operation. To be honest, the first attempt to form this group got bogged down in administrivia and arguments over how the task force would operate, be governed and tasks and publications suitably monitored. I believe there are many social issues that can be addressed, in part, through the voluntary cooperation of the ISOC chapters and members. More access to Internet is high on my list of agenda items.

What surprises you most about how the Internet is used today?

The things that surprise me most include:

1. The use of the Internet for proxy voting at annual meetings.
2. Instant messaging and its use during voice conference calls.
3. The amount and variety of information-sharing that goes on, not even counting Napster. For example, the sharing of information via personal web pages.
4. The popularity of online role-playing games (including Sims, Everquest, etc.)
5. The failure to effectually apply the Internet for health care paperwork.
6. The slow process by which Education has made use of the Internet.
7. The increasing popularity of streaming audio (and video where speeds allow).

Do you have any advice for students studying IT?

Think outside the limitations of existing systems—imagine what might be possible; but then do the hard work of figuring out how to get there from the current state of affairs. Dare to dream: a half dozen colleagues and I at the Jet Propulsion Laboratory have been working on the design of an interplanetary extension of the terrestrial Internet. It may take decades to implement this, mission by mission, but to paraphrase:

"A man's reach should exceed his grasp, or what are the heavens for?"

interview

VINTON G. CERF

part 2

ALGORITHMS AND DIGITIZING INFORMATION

introduction

Having now become more skillful with information technology, it is time to learn a few of the underlying concepts that make IT possible. Like black holes in astronomy or natural selection in ecology, the underlying phenomena of IT are interesting to learn about. The difference is, IT concepts can have direct applicability to your daily use of IT.

In Part II we learn about how information is represented, from basic bits through sound and video to virtual reality. We also explain what a transistor is, and how a few million of them could process information. And we introduce the fundamental idea of an algorithm, though you've already seen several in Part I. At the end you will have a basic idea of what's happening inside a computer and how it stores your information.

In your experience so far, you have known the frustration when some aspect of IT is not working the way you want. So, you know that figuring out what's wrong is one of the most important capabilities a computer user can possess. Though we cannot give you a guaranteed, works-every-time algorithm to debug your problems, we do give useful guidelines that can help you more quickly solve any IT mystery.

chapter

7 TO ERR IS HUMAN

An Introduction to Debugging

learning objectives

> Explain how ordinary precision differs from precision required in IT

> Describe the five-step strategy for debugging
  - Explain the purpose of each step
  - Give an example of each step

> Apply the five-step strategy for debugging the HTML code for a Web page
  - State what changes you made during debugging
  - State what changes were unnecessary

> Learn how to approach debugging when you don't understand the system

One item could not be deleted because it was missing.

—MAC OS SYSTEM 7.0 ERROR MESSAGE

You are not thinking. You are merely being logical.

– NEILS BOHR TO ALBERT EINSTEIN

A COMMON saying among computer users is "To err is human, but to really foul things up takes a computer." One characteristic that makes a computer so useful—and sometimes so frustrating—is that it does exactly what it is told to do, and nothing more. Because it will follow each instruction "to the letter" and continually check itself, it operates almost perfectly. So, in truth, the computer doesn't foul things up at all. We humans—those of us who write the software and those of us who use it—are not perfect, of course. And that combination *can* really foul things up. So we have to learn how to discover what's wrong and to get ourselves out of our difficulties. Learning debugging techniques—the subject of this chapter—is perhaps the best way to deal successfully with mistakes and errors, and to avoid the foul-ups in the first place.

The first goal of this chapter is to recognize that the greatest, most common source of problems is our lack of precision. Computers never get what we *mean*, only what we *say*. So we must say exactly what we mean. The next objective is to understand what debugging is in modern IT systems. We then introduce the debugging process using a student/parent scenario. This lets us analyze the process during the student/parent interaction. The next goal is to abstract from the story the principles of debugging. The principles do not give a mechanical procedure guaranteeing success, but rather a reliable set of guidelines. We then apply the principles to debugging a faulty Web page design. This detective work will not reveal *who*dunit because we're the most likely "perps," but rather *what*-dunit, our error. The final objective is to illustrate debugging a system when we have no idea how the system works.

PRECISION: THE HIGH STANDARDS OF IT

When using information technology, we must be precise. The standards of accuracy in IT are extremely high, much higher than many people's usual level of precision.

Precision in Everyday Life

In normal conversation, for example, when giving telephone numbers, many North Americans will say "oh" rather than "zero," as in "five-five-five-oh-oh-one-two" for 555-0012. Of course, the listener knows that phone numbers are all numeric, and simply makes the mental conversion. A computer does not know that fact unless it has been specifically programmed to know it and to make the conversion. The "oh" and "zero" are different (bit sequences) to a computer. So, if we type "oh" for "zero," a computer would simply accept the input, try to use it literally, and cause an error.

> FITBYTE
>
> **Merrily Mistaken.** Sometimes we use this confusion on purpose, as in Canada's alternating letter-numeral postal code for Santa Claus, H0H 0H0.

The "oh" for "zero" substitution is probably used by North Americans because it is easier to say, having only one syllable. (Other English speakers say "*naught*" for "*zero.*") It is probably not the sort of error we would make if we were asked to type a phone number into a database system or modem software. And, even if it were, the software would catch the error, because some software systems *have* been programmed to know that phone numbers are all numeric. Rather than converting "oh" to "zero," however, they usually just object to being given nonnumeric input. But there are many cases in which the computer cannot help us when we make an error.

EXACTLY HOW ACCURATE IS "PRECISE"?

New email or Web users often type in an incorrect email address or URL. A common error is to confuse "oh" and "zero," or "el" and "one," though there are many other mistakes new users can make. If computers can catch mistakes like "oh" for "zero" in modem software or databases, why can't they catch them in email addresses and URLs? The reason is simple: Although "oh" and "el" are illegal in all phone numbers, they are not illegal in all email addresses or URLs. For example, `flo@exisp.com` and `f10@exisp.com` could both be legitimate email addresses. If the software made "zero" for "oh" and "one" for "el" substitutions, poor Flo would never get any email. So, computers must accept the letters or numbers as typed for email addresses or URLs. Corrections are not possible. Users must be as precise as they can be when entering such information.

FITCAUTION

Be Sensitive. Be alert to case sensitivity—the difference between lower- and uppercase—in email addresses and URLs. To computers, *C* and *c* are different in some cases, and in others they have been programmed to ignore case. For example, case does not matter in Internet domain names—`flo@exisp.com` and `flo@ExISP.COM` are the same—because case is normalized for DNS lookup. But frequently the "local" information in URLs—that is, the text after / symbols—is case sensitive because it is processed by the destination Web server. So, `www.exisp.com/flo/home/` and `www.exisp.com/FLO/HOME/` may be different. When in doubt, assume that case matters.

Lexical Structures

The general principle operating is this: Call the kinds of inputs just discussed **field inputs** because they are the sorts of information that are entered into boxes on forms that are used for names, code numbers, user IDs, files, folder names, and so on. All such field inputs are governed by some **lexical structure**, rules about the legal form for input fields. The lexical structure limits the symbols that can be used in specific positions, possibly how many symbols can be used (i.e., a length limit), and possibly which punctuation symbols can be used. Lexical constraints can be very restrictive. For example, the lexical structure for inputting course grades is limited to at most two symbols: the first symbol must be chosen from {A, B, C, D, F} and the second symbol must be chosen from {+, –, ƀ}. (The ƀ denotes *blank*.) So, A+ is OK, but C++ is wrong. Lexical constraints can be loose, too, allowing any sequence of symbols of any length. Computers check to see that the lexical constraints are met, preventing lexical errors. But if the lexical structure permits both alternatives of a commonly confused symbol, no check can be made. Both alternatives are legal, as in UserIDs. Precision is essential.

FITTIP

Spacing Out. The ƀ represents blank or space. This solves the problem that spaces must be visible in some cases so that we know that they're there. "Multiplication dots," ·, are used by word processors (Chapter 2), but when they are easily confused with other symbols, we use ƀ to represent blank.

Because we have to be accurate when supplying any input to a computer, we can avoid considerable grief by being as exact as we possibly can be. It is obviously faster and less frustrating to enter information exactly than to be sloppy, to have to find the mistake and enter it correctly.

DEBUGGING: WHAT'S THE PROBLEM?

Debugging is the method of figuring out why a process or system doesn't work properly. Debugging is usually applied to computer or communication systems, especially software, but the techniques are the same whether the systems are mechanical, architectural, business, or others. Though debugging relies on logical reasoning and is usually "learned from experience," there are debugging principles and effective strategies that we can learn. Knowing these techniques is important in information technology because a major part of using IT systems is figuring out why things are not working properly.

Debugging in Everyday Life

People debug or **troubleshoot** all the time. When their cars don't start, they figure out whether the battery is dead or whether there is no fuel in the tank. Faults and failures in everyday life usually involve correct, working systems with a broken or worn-out part. That is, the system is properly designed and constructed, but some part failed. The car's dead battery keeps it from starting, for example. When the part is replaced, the system works.

Debugging in Information Technology

Debugging an information system is slightly different. In information systems, we might have entered wrong data or wrong configuration information in a working system. When it's corrected, the system works. But another possibility with information systems is that they might have a **logical design error.** An analogy in car design would be if the backup lights, which should only work when the car is in reverse, come on when we step on the brakes. This would be a design or construction error. In software, such logical errors are quite possible even in commercial software, and users must be aware that a correct, working system cannot always be relied upon. Despite that fact, we will always first assume we have a "correct, working system."

Wrong Data or Wrong Command?

Remember that when we are debugging an information system, we are generally part of the problem. In an information system, we command the computer to do a task, and give it input. When this input gets the computer into an error state despite our belief that the input should have worked, the two possibilities—wrong data or command—involve us. Our commands or data led to the problem, and so we'll have to fix it. Computers cannot debug themselves, though they do detect and correct low-level errors such as memory errors. The two types of mistakes are treated differently.

Fixing Wrong Data. When our wrong data creates an error, either we *understand* the system and just goofed up, or we *don't understand* the system and goofed up. If we understand the system, we just begin afresh and navigate through the data entry again, being more careful. Typically, in these cases, we have some idea where we might have made the mistake, and fixing it is easy. If we don't understand the system, the problem is almost certainly *our* conceptual error. In such cases, debugging will rely more on the how-to-learn-a-new-system guidelines given in Chapter 2 than on the debugging guidelines here, though we'll probably need the debugging principles, too. Of course, the situation is not always so neatly divided. Often we *think* we understand the system, but don't. Then we still have a conceptual error, but the conceptual error is with our understanding.

Fixing a Wrong Command. When a command is at fault, we must debug the system, even if we didn't make the system. We will follow the steps outlined in this chapter, but we also need precision in typing and thinking so that we don't create new errors. Introducing new errors simply makes the problem worse, usually much worse, so it is a good idea to rivet our attention on debugging the immediate problem, putting aside distractions and other concerns until later.

{GREATFITMOMENTS}

Computer Pioneer Grace Hopper > >

Rear Admiral Grace Murray Hopper, a computer pioneer, coined the term bug for a glitch in a computer system while she was working on the Harvard Mark I in the 1940s. When the Mark II computer got a moth jammed in one of its relays (electro-mechanical switches), bringing the machine down, technicians taped the bug into the machine's logbook (Figure 7.1).

Hopper was one of the inventors of a kind of software known as a compiler, which translates a programming language into machine instructions (see Chapter 9), and she greatly influenced the development of the programming language Cobol. Conscious of the physical limitations on computing, Hopper used a length of copper wire (approximately one foot long) to illustrate a "nanosecond" (1/1,000,000,000th of a second), because it is the distance electricity can travel in that time.

A Navy ship was named in her honor.

FITBYTE

A Bug's Life. What insect was jokingly called the first bug? On a recent TV game show, answering this question correctly was worth $1 million. The answer? A moth.

Figure 7.1. *The Harvard Mark II logbook noting "First actual case of bug being found," from the Smithsonian Institution.*

Using the Computer to Debug

Finally, not only is the computer unable to debug itself, we can't debug it directly, either. That is, the error is internal to the computer, either in the data stored or in the logic of the software. To get information about the error, we have to ask the computer to tell us what data it has stored, to run the faulty software, and so forth. We are one step removed from the failure and what's causing it, and we need the computer to help us find the problem.

A modern version of the 1960s slogan "If you're not part of the solution, you're part of the problem" is: "If it's not part of the solution, it can't be part of the problem." That is, if you can find a solution without using a problem (faulty) part of the system, you've achieved your goal. This idea of bypassing an error with an alternative approach is called a **workaround**. Workarounds are essential when you are using commercial software. Bugs in commercial systems are usually not fixed until the next version, so we have to work around them until then.

A DIALOG ABOUT DEBUGGING

Consider the following scenario:

You and your friends have made a video spoofing college life. You showed it to your cluster in the dorm, and everyone thought it was hilariously funny. You sent a copy to your parents, hardly able to wait to hear their praise of your cleverness, but you heard nothing. Eventually you phoned them to ask if they got the tape, and they replied, "Yes. We tried it in the VCR player, but something's wrong." Your impulse is to say, "Fix it!" but you ask brightly, "What's wrong?"

You are about to debug your parents' VCR. What you know is that your parents have tried the videotape in their VCR player—which you're very familiar with, having spent most of last vacation watching movies on it—and it didn't play the tape. That's all the information you have, and it's typical.

Debugging is solving a mystery, and just as we watch detectives solve mysteries in whodunits, we should watch ourselves solving the mystery when debugging. Why? Because this approach will probably get us to a solution faster than if we aimlessly "try stuff." By purposely asking questions such as, "Do I need more clues (inputs)?"; "Are my clues reliable?"; and "What is the theory to explain the problem?" we will focus better and discover a solution faster.

The first step in debugging is to check that the error is reproducible. Computers are deterministic, which means that they will do exactly the same thing every time if given the same input. But there is a tiny possibility that a one-time transient glitch caused the problem, so start by trying to re-create the problem.

You ask your folks,

> "Can you try the tape again?"

And, as the scenario unfolds, your parents report that there is nothing showing on the TV.

The next step is to be sure that you know exactly what the problem is. Mystery novels usually have a dead body, making the problem clear. The mystery is who murdered the person, not why the dead person failed to show up for work the next morning. But in information technology, the computer may perform a sequence of operations *after* an error, and they must be eliminated first as the focal point of the debugging. For example, the reason there are no mailing labels coming out of the printer may be due to a printer problem, but it could be a problem with the word processor or database that is sending the labels to the printer, or it could be that the file containing the addresses is empty; that is, there are no addresses to print. We don't want to be debugging the printer when the problem is an empty file. So, finding out what exactly is the problem is critical.

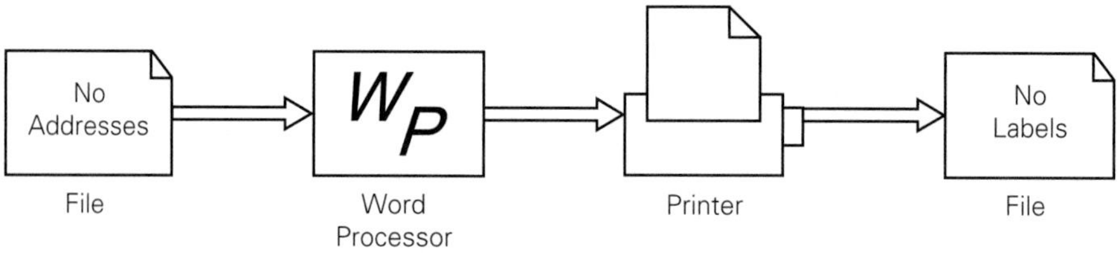

Your parents should be a little more specific about the problem. You patiently ask,

"What's on the screen?"

"Nothing."

"Is it black nothing, blue nothing, or snow nothing?"

"Snow."

A standard next step is to check all of the "obvious" sources of error. Of course, if the error were all that obvious, you wouldn't be debugging—you'd have fixed the problem and be on your way. What kinds of errors are obvious depends on the problem being debugged, naturally, but checking inputs, connections, links, and so on is standard.

Ask your parents to check all of the obvious causes:

"Is there power to the VCR?" (The TV obviously has power.)

"Yes."

"Is the tape in the machine?" (It couldn't be upside down because the drive mechanism doesn't allow that.)

"Yes."

"Is the tape rewound?"

"Yes."

"Have you clicked Play?"

"Yes."

"Is the tape advancing?"

"Sounds like it."

"What happens?"

"Snow reigns."

Clearly the VCR is pretty much as you left it. Except it isn't playing your hilarious tape.

It's now time to apply a basic strategy of debugging: isolate the problem by dividing the operation into those parts that are working and those that are not. This means coming up with a theory about where the problem is located, and possibly gathering more information. At this point you should take nothing for granted. Limit the number of untested assumptions you make. The error could be anywhere. The goal is to eliminate as many possibilities as you can, or to focus in on the failing part.

In the case of your parents' VCR, the system has two basic units, the TV and the VCR player. The data, which is on the tape, is read by the player and sent to the TV for display. You ask yourself, can either of them be eliminated from consideration? If the VCR were OK and the TV were faulty, the TV probably wouldn't show regular programs. You ask your parents:

"Do you get normal TV programs?"

"Define normal."

"You know what I mean . . . ABC?"

"Yes."

So, if the TV is OK, the VCR must be broken, though it seems from the earlier conversation that it is working mechanically; that is, the videotape is running through it. So, if it's OK, what other parts are there? There's the cable connecting the VCR to the TV.

"Are the TV and VCR connected?"

"Didn't look, but it's the way it's always been."

So, they're connected as you left them when you left for college. And there are no other parts.

Everything seems to check out. This is a common situation in debugging. You analyze the problem, perhaps getting more data, and conclude that everything is OK. Except it's not. There is a bug somewhere. Though it is natural to become frustrated, the best response is to review your analysis. You've made some assumptions, gathered data, made some tests, interpreted the results, and made some deductions. Ask yourself, "Is there a wrong assumption?" "Am I misunderstanding what the data mean?" "Did I make a wrong deduction?" It's important at this point to think objectively about the process. *A good approach is to step through the process from beginning to end, comparing what should be happening with what is happening.*

So, starting from the beginning, you ask your parents to put in a different tape.

> "OK, we put in the tape of your sister's wedding, but it's the same thing. Snow."

You know that tape works. You had to sit through the whole two tedious hours of it last summer.

> "Is it rewound?"

> "Yes. Just did it."

> "When you clicked on Rewind, was the screen blue and the letters R-E-W displayed?"

This is a prediction you make about how the TV/VCR system is supposed to operate based on your knowledge or experience with it.

> "No, it's still snow."

At this point you have a prediction that doesn't match the facts. That's what you're looking for. Why would the VCR not be telling the TV that it is rewinding the tape? Maybe because they're not connected.

> "Can you check if the cable from the VCR is plugged into the back of the TV?"

And now you know the problem. As you're waiting for your parents to verify that the cable is not connected to the back of the TV, you recall last summer when the Women's World Cup Soccer final was on and how a bunch of your friends came over to watch the game and you carried the TV out to the patio. Everyone sat around eating pizza and cheering. It was late when you carried the TV back into the house, and you postponed plugging in the VCR cable until morning. And forgot. When you left for college they were still unconnected.

> "Nope, the cable wasn't plugged into the TV. It's working now. How'd you figure that out?"

> "Got lucky, I guess. Hope you like the video."

DEBUGGING RECAP

The key point of the debugging illustration is not that debugging occasionally reveals embarrassing errors, but rather that there is a semi-organized process to follow to find out what's wrong. The key points were

- Make sure that you can reproduce the error.
- Determine exactly what the problem is.

> Eliminate the "obvious" causes.

> Divide the process, separating out the parts that work from the part that does not.

> When you reach a dead end, reassess your information, asking where you may be making wrong assumptions or conclusions; then step through the process again.

> As you work through the process from start to finish, make predictions about what should happen and verify that the predictions are fulfilled.

This is not a recipe, but it is a useful set of guidelines. Debugging requires tough, logical reasoning to figure out what's wrong. But, it's possible to do, and though it is not as entertaining as deducing whodunit from the few clues in a mystery novel, there is a certain satisfaction to figuring it out

FITBYTE

Closer Examination. Watching yourself debug as though you were a mystery detective is important. It helps you be more objective—is the debugger (you) chasing the wrong lead?—and it helps you separate yourself from the process, reducing frustration. Thinking about what you are doing is a good idea generally, of course. After all, Socrates said, "The unexamined life is not worth leading."

BUTTERFLIES AND BUGS: A CASE STUDY

To illustrate the debugging principles in action, we develop a small table in HTML. Our goal page is shown in Figure 7.2. The HTML code we've written is shown in Figure 7.3, together with the Netscape browser's interpretation of it. Obviously, there is an error somewhere. We could study the HTML very, very closely and "brain out" where the error is, or we could use the debugging strategy. Follow along online; the file is at `www.aw.com/snyder`.

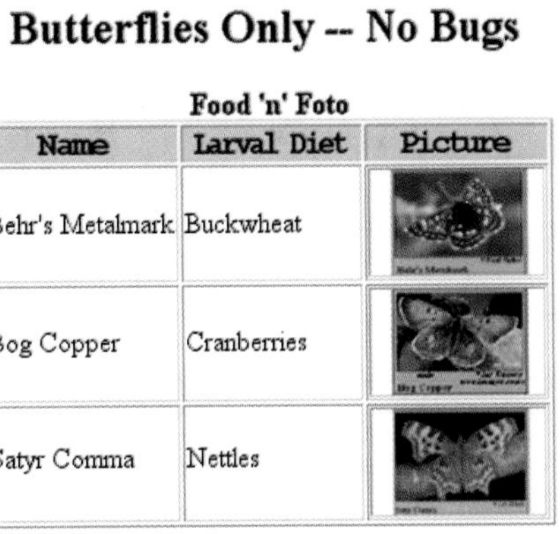

Figure 7.2. *The intended HTML table.*

```
<html>
 <head>
  <title>Butterflies</title>
 </head>
<body>
<h1> Butterflies Only — No Bugs</h1>

 <table border width="50%">
 <caption><b>Food 'n' Foto</b></caption>
  <tr bgcolor="silver">
    <td> Name </td>
    <td> Larval Diet</td>
    <td> Picture </td> </tr>

    <td>Behr's Metalmark</td>
    <td>Buckwheat</td>
    <td align="center"> <img src="butterflies/Apodvirg.jpg
        width="80" height="60"></td>

    <td>Bog Copper</td>
    <td>Cranberries</td>
    <td align="center"> <img src="butterflies/Bog.jpg
        width="80" height="60"></td>

    <td>Satyr Comma</td>
    <td>Nettles</td>
    <td align="center"> <img src="butterflies/Satyr.ipg"
        width="80" height="60"></td>
  </tr>
 </table>
</body>
</html>
```

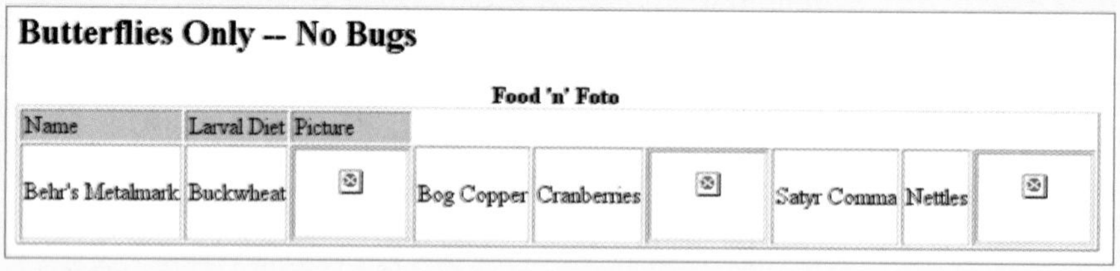

Figure 7.3. Faulty HTML text and its rendering in the browser.

Applying the Steps in Debugging HTML

As we begin, watching ourselves debugging the HTML, we recall that the first step is to be sure we can re-create the error.

Reproduce the Error. So, we close Netscape and reopen our file using a "fresh" copy of that browser. Unfortunately the results are the same. In fact, Internet Explorer produces the same result, so it is definitely a problem with our HTML.

Determine the Problem Exactly. The next step is to determine the problem exactly. In the case of debugging HTML, identifying the problem is simple: just look at the page. We have a table with no pictures and nine columns, so there seem to be two bugs here. There could be more, but we focus on these, guessing that problems like the caption that is supposed to be centered over the table, and is now centered over the broken table, will be in the right place when the table is right. So, we focus on the two problems: too many columns and missing images.

Eliminate the Obvious. Once we know what the problem is, we look for the "obvious" errors. The most obvious HTML error is to forget to close a tag; that is, to forget the matching "slash-tag." Checking the HTML, we see that every tag is matched. However, we do get lucky. In reading the HTML text, we notice that our triples of cell data are not all surrounded by the row tags, `<tr>` and `</tr>`. We have row tags around the heading row—the silver background of the heading proves that—but not around the others. Surrounding them with row tags produces the result in Figure 7.4, a definite improvement. As we predicted, the caption is now centered over the table. Notice that although we described the problem as too many columns, the actual bug was too few rows.

Figure 7.4. Page with row tags added.

With one bug swatted, we focus on why there are no pictures. Another obvious error in HTML is to get the relative pathnames wrong, and when checking our `butterflies` directory (see Figure 7.5), we notice that we indeed have an inconsistency.

Figure 7.5. Files in the `butterflies` *folder.*

The names are capitalized in the HTML and they are lowercase in the directory. Though we may not know whether case matters for this computer, we make the change anyway. And when we try out the revised page, it looks no different from Figure 7.4. Apparently the change didn't hurt the program, but it didn't help either. There must be a different error. Because the relative pathname directs the browser into a directory to find the file, it could still be wrong. Removing the indirection—that is, the use of the subdirectory to store the images—may help. So, we move the butterfly images into the same directory as the HTML for our page, and rewrite the `<img...>` tags to remove the `butterflies/` directory level. The table data for the Metalmark becomes

```
<td align="center"> <img src="apodvirg.jpg width="80"
    height="60"></td>
```

But there is no improvement. What else is there to check?

Divide Up the Process. Having run out of obvious errors and with everything checking out, we move on to the next step of debugging, which is to divide the system to focus on the faulty parts. Again, HTML is relatively easy because the page shows visually where the error must be. It almost certainly must be in the `<img...>` tags. Ignoring the rest of the HTML, we carefully analyze that text, using the **View > Page** `Source` feature of the Web browser. The source display shows, using color and different fonts, how the browser interprets our HTML. Netscape displays the line as

```
<td align="center"> <img src="apodvirg.jpg width="80"
    height="60"></td>
```

whereas Internet Explorer shows it as

```
<td align="center"> <img src="apodvirg.jpg width="80"
    height="60"></td>
```

Our simplified relative pathname attribute is displayed, but its coloring is strange. The browser shows that the blue file name includes the word `width`, which is wrong. We then notice that there is no closing quote mark after the file name. With no closed quote, the pathname spills into the `width` specification. Fixing only this line produces the result shown in Figure 7.6.

The fact that this row is improved indicates that this is the fix, so we change the other two lines, producing the result shown in Figure 7.7. Focusing our attention on the `<img...>` tags has helped, but apparently not quite enough.

If we compare Figures 7.6 and 7.7, we see that although adding a closed quote didn't display the Satyr Comma's image, it did change the spacing. So, the quote was the problem, and we infer that perhaps there is something wrong with the file. We can see the thumbnail image (Figure 7.5), but that doesn't mean there isn't a problem. Sometimes, derived data (thumbnail) is OK, but the file has some other error. One debugging strategy is to run an experiment, so we try to use the `satyr.jpg` file in another application. And it works fine. What can the problem be?

Butterflies Only -- No Bugs
Food 'n' Foto
Name | Larval Diet | Picture
Behr's Metalmark | Buckwheat
Bog Copper | Cranberries
Satyr Comma | Nettles

Figure 7.6. *The result of revising one row of HTML.*

Butterflies Only -- No Bugs
Food 'n' Foto
Name | Larval Diet | Picture
Behr's Metalmark | Buckwheat
Bog Copper | Cranberries
Satyr Comma | Nettles

Figure 7.7. *The result of including quotes after all pathnames.*

`Assess, then Step through the Process.` Let's review our progress so far: We have corrected the capitalization, so that can't be a problem. We have changed the relative pathnames so that they don't involve the directory **`butterflies`**, and that works, which we know because two pictures do display. We have fixed the quote, so now the table cells match in all cases. We have checked the Satyr Comma image file and it works in another application. Basically, the HTML should work. We must be making a wrong assumption or misunderstanding the evidence.

Focusing on the **`<img...>`** tag must be the right strategy. We assumed that the "quotation mark fix" corrected the names for each file. That's certainly right for the first two butterflies, and we thought it was right for the Satyr Comma, based on the fact that it fixed the table spacing. But maybe not. Reviewing the third image tag using the browser's **Source View** again,

```
<td align="center"> <img src="satyr.ipg" width="80"
    height="60"> </td>
```

we see that indeed all of the parameters to the attributes (blue) are interpreted correctly. However, there is one tiny mistake: the file extension has been written `ipg` rather than `jpg`. It's not particularly visible in Figure 7.3, but it's there. So, we had jumped to conclusions about the "quotation mark fix." It helped, but it didn't eliminate the third `<img...>` tag from consideration. When we correct the extension, the result is as shown in Figure 7.8. This solves the problem, but when we compare it to the goal page, we notice there is still a small difference.

The column headings are not correct. Reviewing the figures, we see that it's obvious this has been a problem the whole time. It just wasn't particularly noticeable, given the other problems. And thinking about it, it's clear what the problem is. Tables in HTML should have a **table heading** tag, `<th>` and `</th>`, rather than a table data tag. Correcting that detail gives the goal page, completing the debugging task. The column headings are now bold and centered. We revise the text to restore the relative pathnames to use the `butterflies` subdirectory, as we originally intended.

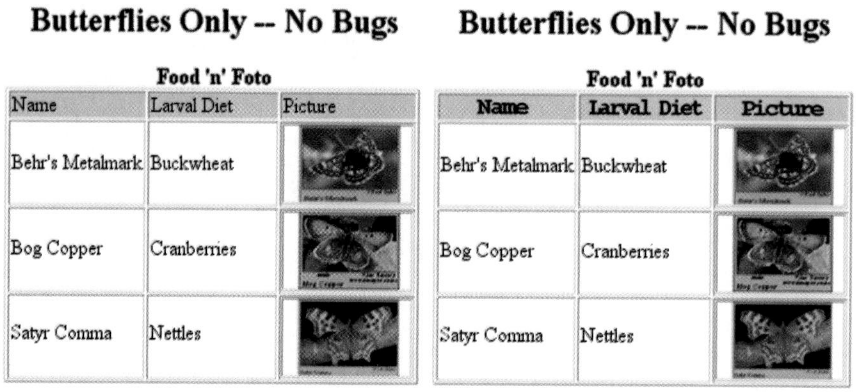

Figure 7.8. *The corrected file extension page, left, and the goal page, right.*

Butterflies and Bugs Postmortem

The bugs in the HTML text have been crushed. In the process we made a series of conjectures, tried different changes to the program, ran a couple of experiments, and drew conclusions. How did we do? Certainly the result turned out fine.

Changes Made. For the record, we made the following changes to the HTML during the debugging process:

1. Enclosed the table rows with `<tr> </tr>` tags.
2. Corrected the capitalization of the file names.
3. Simplified the pathnames to avoid referring to the `butterflies` subdirectory.
4. Corrected the quotation mark problem.

5. Corrected the file extension problem for the Satyr Comma.
6. Fixed the `<th> </th>` tags for the first row.
7. Restored the pathnames to allow the images to be kept in the `butterflies` directory.

Unnecessary Changes. Of these seven changes, only 1, 4, 5, and 6 were necessary to fix the program. The other changes were not needed: change 2 was not needed because the file names are not case sensitive; change 3 was not needed because there was no problem with the relative pathnames; and change 7 reversed change 3. The unnecessary changes were introduced when we made wrong conjectures about the cause of the error. Making changes that are unnecessary is quite typical, because making incorrect conjectures is also quite typical. Luckily these changes didn't make the situation worse, but it is possible to introduce new errors when following the wrong logical path.

Hiding Other Errors. When we first described the errors, we thought we had two: too many columns and no pictures. In fact, we had four errors:

1. Too many columns, which was actually not enough rows.
2. No pictures, because of a consistent error of leaving out the closing quote.
3. No Satyr Comma picture, because of a mistyped extension.
4. Wrong heading tags.

Error 3 was hidden by error 2, and we simply didn't notice error 4 at first. One error hidden by another is also typical. Though this hidden error didn't have any effect on the other errors here, hidden errors often do have an effect, which can make bugs hard to find. Interacting errors can be very difficult to track down because they can make the data seem very confusing. For that reason, we must always remember that more than one error could be causing the observed problems.

Viewing the Source. Notice that the most effective technique in our debugging exercise was to use the browser's **Source View** feature. Seeing the color- and font-coded HTML source told us how the browser interpreted our page. This revealed an error and then confirmed that it had been corrected. In general, one of the most powerful debugging techniques is to find ways for the computer to tell us the meaning of the information it stores or the effects of the commands it executes. Having the computer say how it's interpreting the instructions can separate the case in which we tell it to do the wrong thing from the case in which we command it correctly but the computer is doing it wrong. This is an important difference for finding a bug.

Little Errors, Big Problems. Finally, the errors in the HTML code were—with the exception of forgetting the row tags—quite tiny: three missing quotation marks, a wrong character in the file extension, and a wrong character in table heading tags. Of the 582 non-space characters in the original file, the 27 row tags (27=3(4 + 5)) and three quotes represent a 5 percent addition. The four character corrections are less than 1 percent. But, as we've seen, a single missing or erroneous character can ruin the HTML source. The conclusion: We must be extremely precise.

NO PRINTER OUTPUT: A CLASSIC SCENARIO

Though debugging HTML is possible because we know and write HTML, we don't create most computer systems, and they are extremely complex, way beyond our understanding. A standard personal computer and its software are more complex in several ways than the (noncomputer parts of the) space shuttle. As users, we have no idea how something so complex works, so how is it possible to troubleshoot a system we do not understand?

Of course, we cannot debug software and information systems at the detailed level used by programmers or engineers. If there is a basic, conceptual error in the system, users probably won't find it. But we don't have to. Before we ever come in contact with a system, it has been extensively tested. This testing doesn't eliminate all errors, but it probably means that the "standard operations" used by "average" users have been run through their paces many times. They should be bug-free, and we should be able to depend on the software.

FITBYTE

Putting It to the Test. As noted in Chapter 2, "getting out and getting back in" often works when an application is not operating correctly. The reason this tends to work is related to how software is tested. Beginning with a fresh configuration, the testing proceeds "forward" into the application, with the common operations getting the most attention. So the most stable part of a system is the part that is reachable from an initial configuration—the part you first meet when you're "getting back in."

To illustrate debugging a system without understanding it, consider a classic debugging scenario: You try to print a document and nothing comes out of the printer. This problem happens often to all users. In many ways this situation is like our videotape example. Like the TV/VCR system, the computer/printer system is connected by a cable, part of the system is mechanical, the flow of information is from one device to the other, and the system has worked in the past.

Applying the Debugging Strategy

The printing problem is solved just as the videotape problem was solved: *reproduce the error, understand the problem, and check the obvious causes*. These steps include checking the printer's control panel, the paper, the cartridges, the cable connections, the file to be printed, the installation of the printer driver (the correct printer dialog box comes up when the print command is issued), whether others can print if this is a shared printer, and whether you can print a different document. If all this has not solved the problem, you may think it's time to ask for help. You've already gone further than most users, so this wouldn't be embarrassing, but you can do more.

Pressing On

You can take the next step in the debugging strategy: *try to isolate the problem*. But this is daunting because you don't really understand how printing works. Not to worry. It's still possible to make progress.

Because you have printed before, you know your computer is configured correctly. You try printing a simple document like a text file, but it's the same story: The printer driver's dialog box comes up, asking how many copies you want, and so forth—you reply `1`, click **Print**, and the machine appears to compute for a moment, but when you check the printer, nothing's there. What could be happening to your output?

Thinking through what you imagine to be the process, you guess that when you click **Print**, the printer driver must convert the file into the form suitable for the printer. Because the computer runs briefly after you click **Print**, it's a safe bet that it's doing something like a conversion. Then your computer must send the converted file to the printer. Does it go? Surely, if the computer tried to send the file to the printer and the printer didn't acknowledge getting it, the computer would tell you to plug in the printer. Or would it? Suppose you unplugged the printer from the computer and tried again to print. You run this experiment and the same thing happens! The printer couldn't even receive the converted file, and there were no complaints. What's happening? Where is the file?

Perhaps the computer is saving the converted file. Why? Shouldn't it print if it's told to print? This is a little odd, because it's not asking you to plug in the printer. Could the other files you tried to print be waiting too, even though the printer was plugged in earlier? So, you start looking around for the stranded file(s). You locate the printer driver's printing monitor (**Start > Settings > Printers** on the PC; among the active programs on the Mac). When you open up this monitor, what you find is a list of all the files you've tried to print recently. They're not printing—they're just listed. (See Figure 7.9.)

The Print Queue

What you have discovered is the "print queue" for your machine. You didn't even know that computers *have* print queues, but they apparently do. Not being a computer scientist, you don't know why they have them, either. But it's obvious that your printing is stalled in the queue. As described in Chapter 2 under "Clicking Around," you explore the monitor application, discovering that the queue is "turned off" or possibly "wedged." (The actual description for "turned off" varies from system to system; for the PC it is **Use Printer Offline**, which is set under **File**; for Macs the Print Queue button is configured to **Start Print Queue**; shared printers are different still.) Though machines are different, the situation is the same: The computer's settings tell it to queue your converted files rather than print them immediately. How it got into this state you may never know. The best approach is to cancel or trash all of the jobs in the queue, because there are probably many duplicates, and restart the queue. That is, configure it so that it tries to print your files rather than queuing them. Your printing problem may be solved! Or have you forgotten to recable your printer?

> FITBYTE
>
> **Sleep on It.** One fact that professionals know about debugging is that when they can't solve a bug, it's good to take a break. Whether your mind keeps working on the problem subconsciously or returning to the problem refreshed just clears your thinking, briefly getting away helps.

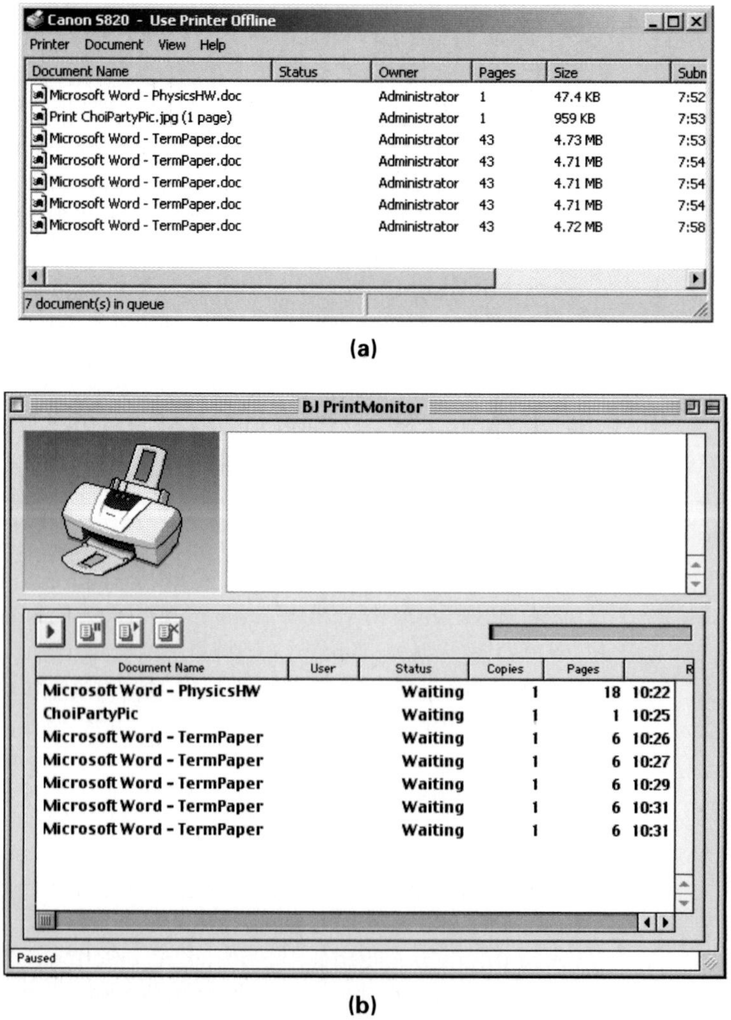

Figure 7.9. *Printer queues for Windows (a), and Mac operating systems (b).*

Calling Tech Support?

Summarizing the situation, you have debugged the printing operation in spite of the fact that it's complicated and you know almost nothing about how computers print. A key assumption was that the software is correct. You discovered that computers use a print queue, though it's a mystery why. The queue can become stopped or stalled, but by using the print monitor you can restart it. Locating the problem was just the standard debugging strategy applied with courage and common sense. The results were successful. Though there are obviously many problems that will not be solved by this approach—that actually require some technical knowledge—you should always assume that the standard debugging strategy will work. When you've applied it without success, it's time to call Tech Support.

SUMMARY

This chapter began by emphasizing why being precise is so important when using computers. The standard of precision is higher than in most other situations, so being careful and exact makes using computers easier. Next we looked at what debugging is and why we need to know how to do it. Then we introduced the basic strategy of debugging by helping virtual parents watch their college student's video spoof. That let us discuss the whys and hows of debugging. The principles that form the debugging strategy were abstracted into a tidy list to prepare for using them in debugging a Web page. We debugged a Web page, thanks in part to the **Source** view of the document that showed how the computer was interpreting the HTML. Analyzing our performance, we noted that debugging involves both correct and incorrect conjectures about the cause of a problem. Acting on incorrect guesses can result in unnecessary changes or, worse, harmful changes. Finally, we emphasized that it is possible to debug a sophisticated system like a computer's printing facility with little more than a vague idea of how it works, using our standard debugging strategy, applied with common sense and courage.

EXERCISES

Multiple Choice

1. An example of an understanding error is a:
   A. memory error
   B. data entry error
   C. design error
   D. none of the above
2. The best way to solve an understanding error is to:
   A. restart the system
   B. change software
   C. try again
   D. all of the above
3. The first step in debugging is to:
   A. check for obvious errors
   B. try to reproduce the problem
   C. isolate the problem
   D. find exactly what the problem is
4. The debugging process can be described as a(n):
   A. recipe
   B. road map
   C. set of guidelines
   D. list
5. The last step in the debugging process is to:
   A. look again to identify the mistake
   B. re-create the problem
   C. divide up the process
   D. determine the exact problem

Short Answer

1. ______ are information that is entered into boxes on a form.
2. A ______ is a set of rules that determine what is legal for field input.
3. Use a ______ to represent a space on the computer.
4. ______ and debugging mean essentially the same thing.
5. A glitch in a computer system is called a(n) ______.
6. A(n) ______ is an error in the way a system was developed.
7. An alternative approach to get around a problems is called a(n) ______.

Exercises

1. You walk into a room and flip the light switch. Nothing happens. Describe the debugging process you use to solve the problem.
2. What advantages does an organized approach have over a trial and error approach?
3. Draw a schematic of the debugging process. Apply this to the debugging process for question 1.
4. How would you say "Room 309"? Did you say "zero" or "oh"? How about a ZIP code? Try 57026.
5. What is the lexical structure for entering dates into the computer? Use the standard American format for a two-digit month, a separator, a two-digit day, a separator, and a four-digit year.
6. Devise a lexical structure for entering a phone number into the computer. What characters are allowed and when? Do the same thing for ZIP codes.
7. Think "outside the box" to solve a problem. You have a quiz in an hour and you're stranded. You must contact the professor before the quiz or you'll get a zero. How do you contact the professor? List multiple alternatives.
8. You've been doing debugging since you learned how to check your math back in grade school. Check the math on this problem.

   $N = -((12 + 6) - 7 \times 4 + ((9 - 2) \times 3) / 7)$
   $N = 18 - 7 \times 4 + 7 \times 3 / 7$
   $N = 11 \times 4 + 21 / 7$
   $N = 44 + 25 / 7$
   $N = 49 / 7$
   $N = 7$

9. Design several workarounds for the computer printing error. Pretend it's your term paper and it has to be printed. How would you get around the problem that that computer and the printer aren't printing?
10. Here is the HTML for a simple Web page. Find the errors in it and get the page to display properly. Test the page to be sure it works properly.

```
<html>
<head>
<title>My Favorites</title>
</head>
<body>
<ol>
   <li>Movies</li>
</ol>
<ul>
   <li><i>Grease</i></li>
   <li><i>Road to Perdition</i></li>
   <li><i>Titanic</i></li>
```

```
</ul>
<ol>
   <li>Shows</li>
   <li><i>Survivor</i></li>
   <li><i>American Idol</i></li>
   <li><i>Everybody Loves Raymond</i></li>
   <li>Stars</li>
</ol>
<ol>
   <li>Matt Damon</li>
   <li>Kate Hudson</li>
   <li>Lucy Lui</li>
</ol>
</body>
</html>
```

chapter

8 BITS AND THE "WHY" OF BYTES

Representing Information Digitally

learning objectives

- > Explain the link between patterns, symbols, and information
- > Compare two different methods of encoding
- > Determine possible PandA encodings of a physical phenomenon
- > Give a bit sequence code for ASCII; decode
- > Explain how structure tags (metadata) encode the *OED*

Before heaven and earth had taken form all was vague and amorphous. Therefore, it was called the Great Beginning. The Great Beginning produced emptiness and emptiness produced the universe. . . . The combined essences of heaven and earth became the yin and yang, the concentrated essences of the yin and yang became the four seasons, and the scattered essences of the four seasons became the myriad creatures of the world.

—HUAI-NAN TSU, 2ND CENTURY, B.C.

MOST PEOPLE know that computers and networks record and transmit information in *bits* and *bytes*. From basic English, you can guess that whatever bits are, they probably represent little pieces of information. But what are bytes? And why is "byte" spelled with a y? In this chapter we confirm that bits do represent little pieces of information, we define what bytes are, and, by the very end, we explain the mysterious *y*. But the chapter is much more fundamental than even these basic concepts. It describes how bits and bytes—the atoms and molecules of information—combine to form our virtual world of computation, information, and communication. (Multimedia is covered in Chapter 11.) We even explain how information exists when there is nothing, as when Sherlock Holmes solves the mystery using the information that "the dog didn't bark in the night."

The first goal of this chapter is to establish that digitizing doesn't require digits—any set of symbols will do. We explore encoding information using dice, learn how pattern sequences can create symbols, and discover that symbols can represent information. Our next goal is to learn the fundamental patterns on which all information technology is built: the presence and absence of a phenomenon. Called PandA encoding here, this meeting of the physical and logical worlds forms the foundation of information technology. We then define bits, bytes, and ASCII. And, finally, we describe the digitization of the *Oxford English Dictionary* (*OED*) to show how metadata is added to content so the computer can help us use it.

DIGITIZING DISCRETE INFORMATION

The dictionary definition of *digitize* is to represent information with digits. In normal conversation, *digit* means the ten Arabic numerals 0 through 9. Thus digitizing uses whole numbers to stand for things. This familiar process represents Americans by Social Security numbers, telephone accounts by phone numbers, and books as ISBN numbers. Such digital representations have probably been used since numerals were invented. But this sense of *digitize* is much too narrow for the digital world of information technology.

> FITBYTE
>
> **Digital Man.** The first person to apply the term digital to computers was George Stibitz, a Bell Labs mathematician. While consulting for the U.S. military, he observed that "pulsed" computing devices would be better described as digital because they represent information in discrete (that is, separate) units.

Limitation of Digits

A limitation of the dictionary definition of *digitize* is that it calls for the use of the ten digits, which produces a whole number. But in many cases the property of being numeric is unimportant and of little use. The benefit of numbers is that they quantify things and they enable us to do arithmetic. But Social Security numbers, phone numbers, and ISBN numbers are not quantities. You are not better than someone else is if you have a larger telephone number. And it doesn't make sense to multiply two ISBN numbers together. So, when we don't need numbers, we don't need to use the digits. But what else can we use to digitize?

Alternative Representations

Digitizing in information technology can use almost any symbols. For example, the North American telephone number `888 555 1212` could be represented as `*** %%% !@!@`. This encoding, rather than using {`1, 2, 3, 4, 5, 6, 7, 8, 9, 0`}, uses the symbol set `{!, @, #, $, %, ^, &, *, (, )}`. These symbols are simply the uppercase digit characters on a keyboard. If we use the symbol set { ▸, ▾, ◂, ⏩, ■, ⏪, ⏭, ▴, ⏮, ⏸ } the phone number is represented as: ▴ ▴ ▴ ■ ■ ■ ▸ ▾ ▸ ▾. This could be called **player encoding** because it uses the standard symbols from tape and disc players. These symbols work just as well as the digits as long as the telephone keypad is relabeled, as shown in Figure 8.1. The reason the encoding works is that a phone number's digits just tell us which sequence of keys to press. Any ten distinct symbols will work as long as the keypad is labeled properly.

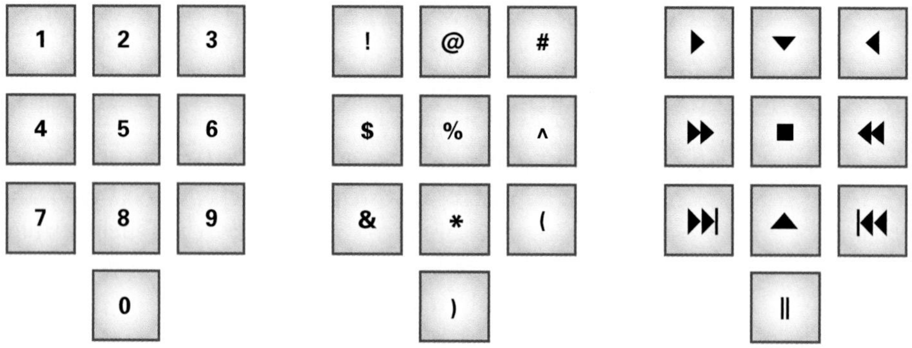

Figure 8.1. *Three symbol assignments for a telephone keypad.*

Symbols, Briefly

One practical advantage of digits over other less familiar symbols is that digits have short names. Imagine speaking your phone number as "asterisk asterisk exclamation point closing parenthesis exclamation point. . . ." In fact, as information technology has adopted these symbols, they are getting shorter names. For example, computer professionals often say exclamation point as *bang* and asterisk as *star*. Instead of saying "eight eight eight five five five one two one two" we could say "star star star per per per bang at bang at," which is just as brief. So, the advantage of brevity is not limited to digits.

Ordering Symbols

One other advantage of digits for encoding information like telephone numbers is that the items can be listed in numerical order. This feature is rarely used for the kinds of information discussed here; for example, telephone books are ordered by the name of the person rather than by the number. But, sometimes ordering items is useful.

To place information in order by using symbols (other than digits), we need to agree on an ordering for the basic symbols. This is called a **collating sequence**. In the same way that the digits are ordered

```
0 < 1 < 2 < 3 < 4 < 5 < 6 < 7 < 8 < 9
```

the player symbols could be ordered

⏸ < ▶ < ▼ < ◀ < ⏩ < ■ < ⏪ < ⏭ < ▲ < ⏮

Then, two coded phone numbers can be ordered based on which has the smaller first symbol, or if the first symbol matches, then on which has the smaller second symbol, or if the first two symbols match, which has the smaller third symbol, and so on. For example,

▲ ⏸ ⏸ ■ ■ ■ ▶ ▼ ▶ ▼ < ▲ ▲ ▲ ■ ■ ■ ▶ ▼ ▶ ▼

Today, digitizing means *representing information by symbols*—not just the ten digit symbols. But which symbols would be best? Before answering that question, we should consider how the choice of symbols interacts with the things being encoded.

ENCODING WITH DICE

Because information can be digitized using any symbols, consider a representation based on dice. A single die has six sides, and the patterns on the sides of the dice can be used for this digital representation. (The patterns can be interpreted as numbers, of course, but for the moment we ignore that property.)

Consider representing the Roman alphabet with dice.

With 26 letters in the Roman alphabet, but only six different patterns on a die, there are more letters to represent than there are patterns available. This is a typical problem in encoding. So we use multiple patterns to represent each letter. How many will be required? Two dice patterns together produce $6 \times 6 = 36$ different pattern sequences because each of the six patterns of one die can be paired with each of the six different patterns of the other die (see Figure 8.2). Three dice can define $6 \times 6 \times 6 = 216$ different pattern sequences because there are six choices for the first position, six for the second position, and six for the last. More generally, n dice together can produce 6^n different pattern sequences. If instead of six there is some other number, p, of basic patterns, a sequence of n of them produces p^n different pattern sequences. (Recall that p_n means $p \times p \times \ldots \times p$; that is, n copies of p multiplied together.)

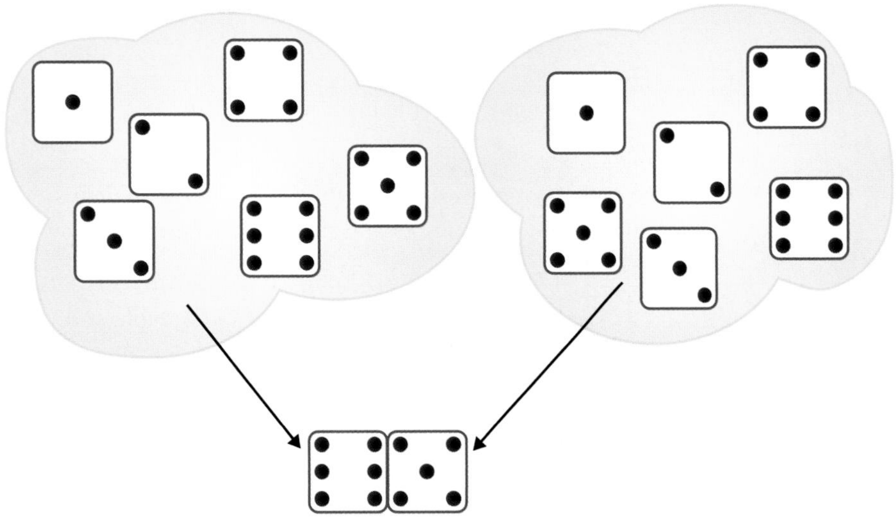

Figure 8.2. *Pairing two dice patterns results in 36 = 6 × 6 possible pattern sequences.*

Returning to the problem of digitizing the alphabet, we can agree to call each of the pattern sequences produced by pairing two dice a symbol. Then we can associate these dice-pair symbols with the letters simply by listing them.

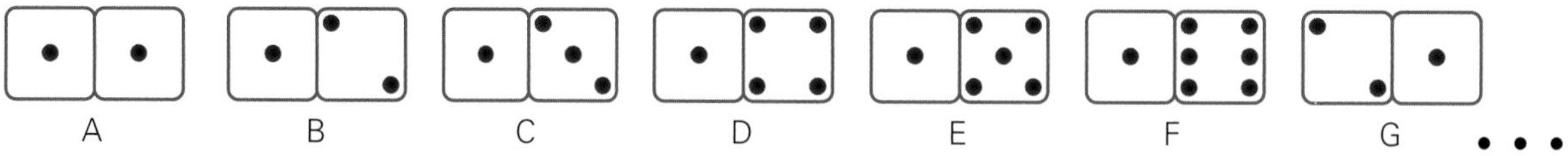

It helps to be systematic when associating the letters with the symbols to make the encoding easier to remember. In fact, because two dice form the symbols, the simplest way to present the association between the symbols and the values they encode (letters) is a table, as illustrated in Figure 8.3.

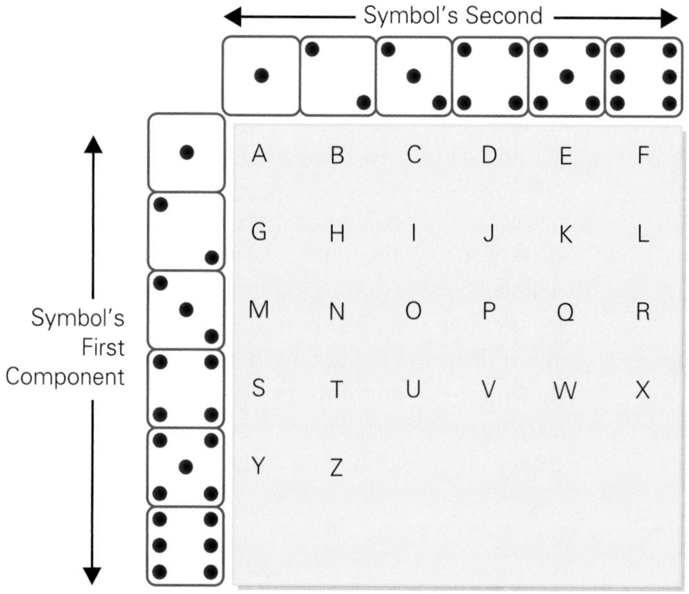

Figure 8.3. *Initial assignment of letters to the dice-pair symbols.*

The table is organized so that the pattern along the left side of the table is the first component of the symbol and the pattern along the top is the second. This makes the digitizing process easy.

> *Encode a letter.* Find the letter in the table and use the pattern of the row as the left half of the symbol and the pattern of the column as the right half.

> *Decode a symbol.* Find the row for the left half of the symbol and the column for the right half; the letter is at the intersection of the row and column.

TRY IT

Use the table (Figure 8.3) to find out what word (acronym) is represented by the three symbols shown.

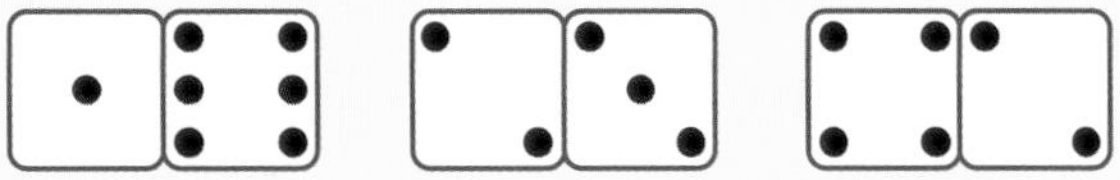

Did you come up with "FIT"?

Extending the Encoding

The representation has associated 26 of the symbols with the Roman letters, leaving ten positions unassigned. If the information to be digitized only uses letters, we're done, because a symbol is associated with each letter. But this rarely happens. A more common situation is that the information uses letters and numerals; many automobile license plates use those 36 characters. In such cases, associating the Arabic numerals to the unassigned symbols of Figure 8.3 would then complete the digitization, as shown in Figure 8.4(a).

But usually the textual information to be digitized includes more than letters and numerals; it also includes punctuation. Including punctuation complicates the dice-pair representation because we need more symbols than we have pairs of dice. Anyone inventing a digitization faces the problem of deciding which items are the most important to represent.

Perhaps the most important character is the space character, because we use it to *delimit* letter sequences, that is, separate words. We cannot use spacing in the digitization (that is, separations in our arrangement of dice-pairs) to indicate word separations in the text because we have no control over how the digital form will be used. For example, using the Figure 8.4(a) digitization, two people could communicate in a noisy environment with a single pair of dice by spelling out words one letter at a time. But with only one pair of dice, there is no way to "separate the pairs" to indicate the end of a word. The point is that the digitization must encode all the information, and the spaces separating words are part of the information. So space must be assigned to some symbol. After that the nine remaining symbols are not enough to represent the digits, so we'll use them for more punctuation. A representation of this type is shown in Figure 8.4(b).

Figure 8.4(b) has the advantage of representing space and other punctuation, but it doesn't represent the numerals. In some cases, this might not be a serious problem because we can find other ways to represent these characters. For example, the two people communicating in a noisy environment with a pair of dice might simply spell out each numeral. There would be no single symbol for zero, for example, but it could be presented as

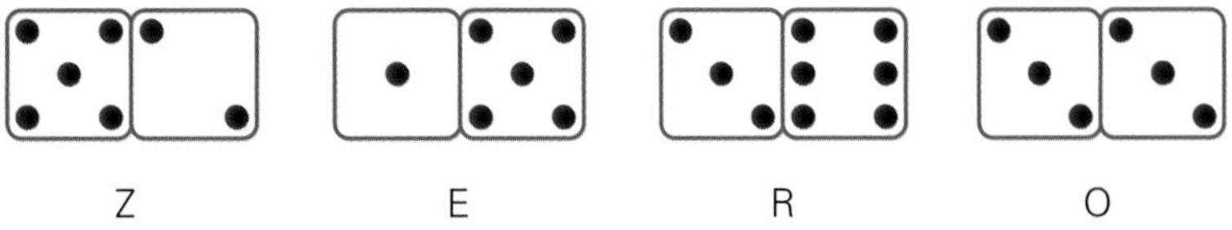

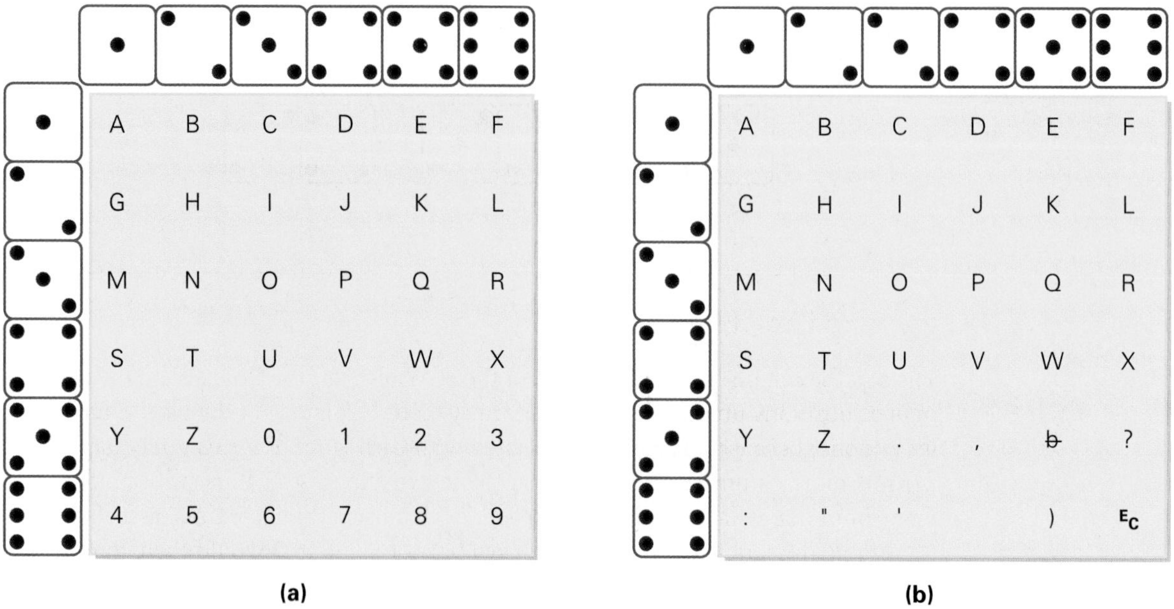

Figure 8.4. *Two complete dice-pair representations.* (Note: ƀ *indicates a space.)*

But spelling out numerals limits how this digital representation can be used, and we want to avoid limitations if we possibly can. Though it appears that we need to use dice triples, there is an alternative.

The Escape: Creating More Symbols

In Figure 8.4(b) the "boxcars" symbol (double sixes) has been associated with an unfamiliar character, Ec. This character, which is not a letter, numeral, or punctuation character, will be called *escape*. It has been included to illustrate how to extend a representation. Because escape does not match any legal character, we will never need it in the normal process of digitizing text. So we can use it to indicate that the digitization is "escaping from the basic representation" and applying a secondary representation. In this way, more symbols can be represented because pairing escape with another symbol doubles the number of representations, though the new symbols are twice as long.

To illustrate the idea, let's encode the numerals by pairing the escape symbol with each of the first ten symbols of the encoding, that is, those assigned to A through J. Each symbol pair, that is, four dice, is assigned to a numeral in order. Thus the symbol pair

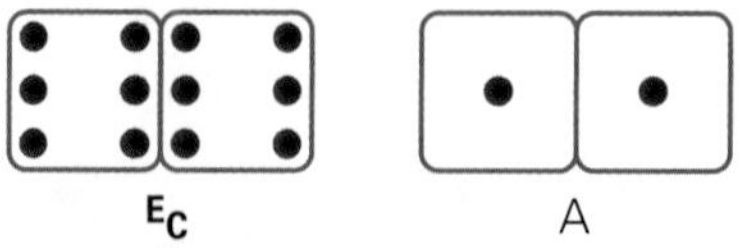

0

which is escape-A, represents 0. Escape-B represents 1, and so on. Notice that the escape symbol precedes the letter. So, 10 is represented as

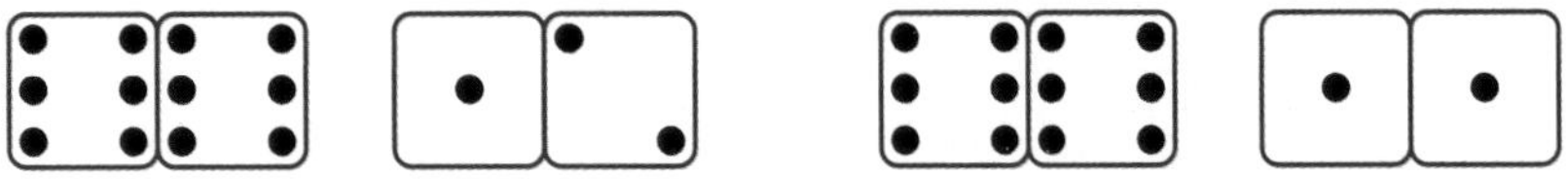

1 0

There can be no "group discount" here: We can't place escape before the first of a whole string of digits because the decoder would not know when the string ended and the base encoding (non-escape characters) resumed. So, a ten-digit number needs 20 symbols in this dice-pair encoding extended by escape.

FITBYTE

Shifty. The escape technique is familiar. The Shift keys are used as an escape for the keyboard; they double the encoding, giving uppercase characters. Control works this way, too.

Double Escape

Using this escape gives 35 basic symbol assignments because the E_C takes up the boxcars symbol. But, escape gives an equal number of two-symbol assignments. These secondary assignments should probably be associated with the less frequently used values because the encoding is less efficient. Of course, the idea can be continued because we could use $E_C E_C$ as another escape for yet another alternate set of symbols. But there are other, more sophisticated ways to use the escape symbol. The point is that in digitizing information, do not associate all symbols with legal information, as was done in Figure 8.4(a), but rather reserve one symbol as an escape, as shown in Figure 8.4(b). The escape gives flexibility to a representation.

Notice that when the 36 symbols created from two dice weren't enough for the letters, numerals, and punctuation, we could have used three dice pattern sequences. That would have given $6^3 = 216$ symbols. The advantage is that numerals would have been encoded with three dice rather than four. The disadvantage is that the letters and punctuation would have been encoded with three dice rather than two. If numerals make up less than half of the values we wish to encode, our "two plus escape" uses fewer dice than the "triples" solution.

To summarize, digitizing involves associating symbols with values, which in the case of text are the keyboard characters. The method of constructing symbols—combining base patterns—creates a fixed-size set of symbols. The symbol set must be large enough to represent each value. Saving one symbol for escape allows the encoding to be extended.

THE FUNDAMENTAL REPRESENTATION OF INFORMATION

The six base patterns of a die are familiar, but not fundamental. The fundamental patterns used in information technology come when the physical world meets the logical world. In the physical world, the most fundamental form of information is the presence or absence of a physical phenomenon:

> Does matter occupy a particular place in space and time, or not?

> Is light detected at a particular place and time, or not?

> Is magnetism sensed at a particular place and time, or not?

The same goes for pressure, charge, flow, and so on. In many cases, the phenomena have a continuous range of values. For example, light and color have a smooth range of intensities

while others like clicking and drumming are discrete

(The continuous case is discussed in Chapter 11.) From a digital information point of view, the amount of a phenomenon is not important as long as it is reliably detected—whether there is some information or none; whether it is present or absent.

In the logical world, which is the world of thinking and reasoning, the concepts of *true* and *false* are all important. Propositions such as "Rain implies wet streets" can be expressed and combined with other propositions such as "The streets are not wet" to draw conclusions such as "It is not raining." Logic is the foundation of reasoning, and it is also the foundation of computing. *By associating true with the presence of a phenomenon and false with its absence, we can use the physical world to implement the logical world. This produces information technology.* In this section, we make that association.

The PandA Representation

PandA is the name we use for the two fundamental patterns of digital information based on the presence and absence of a phenomenon. PandA is mnemonic for "presence and absence." A key property of the PandA representation is that it is black and white; that is, the phenomenon is either present or it is not; the logic is either *true* or *false*. Such a formulation is said to be *discrete*, meaning "distinct" or "separable"; it is not possible to transform one value into the other by continuous gradations. There is no gray.

A Binary System. The PandA encoding has just two basic patterns—Present and Absent—making it a **binary system**. The names Present and Absent are not essential to our use in digitization, so we often use other words that suggest the discrete, black-and-white nature of the two patterns (see Table 8.1). The assignment of these names to the two patterns is also arbitrary. There is no law that says that in all cases and forever and ever *On* means "Present" and *Off* means "Absent." We could agree to assign the names the other way around, and engineers deep into a design often do. As long as all of the information encoders and decoders agree, any assignment works. The associations given in the table seem reasonable, however, and they are probably the most common. But the entries are only names for the two fundamental patterns.

Table 8.1. *Possible interpretations of the two PandA patterns*

Present	Absent
True	False
1	0
On	Off
Yes	No
+	–
Black	White
For	Against
Yang	Yin
Lisa	Bart
...	...

Bits Form Symbols. The unit that can assume the different patterns can vary. In the dice representation, the unit was the top of a single die. This unit could be set to any of six patterns to encode letters. In the same way, in the PandA representation the unit is a specific place (in space and time), where the presence or absence of the phenomenon can be set and detected. The PandA unit is known as a *bit*, which can assume either of the two PandA patterns, Present or Absent. *Bit* is a contraction for "binary digit." (The term *bit* was originally adopted because early computer designers interpreted the two patterns as 1 and 0, the digits of the binary number system.) Though bit sequences can be interpreted as binary numbers, the key idea is that bits form *symbols*. Encoding numbers is a particularly useful application of symbols, but the idea is more general.

FITBYTE

Coincidence? Though *bit* means "small piece" in English, the term came from a contraction of *binary* and *digit*. Of course, bits represent small pieces of information, suggesting the choice may not have been a coincidence.

Bits in Magnetic Media

The two patterns are called the **states** of the bit when they are part of a storage medium. To illustrate bits in the physical world, consider the magnetic encoding of information as might be used on tapes, floppy disks, or hard disks. Like audiocassette tapes, these media are made out of a material containing iron that can be magnetized. Figure 8.5 shows a sequence of positions, some of which are positively magnetized and some of which are not.

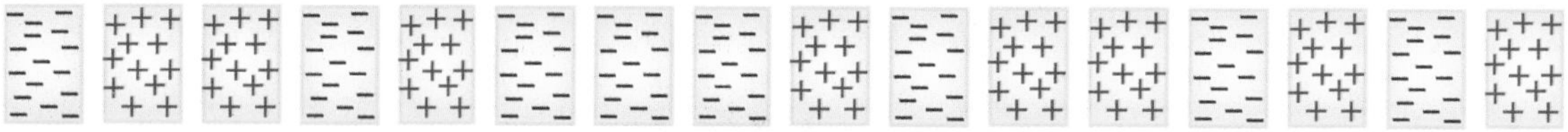

Figure 8.5. *Schematic diagram of a sequence of bit positions on a magnetic medium. The boxes illustrate a position where magnetism may be set and sensed; pluses (red) indicate magnetism of positive polarity, interpreted as "present" and minuses (blue) indicate magnetism of negative polarity, interpreted as "absent."*

Each position can represent a bit because it can be configured into both states, positively magnetized or not—that is, the two PandA patterns. For example, the 16 positions shown in Figure 8.5 encode the 16 bits.

absent-present-present-absent-present-absent-absent-absent-
present-absent-present-present-absent-present-absent-present

or, more briefly,

0110 1000 1011 0101

It is obvious why computer scientists and engineers prefer the names 1 and 0 to Present and Absent, even when the information is not numbers. Ones and zeros are simpler to read, write, and say.

FITBYTE

Positive Presence. The use of physical phenomena to represent information sometimes poses problems because there might be more than two alternatives. For example, a magnetic material might not be magnetized at all, or it could have positive or negative polarity; that is, there seem to be three possibilities. In such situations, engineers adopt one state such as positive polarity to mean "present" and all other states to mean "absent."

Bits in Computer Memory

Inside the computer the memory is arranged in a very long sequence of bits. That is, places where a phenomenon can be set and detected.

Analogy: Sidewalk Memory. To illustrate how memory works, imagine a sidewalk made of a strip of concrete with lines (expansion joints) across it forming squares, and suppose it has been swept clean. We agree that a stone on a sidewalk square corresponds to 1 and the absence of a stone corresponds to 0. This makes the sidewalk a sequence of bits. (Figure 8.6.) Sidewalk memory can encode information just like computer memory. But, it is not as economical of space!

Figure 8.6. *Sidewalk sections as a sequence of bits (1010 0010).*

The bits can be set to write information into the memory, and they can be sensed to read the information out of the memory. To write a 1 the phenomenon must be made to be present; for example, put a stone on a sidewalk square. To write a 0, the phenomenon must be made to be absent; for example, sweep the sidewalk square clean. To determine what information is stored at a specific position, sense whether the phenomenon is present or absent. So, if a stone is on a square, the phenomenon is present (1); otherwise, it is absent (0).

Alternative PandA Encodings. There is no limit to the number of ways to encode two states using physical phenomena, of course. Remaining just in the world of sidewalks, we could use stones on all squares but use white stones and black stones for the two states. Black could be chosen as present and not black as absent. Or, we could use multiple stones of two colors per square, saying that more white stones than black means 1 and more black stones than white means 0. (We must take care that the total number of stones on each sidewalk square is always odd.) Or we could place a stone in the center of the square for one state and off center for the other state. And so forth. These are all PandA encodings, provided the "phenomenon" is chosen properly: presence of black, presence of majority of white, presence of a centered stone.

FITBYTE

No Barking. Sherlock Holmes used one bit of information to solve the disappearance of a prize racehorse in the story "Silver Blaze." In the vicinity of the stable during the night [place and time], the phenomenon [barking watchdog] was not detected [absent], implying to Holmes the dog knew the thief, which meant the thief had to be Simpson, the owner. Holmes's deduction used information [perpetrator known to the household] represented by the absence of a phenomenon, that is, the dog was *not* barking.

Combining Bit Patterns. Like the sides of a die, the two bit patterns alone only give us a limited resource for digitizing information. If the information has only two alternative values—that is, it's binary information, such as votes (*aye*, *nay*), personality types (*A*, *B*), Mariners baseball games (*won*, *loss*)—one bit is enough. But usually the two patterns must be combined into sequences to create the necessary symbols. As we learned in the last section, if there are $p = 2$ patterns, as in the PandA representation, arranged into n-length sequences, we can create 2^n symbols. Table 8.2 relates the length of the bit sequence to the number of possible symbols.

Table 8.2. *Number of symbols when the number of possible patterns is two*

n	2^n	Symbols
1	2^1	2
2	2^2	4
3	2^3	8
4	2^4	16
5	2^5	32
6	2^6	64
7	2^7	128
8	2^8	256
9	2^9	512
10	2^{10}	1024

The 16 symbols of $n = 4$ length bit sequences are shown in Table 8.3.

The PandA encoding is the fundamental representation of information. By grouping bits together, we can produce enough symbols to represent any number of values. By creating symbols using the two PandA patterns, we can record and transform information using resources from the physical world. Information and computation are abstract without physical form, but the miracle of information technology is that they can be made real. With machines and networks doing the work, our lives are simplified.

HEX EXPLAINED

Before using PandA to represent text, let's solve a mystery from Chapter 4. Recall that when we specified custom colors in HTML—`<font color="#FF8E2A">` as shown in Figure 4.2—we used **hex digits**, short for hexadecimal digits, or base-16. We didn't explain hex at the time but simply presented Table 4.4, so we could convert back and forth between decimal and hexadecimal.

Table 8.3. *The basic PandA encoding of length four symbols and the associated bits*

Sixteen Symbols of the 4-Bit PandA Representation

Symbol	Binary	Physical Bits	Hex	Symbol	Binary	Physical Bits	Hex
AAAA	0000	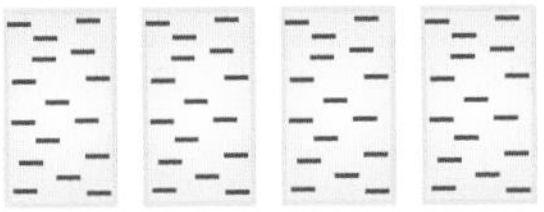	0	PAAA	1000	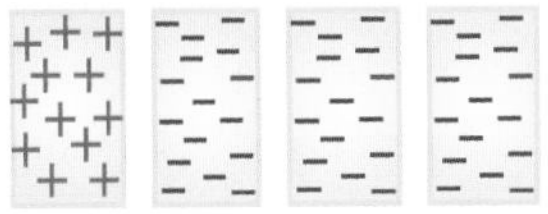	8
AAAP	0001	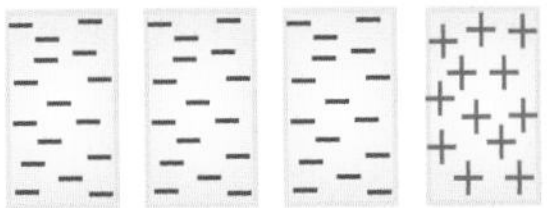	1	PAAP	1001	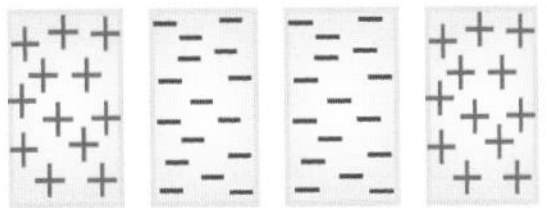	9
AAPA	0010	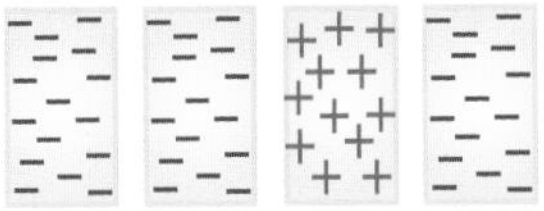	2	PAPA	1010	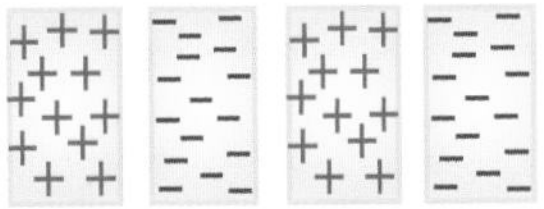	A
AAPP	0011	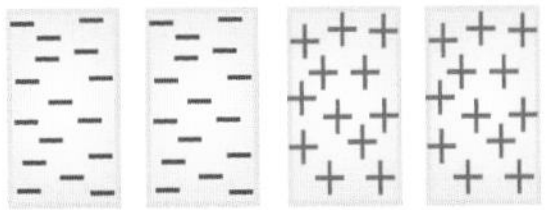	3	PAPP	1011	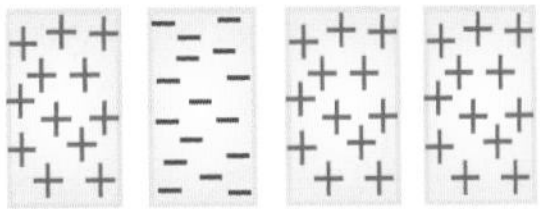	B
APAA	0100	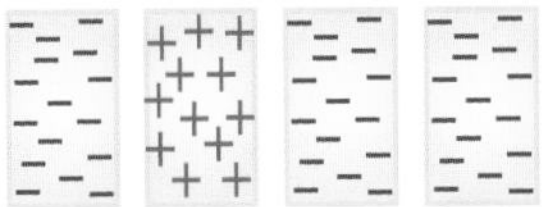	4	PPAA	1100	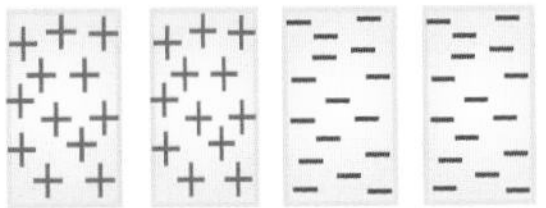	C
APAP	0101	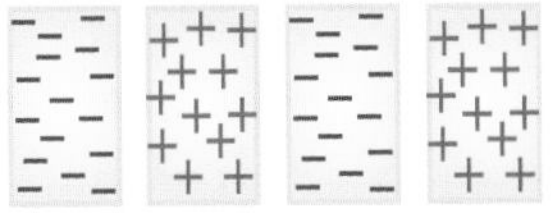	5	PPAP	1101	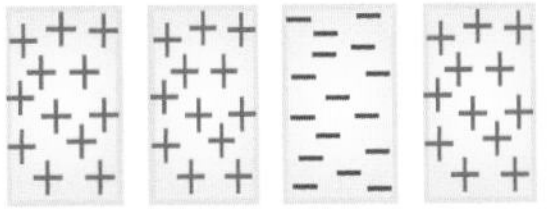	D
APPA	0110	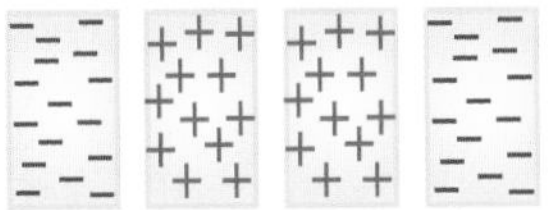	6	PPPA	1110	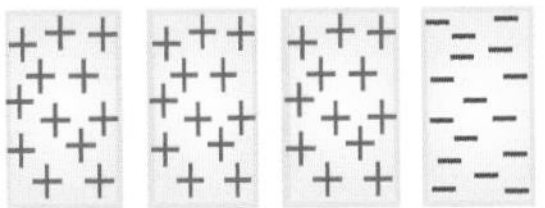	E
APPP	0111	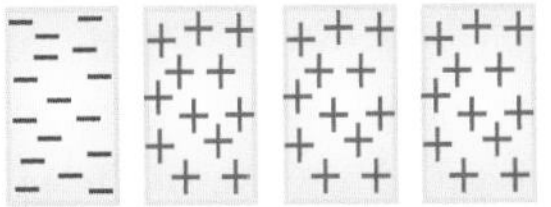	7	PPPP	1111	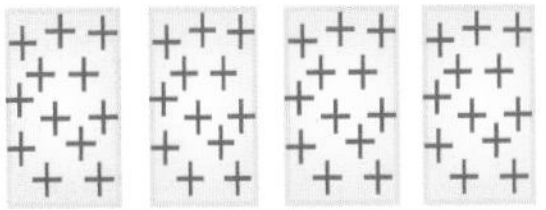	F

The reason for using hexadecimal is as follows. When we specify an RGB color or other encoding using bits, we must give the bits in order. The bit sequence might be given in 0's and 1's,

`<font color="#1111111110011000111000101010">` *Illegal HTML tag*

but writing so many 0's and 1's is tedious and error prone. Computer professionals long ago realized that they needed a better way to write bit sequences, and so began using hexadecimal digits.

The 16 Hex Digits

The digits of hex are `0`, `1`, . . . , `9`, `A`, `B`, `C`, `D`, `E`, `F`. Because there are 16 digits, they can be represented perfectly by the 16 symbols of 4-bit sequences. In Table 8.3, the binary column is associated with the hex column. So bit sequence 0000 is hex 0, bit sequence 0001 is hex 1, and so forth, up to the bit sequence 1111, which is hex F. (This is simply a numeric interpretation of the bits, which will be explained in Chapter 11.)

Changing Hex Digits to Bits and Back Again

Because each hex digit corresponds to a 4-bit sequence, and vice versa, we can translate between hex and bits easily: given hex, write down the associated groups of 4 bits. Given a sequence of bits, group them into sequences of four, and write down the corresponding hex digit. Thus,

```
0010 1011 1010 1101 = 2BAD
```

and

```
1B40 = 0001 1011 0100 0000
```

So, in HTML when we specify the color white as **`"#FFFFFF"`**, we are effectively setting each bit of the RGB specification bits to 1.

TRY IT

> What is ABE8 BEEF as a bit sequence? To find the answer, check Table 8.3. Find each letter in the hex column, and write down the corresponding 4-bit sequence from the binary column. For example, A is in the second column and corresponds to the bits: 1010.
>
> *Answer:* *1010 1011 1110 1000 1011 1110 1110 1111*

DIGITIZING TEXT

The two earliest uses of the PandA representation were to encode numbers and keyboard characters. These two applications are still extremely important, though now representations for sound, images, video, and other types of information are almost as important. In this section we talk about how the text is encoded; we discuss how numbers are encoded in Chapter 11.

Remember that the number of bits determines the number of symbols available for representing values: n bits in sequence yield 2^n symbols. And, as we've learned, the more characters we want encoded, the more symbols we need. Roman letters, Arabic numerals, and about a dozen punctuation characters are about the minimum needed to digitize English text. We would also like to have uppercase and lowercase letters, and the basic arithmetic symbols like +, –, *, /, and =. But, where should the line be drawn? Should characters not required for English but useful in other languages like German (ö), French (é), Spanish (ñ), and Norwegian (ø) be included? What about Czech, Greek, Arabic, Thai, or Cantonese? Should other languages' punctuation be included, like French (« ») and Spanish (¿)? Should arithmetic symbols include degrees (°), pi (π), relational symbols ($\leq$), equivalence ($\equiv$), for all ($\forall$)? What about business symbols: ¢, £, ¥, ©, and ®? What about unprintable characters like backspace and new-line? Should there be a symbol for smiley faces (☺)? Some of these questions are easier to answer than others. Though we want to keep the list small so that we use fewer bits, not being able to represent critical characters would be a mistake.

Assigning Symbols

The 26 uppercase and 26 lowercase Roman letters, the 10 Arabic numerals, a basic set of 20 punctuation characters (including blank), 10 useful arithmetic characters, and 3 nonprintable characters (new-line, tab, backspace) can be represented with 95 symbols. Such a set would be enough for English and the keys on a basic computer keyboard. To represent 95 distinct symbols, we need 7 bits because 6 bits gives only $2^6 = 64$ symbols. Seven bits give $2^7 = 128$ symbols, which is more than we need for the 95 different symbols. Some special control characters must also be represented. These control characters are used for data transmission and other engineering purposes. They are assigned to the remaining 33 of the 7-bit symbols.

An early and still widely used 7-bit code for the characters is **ASCII**, pronounced *AS·key*. ASCII stands for American Standard Code for Information Interchange. The advantages of a "standard" are many: computer parts built by different manufacturers can connect together; programs can create data and store it so that different programs can process it later; and so forth. In all cases, there must be an agreement as to which character is associated with which symbol (bit sequence).

Extended ASCII: An 8-bit Code

As the name implies, ASCII was developed in the United States. But by the mid-1960s, it became clear that 7-bit ASCII was not enough because it could not fully represent text from languages other than English. So IBM, the dominant computer manufacturer at the time, decided to use the next larger set of symbols, the 8-bit symbols, as the standard for character representation. Eight bits produce $2^8 = 256$ symbols, enough to encode English and the Western European languages, their punctuation characters, and a large set of other useful characters. The larger, improved encoding was called **Extended ASCII**, shown in Figure 8.7. The original ASCII is the "first half" of Extended ASCII; that is, 7-bit ASCII is the 8-bit ASCII representation with the leftmost bit set to 0. Though Extended ASCII does not handle all natural languages, it does handle many languages that derived from the Latin alphabet. Handling other languages is solved in two ways: recoding the second half of Extended ASCII for the language's other characters; and using the escape mechanism mentioned earlier.

ASCII	0000	0001	0010	0011	0100	0101	0110	0111	1000	1001	1010	1011	1100	1101	1110	1111
0000	NU	SH	SX	EX	ET	EQ	AK	BL	BS	HT	LF	YT	FF	CR	SO	SI
0001	DL	D1	D2	D3	D4	NK	SY	EΣ	CN	EM	SB	EC	FS	GS	RS	US
0010		!	"	#	$	%	&	'	(	)	*	+	,	-	.	/
0011	0	1	2	3	4	5	6	7	8	9	:	;	<	=	>	?
0100	@	A	B	C	D	E	F	G	H	I	J	K	L	M	N	O
0101	P	Q	R	S	T	U	V	W	X	Y	Z	[	\	]	^	_
0110	`	a	b	c	d	e	f	g	h	i	j	k	l	m	n	o
0111	p	q	r	s	t	u	v	w	x	y	z	{	|	}	~	DT
1000	80	81	82	83	IN	NL	SS	ES	HS	HJ	YS	PD	PV	RI	S2	S3
1001	DC	P1	PZ	SE	CC	MM	SP	EP	Q8	QQ	QA	CS	ST	OS	PM	AP
1010	AO	¡	¢	£		¥	¦	§	¨	©	♀	{{	¬	-	®	¯
1011	°	±	²	³	´	µ	¶	·	¸	¹	♂	}}	¼	½	¾	¿
1100	À	Á	Â	Ã	Ä	Å	Æ	Ç	È	É	Ê	Ë	Ì	Í	Î	Ï
1101	Ð	Ñ	Ò	Ó	Ô	Õ	Ö	×	Ø	Ù	Ú	Û	Ü	Ý	Þ	β
1110	à	á	â	ã	ä	å	æ	ç	è	é	ê	ë	ì	í	î	ï
1111	ð	ñ	ò	ó	ô	õ	ö	÷	ø	ù	ú	û	ü	ý	þ	ÿ

Figure 8.7 *ASCII, The American Standard Code for Information Interchange*

Note: The original 7-bit ASCII is the top half of the table; the whole table is known as Extended ASCII (ISO/IEC8859-1). The 8-bit symbol for a letter is the four row bits followed by the four column bits (e.g., female (♀) = 10101010, while male(♂) = 10111010). Characters shown as two small letters are control symbols used to encode nonprintable information (e.g., BS = 00001000 is backspace). The bottom half of the table represents characters needed by Western European languages, such as Icelandic's eth (ð) and thorn (Þ).

IBM's move to 8 bits was bold because it added the extra bit at a time when computer memory and storage were extremely expensive. IBM gave 8-bit sequences a special name, **byte**, and adopted it as a standard unit for computer memory. Bytes are still the standard unit of memory, and their "8-ness" is noticeable in many places. For example, recent computers have been "32-bit machines," meaning their datapath widths (the size of information processed by most instructions) are 4 bytes.

FITBYTE

The Ultimate. Though ASCII and its variations are widely used, the more complete solution is a 16-bit representation, called *Unicode*. With 65,536 symbols, Unicode can handle *all* languages.

ASCII Coding of Phone Numbers

Let's return to the phone number, `888 555 1212`, whose representation concerned us at the start of the chapter. How would a computer represent this phone number in its memory? Remember, this is not really a number, but rather, it is a keying sequence for a telephone's keypad represented by numerals; it is not necessary, or even desirable, to represent the phone number as a numerical quantity. Because each of the numerals has a representation in Extended ASCII, we can express the phone number by encoding each digit. The encoding is easy: Find each numeral in Figure 8.7, and write down the bit sequence from its row, followed by the bit sequence from its column. So the phone number 888 555 1212 in ASCII is

```
0011 1000   0011 1000   0011 1000   0011 0101   0011 0101   0011 0101
0011 0001   0011 0010   0011 0001   0011 0010
```

You can use Figure 8.7 to check this encoding. This is exactly how computers represent phone numbers. The encoding seems somewhat redundant because each byte has the same left half: 0011. The left halves are repeated because all of the numerals are located on the 0011 row of the ASCII table. If only phone numbers were to be represented, fewer bits could be used, of course. But there is little reason to be so economical, so we adopt the standard ASCII.

FITBYTE

Two bits, four bits . . . The term *byte* has motivated some people to call 4 bits—that is, half a byte—a *nibble*.

Notice that we have run all of the digits of the phone number together, even though when we write them for ourselves we usually put spaces between the area code and exchange code, and between the exchange code and the number. The computer doesn't care, but it might matter to users. However, it is easy to add these spaces and other punctuation.

TRY IT

Encode the phone number (888) 555-1212 in Extended ASCII, that is, insert the punctuation. (Notice that there is a space before the first 5.)

To find the answer, locate each character in Figure 8.7 and write down the four bits at the left of the row and the four bits at the top of the column. For example, the open parenthesis (is in the third row and corresponds to `0010 1000`.

Answer:

0010 1000   0011 1000   0011 1000   0011 1000   0010 1001
0010 0000   0011 0101   0011 0101   0011 0101   0010 1101
0011 0001   0011 0010   0011 0001   0011 0010

NATO Broadcast Alphabet

Finally, although we usually try to be efficient (use shortest symbol sequences) to minimize the amount of memory needed to store and transmit information, not all letter representations should be short. The code for the letters used in radio communication is purposely inefficient in this sense, so they are distinctive when spoken amid noise. The NATO broadcast alphabet, shown in Table 8.5, encodes letters as words; that is, the words are the symbols, replacing the standard spoken names. For example, *Mike* and *November* replace "em" and "en," which can be hard to tell apart. This longer encoding improves the chances letters will be recognized when spoken under less-than-ideal conditions. The digits keep their usual names, except nine, which is frequently replaced by *niner*.

Table 8.5. *NATO broadcast alphabet designed not to be minimal*

A	Alpha	G	Golf	M	Mike	S	Sierra	Y	Yankee
B	Bravo	H	Hotel	N	November	T	Tango	Z	Zulu
C	Charlie	I	India	O	Oscar	U	Uniform		
D	Delta	J	Juliet	P	Papa	V	Victor		
E	Echo	K	Kilo	Q	Quebec	W	Whiskey		
F	Foxtrot	L	Lima	R	Romeo	X	X-ray		

FITBYTE

It's Greek to Me. There are dozens of phonetic alphabets for English and many other languages. The NATO alphabet, used for air traffic control, begins with "alpha," raising the question, "What is the first letter of the Greek phonetic alphabet?" Alexandros.

THE *OXFORD ENGLISH DICTIONARY*

Representations like Extended ASCII encode text directly, 8 bits per letter, with more characters available using the escape technique. But most documents have more than just text. For example, one might need to format information, such as font, font size, justification, etc. We could add formatting characters to ASCII—for example, Escape A might represent the Times Roman font—but this is a poor idea for several reasons. The most serious problem is that it mixes the content (i.e., the text) with the description of its form. The descriptive information—it's called **metadata**—specifies the content's formatting or structure, and should be kept separate from the text. So, we specify metadata by using tags, as we have seen in the searching discussion (Chapter 2) and HTML (Chapter 4). Tags use the same character representation as the content itself, which simplifies the encoding, and they are much more versatile. In this section we illustrate how tags encode the structure of a document, by describing the digitization of the *Oxford English Dictionary*.

Encoding Bits on a CD ROM > >

The compact disc read-only memory (CD-ROM) is the technology of the familiar audio CD applied to storing programs and data. Developed jointly by the Phillips and Sony Corporations, the CD was originally intended only for recorded audio and video. But the two companies engineered the technology so cleverly that CDs are almost error free, making them perfect for storing data and software. Here's how CDs work.

CDs are made of clear plastic that is forced into a round mold, something like a round waffle iron, having a smooth bottom and a bumpy top. When the plastic has hardened and been removed from the mold, the topside bumpy pattern is covered with aluminum to make it shiny. A protective layer is put over the aluminum and the "label" is printed on the top.

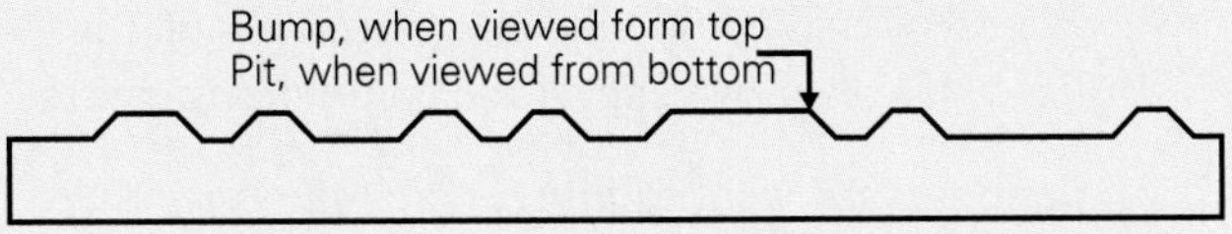

The bumps encode the information. But because they are read from the bottom of the CD, the bumps are called *pits*. The region between the pits is called the *land*. A laser beam is focused up through the CD onto the pitted surface. The beam reflects off of the aluminum and back to a sensor that can detect whether the beam is striking a pit, a land or a diagonal in between.

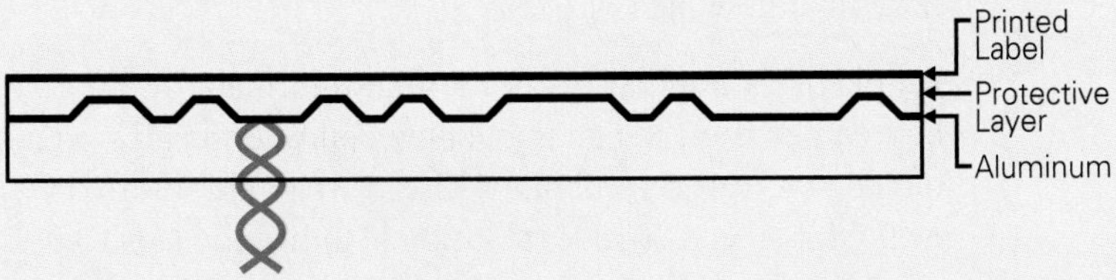

The pits are arranged in a line that begins at the *inner* edge of the CD and spirals out to the *outer* edge. (Notice that inside-out is the opposite of vinyl records.) The first part of the spiral is used for calibrating the laser reading device; then comes an index (track list) for locating specific positions on the CD; and finally the actual information (music or software) in binary.

In addition to CD ROMs, which are manufactured with the information already stored on them, there are CD Recordable (CR-R) discs and CD ReWriteable (CD-RW) discs. Both types are blank to begin with and use somewhat different materials. CD-R disks can be written once and read thereafter; CD-RW disks can be written and rewritten.

Using Tags to Encode

The *Oxford English Dictionary* is the definitive reference for every English word's meaning, etymology, and usage. Because it is so comprehensive, the OED is truly monumental. The printed version is 20 volumes, weighs 150 pounds, and fills 4 feet of shelf space. In 1857, the Philological Society of London set the goal of producing a complete listing of all English words. They expected that the completed dictionary would have 6400 pages in four volumes. By 1884, with the list completed only up to *ant*, it became clear to James Murray, the lexicographer in charge, that the effort was much more ambitious than originally thought. The first edition, completed in 1928, long after Murray's death, filled 15,490 pages and contained 252,200 entries. In 1984, the conversion of the *OED* to digital form began.

Now imagine that you have typed in the entire *OED* as a long sequence of ASCII characters from A through the end of the definition for *Zyxt*, the last word in English. That would take one person about 120 years. Once the dictionary is digitized, however, we expect the computer to help us use it. Can it help?

Suppose you want to find the definition for the verb *set*, which has the longest entry in the *OED*. The searching software—as described in Chapter 2—would look for *s-e-t* and find it thousands of times. This is because *set* is part of many words, like be*set*, cas*set*te, and *set*tle, and *set* is used in many definitions; for example, "*match-point* in tennis is the final score ending the present game, *set* and match."

We can solve the first problem—avoiding *s-e-t* within words—by ignoring all occurrences that do not have a punctuation character or space before and after the *s-e-t*. The software can do that. But how does it find the definition for *set* among the thousands of true occurrences of the word *set* in other definitions? The software processing the text file, unable to understand the dictionary's contents, would have no clue which one that is.

People use a number of cues to find information in the dictionary, such as alphabetic order and the fact that a new definition begins on a new line, and the defined word is set in bold. Though we could insert HTML-like tags for new lines or boldface type, a better solution is to use the tags to describe the *structure* of the dictionary's content.

Structure Tags

For specifying the *OED*'s **structure**, a special set of tags was developed. For example, `<hw>` is the *OED*'s tag for a *headword*, the word being defined. As usual, because tags surround the text like parentheses, there is a closing *headword* tag, `</hw>`. Thus, the place in the *OED* where the verb *set* is defined appears in the tagged text file of the dictionary as

```
<hw>set</hw>
```

Other tags label the pronunciation `<pr>`, phonetic notations `<ph>`, the parts of speech `<ps>`, the homonym number `<hm>` for headwords that sound the same, and so forth. There are also tags to group items, such as `<e>` to surround an entire entry and `<hg>` to surround a head group (that is, all of the information at the start of a definition). In the *OED* the first entry for the verb set begins

set (sɛt), *v.*[1]

giving the word being defined, the pronunciation, the part of speech (verb), and the homonym number (1). We expect it must be tagged as

```
<e><hg><hw>set</hw> <pr><ph>s&epsilont</ph></pr>, <ps>v</ps>.
<hm>1</hm></hg>
```

Notice the use of the escape code (`&epsilon`) for the epsilon character in the pronunciation. Also, the `</e>` is not shown because it must be at the very end of the entry.

With the structure tags in the dictionary, software can find the definition of the verb *set* easily: Search for occurrences of `<hw>set</hw>`, which indicate a definition for set, check within its head group for `<ps>v</ps>`, which indicates that it is a verb form of set being defined, and then print out (formatted) all of the text within the `<e>`, `</e>` tags.

Of course, the tags are not printed. They are included only to specify the structure, so the computer knows what part of the dictionary it is looking at. But in fact, structure tags are very useful for formatting. For example, the boldface type used for headwords can be automatically applied when the dictionary is printed based on the `<hw>` tag. In a similar way, italics typeface can be applied in the part of speech. The parentheses surrounding the pronunciation and the superscript for the homonym number are also generated automatically. Thus, knowing the structure makes it possible to generate the formatting information.

The opposite is not true. That is, formatting tags do not usually tell us enough about a document to allow us to guess its structure. In the *OED* example, though boldface is used for headwords, it is also used for other purposes, meaning that just because a word is boldface does not mean it is a headword. In fact, because some formatting information, like italics, has both structural and nonstructural occurrences, the *OED* digitization includes some formatting information with the structural information. Thus, structure is more important, but most complex documents use both types of tags. (We discuss structure tags further in the XML discussion of Chapter 16.)

Sample OED Entry

Figure 8.8 shows the entry for *byte*, together with its representation, as it actually appears in the file of the online *OED*. At first the form looks very cluttered, but if you compare it with the printed form, you can make sense out of the tags. The tags specify the role of each word of the dictionary. So, for example, to find the first time the word byte was used in print, the software will search for **<hw>byte</hw>**, then look for the quote date tags, **<qd>,</qd>**, to find that the first use was 1964. Structure tags help the software help the user.

byte (baIt). *Computers.* [Arbitrary, prob. influenced by bit sb.[4] and bite sb.] A group of eight consecutive bits operated on as a unit in a computer.

1964 ***Blaauw*** & ***Brooks*** in *IBM Systems Jrnl.* III. 122 An 8-bit unit of information is fundamental to most of the formats [of the System/360]. A consecutive group of *n* such units constitutes a field of length *n*. Fixed-length fields of length one, two, four, and eight are termed bytes, halfwords, words, and double words respectively. **1964** *IBM Jrnl. Res. & Developm.* VIII. 97/1 When a byte of data appears from an I/O device, the CPU is seized, dumped, used and restored. **1967** ***P. A. Stark*** *Digital Computer Programming* xix. 351 The normal operations in fixed point are done on four bytes at a time. **1968** *Dataweek* 24 Jan. 1/1 Tape reading and writing is at from 34,160 to 192,000 bytes per second.

```
<e><hg><hw>byte</hw> <pr><ph>baIt</ph></pr></hg>. <la>Computers
</la>. <etym>Arbitrary, prob. influenced by <xr><x>bit</x></xr>
 <ps>n.<hm>4</hm></ps>and <xr><x>bite</x> <ps>n.</ps></xr></ety
m> <s4>A group of eight consecutive bits operated on as a unit
 in a computer.</s4> <qp><q><qd>1964</qd><a>Blaauw</a> &amp. <
a>Brooks</a> <bib>in</bib> <w>IBM Systems Jrnl.</w> <lc>III. 1
22</lc> <qt>An 8-bit unit of information is fundamental to most
 of the formats <ed>of the System/360</ed>.&es.A consecutive gr
oup of <i>n</i> such units constitutes a field of length <i>n</
i>.&es.Fixed-length fields of length one, two, four, and eight
are termed bytes, halfwords, words, and double words respective
ly. </qt></q><q><qd>1964</qd> <w>IBM Jrnl. Res. &amp. Developm.
</w> <lc>VIII. 97/1</lc> <qt>When a byte of data appears from a
n I/O device, the CPU is seized, dumped, used and restored.</qt
></q> <q><qd>1967</qd> <a>P. A. Stark</a> <w>Digital Computer P
rogramming</w> <lc>xix. 351</lc> <qt>The normal operations in f
ixed point are done on four bytes at a time.</qt></q><q><qd>
1968</qd> <w>Dataweek</w> <lc>24 Jan. 1/1</lc> <qt>Tape reading
and writing is at from 34,160 to 192,000 bytes persecond.</qt>
</q></qp></e>
```

Figure 8.8. *The OED entry for the word* byte, *together with the representation of the entry in its digitized form with tags.*

Because the tag characters are included with the content characters, they increase the size of the file compared with plain text. The entry for *byte* is 841 characters, but the tagged code is 1204 characters, an almost 50 percent increase.

Why "Byte"?

As informative as the OED definition is, it doesn't answer that nagging question: Why is *byte* spelled with a *y*? To understand the charming nature of the answer, we need to know that computer memory is subject to errors (a zero changing to a one, or a one to a zero), caused by such things as cosmic rays. Really. It doesn't happen often, but often enough to worry computer engineers, who build special circuitry to detect and correct memory errors. They often add extra bits to the memory to help detect errors—for example, a ninth bit per byte can detect errors using parity.

Parity refers to whether a number is even or odd. To encode bytes using **even parity**, use the normal byte encoding and then count the number of 1's in the byte; if there is an even number of 1's, set the ninth bit to 0; if there is an odd number, set the ninth bit to 1. The result is that all 9-bit groups will have even parity, either because they were even to begin with and the 0 didn't change that, or they were odd to begin with, but the 1 made them even. Any single bit error in a group causes its parity to become odd, allowing the hardware to detect that an error occurred, though not which bit is wrong.

So, why is *byte* spelled with a y? The answer comes from Werner Buchholz, the inventor of the word and the concept. In the late 1950s, Buchholz was the project manager and architect for the IBM supercomputer, called Stretch. For that machine, he explained to me, "We needed a word for a quantity of memory between a bit and a word." (A "word" of computer memory is typically the amount required to represent computer instructions and the "usual" integer numbers. On modern computers, a word is 32 bits.) Buchholz continued, "It seemed that after 'bit' comes 'bite.' But we changed the 'i' to a 'y' so that a typist couldn't accidentally change 'byte' into 'bit' by the single error of dropping the 'e'. " No single letter change to *byte* can create *bit*, and vice versa. Buchholz and his engineers were so concerned with memory errors that he invented an error-detecting *name* for the memory unit!

SUMMARY

We began by learning that digitizing doesn't require digits—any symbols will do. Using dice as a source of patterns, we considered problems of encoding keyboard characters. We solved these problems by using sequences of dice, by assigning a special escape symbol, and by deciding not to encode certain characters. Then we introduced PandA encoding, the fundamental representation of information, which is based on the Presence and Absence of a physical phenomenon. PandA patterns are discrete; that is, they form the basic unit of a bit. And their names—most often 1 and 0—could be any pair of opposite terms. The term bit is a contraction for binary digit, but bits are used for more than just representing numbers. Next, we learned about 7-bit ASCII, an early, and still useful, assignment of bit sequences (symbols) to keyboard characters. Extended ASCII is now the standard. Once there is an encoding for keyboard characters, documents like the *Oxford English Dictionary* can be encoded. There, we learned that tags associate metadata with every part of the OED. Using that data, a computer can easily help us find words and other information, because every part of every entry has been identified. Finally, we resolved the mystery of the *y* in *byte*.

EXERCISES

Multiple Choice

1. Without an escape sequence, a pair of dice can encode ______ symbols and three dice can encode ______ symbols.
   A. 36, 72
   B. 36, 256
   C. 36, 216
   D. 72, 216
2. How many characters could be represented by two eight-sided dice?
   A. 16
   B. 36
   C. 64
   D. 256
3. Which of the following is not an example of an escape key?
   A. Control
   B. Alt
   C. Shift
   D. Tab
4. Using just the letter keys and the Shift, Alt, and Control modifier keys, how many possible combinations are there?
   A. 29
   B. 78
   C. 104
   D. 256
5. Which of these is not digital?
   A. a clock with hands
   B. a calendar
   C. a checkbook balance
   D. a television channel
6. PandA is a combination of:
   A. true and false
   B. on and off
   C. yes and no
   D. all of the above
7. Finish this: I like cats. Fluffy is a cat. Therefore:
   A. Fluffy is not a dog.
   B. I don't like dogs.
   C. Cats don't like dogs.
   D. I like Fluffy.

8. A binary system:
   A. consists of only two possible items
   B. uses discrete data
   C. can be represented by PandA
   D. all of the above
9. The medium used for storing data on a disk is made from:
   A. iron
   B. plastic
   C. magnetism
   D. light
10. On the computer, PandA is represented by:
    A. 1 and 0
    B. 0 and 1
    C. bits and bytes
    D. off and on

Short Answer

1. If bits are to atoms, bytes are to ______.
2. To ______ is to represent information with digits.
3. PandA is short for ______.
4. When data are ______, they are separate and distinct and cannot be transformed into another value by gradations.
5. A(n) ______ is an agreed upon order for basic symbols.
6. A(n) ______ is another name for a separator.
7. A(n) ______ is a character that is not a letter or numeral or punctuation character.
8. All the values in a PandA formulation are ______.
9. ______ is short for binary digit.
10. The ______ of a bit is its storage pattern in the physical world.
11. ______ is short for hexadecimal.
12. Base-16 is also called ______.
13. Letters, numbers, and symbols are represented on the computer using the ______.
14. All computer systems share a ______ set of symbols used to represent characters.

Exercises

1. Make a list of the numbers you use that are not treated as numbers. (For example, you do not perform math on them.)
2. What is a bit and how was the word created?
3. What does PandA stand for and what does PandA name?
4. Come up with a list of ten different PandA items.
5. What North American telephone number is: 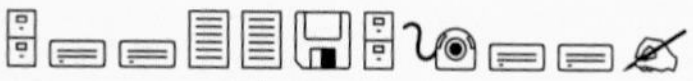
6. Encode (888) 555-1212 in Extended ASCII, including punctuation.
7. You bought a mosaic coffee table in Santorini, Greece, last summer called "Animals of Atlantis." While listening to a boring story about your friend's visit home, you notice the table is eight tiles across, which could be the bits of a byte. What ASCII message did the Greeks encode, using the obvious PandA encoding?

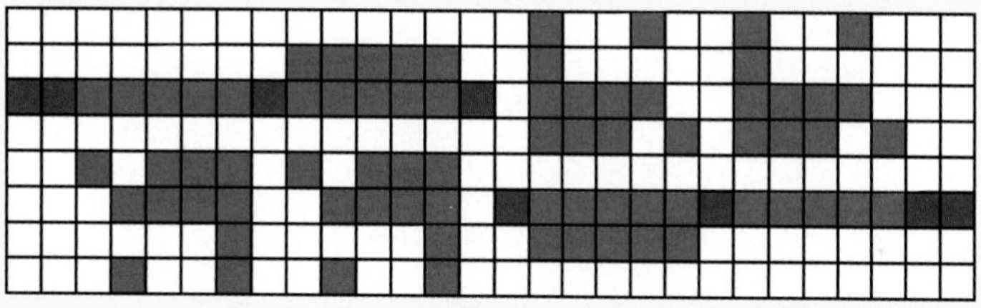

8. The Hawaiian alphabet has 18 symbols. Discuss the symbols you would use for their character set and how many bits would be needed for it.
9. Translate the following into binary and then into English.

   68 65 78 61 64 65 63 69 6D 61 6C

10. Change the letters of the sentence "THE APPLE LOGO HAS A BYTE MISSING" into NATO broadcast code (ignore spaces in all cases) and then represent the result with ASCII. How many bytes are required for each?

chapter 9

FOLLOWING INSTRUCTIONS

Principles of Computer Operation

learning objectives

- Describe how the Fetch/Execute Cycle works
  - List the five steps
  - Give an example (from the Ice Classic analogy) of each of the five steps
- Explain the function of the memory, control unit, ALU, input unit and output unit, program counter
- Explain why integration and photolithography are important in integrated circuits
- Discuss the purpose of an operating system
- Describe how large tasks are performed with simple instructions

Worthless.

—REPLY BY THE BRITISH ASTRONOMER ROYAL, SIR GEORGE BIDDELL AIRY, 1842, RESPONDING TO A QUERY BY THE CHANCELLOR OF THE EXCHEQUER, WHO WAS CONSIDERING FUNDING CHARLES BABBAGE'S ANALYTICAL ENGINE, A MECHANICAL CALCULATOR AND PREDECESSOR OF MODERN DIGITAL COMPUTERS.

Where . . . ENIAC is equipped with 18,000 vacuum tubes and weighs 30 tons, computers in the future may have 1,000 vacuum tubes and perhaps weigh just ½ tons.

– POPULAR MECHANICS, 1949

There is no reason why anyone would want to have a computer in their home.

—KEN OLSEN, PRESIDENT OF DIGITAL EQUIPMENT CORPORATION, 1977

THIS CHAPTER introduces two key inventions in information technology that rank among the top technological achievements of all time: computers and integrated circuits (ICs). Naturally they are both complex and sophisticated topics, so specialized in fact that a Ph.D. degree is not enough training to understand current practice fully. Making today's computers and chips each requires large teams of specialists. If an expert can't completely understand computers and integrated circuits, is there hope for the rest of us?

Both topics are based on easy-to-understand ideas. What makes the technology so sophisticated and complex is pushing the basic ideas to their limit, and that is definitely beyond our needs. But we should learn the main ideas, because the same basic processes of instruction execution used by computers come up often in information technology. Web browsers process Web pages using instruction execution that is just like computer operation. Spreadsheets use the same ideas. You are even an instruction executer when you prepare your income taxes. This idea is fundamental to processing information and a key concept of IT.

First, we discuss the Fetch/Execute Cycle. Next, we describe the parts of a computer, how they're connected, and briefly what each does. We then outline how these parts can execute instructions. We give a detailed example that shows that computers operate in a straightforward way. Next, we discuss software and operating systems to explain how a computer's primitive abilities can achieve such impressive results. Finally, we explain the "big ideas" behind integrated circuits and how semiconductor technology works.

FITBYTE

World Domination. During the 1950s and 1960s, as computers were leaving the lab and entering business, there was concern in the popular press about "computers taking over the world." People worried because computers could do some tasks amazingly well, for example, adding 100,000 numbers in a second. There were grim stories of tyrannical computers enslaving people. When it finally happened—when life as most people knew it *depended* on computers—no one apparently noticed.

INSTRUCTION EXECUTION ENGINES

Before dissecting a computer, consider what a computer actually does. The obvious answer, "It computes," does not say very much to those of us who use modern information processing applications. These applications—Web searching, downloading MP3 tunes, word processing—are very complex and sophisticated. They work by piling layers and layers of powerful software on the basic processing capabilities of the computer's hardware, hiding its fundamental characteristics. Beneath all of this software is the basic computer. What is it doing?

What Computers Can Do

As a definition, **computers** deterministically perform or execute instructions to process information. Another term for *computer* would be "instruction execution engine." The most important aspect of this definition is that the computer is doing what it is told—following instructions—so obviously someone or something else must have decided what those instructions should do. Programmers do that, of course. So, if the instructions don't do what we want them to do, it's certainly not the computer's fault. It's just following instructions.

What Computers Can't Do

A key feature of the definition is the term *deterministically*. This means that when it comes time for the computer to determine which instruction to execute next, it is required by its construction to execute a specific instruction based only on the program and the data that it has been given. It has no options. As compared to people, computers are very methodical:

- Computers have no imagination or creativity.
- Computers have no intuition.

{GREAT FIT MOMENTS}

No. 1 Computer >>

Credit for inventing the first electronic computer is in dispute, but most people give the credit to J. Presper Eckert and John Mauchley of the University of Pennsylvania. Named **ENIAC** for Electronic Numerical Integrator And Calculator, the Eckert/Mauchley machine was built for the U.S. Army in 1946. ENIAC is in many ways the intellectual antecedent of present day computers. Another academic, John V. Atanasoff of Iowa State University, developed ideas used by Eckert and Mauchley, and at about the same time built the **ABC**, Atanasoff Berry Computer, with graduate student Clifford E. Berry. In an epic patent infringement lawsuit, Judge Earl Larson decided on October 19, 1973 that Atanasoff's prior invention invalidated the Eckert/Mauchley patent on the computer.

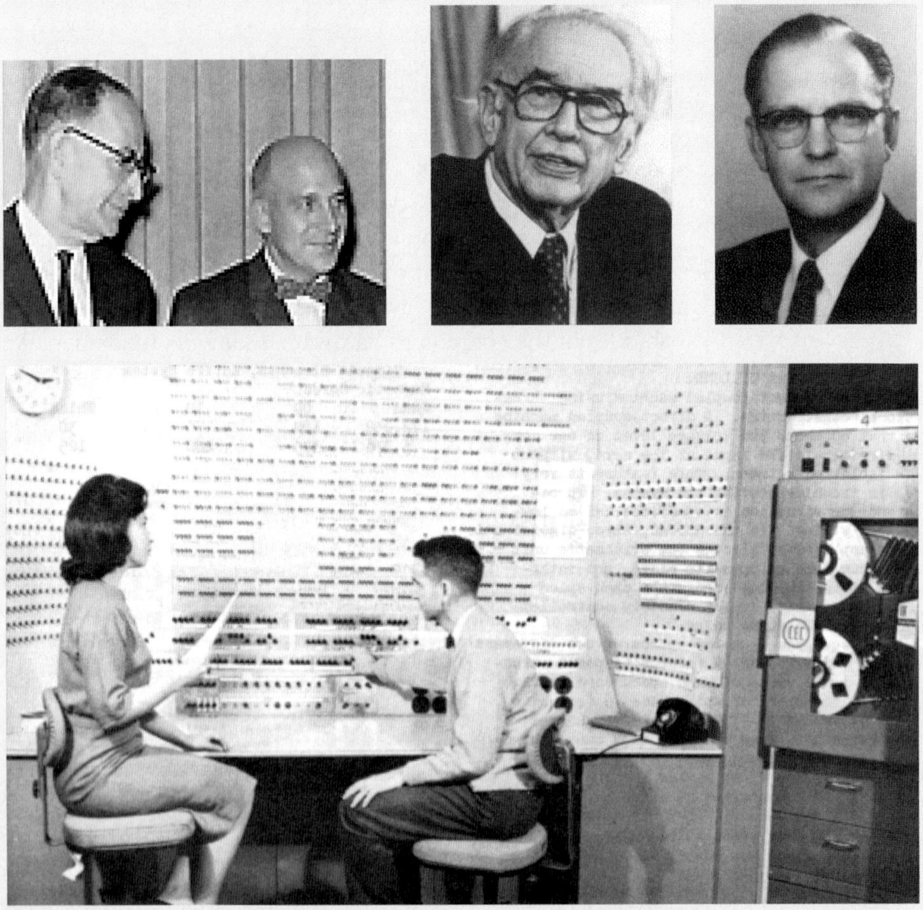

Clockwise from top left: J. Presper Eckert and John Mauchley, John V. Atanasoff, Clifford E. Berry, the ENIAC with operators.

> Computers are literal, with no sense of irony, subtlety, proportion, or decorum.

> Computers don't joke or have a sense of humor.

> Computers are not vindictive or cruel. (Admittedly some frustrated users will find these assertions far-fetched.)

> Computers are not purposeful.

> Computers have no free will.

They only execute instructions. Deterministically. One result of determinism is that rerunning a program with the same data produces exactly the same result every time.

THE FETCH/EXECUTE CYCLE

Calling a computer an "instruction execution engine" suggests the idea of a machine cycling through a series of operations, performing an instruction on each round. And that's pretty much the idea. Computers implement in hardware a process called the **Fetch/Execute Cycle**. The Fetch/Execute Cycle consists of getting the next instruction, figuring out what to do, gathering the data needed to do it, doing it, saving the result, and repeating. It's a simple process, but repeating it billions of times a second can accomplish a lot.

A Five-Step Cycle

The five steps of the Fetch/Execute Cycle have standard names, and because these operations are repeated in a never-ending sequence, they are often written with an arrow from the last step to the first showing the cycle (see Figure 9.1). The step names suggest the operations described in the previous paragraph. But the Fetch/Execute Cycle is a little more complicated than that. What is an instruction like? How is the next instruction located? When instructions and data are fetched, where are they fetched from, and where do they go?

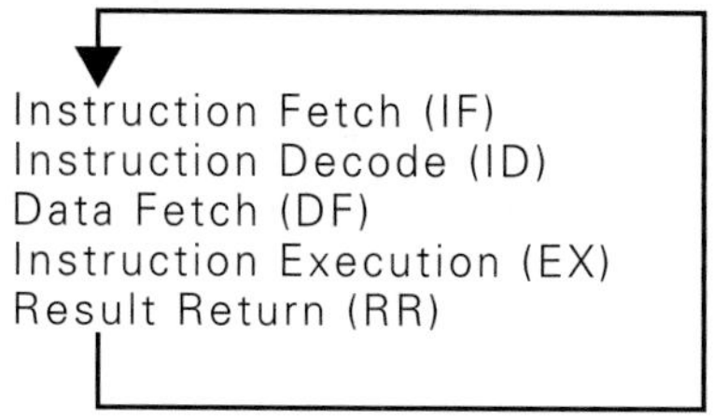

Figure 9.1. *The fetch/execute cycle.*

The Ice Classic Analogy

To help answer these questions, consider an analogy based on the person who opens the mail at the Nenana Ice Classic, a lottery run by the town of Nenana, Alaska (pop. 449). People worldwide buy $2 tickets to guess the exact minute in springtime when the ice will break up on the town's river, the Tananah, and flow downstream. In 2001, breakup was exactly 1:00 P.M., May 8, and the jackpot, split among eight winners, was $308,500. After competition is closed, but before breakup, the town publishes a thick book listing the names of all the contestants organized by the date and time of their guesses. The process of compiling the data for this book is like the Fetch/Execute Cycle.

Imagine in the office at Ice Classic Headquarters a table with trays containing a few thousand 3 × 5 cards, each labeled with a month, day, hour, and minute. The card records the names of contestants guessing that time. For example, the 2001 winners' names would have been listed on the card labeled 5/08-13:00. The cards are filed in time order in several long trays so the card for each date and time can be easily found. Also, imagine a tray of unopened envelopes.

The Ice Classic volunteer, a human version of the Fetch/Execute Cycle, proceeds as follows:

> **Instruction Fetch (IF)** He or she *fetches* the first envelope, opens it, and removes its contents, setting aside the $2 fee in the cash drawer. What comes out of the envelope is an instruction to the volunteer to enter the contestant's guess of a particular date and time.

> **Instruction Decode (ID)** The volunteer *decodes* the instruction, finding the contestant's name and the day, hour, and minute that the contestant predicts for the ice breakup. The key part of the decoding operation is finding the day and time guessed, because together they determine which card is needed.

> **Data Fetch (DF)** The volunteer then *fetches* the proper card. This Data Fetch retrieves the list of the other people, if any, who have already guessed that same day and time.

> **Instruction Execute (EX)** The volunteer then *executes* the instruction by entering the person's name and address on the card. If the space is full, the volunteer simply stores the card in a safe place, gets a blank card, labels it with the same month, day, hour, and minute, and begins using it; the cards will be merged later to create the contestants book.

> **Result Return (RR)** When the entry has been made, the volunteer *returns* the card to its proper place in the tray, which is the human version of the Result Return step of the Fetch/Execute Cycle.

The tireless volunteer then picks up another envelope and repeats the process.

The Ice Classic analogy helps us understand the steps of the Fetch/Execute Cycle. We will refer back to it as we explain how a computer is organized.

Hello, Nenana!
I'm sure breakup will be on May 4 at 12:04PM *** Find $2 enclosed.
61 River St.
Circle, AK

ANATOMY OF A COMPUTER

Now that we know how the Fetch/Execute Cycle works, we need to know how a computer's parts are arranged to fetch and execute instructions. All computers, regardless of their implementing technology, have five basic parts or subsystems: memory, control unit, arithmetic/logic unit (ALU), input unit, and output unit. These are arranged as shown in Figure 9.2. *Caution:* It is just a coincidence that there are five steps to the Fetch/Execute Cycle and five subsystems to a computer—they're related, of course, but not one-to-one.

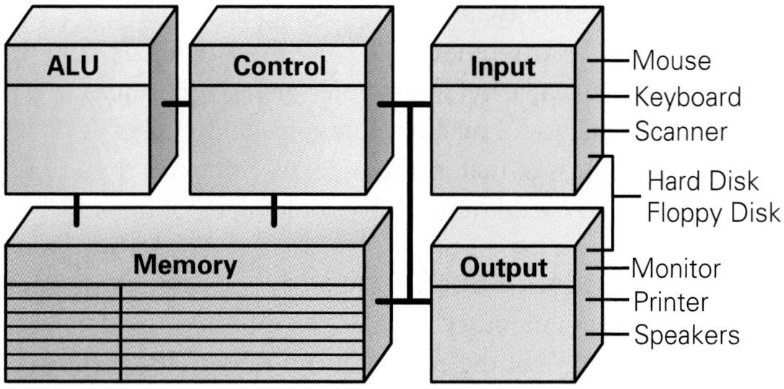

Figure 9.2. *The principal components of a computer.*

The five parts of a computer have the following characteristics.

Memory

Memory stores both the program, while it is running, and the data on which the program operates. In the Ice Classic analogy, the instruction memory is the tray of envelops, and the data memory is the sequence of cards on which the names are written. Memory has the following characteristics:

> **Discrete locations.** Memory is organized as a sequence of discrete locations, like the cards in the Ice Classic analogy. In modern memories, each location is composed of 1 byte (that is, a sequence of 8 bits).

> **Addresses.** Every memory location has an address, like the month/day/hour/minute card labels in the analogy, although computer memory addresses are just whole numbers starting at 0.

> **Values.** Memory locations record or store values, like the cards that record the contestants' names.

> **Finite capacity.** A memory location has finite capacity—limited size—like the cards in the tray. So programmers must keep in mind that the data may not "fit" in the memory location.

Byte-Size Memory Location. These characteristics motivate a commonly used diagram of computer memory (see Figure 9.3). The discrete locations are represented as boxes. The address of each location is displayed above the box. The value or contents of the memory locations are shown in the boxes.

0	1	2	3	4	5	6	7	8	9	10	11	
100	T	h	a	N	K	$	*	4	~~b~~	d	a	...

Figure 9.3. *Diagram of computer memory illustrating its key properties.*

The 1-byte size of a memory location is enough to store one ASCII character (letter or numeral or punctuation symbol) or a number less than 256. Obviously a single computer memory location, unlike the 3 × 5 cards in our analogy, would not be large enough to store the names of several contestants. To overcome the small capacity of computer memory locations, a programmer simply uses a sequence of memory locations and ignores the fact that they all have separate addresses; that is, the programmer treats the address of the first location as if it were the address of the whole block of memory.

Random Access Memory. Computer memory is often called **random access memory** (RAM). The modifier "random access" is out-of-date and simply means that the computer can refer to the memory locations in any order. RAM is most often measured in megabytes, abbreviated MB. A large memory is generally preferable to a small memory because there is more space for programs and data.

FITBYTE

Free Memory. *Mega-* is the prefix for "million," so a megabyte should be 1,000,000 bytes of memory. In fact, a megabyte is 1,048,576 bytes. Why such a weird number? Computers need to associate a byte of memory with every address. A million addresses require 20 bits. But with 20 bits, 2^{20} = 1,048,576 addresses are possible with binary counting. So, to ensure that every 20-bit address has its byte of memory, the extra 48,576 bytes are included "free."

In summary, memory is like a sequence of labeled containers known as locations: The address is the location's number in sequence; the value or the information stored at the location is the container's contents; only so much can fit in each container.

Control Unit

The **control unit** of a computer is the hardware implementation of the Fetch/Execute Cycle. Its circuitry fetches an instruction from memory and performs the other operations of the Fetch/Execute Cycle on it. In the Ice Classic analogy, the tireless volunteer is the control.

Computer instructions are more primitive than the "Enter my name . . ." instructions of the Ice Classic analogy. A typical machine instruction has the form

```
ADD 2000, 2080, 4000
```

which appears to be commanding that three numbers, 2000, 2080, and 4000, be added together, *but it does not*. Rather, the instruction asks that the two numbers stored in the memory locations 2000 and 2080 be added together, and that the result be stored in the memory location 4000. So the Data Fetch step of the Fetch/Execute Cycle must get the two values at memory locations 2000 and 2080, and after they are added, the Result Return step will store the answer in memory location 4000.

We must emphasize a fundamental property of computer instructions. The instruction `ADD 2000, 2080, 4000` does not command the computer to add together the numbers 2000 and 2080—the answer is 4080 and it is pointless to program a computer to do a task we know the answer to. Rather, the instruction commands the computer to add together the numbers *stored in memory locations* 2000 and 2080, whatever those numbers may be. Because different values can be in those memory locations each time the computer executes the instruction, a different result can be computed each time. The concept is that computer instructions encode the memory addresses of the numbers to be added (or subtracted or whatever), not the numbers themselves, and so refer to the values *indirectly*. The indirection means that a single instruction can combine any two numbers simply by placing them in the referenced memory locations (see Figure 9.4). Referring to a value by referring to the address in memory where it is stored is fundamental to a computer's versatilitiy.

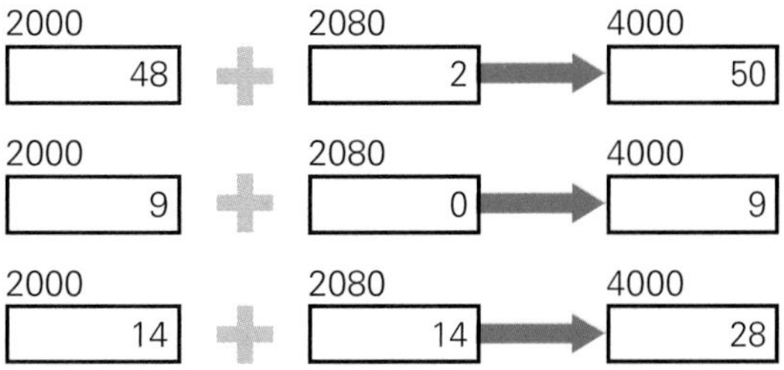

Figure 9.4. *Illustration of a single ADD instruction producing different results depending on the contents of the memory locations referenced in the instruction.*

Arithmetic/Logic Unit (ALU)

As its name suggests, the arithmetic/logic unit (ALU) performs the "math." The ALU is the part of the computer that generally does the work during the Instruction Execute step of the Fetch/Execute Cycle. So, for the example instruction `ADD 2000, 2080, 4000`, the ALU does the actual addition. A circuit in the ALU can add two numbers—an amazing capability when you think about it. There are also circuits for multiplying two numbers, circuits for comparing two numbers, and so on. You can think of an ALU as carrying out each machine instruction with a separate circuit, though modern computers are so sophisticated that they can combine several operations into one circuit.

In the Ice Classic analogy, the ALU corresponds to the office calculator. The instruction execution in the analogy didn't require any arithmetic, just writing names on the card. The calculator (the ALU) doesn't come into the process until the volunteer performs the instruction "Add the amount in the cash drawer to the amount previously received to compute the total receipts." This is true for computers, too: Some instructions use the ALU and others do not. Computers sometimes **transform** information (using the ALU) and sometimes **transfer** information. Both transforming and transferring are included in the term **information processing**.

For instructions that use the ALU, it is now clear what the Data Fetch and Result Return steps of the Fetch/Execute Cycle must do. Data Fetch gets the values from memory that the ALU needs to perform operations like `ADD` and `MULTIPLY`. These values are called **operands**. The instruction includes the addresses where the data is to be found. The Data Fetch step delivers these values to the ALU. When the ALU completes the operation, producing a sum or product or other value, the Result Return step moves that answer from the ALU to the memory at the address specified in the instruction.

Input Unit and Output Unit

These two components, which are inverses of each other, and so can easily be discussed together, are the wires and circuits through which information moves into and out of a computer. A computer without input or output—that is, the memory, control, and ALU sealed in a box—is useless. Indeed, from a philosophical perspective, we might question whether it can even be said to "compute."

The Peripherals. As shown in Figure 9.2, many kinds of devices—called **peripherals**—connect to the computer **input/output (I/O)** ports, providing it with input or receiving its output. The *peripherals* are not considered part of the computer, but rather they are specialized gadgets that encode or decode information between the computer and the physical world. The keyboard encodes the keystrokes we type into binary form for the computer. The monitor decodes information from the computer's memory, displaying it on a lighted, color screen. In general, the peripherals handle the physical part of the operation, sending or receiving the binary information the computer uses.

The cable from the peripheral to the computer connects to the input unit or the output unit. These units handle the communication protocol with the peripherals. As a general rule, think of the input unit as moving information from the peripheral into the memory, and the output unit as moving information from the memory and delivering it to the outside world. (The real details are much more complicated.)

Floppy Disks and Hard Drives. Some peripherals, such as floppy disks and hard disks, are used by computers for both input and output. That makes them storage devices, places where the computer files away information when it is not needed (an output operation) and where it gets information when it needs it again (an input operation). The hard disk is the *alpha-peripheral,* being the most aggressively engineered and the device most tightly linked to the computer. Why? Because although programs and their data must reside in the computer's memory when programs run, they reside on the hard disk the rest of the time because that's where there is more permanent space. In that sense, the hard disk is an extension of the computer's memory, but typically it is a hundred times larger and several thousand times slower.

A Device Driver for Every Peripheral. Most peripheral devices are "dumb" in that all they provide is basic physical translation to or from binary signals. They rely on the computer for any further processing, which is almost always required to make the peripheral operate in an "intelligent way." So, as I type the letters of this sentence, signals are sent from the keyboard to the computer indicating which keys my fingers depress. When the computer receives information that I've pressed the *w* and the *Shift* key at the same time, the computer—not the keyboard—converts the *w* keystroke to a capital *W.* Similarly, keys like *Ctrl* and *Backspace* are just keys to the keyboard. It is the added processing by a piece of software called a **device driver** that gives the keyboard its standard meaning and behavior. Every device needs a device driver to provide this added processing. Naturally, because the peripheral device may have unique characteristics, a device driver will be specialized to only one device.

FITTIP

New Toys. Many users are excited about getting a new peripheral such as a printer, scanner, or CD-ROM. They plug it into their computer, but forget that it needs a device driver before it can run. This is partly because computers often come loaded with standardized or popular device drivers, and so users don't know that peripherals need them, or they forget. A floppy disk or a CD containing the device driver(s) should come with the peripheral, or the driver can be downloaded from the manufacturer's Web site.

Ice Classic Analogy: Input and Output. In the Ice Classic analogy, the output device is the printing company in Fairbanks that prints and binds the list of contestants. When all of the entries have been received, the data for the list will have been recorded in the memory (3 × 5 cards), once all of the filled-up cards are merged back in the tray in the right order. Of course, the printing company doesn't want to deal with trays of cards, so the tireless volunteer becomes the device driver, converting the information on the cards into the right form for the printing company. This might mean putting 6–8 cards on the copier glass, and photocopying them to create a page that the printer can use, maybe including cards with headings for each day. The copier is like the output unit, because it takes the data from memory (the cards) and prepares it for the output device, the printer. When the pages are done, they are transmitted to the company in Fairbanks to produce the user-readable output: the list of contestants.

THE PROGRAM COUNTER: THE PC'S PC

The final question is how a computer determines which instruction to execute next. In the Ice Classic analogy, the volunteer simply removes letters from a tray of mail to get the next "instruction." The order doesn't matter with mail, so any letter will do. In computers, the order in which instructions are executed is critical.

Address of the Next Instruction

Recall that when the Fetch/Execute Cycle is executing a program, the instructions are stored in the memory. That means every instruction has an address, which is the address of the memory location of the first byte of the instruction. (Instructions of present-day computers use 4 bytes.) Naturally, computers keep track of which instruction to execute next by its address. This address, stored in the control part of the computer, should probably be called the *next instruction address,* but for historic reasons it is actually known by the curious term, **program counter**, abbreviated PC. *(For the rest of the chapter* PC *will mean program counter, not personal computer.)*

The Instruction Fetch step of the Fetch/Execute Cycle transfers the instruction from memory at the address specified by the program counter to the decoder part of the control unit. Once the instruction has been fetched, and while it is being processed by the remaining steps of the F/E Cycle, the computer prepares to process the next instruction. The next instruction is assumed to be the next instruction in sequence. Because instructions use 4 bytes of memory, the next instruction must be at the memory address PC + 4, that is, 4 bytes further along in sequence. Therefore, the computer adds four to the PC, so that when the F/E Cycle gets around to the Instruction Fetch step again, the PC is "pointing at" the new instruction.

Branch and Jump Instructions

This scheme of executing instructions in sequence seems flawed: Won't the Fetch/Execute Cycle blaze through the memory executing all the instructions, get to the last instruction in memory, and "fall off the end of memory," having used up all of the instructions? This won't happen unless the program has a bug in it. The reason is that computers come with instructions called *branch* and *jump* that change the PC. After the control unit has prepared for the next instruction in sequence by adding four to the PC, the Instruction Execute step of the current (branch or jump) instruction can reset the PC to a new value. This overrides the selection of the next instruction in sequence and makes the PC address some other instruction in memory. The next instruction will be fetched from this memory location on the next round of the Fetch/Execute Cycle.

INSTRUCTION INTERPRETATION

The process of executing a program is also called **instruction interpretation**. The term comes from the idea that the computer is interpreting our commands, but in its own language.

To illustrate the idea of interpreting instructions, let's follow the execution of a typical `ADD` instruction. Figure 9.5 shows the situation before the Fetch/Execute Cycle starts the next instruction. Notice that some of the memory locations and the program counter (PC) are visible in the control unit.

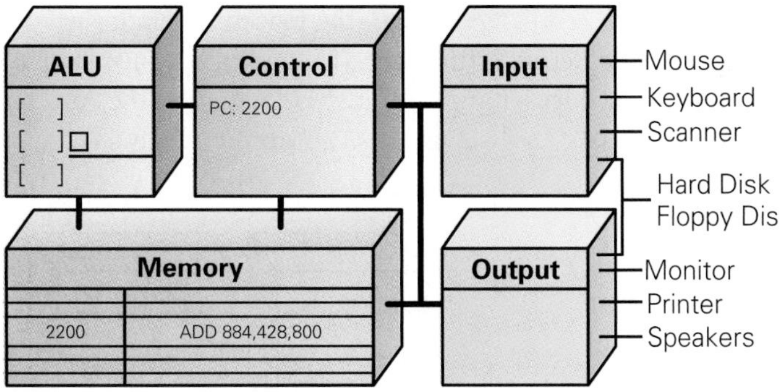

Figure 9.5. *Computer before executing an ADD instruction.*

Instruction execution begins by moving the instruction at the address given by the PC from the memory unit to the control unit. (See Figure 9.6, where the instruction address is 2200 and the example instruction is `ADD 884, 428, 800` .) The bits of the instruction are placed into the decoder circuit of the control unit. Once the instruction is fetched, the PC can be readied for fetching the next instruction. For present-day computers whose instructions are 4 bytes long, 4 is added to the PC. (The updated PC value will be visible in the Data Fetch configuration shown in Figure 9.8 and those that follow.)

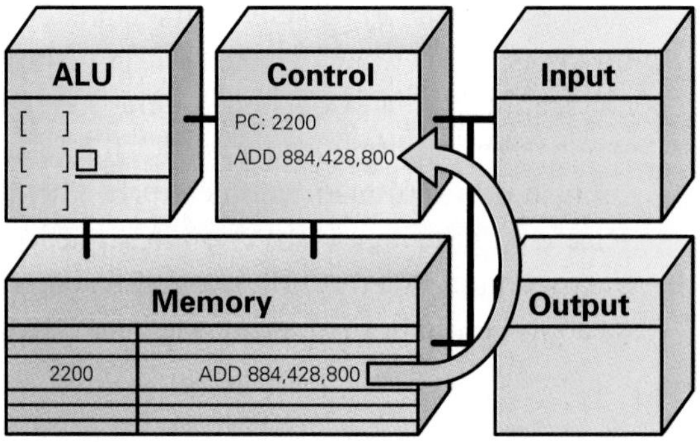

Figure 9.6. *Instruction Fetch: Move instruction from memory to the control unit.*

Figure 9.7 shows the Instruction Decode step, in which the ALU is set up for the operation in the Instruction Execute step. Among the bits of the instruction, the decoder will find the memory addresses of the instruction's data, the *source operands*. Like **ADD**, most instructions operate on two data values stored in memory, so most instructions have addresses for two source operands. These two addresses (**884**, **428**) are passed to the circuit that will fetch the operand values from memory during the next (Data Fetch) step. Simultaneously, the decoder finds the *destination address*, the place in memory where the answer is to be sent during the Result Return step. That address (**800**) is placed in the RR circuit. Finally, the decoder will figure out what operation the ALU should perform on the data values (**ADD**), and set up the ALU appropriately for that operation.

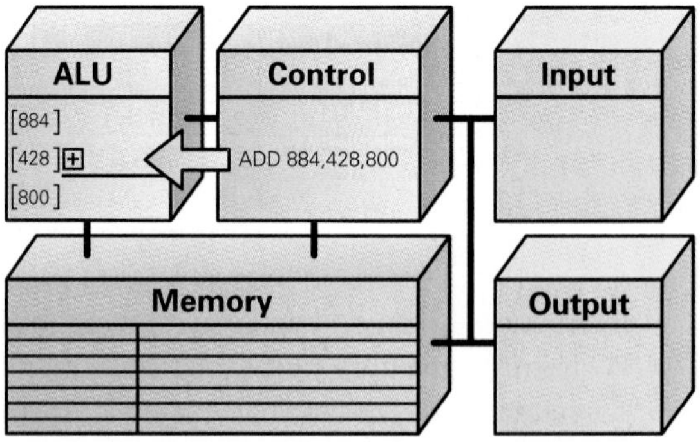

Figure 9.7. *Instruction Decode: Pull apart the instruction, set up the operation in the ALU, and compute the source and destination operand addresses.*

Figure 9.8 shows the Data Fetch step. The data values for the two source operands are moved from the memory into the ALU. These values (**12**, **42**) are the data that the instruction will work on in the next (Execute) step.

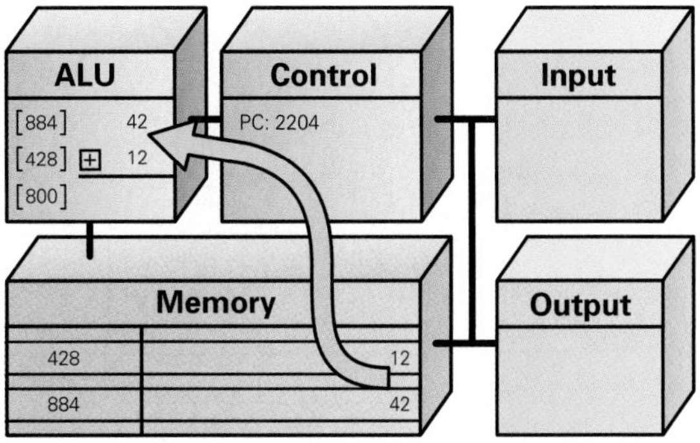

Figure 9.8. *Data Fetch: Move the operands from memory to the ALU.*

Instruction Execution is illustrated in Figure 9.9. The operation—set up during the Instruction Decode step—performs the computation. In the present case, the addition circuit adds the two source operand values together to produce their sum (**54**). This is the actual computation.

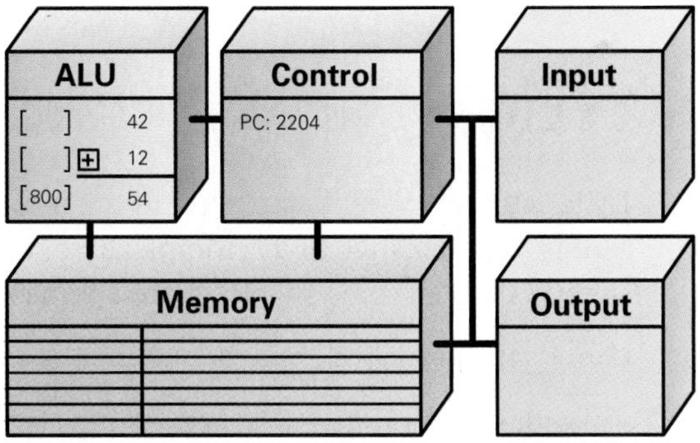

Figure 9.9. *Execute: Compute the result of the operation in the ALU.*

FITBYTE

Micro Computer. In our presentation, Instruction Execution—the "compute" part of the Fetch/Execute Cycle—accounts for only 20 percent of the time spent executing an instruction; it averages even less on real computers. Measured by silicon area, the ALU—the circuitry that does the computing—takes up less than 5 percent of a typical processor chip.

Finally, the Result Return step, shown in Figure 9.10, returns the result of Instruction Execution (**54**) to the memory location specified by the destination address (**800**) and set up during Instruction Decode. Once the result is returned, the cycle begins all over again.

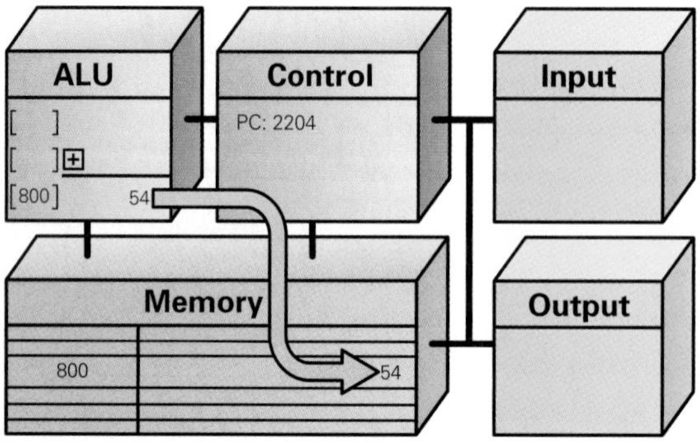

Figure 9.10. *Result Return: Store the result from the ALU into the memory at the destination address.*

FITBYTE

Stop! If the Fetch/Execute Cycle is an infinite loop, how does a computer stop? Early computers actually had Start and Stop buttons, but modern computers simply execute an "idle loop" when there's nothing to do. The instructions keep checking to see if there's anything to do, like process a mouse click or keystroke.

CYCLING THE F/E CYCLE

Using `ADD`, we have illustrated how a computer is able to execute instructions. `ADD` is representative of the complexity of computer instructions—some are slightly simpler, some slightly more complex. There are no instructions like

```
Check_spelling_of_the_document_beginning_at_location 884
```

So, with such primitive instructions, it is surprising that computers can do anything at all. They get their impressive capabilities by executing many of these simple instructions per second, and by programmers translating complex tasks into simple instructions.

The Computer Clock

Computers are instruction execution engines. We have just studied in detail how the Fetch/Execute Cycle carries out one `ADD` instruction. Since the computer does one instruction per cycle, the speed of a computer—the number of instructions executed in a second—depends on the number of Fetch/Execute Cycles it does in a second. The rate of the Fetch/Execute Cycle is determined by the computer's **clock**, and it is measured in **megahertz**, or millions (mega) of cycles per second (hertz). Computer clock speeds have increased dramatically in recent years, resulting in speeds of 1000 MHz or more. A 1000 MHz clock ticks a billion (in American

English) times per second, which is one gigahertz (1 GHz) in any language. (See Figure 9.11 for terms; "giga" is pronounced with hard g's.) Clock speeds are a common feature of computer advertisements, but how important are they

1000^1	kilo-	$1024^1 = 2^{10} = 1,024$	milli-	1000^{-1}
1000^2	mega-	$1024^2 = 2^{20} = 1,048,576$	micro-	1000^{-2}
1000^3	giga-	$1024^3 = 2^{30} = 1,073,741,824$	nano-	1000^{-3}
1000^4	tera-	$1024^4 = 2^{40} = 1,099,511,627,776$	pico-	1000^{-4}
1000^5	peta-	$1024^5 = 2^{50} = 1,125,899,906,842,624$	femto-	1000^{-5}
1000^6	exa-	$1024^6 = 2^{60} = 1,152,921,504,606,876,976$	atto-	1000^{-6}
1000^7	zetta-	$1024^7 = 2^{70} = 1,180,591,620,717,411,303,424$	zepto-	1000^{-7}
1000^8	yotta-	$1024^8 = 2^{80} = 1,208,925,819,614,629,174,706,176$	yocto-	1000^{-8}

Figure 9.11. *Standard prefixes from the Système International (SI) convention on scientific measurements. Generally a prefix refers to a power of 1000, except when the quantity (for example, memory) is counted in binary; for binary quantities the prefix refers to a power of 1024, which is* 2^{10}.

FITTIP

Beauty of Prefixes. Prefixes "change the units" so that very large or small quantities can be expressed with numbers of a reasonable size. A well-known humorous example concerns Helen of Troy from Greek myth "whose face launched 1000 ships." The beauty needed to launch one ship is one-thousandth of Helen's, that is, 0.001 Helen, or 1 MilliHelen.

One Cycle per Clock Tick

A computer with a 1 GHz clock has one billionth of a second—one nanosecond—between clock ticks to run the Fetch/Execute Cycle. In that short time, light can travel only about a foot (30 cm). Is it really possible to add or multiply that fast? No. In truth, modern computers try to *start* an instruction on each clock tick. They pass off finishing the instruction to other circuitry, like a worker on an assembly line. This process, called *pipelining*, frees the fetch unit to start the next instruction before the last one is done. As shown in Figure 9.12, if the five steps of the Fetch/Execute Cycle take a nanosecond *each*—which is still extremely fast—it is possible to finish one instruction on each clock tick as long as there is enough circuitry for five instructions to be "in process" at the same time. That way the computer finishes instructions at the starting rate of one per tick. Of course, to execute 1000 instructions in a five-stage pipeline takes 1004 clock cycles—1000 to start each instruction, and 4 more for the last four steps of the last instruction. So it is not quite true that 1000 instructions are executed in 1000 ticks. But that's probably close enough.

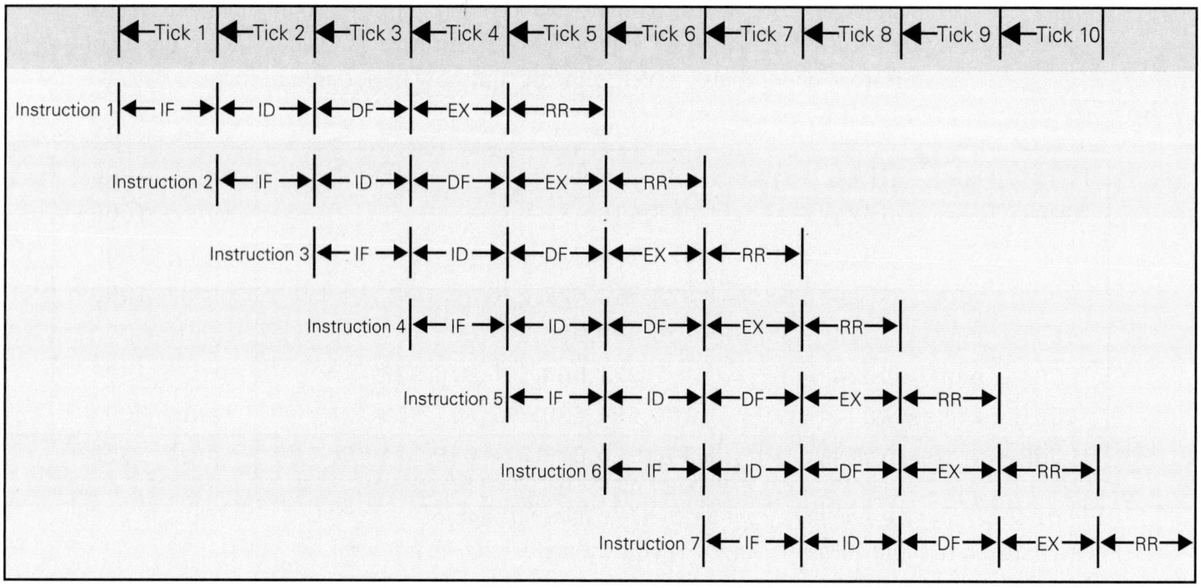

Figure 9.12. *Schematic diagram of a pipelined Fetch/Execute Cycle. On each tick, the IF circuit starts a new instruction, and before the time runs out, it passes it along to the ID (Instruction Decode) unit; the ID unit works on the instruction it receives, finishing just in time to pass it along to the DF (Data Fetch) circuit, and so on. When the pipeline is filled, five instructions are in progress, and one instruction is finished on each clock tick, making the computer appear to be running one instruction per clock tick.*

A Billion Instructions per Second?

So, does a computer with a 1 GHz clock execute a billion instructions per second? Computer salespeople would like you to believe it's true, but it's not. We said that computers *try* to start an instruction on each clock tick, but there is a long list of reasons why it's not always possible. If the computer cannot start instructions on each clock tick, its execution rate falls *below* one billion instructions per second. But the situation is even more complicated. Computer engineers have figured out how to start more than one instruction at a time, even though instructions are supposed to be executed sequentially—that is, the next one isn't started until the current one is finished. If several instructions can be started at the same time often enough, they can make up for not starting instructions at other times. Thus the rate could be *above* one billion per second. It is extremely difficult—even for experts—to figure out how fast a modern computer runs. As a result, the one-instruction-per-cycle guideline—which was once dependable—is no longer correct.

FITBYTE

Speed of Fluency. This book was written on two new laptops with different processors that were the same in most ways except clock speed: one machine's clock was twice as fast as the other's. However, the "slower machine" regularly ran applications faster than the "faster machine," because performance depends on many features: instruction set, memory size and design, other system components like cache, software quality, and so on. The lesson: Clock speed alone doesn't tell you how fast a computer runs.

MANY, MANY SIMPLE OPERATIONS

Computers "know" very few instructions. That is, the decoder hardware in the controller recognizes, and the ALU can perform, only about 100 or so different instructions. And there is a lot of duplication. For example, different types of data usually have different kinds of **ADD** instructions, one for adding bytes, one for adding whole numbers, one for adding "decimal" numbers, and so on. *Everything* that computers do must be reduced to one of these primitive, hardwired instructions. They can't do anything else. We return to this idea in Chapter 23.

The **ADD** instruction has about average complexity, and **MULT** (multiply) and **DIV** (divide) are at the screaming limit of complexity. Examples of other instructions include:

- Shift the bits of a word (4 bytes) to the left or right, filling the emptied places with zeros and throwing away the bits that fall off the end. (Where do they go?)
- Compute the logical **AND**, which tests if pairs of bits are both true (1), and the logical **OR**, which tests if at least one of two bits is true.
- Test if a bit is zero or nonzero, and jump to a new set of instructions based on the outcome.
- Move information around in memory.
- Sense the signals from input/output devices.

Computer instructions are very primitive. There is no DRAW_A_BUTTON or SPELL_CHECK.

Converting Complicated Tasks into Simple Instructions

Computers tirelessly perform their simple instructions very fast, and that is the secret of getting them to do tasks that are more interesting than adding two numbers together. If we can figure out how to describe a more complex operation as a sequence of the primitive hardwired instructions, each time we want the more complex operation done, we simply instruct the computer to follow the sequence. It will *appear* that the computer knows the more complex operation, especially if it does the sequence blazingly fast. Once we have instructed the computer to do more complex operations, we can use them to describe still more complex operations and whole tasks. This is *programming*, of course, and it is key to expanding a computer's abilities. In later chapters, we describe how to build more complex operations from simpler ones.

Think of writing a term paper with a word processor and the thousands of operations that a computer does for you, from recognizing which keyboard key you pressed to spell checking. In order for the computer to do all these things, each

{GREATFITMOMENTS}

Programming Pioneers >>

Programming Pioneers. The first programmers, who wrote and ran the programs on the ENIAC, were all women: Kathleen McNulty Mauchley Antonelli, Jean Jennings Bartik, Frances Snyder Holberton, Marlyn Wescoff Meltzer, Frances Bilas Spence, and Ruth Lichterman Teitelbaum. They were recruited from the ranks of "computers," humans who used mechanical calculators to solve complex mathematical problems before the invention of electronic computers.

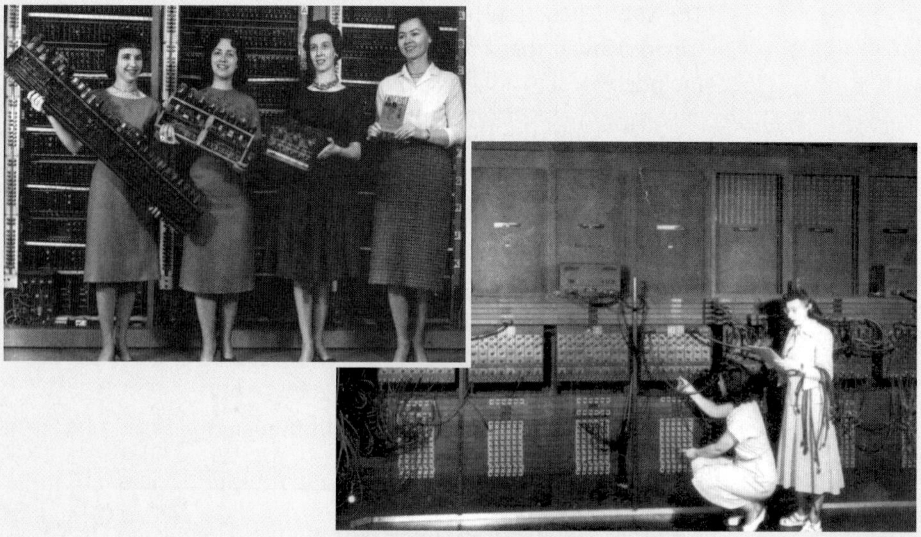

task had to be converted into a sequence of the primitive hardwired instructions—machine instructions—because none of these word processing operations is primitive. This is programming, but the programmer's job would be tediously boring if the translation to primitive instructions had to be done by hand. If that were the case, no one would be a programmer no matter how much he or she was paid.

Fortunately, one "complex" task that computers can be programmed to do is translate complicated operations into the simpler primitive instructions that they understand. Of course, some programmer had to tell the computer how to do this the first time, but after that the computer can do the translation for itself. This automatic translation—there are actually several levels of translation—helps keep programming interesting. The only role for the programmer is to figure out how to do a complex task in a high-level programming language. High-level languages are expressive, meaning it takes fewer commands to write a complex program. That specification is the *program*. From then on, the computer does the rest.

Forms of Translation: Compiling and Assembling

Computers only understand instructions written in binary digits. Writing a string of 32 or more 0's and 1's is so tedious that the earliest computer builders developed a more convenient form for instructions called **assembly language**. The `ADD` instruction `ADD 2000, 2080, 4000` is an example of *assembly language, because it is a machine instruction written using letters and numerals rather than binary*. The process of converting from assembly instructions to binary machine instructions is called **assembling**. But these instructions are still too primitive to be of much use to humans. So, computer scientists invented high-level programming languages like Fortran (1958) and Basic (1965) to help programmers express complex tasks more easily. Still more expressive languages such as C, Smalltalk, C++, and Java can do even more than these early programming languages. The translation process from a programming language to an assembly language is called *compilation*. Because the languages are expressive, a single statement in one of these programming languages may convert into dozens of assembly instructions, which are then converted into binary machine instructions. Figure 9.13 summarizes the process.

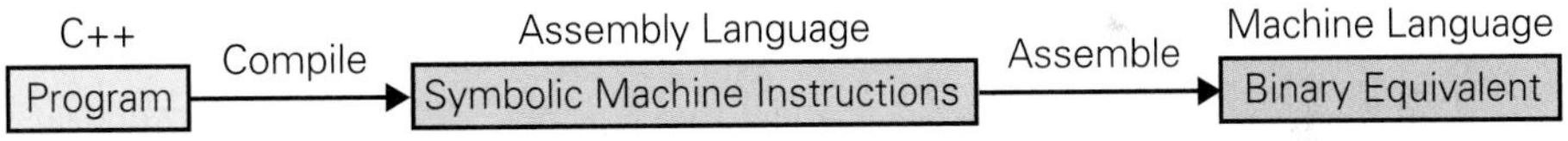

Figure 9.13. *The translation from high-level language to machine instructions.*

Many programmers work in development environments such as Visual C++ in which they simply combine already-written programs, possibly with small amounts of their own code written in the programming language. This is an even more powerful way to instruct a computer.

The Operating System

None of the operations that a computer needs to start up and keep running are hardwired primitive instructions. Because processors are so primitive, programmers must develop a large set of small but complicated procedures to get the computer to start and perform useful work. The result is an operating system. An **operating system** (**OS**) is software that extends the hardwired operations of a processor with general-purpose facilities to start up (**boot**), manage its memory and applications, and interact with its peripheral devices. These are general-purpose facilities that are performed for applications when needed. For example, device drivers are considered operating system software, so when your word processor prints your term paper, it invokes (runs) the print driver and other parts of the operating system to send your crisp prose from the computer memory onto paper.

The three most common operating systems are Windows, MacOS, and UNIX (including Linux). Each system has several variations. Dozens of others have been created, but these three are the state of the art. The question is not which one is best—they all have their technical triumphs and tragedies—but why do we have them at all? The answer can be found in the list of primitive instructions that are hardwired into computers.

Memory Management. Memory management is a basic service of operating systems. When you begin to write your term paper, the word processor program is on the hard disk where the operating system put it when the application was installed. The operating system gives you a way to start the word processor—double clicking on the application's icon, perhaps. The OS locates the start of the program on the hard disk, loads the first part of it into memory, and starts it executing. Most modern computers use virtual memory and demand paging, so that it doesn't much matter where in the memory the OS puts the first part of the program or how much it loads. The computer executes the instructions that are available in memory, and when it tries to execute instructions that are still on the disk, it **page faults**, meaning it stops, waiting for the next page of instructions. A page fault is a hardware "wake up," called an **interrupt**, to the operating system, which may not have been active while the word processing application was running. The OS finds the needed page on the disk, loads it, and tells the computer to resume executing your application. And so it goes, the computer faulting when the next page of instructions or data is not in the memory, the OS finding them and loading them in. It happens so fast that we don't even notice that the program keeps stopping and starting.

Other OS Services. Printing and managing memory are not the only help your word processor application is getting from the OS. There's also everything happening on the monitor—menus, scroll bars, and so on. The OS manages the mouse and creates the mouse pointer fiction. When you click on **Save**, the application asks the OS to write your term paper to the hard disk. In fact, the OS does all sorts of tasks like this, so they don't have to be programmed for each application.

FITBYTE

No Fault. How often have we heard "It was a computer error," as an explanation for a billing or other mistake? As we've often said, true computer errors are extremely rare. A better explanation would be "There was a billing system error caused perhaps by one of the many people who worked on the application software or OS, installed and configured the system, entered the data, or modified or configured the database system; it could be the result of fraud, data transmission or network errors, or failed checkpoint recovery; oh, . . . and there's a tiny chance it was a computer error." In other words, "It probably wasn't a computer error, but an problem with some other part of this complex system."

INTEGRATED CIRCUITS

Integrated circuits (**ICs**) are important because the technology allows extremely complex devices to be made cheaply and reliably. Two characteristics of ICs make this possible: integration and photolithography. Oh, yes. Integrated circuits are also very small.

Miniaturization

One reason that modern computer clocks can run at GHz rates is that the processor chips are so tiny. The farthest electrical signals can travel in a nanosecond is about 1 foot, and in a computer much more has to happen to the signals than simply being transmitted. One reason early computers, which filled whole rooms, could never have run as fast as modern computers is that their components were farther apart than a foot. Making everything smaller has made computers faster by allowing for faster clock rates.

Integration

But the real achievement of microchip technology is not miniaturization, but **integration**. It is impossible to overstate its significance. T. R. Reid in his book *The Chip* called the invention "a seminal event of postwar science: one of those rare demonstrations that changes everything."

To appreciate how profound the invention of integrated circuitry is, understand that before integration, computers were made from separate parts (discrete components) wired together by hand. The three wires coming out of each transistor, the two wires from each resistor, the two wires from each capacitor, and so on, had to be connected to the wires of some other transistor, resistor, or capacitor. It was very tedious work. Even for printed circuit boards in which the "wiring" is printed metallic strips, a person or machine had to "populate" the board with the discrete components one at a time. A serious computer system would have hundreds of thousands or millions of these parts and at least twice as many connections, which are expensive and time consuming to make, error prone, and unreliable. If computers still had to be built this way, they would still be rare.

FITBYTE

Cray's Limit. Seymour Cray, who designed and built more huge computers than anyone else, once said that there is a "manufacturing complexity limit" of about six million connections. Beyond that a system becomes too complicated to produce, test, and maintain. The fact that the Space Shuttle has (approximately) six million parts is probably independent verification of Cray's limit.

The "big idea" behind integrated circuits is really two ideas working together. The first idea is that the active components—transistors, capacitors, and so forth—and the wires that connect them are all made together of similar materials by a single (multistep) process. So, rather than making two transistors and later connecting them by soldering a pair of their wires together, IC technology places them side by side in the silicon and at some stage in the fabrication process—perhaps while some of the transistor's internal parts are still being built—a wire connecting the two is placed in position. The crux of integration is that the active and connective parts of a circuit are built together. Integration saves space (promoting speed), but its greatest advantage is to produce a single monolithic part for the whole system all at once without hand wiring. The resulting "block" of electronics is extremely reliable.

{GREATFITMOMENTS}

IC Man >>

Jack Kilby shared the 2000 Nobel Prize in Physics for inventing the integrated circuit. Kilby worked for the electronics firm Texas Instruments. New to the staff, Kilby hadn't accrued summer vacation time, so while the other employees were away on their holidays, he invented integrated circuits.

Using borrowed and improvised equipment, he conceived of and built the first electronic circuit in which all of the components, both active and connective, were fabricated in a single piece of semiconductor material. On September 12, 1958, he successfully demonstrated in his laboratory the first simple microchip, which was about half the size of a paper clip. Kilby went on to pioneer applications of microchip technology. He later co-invented both the hand-held calculator and a thermal printer used in portable data terminals.

For perspective, the worldwide integrated circuit market in 2000 had sales of $177 billion.

Photolithography

The second idea behind integrated circuits is that they are made with **photolithography**, a printing process. Here's how it works. Making a chip is like making a sandwich. Start with a layer of silicon and add layers of materials to build up the transistors, capacitors, wires, and other features of a chip. For example, wires might be made of a layer of aluminum. But the aluminum cannot be smeared over the chip like mayonnaise covers a sandwich; the wires must be electrically separated from each other and must connect to specific places. This is where photolithography comes in.

The aluminum smear is covered with a layer of light-sensitive material called a *photoresist.* A mask is placed on the chip. The mask—it's like a photographic negative—shows the pattern of the wires. When (ultraviolet) light shines on the mask, it passes through at places to react with the photoresist (see Figure 9.14). The mask is then removed and the changed-by-light resist—and the aluminum it covers—are etched away. Next, the remaining photoresist, but not the aluminum beneath it, is etched away (see Figure 9.15). What remains is the pattern of aluminum that matches the dark pattern on the mask—that is, the wires!

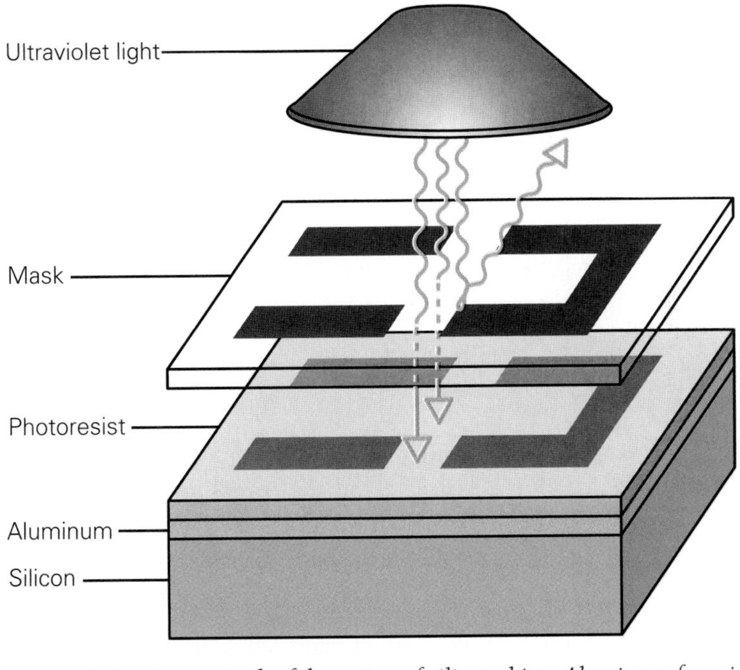

Figure 9.14. *A step in the fabrication of silicon chips. Aluminum for wires is deposited onto the silicon and covered with a layer of photoresist. A mask with the wire pattern is placed over the photoresist. Ultraviolet light passes through light areas of the mask reacting with the photoresist.*

The key aspect of photolithography is that regardless of how complicated the wiring is, the cost and amount of work involved are the same. Like a page of a newspaper, which costs the same to print whether it has 5 words or 5000 words, the cost of making integrated circuits is not related to how complicated they are. Thanks to the photolithographic process, computers and other electronics can be as complicated as we wish.

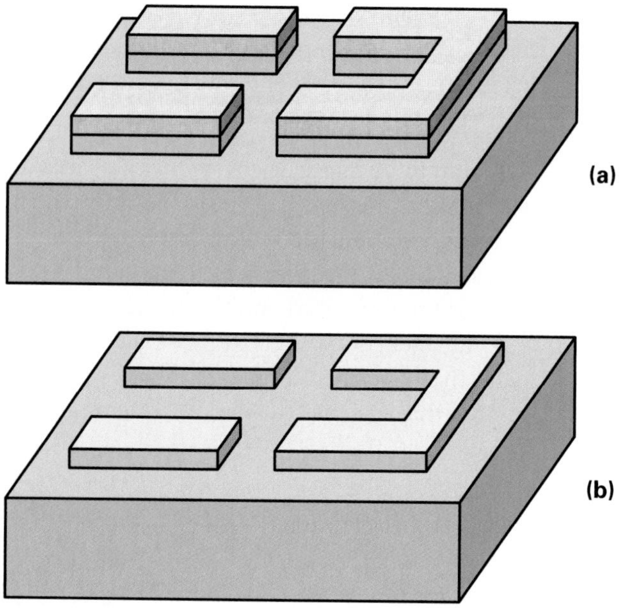

Figure 9.15. *The next step (after Figure 9.14) in the fabrication of silicon chips. The changed-by-light photoresist and its underlying aluminum are etched away, leaving a resist/aluminum pattern corresponding to the dark places on the mask. The remaining resist is removed, leaving the pattern of wires.*

HOW SEMICONDUCTOR TECHNOLOGY WORKS

Silcon is a **semiconductor**, meaning just what its name implies—it sometimes conducts electricity and sometimes does not. The ability to control when semiconductors do and don't conduct electricity is the main tool in constructing computers. To make this point clear, consider an example.

In Chapter 5 we used the **AND** operation when searching for Thai restaurants. The Web pages we wanted had to have both keywords. Inside the Google computer, a test was made to see if "Thai" was on a given page and a test was made to see if "restaurants" was on the same page. When the results of the two tests were known, an instruction in the Google computer **AND**ed them together. How could that be done with electricity?

The On-Again, Off-Again Behavior of Silicon

Imagine that we have a wire with two gaps in it. We fill each gap with specially treated semiconducting material (see Figure 9.16). We send an electrical signal along the wire, which we will interpret as yes, both "Thai" and "restaurants" appear on the page. At the other end of the wire we detect whether the "yes" is present, an application of the PandA encoding from Chapter 8. In between we control (details below) the conductivity of the semiconducting material using the outcomes of the two tests. We make the material in the first gap conduct if "Thai" was found, and the material in the second gap conduct if "restaurants" was found. If the material conducts electricity, the signal can pass to the other end of the wire. So, if "yes" is detected at the output end, both gaps must be conducting; that is, both outcomes are true. If "yes" is not detected, then one or the other (or possibly both) of the two semiconducting points must not be conducting, which means "Thai" and "restaurants" were not both found.

This simple principle—the setting up of a situation in which the conductivity of a wire can be controlled to create the logical conclusion needed—is the basis of all of the instructions and operations of a computer. In the hardware of the computer where this test was done, the two semiconducting points of the **AND** circuit are not limited to the specific question of whether "Thai" **AND** "restaurants" is true; instead the circuit computes *x* **AND** *y* for any logical values *x* and *y*. Such a circuit is part of the ALU of Google's computer (and yours), and it performs the Execute step of all of the **AND** instructions.

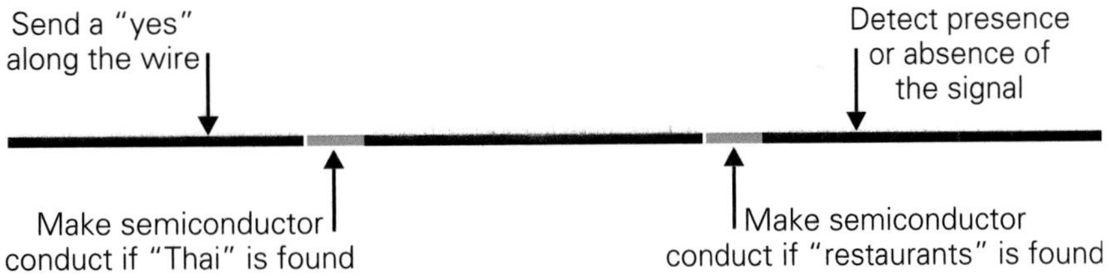

Figure 9.16. *Computing* `Thai AND restaurants` *using a semiconducting material.*

The Field Effect

So how do we control the conductivity of a semiconductor? The answer is we use the field effect. As we all know from combing our hair with a nylon comb on a dry day, objects can become charged positively or negatively. The comb strips off electrons from our hair, leaving the comb with too many electrons and the hair with too few. Because like-charges repel, our hair "stands on end" as each hair pushes away from its neighbors; but opposites attract, so the comb pulls the hair toward it. This effect that charged objects have on each other without actually touching is the field effect. We can use the field effect to control a semiconductor.

Here's how to control a semiconductor using the field effect. The gap between two wires is specially treated to improve its conducting and nonconducting properties, that is, when it conducts it conducts better than pure silicon (see Figure 9.17). This part of the semiconductor is called a *channel*, because it makes a path for electricity to travel along between the two wires. An insulator such as glass, silicon dioxide, covers the channel. Passing over the insulator (at right angles) is a third wire called the *gate*. The gate is separated from the semiconductor by the insulator, so it does not make contact with the two wires or the channel. Thus, electricity cannot be conducted between the two wires unless the channel is conducting. But how does the channel conduct?

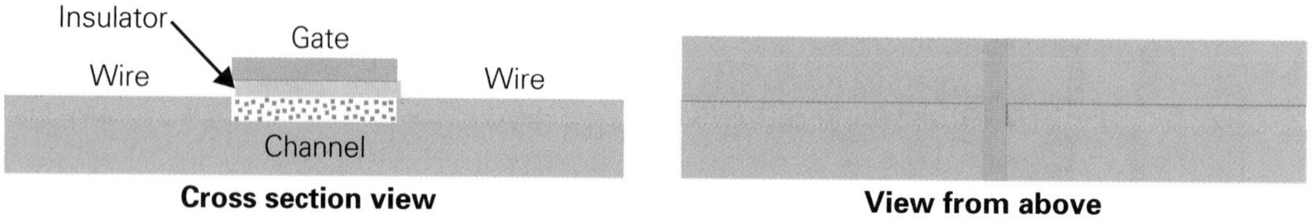

Figure 9.17. *A field-effect transistor. The channel is specially treated to improve its conducting/nonconducting properties.*

Because it has been specially treated, the silicon in the channel can conduct electricity when it is in a charged field. The conductivity is the result of electrons being attracted or repelled in the silicon material, depending on the type of treatment (see Figure 9.18). So, by charging the gate positively we create a field over the channel; electrons are attracted from the silicon material into the channel causing it to conduct electricity between the two wires. If the field is removed, the electrons disperse into the silicon, the channel doesn't conduct, and the two wires are isolated. Of course, the gate is simply another wire, which is or is not conducting (charged) under the control of other gates, and so on.

Transistors

Our example illustrates a **field effect transistor**. A **transistor** is simply a connector between two wires that controls whether or not they are electrically connected. The transistor described is an MOS transistor, where **MOS** stands for **metal, oxide, semiconductor**. Those three terms refer to the materials in the cross-section of the transistor from top to bottom: the gate is metal, the glass insulator is oxide, and the channel is the semiconductor. Modern computers are made out of **CMOS** technology, which stands for "complementary MOS" and means two different, but complementary, treatments for the channels.

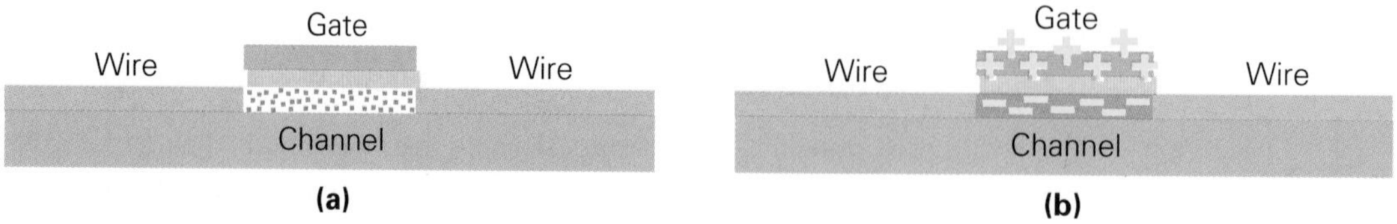

Figure 9.18. *Field effect transistor (a) with the gate at neutral causing the channel not to conduct, isolating the wires, and (b) with the gate charged, causing the channel to conduct, connecting the wires.*

COMBINING THE IDEAS

Let's put these ideas all together. We start with an information-processing task. The task will be performed by an application implemented as a large program written by a programmer in a programming language like C or Java. The program performs the specific operations of the application, but for standard operations like **Print** or **Save**, the application program uses the OS. The program's commands, written in the programming language, are compiled into many simple assembly language instructions. The assembly instructions are then translated into more primitive binary form, the machine instructions, that the computer understands directly.

The application program's binary instructions are stored on the hard disk. When we click on the application's icon, the OS brings the first few pages of the program's instructions into the computer's memory and tells the computer to begin executing them. When more instructions are needed, the OS brings in more pages.

The Fetch/Execute Cycle, a hardwired sequence of five steps that are repeated over and over, executes the instructions:

1. (IF) Fetch the instruction stored at the memory location specified by the PC and place it in the control part of the computer. The PC is advanced to reference the next instruction after the fetch.
2. (ID) Decode the instruction. That is, decide what the operation is, where the data values (operands) are, and where the result should go.
3. (DF) Fetch the data from memory while the arithmetic/logic unit is set up to perform the operation.
4. (EX) The ALU performs the operation on the data values.
5. (RR) Store the result back in memory.

The cycle is repeated endlessly.

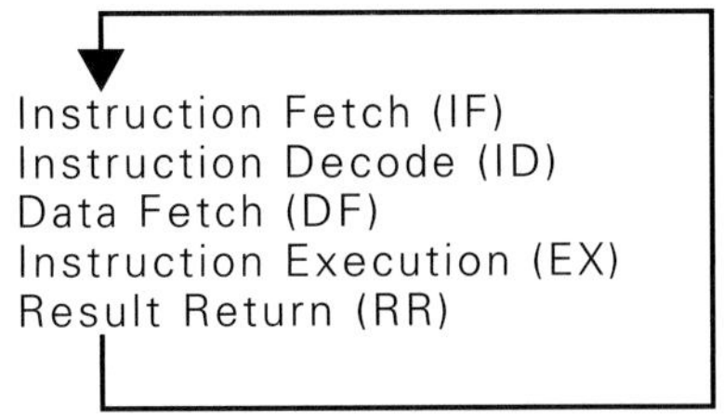

All of the computer's instructions are performed by the ALU circuits. The `AND` instruction, for example, is implemented with MOS technology by breaking a wire in two places and filling the gaps with the semiconducting material of a field effect transistor forming channels connecting the wires. An oxide insulator and a metal gate cover each semiconductor channel. If, for example, the instruction is `ADD 4040, 4280, 2020`, then the data value fetched from memory location

4040 would control the gate on the first MOS transistor, and the data value fetched from memory location 4280 would control the gate on the second MOS transistor. A true operand value creates a field, causing the channel to conduct, and a false operand value is neutral, preventing the channel from conducting. An electrical signal interpreted as "yes" is sent down the wire. If the "yes" is detected at the output end of the wire, both transistors are conducting, and the result is true; otherwise the result is false. Either way, the result is returned to memory location 2020.

That's it, from applications to electrons. It is a sequence of interesting and straightforward ideas working together to create computation. No single idea is *the* key idea. They all contribute. The power comes from applying the ideas in quantity: Application programs and operating systems are composed of millions of machine instructions, the control unit executes billions of cycles per second, memories contain billions of bits, processors have hundreds of millions of MOS transistors, and so on in an impressive process.

Ours has been a simple, but accurate description of a computer. This description mirrors the design and operation of many early computers built in the days before silicon technology had advanced to the microprocessor stage; that is, before everything in Figure 9.2 fit on a chip. Once silicon technology had matured to that stage, computer architects—the engineers that design computers—became very aggressive. By applying integrated circuitry to its fullest, they have optimized the Fetch/Execute Cycle and the simple structure of Figure 9.2 almost beyond recognition. To achieve their impressive speeds, today's computers are dramatically more complex than explained here. But the abstraction—the logical idea of how a computer is organized and operates—is as presented

SUMMARY

We began by describing the Fetch/Execute Cycle, the instruction interpretation engine of a computer system. The process, repeated over and over, is one of fetching the next instruction (indicated by the PC), decoding the operation to be performed and on what data, getting the data, doing the operation, and storing the result back into the memory. This process is hardwired into the control subsystem, one of the five components of a processor. The memory, a very long sequence of bytes, each with an address, stores the program and data while the program is running. The ALU does the actual computing. The input and output units are the interfaces for the peripheral devices attached to the computer.

A key point about machine instructions is that they do not refer to the data (operands) directly, but rather indirectly. Thus, different computations can be done with only one instruction, just by changing the data in the referenced memory locations. Because the instructions are so few and so simple, programmers must create complex computations by software layers, building up simple operations from the base instructions, more complex operations from the simple ones, and so forth. Programmers use sophisticated programming languages to create operating systems as well as the complex applications software.

Finally, the basic ideas of integrated circuits—integrating active and connective components, fabrication by photolithography, controlling conductivity through the field effect—were explained in detail.

EXERCISES

Multiple Choice

1. Which of the following is a characteristic of a computer?
   A. literal
   B. free will
   C. creativity
   D. intuition
2. There are ______ steps in the Fetch/Execute Cycle.
   A. 3
   B. 4
   C. 5
   D. 6
3. The Fetch/Execute Cycle operates:
   A. once a second
   B. thousands of times a second
   C. hundreds of thousands of times a second
   D. hundreds of millions of times a second
4. One byte of memory can store:
   A. any number
   B. one word
   C. one character
   D. one block
5. The ALU is used in the:
   A. Instruction Fetch, Instruction Execution, and Result Return steps
   B. Instruction Fetch, Instruction Execution, and Data Fetch steps
   C. Instruction Execution and Result Return steps
   D. Instruction Decode and Instruction Execution steps
6. Which of the following is used for input and output?
   A. keyboard
   B. hard disk
   C. mouse
   D. printer
7. The program counter is changed by instructions called:
   A. Fetch and Execute
   B. Branch and Jump
   C. Input and Output
   D. Now and Next
8. When there are no instructions for the Fetch/Execute Cycle, the computer:
   A. crashes
   B. executes an idle loop
   C. sends an empty instruction to processing
   D. always has instructions to execute

9. From smallest to largest, the correct order is:
   A. giga, kilo, mega, terra
   B. kilo, mega, giga, terra
   C. terra, kilo, mega, giga
   D. kilo, mega, terra, giga
10. Modern computers know:
    A. only a handful of instructions
    B. a couple of dozen instructions
    C. about a hundred instructions
    D. thousands of instructions

Short Answer

1. ______ deterministically perform or execute instructions to process information.
2. Computers operate under a set of operations called the ______.
3. ______ is an acronym for the name of the location where computer programs run and data is stored.
4. The ______ part of the computer is the hardware part of the Fetch/Execute Cycle.
5. Computers operate ______, that is, they follow instructions exactly based on the program and data they have been given.
6. The math in the computer is done by the ______.
7. Transferring and transforming information is called ______.
8. ______ are the devices that connect to the computer.
9. The ______ encodes keystrokes into binary form for the computer.
10. The computer's clock is measured in ______.
11. ______ is the task of creating complex instructions for the computer to follow from a set of simple instructions.
12. Computers keep track of the next instruction to execute by its ______.
13. ______ is the technical term for the process of executing a program.
14. A(n) ______ sometimes conducts electricity and sometimes doesn't.
15. The flow of electricity in a channel in a semiconductor is controlled by a(n) ______.

Exercises

1. Break the process of brushing your teeth into separate steps. Be as specific as possible.
2. How many bits in a kilobyte? megabyte? terabyte?

3. Find out how much memory your computer has. Calculate exactly how many bytes it has.
4. If a 1 GHz computer can start four instructions per second and can start a new instruction on 80 percent of its cycles, how many instructions can it complete in a second? in a minute?
5. If the mouse cable is five feet long, how long does it take the current generated by a mouse click to travel from the mouse to the computer?
6. If the cable connecting the hard disk to the computer is six inches long, what effect would it have on performance if the length was cut in half? doubled?
7. Explain why the keyboard and the mouse are input devices and the monitor is an output device.
8. Explain how a complicated process like driving can be accomplished as a series of simple steps.
9. Explain how a system that can do only a limited number of very simple tasks can accomplish an almost unlimited number of complicated tasks.
10. Do an online search to find an explanation of how computer circuits are made.
11. Locate a computer circuit and take a close look at it. Describe what it looks like.
12. Using the Fetch/Execute Cycle, describe how you'd answer a true/false question.

chapter

10

WHAT'S THE PLAN?

Algorithmic Thinking

learning objectives

- List the five essential properties of an algorithm
- Describe the difference between an algorithm and a program
- Use the *Alphabetize CDs* algorithm to illustrate algorithmic thinking:
  - Follow the flow of the instruction execution
  - Follow an analysis to pinpoint assumptions
  - Explain the function of loops and tests
- Demonstrate algorithmic thinking by being able to:
  - Explain what the *Beta* sweep abstraction does
  - Explain what the *Alpha* sweep abstraction does

The process of preparing programs for a digital computer is especially attractive, not only because it can be economically and scientifically rewarding, but also because it can be an aesthetic experience much like composing poetry or music.

—DONALD E. KNUTH, 1970

Solving a problem means finding a way out of a difficulty, a way around an obstacle, attaining an aim which was not immediately attainable. Solving problems is the specific achievement of intelligence, and intelligence is the specific gift of mankind: solving problems can be regarded as the most characteristically human activity.

—GEORGE POLYA, 1981

The most beautiful thing we can experience is the mysterious. It is the source of all true art and science.

—ALBERT EINSTEIN, 1930

AN ALGORITHM is a precise, systematic method for producing a specified result. We know algorithms as recipes, assembly instructions, driving directions, business processes, nominating procedures, and so on. Algorithms are key to processing information, of course, and we've already met several in this book. There are three main reasons to learn more about algorithms. First, we must create algorithms so that other people or computers can help us achieve our goals. If they are to be successful, the algorithms must "work." This chapter explains how to create effective algorithms. Second, we will find ourselves following algorithms created by others. If we know the "dos" and "don'ts" of algorithm design, we can pay better attention to the details and be alert to errors in other people's instructions. Finally, learning about algorithms will complete the picture begun in Chapter 8 of how computers solve problems. Understanding this process will make us better computer users, better debuggers, and better problem solvers—that is, more Fluent.

The goals of this chapter are to understand what algorithms are and to learn to think algorithmically. We begin by looking at everyday algorithms. Next, we introduce and illustrate the five fundamental properties of algorithms. We explain the role of *language* in specifying algorithms and the value of a formal language. Next, we discuss the relationship between algorithms and programs. Guidelines—useful for writing out driving directions—help us understand the role of context in executing algorithms. We create an algorithm for alphabetizing our audio CD collection, which helps us discover how and why algorithms are structured as they are. We execute the algorithm; that is, we sort a five-slot rack of our favorite CDs, watching the progress of the algorithm. Then, perhaps most important, we analyze the algorithm to extract key concepts in algorithmic thinking.

FITBYTE

Weird Word. *Algorithm* seems to be an anagram of logarithm, but it comes from the name of a famous Arabic textbook author, Abu Ja'far Mohammed ibn Mûsâ al-Khowârizmî, who lived about AD 825. The end of his name, al-Khowârizmî, means *native of Khowârism* (today Khiva, Uzbekistan). It has been corrupted over the centuries into *algorithm*.

ALGORITHM: A FAMILIAR IDEA

In Chapter 1 we defined an algorithm as a precise and systematic method for producing a specified result. Algorithms are familiar—we've already seen several of them so far in this book:

> **Recognition of a button click.** In Chapter 1, after describing how computers draw buttons on the screen, we explained how the button is "clicked." The systematic method described how, when the mouse is clicked, the computer can look through the list of buttons it has drawn on the screen, and for each button, check to see if the cursor is inside the square defining the button.

> **Placeholder technique.** In Chapter 2 we described a three-step process to eliminate short letter sequences (for example, new-lines), which can also be parts of longer strings (for example, double new-lines), without also eliminating them in the longer strings.

> **Hex to bits.** In Chapter 8 we used algorithms to convert back and forth between hexadecimal digits and bits.

We use algorithms every day. The arithmetic operations—addition, subtraction, multiplication, division—we learned in elementary school are algorithms. Making change is an algorithm, as are looking up a number in a telephone book, sending a greeting card to our parents, and balancing a checkbook. Changing a tire is algorithmic, too, because it is a systematic method to solve a problem (replace a flat tire). Usually, though, *algorithm* means a precise method in information processing.

Algorithms in Everyday Life

Most of the algorithms that we know, like arithmetic, we learned from a patient teacher or we figured out for ourselves, like how to look up a phone number. Because we are the ones performing the operations, we don't think much about algorithms as an explicit sequence of instructions. We simply *know* what to do. Other algorithms—recipes, assembly instructions for a bicycle, driving directions to a party, or income tax filing rules—are written out for us. Written algorithms are of interest here because we want to be able to think up an algorithm, write it out, and have some other agent—another person or a computer—perform its instructions successfully. It's not a matter to be taken lightly.

The specification of an algorithm must be "precise." The algorithms just mentioned from the earlier chapters, though possibly clear enough for a person to follow, were not precise enough for a computer. Computers, as we saw in Chapters 7 and 9, are so clueless and literal that every part of a task must be spelled out in detail. To write a precise algorithm, we need to pay attention to three things:

> **Capability.** Make sure that the computer knows what and how to do the operations.

> **Language.** Ensure that the description is unambiguous—that is, it can only be read and understood one way.

> **Context.** Make few assumptions about the input or execution setting.

These issues are not only crucial when our algorithms are for computers; they're just as important when we're writing for other people. Though we expect people to use their heads and make up for any weaknesses in our descriptions, sometimes they can be clueless and literal, too, especially when dealing with unfamiliar situations. So, it's always in our best interest to make our instructions precise, avoid ambiguity, be sure they know what to do, and minimize assumptions no matter who performs the algorithm.

Five Essential Properties of Algorithms

To write algorithms that are specified well enough for a computer to follow, make sure every algorithm has five essential properties:

> Inputs specified

> Outputs specified

> Definiteness

> Effectiveness

> Finiteness

`Inputs specified.` The **inputs** are the data that will be transformed during the computation to produce the output. We must specify the type of the data, the amount of data, and the form that the data will take. Suppose the algorithm is a recipe. We must list the ingredients (type of inputs), their quantities (amount of input), and their preparation, if any (form of inputs), as in, "1/4 cup onion, minced."

`Outputs specified.` The **outputs** are the data resulting from the computation, the intended result. Often the description is given in the name of the algorithm, as in "Algorithm to compute a batting average." As with inputs, we must specify the type, amount, and any form of the outputs. A possible output for some computations is a statement that there can be no output—that is, no solution is possible. Recipes specify their outputs too, giving the type, quantity, and form of food, as in, "3 dozen 3-inch chocolate chip cookies."

`Definiteness.` Algorithms must specify every step. **Definiteness** means specifying the sequence of operations for transforming the inputs into the outputs. Every detail of each step must be spelled out, including how to handle errors. Definiteness ensures that if the algorithm is performed at different times or by different agents (people or computers) using the same data, the output will be the same. Similarly, recipes should be definite, but because they often rely on the judgment, practicality, and experience of the cook, they can be much less definite than computer algorithms and still be successful. And where they are not definite—"salt and pepper to taste"—it's usually a good thing.

`Effectiveness.` It must be possible for the agent to execute the algorithm mechanically without any further inputs, special talent, clairvoyance, creativity, help from Superman, and so on. Whereas definiteness specifies which operations to do, **effectiveness** means that they are doable. Examples of ineffectiveness abound: "Enter the amount of income you would have received this year had you worked harder," and "Print the length of the longest run of 9s in the decimal expansion of π."

`Finiteness.` An algorithm must have **finiteness**; it must eventually stop, either with the right output or with a statement that no solution is possible. If no answer comes back, we can't tell whether the algorithm is still working on an answer or is just plain "stuck." Finiteness is not usually an issue for noncomputer algorithms because they typically don't repeat instructions. But, as we shall see, computer algorithms often repeat instructions with different data. Finiteness becomes an issue because if the algorithm doesn't specify when to stop the repetition, the computer will continue to repeat the instructions forever.

Any process having these five properties will be called an algorithm.

FITBYTE

Work Without End. "Long" division is an algorithm in which finiteness is important. For example, divide 3 into 10. As we add each new digit (3) to the quotient, the computation returns to a situation—call it a *state*—that it has been in before. When should the algorithm stop?

```
     3.33
  3)10.00
    9
    ----
    1.00
      9
     ---
      10
      ...
```

Language in Algorithms

Because algorithms are developed by people, but executed by some other agent, they must be written in some language. The most important requirement of the language is that the person who creates the instructions and the agent that performs them both interpret the instructions the same way.

Natural Language.

If the agent is a person, we use a natural language, such as English. Although we usually assume all speakers understand every sentence of a language alike, it's not true. In fact, it's probable that no two people understand a language exactly the same way. So, an instruction may mean one thing to the writer and something else to the agent. Ambiguity is very common in natural languages, of course, but ambiguity is not so much the problem as the fact that natural languages are not very precise. So, for example, recipe writers must choose their words carefully to guide the cook—rather than stir they choose *fold in* or *beat*—but there are only a few terms to control how to mix ingredients. Generally, a natural language is an extremely difficult medium in which to express algorithms.

Programming Language.

Since natural languages don't work well, we use a programming language when the executing agent is a computer. Programming languages are **formal languages**, and they are called synthetic instead of natural because they were designed just to express algorithms. They are precisely defined. Programming languages are rarely ambiguous, and the precise definition ensures that the programmer and the computer agree on what each instruction means. So, programmers know that what they tell the computer to do is exactly what it will do. Of course, programmers may make mistakes, but at least they can be sure that if the computer does something wrong, the problem is with their design of the algorithm, not with the way the computer interprets the algorithm.

The Difference between an Algorithm and a Program

A program is an algorithm that has been customized to solve a specific task under a specific set of circumstances in a specific language. Making change—subtracting an amount of money, *x*, from a larger amount paid, *y, and* returning the result as coins and currency—is an *algorithm*, but making change in U.S. dollars is a *program*. The program uses the "making change" algorithm specialized to the denominations of coins (1¢, 5¢, 10¢, 25¢, 50¢, $1) and paper currency ($1, $2, $5, $10, . . .) of the United States. Making change in New Zealand dollars is a different program; it also uses the making change algorithm but with the New Zealand coins (5¢, 10¢, 20¢, 50¢, $1, $2) and paper currency ($5, $10 $20, . . .). From our point of view, whether the method is general (algorithm) or specialized (program) makes no difference. The issues are the same.

The Context of a Program

A program can fulfill the five properties of an algorithm (inputs specified, outputs specified, definiteness, effectiveness, and finiteness), and be unambiguous, and still not work right because it is executed in the wrong **context** (the assumptions of the program are not fulfilled). For example, a form that asks you for your *Last Name* may mean your family name or surname, as is the case for Western names. The request has the right result in the United States, but perhaps not in countries like China where the family name is given first. Good algorithm designers reduce the dependence on context by asking for *Family Name* rather than *Last Name*, and *Given Name* rather than *First Name.*

Context Matters: Driving Instructions. Consider driving directions, another example where context matters. For example, the instruction

> From the Limmat River go to Bahnhof Strasse and turn right.

seems reliable, but it may not be. The "turn right" instruction assumes that you are traveling in a specific direction. If you are traveling east, the instruction works, because you are in the context the instruction writer assumed. But if you are traveling west, you will need to turn left on Bahnhof Strasse and the instruction doesn't work (see Figure 10.1). You are following the instructions in a context the writer didn't expect. Turning right will send you north if you approach from one direction and send you south if you approach from the other direction.

The context in which to apply the algorithm—the point of departure in this case—must be considered. Such conditions can be written as input conditions or they can simply be avoided. The best solution is not to use words like *right* that depend on orientation until you've specified it. Terms like *north* that are orientation independent are better.

When you develop algorithms and programs, you need to think ahead to make sure your algorithm works in any context.

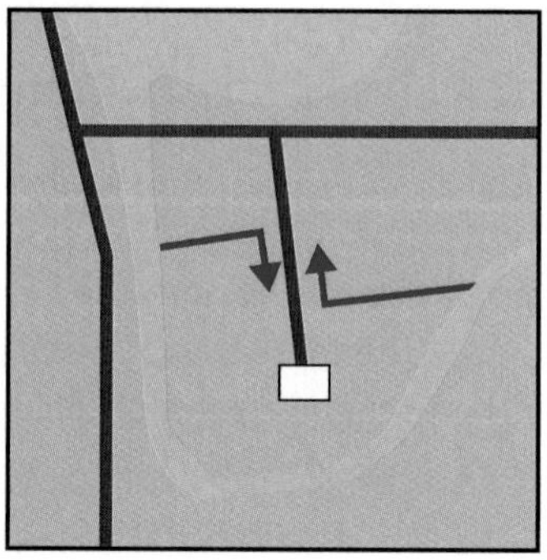

Figure 10.1. *Diagram of approaching a street (Bahnhof Strasse) from different directions, resulting in the instruction "turn right" having different meanings.*

CHECKLIST>>

Travel Directions: To give better travel directions, follow these rules to reduce the dependence on context.

- *Give the* starting point, *"From Place de la Concorde. . . ."*
- *State the* direction *of travel, "Going west on Route 66. . . ."*
- *Give* landmarks, *especially when turning, "Turn left; you'll see a temple (Todai-ji) on your right. . . ."*
- *Give* measured distances *(2.3 miles) instead of blocks, cross streets, or traffic lights, which can be ambiguous.*
- *Include an* "overshot" test, *"If you cross Via Giuseppi Verdi, you've gone too far."*

AN ALGORITHM: *ALPHABETIZE CDS*

It's time for an example algorithm. Though most of the algorithms in later chapters use a programming language to ensure precision, our first algorithms will be written in English.

Imagine that your audio CD collection, which fills a large, slotted rack, is completely disorganized. You've decided that it's time to get your CDs in order, and you want to alphabetize them by the name of the group, the performing musician, or perhaps the composer. How would you go about solving this problem?

Here is an algorithm for alphabetizing CDs:

ALPHABETIZE CDS

Input: An unordered sequence of CDs filling a slotted rack
Output: The same CDs in the rack in alphabetical order
Instructions:

1. Use the term *Artist_Of* to refer to the name of the group or musician or composer on a CD.

2. Decide which end of the rack is to be the beginning of the alphabetic sequence and call the slot at that end the *Alpha* slot.
3. Call the slot next to the *Alpha* slot the *Beta* slot.
4. If the *Artist_Of* the CD in the *Alpha* slot comes later in the alphabet than the *Artist_Of* the CD in the *Beta* slot, swap the CDs; otherwise, continue on.
5. If there is a slot following the *Beta* slot, begin calling it the *Beta* slot and go to Instruction 4; otherwise, continue on.
6. If there are two or more slots following the *Alpha* slot, begin calling the slot following the *Alpha* slot *Alpha* and begin calling the slot following it the *Beta* slot, and go to Instruction 4; otherwise, stop.

In the next sections, we'll check to see that the properties of definitiveness, effectiveness, and finiteness hold true; in other words, we'll check that we truly have an algorithm.

How does this algorithm work? Follow Figure 10.2 as we go through the process.

Instruction 1. *Use the term* Artist_Of *to refer to the name of the group or musician or composer on a given CD.* This instruction gives a name to the operation of locating the name used for alphabetizing. (*Artist_Of* is shorthand for extracting the name of the performer, simplifying Instruction 4; it could be eliminated at the expense of a wordier Instruction 4.)

Instruction 2. *Decide which end of the rack is to be the beginning of the alphabetic sequence and call the slot at that end the* Alpha *slot.* The purpose of this instruction is to give the process a starting point. It also gives the initial meaning to the word *Alpha*. In the algorithm, *Alpha* refers to slots in the rack. At the start, *Alpha* refers to the first slot in the alphabetic sequence. As the algorithm progresses, it refers to successive slots in the rack.

Instruction 3. *Call the slot next to the* Alpha *slot the* Beta *slot.* This instruction gives the word *Beta* its initial meaning. The names *Alpha* and *Beta* have no inherent meaning; the programmer needs to name slots in the rack and just chose these two words.

Instruction 4. *If the* Artist_Of *the CD in the* Alpha *slot comes later in the alphabet than the* Artist_Of *the CD in the* Beta *slot, swap the CDs.* This is the workhorse instruction of the algorithm. It compares the names of the recording artists of the CDs in the slots *Alpha* and *Beta* and, if necessary, exchanges them so that they are in the proper order. It may not be necessary to swap if the CDs are already positioned properly. But either way, the alphabetically earlier CD is in the *Alpha* slot when this instruction is done.

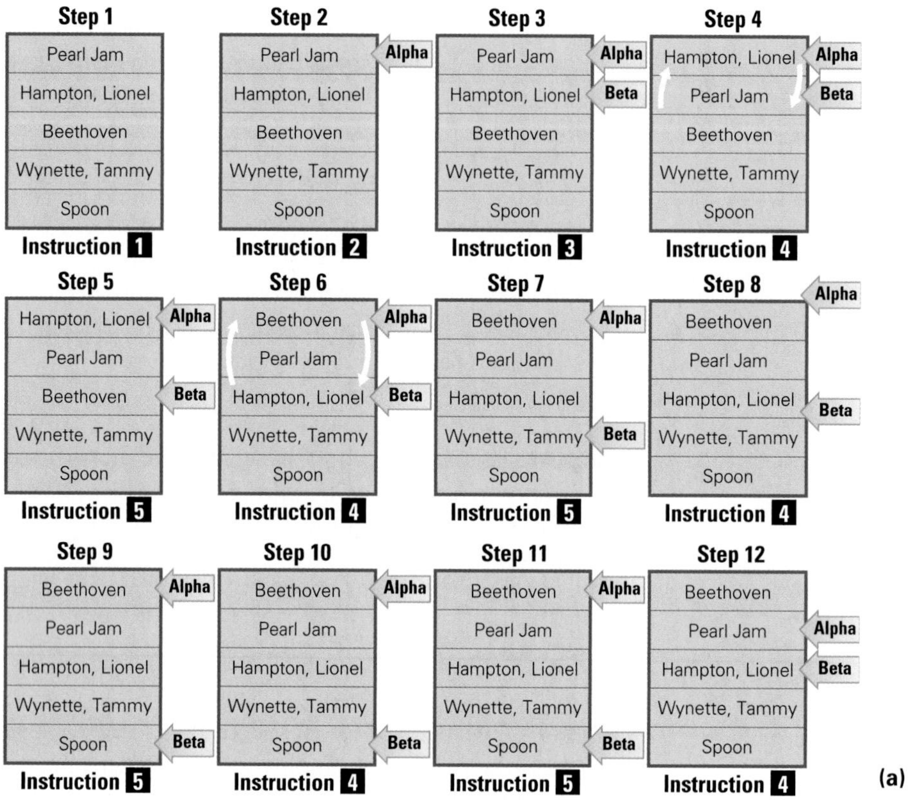

Figure 10.2. The steps of Alphabetize CDs. A snapshot of the CD rack is shown at the completion of each instruction. The pair of numbers in the boxes gives the instruction from the algorithm and step in the overall execution just completed. For example, Instruction 5, Step 9 means "the ninth step of the computation is to perform instruction 5 of the algorithm." Notice how Beta *sweeps through all of the slots following* Alpha. *After the first 11 steps, the alphabetically earliest CD, Beethoven, is in the* Alpha *slot.*

Instruction 5. *If there is a slot following the* Beta *slot, begin calling it the* Beta *slot and go to Instruction 4; otherwise, continue on.* This instruction gives a new definition for the *Beta* slot so that it refers to the next slot in the sequence, if there is one. With this new definition of *Beta*, Instruction 4 can be executed again, comparing a different pair of CDs. One of the pair, the CD in the *Alpha* slot, was compared the last time Instruction 4 was executed, but because *Beta* refers to a new slot, the pair of CDs is "new." If all slots have been considered—that is, there is no next slot for *Beta* to refer to—the algorithm continues on to Instruction 6 instead of returning to Instruction 4.

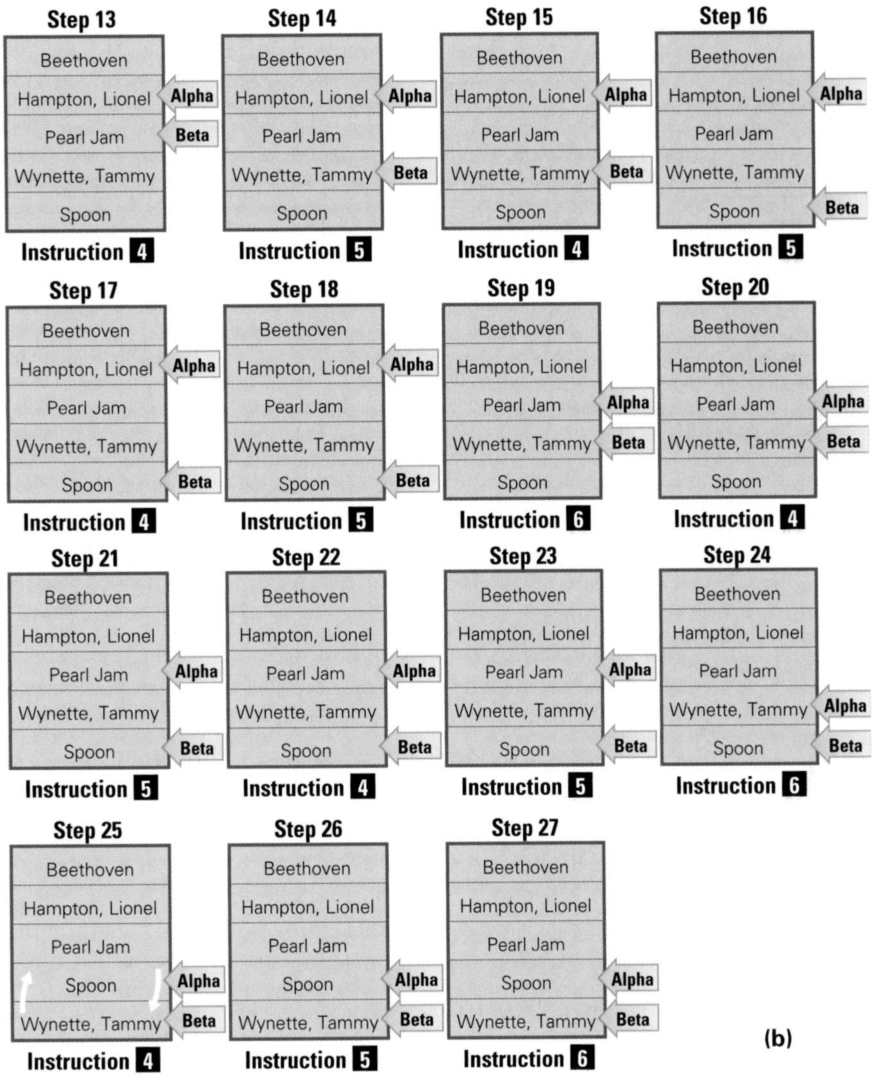

(b)

`Instruction 6.` *If there are two or more slots following the* Alpha *slot, begin calling the slot following the* Alpha *slot* Alpha *and the slot following it the* Beta *slot, and go to Instruction 4; otherwise, stop.* By the time we get to this instruction, the alphabetically earliest CD is in the *Alpha* slot, thanks to the combination of Instructions 4 and 5. The idea now is to advance *Alpha* to the next slot and to sweep through the last of the rack again locating the alphabetically next-earliest CD with the Instruction 4–5 combination. Then *Alpha* moves again, the Instruction 4–5 combination is repeated again, and so on. Each time, the CDs in slots up to and including *Alpha* will be alphabetized. When there are no longer enough slots to call one *Alpha* and the next one *Beta*, the whole rack has been alphabetized and the algorithm stops.

The *Alphabetize CDs* approach is better than dumping the CDs on the floor, and trying to return them to the rack in order. Though it keeps the CDs in the rack while it orders them, that's not the property that makes *Alphabetize CDs* an algorithm. It could be rewritten to work with the CDs spread out on the floor. Rather, it is the fact that *Alphabetize CDs* uses a method to find the alphabetically first CD, then the next, then the next after that, and so forth until the alphabetically last CD is found. That is, *Alphabetize CDs* is systematic.

ANALYZING *ALPHABETIZE CDS* ALGORITHM

The *Alphabetize CDs* example illustrates the five basic properties of algorithms. The inputs and outputs were listed. Each instruction was described precisely—or as precisely as English allows—fulfilling the definiteness requirement. The operations of the algorithm are effective because actions like selecting the next slot and counting to see if there are at least two slots left are simple and doable mechanically. The most complicated operation, deciding which of two artists' names is earlier in the alphabet, is also a completely mechanical process. We need only compare the first two letters of the names, and the one closer to *A* is the earlier; if the two letters are the same letter, we compare the second letters, and so forth. So, our algorithm has the effectiveness property. Finally, the algorithm is finite. Because Instructions 4, 5, and 6 are repeated, this property is not so obvious. However, notice that each time Instruction 4 is repeated, *Alpha* and *Beta* refer to a different pair of slots that has not previously been considered. Because slots can be paired in a rack in only a finite number of *different* ways, Instruction 4 cannot be repeated forever. Instructions 5 and 6 cannot be repeated forever without repeating Instruction 4 forever. Hence, the program satisfies the finiteness property.

A Deeper Analysis

We have shown that *Alphabetize CDs* meets the requirements of an algorithm, but there are other, more interesting aspects to discover.

Structural Features. The algorithm has two instructions, 5 and 6, in which the agent is directed to go back and repeat instructions. Such instructions create **loops** in the algorithm. Loops are instruction sequences that repeat, and they are more obvious when the instructions are given in a form other than English. Consider the flowchart in Figure 10.3. Loops are fundamental to algorithms because they cause parts of the computation to be performed as many times as there are data items. So, the loops in the *Alphabetize CDs* algorithm repeat instructions as many times as there are slots, or CDs.

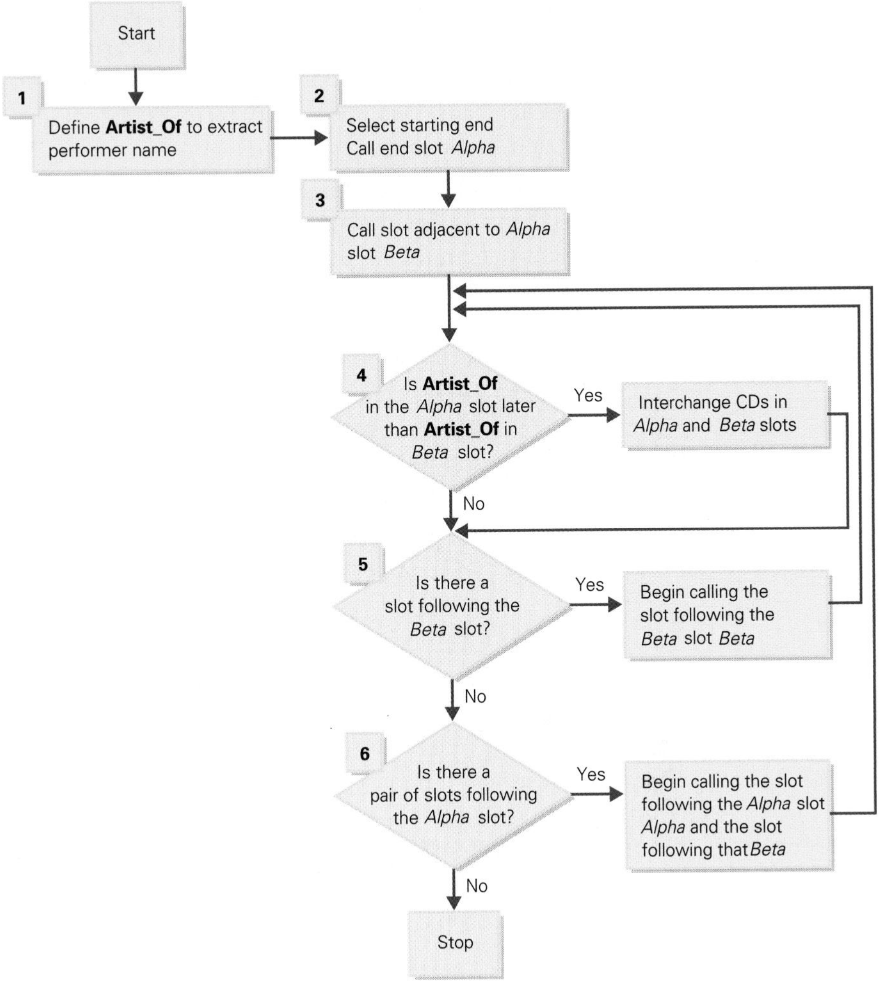

Figure 10.3. *Flowchart of* Alphabetize CDs. *Operations are shown in rectangles; decisions are shown in diamonds. Arrows indicate the sequencing of the operations.*

Loops and Tests. A loop must include a **test** to determine whether the instructions should be repeated one more time. As Figure 10.3 shows *Alphabetize CDs* has two loops. Instruction 5 tests whether there are slots following the *Beta* slot; if so, Instruction 4 will be repeated; if not, that repetition of the inner loop will end. Instruction 6 tests whether there is at least a pair of slots after the *Alpha* slot. If so, Instructions 4 and 5 will be repeated; if not, the outer loop ends. These tests cause the loop to complete and ensure the finiteness property.

FITBYTE

Failed Test. Requiring a test to determine when to stop repeating instructions may seem obvious, but some shampoo directions read "Wet hair, massage in shampoo, rinse, repeat," failing the finiteness test. Does the shampoo run out before the shower's hot water?

Notice that for the loop to continue at Instruction 5, *Beta* must move to the next slot. Similarly, Instruction 6 moves *Alpha* to the next slot and resets *Beta* to follow it. These moves ensure that on the next test *Beta* and *Alpha* refer to different slots. If there are no changes between the two consecutive tests, the outcome must be the same, and so the loop would never stop.

Assumptions. Assumptions are made in specifying *Alphabetize CDs*. First, we assume (and state in the Input specification) that the CD rack is full. This matters because the instructions do not handle the case of empty slots in the rack. (For example, if *Beta* were an empty slot, how would Instruction 4 operate?) The algorithm requires that the *Artist_Of* two CDs be compared, but if one or both of the slots are empty, the agent might not know what to do. The specification is correct because it states that it expects a full CD rack as input. But a better solution would explain what to do if the rack is not full. Then the "full" requirement could be dropped.

"Following" an Assumption. When the *Beta* slot is first set in Instruction 3, only one slot is next to *Alpha* because in Instruction 2 *Alpha* was chosen to be an end slot. This ensures that there is a unique slot *following Alpha* for *Beta* to refer to, and so the specification is effective. There is an assumption in the use of the term *following* in Instructions 5 and 6. Instruction 5 refers to a slot "following" *Beta,* which means a slot further from the end chosen in Instruction 2. Similarly, Instruction 6 refers to a pair of slots "following" *Alpha,* meaning the slots further from the end chosen in Instruction 2. But, nowhere is the term *following* defined. This makes the orientation of the term *following* an assumption. The orientation can be defined—and would have to be for a computer to execute the algorithm—but people know what "following" means.

The Exchange Sort Algorithm

The *Alphabetize CDs* example illustrates a well-known algorithm called **Exchange Sort**. In the *Alphabetize CDs* example, we used the Exchange Sort algorithm to alphabetize CDs based on the names of the musicians. The Exchange Sort algorithm is the idea of comparing pairs of items chosen in a particular way, exchanging them if they are out of order, and continuing to sweep through the items to locate the next minimal item.

A different program based on the Exchange Sort algorithm might alphabetize CDs based on their titles, and another might alphabetize CDs based on the recording company's name (label). The Exchange Sort algorithm can be specialized into programs for alphabetizing books by their authors, ordering books by their ISBNs, ordering canceled checks by date, and so on. When we choose the kind of item (e.g., CDs), the criterion for "order" (e.g., alphabetically ordered by musician's name), and specific names for keeping track of the items (e.g., *Alpha* and *Beta*), we have created a program based on the algorithm. The algorithm is a systematic process, and the program is that process formulated for a particular situation. An algorithm continues to be an algorithm even when it is specialized into a program.

Are there other ways to alphabetize CDs? Of course. There are dozens of sorting algorithms, and most of them could be the basis of programs for alphabetizing CDs. Why one algorithm might be better than another is the sort of question computer scientists worry about. It need not concern us.

{GREATFITMOMENTS}

Impossible Dream >>

At the start of the twentieth century, German mathematician David Hilbert listed several great problems worthy of study in the new century. His tenth problem was to develop an algorithm to decide whether logical propositions were true or false. Algorithmically testing truth seemed like a great goal. Logicians Bertrand Russell and Alfred North Whitehead began setting down axioms and logic rules for mathematics in their three volume *Principia Mathematica*. But in 1931 Slovak-American logician Kurt Gödel astonished everyone by proving it wasn't going to be possible. Soon American logician Alonzo Church and English mathematician Alan M. Turing extended Gödel's work, proving there can be no algorithm to decide truth and laying the foundations for theoretical computer science.

ABSTRACTION IN ALGORITHMIC THINKING

The *Alphabetize CDs* example seems very complicated when described in so much detail, but it is easier to understand than it may first appear. This is because we can think of parts of the algorithm's behavior as whole units rather than as individual instructions. This is abstraction, as defined in Chapter 1.

Beta Sweep Abstraction

For example, the "*Beta* sweep" of Instructions 4 and 5 can become a single concept in our minds. That is,

> ***Beta* Sweep:** While *Alpha* points to a fixed slot, *Beta* sweeps through the slots following *Alpha*, in sequence, comparing each slot's CD with the CD in the *Alpha* slot, and swapping them when necessary.

FITCAUTION

Know the Score. The ideas in this section may be difficult to comprehend by just reading them. They are much easier to understand if, using five of your favorite CDs, you first follow the instructions of *Alphabetize CDs* to sort them.

The idea of treating parts of the algorithm's behavior as a unit—not the instructions themselves, but the behavior the instructions define—is key to algorithmic thinking. We want to discipline ourselves to think about algorithms this way.

The unit of behavior is an *abstraction,* an idea or concept extracted from a specific situation. For example, the "*Beta* sweep" considers in order all CDs following a specific *Alpha.* The sweep process tick-tick-ticks through the following slots, comparing artists, and swapping them when necessary.

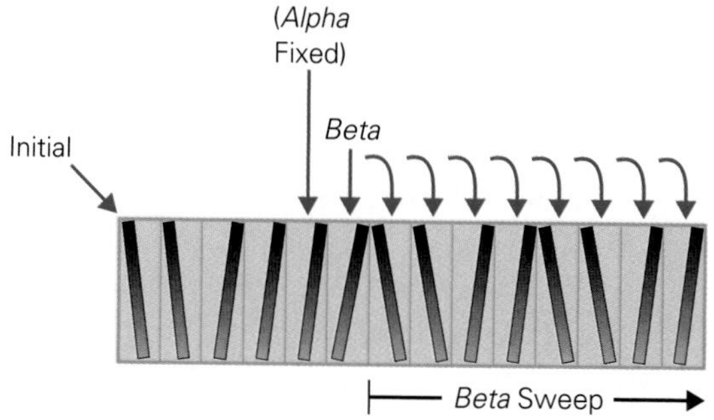

Properties of *Beta* Sweep Abstraction. When we think of the *Beta* sweep abstraction, we can recognize some of its important properties. The *Beta* sweep is

1. **Exhaustive.** It considers all CDs from the *Alpha* slot to the end of the rack, making sure that none is left out.
2. **Nonredundant.** It considers each slot following *Alpha* only once, and so never considers the same pair of CDs twice, which ensures that the sweep will stop.
3. **Progressive.** At any given time, the alphabetically earliest CD seen so far in this sweep is in the *Alpha* slot.
4. **Goal-achieving.** After the sweep completes, the alphabetically earliest CD among all CDs considered in this sweep (including *Alpha*) is in *Alpha.*

These are not general properties that all algorithms have. These are only specific properties of the *Beta* sweep abstraction of the *Alphabetize CDs* program. (They are also properties of the "inner loop sweep" of the Exchange Sort algorithm if we make them general, so as not to refer to "CDs," "slots," "*Alpha,*" "*Beta,*" etc.).

Where did the four properties of the *Beta* sweep abstraction come from? We noticed them when we analyzed how the *Alphabetize CDs* algorithm works. (They are all mentioned in the discussion in the "Analyzing Alphabetize CDs Algorithm" section.) Though they have been listed here so that we can discuss them, they are examples of the features we should notice about the behavior of an algorithm when we study how it operates. Why? Because these properties (together with the *Alpha* sweep properties below) will convince us that the algorithm actually works, that it achieves its goal of alphabetizing.

To see how the properties of the *Beta* sweep can convince us that the algorithm works, first note that properties 1 through 3 imply property 4. That is, the *Beta* sweep considers all CDs once and keeps the alphabetically earliest in *Alpha* at all times. That behavior after processing all CDs in a sweep ensures that the alphabetically earliest CD is in *Alpha*, which is part of the answer.

Alpha Sweep Abstraction

For the rest of the answer, consider the *Alpha* sweep abstraction:

> ***Alpha* Sweep:** *Alpha* sweeps from the slot where the alphabetization begins through all slots (except the last) performing the *Beta* sweep instructions each time.

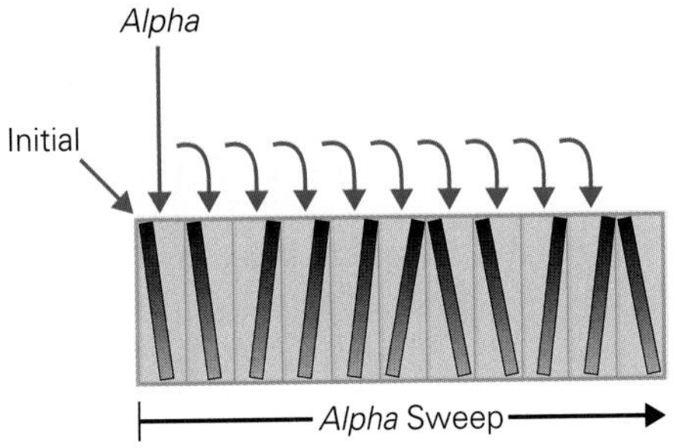

Properties of *Alpha* Sweep Abstraction. We can list properties that we notice about the *Alpha* sweep abstraction. The *Alpha* sweep is

1. **Exhaustive.** It considers all CDs from the first to (but not including) the last.
2. **Nonredundant.** No slot is assigned to *Alpha* more than once, so the process stops if the *Beta* sweep stops, and it does by property 2 of the *Beta* sweep abstraction.
3. **Progressive.** At the end of each *Beta* sweep, the alphabetically next earliest CD is in *Alpha*.
4. **Complete.** When the last *Beta* sweep is completed, the CD in the last slot is later in the alphabet than the CD in the next-to-last slot because the last *Beta* sweep involved these last two slots and it is property (3) of the *Beta* sweep. (Refer to Figure 10.2, Step 25.)
5. **Goal-achieving.** The alphabetically earliest CD is in the first slot at the end of the first *Beta* sweep, by its property (4) and the fact that all CDs are considered; and thereafter in every new position for *Alpha*, the *Beta* sweep assigns the next earliest CD. The program alphabetizes.

Property (5) of the *Alpha* sweep says this program works. We stated that it did originally, but by noticing these properties of the two abstractions—*Beta* sweep and *Alpha* sweep—we can see *why* it works. When we create computer solutions, knowing why our solution works is the only way to be sure the solution does work, achieving our IT goal. Algorithmic thinking involves inventing algorithms that achieve our goals, and understanding why they work.

Abstracting for Other Algorithms and Programs

It must be emphasized that the *Alpha* sweep and *Beta* sweep abstractions are *specific* to the Exchange Sort algorithm and to programs like *Alphabetize CDs* derived from it. Other algorithms and programs will exhibit different behaviors and require different abstractions based on the way they solve their problem. Further, those abstractions will have properties different from (but analogous to) the four properties of the *Beta* sweep and the five properties of the *Alpha* sweep. Every situation is different, but the approach—abstracting the behavior and understanding the properties—is always the same.

Looking to the Future

This chapter has introduced many deep ideas. The reward for the reader who has reached this point with an understanding of these concepts is the satisfaction of having seen nearly all of the basic ideas underlying algorithms and programming. With perhaps two exceptions, every programming idea covered in this book appears in this chapter. All that is left is elaborating on these ideas and mastering them. This isn't trivial, of course, but it won't require many more ideas.

Because we have spent a lot of time understanding these complex ideas, it is worth our while to spend a moment naming them, especially since we will run into them again in later chapters:

- **Variables.** *Alpha* and *Beta* are variables in the *Alphabetize CDs* program.
- **Locations.** The slots in the CD rack are like a computer's memory locations.
- **Values.** The CDs are the values stored in the locations.
- **Function.** *Artist_Of* is a function for locating the name of the group or performer on a CD (a value).
- **Initialization.** Instructions 2 and 3 initialize the variables *Alpha* and *Beta*, respectively.
- **Loops.** The Instructions 4 and 5 form a loop; the Instructions 4 through 6 also form a loop.
- **Array.** The rack is a (linear) array.

We will be studying these terms more completely in the future.

SUMMARY

In this chapter we introduced one of the most fundamental forms of thinking. We learned that recipes and other everyday algorithms can be poor because we write them in an imprecise natural language. The five fundamental properties of algorithms were introduced and explained, and then the role of language in making the specification precise was reviewed. A discussion of being sensitive to context followed. We then presented an algorithm for alphabetizing the audio CDs in a filled rack. This was a six-instruction program that named two slots, *Alpha* and *Beta,* and made repeated sweeps over the remaining CDs. Each instruction was explained, as were several of the general properties of the process. We noted that *Alphabetize CDs* is a program built using the Exchange Sort algorithm. Finally, we abstracted the processing of *Alphabetize CDs,* recognizing two interacting behaviors: the *Beta* sweep and the *Alpha* sweep. These two abstractions have several properties, which explain why the algorithm produced an alphabetized sequence. These sorts of abstractions and their properties are the essence of algorithmic thinking. With a little practice, algorithmic thinking can become second nature, making us much more effective problem solvers.

EXERCISES

Multiple Choice

1. An algorithm has ______ basic requirements
   A. three
   B. four
   C. five
   D. seven
2. An algorithm must be:
   A. precise
   B. approximate
   C. concise
   D. general
3. Which of the following does not fit?
   A. natural language
   B. formal language
   C. synthetic language
   D. programming language
4. A computer program must:
   A. complete a specific task
   B. work in a specific set of circumstances
   C. be written in a specific language
   D. all of the above
5. Which instructions are repeated in the Alphabetizing CDs algorithm on pages 283–285?
   A. all of them
   B. 4 and 5
   C. 4 to 6
   D. 3 to 5
6. If you saw a monitor, keyboard, mouse, printer, and CPU, you would assume these parts formed a computer. This is an example of:
   A. abstraction
   B. encapsulation
   C. utilization
   D. algorithm
7. You notice that the only item in alphabetical order after the *Alpha* sweep of an Exchange Sort is the first item. This is an example of:
   A. abstraction
   B. encapsulation
   C. utilization
   D. algorithm

8. In an Exchange Sort:
   A. the *Alpha* sweep points to every slot except the last
   B. the *Beta* sweep points to every slot on every sweep
   C. the *Alpha* points to the first slot of the sweep and the *Beta* points to the rest
   D. the *Alpha* points to the first slot and the *Beta* points to the last slot

9. The differences between the *Alpha* sweep and the *Beta* sweep in an Exchange Sort include all of the following except:
   A. the *Alpha* sweep must be made first and the *Beta* sweep is made next
   B. the *Beta* sweep is repeated while the *Alpha* sweep is not
   C. the *Beta* sweep organizes every item except the first one, while the *Alpha* sweep organizes just the first item
   D. the *Alpha* sweep organizes one item at a time, while the *Beta* sweep does not

10. Following an *Alpha* sweep, how many items are you sure are in the correct order?
   A. 0
   B. 1
   C. 2
   D. all of them

Short Answer

1. An explicit set of instructions is a(n) ______.
2. A programming language is a(n) ______ language because it is precisely defined.
3. A(n) ______ is a generalized method while a(n) ______ is a specialized solution.
4. The ______ of an algorithm defines the setting for its use.
5. A(n) ______ finds the item in a list that is next in order to the *Alpha* item.
6. In a Beta sweep, the ______ property makes sure every item in the list is considered.
7. In a Beta sweep, the ______ property makes sure the sweep is finite.
8. The *Alpha* and the *Beta* in the *Alphabetize CDs* program are called ______.
9. A(n) ______ is the computer term of a set of instructions that repeat.
10. The memory locations of a computer store items, but the contents of these locations contain the ______ of the items.

Exercises

1. Describe the process for subtracting a four-digit number from a five-digit number.
2. Why aren't natural languages such as English good for programming?
3. Using the *Alphabetize CDs* algorithm, define the five properties of an algorithm.
4. Does the instruction "go downhill" have the same problems as "go right"? Explain.
5. What is the purpose of the *Artist_Of*, Step 1, of the *Alphabetize CDs* algorithm?
6. Given the following artists, write down the instructions and steps to put these in order.

   Newton-John, Olivia
   Hill, Faith
   Incubus
   Chapman, Steven Curtis
   Mendelssohn, Felix
7. What would you need to do to arrange the CDs in reverse order instead of alphabetical order? What would you need to do to arrange them in order by copyright?
8. Discuss what you would need to add to the *Alphabetize CDs* algorithm to alphabetize the CDs of Juice Newton, Wayne Newton, and Olivia Newton-John.
9. Explain why *Alpha* doesn't have to reference the last slot.
10. Write a version of the Exchange Sort algorithm to alphabetize CDs in a slotted rack, from last to first order; that is, that has the same result as *Alphabetize CDs*, but from the back end forward.

DIGITIZING COLOR

When we discussed the binary encoding of keyboard characters to create the ASCII representation (Chapter 8), we (and the creators) didn't pay much attention to which bit patterns were associated with which characters. It's true that in ASCII the numerals are encoded in numeric order, and the letter sets are roughly in alphabetical order, but the assignment is largely arbitrary. The specifics of the keyboard character encoding don't matter much (as long as everyone agrees on them) because the bytes are used as units. We rarely manipulate the individual bits that make up the pattern for the characters. For other encodings, however, manipulating the individual bits is essential.

RGB Colors: Binary Representation

Recall that giving the intensities for the three constituent colors—red, green, and blue (RGB)—specifies a color on the monitor. Each of the RGB colors is assigned a byte (8 bits) to record the intensity of that color. But the color intensities are not assigned arbitrarily, like the letter characters in ASCII. Instead, color intensity is represented as a quantity, ranging from 0 (none) through 255 (most intense); the higher the number, the more intense the color. When we want to change the intensity, we just add to or subtract from the values, implying that the encoding should make it simple to perform arithmetic on the intensities. So, RGB intensities are encoded as binary numbers.

Binary Numbers Compared with Decimal Numbers. Binary numbers are different from decimal numbers because they are limited to two digits, 0 and 1, rather than the customary ten digits, 0 through 9. But that is really the only difference. The other features distinguishing binary from decimal relate to that one difference.

For example, in decimal numbers, we use a **place value** representation, where each "place" represents the next higher power of 10, starting from the right.

Place Value in a Decimal Number. Recall that to find the value of a decimal number, the digit in a place is multiplied by the place value and the results are added up. So, in Figure 11.1, for example, the result is one thousand ten, found by adding from right to left: the digit in the 1s place (0) is multiplied by its place value (1), plus the digit in the 10s place (1) is multiplied by its place value (10), and so on: $0 \times 1 + 1 \times 10 + 0 \times 100 + 1 \times 1000$.

Place Value in a Binary Representation. Binary works in exactly the same way except that the base of the power is not 10 but 2, because there are only two digits, not ten. As usual if given a binary representation, we can find the (decimal) value if we multiply the digit times the place value and add the results. See Figure 11.2, which shows that 1010 in binary has the value 10 in decimal: $0 \times 1 + 1 \times 2 + 0 \times 4 + 1 \times 8$.

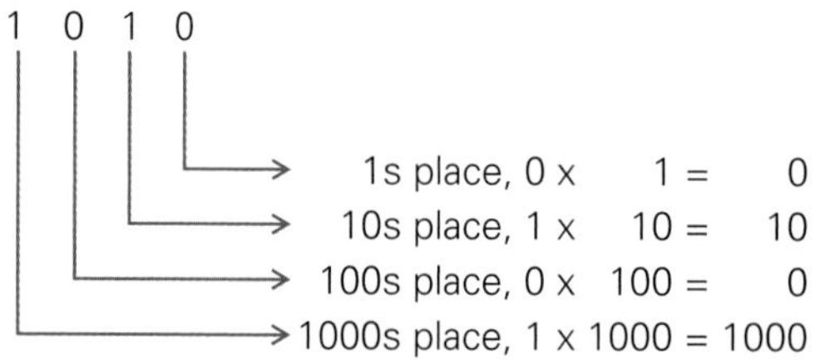

Figure 11.1. *Diagram of the decimal number 1010 representing one thousand ten = 10 + 1000.*

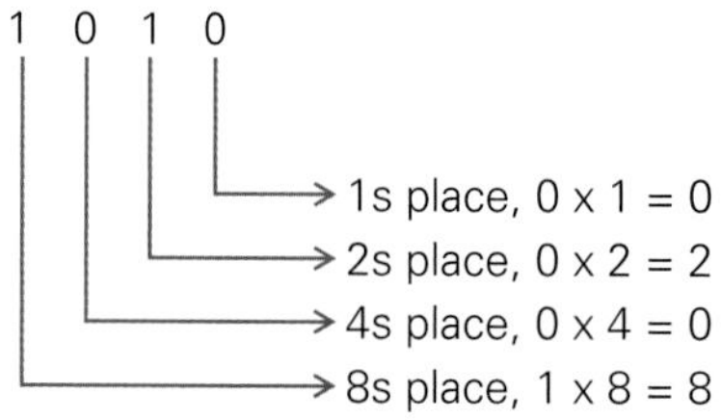

Figure 11.2. *Diagram of the binary number 1010, representing the decimal number ten = 2 + 8.*

> FITBYTE
>
> **2nd Base.** The "base" of a numbering system, 10 for decimal and 2 for binary, is also called its radix.

Because powers of 2 don't increase as fast as powers of 10, binary numbers need more digits than decimal numbers to represent the same amount. So, for example, representing the decimal number 1010 as a binary number requires ten digits: $0 \times 1 + 1 \times 2 + 0 \times 4 + 0 \times 8 + 1 \times 16 + 1 \times 32 + 1 \times 64 + 1 \times 128 + 1 \times 256 + 1 \times 512$. Compare Figure 11.3 with Figure 11.1.

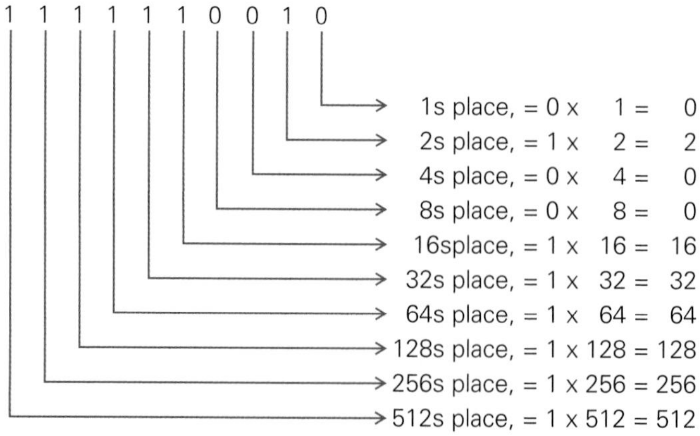

Figure 11.3. *Binary representation of the decimal number one thousand ten = 2 + 16 + 32 + 64 + 128 + 256 + 512.*

Converting a Binary Number to a Decimal Number. Because the digit is either 0 or 1, the "multiply the digit times the place value" rule is especially easy in binary—a 1 means include the place value and a 0 means "forget it." So, to convert a binary number to its decimal equivalent, just add the place values for the places with 1s. Thus, in Figure 11.3, if we start with the highest place value, we have 512 + 256 + 128 + 64 + 32 + 16 + 2 = 1010.

> FITTIP
>
> **Spacing Out.** When writing long decimal numbers, North Americans usually separate groups of three digits with a comma for readability. Binary numbers, which are usually even longer, are usually grouped in four-digit units, separated by a *space*.

Black and White Colors

Returning to the representation of color, the fact that a byte—8 bits—is allocated to each of the RGB intensities means that the smallest intensity is 0000 0000, which is 0, of course, and the largest value is 1111 1111. Figuring out what decimal number this is, we add up the place values for the 1s,

$$\begin{aligned} 1111\ 1111 &= 2^7 + 2^6 + 2^5 + 2^4 + 2^3 + 2^2 + 2^1 + 2^0 \\ &= 128 + 64 + 32 + 16 + 8 + 4 + 2 + 1 \\ &= 255 \end{aligned}$$

which explains why the range of values is 0 through 255 for each color.

As we learned in Chapter 4, black is no color,

0000 0000	0000 0000	0000 0000	*RGB bit assignment for black*
red byte	green byte	blue byte	

whereas white

1111 1111	1111 1111	1111 1111	*RGB bit assignment for white*
red byte	green byte	blue byte	

has full intensity for each. Between these extremes is a whole range of intensity.

Changing a Decimal Number to a Binary Number

As we've seen, to convert a binary number to decimal representation we add up the powers of 2 corresponding to 1 bits. Converting a decimal number x into a binary representation is only slightly harder. Start by finding the largest power of 2 that is less than or equal to the number. For example, for the number 200, the largest power of 2 less than or equal to 200 is $128 = 2^7$ because $256 = 2^8$ is too large.

If the largest power of 2 is 2^d, there will be $d + 1$ digits in the binary result. To find those digits, follow the simple procedure shown in Figure 11.4.

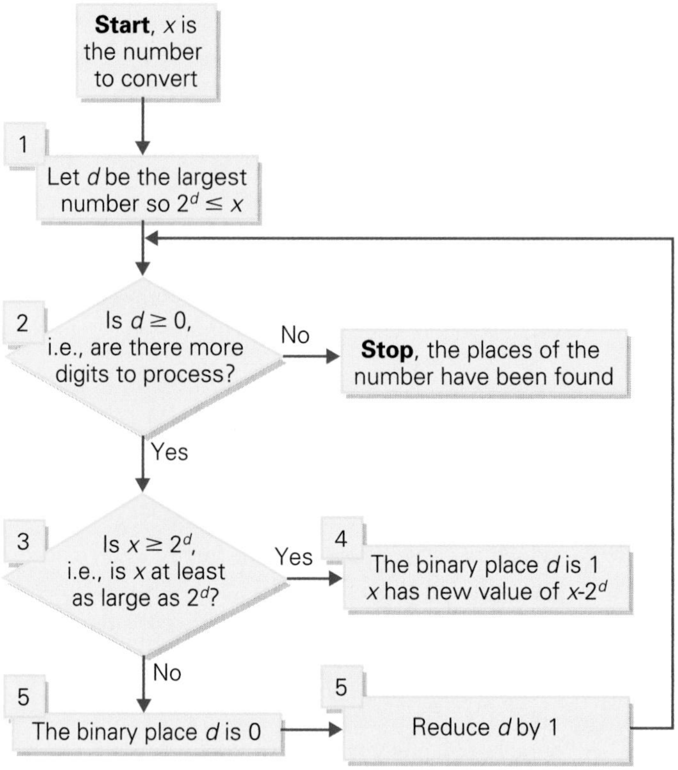

Figure 11.4. *Algorithm to find the bits representing a decimal number x. Begin at Start and follow the operations.*

Build the binary number one place at a time from left to right. At the same time, you are reducing the decimal number by the largest power of 2. The conversion of the decimal number 200 into binary produces the sequence of values shown in Figure 11.5.

Place Number	x	Power of 2	x ≥ 2d	Digit	Comments
7=d	200	$2^7 = 128$	yes	1	Leftmost digit, always 1
6	72	$2^6 = 64$	yes	1	
5	8	$2^5 = 32$	no	0	
4	8	$2^4 = 16$	no	0	
3	8	$2^3 = 8$	yes	1	
2	0	$2^2 = 4$	no	0	
1	0	$2^1 = 2$	no	0	
0	0	$2^0 = 1$	no	0	Rightmost digit

Figure 11.5. *Converting the decimal number 200 into the binary number 1100 1000.*

> **FITTIP** **1 Is First.** The algorithm for converting decimal to binary always produces 1 as its first digit. Why? Because we start at the place corresponding to the largest power of 2 less than the decimal number.

Lighten Up: Changing Color by Addition

Returning to our discussion of color representation, the extreme colors of black and white are easy, but what color does the following represent?

1100 1000	1100 1000	1100 1000
red byte	green byte	blue byte

First we notice that each byte contains the decimal value 200, which we recognize from the conversion in Figure 11.5. So our mystery color is the color produced by the specification `RGB(200, 200, 200)`. In HTML we write this as `#C8C8C8`. Like black and white, our mystery color has equal amounts of red, green, and blue, and it is closer to white than black. In fact, it is a medium gray. All colors with equal amounts of RGB are gray if they are not black or white. It's just a question of whether they're closer to black or white.

To Increase Intensity: Add in Binary

To make a *lighter* color of gray, we obviously change the common value to be closer to white. Suppose we do this by increasing each of the RGB values by 16—that is, by adding 16 to each byte—as shown in Figure 11.6.

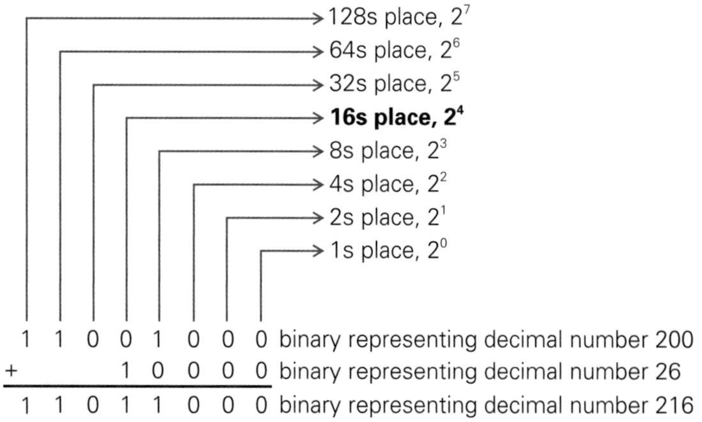

Figure 11.6. *Adding 16 to an RGB value.*

The result in Figure 11.6 is found by simply setting the 16s place value—that is, changing it from 0 to 1. The result

1101 1000	1101 1000	1101 1000
red byte	green byte	blue byte

is a lighter shade of gray.

Lighter Still: Adding with Carry Digits

Imagine that we want the color lighter still by another 16 units of intensity for each RGB byte. Adding another 16 isn't quite as easy this time. The 16s position in the binary representation 1101 1000 of 216 is already filled with a 1. So we "carry" to the next higher place. Thus,

1	← carry digit	
1101 1000	binary representing decimal number	216
+ 1 0000	binary representing decimal number	16
1110 1000	binary representing decimal number	232

So our color intensities are

1101 1000	1101 1000	1101 1000
red byte	green byte	blue byte

Notice that if we'd simply added 32 to 200 originally, we'd have ended up with the same result, the gray with each intensity set at 232 .

The process just illustrated is binary addition. As with other aspects of binary, binary addition is similar to decimal addition. We work from right to left, adding corresponding digits in each place position and writing the sum below. Like decimal addition, there are two cases. Sometimes, we can add the two numbers together and the result is expressed as a single digit. That was the case the first time we added in 16 to the RGB byte: we added 1 + 0 and the result was 1. Other times, when we add two digits together their sum is larger than can be expressed by a single digit, so we must carry to the next higher places. That was the case the second time we added in 16 to the RGB byte: we added 1 + 1 and got 0 with a carry to the next higher digit. Because there may be a carry involved, it is best to think of adding as involving three digits in each place: the two digits being added plus (possibly) a carry.

The rules for binary addtion can be learned using an example for each case.

The first example—called the "no carry-in" case—adds A + B when A is the binary number 1100, which is 12 in decimal, and B is 1010, which is 10 in decimal.

↓↓↓↓	——	Illustrates the "no carry-in" cases
1 0000	←	Carry, shown explicitly
1100	←	A
+ 1010	←	B
1 0110	←	Sum

The four cases of adding binary digits—all combinations of 0 and 1—are illustrated. In each case there is no *carry-in*—that is, no carry from the previous place. The only interesting case is 1 + 1. Of course, in decimal 1 + 1 = 2. But in binary, there is no 2 digit, only 0 and 1, so the result of 1 + 1 cannot be expressed by a single digit. The decimal number 2 is 10 in binary, so we put down the 0 in the first position and carry the 1 to the next higher position. The carry to the next higher digit is called a *carry-out,* and we notice that the carry-out of one place becomes the carry-in of the next higher place. (Verify that the sum is the binary representation of 22 = 12 + 10.)

The second example, the "carry-in" case, adds A + B when A is 1011, which is 11 in decimal, and 111, which is 7 in decimal. Leading 0's will be shown to complete the picture, and the rightmost place adds 1 + 1 to get the "carrying process" started.

```
↓ ↓↓↓──── Illustrates the "carry-in" cases
 1 1110 ← Carry, shown explicitly
 0 1011 ← A
+0 0111 ← B
 ──────
 1 0010 ← Sum
```

The four cases illustrate adding binary digits with a carry-in. Three of the four have the property that the sum of the two digits and the carry are too large to be expressed by a single binary digit, so there is a carry-out to the next higher place. Only the leftmost case, 0 + 0 with a carry-in, can be expressed by a single digit, 1. The new case is the second from right position, which adds 1 + 1 with a carry-in yielding the decimal 3 or binary 11. We write down the 1 in the place and carry-out a 1 to the next higher position. (Verify that the sum is the binary representation of 18 = 11 + 7.)

The rules from the examples are summarized in Table 11.1 We can now apply the rules to add the binary numbers 110 1001 and 110 0011. (What decimal numbers are these?) This time, we follow the usual procedure of showing only the nonzero carries.

```
 11     11    ← Carry
  110 1001    ← A
+ 110 0011    ← B
 ─────────
 1100 1100    ← Sum
```

Binary addition is so easy, even computers can do it.

Table 11.1. *Summary of the rules for binary addition. The carry-in is added to the two operands, A and B, to give the place digit and the carry-out.*

Carry-in	0	0	0	0	1	1	1	1
A	0	1	0	1	0	1	0	1
B	0	0	1	1	0	0	1	1
Place digit	0	1	1	0	1	0	0	1
Carry-out	0	0	0	1	0	1	1	1

Overflow

Because computers use fixed-size bit sequences (for example, a byte is 8 bits long), an interesting question is what happens when there is a carry-out of the most significant bit—that is, the leftmost bit. For example, 255 + 5 in binary is

```
    1111 1111
  + 0000 0101
  -----------
  1 0000 0100
```

But 260 needs 9 bits, one bit too many to fit into a byte. Such situations are called *overflow exceptions*. Computers report them when the computation they're told to perform overflows, and it is up to the programmer to plan for that. Usually programmers try to avoid the situation by choosing large bit fields.

COMPUTING ON REPRESENTATIONS

Though we have focused on binary representation, conversions between decimal and binary, and binary addition, the previous sections have also introduced another fundamental concept of digital representation—the idea of *computing on a representation*. That is, when we made gray lighter, we were showing how digital information—for example, the RGB settings of a pixel—could be changed through computation because we could have made every shade of gray in the image lighter by the same process. Consider a more involved example, for a better understanding of the idea.

Changing the Colors of a Moon Photo

Imagine that you have scanned into your computer a black-and-white photo you took of the moon, similar to Figure 11.7(a). This is a memento from last weekend when you were out with your friends, and you tried connecting your camera to Jaime's telescope. Unfortunately, you only had black-and-white film loaded, so you missed the gorgeous orange of the close-to-the-horizon moon. In the computer, the pixels of your photo form a long sequence of RGB triples. What values do they have?

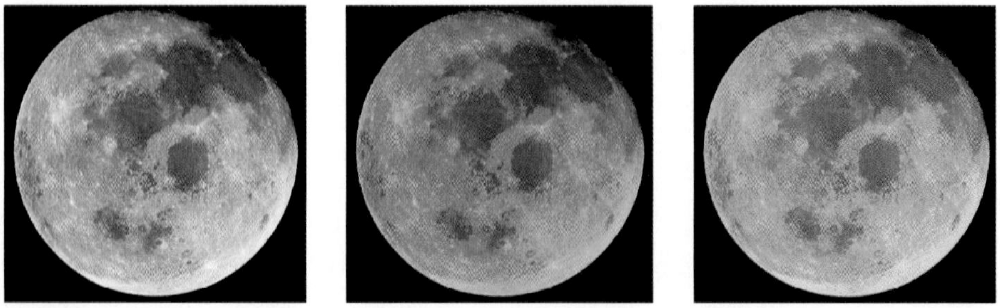

(a) (b) (c)

Figure 11.7. *Moon photographs. (a) The original black-and-white picture, (b) tinted version of original, (c) with boosted highlights.*

Because they are all black, white, or gray, it's easy to guess. There is the (0,0,0) of the black night sky, the (255,255,255) of the brightest part of the moon, some light gray values very close to white—for example, (234,234,234)—of the craters and *marae* of the moon, and some dark gray values very close to black—for example, (28,28,28)—from the smudge left on the glass when someone scanned in a burrito. What you would like to do is email a colorized version of your photo to your friends, similar to Figure 11.7(c).

Removing the Smudges. To create the picture, you must remove the smudges and transform the pixels of the black-and-white image into the colors that you remember. The first task is easy because any value "close" to black can be changed to be true black by replacing it with (0,0,0). But what does *close* mean? The example dark gray value (28,28,28) is represented in binary as

`0001 1100 0001 1100 0001 1100`

Though other dark gray values may be somewhat larger or smaller, it is a safe guess that any dark gray pixel will have the most significant (leftmost) 2 bits of each of its RGB bytes set to 00. That's because, from the binary representation, a byte whose most significant two bits are 00 is less than 64—that is, less than one quarter of the magnitude of full intensity—and any pixel all of whose colors are less than a quarter magnitude must be a darker color.

To change the smudges to pure black, we go through the image looking at each pixel and testing to see if the first 2 bits of each of its bytes are 00. If they are, we set each byte to 0. Recalling our substitution arrow from Chapter 2, we describe this operation as

`00xx xxxx 00xx xxxx 00xx xxxx` ← `0000 0000 0000 0000 0000 0000`

where *x* is a standard symbol for "don't care" or "wildcard"—that is, a symbol matching either 0 or 1. So the substitution statement says "Any three RGB bytes, each of whose first 2 bits are 00, are replaced with all zeros." Making that substitution throughout the image removes the digitized smudge. (Notice that that was an algorithm.)

Making the Moon Orange. Similarly, turning the moon to orange involves changing the white pixels (255,255,255). You decide that the orange of the moon ( ) must be about the color represented by (255,213,132). Changing all of the white pixels to this orange color requires the substitution

`255 255 255` ← `255 213 132`

or, in binary,

`1111 1111 1111 1111 1111 1111` ← `1111 1111 1101 0101 1000 0100`

to produce an orange moon. But it will not change the gray of the craters, because they are not pure white and therefore won't be modified by this replacement. If, like changing the dark gray to black, the very light gray were changed to this orange too, all of the beautiful detail of the craters would be lost. How do we get the white changed to orange and the gray changed to the appropriate orange-tinted gray?

Light Gray into Orange Tint. Though there are many very sophisticated ways to adjust color, the technique that we'll use is to change any light gray into orange in three steps:

> Red byte—leave unchanged

> Green byte—subtract 42 from the green value; that is, reduce the green slightly

> Blue byte—subtract 123 from the blue value; that is, reduce the blue quite a bit

Thus, the light gray color (234,234,234) would be changed into (234,192,111), and the slightly darker light gray (228,228,228) would change into (228,186,105), a slightly grayer orange. These numbers were computed by noting how white (255,255,255) changed into the chosen orange (255,213,132): the red byte was unchanged, the green byte was reduced by 42, and the blue byte was reduced by 123. If all pixels having the most significant bit of each RGB byte equal 1 (that is, the white pixels and all the light gray pixels) are changed by this three-step process, the white areas would become orange and the gray parts would become grayish orange.

You have cleaned up the smudge and colorized the moon, as shown in Figure 11.7(b).

Boosting the Red. Now you inspect your work and decide that the gray parts of the moon are really not as luminous as you remembered. So, you decide to boost the red. If the red in all of the orange pixels is shifted to 255, the moon's craters look too red and "unnatural." But a compromise is to "split the difference." That is, if the current value of the red byte in an orange tint is 234, say, half the difference between it and pure red—(255 – 234)/2 = 10.5—could be added on to get 244. (You need whole numbers, so drop the "point 5.") Thus, the two example tints (234,192,111) and (228,186,105) become (244,192,111) and (241,186,105), respectively. This process brightens the craters without making them unnatural, as demonstrated in Figure 11.7(c). The resulting image looks great, and you can attach it to your email to your friends.

Image Processing Summary

Summarizing, we have computed on a digital representation. We have taken a real photograph scanned into the computer and created an artificial image. First, we improved it by removing the smudges. Then, we colorized it by changing white and light gray into orange and corresponding shades of orange-gray. Finally, we boosted the red in the orange-gray tints to make it a little brighter. We discussed these changes as if you were writing a program, which you could do, but image processing software like Photoshop lets you do this through menu choices like Saturation, Brightness, Hue, and so forth. Such software manipulates the pixels with transformations like those described here, as well as in much more sophisticated ways. The result is not the photograph you would have taken had there been color film in the camera, but rather a different image, a synthetic image closer to what you remember or prefer. It is definitely not reality . . . because we could have just as easily made "the man in the moon" smile.

DIGITIZING SOUND

In this section we learn about digitizing, though this time we focus on digitizing sound rather than images because it is slightly easier and equally interesting. The principles are the same when digitizing any "continuous" information.

An object—think of a cymbal—creates sound, as we know, by vibrating in some medium such as air. The vibrations push the air, causing pressure waves to emanate from the object, which in turn vibrate our eardrums. The vibrations are transmitted by three tiny bones to the fine hairs of our cochlea, stimulating nerves that allow us to sense the waves and "hear" them as sound. The force or intensity of the push determines the volume, and the **frequency** (the number of waves per second) of the pushes is the pitch. Figure 11.8 shows a graph of a sound wave, where the horizontal axis shows time and the vertical axis shows the amount of positive or negative sound pressure.

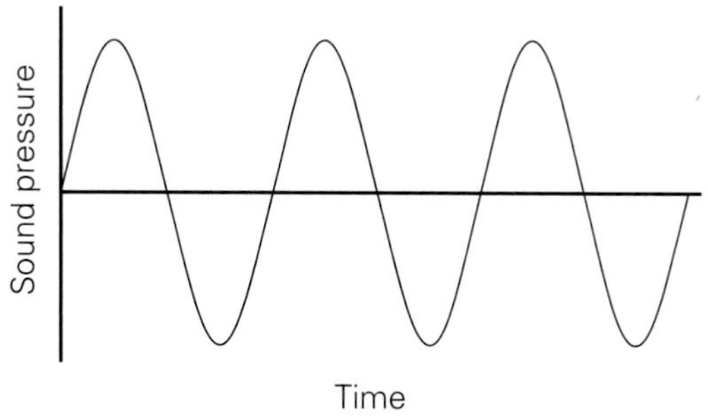

Figure 11.8. *Sound wave. The horizontal axis is time; the vertical axis is sound pressure.*

From a digitization point of view, the key is that the object vibrates *continuously,* producing a continuously changing wave. That is, as the wave moves past, say, a microphone, the measured pressure changes smoothly. When this pressure variation is recorded directly, as it was originally by Edison with a scratch on a wax cylinder, or with the more recent vinyl records, we have a continuous (**analog**) representation of the wave. In principle, all of the continuous variation of the wave has been recorded. Digital representations work differently.

Analog to Digital

To digitize continuous information, we must convert to bits. For a sound wave, we can record with a binary number the amount by which the wave is above or below the 0 line at a given point. But at what point do we measure? There are infinitely many points along the line, too many to record every position of the wave.

Sampling. So, we **sample**, which means we take measurements at regular intervals. The number of samples in a second is called the **sampling rate**, and the faster the rate, the more accurately the wave is recorded (see Figure 11.9).

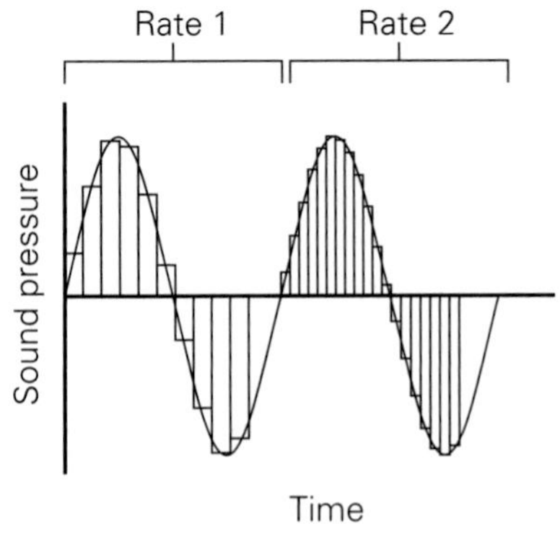

Figure 11.9. *Two sampling rates; the rate on the right is twice as fast as that on the left.*

How Fast a Sampling Rate? To get a good recording of the wave, we need a sampling rate that is related to the wave's frequency. For example, if a sampling were too slow, the sound wave could "fit between" the samples: we'd be missing important segments of the sound.

Fortunately, we have guidelines for the sampling rates. In electrical engineering, the Nyquist Rule says that a sampling rate must be at least twice as fast as the fastest frequency. And what is the fastest frequency we should expect? Because human perception can hear sound up to roughly 20,000 Hz, a 40,000 Hz sampling rate fulfills the Nyquist Rule for digital audio recording. For technical reasons, however, a somewhat faster-than-two-times sampling rate was chosen for digital audio, 44,100 Hz.

ADC, DAC. The digitizing process works as follows: The sound is picked up by a microphone, called a transducer because it converts the sound wave into an electrical wave. This electrical signal is fed into an **analog-to-digital converter** (ADC), which takes the continuous wave and samples it at regular intervals, outputting for each sample binary numbers to be written to memory.

The process is reversed to play the sound: The numbers are read from memory into a **digital-to-analog converter** (DAC), which creates an electrical wave by interpolation between the digital values—that is, filling in or smoothly moving from one value to another. The electrical signal is then input to a speaker, which converts it into a sound wave, as shown in Figure 11.10.

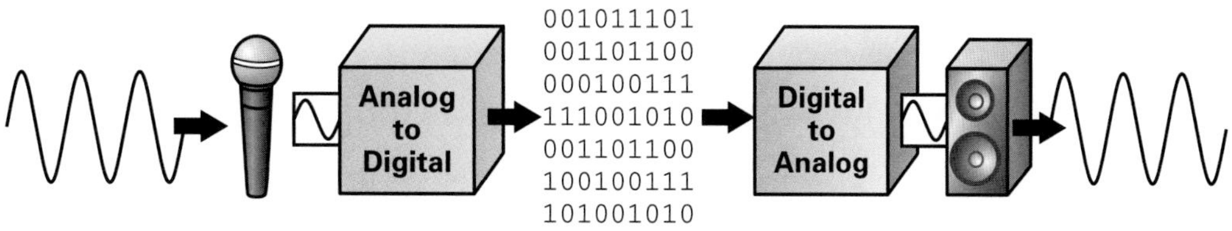

Figure 11.10. *Schematic for analog-to-digital and digital-to-analog conversion.*

`How Many Bits per Sample?` The problem of digitizing is solved except for describing how accurate the samples must be. To make the samples perfectly accurate, we would need an unlimited number of bits for each sample, which is impossible. But to start, we know that the bits must represent both positive and negative values, because the wave has both positive and negative sound pressure. Second, the more bits there are, the more accurate the measurement will be. For example, with only 3 bits, one of which is used to indicate whether the sign is + or –, we could encode one of four positions in either direction (they align at 0). With so few bits, we can only get an approximate measurement, as shown in Figure 11.11(a). If we used another bit, the sample would be twice as accurate. (In Figure 11.11(b), each interval is half as wide, making the illustrated crossing in the "upper" half of the interval.)

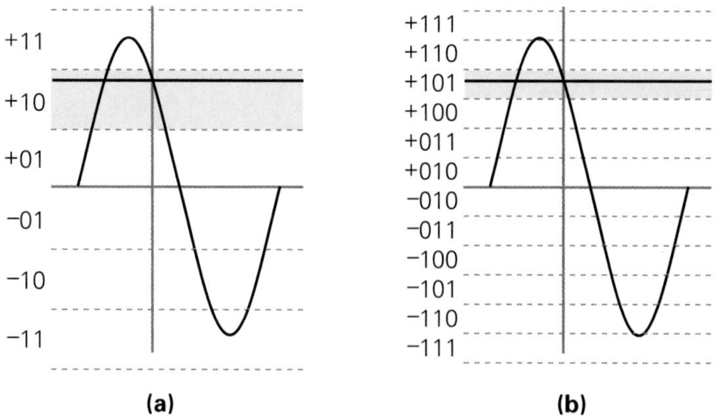

Figure 11.11. *(a) Three-bit precision for samples requires that the indicated reading be approximated as +10. (b) Adding another bit makes the sample twice as accurate.*

Using more bits yields a more accurate digitization. The digital representation of audio CDs uses 16 bits, meaning that 2^{16} = 65,536 levels are recorded, 2^{15} = 32,768 for positive values and 32,768 for negative values.

FITBYTE

Unforgiving Minute. How many bits does it take to record a minute of digital audio? There are 60 seconds of 44,100 samples of 16 bits each, times 2 for stereo. That's 84,672,000 bits, or 10,584,000 bytes, more than 10 megabytes! An hour is 635 MB!

Advantages of Digital Sound

A key advantage of digital information (as demonstrated in the last section) is that we can compute on the representation.

MP3 Compression. One computation of value would be to *compress* the digital audio; that is, reduce the number of bits needed to represent the information. For example, an orchestra produces many sounds that the human ear can't hear—some too high and some too low. Our ADC still encodes these frequencies—not to annoy our dog, but simply as part of the encoding process. By computing special functions on the digital audio representation, it is possible to remove these waves without harming the way the audio sounds to us. This is the sort of compression used for MP3. In MP3 we typically get a **compression ratio** of more than 10:1, which means that the number of bits has been reduced to less than one-tenth what it was. So a minute of MP3 music typically takes less than a megabyte to represent. This makes MP3 popular for Internet transmission, because it has lower bandwidth requirements. We discuss bandwidth—the rate at which bits are transmitted—shortly.

We can "fix" a recording in the same way we "fixed" our moon picture. If someone coughs during a quiet moment of Verdi's *Requiem*, we can remove the offending noise from the recording. Performances can be sped up or slowed down without affecting pitch, and so on.

FITBYTE

MP3. The "sound track" of a digital video in the MPEG representation is known as MPEG level 3, or MP3.

Reproducing the Sound Recording. Another key advantage of digital representations over analog is that they can be reproduced exactly. We can copy the file of bits that make up an audio performance, without losing a single bit of information. Further, when the original and the copy are played by the same system, they will sound exactly the same. With analog storage, the copy is never as exact as the original, and a second (or third or hundredth) playing of the same version is never as good as the first because of wear. Digital recordings never have these problems as long as the bits remain stable.

FITBYTE

Word Search. Searching digital audio for a segment of sound, though possible in principle, is impossible in practice because we have to specify the search string. Thus, in Chapter 6, we searched Fuller's *Everything I Know* recordings not by searching the audio, but by searching the textual transcript of the audio.

DIGITAL IMAGES AND VIDEO

Recall from our discussion of the moon picture that an image is a long sequence of RGB pixels. Of course, the picture is two-dimensional, but we think of the pixels stretched out one row after another in memory, which is one-dimensional. How many pixels are there? For an 8 × 10 image scanned at 300 pixels per inch, there are 80 square inches, each requiring 300 × 300 = 90,000 pixels for a grand total of 7.2 megapixels. At 3 bytes per pixel, it takes 21.6 MB of memory to store one 8 × 10 color image. That's more memory than personal computers came with until recently. Sending such a picture across a standard 56 Kb/s modem—that's kilo*bits* per second—would take at least 21,600,000 × 8 / 56,000 = 3085 seconds, or more than 51 minutes (longer than the average college class). So, how can we see screen-size pictures in seconds when we're surfing the Web?

JPEG Compression

First, a typical computer screen has only about 100 pixels per inch, not 300, which is a factor of 9 savings in memory. But this isn't quite the simplification we need, first because a picture that size still takes more than five and a half minutes to send, and second because once received, we might want to print the picture out, requiring the resolution again. Luckily, electrical engineers invented the **JPEG** compression scheme. *JPEG* stands for "Joint Photographic Experts Group," a nickname for an International Standards Organization (ISO) team that guides the development of digital representation of still photographs.

Compression means to change the representation to use fewer bits to store or transmit information. For example, faxes are usually long sequences of 0's and 1's encoding where the page is white or black. Rather than sending all of the 0's and 1's, we can use run-length encoding to take advantage of the fact that there are long sequences of 0's and 1's. **Run-length encoding** uses binary numbers to specify how long the first sequence (run) of 0's is, then how long the following sequence of 1's is, then how long the following sequence of 0's is, and so on. This works best for long, not short, sequences of 0's and 1's, and most of the time run-length compression is a big win. Run-length encoding is a **lossless compression** scheme, meaning that the original representation of 0's and 1's can be exactly reconstructed. The opposite of lossless compression is **lossy compression**, meaning that the original representation cannot be exactly reconstructed from the compressed form. MP3 is lossy because the high notes cannot be recovered—but it doesn't matter since we can't hear them.

JPEG compression is used for still images. Our eyes are not very sensitive to small changes in hue (chrominance), but we are quite sensitive to small changes in brightness (luminance). This means we can store a less accurate description of the hue of a picture (fewer bits) and, though this compression technique is lossy, our eyes won't notice the difference. With JPEG compression we can get a 20:1 compression ratio or more, compared to an uncompressed still image, without being able to see a difference. For example, if there is a large area of very similar hues (for example, sky), they can all be "lumped together" as the same hue without our noticing. Then, we can apply run-length compression, which wouldn't have worked well with many slight variations in hue, to get further compression. The handy feature of JPEG compression is that we can control the amount of compression: Image compression software will give us a control—a slider or dial, say—so we can choose the amount of compression. Fiddling with the control allows us to determine visually how much more compression can be applied without seriously affecting the look of the image.

MPEG Compression Scheme

MPEG, the compression scheme of the Motion Picture Experts Group of the ISO, is the same idea applied to motion pictures. On the one hand, it seems like an easier task because each image—each frame—will not be seen for very long, so we should be able to get away with even greater levels of single-image compression. On the other hand, the problem seems worse because it takes so many stills to make a movie. In MPEG compression, JPEG-type compression is applied to each frame, but then "interframe coherency" is used. That is, because two consecutive video images will usually be very similar, MPEG compression only has to record and transmit the "differences" between frames. This results in huge amounts of compression, so MPEG only needs moderate amounts of bandwidth.

OPTICAL CHARACTER RECOGNITION

On toll roads now, computers watch cars going by, read their license plates, find accounts for the car in a database, and deduct the toll from the "car's" account. It sure beats stopping every few miles to pay a few more coins! The interesting aspect of this technology is that there is no bar code or electronic transponder; a computer simply recognizes the letters of the license plate. Reading license plates is very easy for humans, but it's a big deal for computers.

Consider some of the difficulties. First, the computer needs an image of the license plate, but the camera is pointed at the highway, getting many images that are not license plates—the scene, parts of cars, trailers, litter, road-kill before it is road-kill, and so on. An electronic device called a **frame grabber** recognizes when to "snap" the image and ship it to the computer for processing. Assuming a frame with a license plate in it has been snapped, the computer must next figure out where in the image it is, because there is no standard location for a license plate on a vehicle, and even if there were, the vehicle could be changing lanes. Looking for letters and numbers doesn't work, because some vehicles display bumper stickers or advertising. Once the license plate is found, recognizing its characters is the most significant challenge, because they're not yet characters, but thousands of pixels.

Happily, license plate colors are chosen to be high contrast, for example, dark letters on a light background. The computer scans groups of pixels looking for edges where the color changes. It forms these into features. A *feature* is a part of a character to be recognized. For example, a *P* might be described by the features of a "vertical stroke" and a "hole" at the top of the stroke, because lines and holes are patterns that could be recognized by noting where color changes. Given the features, a **classifier** matches the features to the alphabet to determine which are close, perhaps finding a strong correlation with *P*, a weaker one with *9*, and a still weaker one with *D*. Finally, after picking the most likely characters, an optical character recognizer usually checks the context, trying to decide if the combination makes sense; for example, has a license been issued with that combination of letters? Finding the number in the database, the computer figures it has read the plate right and debits the account.

FITBYTE

Beginning Reader. In 1954, J. Rainbow demonstrated an optical character reader that could recognize uppercase typewritten characters at the rate of one letter per minute.

OCR Technology

Optical character recognition (*OCR*) is a very sophisticated technology that enables a computer to "read" printed characters. OCR's business applications are sorting mail and banking. The U.S. Postal Service uses a system that locates the address block on an envelope or card, reads it in any of 400 fonts, identifies its ZIP code, generates a nine-digit bar code, sprays the bars on the envelope, sorts it, and, with only a 2 percent error rate, processes up to 45,000 pieces of mail per hour. In banking, where the magnetic numbers at the bottom of the check have been read by computers since the 1950s, OCR is now used to read the *handwritten* digits of the numeric check amount to verify that a data entry person has interpreted the amount correctly.

VIRTUAL REALITY: FOOLING THE SENSES

The ultimate form of digital representation is to create an entire digital world. The idea has become known as virtual reality (VR). So far, VR has less to do with representing the world and more to do with fooling our senses into perceiving something that doesn't exist.

Rapidly displaying still images is a standard way to fool our eyes and brain into seeing motion. Virtual reality applies that idea to our other senses and tries to

{GREAT FIT MOMENTS}

Text-to-speech technology >>

Perhaps the most significant application of optical character recognition, however, is Raymond Kurzweil's text-to-speech reading machines developed for the blind and partially sighted. Produced in 1976, the reading machine uses a flatbed scanner—a technology originally developed by Kurzweil—to scan reading material, recognize it as text, and then speak it using a voice synthesizer. Scanning, font-independent optical character recognition, large-vocabulary dictionaries, and speech synthesis are by now standard technologies that Kurzweil had to create for his devices. For the disabled, the reader, and its inverse, the speech-to-text machine, have dramatically improved personal lives and career opportunities. Says the blind musician Stevie Wonder, who credits the reader with changing his life, "It gave blind people the one life goal that everyone treasures, and that is independence."

Raymond Kurzweil received the National Medal of Science and the Lemelson–MIT Award for Innovation, which is like a Nobel Prize for inventors.

eliminate the cues that keep us grounded in reality. For example, when we see a TV scene of a train coming toward us, we know by various cues, such as peripheral vision, that we're watching a TV; we see the motion but we're not fooled. However, if we're wearing a helmet with a TV in front of each eye that shows the train in a complete scene, gives us three-dimensional vision, and fills in our peripheral vision as well so that when we move our head we can look at other parts of the scene, the cues are reduced or eliminated. Add high-quality audio in each ear and a treadmill so that we seem to be walking or running through the scene, and it's easy to imagine how a computer could effectively fool us into thinking the train is chasing us.

Haptic Devices

Certain deceptions are more useful. **Haptic devices** are input/output technology for interacting with our sense of touch and feel. For example, a haptic glove enables a computer to detect where our fingers are and to apply force against them. When we bring our fingers close enough together, the glove stops their movement, leaving us with the feeling of holding something. With haptic gloves and the VR helmet, a computer can show us Legos in space, which, when we grab them, gives us the sensation of holding them and makes us think we are assembling them. When the glove pulls down on our fingers, we think the Legos are heavy, perhaps made of metal. Though the world is virtual, it is credible to us. Such technology can be used to train surgeons for complex operations, for example.

FITBYTE

Virtual Meaning. The term *virtual* is used often in IT—for example, virtual memory—because the computer produces a believable illusion of something that doesn't exist. *Virtual* means "not actually but just as if."

The Challenge of Latency

The challenge with virtual reality and other sophisticated output devices like video is for the system to operate fast enough and precisely enough to appear natural. We know that when still images are presented in an animation too slowly, the illusion of motion is lost. When that happens in a VR system—when we turn our head but the scene doesn't smoothly change—we can get dizzy, maybe even sick. Our sensation of touch and feel actually operates faster than the 30 Hz standard for visual perception, closer to 1000 Hz. Thus, when we "see" our virtual hand going to pick up a virtual Lego, we must "feel" it before we "see" it if the illusion is to work.

This phenomenon is called **latency**—the time it takes for information to be delivered. We are familiar with long latencies when Web pages are not delivered instantly, but the phenomenon arises wherever information must be transmitted or generated. In most cases, as with Web pages, long latencies just make us wait, but in video, VR, voice communication, and so on, long latency can ruin the medium. Reducing latency is a common engineering goal, but there is an absolute limit to how fast information can be transmitted: the speed of light. Eventually, the virtual world is constrained by the physical world.

The Challenge of Bandwidth

Closely related to latency is **bandwidth**—a measure of how much information can be transmitted per second. Bandwidth is related to latency in that a given amount of information (for example, 100 KB) transmitted with a given bandwidth (for example, 50 KB/s) determines the (best) latency by dividing the amount by the bandwidth; in this case, 100 / 50 = 2, or 2 seconds of latency. Other delays can extend the latency beyond this theoretical best. Higher bandwidth usually means lower latency. (The rule eventually fails for speed-of-light and switching-delay reasons.) So, faster modems mean that Web pages load faster.

VR is a developing technology. It is still challenged by both latency and bandwidth limitations—it takes many, many bytes to represent a synthetic world. Creating them and delivering them to our senses is a difficult technical problem. Nevertheless, it is an exciting future application of IT.

BITS ARE IT

Looking back over this and previous chapters, we have seen that 4 bytes, say, can represent many kinds of information from four ASCII keyboard characters to numbers between zero and about 4 billion. This is not an accident, but rather a fundamental property of information, which we will summarize in this principle:

> **Bias-free Universal Medium Principle:** Bits can represent all discrete information; bits have no inherent meaning.

Bits: The Universal Medium

The first half of the principle—all discrete information can be represented by bits—is the universality aspect. Discrete things—things that can be separated from each other—can be represented by bits. At the very least, we can assign numbers to each one and represent those numbers in binary. But, as we saw with color, it is possible to be far smarter. We assigned the RGB colors so the intensity could be increased or decreased using binary arithmetic. This representation of color is much more organized than simply saying, "Black will be 0, purple will be 1, yellow will be 2, puce will be 3," and so on. As a result of organizing the representation in a sensible way, we can *easily* compute on it, making changes like brightening the image. Of course, if the information is continuous—that is, if it is analog information like sound—it must first be made discrete by an analog-to-digital conversion. But once digitized, this information, too, can be represented by bits.

Bits: Bias-Free

The second half of the principle—bits have no inherent meaning—is the bias-free aspect. Given a bit sequence

0000 0000 1111 0001 0000 1000 0010 0000

there is no way to know what information it represents. The meaning of the bits comes entirely from the *interpretation* placed on them by us or by the computer through our programs. For example, the 4 bytes could be a zero byte followed by the RGB intensities (241,8,32) ■. Or, the 4 bytes could be an instruction to add two binary numbers. As a binary number, the bits work out to 15,796,256.

So, bits are bits. What they mean depends only on how the software interprets them, which means they work for any kind of information. Storage media need only store one pair of patterns: 0 and 1. The principle explains why, for example, a single transmission medium—the TCP/IP packet—is all that's needed to deliver any kind of information across the Internet to your computer: text, photos, MP3 tunes.

Bits Are Not Necessarily Binary Numbers

Since the public first became aware of computers, it's been "common knowledge" that computers represent information as binary *numbers*. Experts reinforce this view, but it's not quite right. Computers represent information as bits. Bits can be *interpreted* as binary numbers, as we've seen, which is why the experts are not wrong. But the bits do not always represent binary numbers. They can be interpreted as ASCII characters, RGB colors, or an unlimited list of other things (see Figure 11.12). Programs often perform arithmetic on the bits, as we saw when we modified the moon image; but often they do not, because it doesn't make sense with the intended interpretation of the information. Computers represent information with bits. They are an amazing medium.

0000 0000 1111 0001 0000 1000 0010 0000 = 15,796,256 interpreted as a binary number
= ■ interpreted as an RGB(241,8,32) color (last 3 bytes)
= ADD 1,7,17 interpreted as a MIPS machine instruction
= NU BS ƀñ interpreted as 8-bit ASCII— null, backspace, n-tilde, blank
= L: +241, R: +280 interpreted as sound samples
= 0.241.8.32 interpreted as an IP address
= 00 F1 08 20 interpreted as a hexadecimal number

Figure 11.12. *Illustration of the principle that "bits are bits."*
The same 4 bytes shown can be interpreted differently depending on context.

SUMMARY

In this chapter we have considered how different forms of information are represented in the computer. In the case of RGB color, we learned that each intensity is a 1-byte numeric quantity represented as a binary number. Binary representation and binary arithmetic are like decimal but are limited to two digits. We found the decimal equivalent of binary numbers by adding up their powers of 2 corresponding to 1's; and by using a simple algorithm, we did the reverse to find binary from decimal. We used arithmetic on the intensities to "compute on the representation," making gray lighter and colorizing a black-and-white picture of the moon. Much more exotic computations on images are possible in photographic software, but the principles are the same.

Next we considered how to digitize sound as an illustration of all analog-to-digital conversion. Sampling rate and measurement precision determine how accurate the digital form is; uncompressed audio requires more than 80 million bits per minute. We learned how compression makes large files manageable: JPEG for still pictures and MPEG for video. These more compact representations work because they remove information people don't miss. We took a quick look at optical character recognition, and noted that it is a technology that makes the world better. Our discussion of virtual reality illustrated the complexities of conveying information to all of our senses at once. Finally, we emphasized that much of the magic of computers is embodied in the universality of bit representations and the unbiased way they encode, the Bias-free Universal Medium Principle.

EXERCISES

Multiple Choice

1. Each RGB color intensity ranges from:
   A. 0-15
   B. 0-255
   C. 1-16
   D. 1-256
2. The RGB setting for blue is (0 is off, 1 is on):
   A. 0000 0000 0000 0000 0000 0000
   B. 1111 1111 0000 0000 0000 0000
   C. 0000 0000 1111 1111 0000 0000
   D. 0000 0000 0000 0000 1111 1111
3. Analog information is:
   A. discrete
   B. continuous
   C. random
   D. digital
4. According to the Nyquist Rule, the sampling rate of sound is roughly:
   A. half of what humans can hear
   B. the same as what humans can hear
   C. twice what humans can hear
   D. three times what humans can hear
5. The accuracy of a digitized sound is determined by:
   A. the sampling rate
   B. the bit rate
   C. the size of the digitized file
   D. all of the above
6. A digital-to-analog converter:
   A. changes digital information to analog sound
   B. converts continuous sound to digital sound
   C. converts sound to an electrical signal
   D. sets approximated values
7. MP3 is the sound information of
   A. MPEG movies
   B. all digital movies
   C. all computer sound
   D. all digital computer sound

8. Jessica Simpson's "A Little Bit" is 3 minutes 47 seconds long. How many bits is that?
   A. 1,411,200
   B. 40,042,800
   C. 84,672,000
   D. 320,342,400

9. OCR is used in all of the following areas except:
   A. text-to-speech recognition
   B. ZIP code recognition
   C. supermarket checkout
   D. bank account recognition

10. Raymond Kurzweil is known as the inventor of:
    A. OCR
    B. text-to-speech recognition
    C. image compression
    D. virtual reality

Short Answer

1. When all the RGB color settings are set to 0, the color displayed is ______.
2. The first digit of a binary number is always ______.
3. ______ is the term used when digital values are converted to create an analog sound.
4. ______ sound removes the highest and lowest samplings as part of its compression algorithm.
5. A(n) ______ is used to convert analog sound to digital values.
6. ______ is a compression scheme for digital video while ______ is the scheme for digital images.
7. ______ is the group that oversees the development of digital media standards.
8. On the computer, ______ means to store or transmit information with fewer bits.
9. A process that allows the computer to "read" printed characters is called ______.
10. Conversion of the written word to speech is called ______.
11. The creation of a digital representation of the world is called ______.
12. JPEG is to still images what ______ is to motion pictures.
13. ______ are used with computers to control a person's sense of touch.
14. ______ is the time it takes information to be delivered.
15. The ______ states that bits can represent all discrete information even though the bits have no meaning of their own.

Exercises

1. Write the algorithm for converting from decimal to binary.
2. Write the algorithm for converting from binary to decimal.
3. Add 1492 and 1776 in binary and display the answer in binary.
4. In binary, add 1011, 1001, 110, and 1100.
5. Convert RGB 200, 200, 200 to hex C8C8C8 by converting it to binary and then to hex.
6. Add 168 and 123 in binary. How many bytes does it take to represent each number? How many bytes are needed for the answer? What happens if there aren't enough bytes to store the answer?
7. Software is now in use that can let you "try on" a dress virtually. What process would be used to change that bright red, taffeta dress into a soft pink? What would be needed to change it to sea foam (light green)? What would it take to turn it into a color to match your eyes?
8. Explain how a picture at 300 pixels per inch could be converted to a picture with 100 pixels per inch.
9. Most music is now sold on CD-ROM. Explain how a singer's voice in the recording studio goes to the earphones on your computer? Why are both processes needed for this to succeed?
10. Digitally, what would need to be done to raise (or lower) a singer's voice an octave?
11. Why are JPEG, MPEG, and MP3 considered algorithms?
12. To the computer, bits are bits. To a page, letters are letters. Use this to explain the meaning of the Bias-free Universal Medium Principle.

RAY KURZWEIL was the principal developer of the first omni-font optical character recognition, the first print-to-speech reading machine for the blind, the first CCD flat-bed scanner, the first text-to-speech synthesizer, the first music synthesizer capable of recreating the grand piano and other orchestral instruments, and the first commercially marketed large-vocabulary speech recognition. Ray has successfully founded and developed nine businesses in OCR, music synthesis, speech recognition, reading technology, virtual reality, financial investment, medical simulation, and cybernetic art. In addition to scores of other national and international awards, Ray was inducted into the National Inventors Hall of Fame, and received the 1999 National Medal of Technology, the nation's highest honor in technology, from President Clinton. Ray's Web site, KurzweilAI.net, is a leading resource on artificial intelligence.

Do you have a "favorite story" to tell about one of your inventions?

We announced the Kurzweil Reading Machine, which was the first print-to-speech reading machine for the blind, on January 13, 1976. I remember this date because Walter Cronkite, the famous news anchor for CBS News, used it to read his signature sign-off that evening "And that's the way it was, January 13, 1976." It was the first time that he did not read this famous phrase himself.

I was subsequently invited to demonstrate this new reading machine on the *Today Show*. We only had one working model and we were nervous about demonstrating it on live television since there was always the possibility of technical glitches. They responded that it was live or nothing.

We arrived at the Today Show studio very early in the morning and set up the reading machine. Sure enough, it stopped working a couple of hours before show time. We tried various easy fixes which failed to rectify the problem. So our chief engineer frantically took the machine apart. With electrical pieces scattered across the studio floor, Frank Field, who was to interview me, walked by, and asked if there was a problem. We said that we were just making a few last minute adjustments.

Our chief engineer put the machine back together, and it still was not working. Then, in a time honored tradition of repairing delicate technical equipment, he picked up the machine and slammed it into the table. It worked perfectly from that moment on, and the live demonstration and interview went without a hitch.

Stevie Wonder happened to catch me on the broadcast, and called our office wanting to stop by and pick up his own reading machine. Our receptionist did not believe it was really the legendary musical artist, but she put him through anyway. We were just finishing up our first production unit, so we rushed that to completion. Stevie stopped by, stayed several hours to learn how to use it, and went off with his new Kurzweil Reading Machine in a taxi. That was the beginning of a nearly thirty-year friendship which continues to this day. A few years later, Stevie was instrumental in my launching Kurzweil Music Systems, Inc.

`Your inventions range from the Kurzweil 250 to a nutritional program that cured you of type II Diabetes. Is there a tie that binds your many inventions?`

My original, and still primary, area of technology interest and expertise is a field called "pattern recognition," which is the science and art of teaching computers to recognize patterns. It turns out that the bulk of human intelligence is based on our remarkable ability to recognize patterns such as faces, visual objects, speech and music. Most of my technology projects are related to recognizing patterns, for example character recognition and speech recognition. Even my work in music synthesis was influenced by pattern recognition. We had to answer the question as to what patterns cause humans to recognize sounds as coming from a particular type of instrument, such as a grand piano.

I quickly realized that timing was important for my inventions, and began to develop mathematical models of how technology develops over time. This endeavor took on a life of its own. By using these models, I was able to make predictions about technologies ten to thirty years into the future, and beyond. From these efforts, I realized that the twenty-first century was going to be an extraordinary time in advancing human civilization. This insight has been a major motivation for me to find the means to live long enough, and in good health, to experience this remarkable century.

I also realized that one of the areas of technology that is accelerating is health and medical technology. Therefore the tools we will have to keep ourselves healthy will grow in power and sophistication in the years ahead. It is important, therefore, to keep ourselves healthy using today's knowledge so that we are in good shape to take advantage of the full flowering of the biotechnology revolution, which is now in its early stages.

`Many of your past predictions about the future of technology have "come true". How is it that you are able to make such specific and accurate predictions?`

Most futurists simply make predictions without a well thought out framework or methodology. I have been studying technology trends for at least a quarter century, and have been developing detailed mathematical models of how technology in different fields evolves. I have a team of people gathering data to measure the key features and capabilities of technologies in a wide array of fields, including computation, communications, biological technologies, and brain reverse engineering. From this work, it has become clear that technologies, particularly those that deal with information, are growing at a double exponential rate (that is the rate of exponential growth is itself growing exponentially). Typically, an information-based technology at least doubles its capability for the same unit cost every year.

The other important issue is that very few people realize that the pace of technical change, what I call the paradigm shift rate, is itself accelerating. We are doubling the pace of technical change every decade. I spoke recently at a conference recently celebrating the fiftieth anniversary of the discovery of the structure of DNA. We were all asked what changes we foresaw for the next fifty years. With very few exceptions, the other speakers used the amount of change in the last fifty years as a guide to the amount of change we will see in the next fifty years. But this is a faulty assumption. Because the rate of change is accelerating, we will see about thirty times as much change in the next fifty years, as we saw in the last half century.

`In your book The Age of Spiritual Machines, you foresee a future where computers have exceeded human intelligence. How and when do you expect this to come about?`

We can separate this question into two questions: when will computers have the computational capacity (the "hardware" capability) of the human brain? Secondly, when will we have the content and methods (the "software") of human intelligence?

In my book, *The Age of Spiritual Machines*, which came out in 1999, I said we would achieve the computational capacity of the human brain for about $1,000 by 2019. I estimate this capacity to be about 100 billion neurons, times about 1,000 interneuronal connections per neuron, times 200 calculations per second per connection, or about 20 million billions calculations per second. This was considered a controversial projection in 1999, but there has been a sea change in perspective on this issue since that time. Today, it is a relatively mainstream expectation that we will have sufficient computational resources by 2019. Computers are at least doubling their speed and memory capacity every year, and even that rate is accelerating.

The more challenging issue is the software of intelligence. A primary source of what I call the "templates" of human intelligence is the human brain itself. We are already well along the path of reverse engineering the brain to understand its principles of operation. Here also we see exponential advance. Brain scanning technologies are doubling their resolution, bandwidth, and price-performance every year.

Knowledge about the human brain, including models of neurons and neural clusters, is doubling every year. We already have detailed mathematical models of several dozen of the several hundred regions that comprise the human brain. I believe it is a conservative projection to say that we will have detailed models of all the regions of the brain by the mid 2020s.

By 2029, we will be able to combine the subtle powers of pattern recognition that the human brain excels in, with several attributes in which machine intelligence already exceeds human capabilities. These include speed, memory capacity, and the ability to instantly share knowledge. Computers circa 2029, possessing human levels of language understanding, will be able to go out on the web and read and absorb all of the available literature and knowledge.

`Will these computers of the future have human emotions?`

Indeed, they will. Emotional intelligence is not a side issue to human intelligence. It is actually the most complex and subtle thing we do. It is the cutting edge of human intelligence. If a human had no understanding of human emotions, we would not consider that person to be operating at a normal human level. The same will be true for machines. Already, there is significant interest in teaching computers about human emotions: how to detect them in humans, and how to respond to them appropriately. This is important for the next generation of human-machine interfaces. As we reverse engineer the human brain, and understand how the different regions process information, we will gain an understanding of what our emotions mean. A very important benefit of this endeavor will be greater insight into ourselves.

What drawbacks do you foresee for the future you envision?

Technology is inherently a double-edged sword. All of the destruction of the twentieth century (for example, two world wars) was amplified by technology. At the same time, we are immeasurably better off as a result of technology. Human life expectancy was 37 years in 1800 and 50 years in 1900. Human life was filled with poverty, hard labor, and disease up until fairly recently.

We are now in the early stages of the biotechnology revolution. We are learning the information processes underlying life and disease, and are close to developing new treatments that will overcome age-old diseases, such as cancer, heart disease, and Diabetes. This same knowledge, however, can also empower a terrorist to create a bioengineered pathogen. There is no easy way to separate the promise from the peril, as both stem from the same technology. We will see similar dilemmas with nanotechnology (technology in which the key features are less than 100 nanometers) and with artificial intelligence.

The answer, I believe, is to substantially increase our investment in developing specific defensive technologies to protect society from these downsides. We can see a similar battle between promise and peril in the area of software viruses. Although we continue to be concerned about software viruses, the defensive technologies have been largely successful. Hopefully we will be able to do as well with biotechnology and other future technologies.

Could you offer some advice to students with regard to keeping pace with information technology and perhaps with regard to inventing it?

This is a very exciting time to be embarking on a career in science and technology. The pace of change and the expansion of new knowledge is greater than at any time in history, and will continue to accelerate. The impact of science and technology goes substantially beyond these subjects themselves. Ultimately, new technological advances will transform every facet of human life and society.

I would advise students to:

1. Obtain a strong background in math, as this is the language of science and technology. Math also represents a way of thinking that leads to discovery and understanding.
2. Become an ardent student of technology and technology trends. Build your inventions for the world of the future, not the world you see in front of you today.
3. Focus on a particular area of science or technology that particularly fascinates you. The days when one person could master all of science and technology are long gone. However, as you focus, don't put on the blinders to what is going on in fields around you.
4. Follow your passion.

interview

RAY KURZWEIL

part 3

DATA AND INFORMATION

introduction

Our understanding of IT has deepened as we have become more versatile users. With greater knowledge and wider experience, it is now wise to consider the bigger picture, noticing how information technology can be used and abused. Topics such as netiquette (etiquette for network users), viruses, and passwords will concern us in this part.

Much of our focus will be on databases—how they store information, structure information, and deliver information that interests us. Knowing how to create our own databases will help us organize our own information, but it will also make us more effective at accessing other databases.

Two important topics covered in Part III are especially active in the "public debate" about IT: privacy and security. We present the technical description of each topic as well as both sides of the debate. Both privacy and security are of personal interest to every user of IT. It is important to be informed.

chapter

12 COMPUTERS IN POLITE SOCIETY

Social Implications of IT

learning objectives

- > Describe several tips associated with netiquette and explain the benefit of following each tip
- > Explain the phrase "expect the unexpected" and how that advice helped in handling an email bug
- > List some ways in which your computer can become infected with a virus or a worm
- > Name three permitted/not permitted uses of licensed software
- > Explain what rights are granted to material that is copyrighted
- > Discuss some issues related to safety-critical applications

While modern technology has given people powerful new communications tools, it apparently can do nothing to alter the fact that many people have nothing useful to say.

—LEE GOMES, SAN JOSE MERCURY NEWS

WHEN COMPUTERS moved out of the lab and onto our desks, laps, and palms, they became part of our social interactions. Usually they are passive tools, being a means of communication and an aid to our work. But a tool can be used crudely or skillfully. By using it skillfully, we smooth our social interactions and make life more pleasant for one another. In this chapter, we break from our usual theme of becoming better computer users to become more considerate computer users.

The chapter begins with three sections on email. Our first goal is to understand the limitations of email, so that we can use it in the right situations and express ourselves well. Next, we look at a set of guidelines called *netiquette,* etiquette for the Internet. Then we introduce an important problem in applying IT—the problem of expecting the unexpected. Unexpected things can happen in any situation, of course, but email is so familiar that it gives us a good context for discussing the issues. The next three topics concern familiar situations in our everyday use of computers and information: passwords, viruses, and copyright law. The "Creating Good Passwords" section discusses the basics of creating good passwords as well as managing them. The "Viruses and Worms" section explains how viruses and worms work, and how you can protect your information. And the "Copyright: Protecting Intellectual Property" section helps you decide when you can and cannot legally copy programs and information. The final section discusses how completely we can trust computer systems, especially their software, in safety-critical applications. If a computer runs a life-support system, how do we know there are no bugs in the program?

IMPROVING THE EFFECTIVENESS OF EMAIL

For many, email has become as routine as telephone communication. In fact, email often replaces the telephone or face-to-face conversation. Is this progress? Certainly the fact that email is asynchronous—the other person doesn't have to be receiving the communication while it is being created and sent—makes it very convenient. And its multicast property—you can send many people a message as easily as you can send it to one person—has its value. So, we use email for much factual communication, like "The next meeting has been postponed until Tuesday at 1:30." But should we use it for everything, like "Your brother died at 4:00 this morning"?

When is email appropriate and when is it not? We cannot give an algorithm for deciding, so our approach will be to identify some of the weaknesses of email.

Problems with Email

The five problems considered here are

> Conveying emotion
> Emphasis
> Conversational pace
> Ambiguity
> Flame-a-thons

Keep these weaknesses in mind as you decide when and how to use email.

Conveying Emotion. It is difficult to convey sympathy, grief, and other subtle emotions using email. The problem is not the writing—sympathy cards convey emotional content as text (and graphics), for example. Rather, it seems that email is too informal, too impersonal, and often too casually written. Even simple feelings like happiness or sadness often don't come across in email because it is treated as a chatty conversation. We type words that in conversation would come with cues such as tone of voice, inflection, stress, pacing, intensity, volume, pauses, and other sounds such as chuckling, and though the words may have those cues in our minds, they don't on the screen. Without the cues, the reader might interpret the words in a way we do not intend. This is why **emoticons**—for example, characters forming smiley faces **:)**—have become so popular in email. The emoticon tags a sentence indicating the emotion we mean to express. In general, expressing sympathy, grief, and so on with email is so difficult that it is inappropriate in almost all cases. In regular email we should be aware of emotional content, sometimes rewriting to make our feelings clear.

Emphasis. At an even more primitive level, the simple act of typing for emphasis can convey the wrong message. Readers could interpret text in all capitals as yelling. For example, "Do you know you forgot my birthday?" has a different sense than "DO YOU KNOW YOU FORGOT MY BIRTHDAY?" Generally, stress must be used with care because email is still largely ASCII-text-based and often does not make the standard indicators of emphasis like italics or underlining available to the writer. A common way to express emphasis is with special symbols like *asterisks* or _underscores_ on both sides of the word. So you could write, "Do you know you forgot my _birthday_?" to give some emphasis. Certain email reading programs convert to *bold* and _italics_, but others do not. Because you probably don't know what email reader your correspondent uses, typing the asterisks and underscores is wise. And it's best to avoid uppercase letters unless you intend to yell.

Conversational Pace. It's difficult to have a dialog (a rapidly alternating communication) asynchronously. This is one reason why chat room "conversations" are often so inane. If the purpose of the communication is interactive, say, a negotiation, the telephone is a better choice because it replaces the asynchronous compose/send/wait/receive cycle of email with synchronous conversation that switches quickly. The ability to alternate rapidly not only speeds up the pace of the communication, but it helps us recognize confusion or misunderstanding through audio cues, such as the feedback of long pauses (cluelessness) rather than periodic "uh huhs" (understanding). Of course, email is useful for setting the time for a phone conversation and exchanging phone numbers.

Ambiguity. Expressing ourselves is difficult, but it's even worse when our text is taken in a way that we did not intend. Ambiguity is a problem with natural language generally, and therefore all writing that is not programming or mathematics. But ambiguity seems to happen even more in email, because email is more casual than most other writing. Some people apparently don't even proofread what they write, much less take time to consider carefully how their writing might be misinterpreted. If you write, "I cannot recommend saffron rice too highly," you might mean that the dish is so good that you will not overstate your praise, but your reader may interpret the sentence as saying that there is little that you can say that is good about saffron rice. If there are no other cues, your reader may get the wrong idea. It is always a good idea to proofread carefully and to look for ambiguities.

FITCAUTION

Universal Mistake. It is nearly impossible to be sarcastic in email and not offend some readers. Many writers try to be funny by being sarcastic, but it rarely works unless you know the recipient well. A good rule: Do not use sarcasm in email you are sending to more than one person.

Flames. Perhaps the worst abuse of email is the phenomenon known as a **flame-a-thon** or **flame war**, an email battle named after the computer slang flame for "inflammatory email." It's hard to generalize on how flame-a-thons begin, but they continue for the same reason conflicts continue in some parts of the world: Neither side wants to quit without getting revenge for the most recent attack. The main reason that flame-a-thons occur and continue seems to be email's immediacy. Email written in anger and sent immediately gives the sender no time for reflection. Including a cc list, of course, makes it worse. If, like snail mail, email had to be addressed to only one person and then carried to the post office or a mailbox, most of us would probably cool down before we dropped the envelope through the slot. No one wins a flame-a-thon. Clearly the best response when you are angered by email is to delay answering it until you've cooled down, and consider a different form of communication with the other person.

Generally, email is a very handy medium. It is most effective when we are sensitive to its weaknesses.

Netiquette

There are a few rules, popularly known as **netiquette**, that promote civilized email usage. The world won't end if you don't follow them any sooner than it will end if you chew with your mouth open, but if you do follow them, at least people won't think you're a boor.

Ask about One Topic at a Time. An email message that requires a response from the receiver should treat only one topic. For example, don't ask your parents for money in the same email that you ask if you left your brown sweater at home. Because most of us handle one matter at a time, the reader of a one-topic message can respond to the matter, and then delete or archive the mail. With multiple topics, it is likely that one will be dropped or ignored. For example, you'll find out you did forget the sweater, but the money request might be ignored. The subject line of the email can describe that one topic. Email is cheap, and it costs no more to send two messages than one. But managing one-topic messages is much easier for everyone.

Include Context. An all too common email reply, unfortunately, is "Yes." We all like to get positive email, of course; the unfortunate part is we've forgotten the question. The subject line is no help; it reads, `Re: Question`.

Any email-reading software worth two bits gives you a way to include the original message in a reply. Including the question with the reply is a courtesy. It provides the context for your answer, so you can give a short reply without leaving the receiver clueless. One of the problems with always including the message in a reply, however, is that an email conversation can become lengthy. If every character is typed by one of the two correspondents, however, there is little chance that this history will become gigantic. But it is a courtesy to limit the context to the most recent message or to the most relevant point.

Use an Automated Reply. When you will not be answering email for a long time, it is polite to set up an **automated reply** saying you are away, and perhaps indicating when you expect to be reading email again. The automated reply was called a "vacation message" in the earliest mailers, and is generally available from your mail server. The benefit of using the vacation message is that readers know why you're not answering their mail. Otherwise, they may think they are being ignored or snubbed.

FITTIP

Nor Rain, Nor Heat, Nor Gloom of Night. Email does get lost occasionally, but it is generally quite reliable. If an Internet destination is *not responding* for a given period of time, typically four hours, you are usually notified. Attempts to deliver the message continue for three days, but if they fail, the sender is then notified. So "I never got the message" is a questionable excuse.

`Answer a Backlog of Emails in Reverse Order.` When we keep up with reading our email, we usually answer messages in the order received. But if we haven't been answering email for a while and our inbox is brimming, it is best to answer email in *reverse* order of its arrival. The reason for this is simple. Many of the oldest messages will have, in computer jargon, "timed-out." That is, we may not have to answer a message because a more recent follow-up message supercedes it. Or we may receive a "forget it" message sent by someone who received our vacation message, and realized they couldn't wait for our reply. Not answering such mail saves us time and saves our correspondent aggravation. For example, when your boss sends a message asking for everyone's availability for a meeting next week, it is unnecessary and somewhat embarrassing to reply when a later message sets the time for the meeting. Answering email in reverse time-order allows us to see these resolution messages before seeing the original. There's only one caution: Avoid the temptation to quit and never finish the backlog. After all, one of those unread messages may be telling you that you have won a new car in that $1 raffle you entered.

`Get the Sender's Permission Before Forwarding Email.` As a general rule, most people assume that when they send email, it is private. So it is impolite to forward email without getting the sender's permission. Asking permission to forward email gives the sender a chance to review the mail to decide if there is something in it that should not be passed along. The sender's opinion is important because although the mail may look innocent to you, other readers may react differently and the sender may know that. It is the sender who should decide who should read his or her email. Notice that most email in the United States is *not* a private conversation. Companies, colleges, or other organizations can (under most circumstances) review the email sent or *received* by the members of their organization; that is, *your* personal email account might be private, but your readers' may not be. (See Chapter 17.)

`Use Targeted Distribution Lists.` There are many good reasons, such as changing your address, for mailing dozens of people the same email message. But keeping a single list of all people you've ever exchanged email with and then forwarding the latest lame joke off the Internet is just a bad idea. Not only is it an abuse of one of the benefits of email—that a group of people can be informed simultaneously—but they've doubtless already seen it. It doesn't take long for the recipients of such mass mailings and forwards to start deleting all messages from the sender *unread*. Your correspondents will appreciate it if you only send email targeted to them. So, having short lists like **Brothers** and **Moms_Kin** is better than a list like **Relatives**. Not everything you'd send your brother will interest every member of your family. Smaller, more specific lists mean more effective communication.

CHECKLIST>>

By observing these rules and general courtesy, our email can be more pleasant and effective.

- *Ask about one topic at a time.*
- *Include context.*
- *Use an automated reply.*
- *Answer a backlog of email in reverse order.*
- *Get the sender's permission before forwarding email.*
- *Use targeted distribution lists.*

EXPECT THE UNEXPECTED

Expecting the unexpected is a valuable survival skill both in life and in IT. When something unexpected happens, we not only should notice it, but also ask ourselves "Why did that happen?" or "What's going on?" By wondering about the unexpected event and analyzing what might have caused it, we may discover an advantage, avoid harm, learn something new, or, perhaps most important, save ourselves from looking like total dummies! Because it is difficult to discuss "the unexpected" in general terms, consider a specific situation in which analyzing the unexpected is beneficial.

A Mailing List Handler Has a Bug

Occasionally—meaning every two to three years in my experience—a mailing list application for a large (1000 names or more) mailing list fails. (Another name for a mailing list application is a **list-server**.) The problem could be a bug in the mailing list software, or the list's **moderator**—the person responsible for deciding what is sent out to the mailing list—could have misconfigured it. Whatever the cause, there is a more-or-less typical sequence of messages to everyone on that mailing list that reveals that some people don't expect the unexpected.

The event begins innocuously enough with a message such as

From: "Sue Marie Acker" <smacker@thermalmail.com>
Subject: Re: Topic of most recent mailing to this list
To: Mondo_list

Remove me from this list, please.

A few similar messages of this same type follow. This is an unexpected event. Mailing lists are for sending information from one source, say, an organization, to many receivers. This kind of mail looks like communication from a receiver back to the source, and then back to all receivers. Unexpected.

Though there are many systems for managing mailing lists, and we probably don't understand at all how they work, no software for handling mailing lists should send requests for removal from the list to the entire list. They should probably be sent to the moderator or intercepted by someone else managing the list. Something is wrong here. It could be in the protocol for removing from the list, or it could be something else. *Everyone* on the mailing list should have noticed this and given it some thought. The moderator, especially, should have noticed, and fixed it.

But because he or she didn't fix it, the next message is

From: "A. S. King" <new2net@coolmail.com>
Subject: Re: Re: Topic of most recent mailing to this list
To: Mondo_list

Why am I getting these messages??

> From: "Sue Marie Acker" <smacker@thermalmail.com>
> Subject: Re: Topic of most recent mailing to this list
> To: Mondo_list
>
> Remove me from this list, please.

From this mail we can conclude that the problem is not simply with the "unsubscribe" feature, the facility that removes people from a mailing list. (The fault might have been limited to "unsubscribe" because all previous mail concerned that issue.) Now it is clear that the mailing list handler is reflecting all of the mail it receives. If we send anything to this list, everyone will get it. The moderator is not intercepting replies to the list. So, until someone fixes the problem, the only way to avoid getting more email is if everyone stops sending to this list.

At this point everyone should have figured out the situation, and there should be no further traffic. That is what would happen if everyone were expecting the unexpected. (It would be good if a civic-minded individual sent a private email to the moderator pointing out the problem.) Nevertheless, there follow several more messages of the form

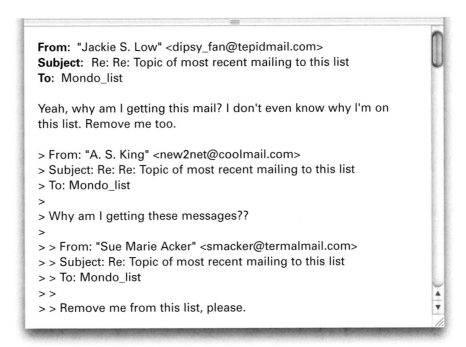

```
From: "Jackie S. Low" <dipsy_fan@tepidmail.com>
Subject: Re: Re: Topic of most recent mailing to this list
To: Mondo_list

Yeah, why am I getting this mail? I don't even know why I'm on
this list. Remove me too.

> From: "A. S. King" <new2net@coolmail.com>
> Subject: Re: Re: Topic of most recent mailing to this list
> To: Mondo_list
>
> Why am I getting these messages??
>
> > From: "Sue Marie Acker" <smacker@termalmail.com>
> > Subject: Re: Topic of most recent mailing to this list
> > To: Mondo_list
> >
> > Remove me from this list, please.
```

After a dozen of these **"Yeah, what's up with this?"** types of messages, someone gets completely frustrated with those who don't seem to be figuring out that continuing to send email to the list prolongs everyone's agony. That person—actually there are usually several—writes

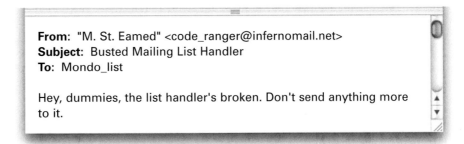

```
From: "M. St. Eamed" <code_ranger@infernomail.net>
Subject: Busted Mailing List Handler
To: Mondo_list

Hey, dummies, the list handler's broken. Don't send anything more
to it.
```

This will be immediately followed by a message of the form

```
From: "Fran K. Lee" <fleet@coldmail.net>
Subject: Re: Busted Mailing List Handler
To: Mondo_list

You just did what you told everyone not to do! - Fleet
> From: "M. St. Eamed" <code_ranger@infernomail.net>
> Subject: Busted Mailing List Handler
> To: Mondo_list
>
> Hey, dummies, the list handler's broken. Don't send anything
> more to it.
```

Or perhaps the message will read, **"I find it offensive getting messages calling me a dummy."** Then other frustrated people will jump in with comments pointing out that any person who sends email to a broken email list claiming to be offended at being called a dummy probably is a dummy, and so on. This can go on for dozens of messages before the person responsible for the mailing list finally gets it fixed. The surprise, perhaps, is that the people sending these messages are on the mailing list because they have something in common, which means that many of them may know each other. How embarrassing!

The point about this email history is that it should have been obvious very quickly (with A. S. King's message) that something unusual was happening. With a moment's thought, people should have realized how to act in a rational manner even though they had no way of knowing exactly what was wrong. Clearly most of the people involved in the event did so or there would have been *much more* such email.

FITCAUTION

Unexpectedly Flaky. Occasionally a familiar application will do something strange, such as slowing down, "forgetting" changes, or failing in other ways. Such behaviors are unexpected, and often come right before a crash. When you notice your software "acting strange," act immediately: save *to a new file name*, exit, and restart. The problem is usually just with the software, but it could be with the instance; a new file name avoids overwriting your previously saved version.

The lesson to be learned is not simply to be alert to mailing list handler bugs, but to be alert to unusual events of any kind at any time. Then, think about them. At the very least, it could save some embarrassment.

CREATING GOOD PASSWORDS

One day electronic hardware may reliably detect who we are when we come in contact with a computer, and there will be no need for **passwords**. Meanwhile, passwords are a key part of our daily interaction with computers. This section considers selecting, changing, and managing passwords as well as password principles that can make your daily computer usage easier. Chapter 17 deals with the related topic of computer security.

The Role of Passwords

Of course, the point of a password is to limit computer or software system access to only those people who know a not-likely-to-be-guessed sequence of keyboard characters. So, obviously, it is necessary to select such a sequence, and choosing a good one is discussed next.

Breaking into a Computer without a Password. But couldn't one computer break into another if we programmed it to try all passwords in an algorithmic way until the true password is found? Computers must surely be fast enough. They probably would be. But they're not that dumb. Or, rather, the software running on them won't let potential users (other computers) try zillions of passwords. The software for the login protocol may include a delay when notifying the user that the password is wrong. The delay is not particularly noticeable to a human user, but it slows down the login protocol to the point that it is too slow to try zillions of passwords. Alternatively, software may notice long sequences of failed attempts to type the correct password and take some action. Of course, humans sometimes produce a sequence of failed attempts because they are agitated or groggy or try to log in using a pencil held in their teeth while holding a coffee cup in one hand and a Danish pastry in the other. So, login protocols allow several password failures before deciding someone is trying to break in.

Forgetting a Password. Another curiosity about passwords is that if we forget ours and go to the system's administrator to find out what it is, he or she can't usually tell us. How could that be? Don't they have complete access—known as **superuser** or **administrator** status—to all of the computers, and so aren't they able to look up passwords? Yes, but the actual password is not stored on the computer.

When a new password is created, it is scrambled or encrypted and then stored in that form. The new password is thrown away. Then, at login, the text given as the password is scrambled using the same algorithm used originally when the new password was set. The two scrambled sequences are then compared. If they are the same, the right password must have been given. If not, the password must have been wrong. This technique is used so that passwords are not stored in "clear text" that someone could steal. How the scrambling is done is explained in Chapter 17. What the superuser does when you ask for your forgotten password is to create a new password and force its scrambled form to replace your old one. You then use the new password.

Guidelines for Selecting a Password

When we receive a new computer account, we are usually given an automatically generated password that is a scramble of letters and digits and possibly special characters: **`rU4Uw2?gR8`**. And we are told to change it. Of course, the motive for asking us to change it is so that we'll select something we can remember. Changing it to our boyfriend's name wouldn't be a good idea because that's too easily guessed, at least by our friends. But what is a good choice?

Passwords are better if they are longer, at least six characters, and if they contain a mix of upper- and lowercase letters, numbers, and, if allowed, punctuation characters. They are better if they are not in dictionaries and have no "obvious" association to us, such as our name. And they are better if we can remember them immediately. Those may seem like difficult constraints to fulfill, but it's still pretty easy to come up with a good password with a few moments' thought.

CHECKLIST>>

Here are a few **heuristics**—guidelines to help solve a problem, which are not algorithmic—that should give good results:

- *Select a personally interesting* topic, *such as a parent, favorite movie, or best travel destination, and* always *select passwords related to that topic. Because you will use many passwords, selecting from one topic area will help you to remember them.*
- *Develop a password from a phrase rather than a single word. The phrase must be memorable to you. It will be compressed according to the next rule.*
- *Encode the password phrase, trying to make it short (6–12 characters) by abbreviating, and by replacing letters or syllables with alternative characters, spellings, or encodings that include numbers and uppercase letters.*

The goal is to create letter strings that are not in dictionaries and are a mixture of numbers and letters.

For example, if you are using your father as the topic and your chosen phrase is his alma mater, Oxford University, then

Oxford University	→ **`OxfordU`**	Shorten standard abbreviation
	→ **`Ox4dU`**	Replace *for* with "4"
	→ **`Ohx4dU`**	Replace *O* with "Oh"

The result doesn't make much sense to someone who hasn't seen the construction process, but it wouldn't be difficult for you to remember.

If your topic is your favorite movie, *Gone With the Wind*, you might use the following process to construct a password:

Gone With The Wind	→ **`GWTW`**	Shorten, standard abbreviation
	→ **`G2uTW`**	Replace *W* with "2u"
	→ **`G2uT2U`**	Replace *W* with "2U"
	→ **`G2uTdosU`**	Replace *2* with Spanish "dos"

The last replacement is not really needed because the password is already pretty obscure, but the use of Spanish emphasizes that passwords can build on any part of your knowledge, heritage, or background.

Finally, if you are using your vacation to Australia as your topic, and your phrase is Surfing in Australia, you might come up with this:

Surfing In Australia	→ `SurfingInOz`	Australia is often abbreviated Oz
	→ `SurfinInOz`	Drop *g* as in slang
	→ `Surf2inOz`	Replace *inIn* with "2in"
	→ `sirf2inOz`	Replace *Sur* with "sir"
	→ `sirF2inOz`	Introduce a capital for variety

It is possible to be too clever, so it's smart to stop the process before your password gets too obscure. After all, you must be able to remember it!

FITTIP

Total Recall. It might seem that remembering such obscure passwords would be difficult, but it usually is not. If you type them daily, they come to mind quickly. It's almost as if your "fingers memorize them." If you use them, say, only monthly for your credit card account, following these heuristics will help you remember how you made them.

Notice the importance of the topic. The topic provides context to narrow the possibilities for us personally, serving as a memory aid. If we're changing from having used `G2uT2U` for a year, a password based on phrases like "Frankly, my dear" or "Rhett and Scarlet," suitably transformed, should be easy to remember. And even if (foolishly) we tell someone our password, and (more foolishly) explain what it means, and (most foolishly) describe the topic from which we select passwords, the topic is probably rich enough that we can still use it. There are probably enough phrases and enough variations on them that we could still create obscure passwords.

This process is intended to produce an obscure password (not in a dictionary) that should be easy to recall without having to write it down. But should it be written down anyway? It's a personal choice. Some people would never be comfortable not having a password written down somewhere. Others are sure they'd be able to remember it under any circumstances, even after an all-night party at a brewery.

Changing Passwords

Passwords should be changed periodically. Organizations often have a policy as to how often a password must be changed, and sometimes there are security intrusions that cause administrators to ask that passwords be changed. Whether you should change your password depends on how likely it is that the password has become known and how important it is to keep the information secure. If you haven't changed your password in a year, it may be time to consider changing it.

Every system that uses passwords has software to change them, though we usually don't notice it when we don't need it. Check the GUI where you enter your password for the option to change it. If that doesn't work, do a search for "password" with the online **Help** facility. These systems typically ask for your current password, your new password, and a second copy of your new password. The second copy is simply a way of checking for a typing error. If they match, the password is changed.

Managing Passwords

People who make extensive use of computers may have to present passwords in dozens of situations. Obviously, if each password is different, it can become a serious challenge to remember them all. But using a single password might create a different headache. If some of them must change often, there is the hassle of having to visit all accounts frequently to update to a new password. One strategy is always to have two current passwords, only one of which you change often. That way you would only ever have to try three or four times to get the right password: the slowly changing one, the quickly changing one, and perhaps the last versions of each in case you hadn't yet gotten around to updating it.

Finally, it is possible to recycle passwords in two ways. First, if you have a good, easy-to-remember password, change it slightly using the process described above to create a new one. So, if you've been using the *Gone With The Wind* password, `G2uT2U`, and need to change it, go for the Spanish version, `G2uTdosU`. This works well for routine changes, but if there is a security concern related to your password, you should pick a totally new one from your topic area. Second, if you have several good passwords, it is probably safe to reuse them over time, especially if they are not variants of each another. Security experts do not like this idea, but most of us don't have top-secret files on our computers either. Just use good judgment in choosing and managing passwords.

> FITTIP
>
> **Risk Assessment.** Use judgment when choosing passwords. For a personal computer kept at home that only you use, even a single-letter password is probably too much. For your online bank account, a password of the type just discussed is a good idea. Assess the risk in each case. Even your girlfriend's name can work in some instances.

VIRUSES AND WORMS

In the 1950s, shortly after computers were invented, scientists created programs that could make exact copies of themselves. Though these programs motivated philosophical discussions about the nature of life, computability, evolution, and so forth, they mostly remained curiosities. Then on November 2, 1988, Robert Tappan Morris, Jr., a computer science graduate student, apparently lost control of a program he wrote, and the general public learned for the first time that programs could replicate themselves. Morris's program was supposed to embed in a computer once and then send copies of itself to other machines. It propagated itself to 6000 machines, or about 10 percent of the Internet at the time. Though it was not designed to do any harm, it had an unfortunate bug in it that caused it to continue to replicate itself on each machine it infected. This quickly filled each machine's memory and hard disk, crashing the machines. The machines had to be manually "cleaned up" at the cost of millions of dollars in wages and downtime. As a result, new security organizations were created to monitor and quickly react to such malicious programs.

FITBYTE

Crime and Punishment. Morris was prosecuted and convicted under the U.S. Computer Fraud and Abuse Act of 1986, sentenced to three years' probation and 400 hours of community service, and fined $10,000. A similar conviction today would doubtless draw a much stiffer punishment.

Getting Infected...

A **virus** is a program that "infects" another program by embedding a (possibly evolved) copy of itself so that when the infected program runs, the virus makes copies of itself, infecting other programs. A virus is transmitted when an infected program or floppy disk is transferred to another computer. A closely related phenomenon is a **worm**, which is an independent program that makes copies of itself from machine to machine across network connections. Morris's program was a worm. The difference—a virus hides in another program, traveling with it, while a worm moves across the network on its own—is not so important from a user's point of view. Rather, what is important is the fact that they can both cause irreparable harm to your computer, such as erasing your files and trashing your software installation.

From Copying Software. Viruses embed in software, so the common way to infect a computer is to copy software from some infected computer. Thus, if a friend's computer is infected, and you copy software from that machine onto your machine—either by using a portable medium like a floppy disk or by a direct transfer—the virus may come with the software. Once you run that software, the virus will then infect your machine. For example, suppose you get your friend's very cool screen saver, which is infected. Then, when the screen saver runs, the virus infects your computer.

A **Trojan horse** is useful and apparently innocent software containing additional hidden code allowing the unauthorized collection, use, or destruction of data. Screen savers are good hosts for Trojan horse code because they run regularly.

From New Software. Notice that any software distribution from **freeware** (software available on the Web at no cost) to **shareware** (software available on the Web that you pay for on the honor system) to standard commercial applications (software you can pay a bundle for) is a potential source of virus-infected code. However, the people who distribute software are *extremely* aware of the risks and take precautions to ensure that the software they publish is clean. Because computers are pretty useless unless we use software other people wrote, we must take a tiny risk when loading new software from these sources, but the risk is generally too tiny to worry about.

From Email Attachments. Recently viruses have been propagated in **email attachments**. For example, if you and a friend both use the same software, say, for word processing, an easy way to work together on a report is to exchange the document file by attaching it to email. When it's your turn to work on the report, your friend attaches the latest version, you receive it, and you open the document with your software. It's very convenient.

Viruses can exploit this process by embedding themselves in documents for widely used software like a word processor. When an unthinking email recipient opens such a document, the software "runs" the virus commands—often in the form of macro instructions—enabling it to do its work. A common behavior for the virus is to locate the user's email address book and to send email to people on the list, along with an attachment into which it has embedded itself. When the next person opens the attachment, the virus infects their computer and can continue its spread. The **Melissa virus** used this process; see "Looking at Melissa."

Obviously, the process doesn't work if no one opens the attachments, but attachments are very tempting. It also doesn't work if the software manufacturer takes greater care to be sure its software can't be so easily compromised. But the best deterrent is an attentive user who is not "trigger happy" about opening attachments and who reads email with a slight skepticism. Is the message a sensible follow-on to the last message from the sender? Is the content of the message something the sender would say to me? Is there a reason for the sender to include an attachment? If you have doubts, be cautious. Do not open the attachments. You can send return email telling the sender you didn't understand his or her last email and asking for clarification. If you believe the email is infected—new worms and viruses are usually reported in the media with much fanfare—simply **Trash** it. You don't need to permanently delete infected email, because viruses are generally harmless as long as the software does not open them.

> FITCAUTION
>
> **It's a Jungle Out There.** Though viruses and worms may not be much in the news at any particular time, they are circulating around the Internet all the time. At `www.wildlist.org` find a list of the currently active viruses, worms, and other malicious programs that are still known to be "in the wild." Three years later the Melissa virus was still at large.

Accidentally Infecting Others

Suppose you accidentally send a virus to the world—what should you do? Having been duped into opening the attachment and assisting the virus's spread is embarrassing to most of us, so we'd like it to go away. But if we discover quickly enough what we have done, there are some useful responses. If we discover it immediately—that is, if our mailer is still sending out virus-infested mail—we may be able to disconnect the computer, say, if the connection is via a dial-up modem, and limit the number of messages sent. If the messages have been sent, but very recently, it may be possible to send follow-up email quickly alerting the recipients

{FITLINK}

Looking at Melissa >>

The Melissa virus, known in security circles as W97M/Melissa, burst onto the Internet on Friday March 26, 1999, embedded in Microsoft Word documents attached to email messages. The original Melissa virus's email message had the form

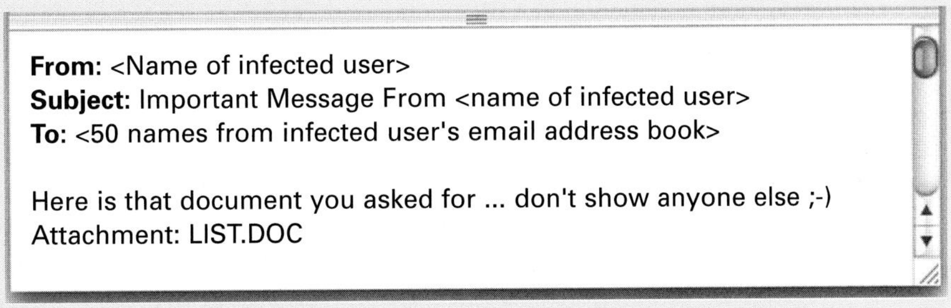

From: <Name of infected user>
Subject: Important Message From <name of infected user>
To: <50 names from infected user's email address book>

Here is that document you asked for ... don't show anyone else ;-)
Attachment: LIST.DOC

The virus was so virulent that many companies, including Microsoft, had to shut down their email servers to limit the spread of the virus. Would this look like a suspicious email if it came from someone you know?

Viruses mutate—hackers who get a copy change them and start them up again. For example, later versions of Melissa had a different attachment file name than LIST.DOC. Also, a variation, known as `W97M/Melissa.I`, used a random-number generator to pick among different subject lines and email bodies, trying to fool people who were alert for the first form of the virus. The eight variations are shown in Table 12.1.

The outcome? David L. Smith pleaded guilty to creating and propagating the Melissa virus. He was sentenced to 20 months in federal prison and fined $5000.

Table 12.1. *Variations of the Melissa Virus Email*

Subject Line	Email Body
Question for you ...	It's fairly complicated so I've attached it.
Check this!!	This is some wicked stuff!
Cool Web Sites	Check out the Attached Document for a list of some of the best Sites on the Web.
80mb Free Web Space	Check out the Attached Document for details on how to obtain the free space. It's cool, I've now got heaps of room.
Cheap Software	The attached document contains a list of web sites where you can obtain Cheap Software.
Cheap Hardware	I've attached a list of web sites where you can obtain Cheap Hardware.
Free Music	Here is a list of places where you can obtain Free Music.
* Free Downloads	Here is a list of sites where you can obtain Free Downloads.

* A randomly selected digit

to the infected mail. (The victims are in the **Sent Mail** file.) It is best if the subject line calls attention to itself somehow, perhaps by being in caps: ALERT! I SENT A VIRUS. This will help email readers who look over their **Inbox** before opening the mail. If, as is likely, the damage has already been done, there is little you can do, except perhaps to commiserate with those who got it and passed it along, too—you'll likely get infected mail back from them! Finally, you will have to disinfect your computer by running commercial antiviral software.

Hoaxes. The catch-22 that complicates protecting yourself from viruses and worms is that there are also virus hoaxes. Some people send around email that warns of a virus, advises some action, and asks that you forward the mail to others. The recommended action may be to uninstall software or to make other serious changes to your computer. Be alert to this kind of mail. Avoid taking any action until you are sure it is necessary. You can get honest information from responsible organizations such the companies that sell virus-checking software.

Virus-checking Software

Because viruses, worms, and other unsavory critters are at large, every computer must have up-to-date **virus-checking software** loaded and running. McAfee, Norton, and Sophos, Inc., are three of the many companies that sell antivirus software. These programs check for the known viruses, worms, and so on, but like biological organisms, new creatures are being created all the time. So, you need to get updates periodically. Typically, owning software from a vendor entitles you to updates that keep the diagnostics current. The task of keeping your computer free of malicious software is yours and it's never ending.

FITBYTE

Colorful Language. Computer security uses many colorful terms (see the CyberGlossary at `www.imms.com/cyberglos/`). An **ankle-biter** is a would-be hacker attacking a system with very little knowledge, and so is ineffective but annoying like a little dog. To **derf** is to use a terminal or computer someone absent-mindedly left logged in. A **Nak Attack**—*nak* is engineering slang for "negative acknowledgment"—exploits a certain operating system weakness to make a computer vulnerable. The **Ping of Death** is a huge message sent to another machine to see if it replies, but instead the other machine chokes.

PROTECTING INTELLECTUAL PROPERTY

Like land or Rover or a Land Rover, information is something that can be owned. Information, including photographs, music, textbooks, and cartoons, is the result of the creative process. The act of creation gives the creator ownership of the result in the United States and most of the world. Sometimes there are multiple forms of ownership. If on her new CD Norah Jones sings a song written by Paul Simon, he owns the words and music, and she owns the performance. If a person creates something while working for a company, the company generally owns the information. All such human creations are called **intellectual property** to distinguish them from real estate, pets, cars, and other stuff that can be owned.

The two forms of intellectual property of interest here are software and copyright on the Web. Each affects how you can use information technology.

Licensing of Software

When you buy software, you load it onto your machine without giving much attention to the legal mumbo jumbo that you agree to by opening the package or downloading the file. (Sure, lawyers probably read it, but the rest of us don't.) If you were to read it, you'd discover a remarkable fact: You didn't buy the software—you're effectively leasing it. That is, **software licenses** tend to give you the use of the software whose ownership remains with the company that is marketing it. (Of course, every license is different, forcing us to discuss the topic generally. To be sure about your particular agreement, check your software license.) Why this is the case is not the issue for us. Rather, what matters it is what such agreements mean for us.

Use the Software. If the agreement allows us to use the software, we can use it on any of our computers, assuming we have more than one. Thus we should be able to install the software on all of our computers. The fact that we use it personally generally means that we use one instance at a time. Installing several instances to make our use of it more convenient should be OK. An analogous situation exists in companies. If a company has several engineers who need a certain specialized software package, they might buy x "site licenses" for that software. The site licenses authorize x engineers to use the software at the same time. The point is not how many hard disks contain a copy of the software, but rather how many people can use the software at once.

Don't Sell It or Give It Away. Because you don't *own* commercial software, you cannot give it to your friend. If you did, you would be violating the terms of the contract that you agreed to when you opened the software package. But even if you simply bought software from a friendly programmer you met in the computer lab, you probably still can't give it away. The programmer created the software—it's his or her intellectual property—and the programmer has full copyright protection. Like a photographer who creates a stunning picture, the programmer's ownership of the software allows copies to be made and sold to people like you. You buy a photograph to frame and enjoy; you buy software to run and enjoy. Unless the programmer gave you the explicit right to make copies and distribute them, you cannot sell the software or even give it away.

Try Before You Buy. Finally, there is shareware, which is software that is usually distributed over the Internet. You can download a copy for free, and you can copy it to your friends. The idea of shareware is that you can try out the software, and if you like it and use it, you pay the person who created it. (The price is listed.) It's a great system both because it gives craftsman programmers a chance to distribute their often well-built and effective software and because you can try it out before paying. But it is an honor system, and if you do use it, you should pay. It would be unethical to download software on the implied promise of paying for it if you use it, and then to use it without paying. Prices are generally very modest, and the software is often exceptionally good.

Copyright on the Web

When a person writes a term paper, builds a Web page, or creates a sculpture, he or she automatically owns the **copyright** on that "work" in the United States and most nations of the world. The creator typically owns the copyright, unless the creation is "work for hire," in which case the owner is the person who paid the creator, usually a company. For example, if you create a personal Web page, you own the copyright, but if you built the Web page as part of your job, the company owns it. Posting information on the World Wide Web is a form of publishing, and though the copyright and other law has not been fully developed yet, it is a good assumption that information on the WWW is owned by someone.

FITBYTE

No © 'em. At one time, to claim copyright, you had to include the phrase "© Copyright *dates* by *author/owner* All Rights Reserved." That's no longer necessary for works produced after March 1, 1989. However, the "© *dates by author*" is still used as a reminder and reference.

What rights are included in a copyright? Obviously the right to copy it, but surprisingly, there are others. Copyright protects the owner's right to

- Make a copy of the work.
- Use a work as the basis for a new work, called creating a derivative work.
- Distribute or publish the work, including electronically.
- Publicly perform the work, as in music, poetry, drama, or to play a video or audio recording or CD-ROM.
- Publicly display the work, as in to display an image on a computer screen.

And it is the very act of creating the intellectual property that creates these rights. No application or approval is required. The work need not carry the © symbol. It's copyrighted the moment it's finished.

Notice the second item in the list, using the work to create a derivative work. This is an important aspect of copyright because it prevents someone from, for example, changing each of the *Simpsons* characters in some small way—aging, for example—and then claiming to have created a new dysfunctional cartoon family. Only their creator, Matt Groening, has the right to change the characters. We might be tempted to bypass copyright law by restating a work in our own words, but if what we create is too much like the original, we've produced a derivative work rather than new intellectual property. Thus, for example, if someone restates this book in different words, I could sue them—and I might.

Free Personal Use. Of course, just because someone else owns a work doesn't mean that you cannot use and enjoy it. Obviously the fact that they've published it on the Web means that you are free to read, view, or listen to it as you wish. Printing it so that you can read it on the bus would be OK, as would filing away a copy on your computer for future *personal* enjoyment. You can mail the URL to your friends, notifying them of the information. Such applications are why the information was published on the Web in the first place.

When Is Permission Needed? Many sites have a written copyright policy. Often the information is placed in the **public domain**, meaning that it is free for use by anyone in any form. This is convenient because it means that we can treat the information as if it were our own. We could even sell it to someone else, if we could find a buyer. Another common situation is that the owners state that they allow the information to be republished or used in other forms, provided that the source is cited. They keep ownership, but we get to use it. All we have to do is take care to follow their guidelines. And, of course, some sites—all of them that don't state otherwise—retain all rights to the Web-published information under the applicable copyright laws. Generally, this means that if you want to use works from such a site in one of the five ways listed earlier, you must get permission from the owners of the information to do so. Using such copyrighted property without permission is illegal, of course. But the fact that a site retains the rights to its information should not keep you from asking for permission. Many sites routinely give permission; their purpose in requiring you to ask for permission is to control the distribution of their works. It takes only a little effort to ask.

The Concept of Fair Use. Between the free personal use and the need to get permission is a gray area in which limited use of copyrighted materials is allowed without getting permission. This is known as the concept of "fair use." **Fair use** is recognized in copyright law to allow the use of copyrighted material for educational or scholarly purposes, to allow limited quotation of copyrighted works for review or criticism, to permit parody, and a few other uses. For example, I can quote Stanley Kubrick's *2001, A Space Odyssey* in

> *One of the most widely known computer instructions is David Bowman's command, "Open the pod bay doors, HAL."*

without getting the permission of Warner Brothers, the present owner, because I am using the quotation for the educational purpose of instructing you about fair use. This is true even though this book is a commercial application of the quoted material. And you would be allowed to use similar brief quotations in class assignments. Indeed, fair use provides many opportunities for using copyrighted material for socially beneficial purposes. The problem is that it can be very unclear just when fair use applies.

FITTIP

No Harm in Asking. When asking for copyright permission, state what works you are interested in, such as "the photograph on your page .../greatpix/elvis/"; how you would like to use the works, such as "put copies on my personal Web page at . . ."; and any other relevant information, such as "I want to colorize his suede shoes so they are actually blue."

To:
Date:

I am writing to you to request permission to use the material described below. This material will be posted on a Web site that receives approximately __________ hits per month. The URL is ________________________ The material will be posted on July 1 and will remain on the Web site for an indefinite period. I am asking permission for the nonexclusive, worldwide right to publish this material.

Description: Include the title and author of the work, the source (if from a book, give the ISBN; if from a Web site, give the complete URL), and a copy of the work if possible (the text or art you want to use).

Full credit will be given to the source. A release form appears below, along with space for indicating your desired credit line.

If you do not control these rights in their entirety, please let me know to whom else I must write. Thank you.

Sincerely,

Your name
Your contact information

I warrant that I have the right to grant the permission to republish the material specified above.
Permission is granted by: ____________________________________
Title: ____________________________________
Address: ____________________________________
Date: ____________________________________
Preferred acknowledgment: ____________________________________

When Is It Fair Use? The following four questions are applied to determine whether a given use of copyrighted information constitutes fair use:

- What is the planned use?
- What is the nature of the work in which the material is to be used?

> How much of the work will be used?

> What effect would this use have on the market for the work if the use were widespread?

What constitutes fair use is complex and subject to disagreements by fair-minded people, lawyers, and even judges. Indeed, a recent two-year Conference on Fair Use (CONFU) struggled mightily with the interpretations and failed to clarify the matter fully. It is beyond the scope of this section to delve into the nuances of deciding fair use. But the University of Texas publishes a very useful guideline:

`www3.utsystem.edu/ogc/IntellectualProperty/copypol2.htm`

Violating the Copyright Law

Finally, many people say that it is all right to use copyrighted material for noncommercial purposes, but that's false. You break the law whether you sell the material or not, though commercial use usually results in larger fines or damages when you get sued. Because the penalties for copyright infringement are substantial—up to $100,000 per act—it pays to be careful. By far the best approach is to think things up on your own—that is, create intellectual property with your own intellect. Not only are you not required to ask for anyone else's permission, you enjoy copyright protection too!

FITTIP **Uncopyrightable Fact.** Facts cannot be copyrighted. For example, "*Uncopyrightable* is the longest English word without repeated letters" is a fact, and so is uncopyrightable.

ENSURING THE RELIABILITY OF SOFTWARE

Anyone who uses information technology regularly knows that software contains bugs, that errors occur routinely, and that even catastrophic errors—crashes—are frustratingly frequent. Most of these errors are just an annoyance. But computers control life-support systems and other medical apparatus, airplanes, nuclear power plants, weapons systems, and so on. Errors in these systems are potentially much more serious—"crash" is no longer a metaphor. How do we know the software running safety-critical systems is perfect? We don't! It's a sobering thought.

Safety-Critical Applications

Any system, whether mechanical or electronic, that supports life or controls hazardous devices or materials should work flawlessly. Accepting anything less would seem reckless. But it is easier to say that we want perfection than it is to achieve it.

Hardware Failures. To understand the issues, distinguish first between hardware failures and software failures. In general, hardware failures can be resolved using techniques such as **redundancy**. For example, three computers can perform all the computations of a safety-critical system and make all decisions based on majority vote. If a failure in one computer causes it to come up with a different answer, the other two overrule it. The chance that the identical error would happen in each computer simultaneously is infinitesimally small. Another technique, dubbed **burn in**, exploits the so-called "infant mortality" property of computer hardware failures caused by manufacturing problems: Most errors show up after only a few hours of operation. A computer that has a record of successful operation is likely to continue to operate successfully. Overall, such techniques can give us confidence that the Fetch/Execute cycle and other hardware will work properly.

Software Failures. Software is another matter. Compared with mechanical and electronic systems, software is amazingly complex. The number of possible configurations that a typical program can define grows exponentially and quickly becomes unimaginably large even for small programs. It is a fact that all states that the software can get into, known as **reachable configurations**, cannot be examined for their correctness. This reality poses a serious problem for programmers and software engineers: How can they be sure their programs work right?

Like all engineers, programmers begin with a **specification**—a precise description of the input, how the system is to behave, and the output to be produced. The specification doesn't say how the behavior is to be achieved necessarily, just what it should be. Using various design methods, programmers produce the program. The program can be tested with sample inputs, and the outputs can be checked against the specification. If they do not match, there is a bug and the program must be fixed. *A program is said to be correct if its behavior exactly matches its specification.*

Though we have a tidy definition for correctness, there are two problems to achieving it, and both are showstoppers. First, it is not possible to know if the specification is perfect. Second, even if it were, it is not possible to establish correctness by testing. These two facts mean that we cannot *know* whether a program is correct, even if it is. Programmers and software engineers have developed many ingenious tools and technologies, including testing, to locate bugs and improve software. These can and do give us confidence that the program closely approximates its specification. But confidence, not certainty, is the best that can be done.

FITBYTE

Hard Fact of Software. Programming pioneer Edsger Dijkstra first stated this fundamental fact: Program testing reveals only the presence of bugs, never their absence.

The Challenge. What can we do about the fact that the software we use cannot be known to be correct? There are two aspects to consider:

> We must accept that software may contain bugs despite Herculean efforts of programmers and software engineers to get it right. So, we must monitor all software usage, alert to unusual behavior that can indicate bugs, and be prepared to limit the harm that they can do.

> Because programmers and software engineers are well aware of this challenge to producing correct software, poorly tested software is simply unprofessional; users should demand software of the highest quality, refuse buggy software, and be prepared to change to better software.

Thus we must be cautious and informed users and take our business to those who produce the best product.

Fail-Soft and Fail-Safe Software

Returning to the problem of software controlling safety-critical systems, what should the standard of quality be? The software could be perfectly correct, but we can never know it. Instead we can put limits on the harm that can result from using the software. If we know that software is safe—that the life-support system does not cause patients to die, and the nuclear power plant software will not cause meltdown—then perhaps we are less concerned about bugs. The idea of **safe software** changes the focus from worry about program correctness to concern about the consequences of errors in the software.

Testing and other techniques can give us confidence that software works "under normal circumstances," so safety focuses on what happens in unusual circumstances. It is difficult to test software under unusual circumstances, as when an earthquake damages a nuclear power plant. So, there are two design strategies known as fail-soft and fail-safe. **Fail-soft** means that the program continues to operate, providing a possibly degraded level of functionality. **Fail-safe** means that the system stops functioning to avoid causing harm. The basic strategy, therefore, is to continue to operate as long as productive service can be safely provided, but when that isn't possible, to avoid negative outcomes by stopping entirely.

Perfectly safe software is just as impossible as correct software, since the only way for the software to avoid all harm is not to do anything at all—don't even start the nuclear power plant. Using software to control potentially dangerous systems means taking a risk, just as crossing a bridge or riding an elevator means taking a risk.

SUMMARY

The chapter began with a discussion of the weaknesses of email. We recognized email's shortcomings in expressing emotion and ideas unambiguously. Problems arise in stressing words, alternation, and using email in anger. But netiquette makes email usage more pleasant. Thoughtful email users limit messages requiring an answer to one topic, include context, and do not forward private messages or broadcast email to everyone they ever met on the Internet. As a courtesy, they use a vacation message when they will not be reading email for a while, and they answer a backlog of email in reverse time order.

Expecting the unexpected is a difficult but useful survival skill. We first recognize the unusual situation, and then think about what it means. "Why is it happening?" "What's going on?" The challenge is to think about the unexpected event, and correctly determine whether and how you should respond.

The next topic was passwords. We gave a set of heuristics for creating an easy-to-remember password. The approach emphasized selecting all of your passwords so they are connected to a common topic. This will help you remember them. It is also a good idea to choose simple passwords where little security is needed and to choose more obscure passwords when there is greater risk.

Risk is also present with viruses and worms. We can reduce the chances that viruses and worms could harm our computer usage by installing and running antivirus software. Copyright infringement poses a legal risk, causing us to take care not to share software or pirate copyrighted information from the Web. Finally, we discussed the reliability of computers and software. Unfortunately, it is practically impossible to have bug-free software. This doesn't mean that we quit using computers or accept bugs. Rather, we must watch for unusual behavior that might be caused by bugs and take precautions to limit the harm that software bugs can cause.

EXERCISES

Multiple Choice

1. Which of the following is not a weakness of email?
   A. conveying emotion
   B. multicasting
   C. emphasis
   D. ambiguity
2. Using ALL CAPS for an email message conveys:
   A. sarcasm
   B. urgency
   C. anger
   D. humor
3. The best way to end a flame war is to:
   A. cc all parties
   B. cool down before you reply
   C. use humor or sarcasm
   D. proofread your message
4. Email:
   A. never fails to be delivered
   B. is usually delivered in four hours or less
   C. notifies you only if your message isn't delivered in three days
   D. is only about 90 percent reliable
5. A list moderator does all of the following except:
   A. configures the list-server for its members
   B. edits all messages sent to the list
   C. maintains a list of members subscribed to the list-server
   D. handles errors and problems for the list-server
6. When you forget your password:
   A. you must apply for a new one
   B. the system administrator looks up your password
   C. the system administrator unscrambles your password and gives it to you
   D. the system administrator assigns a new password for you to use
7. Computer viruses and worms have been around since:
   A. the early days of computers
   B. the early days of the Internet
   C. the late 1980s
   D. the late 1990s
8. Computer viruses are typically spread by:
   A. copying software from an infected computer
   B. receiving email from an infected computer
   C. opening email from an infected computer
   D. sending email to an infected computer

9. Copyrighted material may be used:
   A. only in non-profit instances
   B. only when written permission is granted
   C. if proper credit is given to the owner
   D. without permission in limited circumstances

10. Most software:
    A. contains bugs
    B. is bug-free
    C. contains no known bugs
    D. works exactly as it should in every circumstance

Short Answer

1. ______ is etiquette for the Internet.
2. Email has a ______ property, that is, the ability to send the same message to many people at the same time.
3. Communication with email is ______ while ______ are synchronous.
4. A(n) ______ is a programmed response to your email that's sent when you are away.
5. A(n) ______ is the person that controls a list-server.
6. The individual that controls access to a computer system, including logins and passwords, is called a(n) ______.
7. A(n) ______ is a program that embeds itself in another program, copies itself, and spreads to other computers.
8. A(n) ______ is a program that copies itself from one machine to another across a network.
9. ______ is non-material, human creations that people can claim ownership to.
10. New work created from an existing work is called a(n) ______.
11. Information in the ______ is free for anyone to use.
12. All the possible states in which a piece of software can exist are its ______.
13. A(n) ______ program continues to operate when there is a problem, although its efficiency may be degraded.
14. A(n) ______ program shuts down to avoid causing problems.

Exercises

1. What is this password: `BH9oH2won0`? (Hint: It was a popular '90s TV show.)
2. Devise a year's worth of passwords based on a common theme.
3. Go to www.wildlist.org. Check the current list to see how many viruses are currently considered "in the wild."

4. For each of the following, determine whether the practice is legal, illegal, or iffy. Defend your answer.
   a. You sell a copy of a computer game to your friend.
   b. You exchange computer games with your friend.
   c. You sell your old PC with the software still on it, but you keep the original copies of the software.
   d. You download a piece of shareware but don't pay for it.
   e. You frequently use a piece of shareware but don't pay for it.
   f. You install your company's software on your home computer.
   g. You frequently play a freeware game.
   h. You install software on your computer and the laptop of your college-bound child.
   i. You make a backup CD of a set of originals.
   j. You buy one license but install it throughout a lab.
5. For each of the following, determine whether the practice is legal or illegal.
   a. You create a comical, big-eared cartoon rodent.
   b. You publish a Web page without using the copyright notice.
   c. You write a sequel to *Titanic*.
   d. You include a link to a Web page in your term paper.
   e. You include a paragraph from the *Fluency* text in your term paper.
   f. You put your favorite band's picture on your Web site.
   g. You scan the autographed picture of your favorite band and put it on your Web site.
   h. You put a sound bite from a movie on your answering machine.
   i. You put a sound bite from a movie into your class presentation.
   j. You use parts of your friend's term paper from last semester in your term paper.
6. How many possible eight-character passwords can be created using only uppercase letters and numbers?
7. Use the Web to find rules on netiquette. From these, develop your own list of rules.
8. Describe how computer viruses and worms are like the living kind of viruses. In these same terms, describe how to protect your computer from these synthetic viruses.
9. Describe fail-soft and fail-safe systems on your computer and with your software. Approach the problem from a nontechnical, user standpoint. What safeguards are in place to keep you from damaging or destroying your system, programs, and data?
10. Take a major system such as a commercial airliner or a hydroelectric power plant and describe the fail-soft and fail-safe system they might have.

chapter

13 GETTING TO FIRST BASE

Introduction to Database Concepts

learning objectives

- Explain the differences between everyday tables and database tables
- Explain the ways in which the concepts of structure, entities, and attributes are used in designing a database table
- Explain the use of name, field specifiers, and primary key
- Use the six database operations: **`Select`**, **`Project`**, **`Union`**, **`Difference`**, **`Product`**, **`Join`**
- Explain the way in which the **`Join`** (natural Join) operation differs from the **`Product`** operation

Now that we have all this useful information, it would be nice to do something with it. (Actually, it can be emotionally fulfilling just to get the information. This is usually only true, however, if you have the social life of a kumquat.)

—UNIX PROGRAMMER'S MANUAL

MOST PEOPLE understand a **database** to be a "collection of information." That's correct, but it doesn't say much. It allows almost anything to be a database, including the neighborhood newspaper-recycling bin, which fails as a database for at least two reasons. First, it doesn't record data about any particular thing—we are rarely interested in amorphous collections of text or documents. Second, it is not organized—information must be arranged and structured if it is to be useful for finding specific items. This chapter introduces the basic ideas of organizing information into a relational database.

The chapter begins by comparing what we usually think of as a *table*—an informal concept—with a *table* that we use to build a database. We next introduce the ideas and terminology of relational databases, so we can build sample database tables. (There are other kinds of databases, but because relational databases are the most common, we'll refer to them throughout simply as databases.) Next, we introduce the five fundamental operations of database tables. Finally, we add a sixth operation, `Join`, which simplifies practical table construction. We demonstrate all of these ideas with a rich set of examples.

TABLES: "YOU CAN LOOK IT UP"

Baseball legend Yogi Berra once told a disbelieving listener, "You can look it up" as a challenge to check the record book to verify a claimed fact. A "record book" is a database, and we can imagine—even if we've never seen one—that it is a collection of **tables** like most other archives of factual information. For example, the Olympic record book contains a table for each Olympic event, giving the gold, silver, and bronze medal winners' names and nationalities for each year. (Find them online at `www.olympic.org`.) There are also tables of host countries and of participating nations for each Olympic competition, with the number of athletes competing, and so on.

To "look it up" involves finding the right table and then locating the right entry. Looking through the table of high jump medallists, for example, we can find the world's record jump (2.9 meters!). Many questions, however, do not produce just one answer, but a whole table of answers. So, for example, to find out what athletes from African nations have won medals in the marathon, we look at the table of marathon medallists and select those from Africa. Because more than one person could be a marathon medallist and African, the answer—it's a list of names and countries—is a table. (It is still a table even if there is only one entry, or no entries.)

DATABASE TABLES

There are two important differences between database tables and everyday tables: Database tables specify the sort of information they can contain, and they separate this structure from the actual data; everyday tables do not. Both ideas are straightforward.

Structure

The first and most important difference is that everyday tables show a *picture* (in a tidy format) of the information, while database tables record the structure of the information. Knowing the structure, the computer can produce a picture, too, but the opposite is not possible. The computer can't figure out the structure from the picture. To emphasize the difference, consider the HTML table shown in Figure 13.1.

Though this is a computer specification of a table that *appears* to describe its structure, it only produces a table in the everyday "picture" sense. The HTML specifies how the table entries should look, but it doesn't describe the nature of the data. For example, we know that countries' names are sequences of letters, and so we should expect to find that kind of data in the first column headed Country. But there is no way in HTML to *require* such a characteristic of a table—that is, to specify a property of the data in a column. So the first column entries of the

```
<table border>
 <caption>Country Data</caption>
  <tr>
   <th>Country</th>
   <th>Capital</th>
   <th>Language</th></tr>
  <tr>
   <td>Ecuador</td>
   <td>Quito</td>
   <td>Spanish</td></tr>
  <tr>
   <td>Bolivia</td>
   <td>La Paz</td>
   <td>Spanish</td></tr>
  <tr>
   <td>Brazil</td>
   <td>Brasilia</td>
   <td>Portuguese</td></tr>
</table>
```

Figure 13.1. *HTML specification for a table—but not a database table—giving country information.*

HTML table in Figure 13.2(a) could be replaced with numbers, colors, currency amounts, images, exclamations, and so on as in Figure 13.2(b). It is still an HTML table, but it isn't a database table. It's completely meaningless.

Country Data

Country	Capital	Language
Ecuador	Quito	Spanish
Bolivia	La Paz	Spanish
Brazil	Brasilia	Portuguese

(a)

Country Data

Country	Capital	Language
$54.48	Quito	Spanish
	La Paz	Spanish
Eureka!!	Brasilia	Portuguese

(b)

Figure 13.2. *HTML table (a) made meaningless by replacing table data entries in the first column (b).*

By contrast, database tables record the structure of data, by means of **metadata**, which tell the kind of information stored in the columns. The difference between giving a picture of a table and specifying its structural properties is similar to what we saw in the digitization of the *Oxford English Dictionary* (Chapter 8). There, we could have produced a textual form of the definitions, but instead we defined the structure of the definitions with metadata, enabling the computer to help us search. Our goal with database tables is the same as with the *OED*—we want to specify the information's structure with metadata so the computer can help us use it. Because the types of information are different, the metadata has a variety of forms. For the *OED* we used tags around parts of the text; for databases we use **table descriptions**, as we learn in a later section.

Separate Structure and Content

The second difference between everyday tables and database tables is that in database tables we separate the structure of the information from the information itself. This means we can have a table—that is, the structure—but with no data in it. What would such a table look like? It would have a name and column headings, called **fields**, but no rows, as shown in Figure 13.3(a). This is an **empty table**, and though it's pure structure, it's not such an unusual idea.

Data, Entities, Attributes, and Values

If we can think of the structure without the data, can we think of the data by itself? Yes. In database terminology, information is a set of **entities**. *Entity* is about as vague a word as *thing* or *stuff*. But databases should be able to contain *any* kind of information, so the inventors of relational databases chose a term that could include anything. When we think of a database containing data, the sorts of information most people have in mind are called entities.

What are entities like? They're things with **attributes**; see Figure 13.3(b), which shows five entities. Attributes can be any features people observe about things. Each of an entity's attributes has a **value**. Often, attributes are features that can be measured, such as weight; 36,000 kg might be a value for the attribute weight for a whale. But attributes are very general and can include relationships (such as *aunt*), beliefs (like *Buddhism*), and estimates (like *lifetime earning capacity*). The key point is that entities are synthetic; that is, people invent them, so entities can have any attributes we want. If we can identify a set of things, the features that separate those things from everything else, and from each other, are their attributes.

FITBYTE

A Bright Idea. Though many people contributed to the creation of relational databases—the kind of databases discussed here—E. F. Codd of IBM is widely credited with the idea. He received the Association of Computing Machinery's Turing Award for it, the field's Nobel Prize.

Once we have defined a table's structure, as in an empty table, and have decided on the entities' attributes and the types of the attributes' values, the entities themselves become the rows of the table, called **tuples**; see Figure 13.3(c). A tuple is a set of fields, each field containing the value of one of the attributes of that entity. An important property of tuples and fields is that they are not ordered. Of course, there will be some order when they are printed or displayed—for example, the fields are aligned into columns for each attribute—but in concept there is no order. Since *row* is a more familiar term than tuple, we will use it.

Whales

name	scientific_name	food	weight	length_range	picture

(a)

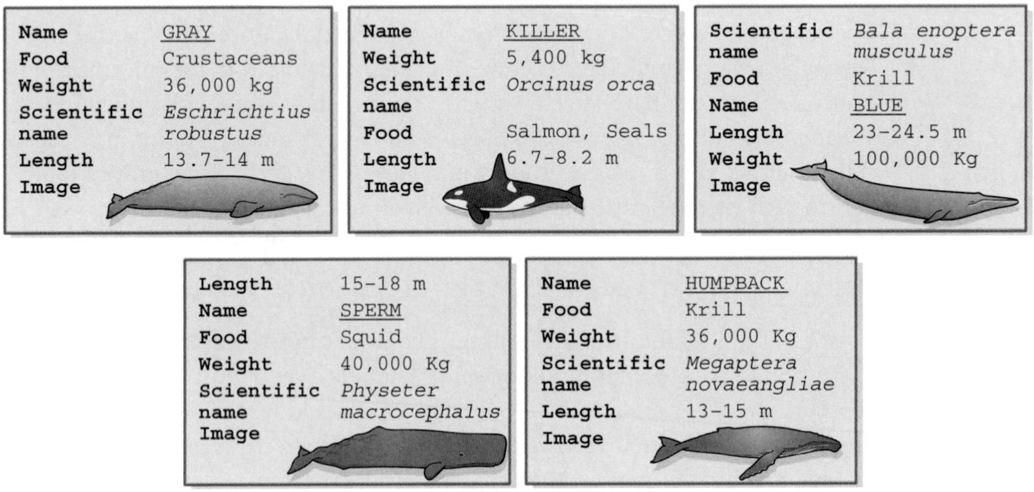

(b)

Whales					
name	**scientific**	**food Source**	**Wt. Kg.**	**length range**	**photograph**
Gray	*Eschrichtius robustus*	Crustaceans	36,000	13.7-14m	
Killer	*Orcinus orca*	Salmon, Seals	5,400	6.7-8.2m	
Blue	*Bala enoptera musculus*	Krill	100,000	23-24.5m	
Sperm	*Physeter macrocephalus*	Squid	40,000	15-18m	
Humpback	*Megaptera novaeangliae*	Krill	36,000	13-15m	

(c)

Figure 13.3. *The constituents of a database table: (a) the table structure, (b) unordered entities with their unordered attributes, (c) the rows of the whale table.*

FITBYTE

Tuples. The sequence of terms *singleton, pair, triple, quadruple, quintuple, sextuple, septuple, . . .* for groups of things motivates the term *tuple*. A group of *n* things is called an *n-tuple*, or just a *tuple*. It conveys the idea of *n* things, grouped together, but without order. *Tuple* is usually pronounced with a short *u*.

Because databases separate a table's structure from its contents, the content can be referred to separately. A specific set of rows is a table **instance**. Figure 13.3(c) shows one instance for the `Whales` table; adding a row for beluga whales produces a different instance, as does removing killer whales.

DEFINING A DATABASE TABLE

In this section, we explain how to define the structure of database tables. We also describe pitfalls to avoid when building the definition of a table.

Components of a Table Definition

The definition of a database table requires three parts: a name, field specifiers, and a primary key.

Name. The name of a database table *describes* the kind of things that are collected together in the table and is the entity's name. We prefer descriptive nouns like *whales* rather than caption-like phrases such as "Rita's Five Favorite Whales," which might contain irrelevant text. *Five*, for example, doesn't work because the number of entities in a table is variable.

Field specifiers. Field specifiers give names to the attributes and describe the type of information that will appear in the columns. Field specifiers are said to **declare** a column of a table using the syntax

field_name *data_format* *optional_comment*

Here *field_name* describes the attribute, *data_format* specifies the type of information to be expected in that field, and *optional_comment* is anything else we want to remember about the attribute. Our options for a *data_format* depend on the database software. The formats usually include numbers, ASCII strings, dates, currency amounts, JPEG or GIF images, Boolean values (i.e., a single bit to represent things like yes/no), and so on. (Because the present discussion is independent of an implementing system, we use any convenient form of data when specifying *data_formats*.) By specifying the *data_format*, we avoid problems like the one illustrated in the meaningless table in Figure 13.2(b).

Databases usually contain many tables, which must all have different field names. It's convenient and legal to reuse field names, because different tables may record similar kinds of data (for example, name, size, address, etc.). Reuse motivates the "dot" notation for fields, *table_name.field_name*, as in `Whales.photo`.

Primary key. A primary key is one or more fields that uniquely identify any row in the table, as explained momentarily.

Notice that although a database table has a single name and a single primary key, it usually has several field specifiers.

FITBYTE

For the Record. *Tuples* is the proper term for entities. *Rows* is used as a synonym; the term *records* is also a synonym. *Record* is a holdover from computing's punch-card days but is still commonly used.

Specifying a Table: The Whale Example

To apply the concepts we just learned, consider the specification of the database table shown in Figure 13.3(a).

```
Whales
  name              text 15    The common English name
  scientific_name   text 30    Genus and species
  food              text 12    Primary food source
  weight            number     Typical max. adult weight,
                               kilograms
  length_range      text 20    Lower-upper adult length
                               range, meters
  image             GIF        Picture of mature adult
Primary Key: name
```

In this specification, the names are at the left, the data formats in the middle, and comments are at the right. In the data format text column, the numbers following `text` refer to a sequence of ASCII symbols—not just letters—of that length. The data format `number` specifies a numerical quantity, and `GIF` specifies a value represented in the Graphic Interchange Format (i.e., a picture).

A Closer Look at Whales

Three aspects of the `Whales` specification need more explanation: descriptive field names, atomic field data, and keys.

Descriptive Field Names. A field name *describes* the attribute in the same way that the table name should describe the entities of the table. Field names are nouns, not the text that would label a column as the heading when the table is printed. For example, `weight` describes the attribute, whereas "Weight, kg" might be used as the printed heading for its column. Notice that we use the comment field to remind ourselves that the measurements are in kilograms. As might be expected, the names have meaning only to us; the computer doesn't know what they mean and would be just as happy with `field0001`, `field0002`, and so on.

Atomic Field Data. One fundamental rule in database design is that the information in a field must be **atomic**, meaning that it cannot be subdivided into separate smaller parts. (We called atomic items tokens in the searching sections of Chapter 2.) For example, scientific names are made up of two words: the genus and the species. Our specification of `scientific_name` was a single 30-letter string of text, enough to give both parts of any scientific name. Because fields must be atomic, the `scientific_name` can be used only in its entirety, not by its two component parts. We can search on the whole entry (e.g., `Orcinus orca`) but not on a part of it (e.g., `orca`).

If we had wanted to treat the genus and species separately, we should have replaced the original specification

```
scientific_name      text 30     Genus and species
```

with

```
genus_name           text 15     Genus
species_name         text 15     Species
```

This would let us search for either the genus or the species name.

Keeping the scientific name together has its advantages, and in the `Whales` example, we chose to treat them as a unit because we do not plan to view or change either name separately. Predicting how information is to be used is a difficult part of database design. Notice that the length range of the whales could also have been broken into two fields: the lower and upper ends of the range. If we were to store the limits separately, we could manipulate them separately, and each part would probably be stored as a number.

Finally, there is the problem of data types such as dates (e.g., 14 July 2003), time (e.g., 12:57:21), and money (e.g., $199.95), which are constructed out of parts (days and months) or have special characteristics (only two decimal places) or both. Strictly speaking, such data should be kept in separate fields, stored in its most basic, atomic unit—seconds or pennies. Doing so is tedious, so database systems create special data types—dates, time, currency—that automatically preserve the atomic property, but that allow us to reference the subfields when we need to. This is a safe way to "cheat" on the atomic property for those few types of information. The problem of atomic data still arises frequently, however, with data such as addresses.

Keys. We need to be able to tell entities apart. That is, if they're like rice grains or amoebas and you can't tell the data items apart, they're not entities. So, another table definition requirement is that the fields chosen for the table contain enough information to make each row different. Usually one or a few of the fields make this property true. A field for which all rows have a different value is known as a **key**. For example, because the English names for whales are unique, the name field is a key for the table in Figure 13.3. The `scientific_name` is also a key. Keys are used to identify a row. For example, we can look up the second row shown in Figure 13.3(c) either by the value `Killer` in the name field or `Orcinus orca` in the `scientific_name` field, because either one uniquely specifies a particular row. Tables often have more than one key, so we pick one of the keys as the **primary key**; it tells the database system that among all the possible keys, this field is the one to use as the key. The uses for keys will be discussed in Chapter 14.

When we specify a key we assert that *as a property of the data* all rows for all time will have different values for that field. That's true for `name` and `scientific_name`, for example. Sometimes we notice a column with different values, for example, `Whales.weight`, but if being different is not a *requirement* of the data—whales could weigh the same, so it's not—then the field is not a key. Thus, selecting a key is an assertion, not an observation.

Database Tables Recap

Summarizing the important points of the last two sections, tables in databases are not simply an arrangement of text (that is, a picture), but rather have a structure that is specified by metadata. The structure of a database table is separate from its contents. A table structures a set of entities—any things we can tell apart by their attributes—by naming fields for the attributes' values and giving the data types for those fields. The entities of the table are represented as tuples. We use **rows** to mean tuples and we use **columns** and fields interchangeably, but we understand that rows and columns are unordered in databases. (Of course, when defining a table or displaying it, we must list them in some order.) Tables and fields should have names that describe their contents, the fields must be atomic (i.e., indivisible), and one field—the primary key—has the property that it will have a different value for every row in any table instance.

OPERATIONS ON TABLES

As we mentioned earlier, the answer to a question about a database table is often a table. That idea motivates us to learn how tables can be used to create other tables. In this section, we illustrate the idea with a database table of the countries of the world that might be used by a travel agency. Its structure and sample entries are shown in Figure 13.4. Using that table, `Nations`, we'll investigate the five fundamental operations that can be performed on tables: `Select`, `Project`, `Union`, `Difference`, and `Product`.

```
Nations
  Name        Character 15   Common rather than official name
  Domain      Character  2   Internet top-level domain name
  Capital     Character 20   Nation's capital
  Latitude    Number         Approx. latitude of capital
  N_S         Boolean        Latitude is N(orth) or S(outh)
  Longitude   Number         Approx. longitude of capital
  E_W         Boolean        Longitude is E(ast) or W(est)
  One_Word    Character 50   A word describing the country
Primary Key: Name
```

Name	Dom	Capital	Lat	NS	Lon	EW	Word
Ireland	IE	Dublin	52	N	7	W	History
Israel	IR	Jerusalem	32	N	34	E	History
Italy	IT	Rome	41	N	12	E	Art
Jamaica	JM	Kingston	17	N	77	W	Beach
Japan	JP	Tokyo	35	N	143	E	Kabuki

Figure 13.4. *The* `Nations` *table definition and sample entries.*

Select Operation

The **Select** operation takes rows from one table to create a new table. Generally we specify the **Select** operation by giving the (single) table from which rows are to be selected and the test for selection. We use the syntax:

Select_from *Table* **On** *Test*

The *Test* is to be applied to each row of the given table to decide if it should be included in the new table. The *Test* is a short formula that tests field values. It is written using field names, constants like numbers or letter strings, and the relational operators <, ≤, =, ≠, ≥, and >. The relational operators just test whether the field has a particular relationship, for example, `Word = 'Beach'` or `Latitude < 45`. If the *Test* is true, the row is included in the new table; otherwise, it is ignored. Notice that the information used to create the new table is a copy, so the original table is not changed by **Select** (or any of the other table-building operations discussed here).

To use the **Nations** table to create a table of countries with beaches, we write a query to remove all rows for countries that have **Beach** as their one-word description. The query would be

Select_from Nations **On** One_Word = 'Beach'

This gives us a new table, shown in part in Figure 13.5. Notice that the information in the last column is constant because the *Test* required the word Beach for that field.

Name	Dom	Capital	Lat	NS	Lon	EW	Word
Australia	AU	Canberra	37	S	148	E	Beach
Bahamas	BS	Nassau	25	N	78	W	Beach
Barbados	BB	Bridgetown	13	N	59	W	Beach
Belize	BZ	Belize	17	N	89	W	Beach
Bermuda	BM	Hamilton	32	N	64	W	Beach

Figure 13.5. *Part of the table created by selecting countries with the Test that the one-word description equals Beach.*

The *Test* can be more than a test of a single value. For example, we can use the logical operations **AND** and **OR** in the way they were used to search in Chapters 5 and 6. So, for example, to find countries whose capitals are at least 60° north latitude, we write

```
Select_from Nations On Latitude ≥ 60 AND N_S = 'N'
```

which should produce a four-row table created from the **Nations** table's rows for Greenland, Iceland, Norway, and Finland.

Project Operation

If we can pick out rows of a table (using **Select**), we should be able to pick out columns too. **Project** (pronounced *pro·JÉCT*) is the operation that builds a new table from the columns of an existing table. All that we must specify are the name(s) of the existing table(s) and of the columns (field names) to be included in the new table. The syntax is

Project *Field_List* **From** *Table*

For example, to create a new table from the **Nations** table without the **capital** and position information—that is, to keep the other three columns—write

```
Project Name, Domain, One_Word From Nations
```

The new table will have as many rows as the **Nations** table, but just three columns. Figure 13.6 shows part of that table.

Name	Dom	Word
Nauru	NR	Beach
Nepal	NP	Mountains
Netherlands	NL	Art
New Caledonia	NC	Beach
New Zealand	NZ	Adventure

Figure 13.6. *Sample entries for a* **Project** *operation on* **Nations**.

`Project` does not *always* result in a table with the same number of rows as the original table. When the new table includes a key from the old table (e.g., `Name`), the key makes each row distinct, the new table will include fields from all rows of the original table, meaning that both tables have the same number of rows. But if some of the new table's rows are the same—which can't happen if key columns are included, but can if there is no key—they will be merged together into a single row. The rows have to be merged because of the rule that the rows of any table must always be distinct. If rows in one table are merged, the two tables will, of course, have different numbers of rows. So, for example, to list the single-word descriptions that travel agents use to describe countries, we create a new table of only the last column of `Nations`:

```
Project One_Word From Nations
```

which produces a one-column table with a row for each descriptive word: `Beach` appears once, `Art` appears once, and so on. Thus the table has as many rows as unique words, but not as many rows as `Nations`.

We often use `Select` and `Project` operations together to "trim" base tables to keep only some of the rows and some of the columns. To illustrate, we define a table of the countries with northern capitals, called `Northern`, and define it with the command

```
Northern = (Select_from Nations On Latitude ≥ 60 AND N_S = 'N')
```

which is the table we created earlier. To throw away everything except the name, domain, and latitude to produce Northland, we write

```
Northland = Project Name, Domain, Latitude From Northern
```

as shown in Figure 13.7.

Name	Dom	Lat
Finland	FI	64
Greenland	GL	72
Iceland	IS	65
Norway	NO	62

Figure 13.7. *`Northland`, the table of countries with northern capitals.*

Another way to achieve the same result is to combine the two operations:

```
Project Name, Domain, Latitude From
     (Select_from Nations On Latitude ≥ 60 AND N_S = 'N')
```

First a temporary table is created with the four countries, just as we did before. Then the desired columns are selected. It might be a slightly more efficient solution if we don't need the `Northern` table for any other purpose, but generally either solution is fine.

Union Operation

Besides picking out rows and columns of a table, another operation on tables is to combine two tables. This only makes sense if they have the same set of attributes, of course. The operation is known as **Union**, and is written as though it were addition:

*Table*1 + *Table*2

The plus sign (+) can be read "combined with." So, if the table of countries with capitals at least 45° south latitude are named **Southern** with the command

```
Southern = (Select_from Nations On Latitude ≥ 45 AND N_S = 'S')
```

then countries where the northern or southern lights should be visible—call it **Aurora**—would be

```
Aurora = Northern + Southern
```

The result is shown in Figure 13.8. This table could also have been created with a complex **Select** command.

Name	Dom	Capital	Lat	NS	Lon	EW	Word
Falkland Is	FK	Stanley	51	S	58	W	Nature
Finland	FI	Helsinki	64	N	26	E	Nature
Greenland	GL	Nuuk	72	N	40	W	Nature
Iceland	IS	Reykjavik	65	N	18	W	Geysers
Norway	NO	Oslo	62	N	10	E	Vikings

Figure 13.8. *The* **Aurora** *table created with* **Union.**

Union can be used to combine separate tables, say, **Nations** with **Canada_Provinces**. (**Canada_Provinces** gives the same data about the provinces as **Nations** does about countries, except the **Domain** field is **CA** for all rows.) For example, had the **Northern** table been defined by

```
Select_from (Nations + Canada_Provinces)
       On Latitude ≥ 60 AND N_S = 'N'
```

Then the Yukon would be included because its capital, Whitehorse, is north of 60°.

Difference Operation

The opposite of combining two tables with **Union** is to remove from one table the rows also listed in a second table. The operation is known as **Difference** and it is written with the syntax

*Table*1 – *Table*2

The operation can be read, "remove from *Table1* any rows also in *Table2*." Like **Union**, **Difference** only makes sense when the table's fields are the same. For example,

```
Nations - Northern
```

produces a table without those countries with northern capitals—that is, without Finland, Greenland, Iceland, and Norway. Interestingly, this same command works just as well if **Northern** had included the Canadian provinces like the Yukon. That is, in a **Difference** command, the items "subtracted away" do not have to exist in the original table.

Product Operation

Adding and subtracting tables is easy. What would multiplying tables be like? The **Product** operation on tables, which is written as

*Table*1 × *Table*2

creates a **super table**. The table has all the fields from *both* tables. So, if the first table has five fields and the second table has six fields, the **Product** table has eleven fields. The rows of the new table are created by **appending** each row of the second table to each row of the first table—that is, putting the rows together. The result is the "product" of the rows of each table. For example, if the first table is **Nations** with 230 rows, and the second table has 4 rows, there will be 230 × 4 = 920 rows because each row of the **Nations** table would be concatenated with each row of the second table to produce a row of the result.

For example, suppose you have a table of your traveling companions, as described in Figure 13.9(a), containing the information shown in Figure 13.9(b).

```
Travelers
   Friend
   Homeland

Primary Key: Friend
```

(a)

Friend	Homeland
Isabella	Argentina
Brian	South Africa
Wen	China
Clare	Canada

(b)

Figure 13.9. *The definition of the* **Travelers** *table (a), and its values (b).*

Then the **Product** operation

```
Nations × Travelers
```

creates a new table with ten fields—eight fields from **Nations** and two fields from **Travelers**—and 920 rows. Some of the rows of the new table are shown in Figure 13.10. For each country, there is a row for each of your friends.

Name	Dom	Capital	Lat	NS	Log	EW	Word	Friend	Homeland
Cyprus	CY	Nicosia	35	N	32	E	History	Clare	Canada
Czech Rep.	CZ	Prague	51	N	15	E	Pilsner	Isabella	Argentina
Czech Rep.	CZ	Prague	51	N	15	E	Pilsner	Brian	South Africa
Czech Rep.	CZ	Prague	51	N	15	E	Pilsner	Wen	China
Czech Rep.	CZ	Prague	51	N	15	E	Pilsner	Clare	Canada
Denmark	DK	Copenhagen	55	N	12	E	History	Isabella	Argentina

Figure 13.10. *Some rows from the* `Super` *table, the product of* `Nations` *and* `Travelers`*; for each row in* `Nations` *and each row in* `Travelers`*, there is a row in the product table that combines them.*

The **`Product`** operation may seem a little odd at first because its approach of using all combinations combines information that may not "belong together." And it's true. But most often, **`Product`** is used to create a super table that contains both useful and useless rows, and then it is "trimmed down" using **`Select`**, **`Project`**, and **`Difference`** to contain only the intended information. This is a powerful approach that we will see many times in this and the next two chapters.

To illustrate, suppose your traveling companions volunteer to tutor students preparing for the National Geographic Society's Geography Bee. Each friend agrees to tutor students "on their part of the world," that is, in the quarter of the planet from which they come. So, Isabella, who comes from Argentina in the southern and western hemispheres, agrees to tutor students on the geography of that part of the world, and so on. Then you can produce a master list of who's responsible for each country. We'll call it the **`Master`** table. It is produced by these commands:

```
Super  = Nations × Travelers
Assign = (Select_from Super On N_S = 'S' AND E_W = 'W'
             AND Friend = 'Isabella')
          +(Select_from Super On N_S = 'S' AND E_W = 'E'
             AND Friend = 'Brian')
          +(Select_from Super On N_S = 'N' AND E_W = 'E'
             AND Friend = 'Wen')
          +(Select_from Super On N_S = 'N' AND E_W = 'W'
             AND Friend = 'Clare')
Master = Project Name, Friend From Assign
```

How do these commands work? The **`Super`** table is the product table discussed earlier with a row for each nation paired with each friend (see Figure 13.10). Then the **`Assign`** table is created by the **`Union`** operation (+) that combines four tables, each created by a **`Select`** operation from **`Super`**. The first **`Select`** keeps only those countries from **`Super`** with Isabella's name that are also in the southern and western hemispheres. The second **`Select`** keeps only those countries from **`Super`** with Brian's name that are in the southern and eastern hemispheres. The same kind of operations are used for Wen and Clare. The resulting **`Assign`** table has

230 rows—the same as the original **Nations** table—with one of your friends' names assigned to each country.

We know that all of the countries are in the **Assign** table because every country is in one of the four hemisphere pairs and in **Super** there is a row for each country for each friend. When the right combination "comes up," the country will be selected. In addition, **Assign** has the property that each person is given countries in "their" part of the world. (Wen seems to have been assigned the greatest amount of work!) Finally, we throw away all of the location information to create our **Master** list, keeping only the names of the countries and the friends responsible for tutoring students about that geography. Part of the result is shown in Figure 13.11.

Name	Friend
Chad	Wen
Chile	Isabella
China	Wen
Christmas Is.	Clare
Cocos Is.	Brian

Figure 13.11. *A portion of the* **Master** *table of your friends' assignments*

FITBYTE

Quotient Intelligence. There *is* a **Divide** operation on tables, but it's complicated and rather bizarre. Because it doesn't give us any new capabilities, we will leave it to the experts.

We have introduced five basic operations on tables. They are straightforward and simple. It is surprising, therefore, that these five are all the operations needed to create any table in the relational database world. In practice, we will rarely use the operations directly. Instead, they will be incorporated into database software in ways so natural that if we are thinking about creating tables from other tables—the point of learning them—we will hardly be aware they are being used.

JOIN OPERATION

Another powerful and useful operation for creating database tables is **Join**. Indeed, it is so useful that although **Join** can be defined from the five primitive database operations of the previous section, it is usually considered a separate operator. **Join** combines two tables, like the **Product** operation does, but it doesn't necessarily produce all pairings. If the two tables have a common field, the new table produced by **`Join`** combines only the rows from the given tables that match *on the common fields*, not all pairings of rows, as does **`Product`**. We write the **`Join`** operation as follows:

`Table1 ⋈ Table2`

The unusual "bow tie" symbol suggests a special form of **`Product`** in which the two tables "match up."

To show how **`Join`** works, recall the **`Northland`** table (Figure 13.7) and the **`Master`** table of your friends' assignments (Figure 13.11). The **`Join`**

`Master ⋈ Northland`

pairs all rows that match on their common field, **`Name`**. Which rows are those? Beginning with the first row of the **`Master`** table (shown here):

Name	Friend
Afghanistan	Wen
Albania	Wen
...	...

the Afghanistan row does not have the same **`Name`** field as any of the four rows of **`Northland`**, so it is not part of the result. Nor is the second row with **`Name`** equal to the Albania part of the result. Indeed, only four rows of **`Master`** have the same **`Name`** field as rows in **`Northland`**: Finland, Greenland, Iceland, and Norway. We combine those four rows with their corresponding rows in **`Northland`** (and remove the repeated **`Name`** field) to produce the four-row result shown in Figure 13.12. As you see, **`Join`** associates the information from the rows of two tables in a sensible way. Thus, **`Join`** is used to create new associations of information in the database.

There are at least two ways to think about the **`Join`** operation. One way is to see it as a "lookup" operation on tables. That is, for each row in one table, locate a row (or rows) in the other table with the same value in the common field; if found, combine the two and eliminate one copy of the common field; if not, look up the next row. That's how we explained it in the last paragraph. Another way is to see **`Join`** as a **`Product`** operation forming all pairs of the two tables and then eliminating all rows that don't match in the common fields, one of which is removed. Both ideas accurately describe the result, and the computer probably uses still another approach to produce the **`Join`** table.

`Join`, as described, is called a **natural Join** because the natural meaning of "to match" is for the fields to be equal. But as is typical of IT, it is also possible to join using any relational operator (<, ≤, =, ≠, ≥, >), not just = to compare the common field. Unnatural or not, a **`Join`** where **`T1.fieldID < T2.fieldID`** can be handy.

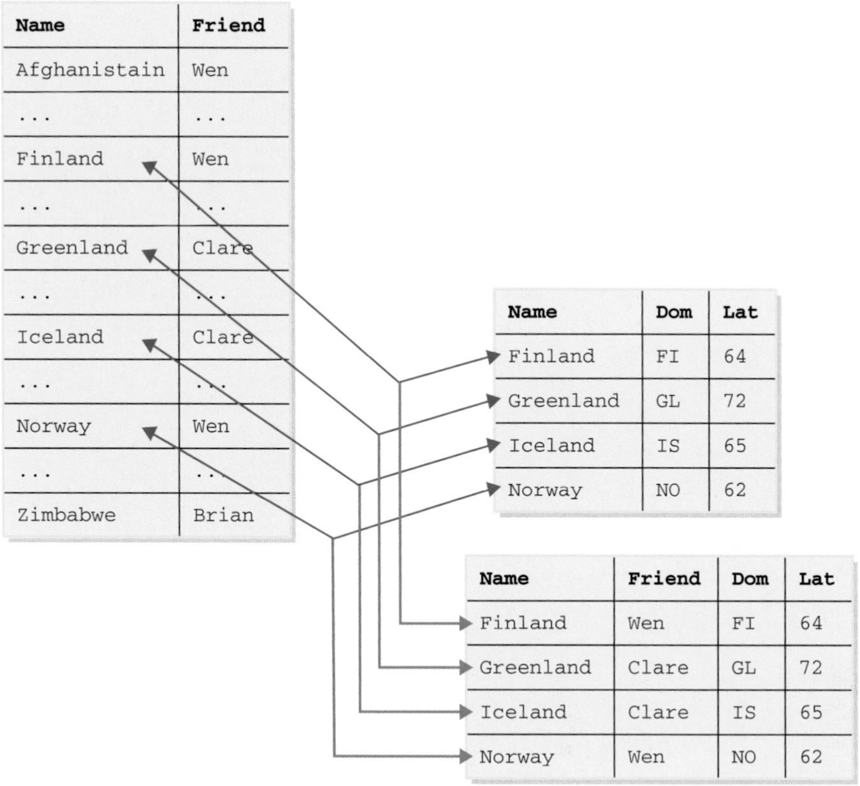

Figure 13.12. *The* `Join` *operation:* `Master ⋈ Northland.`

Because the "matching" operation may not be "=" and because it is often convenient to be able to join on fields with different names, another way to express `Join` is

Table1 ⋈ *Table2* **`On`** *Match*

Here the *Match* specifies the two fields and how they are to be compared. For example, the previous natural Join of `Master` and `Northern` is in this form

`Master ⋈ Northland` **`On`** `Master.Name = Northland.Name`

Consider the following example:

`Nations ⋈ Travelers` **`On`** `Nations.Name = Travelers.Homeland`

This produces a four-row, nine-column table that associates each of your traveling friends with the data for their home country. (Chapter 14 has more on `Join`.)

SUMMARY

The chapter began by introducing the ideas and terminology for tables, and by comparing everyday tables with database tables. Database tables have names and fields that describe the attributes of the entities contained in the table. The data quantitatively recording each property has a specific data type and is atomic. Five fundamental operations on tables—`Select`, `Project`, `Union`, `Difference`, and `Product`—were introduced. These five are the only operations we need to create any new table from a database of tables. `Join` is an especially useful operation that associates information from separate tables in new ways, based on a common field.

EXERCISES

Multiple Choice

1. In database terminology, a set of entities refers to:
   A. fields
   B. columns
   C. tables
   D. information
2. The columns of data in a database are often known as:
   A. fields
   B. records
   C. tables
   D. tuples
3. The definition of a database includes all of the following except:
   A. tuples
   B. name
   C. field specifiers
   D. primary key
4. The type of information stored in a field in a database is described by the:
   A. tuple
   B. field name
   C. data format
   D. record
5. In the field name, `Fall_Schedule.Room`, `Fall_Schedule` and `Room` represent, respectively:
   A. *`table_name`*, *`field_name`*
   B. attribute, entity
   C. row, tuple
   D. *`field_name`*, *`table_name`*
6. A field name:
   A. is identical to its column heading
   B. describes the entities in a table
   C. cannot be subdivided
   D. can only contain letters
7. Which of the following fields could not be a key field?
   A. Social Security number
   B. student ID number
   C. phone number
   D. Web address

8. A Test is used to:
   A. add rows to an existing table
   B. remove rows from an existing table
   C. include rows in a new table
   D. describe rows in any table
9. The `Project` operation is used to:
   A. create a new table from existing rows in a table
   B. create a new table from existing fields in a table
   C. exclude specific rows from a table
   D. remove existing fields from a table
10. Information from two tables can be combined using the:
    A. `Join` operation
    B. `Combine` operation
    C. `Union` operation
    D. `Apply` operation
11. Using the `Product` operation on a table with 4 fields and 9 rows and a table with 7 fields and 6 rows will result in a table with:
    A. 11 fields and 9 rows
    B. 11 fields and 54 rows
    C. 28 fields and 15 rows
    D. 26 fields and 15 rows
12. The `Join` operation can work with the relational operators:
    A. =, ≠
    B. ≤, ≥
    C. <, >
    D. all of the above

Short Answer

1. A(n) ______ is an organized collection of information on a particular topic.
2. Databases are based on information organized in ______.
3. Normal tables show a ______ of the information while a database also shows the ______ of the information.
4. Column headings for a database table are called ______.
5. ______ are the values of an entity in a database.
6. When creating a database, you can ______ a field by specifying the field name and the data format.
7. A(n) ______ is a unique identifier for any row in a database table.
8. The ______ operation takes rows from a table to create a new table.
9. A ______ is used to see if a row should be included in a table.
10. The ______ operation is used to combine information from two tables.

11. Putting the rows of two tables together using the `Product` operation is known as ______.

12. The ______ operation combines two tables and removes the duplicate rows from the resulting table.

13. The `Join` operation works by combining tables based on a(n) ______.

14. The ______ operation is used to remove the contents of one table from another table.

15. A(n) ______ makes use of the multiple tables of related information.

Exercises

1. For the following, either indicate that the field is atomic or divide the field to make the result atomic.

Field	**Contents**
Phone	(212) 555-1212
Name	Larry Snyder
Class	CSE 100
City	Seattle, WA
DOB	September 26, 1948

2. Define the field name, data format, and optional comment needed to create a table that could be used as a datebook.

3. Define the field name, data format, and optional comment needed to create a table that could be used for your college coursework. Include such fields as college courses, credits, prerequisites, major, minor, and elective courses.

4. Write an operation to display the `Name` and `Word` from the `Nations` table on page 361 for those countries with `Beach` and store it in a table called `Vacation`.

5. Write an operation using `Product` and based on the `Word` field to combine the `Tropics` and `Tops` tables.

6. Write an operation to remove `Tops` from `Tropics`.

7. Write an operation to combine the `Vacation` and `Tops` tables into a table called `Sp_Break`.

8. Use the `Join` operation to combine the `Tropics` and `Tops` tables based on `Name`.

chapter

14

A TABLE WITH A VIEW

Database Queries

learning objectives

- Explain the idea of a "relationship" between two database entities
- Give some examples of relationships
- Explain the difference between a physical and logical database
- Explain what a view is and how it is created by a database query
- Describe the structure of an SQL query
- Interpret an entity-relationship (ER) diagram and create one
- Identify a relationship as one-to-one; as many-to-one

Computers are useless. They only give answers.

—PABLO PICASSO

WHEN WE VISIT an airline Web page looking for flights between Istanbul and Frankfurt, we are asking the software to check the flight schedule and return a table of the flights. The Web page software translates our request into a `Select` operation on the schedule table, selecting those rows with field `depart='Istanbul'` and field `arrive='Frankfurt'`. That's a database query, and as we learn in this chapter, we can use queries to create tables and get a view of the database. Views contain customized information, letting users see the data the way that makes the most sense to them.

We begin with the problem of redundancy. Understanding redundancy can save us from creating poor databases. One method for avoiding redundancy leads to identifying connections among entities, which are called *relationships* because they are similar to familiar relationships like *Mother_Of*. Relationships allow us to reconstruct tables that had been split apart to avoid redundancy. This leads us to the ideas of physical and logical databases, queries, and views. After giving examples of these ideas, we introduce Structured Query Language (SQL), which is used in commercial database systems. The chapter closes with entity-relationship diagrams.

DESIGNING THE PHYSICAL DATABASE

Our first topic in database design is the physical database—the tables that are stored on the hard disk. Not every collection of tables is a good database, so we must be careful with our design. Redundancy is one thing to avoid.

Redundancy Is Bad, Very, Very, Very Bad

Databases are usually formed from several tables. A basic rule of database design is: *Never duplicate information*. It is common sense that avoiding duplication, or redundancy, is good, because storing multiple copies of the same information must use more resources (such as disk storage) than storing only a single copy. But that's not really the reason we want to avoid redundancy—disk space is so inexpensive the copies would cost almost nothing.

The main reason to avoid redundancy is to avoid **inconsistency** among the copies. That is, the same information, such as an address, stored in different rows or different tables of the database could differ in its different locations. We might change the information in one place and forget to change it in the other. For example, if one database table stores your home address as 4 Wheel Drive, and another table has it as 1 Supreme Court, the database is inconsistent. Which, if either, is correct?

Inconsistent data, known as **garbage**, is actually worse than having no data at all. With no value for the address, the row could be flagged and someone could contact you, perhaps by email, to find out your address. But inconsistent data "looks good" in each place. Duplication creates the opportunity for inconsistency, which has the potential of converting perfectly good data into garbage. So we adopt the rule: *Never duplicate information*.

Keep Only One Copy of Information

In designing a database, then, we will strive to keep only one copy of information. Avoiding duplication promotes internal consistency in the database, but how do we know that that one copy of information is correct? We do not. The goal of a database is to record and return to the user the information stored in it. If wrong information is stored originally, that is what will be returned.

FITBYTE

It's a Rule. Database designers and administrators emphasize the importance of accurate input by the maxim *garbage in, garbage out*, or GIGO for short.

The problem with asserting that there should be only one copy of any information in a database is that the information may be needed in several places. For example, think of the places at college that need your address:

> The administration needs to send your tuition bills.

> The library needs to send notices of your outstanding books.

> The dean needs to send congratulations on your outstanding grades.

> The sports center needs to send your Outstanding Sportsman certificate.

And a dozen other campus organizations might need to know your address. These organizations, all logically part of a campus database system, could each store a copy of your address. But they don't, or at least they shouldn't because of redundancy. Rather, they only record your student ID number, and when they need your address, they find it in a master list of student addresses keyed to student ID number.

Keep a Separate Table and a Key

This familiar idea, which illustrates a standard approach to avoiding redundancy in a database, can be abstracted as follows: Rather than repeating information in a database (e.g., addresses), keep a separate table of the information (e.g., master address list), keyed with a unique identifier (e.g., student ID). Then, store the unique identifier, called a **foreign key**, wherever the information would have been repeated. Whenever the information is needed, simply look it up in the master list using the unique identifier.

By this indirect reference, we avoid redundancy—there is only one copy of the information—but we can link the information to any other information in the database. This is an important enough idea that we spend the next section illustrating how it is used.

THE DATABASE SCHEMA

The entity descriptions of a database's tables are called its **database schema**, or **database scheme**. Interactive software can help us define a database schema, but, as we saw in Chapter 13, declaring an entity's structure is easy enough to do without software. The database schema is important because it describes the database design. When we want to analyze a database design, we look at its schema.

To illustrate our strategy for removing redundancy, imagine a college having at least two entities defined in its database schema, `Student` and `Home_Base`:

```
Student
  Student_ID     Number         8 digits
  First_Name     Character 25   Single name, starting with a
                                capital
  Middle_Name    Character 2    All other names
  Last_Name      Character 25   Family name
  Birthdate      Date
  On_Probation   Boolean        0 = good standing; 1 = academic
                                trouble

Primary Key: Student_ID
```

```
Home_Base
  Student_ID      Number          8 digits
  Street_Address  Character 100   All address info before city
  City            Character  25   No abbreviations like NYC
  State           Character  25   Or province, canton,
                                  prefecture, etc.
  Country         Character  25   Standard postal
                                  abbreviations OK
  Postal Code     Character  10   Most including ZIP+4 are not
                                  numbers

Primary Key: Student_ID
```

Connecting Database Tables by Relationship

The **Student** entity records the information basic to the person's identity and associates a student with his or her **Student_ID**. This is the college's master record of each student. Part of each student's information is where he or she lives. Though we could put addresses in the **Student** table, we decide not to, so that other campus units can access the address without accessing all of the other information about the student. The addresses are stored in a different table, the **Home_Base** entity. Though these two entities are separate, they are not independent. The **Student_ID** connects each row in **Student** with his or her address in **Home_Base**. We say that there is a **relationship** between the two entities.

The relationship is the direct correspondence between rows of the **Home_Base** table and the rows of the **Student** table. Using the **Student_ID** from the **Student** entity, we can find the student's address in the **Home_Base** table. We name this relationship *Lives_At*. Setting up the tables in this way is largely equivalent to storing the address in **Student**, but not all relationships are so close. This one is especially close because it is based on the **Student_ID**, which is the key for both tables. (Recall that keys are unique, meaning no two rows can have the same value.) So, not only can we find the address for each student, but we can also find the student for each address by using the **Student_ID**. That is, there is a second relationship in the opposite direction, which we could call *Home_Of*, meaning that the home base entry is the address of the student who has that ID. Relationships connect data of one table with data of another.

Some relationships that we encounter everyday are:

- *Father_Of* relationship between a man and his child
- *Daughter_Of* relationship between a girl and her parent
- *Employed_By* relationships between people and companies
- *Stars_In* relationships between actors and movies

Names of database relationships should be meaningful, to help people working with the database, but like all names in computing, the computer doesn't know whether the name makes sense or not.

Relationships are part of the metadata of a database. They state the intended connection between different parts of the database. As with other metadata, the designer specifies relationships so that the computer can help us use the database.

Using the Join Operation

The close correspondence between the information in the **Student** and **Home_Base** tables allows us to **construct** a single table containing the combined information from both tables. How? Using the natural **Join** operation, described in Chapter 13. Recall that the natural **Join** operation creates a table out of two other tables by joining rows that match—it's an equality test—in specified fields. Thus, we write

```
Master_Record = Student ⋈ Home_Base
```

where the match is on the common field of **Student_ID**. The fields of the resulting table are shown in Figure 14.1. A more explicit form of the same natural **Join** specifies

```
Master_Record = Student ⋈ Home_Base
                On Student.Student_ID = Home_Base.Student_ID
```

Student_ID
First_Name
Middle_Name
Last_Name
Birthdate
On_Probation
Street_Address
City
State
Country
Postal_Code

Figure 14.1. *Fields of the* **Master_Record** *table.*

We don't lose anything by storing the basic student information in one table and the addresses in another, because with a simple command, we can create a table that recombines the information just as if it were stored in a single table.

The key idea here is that although we chose to store the information in two tables, we never lost the association of the information because we kept the **Student_ID** with the addresses. The relationship, *Lives_At*, lets us connect each student with his or her address by the **Student_ID**. The approach gives us the flexibility to arrange tables so as to avoid problems of redundancy—though we haven't demonstrated that benefit yet—while keeping track of important information, like where a person lives. We will use this idea routinely in our database designs.

Designing a Database Schema

Consider other entities in the college's database schema that need address information, say, for the dean's office and the sports center:

```
Top_Scholar                      Good_Sport
   Student_ID                       Student_ID
   Nickname                         Locker_Number
   Major                            Deposit_Amt
   GPA                              Sport

Primary Key: Student_ID          Primary Key: Student_ID
```

(We don't bother to define the field information while we are designing the database schema.)

The `Top_Scholar` and `Good_Sport` tables each have a one-to-one relationship with the `Home_Base` table. These relationships are based on the `Student_ID` attribute, just as `Student` was: For each scholar, there is an address in `Home_Base`, as there is for each athlete. Therefore, there is a relationship between the `Top_Scholar` and the `Home_Base` tables, which we'll call *Resides_At*, and between the `Good_Sport` and the `Home_Base` tables, which we'll call *Trains_At*. So, both the dean's office and the sports center have access to student addresses, just as the administration does. Notice that there is no inconsistency, because as these tables are constructed, the computer takes the addresses only from the `Home_Base` entity.

> FITTIP
>
> **Being Discreet.** Including addresses in `Top_Scholar` and `Good_Sport` would create redundancy, but referencing the `Home_Base` table avoids redundancy. It was not necessary to create a separate `Home_Base` table, however, because addresses could have been stored in `Student`. But `Student` contains sensitive information—academic probation status, for example—that should not be widely distributed. Defining a separate `Home_Base` table records the addresses without connecting to sensitive information. It is a better design.

`Student_ID` also connects both `Top_Scholar` and `Good_Sport` to `Student`. This is lucky, because otherwise neither the dean nor the sports center knows the students' legal names, only their IDs. Thus, combined tables can be created for the dean's office or the sports center using one or more natural `Join` operations that associate information from several tables in the schema. We implement these tables in the next section.

Physical vs. Logical Database

We've defined a set of tables that avoid redundancy and that will be stored on the hard disk. These tables are called the **physical database** because they physically exist on the hard disk. From the tables of the physical database we can create other tables, customized to other campus units. These customized tables are called the **logical database**. Because they are logical, or virtual, they do not physically exist.

They are created fresh every time they are needed, using the current values in the physical database. Whenever the dean or the sports center needs to look at their database, they get a fresh one created just for that request. Then, when the application is closed—say, the dean moves on to the alumni database—the current version of the Dean's View vanishes. It will be constructed anew the next time it's needed.

This approach of storing the database in one form but building a different form on demand may seem silly. It seems as if we could save work by storing the logical database on the disk, too. But the logical database is built from information in the physical database. So the logical database tables *contain duplicate information*. If we store them, we create redundancy—there would be a copy in the physical database and a copy in the logical database—violating our principle of no duplication. Suppose one copy were changed but not the other! So, logical databases can only exist in the virtual world of the user's screen. In this way, modern databases always deliver fresh, current data to users.

Separating the logical and physical structure of a database is smart for another reason, too. The logical tables people look at on their screens can be customized to their needs exactly. These personalized logical tables are called **database views**. Thus, to allow every user group to see the database in a different way, the various logical tables are created from the single physical database. Personal considerations guide logical database design, while technical considerations (like avoiding redundancy) guide the physical database design. The idea of separating into physical and logical forms—they're all part of the one database schema—was an intellectual milestone.

QUERIES: CREATING VIEWS

Views are the logical tables constructed by database operations from the physical tables. The operations that create views are called **database queries**. The "master student records" table created by combining `Student` and `Home_Base` using a natural `Join`, was created by a database query:

```
Master_Record = Student ⋈ Home_Base
                On Student.Student_ID = Home_Base.Student_ID
```

The queries creating the views are part of the logical database of the database schema, making them part of the metadata. Thus, *every named table of the database is either a physical table, on the hard disk, or a logical table created by a query*. Let's consider other views and the queries that create them.

Creating a Dean's View

Imagine a table, known as the Dean's View, containing information specific to the dean's unique needs. For example, because the dean is not the person who sends letters to top students telling them they made the "Dean's List," the Dean's View doesn't need the students' full home addresses. (Someone else in the dean's office will need them.) The students' hometowns are enough information for the dean to make small talk at parties in honor of the good students. So the Dean's View will include information selected from the physical tables, as shown in Figure 14.2.

Deans_View	Source Table	
Nickname	Top_Scholar	*Used by the dean to seem "chummy" toward students*
First_Name	Student	*Name information required because*
Middle_Name	Student	*the dean forgets the person's*
Last_Name	Student	*actual name, being so chummy*
Birthdate	Student	*Needs to know if the student is of "drinking age"*
City	Home_Base	*Hometown (given by city, state) is important for small talk, but actual street address not needed by dean*
Major	Top_Scholar	*Indicates what the student's doing in college besides hanging out*
GPA	Top_Scholar	*Needs to know how the student is doing grade-wise*

Figure 14.2. The Dean's View; information from several tables.

Join Three Tables into One. The first step in creating a query for the Dean's View is to note that it contains information from three tables: **Top_Scholar**, the table actually storing the data the dean wants kept; **Student**, the college's permanent record of the student; and **Home_Base**, the college's current address list. The information for each student must be associated to create the Dean's View table, and the **Join** operation is the key to doing it. The expression

```
Top_Scholar ⋈ Student ⋈ Home_Base
```

makes a table that has a row for each student in the dean's **Top_Scholar** table, but it has all of the information from all three tables. The association of each student's row in each table is accomplished by matching on the **Student_ID** attribute. Of course, the **Join** operations are performed in pairs, as the following explicit form shows:

```
Top_Scholar ⋈ (Student ⋈ Home_Base
            On Student.Student_ID = Home_Base.Student_ID)
On Student.Student_ID = Top_Scholar.Student_ID
```

The **Student ⋈ Home_Base** is performed first, producing an intermediate table, say, **T1**, and then **Top_Scholar ⋈ T1** is performed. (The order of operations doesn't matter with **Join**.)

Trim the Table. The resulting table contains too much information, of course, because it has all columns from the three tables, except for the repeated

Student_ID. The dean doesn't want to see so much information. So, the second step is to retrieve only the columns the dean wants to see. The **Project** operation retrieves columns:

```
Deans_View =
    Project Nickname, First_Name, Middle_Name, Last_Name,
      Birthdate, City, State, Major, GPA
    From Top_Scholar ⋈ Student ⋈ Home_Base
```

Notice that the dean doesn't even want to see the **Student_ID**, so it is not shown. But it is essential to creating the table.

In English, the query says, "Save the **Nickname** column, **First_Name** column, and so forth, from the table that is formed by joining—that is, associating on **Student_ID**—the three tables **Top_Scholar**, **Student**, and **Home_Base**." This is precisely what the dean wants. The query defines the **Deans_View** table. Although the dean probably thinks the table exists physically, it is created fresh every time the dean checks it.

The join-then-trim strategy used to create the Dean's View is a standard approach to creating logical tables: a super table is formed by joining several physical tables. These are then trimmed down to keep only the information of interest to the user. The **Deans_View** query used **Project**, but **Select** is also frequently used.

Creating a Sport's Center View

As another example, the sports center (SC) view would join its table **Good_Sport** with the administration's tables. The table of interest to the SC is defined in Figure 14.3. The table can be created by the query

```
SC_View =
   Project Student_ID, First_Name, Last_Name, Birthdate,
      Sport, Locker_Number, Deposit_Amt, Street_Address,
      City, State, zip
   From Good_Sport ⋈ Student ⋈ Home_Base
```

SC_View

Student_ID	Student	*The ID is in each table*
First_Name	Student	*The name is handy, but the*
Last_Name	Student	*middle name is not needed*
Birthdate	Student	
Sport	Good_Sport	
Locker_Number	Good_Sport	
Deposit_Amt	Good_Sport	
Street_Address	Home_Base	*Address information is needed*
City	Home_Base	*to return the locker deposit*
State	Home_Base	
Zip	Home_Base	

Figure 14.3. *The fields and sources for the sports center's view; information drawn from three physical tables.*

And logical tables can be used just like physical tables. So if the sports center wants to create intramural water polo teams, they might use the query

```
Project Student_ID, First_Name, Last_Name, Birthdate
From (Select_from SC_View On Sport="Water Polo")
```

In concept, the computer first creates the logical table **`SC_View`** and then uses it to build the water polo table. In reality, a database system would be much more clever.

A QUERY LANGUAGE: SQL

The relational database concepts introduced so far are abstract and independent of any specific database system. They have been written in **conceptual** form using a notation invented for teaching purposes. Although every database system implements these concepts, each system has its own way of specifying them. So, to have a real database, we must translate our conceptual form into the form used by some commercial software system. For that, we need to learn how to specify the conceptual form for the software.

Fortunately, there is a standard language in wide use, **SQL**, the **Structured Query Language**. As the name suggests, SQL doesn't support arbitrary queries using the full power of the five fundamental relational database operators we learned about in Chapter 13. Instead, it provides a specific query structure that works well for techniques like join-then-trim. Database *users* don't usually need to know SQL, but nearly everyone else involved with databases does. We will learn enough basics of SQL to build simple databases.

Though vendors have their own dialects of SQL—and SQL is complicated to begin with—simple queries like ours are roughly the same no matter which version you're using. SQL's query structure has the following syntax:

`SELECT`	*List of fields*
`FROM`	*Table(s)*
`WHERE`	*Constraints on the rows*

(Confusingly, **`SELECT`** in SQL means *select fields*, and therefore closely approximates **`Project`**, presented in Chapter 13. Unfortunately, these two standard sets of terms conflict.)

SQL's query structure is perfect for the join-then-trim approach to creating tables. **`FROM`** gives the table(s) that the fields are to be taken from, **`SELECT`** says which fields those are, and **`WHERE`** specifies any additional conditions that must be met by individual rows. Typically, the **`FROM`** clause will specify a single super table formed using **`Product`** or **`Join`**. SQL has several kinds of **`Joins`**, but the **`INNER JOIN`** type corresponds to the **`Join`** operation discussed previously. In SQL, the "match fields" must be specified explicitly using an **`ON`** clause.

SQL ON Clause

Recall the **Deans_View** table constructed earlier in the chapter using the conceptual query:

```
Project Nickname, First_Name, Middle_Name, Last_Name, Birthdate,
   City, State, Major, GPA
From Top_Scholar ⋈ (Student ⋈ Home_Base
                 On Student.Student_ID = Home_Base.Student_ID)
     On Student.Student_ID = Top_Scholar.Student_ID
```

This can be expressed in SQL using the following query:

```
SELECT   Top_Scholar.Nickname,Student.First_Name,
         Student_Middle_Name,Student.Last_Name,
         Student.Birthdate,Home_Base.City,Home_Base.State,
         Top_Scholar.Major,Top_Scholar.GPA
FROM Top_Scholar INNER JOIN (Student INNER JOIN Home_Base
                  ON Student.Student_ID=Home_Base.Student_ID)
     ON Student.Student_ID=Top_Scholar.Student_ID
```

The table names have been color-coded blue and the field names fuchsia to make the query easier to read. Notice first that following the **SELECT** is the list of fields that form the Dean's View. Then, the **FROM** field has two **Joins** that have been grouped together (as we did in the earlier conceptual form). First, **Student** and **Home_Base** are joined **ON** equal **Student_IDs**, and then **Top_Scholar** is joined with the result, again **ON** matching **Student_IDs**.

SQL WHERE Clause

There is no **WHERE** clause because the Dean's View doesn't require further limiting. However, if the dean wanted to view only students whose GPA is greater than 3.8, a **WHERE** clause can choose those rows:

```
SELECT   Top_Scholar.Nickname,Student.First_Name,
         Student.Middle_Name,Student.Last_Name,
         Student.Birthdate,Home_Base.City,Home_Base.State,
         Top_Scholar.Major,Top_Scholar.GPA
FROM Top_Scholar INNER JOIN (Student INNER JOIN Home_Base
                  ON Student.Student_ID=Home_Base.Student_ID)
     ON Student.Student_ID=Top_Scholar.Student_ID
WHERE Top_Scholar.GPA > 3.8
```

Interestingly, the **WHERE** clause uses our conceptual **Select** operator. Though the SQL query is longer because the table name must be specified with each field using the dot notation, and the fields **ON** which the match is based must be specified, the result matches the conceptual structure quite well.

Translating into SQL

As a final example, recall that the table of Figure 13.12, associating the northerly countries (**Northland**) with your friends' master tutoring list, had the conceptual form

```
Master ⋈ Northland On Master.Name = Northland.Name
```

which has the SQL form

```
SELECT  Master.Name, Travelers.Friend, Master.Domain,
        Master.Latitude
FROM Master INNER JOIN Travelers
            ON Master.Name = Northland.Name
```

Again, this is a direct translation. The differences between the conceptual form we used in Chapter 13 and the SQL form are small—fields must be listed for SQL that are assumed in the conceptual query by default. And, computer software understands the SQL.

These SQL examples provide just a hint of the enormous capabilities of the query language. Many very handy extras can be included in SQL queries. And learning your system's dialect will be necessary—though not particularly difficult now that you understand the abstract ideas.

ENTITY RELATIONSHIPS DIAGRAMS

To wrap up our discussion of views and queries, we return to the subject of relationships.

Notice that our ability to create new tables involved relationships. When we joined **Top_Scholar**, **Student**, and **Home_Base** to create the Dean's View, we used the **Student_ID**, which embodies associations from named relationships: The first join, between **Student** and **Home_Base**, used the relationship *Lives_At*, and the second join, between **Top_Scholar** and the result of the first join, used the relationship *Resides_At*. This is not an accident. The whole point of identifying relationships in a database schema is to indicate how the information is interconnected and joins make these connections. If the potential for interconnections exists—that is, if there are relationships—then it is likely that they will be applied when building the logical database.

With many entities, attributes, keys, and relationships in a large database, the design can get confusing. So, database administrators and others who work daily with databases diagram the relationships to make the database's structure clearer.

Such a diagram is known as an **entity-relationship diagram**, or an **ER diagram**. In an ER diagram, relationships are drawn as arrows between boxes, which represent entities. For example, in Figure 14.4 the arrow from **Student** to **Home_Base** (addresses) shows the relationship *Lives_At*. The other entities and relationships discussed earlier are expressed in the ER diagram of Figure 14.5 too. As we shall see, ER diagrams help us make sense out of the relationships among the entities.

Figure 14.4. *A diagram showing the Lives_At relationship.*

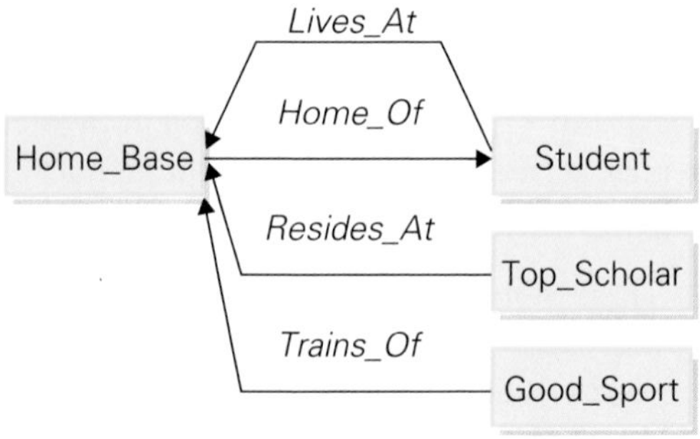

Figure 14.5. *ER diagram for the entities and relationships involving* `Home_Base`.

In its simplest form, the ER diagram uses arrows to represent the relationships between the boxes that represent the entities. But variations on this form can also be helpful. One form typical of database software shows the entity name outside the box and lists the attributes of the entity inside the box (see Figure 14.6).

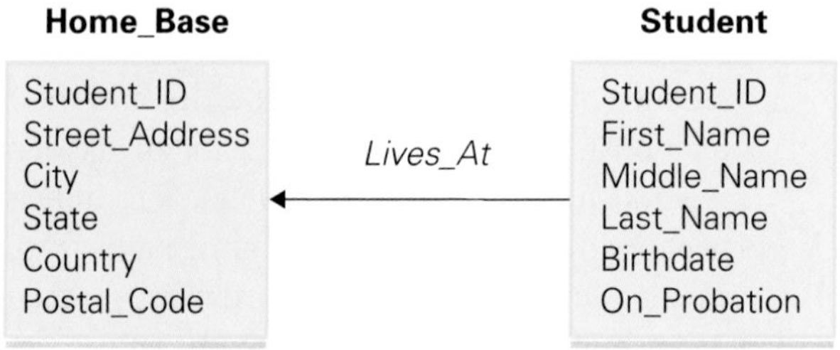

Figure 14.6. *Another form of an ER diagram typical of database software.*

One-to-One Relationships

One more piece of information is usually included in an ER diagram: the type of relationship. The type of a relationship says how the data in the two entities are associated. For example, a one-to-one relationship says that any row in either entity is associated with at most one row in the other entity. The relationships in Figure 14.6 are all one-to-one because the relationships are all based on the `Student_ID` key.

Many-to-One Relationships

A more typical kind of relationship is based on entities that have different keys. When one entity refers to another entity by giving its key, the foreign key, there is generally a **many-to-one** relationship. That is, many of the rows of the first entity can be associated with a single row in the second entity. For example, imagine a `User_Acct` entity that lists all of the campus's student computer users. It has a many-to-one relationship to `Student`, called *Assigned_To*. The `User_Acct` has as its key the student's `User_ID`, and in each row the student's `Student_ID` is no doubt listed. However, since students can have many accounts, many rows in `User_Acct` may be associated by *Assigned_To* with one row in `Student`. For example, if Jean has a personal account as well as an account for his library job and an account for French, his major department, then *Assigned_To* associates those three rows with his row in `Student`. It is a many-to-one relationship.

In ER diagrams the type of the relationship can be shown in different ways. For example, a one-to-one relationship might be shown with one type of arrow, while a many-to-one relationship might use a different kind of arrow. In Chapter 15 we will see how the types of relationships are expressed in commercial database software.

SUMMARY

The secret of modern databases is that many of the tables we see don't actually exist, but rather are logical tables constructed on-the-fly using the physical tables that do exist. Relationships are the key to associating fields of the physical tables. The database administrator—a professional database manager, or you if you create your own databases—carefully designs the database's metadata, the underlying structure of tables and relationships. The design for the physically stored tables is optimized to avoid problems such as redundancy. If the physical tables have been set up properly, it is easy, by using queries, to give users whatever view of the data they want.

A main tool for creating the views of the logical database is the join-then-trim method, which creates a super table by joining physical tables, and then keeps only the interesting information by trimming with the `Select` and `Project` operations. We learned that SQL is "structured" to support this technique, that SQL is the query language of relational database software, and that, despite different meanings for the word "select," SQL and the conceptual database form presented in Chapter 13 are very similar. Finally, we learned the basics of ER diagrams, which give graphical form to a database design and help organize its structure.

EXERCISES

Multiple Choice

1. SQL stands for:
   A. Simple Query Language
   B. Simplified Question Line
   C. Structured Query Language
   D. Stored Question Logic
2. The main reason to avoid duplication in a database is:
   A. the expense of maintaining the information
   B. the added size of the information
   C. inconsistency
   D. incompatibility
3. The intended connection between different parts of a database is controlled by:
   A. entities
   B. relationships
   C. keys
   D. tables
4. Storing information in two tables rather than one:
   A. greatly increases the size of the database
   B. unduly complicates the database design
   C. presents few problems and offers several advantages
   D. is not allowed
5. A one-to-one relationship between tables means:
   A. each row has one field
   B. there is one row in each table
   C. the tables have corresponding rows
   D. the tables share the same fields
6. The design of a physical database is determined by:
   A. security considerations
   B. the need for flexibility
   C. the need to avoid redundancy
   D. all of the above
7. ______ can be physical or logical.
   A. Queries
   B. Tables
   C. Views
   D. all of the above

8. A super table:
   A. is created by joining two or more physical tables
   B. is created by joining two or more logical tables
   C. is a combination of logical and physical tables
   D. none of the above

9. SQL is designed to:
   A. let any user create their own tables
   B. provide a specific query structure for relational databases
   C. eliminate the need for multiple tables
   D. eliminate the need for join and trim commands

10. The SQL `SELECT` clause is similar to the:
    A. `Join` operation
    B. `Union` operation
    C. `Project` operation
    D. `Add` operation

Short Answer

1. The personalized content of a database is called a ______.
2. Connections among entities in a database are known as ______.
3. In a database, the existence of duplicate sets of information is known as ______.
4. Inconsistent data is known as ______.
5. GIGO is short for ______.
6. A(n) ______ is a set of tables that are actually stored on the computer.
7. A(n) ______ is created as needed from tables that are stored on the computer.
8. In SQL, you would chose fields for a query using the ______ clause.
9. To select a table in SQL, you need to use the ______ clause.
10. The ______ clause in SQL is used to find specific rows in a table.
11. The ______ clause in SQL is used to match key fields between tables.
12. A(n) ______ is used to graphically show relationships in a database.
13. A(n) ______ relationship exists when one row in a table is related to at most one row in another table.
14. When one field in a table is related to one or more fields in another table, a(n) ______ relationship exists.

Exercises

1. Why is a relationship needed to link the fields of two tables together?
2. Why is redundancy bad for databases when a backup is good for information?
3. Explain how the use of a foreign key avoids information redundancy.
4. Explain a many-to-one relationship using a company with multiple phone lines as an example.

The following information is used for questions 5–12.

The Digital Alliance of Technical Associates (DATA) has the following tables for its DATA file.

Personal

Last_Name	Text 20	Employee Last Name
First_Name	Text 15	Employee First Name
Emp_ID	Text 10	Employee ID Number
Address	Text 25	Permanent Address
City	Text 20	City
State	Text 2	State Abbreviation
Zip	Text 5	Zip Code
Phone	Text 15	Home Phone
Hire_Date	Date	Date of Hire

Payroll

Emp_ID	Text 10	Employee ID Number
Pay_Rate	Number	Hourly Pay Rate
Deductions	Number	Number of IRS Deductions
Health	Yes/No	Single Health Coverage
Life	Yes/No	Company Life Policy

HR (Human Resources)

Emp_ID	Text 10	Employee ID Number
Dept	Text 15	Assigned Work Dept.
Hire_Date	Date	Date of Hire
Performance	Memo	Comments on Performance
Supervisor	Text 20	Name of Boss
Projects	Text 50	Current Projects Assigned

Softball

Emp_ID	Text 10	Employee ID Number
Throws	Text 1	Right or Left
Bats	Text 1	Right or Left
Position	Text 12	Playing Position

5. What key field connects all the tables in this database? Why is this field preferable to their name or their Social Security number?
6. Where is there redundancy in these tables? How could this be avoided?
7. What tables and fields should the company softball manager have access to? What relationship controls this association?
8. Where is there potential for a many-to-one relationship for the employee?
9. HR needs a list of all employees who are due for their annual review. The annual review is done during the month the employee was hired. What should the table that HR needs look like so they can complete their review?
10. Write the SQL for the logical table created in question 9.
11. The softball manager needs a list of players so they can be contacted about the upcoming season. What should the table look like?
12. Write the SQL for the logical table created in question 11.

chapter

15 HAI! ADVENTURE DATABASE

Case Study in Database Design

learning objectives

- Explain the purpose of a needs analysis
- Construct the tables of a physical database and avoid redundancy
- Given several associated tables, analyze the relationships between them
- Determine the views of a database, given a design in progress
- Express simple conceptual queries for views using SQL
- Describe how and when the GUIs are created

The mind can store an estimated 100 trillion bits of information—compared with which a computer's mere billions are virtually amnesiac.

—SHARON BEGLEY, *NEWSWEEK*, 1986

THIS CHAPTER concerns three college friends, Hon, Amanda, and Ian, who wasted way too much time hanging out together. During their senior year, while jogging in a last-ditch effort to get in shape for spring break, the three hatched a plan to go into business together. Their idea was to rent sports equipment to rich people at resorts in ski areas, tropical islands, and in the mountains, including lessons and guided activities such as dives and climbs. What would make their business different from others is that the employees—they plan to call them *adventure specialists*—would be well trained, knowledgeable, "up," and helpful, giving their customers complete satisfaction so they return again and again to the business. To keep them dedicated and their attitudes positive, the adventure specialists would rotate among several resorts, in both the northern and southern hemispheres, working at different rental shops. The trio planned to call their business HAI! Adventure, knowing that *hai* is Japanese for "yes." Whether HAI! Adventure is a realistic business idea or not is irrelevant—it presents great opportunities for database design.

The major goal of this chapter is to work out the design of a database, using the ideas and principles from Chapters 13 and 14. We start with a needs analysis, which analyzes the nature of the business, and then follows the workflow of the enterprise, asking at each step what the information needs are for that activity. From the analysis will emerge a conceptual design.

Our next goal is to turn the conceptual design into an operational database using standard database software. After we finish the initial design, we consider how the design prepares for other HAI! Adventure business directions.

The final goal of the chapter is to extend the database design to handle business activities such as lessons and guided tours. As before, we create a conceptual design for the database before trying to implement it. But when we reach the lessons and guided tours extension, we will discuss the pitfalls of alternative designs. The practical implementation follows. Our overall objective is to illustrate how a significant database can be designed at a high conceptual level before all of the details of implementation are considered.

STRATEGY FOR BUILDING A DATABASE

Though this chapter focuses on the design for the HAI! Adventure database, the strategy we'll use can be applied to database design in general. Pay attention to the "big picture" of this example to learn how to create your own databases. Like most design activities, however, it is not possible to give an algorithm for creating a database. The steps used here can only be guidelines—heuristics—for other designs, because every case is different.

Follow this general pattern in constructing a database:

1. **Perform a needs analysis.** Understand how the database will be used, and list the kinds of data the users will need to input to the database as well as the kinds of information the database will need to output to the users. It is often helpful to study the information "flow" through the organization or business. A needs analysis helps us understand the goals of the database design.

2. **Approximate and revise a physical design.** One approach to creating any design is to construct a rough solution and then to revise it. Once we have created a rough solution, we can assess it to see how well it fulfills the needs, and where it fails, we can revise the solution. Because it is difficult to create the perfect design the first time, this iterative approach often works well. The criteria for success include goals such as avoiding redundancy and meeting the users' needs. We create the design "on paper"—often using ER diagrams—making it easy to revise.

3. **Implement the physical design.** At some point, we stop making revisions and decide our design is "optimal," the best we can do up to this point. We will have defined the physical tables and established the relationships. If the process has been done thoughtfully, the physical database is finished and can be implemented. It is often a good idea to implement the physical tables using commercial database software and fill them with some sample values. The process can reveal oversights or errors.

4. **Design the logical database.** Next we create the logical database. We consider who must interact with the database. Identifying the users will help us decide how many views we need. We decide what data each user group will enter into the database, and what data they must see from the database. The view will generally be the combination of these two types of information. Then, we create the queries using the join-and-trim approach we learned in Chapter 14, assess how the groups will be served by the views, and possibly revise the design.

5. **Implement the logical database.** With the views conceptually defined (and the physical tables and relationships already programmed), we implement the views in SQL. If the join-and-trim technique has been used, translating to SQL is usually very easy.

6. **Implement the GUIs.** Finally, it is time to complete the implementation. We create the GUIs the users will interact with. Though the process can be tedious and detail oriented, the software helps make it easier.

7. **Evaluate the usefulness and (possibly) revise.** Like all designs, the database must be evaluated to be sure it fulfills the users' needs. Though the design process should produce a very useful database, it is almost always possible to think of improvements. The design can be revised to add more functionality.

THE HAI! ADVENTURE BUSINESSES

We're going to design the database for HAI! Adventure, a business founded by three college friends. The business, when it is fully up and running, will have shops at resort locations around the world. Each shop will offer equipment for a single activity such as skiing, wind surfing, scuba diving, mountain climbing, or kayaking. The shop will rent high-quality equipment, and the company plans to run organized activities such as lessons and guided tours. These activities—dives, climbs, bungee jumping, paragliding—will involve one or more customers and a guide, leader, or instructor. Though the business will have other data processing needs such as payroll, receivables, taxes, and equipment management, we won't include those in this design. We're only interested in the rentals and activities like lessons and tours.

The ideal HAI! Adventure employees—adventure specialists—will be active, outdoorsy people who like to travel. They will have some training in an active sport to qualify them to rent equipment such as scuba gear, and to serve as instructors or guides. It is a benefit of the job that the adventure specialists will change locations and activities from time to time. (Working for such a company is like being on a permanent vacation!)

All businesses need to start small, so the first HAI! Adventure business is a ski rental shop at a resort in the Canadian Rockies, The Snow Machine Ski Rental Shop (Snow Machine). The shop rents downhill skis and snowboards. The Snow Machine business has four rooms—a large Entry Room through which the customers enter and leave, a large Fitting Room in which the customers get their equipment, an Equipment Room behind the Fitting Room where the gear is stowed and maintained, and a small Staff Room. A typical customer proceeds through the following stages:

- **Selection.** The customer comes into the store and is greeted by the receptionist. The equipment and services available and their prices are posted on the wall. Having decided to rent equipment, the customer gives the receptionist his or her name, address, and local contact information. The receptionist enters this information into the database.
- **Fitting.** The customer goes to the Fitting Room, where a specialist will get information needed to set the bindings of the skis, for example, weight, and skiing ability. The equipment is selected and its equipment identification numbers are recorded. The equipment is adjusted, the settings are recorded, and the gear is given to the customer.
- **Payment.** On the way out, the customer returns with the equipment to the Entry Room to sign the rental agreement—a legal contract stating the personal data about the person, what gear the person rented, the specialist's name who set the gear, and all of the legal mumbo-jumbo required to rent equipment for a life-threatening activity like skiing. The receptionist also collects payment from the customer.

When the skis are returned, they are inspected by the specialist and stowed in the Equipment Room.

PERFORM A NEEDS ANALYSIS

Now we must decide how to organize the database to support HAI! Adventure's ski rental shop. Perhaps the best way to approach the matter is to consider what information is *created* and what information is *needed* to transact the business. The information that is being created is the documentation on the customer (personal information), and the data on the equipment rented and adjustments set (technical information from the specialist). The information needed for the rental is the content of the rental agreement document, which the customer must sign before taking the equipment. The rental is the association of the customer's personal data with the technical data of the equipment, most of which must be in the rental agreement.

The first idea might be to define a **`Rentals`** table, with a field for each kind of information needed for the contract. Then each row of the table would represent one rental. This is a good place to begin the design, but the **`Rentals`** table as described may not be perfect. So, before adopting it, we must think about the design's usefulness.

Specifically, the contract needs to contain the customer's name, address, and phone number, implying that this information will be in the table. But if the HAI! Adventure business plan works out, customers will return repeatedly to the shop, which means that their names, addresses, and phone numbers will be repeated in the **`Rentals`** table several times. As we learned in Chapter 13, having the same information stored in several places in a database is called *redundancy* and should be avoided. So we decide that we need a table of customers, **`Clients`**, so that their personal data will be in the database only once.

There is a similar problem with the adventure specialists. The **`Rentals`** table needs to record which specialist adjusted the bindings, for legal reasons. (The bindings hold the skis to the ski boots, and release when the skier falls in order to avoid injuries such as broken legs. The setting specifies the amount of force required to cause the bindings to release; it is affected by the skier's weight and ability.) Because making binding adjustments requires training, the specialist's credentials for performing the operation should be available online. The credentials don't have to be in the contract—only the specialist's name—so they shouldn't be stored in the **`Rentals`** table. This means there should be another table for the specialists' credentials, the Adventure Specialist Team table, or **`ASTeam`** for short.

With the customers' and specialists' data moved to their own tables, referenced by keys, what remains in the **`Rentals`** table? Plenty. The table still records the date of the transaction, equipment rented, adjustments, and a record of any special information that the specialist gave the customer.

The database so far includes three tables:

> **`Clients`**—the table of customers' personal information

> **`ASTeam`**—the table of adventure specialists, including their training records and certification, as appropriate

> **`Rentals`**—the table of rentals, giving the gear rented and the customer information such as level of skiing ability, weight, and settings

Relationships will exist between the **`Clients`** and **`Rentals`** tables, and the **`ASTeam`** and **`Rentals`** tables, reflecting the fact that a customer and a specialist participate in the rental, but their specific information is stored in other tables.

APPROXIMATE/REVISE THE DB DESIGN

Next we specify the details for the tables required by the HAI! Adventure's Snow Machine physical database. By being explicit about the design, we can work out additional details conceptually before trying to implement them.

Specify the Clients Table

The **`Clients`** table is straightforward. It includes the customer's name, home and local addresses, and contact information. Although we expect repeat customers, we do not have to worry about the problems of frequent address changes, like colleges do. Customers will probably not be changing their permanent addresses while on vacation, so a single record will do for a single season. If the customer returns the following year, a new record will be created.

So, all of the personal information about a customer will be stored in this table. We recognize the following fields, data types, and field sizes:

```
Clients
  Customer_ID      Integer          Unique identifier
  First            Character, 20    Given name
  Middle           Character, 15    Middle name
  Last             Character, 30    Family name
  Birthdate        Date             Date of birth
  Street           Character, 30    Home address
  City             Character, 20
  State            Character,  2    State/Province abbreviation
  ZIP              Character, 10    Postal code
  Country          Character, 10
  Home_Phone       Character, 20    Phone at residence
  Mobile_Phone     Character, 20
  Email            Character, 40
  Local_Contact    Character, 40    Where staying locally
                                    (hotel)

Primary Key: Customer_ID
```

The key for this relation is **Customer_ID**, a computer-produced unique number, since none of the other fields is guaranteed to give uniqueness to the rows of the table.

Specify ASTeam Table

The employees of HAI! Adventure do move around, and they have both local addresses and permanent addresses. So we will manage these addresses by setting up an employee contact schema. Recall that a **schema** is the abstract structure of an entity or entities.

```
Contact
   Contact_ID      Integer           Unique identifier
   Street          Character, 30
   City            Character, 20
   State           Character,  2     State/Province abbreviation
   ZIP             Character, 10     Postal code
   Country         Character, 10
   Phone           Character, 15     Phone at this address

Primary Key: Contact_ID
```

The schema will be used to set up two tables, **AS_Home** and **AS_Local**, recording permanent and local address information, respectively. The tables are, therefore, two instances of the schema—that is, separate tables with the same structure.

The **Contact** schema could have been used for the customers as well, but it's not necessary. The customers will not likely move in one season, and because we will probably archive and delete all of the **Clients** records after each season, the addresses don't have to be carried across several years. The employee data must be kept over a longer period of time. Such differences in the characteristics of the data motivate keeping the employee addresses separate.

The full **ASTeam** table will record employment information, such as Social Security number, and professional information, such as certification data. All employees will use the same table, though some, like the receptionist, may not need the certification fields. The table contains the following fields:

```
ASTeam
   Nickname        Character, 10     Unique identifier
   First           Character, 20
   Middle          Character, 15
   Last            Character, 30
   Birthdate       Date
   SS_Number       ddd-dd-dddd
   Home_Addr       Number            AS_Home.Contact_ID
   Local_Addr      Number            AS_Local.Contact_ID
```

```
  Mobil_Phone     Character, 20
  Email           Character, 40
  Certified       Y/N                Is the specialist
                                     certified?
  Cert_Expire     Date               When does certification
                                     expire
  Cert_Detail     Character, 255     Description of
                                     certification type

Primary Key: Nickname
```

The HAI! Adventure team is an informal, tight-knit group, who know each other by nicknames like Sissy and Chip. They prefer to use these names around the office rather than an employee ID. So the database software will use the **`Nickname`** field as a key for **`ASTeam`**, even though the uniqueness requirement forces any two employees who go by the same name—say, Chip—to use different versions of that name—ChipR and ChipS. The Social Security number field also makes the entries unique, but by law the Social Security number can be used only for payroll and tax purposes.

Because there will be different kinds of certification, the ASTeam table has fields for whether the person is certified at all, when the certification expires, and the details of the certification, such as where, when, what type, and certifying organization. This information must be recorded, but it will probably not be used very often.

Specify the Rentals Table

The fields of the **`Rentals`** table are straightforward. They include both the customers' and the specialists' keys to refer to the **`Clients`** and **`ASTeam`** tables, and details about the gear rented. If the customer rents skis and therefore must have bindings set, the **`Ski`**? field is checked. If this field is checked, **`Weight`** must be filled in, **`Ability`** must be filled in, and the two settings fields must be filled in. The implementation will enforce these constraints.

The table that records a rental has the following fields:

```
Rental
  Rental_ID       Integer            Unique identifier
  Date            Date
  Customer        Integer            Clients.Client_ID
  ASTeamer        Character, 10      ASTeam.Nickname
  Boot_Serial     Character, 10      Serial number of boots
                                     rented
  Gear_Serial     Character, 10      Serial number applies to
                                     skis and boards
```

```
   Ski?              Y/N              Yes, specifies skis and
                                      bindings
   Ability           Character, 12    Beginner/Intermediate/
                                      Expert
   Weight            Integer          Skier weight
   Binding_Set_L     Character, 5     Setting for left binding
   Binding_Set_R     Character, 5     Setting for right binding
   Poles             Character, 5     Mfr abbrev and length
   Out_Remarks       Character, 255   Cautions or directives to
                                      customer

Primary_Key: Rental_ID
```

The **Out_Remarks** field can be used for any comments that the specialist thinks are important to the rental, such as comments made to the skier or observations about the equipment. Notice that the **ASTeamer** field name was chosen to differ from the table name **ASTeam**.

Summarizing, we have designed five database tables of the physical database to support the activity of the ski rental shop. Two of the entities—**Clients** and **ASTeam**—record information about people, and two other entities—**AS_Home** and **AS_Local**—record information about places. These tables record facts about physical phenomena. But the **Rentals** table records information not about a physical object, but about an event. The event occupies time in the same way the physical objects occupy space. Different types of entities are thus possible with a database.

Specify the Relationships

The **Rentals** table references the **Clients** and **ASTeam** tables. That is, **Rentals** has fields, **Customer** and **ASTeamer**, that contain keys for **Clients** and **ASTeam** tables. Additionally, **ASTeam** has fields with keys referencing the **AS_Home** and **AS_Local** tables. These references establish relationships, and though they have been expressed clearly in our explanation, we must specify their characteristics for the implementation, too.

The relationships are all one-to-many relationships. That is, each relationship associates the key of one table (the "one" side) with rows in the other table (the "many" side). We name the relationships as follows:

> *Rents*, the **Clients:Rentals** relationship—In the **Rentals** table, customers are referred to by their key (**Customer_ID**) in the **Clients** table.

> *Serves*, the **ASTeam:Rentals** relationship—In the **Rentals** table, specialists are referred to by their key (**Nickname**) in the **ASTeam** table.

> *Home_Of*, the **AS_Home:ASTeam** relationship—In the **ASTeam** table, the specialist's permanent address is referred to by its key (**Contact_ID**) in the **AS_Home** table.

> *Sleeps_At*, the **AS_Local:ASTeam** relationship—In the **ASTeam** table the specialist's local address is referred to by its key (**Contact_ID**) in the **AS_Local** table.

By specifying these relationships, we make our intent clear as to how the information of the tables is interconnected.

At this point, the conceptual design of the Snow Machine database's physical components is done. The entities and relationships have been defined. The design could be implemented using any of the many database software systems, all of which support the relational database concepts used here. But before investing our time in the detailed and time-consuming work of implementing the design, we should assess it.

Revise the Physical Design?

As with any design, we assess this table organization to see how well it fulfills the needs of the Snow Machine shop. We notice that there is little redundancy because of the use of the **Clients**, **ASTeam**, **AS_Home**, and **AS_Local** tables. As a result, the fields of the **Rentals** table concern only the details of a single ski rental, plus links to the customer and specialist that participated in it. The design is sound. Is this the best design?

From the point of view of The Snow Machine Ski Rental Shop, the design will probably meet its needs well. But from the point of view of the HAI! Adventure business, it might not. Why? The entrepreneurs who formed HAI! Adventure expect to grow, renting sports gear of many kinds at many sites. The ideas behind the Snow Machine database design can apply to equipment rentals for scuba diving, wind surfing, kayaking, and mountain climbing equipment rentals as well because these sports all have a similar set of requirements. How would the five tables and four relationships of the design translate to another business unit?

Table	Changes
Clients (Customer data)	None
AS_Home (Employee permanent address)	None
AS_Local (Employee local address)	None
ASTeam (Employee profile)	None, though the info entered in Cert_detail will differ
Rentals (Transaction)	Revise equipment detail for the specialized activity
Relationships	
Rents (**Clients:Rentals**)	None
Serves (**ASTeam:Rentals**)	None
Home_Of (**AS_Home:ASTeam**)	None
Sleeps_At (**AS_Local:ASTeam**)	None

Though **Rentals** changes because a different kind of equipment is being rented, it is only the ski equipment–related fields that change.

Analyze the Tables. Imagine that another HAI! Adventure business unit, say Fat Daddy's Dive Shop on Grand Cayman Island, modifies the **Rentals** table for renting scuba diving gear. Only the first four fields would be the same, and possibly the last. All others change. Though this is not a hard technical task, it means that the Fat Daddy's **Rentals** table and the Snow Machine **Rentals** table are different. The rentals of the scuba shop and rentals of the ski shop cannot be part of the same table because of these different fields. It's not a problem for the two shops—they're thousands of miles apart and never interact. But from the point of view of the main company, HAI! Adventure, they're all rentals. The fact that different equipment is being rented is unimportant in many circumstances. It would be desirable to be able to think of all such transactions as *rentals*, each of a different kind of equipment. Is this possible? Of course, anything's possible.

What is the solution? In the same way that customer information has been recorded in a separate table, the details of the equipment rental can also be recorded in another table. Call it **Gear**. But **Gear** is different from **Clients** in one important way. Customers could rent several times, and the details of the equipment are different for each rental. That is, each **Rentals** tuple will be associated with exactly one **Gear** tuple, and vice versa. This is a one-to-one relationship like those we saw in Chapter 14 based on **Student_ID**. Because we want a one-to-one relationship between **Rentals** and **Gear**, we will associate **Rental_ID**, the key of **Rentals**, with the key of **Gear**.

The **Gear** table for the Snow Machine's ski rentals has the following fields:

Gear

Equip_ID	Integer	*Key of rental (Rental_ID)*
Boot_Serial	Character, 10	*Serial number of boots rented*
Gear_Serial	Character, 10	*Serial number applies to skis and boards*
Ski?	Y/N	*Yes, specifies skis and bindings*
Ability	Character, 12	*Beginner/Intermediate/ Expert*
Weight	Integer	*Skier weight*
Binding_Set_L	Character, 5	*Setting for left binding*
Binding_Set_R	Character, 5	*Setting for right binding*
Poles	Character, 5	*Mfr abbrev and length*
Out_Remarks	Character, 255	*Customer/Specialist conversation*

Primary_Key: Equip_ID

These are simply the fields from the first version of **Rentals**.

The new **Rentals** table is simply the previous structure with the skiing details removed:

```
Rentals
   Shop_ID          Character, 10    Short name of the shop
   Rental_ID        Integer          Unique identifier
   Date             Date
   Customer         Integer          Clients.Client_ID
   ASTeamer         Character, 10    ASTeam.Nickname
   Payment          Currency         Amount received for rental

Primary_Key: Shop_ID, Rental_ID
```

`Ensure Unique Fields.` This structure can apply to any of HAI! Adventure's shops. Notice that a **Shop_ID** field has been added to identify which shop made the rental. Entries in this field might be **SnoMachine** or **FatDaddys**, or we could use store numbers. The reason for this field is to create unique records when the rentals of multiple stores are **Union**ed together. (Recall from Chapter 13 that Union combines the rows of two tables that have the same fields.) That is, each store uses its own sequence of **Rental_ID** numbers, but to avoid disaster if two stores use the same number, we make the rows unique by using the store name as a prefix. Thus the primary key (from the point of view of the main company) is the composition of **Shop_ID** and **Rental_ID**. Finally, we've added a **Payment** field because HAI! Adventure's founders may be interested in that information, too.

`Introduce New Relationships.` By splitting up the original **Rentals** table into the core activity of renting (the new version of **Rentals**) and a table for the specific equipment rented (**Gear**), we introduced two more relationships, the opposite sides of the one-to-one relationship between the two tables:

> *Equips*, the **Gear:Rentals** relationship—In the **Rentals** table, the specific equipment in **Gear** is referred to by its key (**Rental_ID**).

> *Package*, the **Rentals:Gear** relationship—In the **Gear** table, the supplied equipment in **Rentals** is referred to by its key (**Rental_ID**).

These are one-to-one relationships.

Now it will be possible for any HAI! Adventure shop to use the **Rentals** table unchanged, though different recreations will refer to different **Gear** tables. For example, Fat Daddy's rental will refer to a **Gear** table customized to scuba equipment. Of course, all shops renting the same kind of gear can use the same **Gear** table design.

IMPLEMENT THE PHYSICAL DB DESIGN

Having completed the approximate-and-revise process, we now have a physical database that meets our needs and we know the relationships among its tables. More revisions are possible, but further changes might not produce a better design. We need some experience with the design to see how well it works. So we stop the revision process and go with what we have—in other words, we "freeze" the design. We will implement it in a commercial database system and store some sample data. We will also specify the relationships in the database system. These physical tables will be the basis for the next design steps, and eventually will allow us to produce our first working system. Experience with the system may indicate that we need more changes to the physical database tables, so the revision process is not necessarily complete. But at this point we need some experience.

Define the Tables

All database systems support the concepts used in the design. For our example we'll use the Microsoft Access system.

The first step in the implementation is to define the tables. Defining tables is basically typing into the database system the information outlined above. It is tedious, but easy. We implement the tables at this stage to fill them with sample data in hopes of finding mistakes. Some of the Snow Machine tables are shown in Figure 15.1.

Define the Relationships

The next step is to define the relationships to connect the parts of the database. Again, the database systems give us easy-to-use software tools for defining the relationships. The specification of these relationships is shown in Figure 15.2.

DESIGN THE LOGICAL DATABASE

Having defined the physical database, it is time to create the logical database. Though we have stored the information in a particular way (for example, to avoid redundancy), the users will want to look at it differently. Different users want different views of the database customized to their needs, as discussed in Chapter 14.

Giving users views of the database is easy. Just use a five-step approach:

1. Analyze the business activity to identify the information inputs and outputs—these are the needed views.
2. Determine what information the specialists need from each view and where it is stored in the tables.

Clients : Table

Field Name	Data Type	
Customer_ID	AutoNumb	Unique identifier
First	Text	First Name
Middle	Text	Middle Name
Last	Text	Last Name
Birthdate	Date/Time	Date of Birth
Street	Text	Street address
City	Text	City
State	Text	State/Province/Canton/Prefecture
ZIP	Text	Postal Code
Country	Text	Country of Residence
Home_Phone	Text	Phone at Residence
Mobile_Phone	Text	Cell
Email	Text	Email Address
Local_Contact	Text	Hotel or local phone number

ASTeam : Table

Field Name	Data Type	
Nickname	Text	Unique Identifier
First	Text	First Name
Middle	Text	Middle Name
Last	Text	Last Name
Birthdate	Date/Tim	Date of Birth
SS_number	Text	ddd-dd-dddd
Home_Addr	Number	Key into AS_Home
Local_Addr	Number	Key into AS_Local
Mobile_Phone	Text	Cell
Email	Text	Email address
Certified	Yes/No	Any relevant certification?
Cert_Expire	Date/Tim	Expiration date
Cert_Detail	Text	Details of when, where, etc.

Rentals : Table

Field Name	Data Type	
Store_ID	Text	Unique store name
Rental_ID	AutoNumber	Unique number for each rental
Date	Date/Time	Transaction Date
Customer	Number	Key into Clients
ASTeamer	Text	Key into ASTeam
Payment	Currency	Amt received for rental

Gear : Table

Field Name	Data Type	
Equip_ID	Number	Key from Rentals table
Boot_Serial	Text	Serial Number for boots
Gear_Serial	Text	Serial Number for skis or board
Ski?	Yes/No	Are bindings involved?
Ability	Text	Beginner/Intermediate/Exper
Weight	Number	Weight of skier
Binding_Set_L	Text	Binding setting, left
Binding_Set_R	Text	Binding setting, right
Poles	Text	Mfr Abbrev + length
Out_Remarks	Text	Comments about rental or to customer

Figure 15.1. *Four of the six tables required for the revised Snow Machine physical database. The* `AS_Home` *and* `AS_Local` *tables are identical and are composed only of address fields, like fields 6–11 of* `Clients`.

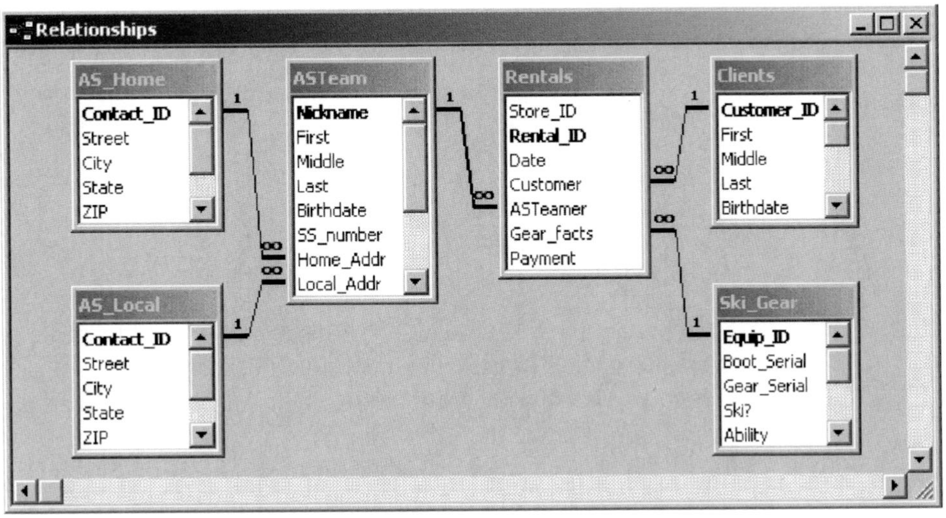

Figure 15.2. *The relationships of HAI! Adventure's Snow Machine database. The one-to-many relationships are shown with the "one" side (shown as the symbol "1") as a primary key to the relationship, and the many side (shown as a small infinity symbol "∞") as a position where the key is used as a reference.*

3. Define a conceptual query for a new table as a join-then-trim process from existing tables.

4. Implement the conceptual query in SQL.

5. Define a GUI to display the information for the specialists.

To begin, we analyze the business activity. The adventure specialists interact with the Snow Machine database three times: at sign-in; at the fitting of gear; and at the signing of the rental agreement. Thus, there are three customer-related views:

> **Sign-in.** After the receptionist has greeted the customer and the customer has decided on what to rent, the receptionist records the customer's personal information. That is, the receptionist establishes a new rental, and enters data on the customer into the **`Clients`** table. In addition, the receptionist specifies whether ski or snowboarding gear is being rented.

> **Fitting.** The customer moves to the Fitting Room, where an adventure specialist helps the customer select and fit the gear. The specialist must enter information into the **`Rentals`** (his or her name) and **`Gear`** tables (equipment).

> **Agreeing.** The customer takes the gear and stops at the receptionist's station to sign the rental agreement and pay for the rental. The price is entered at this point. For the rental agreement contract, the information in the **`Clients`**, **`Gear`**, **`ASTeam`**, and **`Rentals`** tables must be combined into a contract and printed.

In addition to these three customer-related views, there is one employee-related view:

> **Hiring.** When new adventure specialists are hired, their information must be entered into the database. That is, information must be entered into three tables: **`ASTeam`**, **`AS_Home`**, and **`AS_Local`**.

Notice that Sign-in, Fitting, and Hiring are "input views" and Agreeing is an "output view" in which database information is displayed.

Analyze the Tables for the Views

To present these four views of the database, we need to create the tables that correspond to them. These will not be stored tables, but rather logical tables computed by queries. What data is in the new tables depends on what information the user must see. Analyze the four views:

> **Sign-in.** Begins a rental, and so requires fields **`Rental_ID`** and **`Customer`** from **`Rentals`**. It should also include the **`ASTeamer`** field so that the receptionist can send the customer to a particular specialist, if one is requested. All of the fields of **`Clients`** are required because the customer may be new to the store. Finally, the view must include the **`Ski`**? field from the **`Gear`** table.

> **Fitting.** Requires all the fields from **`Gear`**. It also requires the **`Rental_ID`** and **`ASTeamer`** fields from **`Rentals`**, so the specialist can sign in if no particular specialist was requested. In addition, so that the specialist can call the customer by name, the two fields **`First`** and **`Last`** from the **`Clients`** table are also required.

> **Agreeing.** Requires all of the fields from **`Rentals`**, **`Clients`** (except **`Email`** and **`Local_Contact`**), and **`Gear`** and the name of the specialist from the **`ASTeam`** table.

> **Hiring.** Requires all of the fields from **`ASTeam`**, **`AS_Home`**, and **`AS_Local`** for signing in new specialists or updating their records.

This information is shown in Table 15.1.

Table 15.1. *Summary of the fields required for the* **`Snow Machine`** *database views*

View	Clients	ASTeam	Gear	AS_Home	AS_Local	Rentals

`Sign-In`	*All*		`Ski?`			`Rental_ID`
						`Customer`
						`ASTeamer`

`Fitting`	`First`
	`Last`
			All			`Rental_ID`
						`Customer`
						`ASTeamer`

`Agreeing`	*All—except*
	`Email`
	`Local_Contact`
		`First`
		`Middle`
		`Last`
			All			*All*

`Hiring`		*All*		*All*	*All*	

Create the View Queries

The views will be created using *queries*, commands formed from the basic table-manipulating operations using the join-then-trim approach described in Chapter 14: *Combine the base tables into a super table, and then retrieve the fields needed for the view.* Consider each query in turn.

Sign-in query. The Sign-in view begins a rental, so we should think of it as establishing a new **`Rentals`** row; specifically, the fields **`Rental_ID`** and **`Customer`**. **`ASTeamer`** from **`Rentals`** may also be defined if a customer asks for a specific adventure specialist. All of the fields from **`Clients`** are required, though they may have been entered on an earlier visit. Only **`Ski?`** is needed from **`Gear`**. The form for the query is

```
Project Customer_ID, First, Middle, Last, Birthdate,
     Street, City, State, ZIP, Country, Home_Phone,
     Mobile_Phone, Email, Local_Contact, Rental_ID,
     Customer, ASTeamer, Ski?

From (Clients ⋈ Rentals) ⋈ Gear
```

The first join relies on the *Rents* relationship between **Clients** and **Rentals**, matching whenever `Customer_ID = Customer`, and the second join relies on the *Equips* relationship between **Gear** and **Rentals**, matching whenever `Equip_ID = Rental_ID`.

Fitting query. The Fitting view needs data from three tables, **Rentals**, **Gear**, and **Clients**. From **Rentals**, only the `Rental_ID`, `ASTeamer`, and `Customer` fields are needed. The `Customer` field is needed to retrieve the customer's first and last name from **Clients**. All of the fields of **Gear** are needed. The query is

```
Project Rental_ID, ASTeamer, Customer, First, Last,
     Equip_ID, Boot_Serial, Gear_Serial, Ski?, Ability,
     Weight, Binding_Set_L, Binding_Set_R, Poles,
     Out_Remarks
From (Rentals ⋈ Clients) ⋈ Gear
```

The super table is like the Sign-in view, relying on the *Rents* relationship and the *Equips* relationship.

Agreeing query. The contract will need information from the **Rentals**, **Clients**, **Gear**, and **ASTeamer** tables. It needs all of the fields (except `Clients.Email` and `Clients.Local_Contact`) from the first three tables, and the name fields from **ASTeamer**. Though straightforward, listing all of the fields is rather lengthy:

```
Project Shop_ID, Rental_ID, Date, Customer, ASTeamer,
     Payment, Customer_ID, Clients.First, Clients.Middle,
     Clients.Last, Birthdate, Street, City, State, ZIP,
     Country, Home_Phone, Mobile_Phone, Equip_ID,
     Boot_Serial, Gear_Serial, Ski?, Ability, Weight,
     Binding_Set_L, Binding_Set_R, Poles, Out_Remarks,
     NickName, ASTeamer.First, ASTeamer.Middle,
     ASTeamer.Last
From (((Rentals ⋈ Clients) ⋈ Ski_Gear) ⋈ ASTeamer)
```

The three relationships used for the joins are *Rents*, *Equips*, and *Serves*. We've seen the *Rents*- and *Equips*-based equality tests before. The join based on *Serves* creates rows whenever `ASTeamer = NickName`.

Hiring query. The *Hiring* view is more direct. It uses all of the fields from the three tables, **ASTeam**, **AS_Home**, and **AS_Local**. Because all of the fields are needed, no project operation (trimming) will be required. The query is simply the three joins:

```
(ASTeam ⋈ AS_Home) ⋈ AS_Local
```

The first join relies on the *Home_Of* relationship, combining rows whenever `Home_Addr = AS_Home.Contact_ID`. The second join relies on the *Sleeps_At* relationship, forming rows whenever **Local_Addr = AS_Local.Contact_ID**. All of the fields are kept.

Having defined the views that the Snow Machine personnel will use to interact with the database, it's time to set up the interfaces to the views.

IMPLEMENT THE LOGICAL DATABASE DESIGN

Naturally the view queries can be implemented in database system software. With the tables and relationships already implemented, specifying the queries for the views is easy. We translate the conceptual queries directly into SQL. The best place to begin is with the *Hiring* query, because specialists must be added to the database before any customers can be processed.

Encode the Hiring Query

The *Hiring* query (**Hiring_Q**) is especially easy because it is just the join of three tables:

```
(ASTeam ⋈ AS_Home) ⋈ AS_Local
```

The three key points to remember about the translation from our conceptual form of the query to SQL are as follows:

- The conceptual natural **Join** produces a table with all (unique) fields in it, but in SQL it is necessary to specify which fields should be included. Rather than picking out the fields with the operation **Project** … **From**, we use the command **SELECT** … **FROM**.
- Rather than the natural **Join** operator, ⋈, we use the operator **INNER JOIN**.
- We must give the equality test that is the basis for the **INNER JOIN**.
- In addition, all references to fields use the *table name.field name* syntax.

Keeping those differences in mind, the translation of the *Hiring* query into SQL is

```
SELECT  ASTeam.Nickname, ASTeam.First, ASTeam.Middle,
        ASTeam.Last, ASTeam.Birthdate, ASTeam.SS_number,
        ASTeam.Home_Addr, ASTeam.Local_Addr, ASTeam.Mobile_Phone,
        ASTeam.Email, ASTeam.Certified, ASTeam.Cert_Expire,
        ASTeam.Cert_Detail, AS_Home.Contact_ID, AS_Home.Street,
        AS_Home.City, AS_Home.State,AS_Home.ZIP, AS_Home.Country,
        AS_Home.Phone, AS_Local.Contact_ID, AS_Local.Street,
        AS_Local.City, AS_Local.State, AS_Local.ZIP,
        AS_Local.Country, AS_Local.Phone
FROM    AS_Local INNER JOIN
               (AS_Home INNER JOIN ASTeam
                        ON AS_Home.Contact_ID = ASTeam.Home_Addr)
                ON AS_Local.Contact_ID = ASTeam.Local_Addr;
```

It's an impressive command, but when it's decomposed into its components, it's far less menacing. The command works as promised—the **SELECT** picks out all of the fields from the join of the three tables. Notice that although the order of the **INNER JOIN**'s operands is different from our conceptual form, the parentheses ensure that the operations are done in the same order; that is, **AS_Home INNER JOIN ASTeam** is first, though order doesn't matter when giving joins.

Encode the Sign-in Query

Next we translate the *Sign-in* query directly into SQL. Recall that the query is

```
Project Customer_ID, First, Middle, Last, Birthdate,
     Street, City, State, ZIP, Country, Home_Phone,
     Mobile_Phone, Email, Local_Contact, Rental_ID,
     Customer, ASTeamer, Ski?

From (Clients ⋈ Rentals) ⋈ Gear
```

Following the three guidelines listed above yields the `Sign-In_Q`:

```
SELECT Clients.Customer_ID, Clients.First, Clients.Middle,
       Clients.Last, Clients.Birthdate, Clients.Street,
       Clients.City, Clients.State, Clients.ZIP,
       Clients.Country, Clients.Home_Phone,
       Clients.Mobile_Phone, Clients.Email,
       Clients.Local_Contact, Rentals.Rental_ID,
       Rentals.Customer, Rentals.ASTeamer, Gear.Ski?
FROM   (Clients INNER JOIN Rentals
              ON Clients.Customer_ID = Rentals.Customer)
       INNER JOIN Gear
       ON Rentals.Rentals_ID = Gear.Equip_ID;
```

which is exactly the query required for the Sign-in view.

Encode the Fitting Query

The *Fitting* query is also an easy command to program directly in SQL. Recalling the conceptual form of the query

```
Project Rental_ID, ASTeamer, Customer, Gear_facts, First,
     Last, Equip_ID, Boot_Serial, Gear_Serial, Ski?, Ability,
     Weight, Binding_Set_L, Binding_Set_R, Poles,
     Out_Remarks
From (Rentals ⋈ Clients) ⋈ Gear
```

the `Fitting_Q` query is therefore

```
SELECT Rentals.Rental_ID, Rentals.ASTeamer, Rentals.Customer,
       Clients.First, Clients.Last, Gear.Equip_ID,
       Gear.Boot_Serial, Gear.Gear_Serial, Gear.Ski?,
       Gear.Ability, Gear.Weight, Gear.Binding_Set_L,
       Gear.Binding_Set_R, Gear.Poles, Gear.Out_Remarks
FROM   (Clients INNER JOIN Rentals
              ON Clients.Customer_ID = Rentals.Customer)
       INNER JOIN Gear
       ON Rentals.Rentals_ID = Gear.Equip_ID;
```

Encode the Agreeing Query

Finally, the view query (`Agreeing_Q`) for the rental agreement contract seems to be the most complicated because it involves four tables. But because it uses all of the fields (but two) of three tables, and only three fields of the other, it isn't so difficult in concept.

```
SELECT Rentals.Store_ID, Rentals.Rental_ID, Rentals.Date,
       Rentals.Customer, Rentals.ASTeamer, Rentals.Payment,
       Clients.Customer_ID, Clients.First, Clients.Middle,
       Clients.Last, Clients.Birthdate, Clients.Street,
       Clients.City, Clients.State, Clients.ZIP,
       Clients.Country, Clients.Home_Phone,
       Clients.Mobile_Phone, Gear.Equip_ID, Gear.Boot_Serial,
       Gear.Gear_Serial, Gear.Ski, Gear.Ability, Gear.Weight,
       Gear.Binding_Set_L, Gear.Binding_Set_R, Gear.Poles,
       Gear.Out_Remarks, ASTeam.First, ASTeam.Middle,
       ASTeam.Last
FROM   Gear INNER JOIN
          (Clients INNER JOIN
              (ASTeam INNER JOIN Rentals
                  ON ASTeam.Nickname = Rentals.ASTeamer)
               ON Clients.Customer_ID = Rentals.Customer)
           ON Gear.Equip_ID = Rentals.Rental_ID;
```

In general, translating queries directly into SQL is about as complicated as in these examples. Because SQL is the standard language for database queries in production database systems, anyone expecting to build or be responsible for one (that is, anyone expecting to be a database administrator), should plan on spending a few more minutes learning the details.

{FITRULE}

Query-by-Example > >

Although translating from our conceptual form to SQL is not difficult, there is an even easier way to produce SQL: Query-by-Example (QBE). Developed at IBM in 1975, QBE has been included in Microsoft Access as an alternative to programming SQL directly. The idea is that the user gives an example of the desired table by filling in the fields of a blank table. The software then generates an SQL query to create the example table. Let's see how it works for the Hiring view.

Figure 15.3 shows Access's Query-by-Example facility for defining the `Hiring_Q` query. Notice that there are two windows. The upper window shows the entity-relationship diagram for the tables used in the query, and the relationships used for the joins. These were displayed automatically when the user chose the tables for the example.

The lower window shows (part of) the display of the fields of the intended table. This is an "example" of how the table should look. Each position corresponds to a field of the intended table with the source table and source field shown. It is possible to order the items of the table's column (`Sort`), include them, but not display them (`Show`), or put conditions on them (`Criteria`, `Or`). The software documentation gives more information.

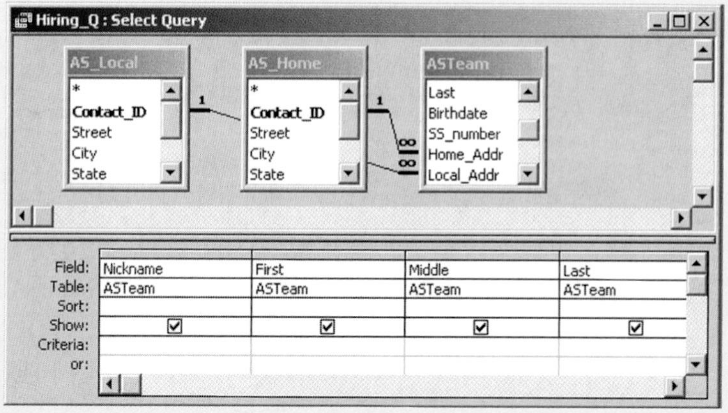

Figure 15.3. *Query-by-example display (from MS Access) showing the tables with the relationships and the first four fields of the* `Hiring_Q` *query.*

The software translates the QBE queries into SQL automatically. It is possible (and informative) to look at the SQL generated by the software: **View > SQL View**. The SQL for `Hiring_Q` generated by the software is identical to the query we wrote.

Figure 15.4 shows the two windows of the QBE interface for the `Agreeing_Q` query. Notice the tables/relationships and example table windows. The three relationships enable the query to assemble the needed information. The query generated by SQL is again exactly the query we wrote.

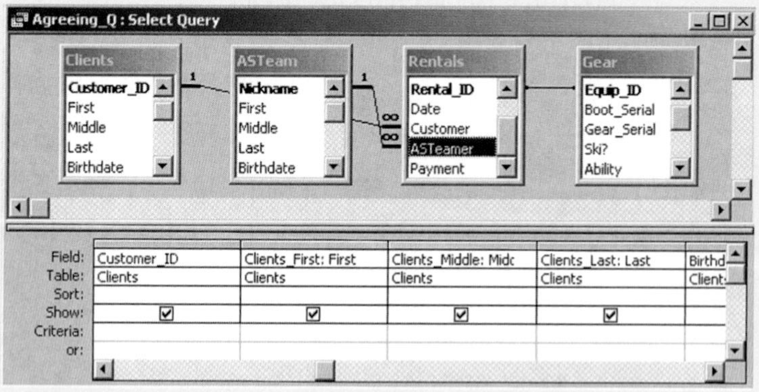

Figure 15.4. `Agreeing_Q` *query in the Query-by-Example window.*

IMPLEMENT THE GUIS

Data can be entered directly into the "tabular sheet" form of the tables, but users expect a GUI to make data entry more pleasant. Such GUIs are also known as *forms*. A GUI should be clear and convenient to use, and pleasant to look at. Though designing pleasing and effective GUIs is an art—a career for those who are talented at it—there are some commonsense guidelines:

- **Arrange information sensibly.** Cluster the fields together in a way that makes sense—names go together, address fields go together, and so on. Also, orient the fields the way the user will expect to see them—perhaps arranging name information horizontally and address information vertically, to follow the most common orientation in which the information is written.
- **Avoid clutter.** Eliminate duplicate fields and avoid unnecessary text, lines, and visual effects. Many believe that sans serif fonts work best onscreen.
- **Preload fields.** Where possible, fill a field with a default value, or if there is a specific format expected, fill the field with the guidelines for its form, as in DD/MM/YY for dates.

Most people who use a data entry GUI probably stop noticing its pleasant or annoying features quickly. Still we should make it the best possible. Use your database system to build the GUIs.

Ta DAH! It's done. The Snow Machine Ski Rental Shop database has been designed and implemented (see Figure 15.5). HAI! Adventure is in business.

EXTENDING A DATABASE: LESSONS AND TOURS

The Snow Machine database has been designed to handle new rental businesses of HAI! Adventure, such as renting scuba equipment and mountain climbing gear. It will be a simple matter to develop new tables for the new equipment types.

The problem for this section is to consider what changes are needed for the HAI! Adventure team to move into the lessons and tours business. How do we handle the fact that some of the adventure specialists will serve as instructors, guides, or leaders for activities related to the shop's sports specialty? Each of these activities includes a set of customers and a guide or instructor. The question is, "How should the present database be extended to handle these new activities?"

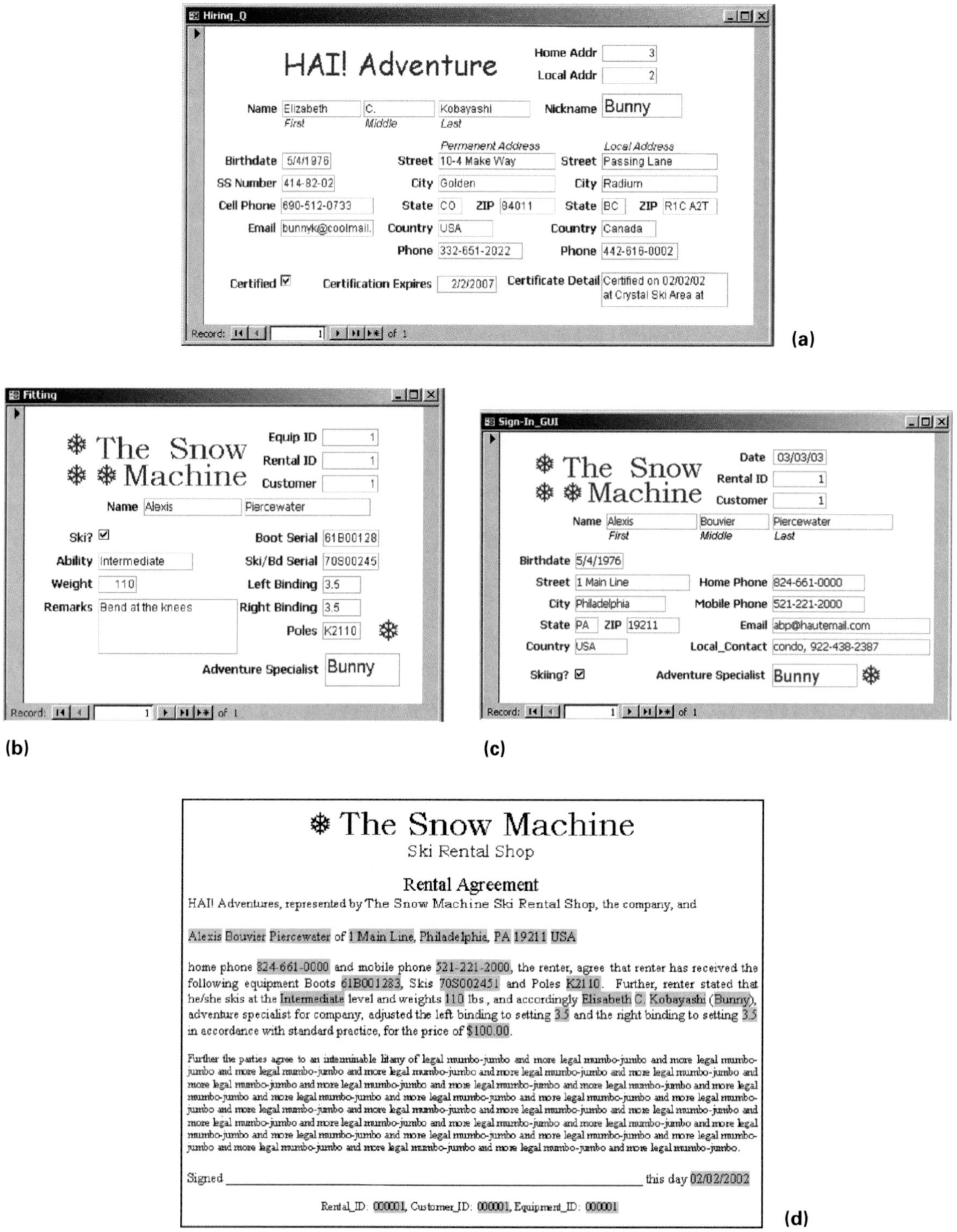

The Snow Machine

Ski Rental Shop

Rental Agreement

HAI! Adventures, represented by The Snow Machine Ski Rental Shop, the company, and

Alexis Bouvier Piercewater of 1 Main Line, Philadelphia, PA 19211 USA

home phone 824-661-0000 and mobile phone 521-221-2000, the renter, agree that renter has received the following equipment Boots 61B001283, Skis 70S002451 and Poles K2110. Further, renter stated that he/she skis at the Intermediate level and weights 110 lbs., and accordingly Elisabeth C. Kobayashi (Bunny), adventure specialist for company, adjusted the left binding to setting 3.5 and the right binding to setting 3.5 in accordance with standard practice, for the price of $100.00.

Further the parties agree to an interminable litany of legal mumbo-jumbo and more legal mumbo-jumbo.

Signed ______________________________ this day 02/02/2002

Rental_ID: 000001, Customer_ID: 000001, Equipment_ID: 000001

Figure 15.5. Sample GUIs for the four Snow Machine views: (a) Hiring view, (b) Fitting view, (c) Sign-In view, and (d) Rental agreement.

An Analogy

When thinking about how to design the tables to incorporate lessons and tours, it is natural to make analogies to familiar situations. We visualize a ski instructor and students, and think about organizing the table as a class list. Because the number of students will be limited, it would seem that a `Class_List` table with the following schema should work:

```
Class_List                              CAUTION – NOT A GOOD DESIGN
   Class_ID         Number              Unique identifier
   Date             mm/dd/yy            Date of event or first
                                        lesson
   Type             Character, 50       Description of the lesson
                                        or tour
   Leader           Character, 10       ASTeam.Nickname value
   Participant1     Number              Clients.Customer_ID
   Participant2     Number              Clients.Customer_ID
   Participant3     Number              Clients.Customer_ID
   Participant4     Number              Clients.Customer_ID
   Participant5     Number              Clients.Customer_ID

Primary Key: Class_ID
```

The idea is that each group has a leader as well as a set of participants. By using the keys for the **`Leader`** and the **`Participants`**, we avoid redundancy. But we make a different mistake. This is *not* the way to extend the database to include lessons and tours, even though the analogy seems right.

The **`Class_List`** table idea has several problems, but mostly the error is binding together data that should be *independent*. That is, participation in the class should not be ordered. But the **`Class_List`** definition implies, for example, that because we've assigned a numbered attribute to each student, being student number 2 is different than being student number 3. This structure implies that we are interested in tuples in a table that are the same in all respects except that the participants are ordered differently, as in Table 15.2. But we don't want to recognize such distinctions. Students in a class should be unordered. This design is faulty.

Table 15.2. *Possible tuples based on the `Class_List` table definition*

Class_ID	Date	Type	Leader	Partic_1	Partic_2	Partic_3	Partic_4	Partic_5
223	2/2/02	Beg'g Skiing	Thor	Jan	John	Jon	Ian	Juan
223	2/2/02	Beg'g Skiing	Thor	Juan	Jan	John	Jon	Ian
223	2/2/02	Beg'g Skiing	Thor	Ian	Juan	Jan	John	Jon

The Activities Table

A better design is to create an entity that includes the common features and properties of the lessons and tours. The "thing" we're trying to describe is a scheduled activity—a lesson at a given time or a dive on a given morning or a climb on a specific day—and a collection of such things would form a table of instances in which each would have the following fields:

Activities

Activity_ID	Number	*Unique identifier*
Date	Date	*Date of activity*
Leader	Character, 10	*ASTeam.NickName*
Description	Character, 50	*Statement describing activity*
Limit	Number	*Upper limit on participation*

Primary Key: Activity_ID

HAI! Adventure plans to offer these activities. Basically this is the **Class_List** schema without the participants. This design not only avoids the problem of ordering the participants, but also regularizes lessons and tours for all sports because the nature of the activity is specified in the **Description** field. Having all lessons "look alike" in the database tables will be important to HAI! Adventure, just as making all **Rentals** look alike was.

Thinking abstractly about the database design for a moment, how *will* we create a class list or tour-participants list? After all, even if it is unwise to implement the class list metaphor directly as a tuple in a table, it is nevertheless a useful document. Thinking about this might guide us to a better solution. And it does.

The Apply Table

From our knowledge of the join-then-trim method, we can expect to construct the class list by creating a query that combines some of the base tables, such as **ASTeam** for the leader. From the resulting super table, we will remove the fields needed for the class list. That's what we did before when the logical database view didn't exactly match the tables of the physical database. So, what should we store so we can create the class list in this way? Obviously, we need a table of students. But we already have that. It's simply our **Clients** table.

Perhaps the activity the customer signs up for could be added to the **Clients** records. When thinking about how we might extend the **Clients** table to include "sign-up" information, however, we realize that the customer might register for several tours or lessons. And as we're imagining adding a series of fields to the **Clients** records—**Activity1**, **Activity2**, and **Activity3**, say—in which to store the **Activity_ID** keys of the lessons—we realize that we're about to make the same mistake as with the class list! The activities should be independent, too.

To solve these problems, think about how your school works. Colleges have students (like HAI! Adventure has **Clients**) and classes (like HAI! Adventure has **Activities**), but for a student to take a class, he or she must *register*. That is, the binding of **Clients** to **Activities** can be done using the concept of registration. What form would the registration take? Because registration binds customers with activities, it will be like **Rentals**, but without the equipment table. It would likely have the following schema:

```
Apply
   Shop_ID          Character, 10    Short name of the shop
   Regist_ID        Number           Unique identifier
   Date             Date
   Activity         Number           Activities.Activity_ID
   Participant      Number           Clients.Customer_ID
   Skill            Character, 255   Skill level description
   Payment          Currency         Amount paid

Primary_Key: Shop_ID, Regist_ID
```

The fields are self-explanatory except perhaps for **Skill**, which is a text description of the participant's qualifications for the activity. The leader will evaluate this field. That is, registration is an *application* to participate, which is why we called the table **Apply**, and the customer must have the right qualifications. Some activities, like skiing, require routine information, "Intermediate Skier"; some activities, like mountain climbing, require detailed information, "Climbed the four highest peaks in the Bugaboos as follows . . . "; and some activities, like bungee jumping, require little information, "Have Mass." Like college, you have to have the prereqs.

Notice that everyone registered for an activity will be in the **Apply** table; that is, the design works for participants of any class or tour. If a person is registered for more than one activity, he or she will have more than one row in **Apply**, and the rows will be independent (unordered). If two **Clients** are signed up for the same class, they are also unordered. If participants cancel their registration, they are given a refund and removed from the table, but they don't leave "holes" in a schedule, as would have happened with the earlier **Class_List** design, because there is not yet any schedule. And, finally, a participants list or class list can be created by joining **Apply**, **Clients**, and **Activities**, as explained later in this chapter. The solution has every positive feature imaginable, except one: Even though there is a registration limit for each of the activities, this scheme doesn't automatically cap the enrollment at that number. Any number of people could register for a three-person trek to Acuncagua. But this problem is easily solved with database software systems, so we won't worry about it.

Establish Relationships between Tables

The creation of the **Activities** and **Apply** tables for the physical data base naturally defines some relationships:

- *Leads*, the **ASTeam:Activities** relationship—In the **Activities** table, specialists are referred to by their key (**Nickname**) in the **ASTeam** table.
- *Offers*, the **Activities:Apply** relationship—In the **Apply** table, lessons and tours are referred to by their key (**Activity_ID**) in the **Activities** table.
- *Registers_For*, the **Clients:Apply** relationship—In the **Apply** table, the participants are referred to by their key (**Customer_ID**) in the **Clients** table.

These are all one-to-many relationships. Figure 15.6 shows the relationships.

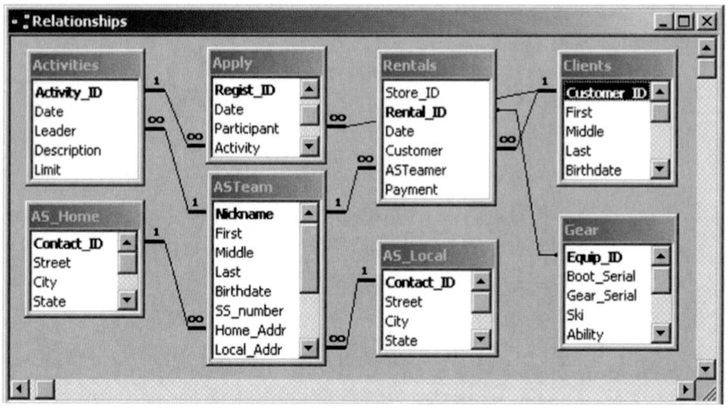

Figure 15.6. *The relationships of the Snow Machine database after adding the Activities and Apply tables, and their induced relationships.*

Creating the participants list or class list for a given activity is straightforward. The **Activities**, **Apply**, and **Customers** tables are joined, and the necessary fields are extracted. For the list, we want all fields from **Activities** and the participants' names from **Clients**. No information is actually needed from **Apply** because the instructor or leader will have already looked over the participants and decided who is qualified. (This requires another view, of course.) So our class list uses the registration table **Apply**, but only for associating **Activities** table entries to **Clients** table entries, as planned. The required Class List view is implemented by the table created by the **Attends_Q** query:

```
Project Activity_ID, Date, Leader, Description, Limit,
     Activity, Participant, Customer_ID, First, Last
From (Activities ⋈ Apply) ⋈ Clients
```

Converting this conceptual query to SQL is direct because it amounts to repeating the field list and testing equality on the fields of the *Offers* and *Registers_For* relationships. The result is

```
SELECT Activities.Activity_ID, Activities.Date,
       Activities.Leader, Activities.Description,
       Activities.Limit, Apply.Participant, Clients.First,
       Clients.Last
FROM   Clients INNER JOIN
              (Activities INNER JOIN Apply
                     ON Activities.Activity_ID = Apply.Activity)
              ON Clients.Customer_ID = Apply.Participant
```

A Class List Report

There's one more thing to do. `Attends_Q` will create a table of *all* the students signed up for *all* of the classes, which isn't quite what we want. What we actually need is the list for one class, or perhaps a list for one day, if there are few enough classes in a day. We can easily do this using `Activity_ID` or `Date` to select the necessary rows from the `Attends_Q` table. Using the conceptual `Select_from... On...` operation discussed in Chapter 13, we can revise the `Attends_Q` query to form the `Class_List_Q` query:

```
Select_from
  Project Activity_ID, Date, Leader, Description, Limit,
        Activity, Participant, Customer_ID, First, Last
  From (Activities ⋈ Apply) ⋈ Clients
On Date = current_date
```

where `current_date` is a system-defined constant. `Select_from` keeps only those rows that satisfy its `On` test, so that `Class_List_Q` produces the list of participants on a given day. To select on `Activity_ID`, the user would be asked for the name of the activity (by a GUI) and the returned value would be matched in the `On`.

To get the SQL `Class_List_Q` query, we only need to add a `WHERE` clause to the `Attends_Q` query that saves only those rows that meet the criterion. Therefore, the `Class_List_Q` query has the SQL form:

```
SELECT Activities.Activity_ID, Activities.Date,
       Activities.Leader, Activities.Description,
       Activities.Limit, Apply.Participant, Clients.First,
       Clients.Last
FROM   Clients INNER JOIN
              (Activities INNER JOIN Apply
                     ON Activities.Activity_ID = Apply.Activity)
              ON Clients.Customer_ID = Apply.Participant
WHERE ((Activities.Date)="Date");
```

An example document produced by the `Class_List_Q` query is shown in Figure 15.7.

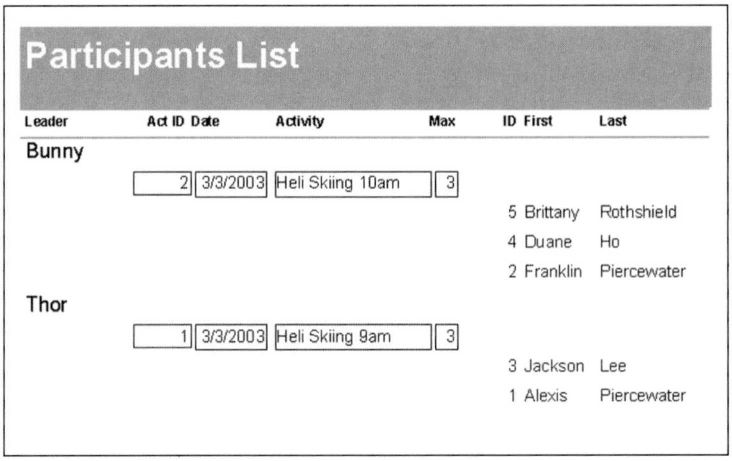

Figure 15.7. *A participants list document displaying the results of the* `Class_List_Q` *query.*

SUMMARY

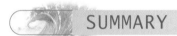

Our design of the HAI! Adventure database was typical of most design efforts. It began with our best guess at a solution, followed by an analysis of how well the solution satisfied our needs. That led to revisions, which were followed by more analysis, and so on. The process of design-then-refine continued until we produced a quality solution. We immediately considered how it could be improved! The result, a long way from our first idea about how the database should be organized, resulted from careful thought about what would make the solution better.

Less abstractly, we began our design process by studying the structure and operation of the Snow Machine Ski Rental Shop. Though we used the physical structure of the shop to help us visualize its operation, the things that affected the database design were the rental process and the allocation of tasks among the employees. The rental process began when the receptionist input the customer's information. The adventure specialist then added data. Then the information had to be brought together into a rental agreement. This originally motivated a "mega" **`Rentals`** table in which all of the relevant information for each rental would be stored in a single row. But such an arrangement introduced the dreaded problem of *redundancy*, so we created smaller tables that collected information in logically related units.

There is no algorithm for formulating tables. It is simply a matter of thinking about the process and the types of information created. Before implementing the tables, we considered whether the Snow Machine database design perfectly fulfilled HAI! Adventure's plans to branch out into other forms of equipment rental. We found that it did not, and revised the design one more time before implementing the tables and relationships.

When the tables and relationships are defined, the physical database is set up the way it will be stored on the hard disk. But that's probably not how the users will want to see it, so we designed database views for the Snow Machine shop. We identified three views for transacting business: Sign-in, Fitting, and Agreeing. Then we worked out the conceptual queries needed to create these view tables. A few tables were combined using `Join`, and then trimmed as needed. Once the conceptual queries were created, it was a simple matter to encode those in SQL.

We created a GUI for the view to make the database convenient for the Snow Machine's adventure specialists. At that point, the basic rental database was done and ready to have the GUIs customized to any of HAI! Adventure's rental businesses.

Finally, we looked at how HAI! Adventure could extend the rental version of its database to lessons and guided tours. The task gave us a chance to illustrate that although reasoning by analogy is a very powerful design and problem-solving technique, it is not perfect. It is possible to use the wrong analogy or metaphor. The class list was used as an example. Quickly, however, we saw the weaknesses of that metaphor, and switched to a registration analogy. So we created the `Activities` and `Apply` extensions. We created a Class List view within the `Activities`, `Apply` structure.

Though the focus of this chapter has been on solving the database problems for HAI! Adventure and its Snow Machine shop, the ideas and approaches used in this case study can be used in any database design. The details of the approach—tables and relationships first, views second, implementation last—also apply to most other design situations. We were successful here simply by working through the process carefully. It's a powerful strategy.

EXERCISES

Multiple Choice

1. The first step in building a database is to:
   A. design the logical database
   B. create the physical design
   C. determine the tables and their relationships
   D. perform a needs analysis

2. In building a database, the creation of ER diagrams would probably occur in the:
   A. needs analysis phase
   B. approximate and revise a physical design phase
   C. implement the physical design phase
   D. implement the logical database phase

Questions 3–12 refer to the HAI! Adventure Database Case Study.

3. In the case study, personal information is stored in the:
   A. **`Rentals`** table
   B. **`Clients`** table
   C. **`ASTeam`** table
   D. **`Activities`** table

4. The key field in the **`Clients`** table is:
   A. **`Birthdate`**
   B. **`Email`**
   C. **`Customer_ID`**
   D. **`Rental`**

5. The Social Security number field cannot be used as a key field because:
   A. it's not unique
   B. it's not long enough
   C. it's illegal to use it for anything but payroll and taxes
   D. fields cannot store the hyphens that are in a Social Security number

6. The **`Clients`** table contains information on clients. The **`Rentals`** table contains information on rentals to clients. The relationship of **`Clients`** to **`Rentals`** is:
   A. one-to-many
   B. many-to-one
   C. one-to-one
   D. brother-to-sister

7. The key field for the **`Clients`** and **`Rentals`** relationship is the:
   A. **`Date`**
   B. **`Rental_ID`**
   C. **`Nickname`**
   D. **`CustomerID`**

8. In the case study, the relationship between **Clients** and **Rentals** is called:
   A. *Rents*
   B. *Serves*
   C. *Home_Of*
   D. *Sleeps_At*

9. In the case study, the relationship between **Rentals** and **Gear** is:
   A. one-to-one based on **Student_ID**
   B. one-to-one based on **Rental_ID**
   C. one-to-many based on **Rentals** and **Gear**
   D. one-to-one based on **Rentals** and **Gear**

10. The field that separates the Rentals table of one store from the **Rentals** table of another store is:
    A. **Rental_ID**
    B. **Shop_ID**
    C. **Equip_ID**
    D. **Customer**

11. To combine the **Rentals** tables from each store into one table, you'd use the:
    A. **Product** operation
    B. **Add** operation
    C. **Union** operation
    D. **Combine** operation

12. Using proper database naming conventions for **ASTeam.First**:
    A. **ASTeam** is the database and **First** is the table
    B. **ASTeam** is the table and **First** is the field
    C. **First** is the table and **ASTeam** is the field
    D. **ASTeam** is the field and **First** is the database

Short Answer

1. A(n) ______ analyzes the nature of a business, its workflow, and its information needs.
2. The ______ of information is the way information travels through a business or organization.
3. The relationship between **Rentals** and **Gear** is a ______ relationship.
4. You ______ a design, that is, you stop making changes to a design, to test it to see how well it works.
5. The ______ is used to depict the many side of a relationship.
6. In SQL, the ______ command is used to tie two tables together based on a relationship between fields.
7. A(n) ______ is the individual who builds, maintains, and is responsible for a database.

8. QBE stands for ______.
9. A(n) ______ is used to make entering data into a table easier.
10. A(n) ______ is the combination of two or more base tables.
11. ______ is the term for removing unneeded fields from a super table.
12. Storing the same data in more than one place is called ______.
13. A(n) ______ can be defined as one-to-one, many-to-one, or one-to-many.
14. Different users need different ______ of a database in order to properly see the information they need.
15. In SQL, the ______ command is used to pick the fields to show from the join of two tables.

Exercises

1. HAI! Adventure wants to expand into white-water rafting in Idaho. Do the needs analysis and physical database design for this plan. What existing tables should be used to build the database for this resort? What new tables would be needed? Could existing tables be modified for this purpose?
2. The white-water rafting has numerous classes each day. Each instructor has classes at varying experience levels. What tables need to be used and what fields need to be included to produce a report showing the clients in each class for each instructor?
3. Sketch what the GUI for the report in exercise 2 would look like.
4. Write the SQL statement needed to display the information for the report in exercise 2.
5. The Accounting department for HAI! wants to add information to the database for each employee. They want to add information on individual taxes and insurance to the `ASTeam` table. Why would you advise against this?
6. What solution would you offer to the Accounting department? What would you name the table? What relationships would you establish?
7. HAI! wants to set up a feedback form for its clients to fill out after an activity. What fields should be included? What should it be called? What relationships should be set up?
8. In preparation for the upcoming ski season, HAI! wants to send out promotional information to last year's clients. What tables and fields are needed to do a mailing?
9. What changes would you make if you decided to send out an email promotion instead of snail mail?
10. Write the SQL statement needed to display the promotional information.

chapter

16 WORKING ONLINE

eCommerce and Interactive Networking

learning objectives

> Describe the client/server structure

> Identify the actions of a client and server when a browser requests a Web page

> Explain the differences between a two-tier and a three-tier system

> Explain the discrete event problem and give an example
  - Describe how cookies are a solution to the discrete event system
  - Explain the role of the cookie domain, name, and value
  - Describe how using a CGI program is a solution to the discrete event problem

> Explain the challenge of handling many, almost simultaneous transactions

> Discuss the importance of standards to interoperability in eCommerce

Software is like Entropy; it's hard to grasp, weighs nothing and obeys the Second Law of Thermodynamics, i.e. it is always increasing.

—NORMAN AUGUSTINE

AT THE END of the second millennium, electronic commerce—eCommerce—"was revolutionizing the economy" so dramatically that "old business rules no longer applied." Amazon.com, whose founder Jeff Bezos was *Time* magazine's "Man of the Year" for 2000, was a model for such businesses. Happily, the hype has died down. What remains are three facts: eCommerce will continue to grow as a significant commercial mechanism; eCommerce is extremely complex from both technical and business points of view; and the methods and techniques of eCommerce have not yet been fully worked out. That is, it's here to stay, it's too complex to learn in one chapter, and it's a moving target. Our best hope is to learn the basics. Then, when the day comes that eCommerce sites are so good that we don't even notice them, we'll at least appreciate the tremendous obstacles these pioneers overcame.

CHALLENGES OF ECOMMERCE

The term eCommerce means conducting business using electronic data communications. Usually the Internet and World Wide Web come to mind, because we think of "shopping on the Web." But eCommerce also includes electronic funds transfer (cash machines), point-of-sale transactions (credit and debit cards), business-to-business activities, networked meetings, and so on. Essentially any business activity using network communication with a computer at one or both ends is eCommerce. Toward our goal of achieving Fluency, we study eCommerce because it embodies all the aspects of complex networked interactions. People and organizations use the same ideas and have the same problems interacting over the Internet regardless of whether or not they're conducting business. Besides eCommerce is interesting, and focuses our study.

Using network communication for business is such a new idea it is developing and changing almost day by day. The process can at times seem very chaotic to the developers and the public. But we can put structure on the topic by considering some of the challenges of working across the network:

- **Variation.** The people, products, and interactive experiences of eCommerce are truly diverse.
- **Structure of the setting.** Interacting with computers across a network has a standard structure.
- **Discrete events.** Unlike person-to-person interactions, eCommerce happens in separate independent units.
- **Transactions do the work.** Many people interact with servers simultaneously, but each person's experience must be coherent and self-contained.
- **Interoperability.** Orchestrating all of the components to work together requires standards.
- **Unreliability.** Life is uncertain, so how does "life go on" after disaster strikes a computer system?

This chapter takes up these challenges and explains how they have been solved thus far.

FITTIP

Don't Accept Crummy. Although eCommerce is new and difficult, it is also competitive. Companies that should know better put up poor sites that are hard to use, slow, repetitive, and crash or fail. Don't accept it! Take your business to sites that work well. Reward those who are trying to make eCommerce a success. After all, consumers have the power.

THE CHALLENGE OF VARIATION

When compared to traditional businesses—the so-called "bricks and mortar" enterprises—eCommerce must deal with much more variation in the types of customers and in the number of business rules, products, and shopping experiences that must be accommodated. In each case, the difference between a bricks-and-mortar business and an eCommerce business is striking.

Global Customers

When most Americans visit a greeting card shop, they probably do not notice that it sells cards for birthdays, graduations, Mother's Day, and so forth, because these are the occasions for which Americans send cards. Nor does it come to their attention that the cards are written in English, may use "beached whale" humorously, generally open on the right, are priced in dollars, are printed on recycled paper, meet the local postal regulations, and so on. But other people would notice that there are no cards celebrating Children's Day, written in Farsi, using the expression "beached whale" respectfully, opening on the left, priced in drachmas, printed on new paper, preprinted with postal code squares, and so on. Enterprises with a physical location can and do stock what the local population wants, in the local language, according to the local customs, biases, and needs. Electronic businesses, which can easily reach customers across the planet, must accommodate the variation among people from all over the world. They need more than just a Web page in a foreign language; they need to respect all of their customers' cultural differences that impact business.

Many Business Rules

The countries of the world exercise their power to define a currency and set import and export controls, tariffs, taxes, and other conditions of business operation. Though crossing a border electronically is easy, learning and respecting all of these business rules and laws is challenging.

A business might try to simplify the problem by limiting itself to only one country, say, the United States, and refuse to honor orders from clients without a mailing address in the country. The tactic reduces the currency to dollars and eliminates import/export controls and tariffs. But it doesn't eliminate taxation as a problem, for example. There are about 7000 taxing authorities in the United States, so collecting the right amount of tax is complicated; but then paying the proper amount to each authority can be even more complicated. There has been a moratorium on collecting taxes on Internet business when a company doesn't have a physical presence in the locality, but that won't last forever. In any case, the moratorium simplifies only one aspect of conducting business on the World Wide Web.

Diverse Products and Information

Physical stores are usually constrained to offer only as many products as they have display space for, and catalog businesses are limited by page space. But in eCommerce the display space is virtual, so there is no limit on the number of products that can be offered. This motivates some businesses to offer a large number of products, especially of different types. But for a customer to buy, shopping must be informed. With no clerks, eCommerce must rely on a computer to provide the proper information customized to each product. The representation and presentation of factual information about shirts, textbooks, and computers varies widely, and though there are common principles, a one-size-fits-all software approach will not satisfy all customers. Even within a single product type—clothing or books—there is still considerable variation that challenges the eCommerce site to deliver all the useful, relevant information for each product.

Diverse Shopping Experiences

Though shoppers entering a physical store can be distracted by their phones, friends, children, and packages, they are usually there to shop. Clerks can watch them, deciding when to offer assistance as they proceed through a more-or-less standard protocol of looking, deciding, selecting, paying, and leaving. Visitors to an Internet site may have all the distractions of a bricks-and-mortar shopper plus they could also be eating breakfast, fixing dinner, trying to work, watching Jeopardy, playing with a pet that might be pawing at the keyboard, communicating over a slow connection, or any of hundreds of other distractions. There is no "standard protocol" under these circumstances, no standard navigation path through the site. There isn't even a guarantee that a single person is doing the navigating. Besides distractions, there is the problem that customers cannot inspect the product beyond seeing a photograph of it or hearing a clip of it. Catalogs have this same problem, but there is always an 800 number that a customer can dial to get informed assistance. Online there's just a computer at the other end.

Each of these differences poses a significant challenge. Taken together they are truly daunting. They explain some of the struggles that eCommerce sites have had to deal with as they have developed online commerce.

STRUCTURE OF THE SETTING

The eCommerce settings considered here share a common form. A customer sits at a personal computer using a Web browser and interacting over the Internet with a business's computer, which is at some unknown location.

The Client/Server Structure

This situation is known as the **client/server structure**: The customer's computer is the client and the business's computer is the server. The term "client" isn't another word for "customer" here; the "client" concept predates eCommerce and it refers to any situation where one computer, the *client*, gets services from another computer, the *server*. Whenever you are browsing, your computer is in a client/server relationship with the remote Web server—which "serves" the Web pages your browser client requests in response to your clicks. Of course, the name "Web server" comes from this relationship, too. Figure 16.1 displays this familiar setup.

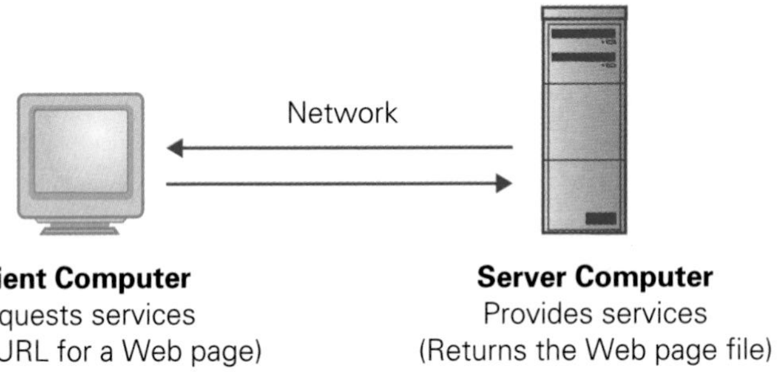

Figure 16.1. *The basic client/server structure, as illustrated by the browser (client) requesting Web pages provided by the Web server.*

Many Brief Relationships

The client/server structure is fundamental to Web interactions. A key aspect of the idea is that, as shown in Figure 16.1, only a single service request and response are involved. It is a very brief relationship, lasting from the moment the request is sent to the moment the service has been provided. Unlike a telephone call, in which a connection is made and held for as long as the call lasts, and during which there are many alternating exchanges, the client/server relationship is very short. It only entails the client asking for a service and receiving it.

An important advantage of this approach is that the server can handle many clients at a time. Typically between two consecutive client requests from your browser—between getting a Web page and asking for the next Web page from the same site—that server could have serviced hundreds or perhaps thousands of other clients. This is a very efficient system, because the server is tied up with you only for as long as it takes to perform your request. Once it's fulfilled, the relationship is over from the server's point of view. But the relationship is over from your viewpoint, too. Your next click could be on the URL for a different server. Between that click and the next time you visit the site, if ever, you and your browser could be clients to hundreds or perhaps thousands of other servers. So, Figure 16.2 shows the client/server relationship over an interval of time.

FITBYTE

Staying Connected. With conventional telephones, callers stay connected even if no one is talking. In a client/server structure, there is no connection. There is a client-to-server transmission for requests, and a server-to-client transmission for replies. But doesn't your computer stay connected to the Internet? Yes, but only to your ISP—that is, to the Internet—not to any Web server.

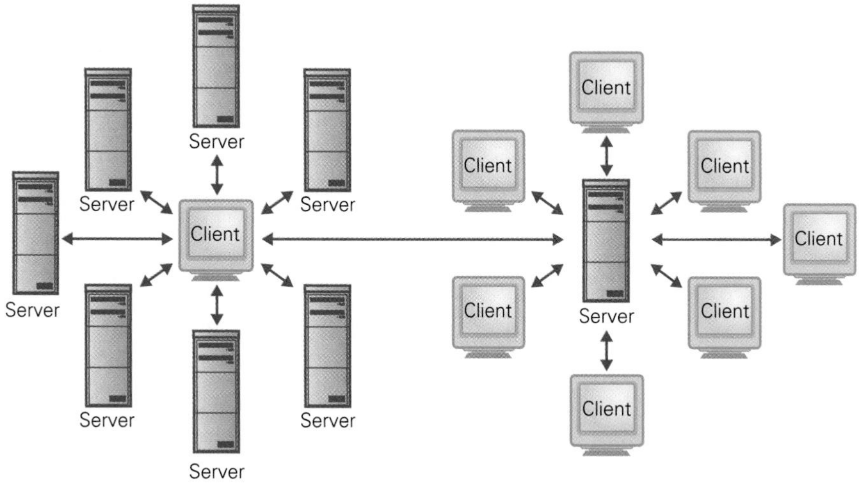

Figure 16.2. *Client/server relationships as they might evolve over time.*

Creating Web Pages On-the-Fly

The client/server structure was a useful starting point for developing Web technology, and it is still an excellent tool for understanding eCommerce, but it is not sophisticated enough to solve all the problems. The basic client/server abstraction is fine for serving up static Web pages in HTML, say, as a college's Web server might do. But in order to handle the challenge of variation, we often need to create customized Web pages **on-the-fly**, customized to each request. For example, a Web page that shows real-time flight arrival and departure times for an airline cannot be based on static, preprogrammed HTML pages. Almost all eCommerce applications require created-for-the-situation Web pages, for these reasons:

- Some or all of the information changes often—once a month or faster.
- There's so much information, we can't possibly build separate Web pages for each item (as in a dictionary).
- The possible combinations of information grows geometrically—for example, for automobiles, options include the model, engine size, transmission type, number of doors, body color, interior color, interior fabric, wheels, tires, and so on.

Middleware

Though servers can and do create Web pages on-the-fly, other components are usually involved, such as a database system (see Chapters 13–15) where all of the information that goes into the Web page is stored. Adding other components means that we must extend the client/server structure. Though the extensions make sense, the words we use for this are rather curious.

To extend the client/server abstraction, the "techies" who create Web software began calling it a **two-tier system**, where the client and the server are each a **tier**, or *layer*. (Think of the tiers as a vertical stack, like layers in a cake.) When the database is added onto a two-tier system, we get a **three-tier system**. The third tier doesn't have to be a database management computer. It only needs to be another logical system component that helps fulfill client requests. This naturally leads to the ***n*-tier system**, meaning systems with several layers. Finally, the amazing term **middleware** refers to the programs running at the center of the three-tier or *n*-tier system. It is middleware that produces the created-on-the-fly HTML pages by getting information from the database and assembling it into Web pages to fulfill the client's request.

FITBYTE

Where Ware? A tech document on the Web describes "middleware" as "software running on the middle end of the system."

DISCRETE EVENTS

As we've discussed, the client/server relationship is brief and so a server can handle many clients. It's very efficient. But there's a catch: Nothing connects consecutive requests produced by one customer. Each client request is a separate event, so how can the server recognize a returning customer, even when events are a few seconds apart?

Businesses engaged in eCommerce need to be able to recognize consecutive events by customers because, for example, they must match a request to purchase a product with the credit card number to pay for it, information that's probably specified in separate client/server events.

The Discrete Event Problem

Think about relating consecutive requests for a moment. Imagine you request a biography of Serena Williams, the tennis star, from a biography site. Then you immediately ask for a biography of Venus. Everyone—though not a Web server—would know that you're asking about Venus Williams, her sister, not the goddess of Roman mythology. The Web server is unaware of the connection between the two requests. Although your requests were consecutive from your point of view, the server handled many other requests in between. It may be that your Serena request wasn't even in the thousand requests before the Venus request, and that a request for Aphrodite was. That is, the more recent relevant context from the server's point of view may not be yours. The biography server delivers biographies as a series of unrelated events. It doesn't remember client requests because there is no (apparent) commercial value in knowing which biographies you've asked for recently.

Consider another factor: The server cannot be sure that two requests came from the same person or session. Imagine asking for the Serena Williams biography in the computer lab, reading it, deciding it's time to go to class, and logging out. Your friend logs on to the same machine and asks for a biography of Venus. He doesn't want Venus Williams, but the goddess. From the point of view of the biography server, the two requests come from the same IP address—that is, the same client. Or suppose you request Serena's bio at home, and then log out; your ISP then assigns the IP address you were using to someone else. Whoever receives it would be surprised if the bio server tried to maintain continuity with your request based on the IP address. The problem of how to treat consecutive requests, which we call the **discrete event problem**, is clearly difficult.

One Solution with Cookies

One solution is to store and retrieve cookies, a computer science concept not widely known before the WWW. A **cookie** is information stored on a client computer by a Web server computer. Cookies were introduced into Netscape 1.0 to solve the discrete event problem. Cookies are stored in a file (Netscape) or directory (IE) called cookies and have a standard structure for each browser. Netscape's cookies have seven parts, named

domain *dom_flag* *path* *secure_flag* *exp_date* *name* *value*

Cookie Domain, Name, and Value.

The three fields we're interested in are *domain* (the server that wrote the cookie), *name* (the cookie's name), and *value* (the information that the cookie is storing). Cookies are typically exchanged between a client and server every time they interact. For example, while I was researching Buckminster Fuller's life for Chapter 6, WNET-TV's Web server placed the following cookie on my computer:

www.WNET.org	FALSE	/	FALSE	1027192661	thirteen_uid	64.10.140.253.171119956565334
domain					name	value

and a related Web server stored

www.thirteen.org	FALSE	/	FALSE	1026961838	thirteen_uid	64.10.140.161.28198995425707131
domain					name	value

The two different domains identify two different servers, but the servers are apparently part of the same site because they use a common cookie name, `thirteen_uid`. The two different values, which seem to begin with four-digit IP addresses, identified my client to these two different servers. (The expiration date, e.g., 1027192661, is a "UNIX date," counting milliseconds since 1 January 1970, 00:00:00 GMT; see Chapter 20.)

The value of a cookie is any information that the domain server needs to store on the client. Usually the value is simply a unique identifier for the client.

How Cookies Work. Here's how a cookie solves the discrete event problem. When a client first visits a site, there is no stored cookie from the server. The server—if it needs to recognize the client later—*creates a cookie and sends it to the client in the header of the Web page*. The client records the cookie, and after that, each time the client communicates with the server, it passes the cookie. The server records in its database whatever information it needs to remember, each time using the unique value as the key (refer to Chapter 13) to find the client among its records. In this way, the server can keep track of the client's requests and visits, as shown in Figure 16.3.

> FITTIP
>
> **Finding Cookies.** Locate the cookies stored on your computer by searching for files and folders containing the string `cookie` or `cookies`. The files can be opened using a basic ASCII text editor like **Notepad** or **SimpleText**. College computers are often "wiped" clean after each session, so you may have to surf for a few minutes before any cookies are stored.

Which Events Are Recorded. Servers could try to keep the whole history of a session, but that might include too many unimportant events. For example, customers might just be browsing the site. The server could try to guess information about the customer from these wanderings, but that's probably too difficult. So, only certain significant events are recorded in the server's database, such as the `Select` request of Figure 16.3. The "shopping cart" abstraction has been used to help customers understand when they are making significant decisions. In such a situation, the server would record a "put in the shopping cart" request, a "buy" request, and the requests needed to close the sale.

Problems with Cookies. The original idea of the Netscape engineers who adopted the cookie solution was that *clients* would store the shopping cart, credit card, and mailing address information rather than having the *server* store it in its database. The approach is smart, for example, because storing credit card numbers on the client removes the responsibility from the server to keep them secure. The idea means that servers would be free to set almost any value on the client. Instead, today cookies have become a unique identifier that the server uses as a key to find client information it keeps in its own database. Meanwhile, privacy experts are worried because there are many ways to abuse cookies, and some companies have apparently done so. The problems with storing cookies are discussed in Chapter 17. For now, cookies solve the difficult problem of maintaining continuity across many discrete events.

Another Solution Without Cookies

Between processing completely unrelated requests and knowing the entire history of the client's contact with the site using cookies, there is a middle ground in which continuity is maintained, but not the exact identity of the client. This is perhaps the most common setting for Web interactions and eCommerce. To under-

```
           Client: c_me                         Server: NetRags.com

To: NetRags.com
Request: Select "Just do IT!" Sweatshirt
         product No. 61-28504
(NetRags Cookie: A1BB22CCC333DDDD4444)
                             To: 201.22.79.101 (c_me@college.edu)
                             Reply: It's selected. Want to buy?
                             To: 22.33.44.55
                             Reply: Blah, Blah, Blah
                             To: 22.34.45.56
                             Reply: Blah, Blah, Blah
                             ...
                             To: 24.35.46.57
                             Reply: Blah, Blah, Blah
To: NetRags.com
Request: Yes.
(NetRags Cookie: A1BB22CCC333DDDD4444)
                             To: 201.22.79.101 (c_me@college.edu)
                             Reply: What size?
                             To: 25.36.47.58
                             Reply: Blah, Blah, Blah
                             To: 26.37.48.59
                             Reply: Blah, Blah, Blah
                             ...
                             To: 27.38.49.60
                             Reply: Blah, Blah, Blah
To: NetRags.com
Request: Large.
(NetRags Cookie: A1BB22CCC333DDDD4444)
                             To: 201.22.79.101 (c_me@college.edu)
                             Reply: Buy "Just do IT!" Sweatshirt
                                    product 61-28504, Size L
                                    Same credit card as before?
                                    xxxx-xxxx-xxxx-9876
                                    Email still: c_me@college.edu?
```

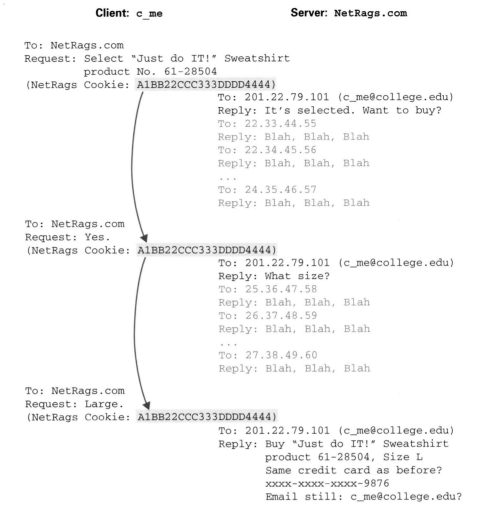

Figure 16.3. *An imaginary interaction between client and server. A cookie stored at the client lets the server connect independent events into a dialog. Notice that the cookie also connects to an earlier session when the customer gave an email address, credit card number, and probably mailing address.*

stand this solution we need to look a bit more closely at the three-tier system's organization.

Imagine a server that supports interactions like those shown in Figure 16.3. Because it must access a database to get information about the clothing products, the system is probably organized in three tiers, as shown in Figure 16.4.

To create the pages that the client sees, the server follows these steps:

1. The server receives the client's request, figures out what to do, and asks a middleware program to do it.

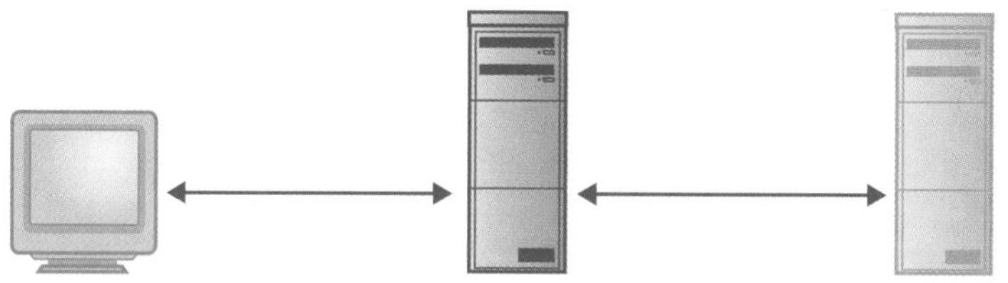

Figure 16.4. *A three-tier system in which backend tasks are performed by CGI.*

2. The middleware program runs, accessing the database and building a Web page with the requested information.
3. The server receives this page from the middleware and returns it to the client.

This processing sequence—in which the middleware program is in the middle at step 2—explains how middleware got its name. It is in the middle of the processing activity when the server needs additional services, like accessing a database. Notice that the system organization in Figure 16.4—showing who communicates with whom—places the computer added as the third tier at the end farthest from the client. Thus there are two ways to look at the situation. In the processing view, the middleware is in the middle. In the communication view, the third computer is at the end because it's farthest removed from the client. (See Figure 16.5.) Seen from these two points of view, the description "middleware is at the middle end of the system" doesn't seem so bizarre, perhaps.

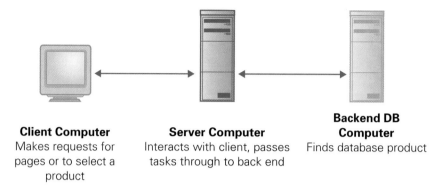

Using a CGI Program. Suppose that our middleware program uses the **Common Gateway Interface (CGI)** mechanism, though there are many other alternatives. The CGI program, running on the server, queries a backend database for product information in response to the client's request. The database system looks up the information and returns text, an image, and other forms of information back to the program. The program then fills in the information on a page form, or **template**, which has headings and other page layout specifications, with placeholders for the actual information. The server returns the new page, which "looks and feels" like a regular page for that Web site, because of the template, but is really customized to the client's requested content. This approach goes a long way to solving the problem of customizing information about a product. Notice that when the CGI program requests information from the database, those two computers are in their own client/server relationship, only now the server has become the client and the database computer is the server.

By using a CGI program, a three-tier system can store repeated information in a request string so that no cookies are needed. For an example of how this happens, consider the Web purchase of a Cairo-Bangkok airline ticket.

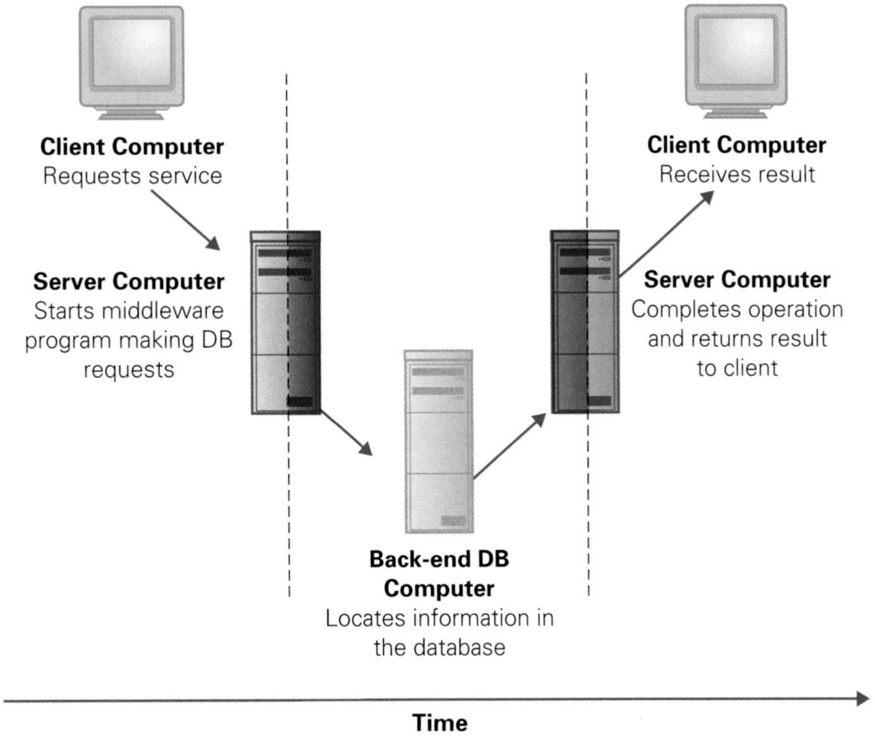

Figure 16.5. *Middleware performs an operation on a three-tier system; the process moves to the right; the Client Computer boxes represent one computer at different points in time; similarly for the Server Computer boxes.*

{FITLINK}

Cairo–Bangkok Travel Information > >

Suppose a customer wants pricing information for a round-trip flight between Cairo and Bangkok. The customer types in `Cairo` or chooses it from a pop-up menu, and does the same for `Bangkok`. (Such menus are not available directly in HTML, but can be written in JavaScript, explained in Chapters 18–22.)

How do the middleware and the CGI program handle the request?

When the client sends its request to the server, it directly calls the CGI program that will find the route information in the database. The call gives the names of the two cities and other information as part of the request string as if it were a long URL. The typical form is

```
.../cgi-bin/find_flights?DEP=CAIRO&ARR=BANGKOK&RET=Y&FARE=ECON&DEP-DATE=...
```

Here `find_flights` is the name of the program, and the text after the ? gives the data for the request. The data is a list of parameters (the departure city, Cairo, and the arrival city, Bangkok, and so forth) separated by `&` and having the form *data_name=data_value* in this example. Each CGI program can have its own format as long as it sticks to a few simple rules—for example, use + instead of blank. (You can see long strings like this in the location window of your browser when you're using many Web sites. For example, in Google the query being searched is encoded after the question mark.) These are requests to the middleware program that performs the service.

When the pricing information comes back from the server, the customer may have to make more decisions, say, picking a departure time. This new data will be added to the end of the next request, so that the CGI program has the data from both queries. And so forth. By accumulating data from many rounds of request and reply, the CGI mechanism helps the server connect client requests, because the data list contains the whole history of the dialog. When the client finally decides to buy the ticket, all the information can be passed off as the data list to the CGI program handling purchases, so it knows about the previous interactions, too. Notice that this solution doesn't use cookies at all.

TRANSACTIONS DO THE WORK

Suppose while one instance of a CGI program is replying to a customer about selecting seat 14C on the flight to Bangkok, another instance of the same program is assigning 14C to a different customer. To avoid strapping two passengers into the same seat, care must be taken to maintain the integrity of the database. When independent **transactions** on a database—operations like finding information and making changes—overlap in time, the changes could corrupt the database, resulting in garbage. To understand the problem better, consider a more detailed example.

Simultaneous Requests

Imagine two people—perhaps husband and wife—with a joint bank account, who have traveled to a distant city, realize they're short on cash, try to use the nearest ATM, and find it is broken. They decide to split up to look for a working machine and agree to return to the hotel in 15 minutes. If neither finds a working machine, they'll develop a plan B; if only one finds a working machine, they've got their cash; and if both find a working machine, they'll have twice as much cash, but the bellman deserves a big tip after struggling with all their bags. Naturally they both find a machine at about the same time. The ATMs send their requests to withdraw $100 from the same account, and two middleware programs, W and H, process the requests (see Figure 16.6). These are two instances of the same program. W and H must get the current balance in the account from the database, check that the balance is more than $100, subtract $100, and store the new balance back in the database. (Of course, if the balance is less than $100, the request is denied.)

Transactions Interleaved

The W and H programs and the database serving their requests should operate as shown in Figure 16.6. However, the transactions are implemented as multistep operations with two requests to the database server: one to get the balance, one to change the balance. They might have been interleaved in time, as shown in Figure 16.7. That is, the ATMs dispensed $200 in cash to the lucky couple, but their account was charged only $100. Maybe they should have gotten even more cash! What happened?

W	Database Account Balance	H
	$500	
Request balance of Acct 02468HW		
Receive reply that it's $500		
Compute. `NewBal = $500 – $100`		
Request set Acct 02468HW Bal to $400		
Tell ATM to give $100 to customer	$400	Request balance of Acct 02468HW
		Receive reply that it's $400
		Compute. `NewBal = $400 – $100`
		Request set Acct 02468HW Bal to$300
	$300	Tell ATM to give $100 to customer

Figure 16.6. *Correct processing of two withdrawals from a bank account.*

W	Database Account Balance	H
	$500	
Request balance of Acct 02468HW		
Receive reply that it's $500		Request balance of Acct 02468HW
Compute. `NewBal = $500 – $100`		Receive reply that it's $500
Request set Acct 02468HW Bal to $400		Compute. `NewBal = $500 – $100`
Tell ATM to give $100 to customer	$400	Request set Acct 02468HW Bal to$400
	$400	Tell ATM to give $100 to customer

Figure 16.7. *Two withdrawal transactions interleaved in time produce the wrong balance —that is, corrupt the database.*

Serialized Behavior: Transactions Happen One at a Time

In the second scenario, the H program's request for the account balance came before the W program had completed its transaction and updated the balance. So, instead of receiving the updated balance of $400, it got the original balance of $500. Because this is a well-known problem in distributed databases, it probably doesn't happen with ATMs. But it can happen in other situations. To handle this problem, any transactions that use common data—the balance, in this case—run so that one completes before the other starts. This is called **serialized behavior**.

Serialized behavior means that the operations are done as if they take place one at a time in some order, so that no two programs are ever working on the same information at the same time. From the time of the first reference to any data involved in the transaction until the last change to any data has been returned to storage, there can be no references to any of the data involved in the transaction—neither reading nor writing—except by the program performing the transaction. The W and H transactions of Figure 16.7 were not serialized, because H referenced the balance before W had completed its transaction. Serialized behavior doesn't prevent references or changes to other parts of the database from happening at the same time, as long as they reference different data. So, other people can be getting money from their accounts simultaneously from other ATMS as long as they are all separate accounts. If the requests refer to the same data—that is, if the bank accounts are the same—serialized behavior keeps transactions from being simultaneous. If the requests are not the same—that is, if the bank accounts are separate—money can be withdrawn from those accounts at the same time.

FITBYTE

A Little Cooperation. A common case where transactions are not serialized, but should be, is when people work cooperatively on a project. Someone finishes a draft of the work and sends it around. Then two or more people work on it without telling the others what they are doing. If they work on separate parts, it's OK; if not, the draft may have incompatible changes—that is, the document is corrupted. The solution is to treat the draft like a library book: send email "checking it out" to change it, and send email "checking it in" to give someone else a chance.

Recall the example of assigning seat 14C on the flight to Bangkok. The seat-assignment middleware programs, which check whether the seat is available and then make the assignment, must not be serialized. Serializing—preventing the Availability Check to a seat while another transaction is checking/assigning that seat—would solve the problem.

THE STANDARDS CASE

Yet another challenge of interactive networking is that every use of a network is a dialog between two computers, and like people they must both speak the same language to communicate. The people of the world have an almost impossible time communicating even though most of them speak one of only a dozen different languages. What's the problem?

Common Language

In a population of speakers of one of n languages, there are $n(n+1)/2$ ways to pair people, but only n of those pairs can have a conversation, that is, speak the same language. For example, with 12 languages, there are 78 different pairs of speakers, but only 12 can communicate. The other 66 cannot. If everyone spoke a common language in addition to their mother tongue, all 78 conversations could take place.

Web Standard Languages

The situation is the same for computers. There are millions of different computers using thousands of different hardware configurations and thousands of different operating system configurations. If each server had to "speak the language" of each of these computers, the Web would never have happened. Period. But it did, thanks to Hypertext Markup Language, HTML, and the processing method of the Hypertext Transfer Protocol, HTTP. Having these standards means that client computers only have to "understand" HTML to display a page to the user, and server computers only have to "understand" HTTP to fulfill the client's request. The client and server can have any hardware, run any operating system, use any file structure, and so on. As long as each can understand the common language of HTML/HTTP, everything works. Using hypertext for networked communication was brilliant, but the genius of the Web was that everyone adopted it as the standard. Standards are fundamental to networking.

FITBYTE

IT's Standard. HTML/HTTP is actually one in a long sequence of standards used in networking. TCP/IP—the packet-level communication of Chapter 3—was the first and most basic of these.

Importance of Standards to Communication

As important as the HTML/HTTP standard is, it only got the World Wide Web started and defined its baseline capability. Splashier media, more dazzling graphic effects, and less stilted interaction require the client and the server to be upgraded. This has already happened. For example, the HTML/HTTP client/server relationship supports the CGI mechanism, mentioned earlier. CGI is an extension of the HTTP protocol, making it another standard. The key point is that standards are essential to the present and future of networked communication. They allow the client and server to be independent, but still communicate.

The Java Language. Java is an important standard that provides a general means for dynamically upgrading a browser's capability. Java is a programming language that browsers can interpret. A server can send a client a small Java program, called an **applet**, a little *appl*ication. The client computer runs the applet because browsers know how to do that. The applet might display data from the server in a splashy way or perhaps help the user in gathering and packaging data to send back to the server. Because Java is a general programming language capable of expressing any algorithm, the server can add any capability to the client side of the interaction so long as it meets Java's security and other limitations.

FITBYTE

What Side Are You On? Facilities like Java enable the server to move some of its work to the client, introducing the need for terms like *client side* and *server side*. The advantage of client-side services like applets is that Internet delays cannot slow them.

In effect, the server can improve its dialog with a client by giving the client more capabilities. Java gives flexibility to both sides of the client/server relationship. The server tells the client how it wants the client upgraded by giving the client the applet program. Then, rather than the server doing work and sending the result to the client—that is, supporting the interaction from the server side—the server simply tells the applet to do the work on the client's side. The client gets better service because the work is done locally instead of over the (perhaps) slow network and on the (possibly) overloaded server. Over time, as programmers improve the applet, the interactions get even better. Further, each server can customize to its own business needs.

`XML, the Extensible Markup Language.` There is one other place besides the basic Web client/server relationship where standards are critical. Remember that in the three-tier system, when the server interacts with the back-end database it becomes the client to the database's server role. In an *n*-tier system, such relationships are quite numerous, and often the server in these cases is some other company's product. For example, an eCommerce site might decide not to try to keep track of 7000 tax rates, but rather to buy a tax rate service from a company specializing in taxation; its middleware accesses the service using the Web. Thus we have many client/server relationships *inside* the site's middleware system, and as before *both ends of each of these client/server pairs* must "speak" the same language. Standards are the key to business flexibility.

In this middleware client/server relationship, complex data structures must be encoded so that they can be exchanged. For basic Web pages, HTML performs this encoding. But HTML focuses only on the presentation, and is rigid and limited. Middleware needs to know how to find specific information in the data sent between a client and server, so describing the presentation is less important than describing the **content**. But content is extremely variable. The new standard is called the **Extensible Markup Language** or **XML**. A forerunner of XML was used for digitizing the *Oxford English Dictionary* in Chapter 8. XML uses tags for metadata as usual. What makes XML significant is that it is a *self-describing* encoding of information: The tags are defined within the description for each client/server relationship. Accordingly, XML can be adapted to the structural needs of any information flowing among the middleware subsystems, making it essentially universal.

For example, in Figure 16.8, the order information, perhaps to be sent to the order processing subsystem as a result of the dialog in Figure 16.3, shows the key information in human-readable and machine-understandable form. When the middleware order-processor gets it, it looks through for the `<ClientCode>` tag and knows that all of the information between it and the `</ClientCode>` tag is the client code. The tag was invented for this specific client/server interaction.

```
<?xml version="1.0"?>
<Order>
  <OrderNum>71442</OrderNum>
  <ClientCode>A1BB22CCC333DDDD4444</ClientCode>
  <PurchaseList>
    <ItemCode color="Blue">64-28741</ItemCode>
    <ItemCode size="L">61-28504</ItemCode>
  </PurchaseList>
</Order>
```

Figure 16.8. *An example XML encoding of order information that might result from the session in Figure 16.3. Notice that it is possible to include attributes that further specify the tag information.*

Agreeing on Standards

So, who decides on the standards? In some cases, a standard is accepted because many people independently decide to follow it. The original HTML became a standard in that way. Many people got a copy of a free browser program, called Mosaic, which allowed them to read HTML that other people had published, and they quickly decided to set up their own Web site. Naturally they chose to follow the HTML/HTTP protocol. But such an anarchic process only works at the beginning. Soon the process must become much more organized. Today a group known as the World Wide Web Consortium (W3C) decides standards like CGI and XML.

REDUNDANCY IS VERY, VERY, VERY GOOD

As the saying goes, "Life is uncertain; eat dessert first." Uncertainty is another challenge of interactive networking, and computer use generally.

Uncertainty results from lightning strikes that cut power, earthquakes and other natural disasters, terrorist attacks, accidents, as well as simple entropy—the tendency of things to "run down." To the list of physical risks, add the potential logical problems of program bugs, operator errors, and computer viruses and worms. Obviously, at any moment, parts of the World Wide Web and the Internet are down (out of service). But because it is decentralized—millions of independent servers with no single point of failure—most of it is up and running most of the time.

You've probably had the experience of a software-crash-before-the-work-is-saved. You know you should save, but you forget until it's too late. Then there's the case of a hard drive crash that destroys all of your files, saved or not. You know you should back up your files to a floppy or CD, but you forget until it's too late. Alas, the consequences in this case are much more serious. When the hard disk starts screeching or smelling like burnt plastic, much more than one session will be lost. A week's, a month's, or even a year's worth of work may be gone in an instant.

In eCommerce, daily backups, off-site storage, a system recovery team, and possibly system redundancy are the same as our personal periodic backups and saving. But responsibility to prepare for disaster cannot depend on remembering about it. No company can remain in business if it ever loses more than a negligible amount of information. Thus, any eCommerce enterprise expecting to survive long enough to make money must solve the "backup and **fault recovery problem**" immediately.

FITTIP

Alternate Superstition. People can be superstitious, believing, for example, that thinking about a disaster can make it happen. Naturally, repressing such thoughts is sensible. But believing a different superstition—that taking precautions against disasters, like saving often, prevents them—may be better in IT. They're both superstitions, of course, but the second one reduces the harm when it turns out to be wrong, and your machine crashes.

A Fault Recovery Program for Business

The solutions to the fault recovery problem become quite technical, beyond the scope of this book, but the basic idea is to keep a full copy of everything written on the system as of some date and time. This is a *full backup*. After that, *partial backups* of the changes since the last full (or partial) backup are created. Eventually there will have been enough changes that another full backup should be made. How often partial backups are performed, such as daily or every eight hours, is usually decided by the cost, and grief, of losing all of the information since the last partial backup. It would be easier to have full backups every few minutes, but that's too much information to copy and save. However, too many partial backups can make reconstruction extremely tedious, so regular full backups are a good idea.

FITTIP

Good Recovery. If disaster strikes, begin by installing the last full backup copy. Then re-create the state of the system by making the changes saved in the partial backups in order. Continue with each partial backup until the most recent.

Backing Up a Personal Computer

Backups aren't just for business. If you work on a computer system that is managed by professional staff (like most college systems), there is little need to worry about backups. The support staff nearly always takes care of backups, though you should check to be sure. However, backing up your own personal computer is your responsibility. There are two important points to think about regarding backups.

How and What to Back Up. First, to back up your own computer, you can buy software for the task. Such programs perform incremental backups, analogous to the full/partial strategy just discussed, and do so automatically. They usually write to your Zip drive or writeable CD. Such software can save a lot of headaches.

FITCAUTION

A Three-Line Sermon. Disasters don't always happen to someone else. (I had a disk meltdown while writing *Fluency*.) Backups are truly important. Further, it is wise to keep the full backups somewhere away from your computer.

Of course, you can do backups manually by simply copying your directories and files to a disk or CD. Remember, you do not have to back up information that:

> Can be re-created from some permanent source, such as software

> Was saved before but has not changed—last year's email archive, for example

> You don't care about, like your Web cache or old versions of term papers

Most of us do not have much to back up if we do so every two or three months.

FITTIP

How Often? No rule says when to back up. Organizations must follow a fixed schedule, but individuals can simply assess the risk of losing everything. Hard use makes laptops more likely to fail than desktops; very new and very old equipment is more likely to fail than a middle-aged system. There is always risk.

Recovering Deleted Information. The second thing about backups is that they prevent "delete from deleting." Here is why. An organization's support staff backs up files regularly, usually daily. They keep the information safe so fires and earthquakes will not harm it. And, they often keep it for a very long time so people can go back to find information that they deleted long ago. If you accidentally delete important files, file restoration is a very desirable and helpful service. So, deleting a file that was archived means that it is not truly gone.

Of course, backups can save evidence of crime or other inappropriate behavior, too. Computer users have hastily deleted incriminating files in hopes of covering up undesirable activity only to learn later that the files can be completely re-created from the backups. (Of course, your own backups can be used in the same way.) Unlike paper files, digital copies of files are easy to create and beneficial to have, but it can be difficult to eradicate all copies of digital information. Perhaps the Information Age will promote better behavior.

FITBYTE

Gone, But Not Forgotten. Emptying trash on a personal computer is another example when delete does not truly delete. Computers keep a free list of available disk storage blocks, and take blocks from it whenever they write. Emptying trash usually adds the trashed files' blocks to the free list, allowing them to be reused but without changing their contents. Experts can recover the information until the blocks are overwritten.

SUMMARY

We've discussed various aspects of interactive networking in general, and eCommerce in particular. We also discussed several challenges of interactive networking, such as variation and discrete events, using Web-based retailing as an example. Web-based enterprises are like any business, except that customers can "walk in" from around the world, and all of the clerks are fast, but rather slow-witted—that is, computers. And interaction with customers comes not from continuous contact typical of shopping, but in brief events, as if the store were all dark and the clerk and customer used a camera's flash to conduct business.

We learned that the standard mechanism for handling eCommerce activities is the client/server structure: One computer, the client, requests that some task be performed by another computer, the server. This structure is used for activities like serving Web pages. It is also used for much more complex processing structures—three-tier and *n*-tier organizations—where a computer might at one time be the server and at another time be the client. The client/server interaction is an event or transaction that lasts only as long as it takes to make, process, and reply to the request. On the World Wide Web, the server has a challenging problem of maintaining the context with a client. (Not all client/server interactions are handicapped in this way.) Two solutions were introduced. In the cookie solution, the server places a unique identifier on the client, which is swapped on all client/server interactions, effectively allowing the client to identify itself and the server to keep a record of the transactions with that client. In the other solution—the CGI approach—the client calls a program of the server and passes it the accumulated information of the successive events.

We learned that distributed transaction processing can trash a database unless the operations are serialized—that is, each transaction is completed before another starts. We also learned that standards, such as HTML, HTTP, and Java, are the key to network communication and the WWW. Finally, we learned that the uncertainties of the world require backups to maintain the integrity of the information and processing of an eCommerce site.

There is much more to say about eCommerce. In Chapter 17 we return to the topic of cookies to maintain the context in a client/server interaction. The possibility that your privacy will be invaded is real.

EXERCISES

Multiple Choice

1. eCommerce includes all of the following except:
   A. electronic funds transfer
   B. database design and development
   C. business to business activities
   D. networked meetings
2. An electronic business must be aware of all of the following except:
   A. language variations of a global customer base
   B. differing monetary systems
   C. incomplete communication structures
   D. cultural variations
3. Static HTML pages and basic client/server structure won't work when:
   A. some or all information changes often
   B. the amount of information is too large to build separate Web pages for all of it
   C. the possible combinations of information is too large for separate Web pages
   D. all of the above
4. Between client requests from a specific IP address, a Web server:
   A. cannot handle requests from another client
   B. can handle requests up to the number of clients specified by the administrator
   C. can handle up to 255 other requests
   D. might handle hundreds or even thousands of requests
5. A cookie:
   A. stays on a client computer until removed by the server
   B. is removed when the client shuts down
   C. has an expiration date
   D. none of the above
6. Middleware got its name from its:
   A. use of midrange computers
   B. use of midpriced software
   C. position between a client and server
   D. position in the middle of a client's request and its result
7. A client/server request handled by a CGI program:
   A. uses the URL string to send and store data for a request
   B. uses cookies to store data for requests
   C. maintains a continuous connection until the transaction is complete
   D. stores requests on the computer that runs the middleware software

8. Java applets can run on:
   A. the server side
   B. the client side
   C. both the client side and the server side
   D. neither side

9. Presentation is not as important to XML as:
   A. structure
   B. formatting
   C. content
   D. context

10. The World Wide Web is:
    A. highly decentralized
    B. highly standardized
    C. tightly integrated
    D. mostly entropic

Short Answer

1. ______ means conducting business using electronic data communications.
2. In a client/server structure, the customer's computer is the ______ and the business's computer is the ______.
3. The basic client/server relationship is a(n) ______ system.
4. A client/server relationship with a database creates a(n) ______ system.
5. A(n) ______ is the inability to maintain the continuity of client requests based solely on IP address.
6. A(n) ______ is information from a Web server that's stored on a client's computer.
7. A(n) ______ program queries a database for information based on a client request and then builds a Web page from the information it receives.
8. Database operations, such as searches and changes, are called ______.
9. ______ requires a database to complete an operation on some data before another operation is allowed to work with the same data.
10. A Java program is called a(n) ______.
11. XML stands for ______.
12. XML information is ______, that is, its tags are defined within the description for each client/server relationship.
13. A(n) ______ is an incremental backup of all changes since the last backup.
14. A(n) ______ is the listing of available blocks that can be used to store files.

Exercises

1. If a different language were spoken in each state in the United States, how many different pairs of conversations could there be?
2. Describe the client/server structure when you use a credit card to purchase a product from a Web site.
3. Are there more client computers or more server computers on the Internet?
4. When posted, the simple Web pages you constructed earlier use a client/server relationship. Why isn't middleware needed for them?
5. Mapquest (`www.mapquest.com`) remembers your home address. How does it know your address?
6. Visit mapquest.com and look up the map of your home. Check the cookie. Can you figure out how it remembers your address?
7. Devise a backup scheme for your personal computer.
8. List Web sites that need to create Web pages on-the-fly.
9. Large Web sites use multiple servers. Explain how cookies prevent problems when a different server could handle each client request.
10. What are the advantages of running applets on the client side?

chapter

17

SHHH, IT'S A SECRET

Privacy and Digital Security

learning objectives

- Explain what is meant by privacy; discuss the issues surrounding privacy of information
- List and explain the meaning of the OECD Fair Information Practices
- Compare privacy in the United States to the European Union privacy practices
- Discuss the issues of disagreement concerning privacy: Opt-in/Opt-out, and compliance/enforcement
- Explain the security methods used in public key cryptosystems (PKCs) and, in particular, in the RSA system
- Perform simple encryption from cleartext to cipher text and perform the reverse decryption

I've never looked through a keyhole without finding someone was looking back.

—JUDY GARLAND,
COMMENTING ON HER LACK OF PRIVACY, 1967

PRIVACY is a fundamental human right. The United Nations' Universal Declaration of Human Rights recognizes privacy in Article 12. The constitutions of Australia, Hungary, and South Africa, among others, state a right to privacy. Though privacy is not explicitly mentioned in the U.S. Constitution, the U.S. Supreme Court has accepted privacy as a right implied by other constitutional guarantees. And privacy is a right that matters to us all. No matter how exemplary our lives may be, all of us have aspects of our life that we would prefer no one else found out about, and which are no one else's business. When those aspects interact with information technology, the issues of electronic privacy and security become important. We have much more than our password that we want to keep to ourselves.

In this chapter we discuss privacy and security. To begin, we consider a business transaction as a basis for understanding the topic of privacy and for considering who has an interest in private information. We consider different definitions of privacy, adopting a clear, but abstract definition. Using the definition, we find that maintaining privacy in the modern world is difficult, because we often are required to or choose to reveal information about ourselves. We look at how private information can be kept private, and we list the principles of privacy, including the principles from the Organization for Economic Cooperation and Development. We then explore the differences between how the principles are followed in the United States and in other countries of the world, including a disagreement between the United States and the European Union over these principles. Finally, we consider how cookies can be abused to compromise Web users' security.

The next topic is encryption. After learning encryption vocabulary, we study a simple encryption example. Public key cryptosystems (PKC) are studied as a means of achieving more convenient security for Internet-related situations. PKC systems seem at first to offer almost no protection, and then they seem to offer so much protection that it's impossible to decrypt what was encrypted. This dilemma is resolved for the RSA public key system. Examples make the whole process clear. Finally, the matter of compromising RSA's security is explored, with the outcome that 100 billion computers wouldn't really help!

PRIVACY: WHOSE INFORMATION IS IT?

Buying a product at a store generates a transaction, which produces information. The data includes the date and time of the purchase, the product, the cost, and possibly information about other products in the same "market basket." Is this information connected to a specific buyer? Paying with cash generally assures anonymity; that is, the buyer is not connected with the purchase, though cash payments in small towns or even in neighborhood stores where "everyone knows everyone" probably aren't anonymous. However, other transactions can certainly link the product with the buyer:

- Paying by check, credit, or debit card
- Purchasing through mail order or on the Internet
- Providing a "preferred customer" number
- Buying a product that must be registered for a service agreement or warranty

If you're buying socks, you probably don't care. If you're buying *Dating for Total Dummies*, you probably do. You want the information to be private.

But what is private? It is not so easy to define, so we wait to give a formal definition until later. For now, we look closer at the *Dating for Total Dummies* transaction.

How Could the Information Be Used?

The book merchant, who accepts your check for *Dating for Total Dummies*, can reasonably claim that gathering this information was a normal part of conducting business (keeping a record until the check clears), and so the information belongs to the store, or at least doesn't belong to you alone. If the bookstore decides, based on the information from this transaction, to send you an advertisement—"*Improve Your Love Life* Spring Sale ♥ All Whitman books and Samplers half price"—the store is using the information for the standard business practice of generating more business. You may even be happy to get the advertisement. But even if you're not, using "buyer profiles" is so established—they've probably been used since merchandizing began—that few would claim the store misused the information. If the merchant sells your name and lovelorn status to the local florists, movie theaters, restaurants, cosmetic surgeons, and so forth, has the information been misused? They are only trying to generate more business, too. Is it misused if the information gets to the campus newspaper, where it is published? Has the store broken the law? (The United States differs from Europe in this respect.) Can't you just be left alone to upgrade your dating skills in peace?

Modern Devices and Privacy

Justice Louis D. Brandeis would have sympathized with you. He described privacy as the individual's "right to be left alone." He also wrote in the Harvard Law Review with Samuel D. Warren,

> *The narrower doctrine [of privacy] may have satisfied the demands of society at a time when the abuse to be guarded against could rarely have arisen without violating a contract or a special confidence; but now that* ***modern devices*** *afford abundant opportunities for the perpetration of such wrongs without any participation of the injured party, the protection granted by the law must be placed upon a broader foundation. [Emphasis added]*

This argues that, in the past, it was hard for people's privacy to be violated without their knowledge, but using *modern devices*, people's privacy can be violated without their knowing it. The amazing thing about Warren and Brandeis's comments is that, although they might have been written about IT, they were written in 1890. The modern devices referred to were the first portable cameras and the faster film permitting short exposure photographs. They continued,

> *While, for instance, the state of the photographic art was such that one's picture could seldom be taken without his consciously "sitting" for the purpose, the law of contract or of trust might afford the prudent man sufficient safeguards against the improper circulation of his portrait; but since the latest advances in photographic art have rendered it possible to take pictures surreptitiously, the doctrines of contract and of trust are inadequate to support the required protection.*

What would Warren and Brandeis have thought about the ever-present surveillance camera? Their important point is that your image—and more generally information about you—deserves "sufficient safeguards against improper circulation." It's a nineteenth-century formulation of a twenty-first-century concern.

Controlling the Use of Information

The *Dating for Total Dummies* problem comes down to, "Who controls the use, if any, of the transaction information?" There is a spectrum spanning four main possibilities:

1. **No uses.** The information ought to be deleted when the store is finished with it (for example, when the check has cleared the bank), because there can be no further use of it.
2. **Approval.** The store can use it for other purposes, but only if you approve the use.
3. **Objection.** The store can use it for other purposes, but not if you object to a use.
4. **No limits.** The information can be used any way the store chooses.

The spectrum, which ranges from No Uses to No Limits, includes other intermediate points, too.

There is also a fifth possibility, call it internal use, where the store can use the information to conduct business with you, but for no other use. "Conducting business with you" might mean keeping your address on file so that you can be sent announcements about book readings. It would not include giving or selling your information to another person or business, but it may not require your approval either.

FITBYTE

Australian Perspective. The Preamble to the Australian Privacy Charter states, "A free and democratic people requires respect for the autonomy of individuals, and limits on the power of both state and private organizations to intrude on that autonomy. . . . Privacy is a basic human right and the reasonable expectation of every person."

If the transaction took place in Europe, New Zealand, Australia, Canada, Hong Kong, or several other countries, the law and standards would place it between (1) and (2), but very close to (1). If the transaction occurred in the United States, the law and standards would place it between (3) and (4), but very close to (4). Perhaps of greater concern, many Americans apparently *assume* that there is a privacy law that is close to the fifth case, internal use. We return to these different standards in a later section, but first we must understand the concept of privacy.

A PRIVACY DEFINITION

As important as it is, privacy is difficult to define. It is more than Brandeis's right "to be left alone." Generally, privacy concerns four aspects of our lives: our bodies, territory, personal information, and communication. Of these only the last two—personal information and communication—are of concern here. We adopt the definition

Privacy: The right of people to choose freely under what circumstances and to what extent they will reveal themselves, their attitude, and their behavior to others.

The definition emphasizes first that it is the person who decides the "circumstances" and the "extent" to which information is revealed, not anyone else. Thus the person has the control. Second, it emphasizes that the range of features over which the person controls the information embodies every aspect of the person—themselves, their attitudes, and their behaviors. Adopting such an inclusive definition is essential to cover situations of importance. For example, buying *Dating for Total Dummies* was an act, covered by behavior, included in our privacy definition. Notice that it doesn't automatically imply the No Uses classification. We may decide that the fact that the book was paid for with a check rather than cash—that is, an identifying as opposed to an anonymous form of payment—was evidence of a willingness by the buyer to reveal the fact of the purchase. Or we could decide that the form of payment has no bearing on whether the information should be revealed; permission to reveal it must be explicitly given.

Threats to Privacy

Now that we have the definition, what are the threats to privacy? There are only two basic threats: government and business. A third threat, private parties snooping or gossiping, will be handled here by security, that is, keeping the information private. Historically, the governmental threat—a regime spying on its citizens—has worried people more, probably because it has happened so often and the consequences have been so serious. The business threat is a more recent worry, and its IT aspects even newer still. There are two types of business threats: surveillance of employees and the use of business-related information, including transaction information, for other purposes.

Voluntary Disclosure

A person could in principle have perfect privacy by simply deciding not to reveal anything to anyone; that is, to be a hermit, though that probably would mean living alone on a remote island, surviving on coconuts and clams. But most of us interact with many people and organizations—businesses, our employer, and governments—to whom it is in our interest to reveal private information. That is, we freely choose to reveal information in exchange for real benefits.

> We tell our doctors many personal facts about ourselves so they can help us stay healthy.

> We allow credit card companies to check our credit record in exchange for the convenience of paying with a card.

> We permit our employer to read the email we send at work knowing that it's the employer's computer, Internet connection, and time we are using to send it, that the email system is there for use in our job, and that we have no need or intent to send personal mail.

> We reveal to the government—though not in the United States—our religion, our parents' names and birthplaces, race and ethnicity, and so on for the purposes of enjoying the rights of citizenship.

How private can we be when we are revealing so much about ourselves, our attitudes, and our behavior?

FAIR INFORMATION PRACTICES

It is possible to reveal information about ourselves and still enjoy considerable privacy, but it depends on what happens to the information after we've revealed it to other people and organizations. If they keep the information confidential, use it only for the purposes for which they gathered it, and protect it from all threats, our privacy has not been seriously compromised. We get the benefits and preserve our privacy. It's a good deal. But if those people or organizations are free to give or sell the information to anyone else, they are also engaged in "revealing," not just us. Our privacy is compromised. It's not enough to trust the people we give the information to. There must be clear guidelines adopted for handling private information, so we have some standard by which to judge whether the trust is warranted. For that we have the Fair Information Practices principles.

Five HEW Fair Information Principles

The first clear principles for the collection and use of private information came in 1972 from a report of the Advisory Committee on Automated Personal Data Systems for the U.S. Department of Health, Education, and Welfare (HEW). The report listed five principles, called the Code of Fair Information Practices:

1. There must be no personal data record-keeping systems whose very existence is secret.
2. There must be a way for a person to find out what information about the person is in a record and how it is used.
3. There must be a way for a person to prevent information gathered for one purpose from being used for other purposes without the person's consent.
4. There must be a way for a person to correct or amend a record of their information.
5. Any organization creating, maintaining, using, or disseminating records of identifiable personal data must ensure the reliability of the data for the intended use and must prevent misuses of the information.

These principles were a good start for a time before personal computers became widely used and when the ARPAnet—forerunner of the Internet—connected only a handful of U.S. universities. But the principles needed to be broader. For example, the principles do not address what happens if the principles are not followed—that is, compliance and enforcement.

OECD Fair Information Practices

In 1980 the Organization of Economic Cooperation and Development (OECD)—an organization of 29 countries concerned with international trade—developed an eight-point list of privacy principles that included the five HEW principles and became the Fair Information Practices. They have become a widely accepted standard, forming a reasonably complete solution to the problems of keeping information private while at the same time revealing appropriate information to businesses and governments. For that reason, the public has an interest in these principles becoming law. The principles also give a standard that businesses can meet as a "due diligence test" for protecting citizens' rights of privacy, thereby protecting themselves from criticism or legal action. The OECD principles are a practical implementation of privacy protection.

The OECD Fair Information Practices principles are as follows.

- **Limited Collection Principle:** There should be limits to the personal data collected about anyone; data should be collected by fair and lawful means; and it should be collected with the knowledge and consent of the person whenever appropriate and possible.
- **Quality Principle:** Personal data gathered should be relevant to the purposes for which it is used, and should be accurate, complete, and up-to-date.
- **Purpose Principle:** The purposes for collecting personal data should be stated when it is collected, and the uses should be limited to those purposes.
- **Use Limitation Principle:** Personal data should not be disclosed or used for purposes other than stated in the Purpose Principle, except with the consent of the individual or by the authority of law.
- **Security Principle:** Personal data should be protected by reasonable security measures against risks of disclosure, unauthorized access, misuse, modification, destruction, or loss.
- **Openness Principle:** There should be general openness of policies and practices about personal data collection, making it possible to know of its existence, kind, and purpose of use, as well as the identity and contact information for the data controller.
- **Participation Principle:** An individual should be able to (a) determine whether the data controller has information about him or her, and (b) discover what it is in a timely manner, in an understandable form, and at a reasonable charge (if any). If the enquiry is denied, the individual should be allowed to find out why and be able to challenge the denial. Further, the individual can challenge the data relating to him or her, and if successful, have the data erased, completed, or changed.

> **Accountability Principle:** The data controller should be accountable for complying with these principles.

Thus the OECD principles fill out the original five HEW principles. An important addition in the OECD principles is the concept of the **data controller**, a person or office that sets the policies, must interact with individuals about their information, if any, and must be accountable for those policies and actions. In 1981 the Council of Europe's Convention for the Protection of Individuals created similar rules.

Despite being a fundamental human right, however, privacy is not enjoyed in much of the world at the OECD standard for both government- and business-held information. This is somewhat surprising because privacy is well understood, its IT implications are clear, and all that's left is to enact laws and to enforce them. What's the problem?

COMPARING PRIVACY ACROSS THE ATLANTIC

Privacy often comes in conflict with private or governmental interests. For example, the United States hasn't adopted the OECD principles, despite being a major player in the OECD and having created the earlier HEW principles in the first place. It can be presumed that this is because many U.S. businesses make their profits gathering and collating information, or by buying and using information in ways that are inconsistent with the OECD principles. Similarly, the Chinese government isn't going to protect the right to privacy when it denies other basic human rights. The rights to privacy for these countries' citizens are thus diminished. Globalization may change that.

In a landmark advancement for privacy, the European Union in 1995 issued the European Data Protection Directive, a benchmark law incorporating the OECD principles. The member countries have enacted this law giving everyone in the E.U. the same level of privacy. (Another directive handles privacy for telecommunication.)

Many non-E.U. countries have also adopted laws based on OECD principles, such as Australia, New Zealand, Canada, Hong Kong, and non-E.U. countries of Europe. This is important because one provision in the Directive requires that data about E.U. citizens be protected by the standards of the law even when it leaves their country. Non-E.U. countries that want information on E.U. citizens must show that they have privacy laws consistent with the Directive, which effectively means consistent with OECD principles. Switzerland, a non-E.U. country, applied and was approved. The United States was not. What sorts of laws protect U.S. privacy?

U.S. Laws Protecting Privacy

The United States has the Privacy Act of 1974, a strong limit on the government's ability to invade people's privacy. (The U.S. Patriot Act of 2002 may have weakened it. This covers half of the privacy problem—interactions with *government*. But the reason the United States failed to meet the requirements of the Directive concerns information stored by *businesses*.

By contrast to the "omnibus" solution of adopting the OECD list, the United States uses an approach called "sectoral," meaning that it passes laws to deal with specific industries (business sectors) or practices. Examples include:

> Electronic Communication Privacy Act of 1986

> Video Privacy Protection Act of 1988

> Telephone Consumer Protection Act of 1991

> Driver's Privacy Protection Act of 1994

To illustrate, the Driver's Privacy Protection Act makes it illegal for motor vehicle registration departments to make information publicly available. Mass marketers once used motor vehicle information to create mailing lists. (Driving an expensive car might imply that you have a large income.) Now, DMVs must *get permission from the registrant* before making the information available for any purpose other than registering cars.

FITBYTE

Don't Ask. When the Supreme Court upheld the constitutionality of the Driver's Privacy Protection Act, the *Wall Street Journal* quoted a mass marketing industry spokesman as saying it was "death to us . . . If you can't use information about a person without permission, that generally means you're not going to have a list of any great substance." That is, using information without permission is essential to mass marketing.

The sectoral approach, though it often provides strong privacy protections in specific narrow cases, leaves much information unprotected. Naturally, then, when an E.U. resident allows a drug company access to his or her medical records for purposes of evaluating the efficacy of a new treatment, that information cannot be transferred to the company's subsidiary office in New York.

Privacy Principles: European Union

The differences in privacy laws between the U.S. and the E.U. is a serious problem for multinational companies, and Internet and Web-based businesses. A company cannot move data from an E.U. country to the United States until the United States meets the OECD principles. (Non-E.U. states subscribing to the OECD principles would probably object, too.) Think of a plane ticket bought from KLM in Holland for a Northwest flight in the United States—how does KLM tell Northwest the customer data? What is a business to do?

FITBYTE

Plain and Simple. Companies that are serious about protecting your privacy can say so simply, without complex and wordy privacy statements. For example, while Expedia.com is searching for flights in its database, it displays to its customers, "We do not lease or sell your information to anyone."

The Federal Trade Commission and the E.U. have been negotiating for years to solve this problem. A tentative agreement was founded on a concept called a Safe Harbor, which means a U.S. company that follows the rules of the agreement can receive information from the E.U. The FTC Safe Harbor guidelines are weaker than the original HEW principles. There are two glaring points of disagreement—Opt-in/Opt-out and compliance/enforcement—that are causing most of the difficulties.

Opt-in/Opt-out distinguishes between approval and objection, as we saw in the *Dating for Total Dummies* example. That is, when can an organization use information it collects for one purpose for a different purpose? "Opt-in" means the business cannot use it unless the person explicitly allows the new use. "Opt-out" means the business can use it unless the person explicitly prohibits the new use. Privacy principles as far back as the five HEW principles have consistently required Opt-in for all changes in use because otherwise the person does not control the use of private information. (Opt-in is actually a longer-standing principle than stated. Warren and Brandeis's concept of a "special confidence" between photographers and their subjects protecting their privacy amounts to Opt-in. That is, the photographer would violate the confidence unless he or she asked for and received permission from the subject first.) It was the Opt-in requirement of the motor vehicle registration act that caused predictions of "death" by the mass marketing spokesman. The FTC guidelines, however, require Opt-in only for highly sensitive information like medical data; Opt-out is the norm for most information.

Compliance/Enforcement means that organizations comply with the principles, that is, fulfill the role of the data controller. The E.U. and other OECD-subscribing countries have introduced offices to perform the duties of the data controller. There is no such person or office in the United States, of course. The FTC proposes that U.S. companies comply voluntarily, as a result of "market pressure." Private firms like TRUSTe and private agencies like the Better Business Bureau would do the monitoring. These private agencies and firms would then report violations to the FTC, but privacy advocates say that such a voluntary process amounts to no enforcement at all. (See the Voluntary Compliance Report Card, Figure 17.1.)

These privacy issues are important to both sides. Without Opt-in and enforcement, the OECD principles are badly eroded. But with those requirements, industries like direct marketing are by their own description mortally affected. At last check, the stalemate continued.

FITBYTE

Voluntary Compliance? Privacy consultant Richard M. Smith discovered in November 1999 that Real Networks' JukeBox software was gathering music taste profiles based on users' unique IDs. The company had a privacy statement, but it didn't mention the unique ID or the profiling activity, *until they got caught*. Further, Real Networks had hired the audit firm TRUSTe.

```
What: The Georgetown Internet Privacy Policy Survey Report
For Whom: Federal Trade Commission
Purpose: Assess "extent to which commercial Web sites have
    posted privacy disclosures based on fair information
    practices."
Sample: 361 .com Web sites, (describing 98.8% of the
    population as of January 1999)
Sampling Dates: March 8-12, 1999
Results:
  Sites collecting …
    Personal identifying information
      (name, email, postal address):                  92.8%
    Demographic information
      (gender, preferences, Zip Code):                56.8%
    Both personal and demographic information:        56.2%
  Sites posting …
    Either a privacy policy disclosure
      or information practice statement:              65.9%
    Both privacy policy disclosure and
      information practice statement:                 36.0%
  Sites collecting information and posting a
      privacy policy following Fair Information
      Practices . . . On the five elements examined
      in the survey (notice, choice, access,
      security, contact):                              9.5%
```

Figure 17.1. *Voluntary Compliance Report Card. Fewer than a tenth of .com Web sites gathering personal information as of March 1999 posted a privacy statement that included five of the Fair Information Practices components. Source: Mary Culnan, Georgetown Internet Privacy Policy Survey, 1999.*

THE COOKIE MONSTER

Cookies are perhaps the most controversial aspect of Internet privacy. As described in Chapter 16, cookies were originally used by Netscape engineers to connect the identity of a client across a series of independent client/server events. These cookies allowed Web servers to store seven-item records on the client's computer. Though the engineers assumed servers would use cookies to record information on the client's computer like mailing address, credit card number, and shopping cart contents—information that is private and rightly should be stored on the client's computer—that's not the way it developed. Today, cookies are simply serial numbers chosen by the server to identify the client uniquely. Every time a client visits the server, whether within a single session or at different times separated by years, the server gets its cookie from the client and can connect the latest visit with any information gathered and saved from earlier visits, based on the serial number. From the point of view of the intended purpose of cookies, as explained in Chapter 16, the serial number variation is entirely equivalent. But there are other ways to use a serial number.

Sharing Cookies

If two companies can match the serial numbers they have stored on a client, they can share the information they've gathered. But matching numbers isn't possible if Web servers only store and retrieve *their own cookies*. This would seem to imply that cookies should be private information shared between you and the site you visit, and the information they have is information you gave them voluntarily, say, to buy a product. But if you check the cookies on your computer, you will probably find cookies from many sites you've never visited or even heard of. How could they get there?

A loophole in the plan works as follows. You browse a site B that displays advertisements for site A. While your browser is building the Web page sent from B, it goes to A's site to get the ads. At that point, A is in a client/server relationship with your computer and is allowed by the only-the-server-can-store-and-receive-its-own-cookies policy to store its cookie on your client. Site B contracting with site A, a third party, to display ads enabled A to place a cookie on your computer. But so what? The cookie uses a few bytes of disk space, sure, but if you never visit A's site, they'll never again see the cookie. Right? Probably wrong.

FITBYTE

Enter Your Salary. In a widely reported incident in 2000, Intuit was sued by customers of its Web-based Quicken mortgage software for disclosing to mass advertiser, DoubleClick, private information gathered when Web users computed mortgages at Intuit's site. Cookies were blamed in the press, which would imply DoubleClick was A and Intuit was B in the preceding scenario. At the time, DoubleClick's ads were displayed on more than 11,000 Web sites.

Third-Party Cookies

Another site C can agree with A to place ads on its page, enabling the same scenario to unfold, although this time A's cookie is already on the client. Now A can match its unique cookie with B and C cookies. There can be a B–A link and a C–A link, and because it's the same unique A serial number, B's information can be linked to C's information; that is, A can make a B–C link. If this were to happen—actually, it almost certainly is happening—the linking takes place on the server side, out of sight and control of you, the client. And, of course, A's connections don't stop at two. So the threat to privacy is not the cookie itself, but the third-party cookies and the opportunity for the second and third parties to link their serial numbers, and hence the associated information.

FITBYTE

Many Double Clicks. Richard M. Smith, the privacy consultant, testified to Congress in June 2000 that in the previous six months his computer had logged 250,000 Internet transactions, roughly 10 percent of which was traffic to DoubleClick, tracking the URLs of the sites he visited.

One reason A places its cookie on the client is so that it can be paid for its advertising. That is, suppose when you visited site B, A was advertising for site D, and later you buy a product from site D. Site D may be obligated by its advertising contract to pay A because you saw the ad. No one knows whether you looked at the ad, but the existence of A's cookie on your client may be evidence that A placed some ad on your machine and that may be enough for D to pay A a commission. It's not much different from including coupons with print ads, a standard business practice for demonstrating the effectiveness of ad placement.

The third-party cookie loophole is a serious flaw that browser manufacturers could easily fix. Privacy advocates have been lobbying for a fix, but strong public support is needed.

Managing Your Privacy

Cookies are not the only way to connect your identity between the B and C sites. Even if there were no cookies, your email address is as unique as a serial number, and so the scenario described earlier applies. Companies can connect their information on you to information others have on you based on your email address.

The issue is not cookies. The issue is the same one that concerned us with *Dating for Total Dummies* and the Opt-in/Opt-out discussions: Do *you* have control over the information you created in a business transaction? Is the law that the business cannot use it for other purposes unless they receive your *approval*, preserving your privacy, or can the business use it for other purposes unless they receive your *objection, compromising your privacy*? The issue is privacy policy, not the technology of matching user information.

FITBYTE

Identity Crisis. Chipmaker Intel introduced a unique ID for each Pentium III processor chip, but removed it under intense criticism. The ID would have greatly simplified the task of matching Web-collected data—it's like all .coms using the same cookie on a given machine.

What is to be done about cookies? There's nothing wrong with cookies themselves. Many organizations that don't gather information—WNET, the *Oxford English Dictionary*, even the E.U. Secretariat—place cookies because they improve Web interaction. All recent browsers let you disable cookies, as well as set other levels of "cookie acceptance," including stopping third-party cookies.

Many users choose to turn off "cookie acceptance". But if you want to benefit from online banking, securities trading, and so on, your browser client will usually have to accept cookies. It's possible to delete the cookies' files—be sure your browser is closed, because while it's running, the cookies are stored in the RAM—but that's like starting over with a new computer. In particular, any "good" cookies that you want for applications like online banking will also be lost. Despite browser warnings not to, it's possible to edit the cookies' files, deleting those you do not want, though it is a rather delicate operation better left to the experienced.

The best response when concerned about cookies is to visit privacy Web sites, which can advise you on how to manage cookies for your browser or direct you to software that will help contain cookies. (Make sure to check if the site is legitimate!) By remaining aware of the risks and the benefits, you can receive useful network services and perhaps preserve some privacy.

ENCRYPTION AND DECRYPTION

The best way to keep electronic information secret is to **digitally encrypt** it—that is, to transform the representation so it is no longer understandable.

Encryption Terminology

We have already seen encryption applied to passwords in Chapter 12. We noted that if we forget our password, the superuser usually cannot tell us what it is because the software stores it in encrypted form—what we called being scrambled. In a **cryptosystem**—a combination of encryption and decryption methods—the password is the **cleartext** or **plaintext**, that is, the information before encryption. The encrypted password would be the **cipher text**, the encrypted form. Passwords use a **one-way cipher**—an encryption technique that cannot be easily reversed—because there's really no need ever to decrypt them: The system encrypts the password the user enters and compares it to the stored version, which is also encrypted. If they don't match as cipher text, they don't match as cleartext either. So, for password scrambling, the simple one-way encryption works.

Information is encrypted so it can be safely transmitted or stored. Transmitting or storing unencrypted information makes it vulnerable to snooping. Eventually, the cleartext must be recovered by reversing the encryption process, or **decrypting** the cipher text. In the diagram of the cryptosystem shown in Figure 17.2, the sender and receiver agree on a key, K_{SR}. The sender uses the key to encrypt the cleartext, and the receiver uses it to decrypt the cipher text. The key can be applied to the letters of the cleartext in various ways.

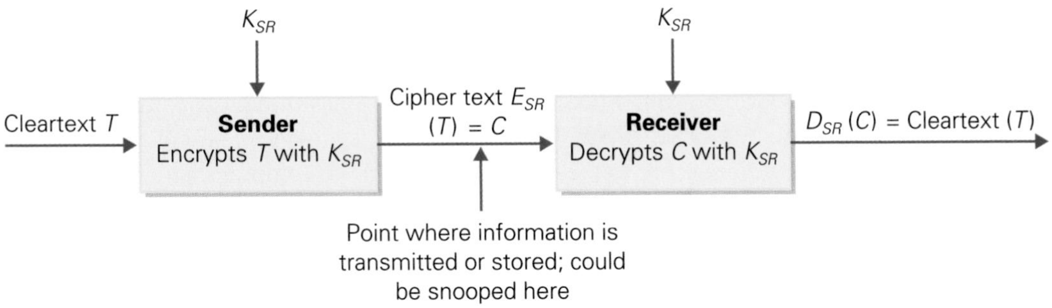

Figure 17.2. *Schematic diagram of a cryptosystem. Using a key K_{SR} known only to them, the sender encrypts the cleartext information to produce a cipher text, and the receiver decrypts the cipher text to recover the cleartext.*

A common way is as follows: ASCII letters are treated as numbers using their bit representation and transformed by some mathematical operation with an inverse, say, multiplication, to produce the cipher text bits. That is, a few letters of the ASCII text are multiplied times the key and the resulting number is sent or stored. The cleartext can be recovered by applying the inverse operation (division by the key, in this case).

XOR: An Encryption Operation

Exclusive OR, known as XOR, is an interesting way of applying a key to cleartext. XOR, which can be described as "*x* or *y* but not both," is written like an addition symbol in a circle, ⊕. It combines two bits by the rule: If the bits are the same, the result is 0; if the bits are different, the result is 1. Thus, if 0101 is the cleartext and 1001 is the key, then

0101	Cleartext
⊕1001	Key
1100	Cipher text

XOR produces **1100** for the cipher text. Applying the key to the cipher text again with XOR produces the original cleartext:

1100	Cleartext
⊕1001	Key
0101	Cipher text

Thus XOR is its own inverse.

Encrypting a Message. To illustrate encryption, imagine two students who have been writing messages to each other on the white board in the computer lab, but now they're worried that other people may be reading them, and so they decide to encrypt them. They agree on a key **0110 0101 1001 1010**, and plan to encode pairs of ASCII letters by transforming them with the key using XOR. Here's what they do. (See Figure 17.3.)

Using the cleartext **Meet @ 12:15 XOX**, they first write down the ASCII representation of these letters in pairs. (The ASCII representation is shown in Table 8.4.) Next, they XOR each of these 16-bit sequences with their key sequence to produce the cipher text, which in this case has the ASCII equivalent of **(ÿNUîEÚE«WAbT¯EÂ*Â**. This is the cipher text—a very strange sequence that should be secure to the causal observer in the computer lab. The cipher text can be easily decrypted using the same technique: XOR each of the ASCII equivalents of the cipher text with the key to produce the cleartext bits of the pairs. Then, look up the letters in the ASCII table. We can see that this scheme must always work by reviewing Figure 17.3 and using two facts:

- If any bit sequence is XORed with another bit sequence (the key) and the result is also XORed again with the key, that result is the original bit sequence.

> With XOR, it makes no difference whether the key is on the left or the right.

These facts mean that encrypting is moving from left to right in the figure, whereas decrypting would move from right to left.

```
      Cleartext                       Key                    Cipher Text
Me 0100 1101 0110 0101                               0010 1000 1111 1111 (ÿ
et 0110 0101 0111 0100                               0000 0000 1110 1110 ᴺᵤî
ƀ@ 0010 0000 0100 0000                               0100 0101 1101 1010 EÚ
ƀ1 0010 0000 0011 0001   ⊕ 0110 0101 1001 1010 =    0100 0101 1010 1011 E«
2: 0011 0010 0011 1010                               0101 0111 1010 0000 Wᴬ₀
15 0011 0001 0011 0101                               0101 0100 1010 1111 T¯
ƀX 0010 0000 0101 1000                               0100 0101 1100 0010 EÂ
OX 0100 1111 0101 1000                               0010 1010 1100 0010 *Â
```

Figure 17.3. *Encrypting the cleartext Meet @ 12:15 XOX, using ASCII encoding of letter pairs, the key 0110 0101 1001 1010, and the operation of exclusive OR to produce the cipher text (ÿ ᴺᵤ îEÚE«Wᴬ₀T¯EÂ*Â. (Decryption works in the opposite direction, as if the "⊕" and "=" symbols of the figure were exchanged.)*

Breaking the Code. How secure is the code? Probably not too secure. It is possible, knowing that XOR is the operation, to guess 6 of the 16 bits of the key in about three minutes (see Exercises), and it probably wouldn't take much fooling around to figure out the others. And this is with only a 16-character cleartext. The longer the text, the easier it is to decode, because once enough letters have been used, it is possible to notice what bit patterns show up frequently. With a large volume of English text, we might notice the patterns

```
0000 0000 xxxx xxxx
xxxx xxxx 1111 1111
```

which correspond to *e* in the first letter position and *e* in the second letter position. (Our key just happened to use the ASCII bit sequence for *e* as the first half of the key, and its complement—the opposite bits—as the second half of the key, but the code breaker will not use that information.)

As we know, *e* is the most common letter in English. Seeing these patterns and guessing that they correspond to *e* bytes, we can begin figuring out the cleartext from the cipher text by replacing each occurrence with *e*s. English's 12 most common letters are e t a o i n s h r d l u. (Curiously, most people who remember this sequence do so by pronouncing it!) Other languages are different, of course. These dozen letters represent about 80 percent of the letters in the average English text. Using these letters, we can replace the dozen most frequently occurring (left and right) patterns. Decrypting that many letters of a cipher text would make decrypting the remainder a simple *Wheel-of-Fortune* endgame. We would have broken the code without ever knowing that the two students had used XOR as the encryption scheme, or what the key was. The only property we used was that the students' code consistently replaced each letter with one of two patterns. Clearly they had better be smarter next time!

FITBYTE

Tse Beht of Tnmeh. The frequency count for English is not fixed, of course. Different sources produce somewhat different results, even for large documents. For example, *A Tale of Two Cities* contains more than half a million letters that are distributed from greatest to least frequency: e t a o n i h s r d l u. That is, *n* and *i* are swapped, and *s* and *h* are swapped from the standard distribution.

Being smarter about byte-for-byte substitutions is easy to do. For example, grouping more than 2 bytes will help our student encoders. The harder problem is that the sender and the receiver have to agree on the key *ahead of time*. That is, they had to meet or at least communicate for the purpose of selecting the key. Of course, if they don't meet, but communicate instead, that communication couldn't be made secure because there is no agreed upon key yet. Key exchange would be a showstopper for applications like Internet commerce, where credit card numbers should be kept secret, but the customer and the company cannot meet, perhaps because they are on opposite sides of the planet. The problem is beautifully solved using public key encryption.

PUBLIC KEY CRYPTOSYSTEMS

In a public key cryptosystem (PKC), people who want to receive information securely publish a key that senders should use to encrypt messages. For example, the key could be published on a Web page. Imagine that the key is 129 digits long and the senders are told to cube 32-byte groups of ASCII letters—yes, treat the bits like a 256-bit number and raise it to the third power—divide the result by the key, and send the remainder (that is, the bits smaller than the key that are left over from the division). The key was chosen so that the receiver, but not the general public or a code cracker, can decrypt it. If we change Figure 17.2 to a public key encryption, we get Figure 17.4.

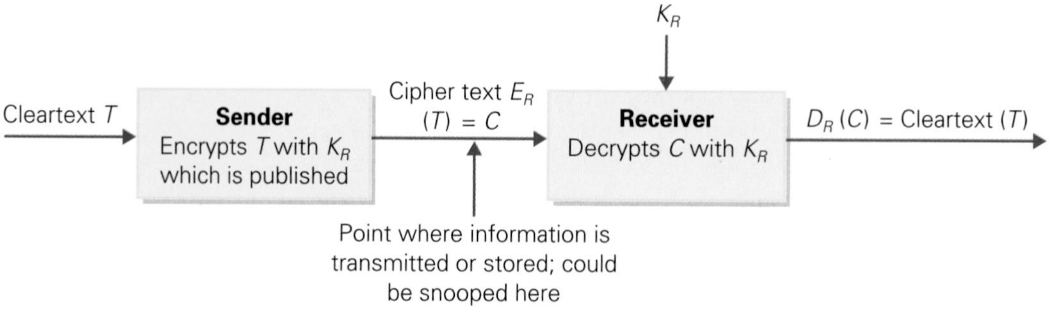

Figure 17.4. *Public key cryptosystem. The sender uses the receiver's public key K_R to encrypt the cleartext, and only the receiver is able to decrypt it to recover the cleartext.*

FITBYTE

Public Spirited. Computer scientists Whitfield Diffie and Martin Helman invented public key cryptosystems in 1976.

Code Cracker's Problem

The bad guy who is trying to snoop the communication by intercepting the cipher text and decrypting it knows the key, too, because it's published on the Web page. And it would seem the bad guy has the same ability to perform arithmetic on the cipher text that the receiver does. How much security can there be when so much information is known?

But cracking the code isn't so easy. All that was sent was the **remainder**—the bits that were left over from the division.

Recall from elementary school that the definition for division, *a/b*, is to satisfy the equation

$$a = b \cdot c + d$$

for *divisor* b, *quotient* c, that is, the result of the division, and *remainder* d. Further, d will be smaller than b. For example, 30/8 becomes

$$30 = 8 \cdot 3 + 6$$

which is the same as saying, "30 divided by 8 is 3 with a remainder of 6." This is called the **quotient-remainder** form of division. Substituting the variables of our encryption situation, the equation becomes

$$T^3 = K_R \cdot c + d$$

for cleartext T and some quotient c that doesn't interest us. Only d, the remainder, is sent.

Snooping and Decrypting

If the code cracker had the quotient c *and* the remainder d, he or she could simply multiply the quotient by the key ($K_R \cdot c$) and add in the remainder to produce T^3. Using a calculator to find the cube root gives the binary number of the 32-byte sequences. Presto! There's the original cleartext, T. But the snooper didn't get both the quotient and the remainder, only the remainder. So snooping is a lot tougher.

But now it doesn't look so good for the receiver. The receiver didn't get the quotient either, only the remainder, so how is he or she supposed to figure out what was sent? It seems that the message is so well encrypted *no one* can figure it out! Happily, Leonhard Euler, an eighteenth-century mathematician, and a few enterprising computer scientists, came to everyone's rescue—except, of course, the cracker.

RSA PUBLIC KEY CRYPTOSYSTEM

The **RSA public key cryptosystem** is the best known of the PKC systems. Named for its inventors, Ron Rivest, Adi Shamir, and Len Adleman, the RSA scheme is basically the same as the PKC scheme we just described. We need to learn enough about how it works to retrieve the original cleartext. *Why* it works relies on very deep mathematics and computer science that will not be described here. But it does work. It has withstood formidable attacks and will continue to as computers get faster. The assaults on RSA are described after we give it a try.

FITBYTE

Secret Prize. Rivest, Shamir, and Adleman were awarded the 2003 Turing Award by the Association for Computing Machinery, computing's Nobel Prize, for their creation of the RSA cryptosystem.

The RSA scheme relies on prime numbers. Recall from middle school that **prime numbers** can only be divided evenly—that is, without a remainder—by 1 and themselves. So, the first few prime numbers are 2, 3, 5, 7, 11, 13, 17, 19, 23, 29, 31, . . .

Mathematicians adore prime numbers because they have amazing properties. The rest of us only know that prime numbers are the basic "atoms" of a whole number: Any number can be **factored** into primes in only one way. The factors of a number x are just numbers that multiply together to give x. So, factors of 30 are

$$1 \times 30 = 30$$
$$2 \times 15 = 30$$
$$5 \times 6 = 30$$
$$2 \times 3 \times 5 = 30$$

but only {2,3,5} are the prime factors of 30.

Choosing a Key

The secret of the RSA scheme, of course, is that the receiver didn't publish any random 129-digit sequence as the public key, K_R. The key has some special properties. Specifically, the public key must be the product of two different prime numbers, p and q,

$$K_R = pq$$

Because multiplying two numbers of roughly equal size produces a number twice as long, p and q must be about 64 or 65 digits long to produce the 129-digit public key of the example. Additionally, p and q, besides being long enough and prime, must also be 2 greater than a multiple of 3. It's a rather strange requirement, but essential, as we'll see in a moment. Many primes have this property. For example, 5 and 11 are 2 larger than multiples of 3, namely, 3 and 9. As a running example, take

$p \ = 5$
$q \ = 11$
$K_R = pq = 55.$

Encrypting a Message

To encrypt a cleartext, divide it up into blocks—we'll use 6-bit blocks of the ASCII encoding for the running example, but they're usually many bytes long—cube the blocks, divide them by the public key, and transmit the remainders from the divisions. (We use 6-bit blocks just to keep the numbers small.)

Thus, to encrypt the amount of a credit card transaction,

```
****$0.02
```

the ASCII characters are expressed in their byte representation

```
0010 1010 0010 1010 0010 1010 0010 1010 0010 0100 0011 0000
0010 1110 0011 0000 0011 0010
```

and grouped into 6-bit blocks,

```
0010 1010 0010 1010 0010 1010 0010 1010 0010 0100 0011 0000
0010 1110 0011 0000 0011 0010
```

shown in white and blue.

Recalling from Chapter 11 that bits can be interpreted in any way that is convenient, our groups are interpreted as numbers

$T = 10, 34, 40, 42, 10, 34, 16, 48, 11, 35, 0, 50$

cubed,

$T^3 = 1000, 39304, 64000, 74088, 1000, 39304, 4096, 110592, 1331, 42875, 0, 125000$

divided by the key $K_R = 55$, and expressed in quotient, remainder form,

$1000 \quad = 55 \cdot 18 + 10$
$39304 \quad = 55 \cdot 714 + 34$
$64000 \quad = 55 \cdot 1163 + 35$
$74088 \quad = 55 \cdot 1347 + 3$
$1000 \quad = 55 \cdot 18 + 10$
$39304 \quad = 55 \cdot 714 + 34$
$4096 \quad = 55 \cdot 74 + 26$
$110592 = 55 \cdot 2010 + 42$
$1331 \quad = 55 \cdot 24 + 11$
$42875 \quad = 55 \cdot 779 + 30$
$0 \quad = 55 \cdot 0 + 0$
$125000 = 55 \cdot 2272 + 40$

And finally, only the remainders are kept to yield the cipher text

C = 10, 34, 35, 3, 10, 34, 26, 42, 11, 30, 0, 40

These numbers are the encrypted message to be sent. (The apparent coincidence that some of the cipher text numbers happened to be the same as their corresponding cleartext occurs because our example numbers (55) are so small. The result is still incomprehensibly scrambled.)

The Decryption Method

How does the receiver reconstruct the cleartext? First, we must compute the quantity

$$s = (1/3)(2(p-1)(q-1) + 1)$$

For our running example, this curious number is

$$s = (1/3)\ (2 \cdot 4 \cdot 10 + 1) = 81/3 = 27$$

It was to make s come out right that we added the requirement of "2 greater than a multiple of 3" when choosing p and q.

The amazing fact is that if the cipher text numbers C are each raised to the s power, C^s—that's right, C^{27} in our example—and divided by the key K_R, the remainders are the cleartext! That is, for some quotient c that we don't care about,

$$C^s = K_R \cdot c + T$$

which is *truly* the key to the RSA scheme.

Decrypting: C = 10. To demonstrate this amazing fact, take the first number of our cipher text

$$C = 10$$

and compute

$$C^s = C^{27} = 10^{27} = 1{,}000{,}000{,}000{,}000{,}000{,}000{,}000{,}000{,}000$$

which is not a binary number, but the huge decimal number of 1 followed by 27 zeros. Divide by K_R = 55 and express the result in the quotient-remainder form

$$\begin{aligned} &1{,}000{,}000{,}000{,}000{,}000{,}000{,}000{,}000{,}000 \\ &= 55 \cdot 18{,}181{,}818{,}181{,}818{,}181{,}818{,}181{,}818 + 10 \end{aligned}$$

Thus, T = 10, so the first 6 bits of the cleartext must be 10 in binary, 001010, as can be checked.

Decrypting: C = 3. The numbers can get very large for us—encryption algorithms actually use several techniques, such as modular arithmetic, to avoid the large intermediate numbers—but let's try another example. The fourth term of the cipher text is

$$C = 3$$

which we can raise to the 27th power with a calculator to get

$$3^s = 3^{27} = 7{,}625{,}597{,}484{,}987$$

Dividing by the public key, K_R and expressing the result in the quotient-remainder form yields

$$7{,}625{,}597{,}484{,}987 = 55 \cdot 138{,}647{,}226{,}999 + 42$$

implying that the fourth block of the text is binary for 42, or 101010, as can be verified. As a third example, we notice that everything works out right for the cipher text $C = 0$.

Why *does* the RSA work? Euler proved the following theorem in 1736. (This is the only occurrence of higher mathematics in this book. It isn't necessary to understand it. Simply accept that Euler's formula makes the RSA scheme work out.)

> **Theorem:** Let p and q be distinct primes, $K = pq$, $0 \le T < K$, and $r > 0$. If $T^{r(p-1)(q-1)+1}$ is divided by K, the remainder is T.

For our use of Euler's formula, $r = 2$, because

$$\begin{aligned}(T^3)^s &= (T^3)^{(1/3)[2(p-1)(q-1)+1]} \\ &= T^{2(p-1)(q-1)+1}\end{aligned}$$

Thus, when the cipher text—that is, the remainders—is raised to the s power and divided by the key, the cleartext is recovered.

Summarizing the RSA System

To summarize, (our example version of the) RSA public key crypto scheme follows these steps:

1. **Publishing.** Select two different prime numbers, p and q, which are 2 larger than a multiple of 3, and define $K_R = pq$, the public key. Compute $s = (1/3)[2(p - 1)(q - 1) + 1]$. Keep p, q, and s secret. Publish K_R where senders can find it.

2. **Encrypting.** Get the public key from the receiver, and break the cleartext bit-sequence into blocks according to the receiver's instructions, but less than K_R. Cube each block, divide each of the cubes by K_R, and send the remainders to the receiver as the cipher text.

3. **Decrypting.** Using the secret value s, raise each number in the cipher text to the s power, divide each result by K_R, and assemble the remainders into the blocks of the bit sequence of the cleartext.

Of course, humans don't do these calculations. Software does. And though the software is extremely sophisticated to perform these operations fast, the principles that the programs implement are embodied in these three steps.

RSA Security Challenge. Can RSA withstand attacks? Could anyone actually break the code? As far as is known, scientifically, a code cracker would have to figure out what *s* was to break the code. Constructing *s* is easy if the two primes *p* and *q* are known.

Factoring the Key. The problem of finding *s* reduces to factoring the public key K_R to discover *p* and *q*. But factoring large numbers is a computationally difficult problem, even for the world's fastest computers. It is that fact—factoring large numbers is so difficult—that keeps the public key encryption schemes secure. Put another way, if the key is large enough, it can be published because there is no known way to factor it into its two prime components in any reasonable amount of time.

{GREAT FIT MOMENTS}

RSA's Challenge >>

In 1977, shortly after inventing their scheme, Rivest, Shamir, and Adleman issued a challenge to the world: Break the small cipher text they encrypted with their public key RSA129—the 129 refers to the number of digits of their key—and win $100. This was a bold challenge because, although there was no known way to factor a 129-digit key quickly, maybe someone could invent a better factoring algorithm. The best-known method at the time wasn't much better than the grammar school technique of dividing consecutive prime numbers into the number, looking for one that divides evenly. If computer scientists were clever enough to come up with public key encryption in the first place, they could probably come up with better ways to factor.

In fact, in 1981 Carl Pomerance did invent a new factoring method that gave some hope, though all the while other computer scientists were trying to prove that the factoring process could never be improved much. Pomerance's algorithm was better, but it didn't crack the code. Eventually, Arjen Lenstra and Mark Manasse organized an effort which in 1994, using better algorithms, the Internet, and the improved speed of computers, cracked the RSA129 cipher. Their strategy took eight months and used nearly a thousand computers from around the world. But this wasn't the end of public key cryptosystems. It only revealed the factors of a *single* public key.

Most of us don't have a thousand computers or eight months to spend trying to snoop a single credit card transaction. Even if the secret is extremely important—a missile code, for example, or the outcome of the final episode of a TV show—and the code cracker has the resources of the U.S. government, the RSA scheme is still secure because all it takes to make things harder for code crackers is to increase the size of the key.

The difficulty of factoring increases dramatically as the key length grows. It has been estimated that increasing the key to 250 digits would increase the cracking time 100,000,000 times. Keys can be increased to 300 or 400 digits or more if one hundred million times harder is not enough. Larger keys do not seriously complicate the problem for the encryption and decryption processes compared to their impact on increasing the factoring time.

When RSA129 was cracked—an effort dubbed the largest computation of all time—everyone was waiting breathlessly to know what the secret message was. It turned out to be THE MAGIC WORDS ARE SQUEAMISH OSSIFRAGE.

Strong Encryption Techniques

Public key encryption techniques are known as **strong encryption**. The term is intended to convey the fact that a communicating party can use the technology to protect their communication so that no one else can read it. Period. From a national defense or crime fighting perspective, complete secrecy is of great concern. Agencies that protect society from internal and external threats have routinely snooped on those people and organizations that may cause harm. Because surveillance would be impossible if the "bad guys" got such technology, the U.S. government has fought a long-running battle since the invention of PKC technology to keep it contained and out of the hands of "bad guys." This has never been a very realistic goal because papers describing the scientific foundations of the technology—including Diffie and Helman's original paper, "New Directions in Cryptography" (*IEEE Transactions on Information Theory* IT(22):644–654)—are published in scientific journals, which anyone with a respectable computer science education can read to build his or her own encryption software. On the other hand, security professionals probably have a point. It could be valuable to spy on people who are in the process of planning crimes or attacks.

Of course, most people don't write their own software—they buy it—and that probably includes most "bad guys." If cryptography software vendors had to give government agencies and law enforcement officials a way to break such codes, perhaps we could have both security and a defense against the "bad buys." How could that be? Doesn't breaking the code require earth-shaking discoveries in factoring? Not from the software vendor's point of view.

Two techniques that could be used are known as **trapdoor** and **key escrow**:

> **Trapdoor.** While the software is encrypting the cleartext, ways might be provided to bypass the security. When the cipher text is sent, the cleartext could also be sent to law-enforcement or security officials. The trapdoor would work like a telephone wiretap in that the "bad guys'" encryption software would be configured without their knowledge. Legal safeguards (court-approved warrant) would be required to do so. Other trapdoor techniques exist.

> **Key escrow.** Knowing the key makes breaking the code easy, so a key escrow system would require encryption software to register the key (actually, the two prime numbers from which the key is created) with a third party, who would hold the key in confidence. Then, if there is ever a need to break a code—law enforcement personnel having a court-approved warrant, for example, or your computer being toasted in a fire—the escrow agent could provide the two primes.

These two schemes could also be abused: Couldn't anyone with (legal or illegal) access to your computer open the trapdoor? Wouldn't the escrow company be a tantalizing target for criminals because it contains everyone's PKC keys? Neither of these schemes has satisfied security and other experts.

SUMMARY

After discussing a privacy scenario, we defined privacy as the right of individuals to choose freely under what circumstances and to what extent they will reveal themselves, their attitudes, and their behaviors. Unfortunately, there are many benefits to giving out personal information. So the people and organizations that receive that information must keep it private. The guidelines for keeping data private have been created by several organizations, including the Organization for Economic Cooperation and Development. But such guidelines often conflict with the interests of business and government, so some countries like the United States have not adopted them. The member states of the European Union and other countries around the world have nevertheless accepted them as the guidelines for business or government or both. The E.U. countries have also required that information on any of its member states' citizens must enjoy the same level of data privacy outside their borders. Because the United States takes a sectoral approach to privacy, adopting laws only for specific business sectors or practices, much of the information collected on U.S. citizens is not protected to OECD standards. This has led to long-running negotiations between the E.U. and the United States regarding privacy standards. The dispute's two main sticking points are Opt-in/Opt-out and compliance/enforcement.

We completed the privacy discussion by taking another look at cookies. Because of the "third-party cookie" loophole, advertisers can place cookies on your computer, which helps them match data they receive from different Web servers. Though cookies are not the only culprits—simple email addresses constitute a decent unique identifier—plugging the third-party cookie loophole would improve Web privacy considerably. The best solution is to have OECD-grade privacy laws.

After introducing encryption terms and giving an example using XOR, we introduced public key cryptography. PKC is a straightforward idea built on familiar concepts. We showed a complete example of the RSA scheme. Though computer scientists have not yet proved the invincibility of the RSA scheme, it can be "made more secure" simply by increasing the size of the key. This has little effect on the encryption and decryption processes, but it greatly increases the problem of finding the prime factors that make up the key. Such strong encryption methods worry defense and law enforcement officials, but to date the conflict between balancing those concerns with the interests of peaceful, law-abiding citizens has not been reconciled.

Both privacy and security are topics that have not been fully resolved in the public forum. Laws and policies regarding both are still under construction. Privacy seems to be waiting for the broad adoption of the OCED safeguards for both business and government information gathering. Security seems to be waiting for a way for parties to communicate securely by mechanisms fully within their control, yet that can be compromised in extraordinary circumstances of public importance. Both pose daunting challenges.

EXERCISES

Multiple Choice

1. For a business, the least restrictive use of private information is called:
   A. No Uses
   B. Approval
   C. Objection
   D. No Limits
2. An individual faces the fewest potential invasions of privacy from the policy called:
   A. No uses
   B. Approval
   C. Objection
   D. No Limits
3. Fair Information Practices forbid:
   A. secret record-keeping systems
   B. information gathering on a person without their consent
   C. denying someone access to his or her own information
   D. collecting information that is not a part of a business transaction
4. The Code of Fair Information Practices lacked:
   A. methods for correcting mistakes
   B. legal penalties
   C. protection for children
   D. rules for data gaining access to your own data
5. You discover that credit information on you is inaccurate. Which principle does this violate?
   A. Limited Collection
   B. Quality
   C. Security
   D. Openness
6. Which Fair Information Practice provides for ways to correct your faulty credit record?
   A. Quality
   B. Purpose
   C. Participation
   D. Accountability
7. Data on E.U. citizens is:
   A. not as secure as data on Americans
   B. protected even outside of the E.U.
   C. not protected by OECD principles
   D. protected in Europe but not outside of it

8. The Driver's Privacy Protection Act:
   A. prevents departments of motor vehicles from releasing private information
   B. prevents departments of motor vehicles from charging for information
   C. prevents departments of motor vehicles from releasing information without permission
   D. allows departments of motor vehicles to sell information, provided the buyer discloses how the information will be used

9. Information from people in E.U. countries can be shared outside of the E.U., providing the business or government follows the principles of:
   A. Don't ask, don't tell
   B. Safe Harbor
   C. Hands-off
   D. Opt-in/Opt-out

10. If the cleartext is 1101 and the XOR key is 1001, the cipher is:
    A. 1011
    B. 0100
    C. 0110
    D. 1110

11. XOR can be described as:
    A. x and y or x or y
    B. x or y
    C. x or y but not both
    D. none of the above

12. Digital encryption is:
    A. only used for passwords
    B. easily broken by computer experts
    C. the use of math to make communication unreadable to snoops
    D. all of the above

Short Answer

1. ______ is the right of people to choose freely under what circumstances and to what extent they will reveal themselves, their attitude, and their behavior to others.
2. In regards to information technology, privacy is primarily concerned with ______ and ______.
3. ______ is an anonymous form of payment.
4. The ______ serve as a guideline for protecting personal privacy in regards to international trade.
5. The ______ provides a benchmark by which businesses can measure how well they are protecting the privacy of individuals.
6. A(n) ______ is responsible for maintaining personal information and is held accountable for it.

7. The ______ is the European Union's law incorporating the OECD principles.
8. In the United States, ______ offers more protection than ______ for protecting personal information.
9. A(n) ______ is a combination encryption and decryption.
10. ______ or plaintext is information before it is encrypted.
11. Passwords generally use a(n) ______ because it's hard to reverse and there's little need to decrypt it.
12. The ______ cryptosystem is the best-known public key cryptosystem.

Exercises

1. What are the two types of business threats regarding privacy?
2. There are several national "sweepstakes" that deliver big prizes to the winners. To be a part of these contests, you must register and provide your address (so they can deliver your check on national TV!). What potential privacy concerns are involved with such contests?
3. Credit card companies track your transactions. How can they abuse this?
4. What flaws exist in a sectoral approach to privacy?
5. Based on existing legislation, who appears to have more influence, business or individuals?
6. Explain how a simple serial number stored in a cookie can be used to store personal information.
7. Is compliance without enforcement effective?
8. Discuss the different approaches to privacy taken by the European Union and the United States.
9. Discuss the loopholes between compliance and enforcement.
10. Using XOR and 10110110, determine the cipher for the ASCII text for THE MAGIC WORDS ARE SQUEAMISH OSSIFRAGE.

ALAN KAY is one of the earliest pioneers of personal computing, and his research continues today. In 1967-9 Alan co-invented the FLEX Machine, one of the earliest modern desktops, and designed the "Dynabook" considered by many to be the prototype for the notebook computer. At Xerox PARC in the early 70s Alan invented Smalltalk, the first complete dynamic object oriented language, development, and operating system. There, he also invented the now ubiquitous overlapping window interface. Most of his contributions have been the result of trying to create better learning environments, mainly for children.

Alan has been a Xerox Fellow, Chief Scientist of Atari, Apple Fellow, and Disney Fellow. He recently joined the Hewlett-Packard Co. as a Senior Fellow at HP Labs.

Alan has his BA in Mathematics and Molecular Biology with minor concentrations in English and Anthropology from the University of Colorado, 1966, and his MS and PhD in Computer Science from the University of Utah, 1968 and 1969.

You started out in show business. What led you to become a computer scientist?

I was a professional jazz musician with quite medium abilities for about 10 years and did some teaching of guitar in that period. My general background included an artistic and musical mother, a scientific and mathematical father, and a grandfather who wrote and illustrated many books. So I grew up interested in many things and didn't make much distinction between what are called the Arts and the Sciences. I came across a number of books about computers and how to build them as a teenager in the 50s and when taking a computer aptitude test in the Air Force was an option, I took it, got a good score on it, and starting programming in the early 60s.

In college I carried full majors in mathematics and biology and supported this by being a programmer at the National Center for Atmospheric Research in Boulder. I was also still playing jazz in clubs at this time.

I wound up at the University of Utah ARPA project for grad school in 1966 as a complete fluke without any planning or knowledge about ARPA. From the moment I got there and met Dave Evans I "got" what ARPA was trying to do and it was a huge stroke of "Romance" that I responded to.

How does the musician in you continue to influence the computer scientist?

Analogies can often be misleading, but there are some interesting ones to be made between music and computing (and mathematics and biology). The big ones for me have been the large aesthetic content of music and math and a wish for computing to always be that beautiful, the textures of different kinds of things interacting over time, the incredible ratio of parsimony to effect, etc.

You are often talking about education and the art of teaching. Did someone in particular inspire your concept of the ideal teacher?

The initial ideas about "teaching people to think better – even qualitatively better" came from a number of science fiction novels, one of which led me to the General Semantics movement started by Alfred Korzybski. I also had one truly fantastic teacher in the 4th grade. She knew how to reach and realize the potential in the many different kinds of children in her classroom "without teaching", and she has been one of the main models for me for how to go about helping people learn.

You have said that "literacy is not just about being able to read street signs or medicine labels. It means being able to deal in the world of ideas." What does it mean to you for someone to be computer literate?

I like Frank Smith's general definition of literacy as something that starts with important ideas, finds ways to write them down in some kind of language, and helps develop more "readers and writers". The computer has ways of "writing" down representation systems of all kinds – it is a simulator and a metamedium. By metamedium, I mean that it is a holder of all the media you can think of, as well as ones you haven't thought of yet. Computer literacy is all about important ideas written and read as simulations. And the writing and reading are actually some kind of programming, where the programs – like mathematics or a musical score or an essay – are a means for expressing a powerful idea.

What many consider to be the prototype for the laptop computer is a machine you designed about 35 years ago, the Dynabook, yet, you often contend that the Dynabook is still a dream...

It is indeed now possible to not just make a physical Dynabook, but one with many more capabilities than my original conception. However, the physical part of the Dynabook is about 5% of the dream. In musical terms, we can now make the body of the violin but we are still struggling with the strings, fingerboard and bow (the user interface that includes authoring) and we still only have a few instances of what the musical expression will be like (the content of the Dynabook). The other difficult part of the design is that we somehow want the early parts of the Dynabook experience to be a lot more value-laden and fun than learning to play the violin usually is. More importantly, we want users to keep experimenting, move on, and not get complacent as many do for example after learning to play 3 chords on the guitar.

What is Squeak?

Squeak is a vehicle for getting to better places in all the areas we've been discussing. It is derived from one of the last Xerox PARC Smalltalks and has been brought forward to 21st century graphics, etc. It contains models of itself, which make it easy to port, and now exists on more than 25 platforms running "bit-identically" (exactly the same). From the computer science standpoint it is a little more interesting than most of the other stuff that is around but pretty much all of its ideas date from the 1970s, so its interesting features are more of a commentary on what didn't happen in computer science in the last 20 years.

We have now done and tested a child's environment that is working out pretty well, and contains a number of new language and structuring ideas. This has been used to implement a much more comprehensive adult/media authoring environment (a kind of super-duper Hypercard) that contains the child's environment as a subset. This is essentially what we think the Dynabook should be like, plus, you can now download it and use it for free.

You have said, "The best way to predict the future is to invent it." What advice do you have for students who are planning a career in the field of technology?

Gain wide perspective by majoring in something else while an undergraduate. Try to find partial answers to Bruner's 3 MACOS questions: What makes humans human? How did we get that way? How can we become more so? In other words, try to understand civilization and the role that representation systems for ideas have played in the journey called "civilization".

interview

ALAN KAY

part 4

PROBLEM SOLVING

introduction

Our study of information technology has already concerned itself with problem solving in several different forms. We have solved problems related to writing HTML, finding accurate information sources, answering research questions about Buckminster Fuller's life, debugging, designing a database for HAI! Adventure, and more. In all cases our main tool was logical reasoning applied to a specific situation. Our goal in this part is to become even more effective problem solvers.

Problem solving requires, naturally, a problem and some medium or mechanism in which to produce a solution. For us, Web pages and familiar applications will provide the problems, and JavaScript will be our solution medium. The important part of our study—the part that transfers to other aspects of our lives—is neither the problems nor the solutions, but the process by which we find them.

Though problem solving is the "high-order bit" (i.e., most significant information), JavaScript is a programming language. Once you see how programs are written, you will have a better idea of how IT works, which will make you more operationally attuned, and so a better user. And, the practical bonus from learning JavaScript is that it allows us to create much slicker Web pages.

chapter

18

GET WITH THE PROGRAM

Fundamental Concepts Expressed in JavaScript

learning objectives

> Tell the difference between name, value, and variable

> List three basic data types and the rules for specifying them in a program

> Explain the way in which the assignment statement changes a variable's value

> Write expressions using arithmetic, relational, and logical operators

> Write conditional and compound statements

Verbing weirds language.

—BILL WATTERSON, *CALVIN & HOBBES*

PROGRAMMING is a profession, yet we need to know something about it to be effective computer users. This is analogous to medicine. Doctors and nurses are professionals, but we need to know something about their specialties—our bodies, disease symptoms, nutrition, first aid, and so forth—to care for ourselves and benefit fully from their care. In neither case do we need an expert's knowledge, and in both cases we could probably survive with near total ignorance. But knowing some of what the professionals know is of unquestionable benefit and worth learning despite its technical nature.

What we need to know about programming is a fuller elaboration of the concepts already discussed in Chapter 10 on algorithms. These concepts are deep and subtle. We cannot expect to understand them fully the first time we meet them. Indeed, our goal is to change our thinking habits to be more "abstract." Just as we need experience writing, reading, and speaking a foreign language in order to acquire it, so too do we need experience writing, reading, and executing algorithms and programs to acquire the thought processes of computation.

OVERVIEW: PROGRAMMING CONCEPTS

Programming is the act of formulating an algorithm or program. It entails developing a systematic means of solving a problem so that an agent—someone other than the programmer and usually a computer—can follow the instructions and produce the intended result for every input, every time. The agent must also be able to perform or execute the program without any intervention from the programmer. This means that all of the steps must be spelled out precisely and effectively, and that all contingencies must be planned for.

Programming actually requires thinking. But thinking alone would make programming very difficult indeed. Instead, in this and other chapters, basic programming concepts developed over the past 50 years will be introduced. These are the tools you will need to formulate any computation. They are used daily by professional programmers. They not only simplify common programming tasks, but also help you write programs that are clear and complete and assist in managing the complexity of writing a program. When you understand all the concepts, programming should be manageable, an interesting intellectual exercise like working a crossword puzzle or figuring out whodunit in a murder mystery. It's really no harder than that.

Trying to program an algorithm precisely using English is hopeless. Natural languages are too ambiguous for directing anything as clueless as a computer. So, programming languages have been developed to help programmers in two ways: they are precise, and they are specialized in using the concepts mentioned in the last paragraph. Using a programming language is actually easier than writing in English. We will use **JavaScript**, a recently developed programming language that is especially effective for World Wide Web applications. Though you will not become a JavaScript expert from reading this chapter, you might learn enough to make your personal Web page fancier.

This chapter introduces the following programming concepts:

> Names, values, variables

> Declarations

> Data types, numbers, string literals, and Booleans

> Assignment

> Expressions

> Conditionals

With just these few concepts, you should be able to write actual programs. The program in Figure 18.1 is an example. It probably looks like gibberish at this moment, but by the end of the chapter you'll be able to read and understand it. (It is presented now to make it clear where we are headed, but it should be skipped if it appears intimidating.)

Finally, in introducing the deep ideas of the chapter, we must set down the practical details of programming. These rules can be as burdensome as a chapter-long list of dos and don'ts. So, the more obvious rules—the ones you would guess intuitively—are skipped, and can be found in Appendix B. This allows us to emphasize the few rules that you could not guess on your own. When in doubt, refer to Appendix B. All of the rules are listed there.

At the Espresso Stand

Espresso is concentrated liquid coffee produced by passing steam through finely ground coffee beans. Some people enjoy drinking espresso straight, but others prefer a café latté, espresso in steamed milk; a cappuccino, espresso in equal parts of steamed milk and milk foam; or an Americano, espresso in near-boiling water. Espresso drinks are sold in three sizes: short (8 oz.), tall (12 oz.), and grande (16 oz.). These drinks come with a single unit of espresso, called a shot, but coffee addicts often order additional shots. The price of additional shots is added to the base price of the drink, and tax is figured in to produce the charge for the drink. The program to compute the price of an espresso drink is:

Input:

`drink`, a string with one of the values: `"espresso"`, `"latte"`, `"cappuccino"`, `"Americano"`
`ounce`, an integer, giving the size of the drink in ounces
`shots`, an integer, giving the number of shots

Output:

`price` in dollars of an order, including 8.7% sales tax

Program:

```
var price;
var taxRate = 0.087;
if (drink == "espresso")
    price = 1.00;
if (drink == "latte" || drink == "cappuccino") {
    if (ounce == 8)
        price = 1.55;
    if (ounce == 12)
        price = 1.95;
    if (ounce == 16)
        price = 2.35;
}
if (drink == "Americano")
    price = 1.10 + .30 * (ounce/8);
price = price + (shots - 1) * .70;
price = price + price * taxRate;
```

Figure 18.1. *Sample JavaScript computation to figure the cost of espresso drinks*

NAMES, VALUES, AND VARIABLES

Though we are familiar with the concepts of a name, the letter sequence used to refer to something, and a value, the thing itself, we tend in normal conversation not to distinguish carefully between the two. Thus, when we use the letter sequences "Julia Roberts" or "Harrison Ford," we mean those specific movie stars. There are many people with those names, of course, and if your friend from Geology class is also named Harrison Ford, that name has one value for you in the context of that class, and another in the context of the movies. People ignore this distinction in everyday conversation. In everyday life we treat names as "bound to" their values.

Names Have Changing Values

Names and values are separable in programming. The best way to think of names and values in programming is to think of names as if they were offices or titles, or other designations purposely selected to have changing values. There are plenty of examples:

Name	Current Value (1/1/2003)	Previous Values
U.S. President	George W. Bush	Bill Clinton, George Washington
U.S. Supreme Court Chief Justice	William Rehnquist	Warren Burger, Earl Warren
James Bond	Pierce Brosnan	Sean Connery, Roger Moore
Queen Of England	Elizabeth II	Victoria I, Elizabeth I
UN Secretary General	Kofi Annan	Butros Butros-Ghali, U Thant

The names used in the right two columns are, of course, the informal usage of names from everyday conversation.

The reason we focus on the case where the values associated with a name can change is because they change in programs. A program is a fixed specification of a process. As the process evolves and the program transforms data to produce new values, the names must refer to these new values. This is a natural result of the fixed specification of the process. So, for example, the U.S. Constitution contains this specification of a process: "The President-elect will be sworn into office by the Chief Justice on the January 20 following the election." The intent of this command is to describe a process that applies no matter who wins the presidential election, that is, the value of "President-elect," and who is the senior justice of the Supreme Court on that date, that is, the value of "Chief Justice." We naturally interpret the U.S. Constitution this way. The names "President-elect" and "Chief Justice" have changing values.

Names used in this way—a single letter sequence with a varying value—are an already familiar concept to us from our previous computing experience. The file with the name **EnglishPaper** changes its value every time you save a version of your composition. In computing, the name is always separable from the value and the value can be changed. It's a basic idea worth thinking about.

Names in a Program Are Called Variables

In programming terminology, the names just discussed are called **variables**, a term that reminds us that their values will *vary*. For example, in the *Alphabetize CDs* program in Chapter 10, two variables, *Alpha* and *Beta*, were used. Nearly every step in that program changed the value of one or the other of those variables. That's typical. The most commonly used programming language operation is the command to change the value of a variable. That command is called **assignment**, and it is discussed in a later section.

FITBYTE

Names and Values. We've seen one other example of names having multiple values over time. Memory locations—their names are called *addresses*—have different values at different times. This is not a coincidence. Variables *are* memory locations in the computer. Variables are simply a more readable and convenient way to reference computer memory than are the actual numerical addresses. The value of the address is the current contents of the memory location, and it is the value of the corresponding variable.

Identifiers and Their Rules

The letter sequence that makes up a variable's name is called the **identifier**. Identifiers in every programming language must have a particular form, though the form is somewhat different from language to language. Generally, identifiers must begin with a letter, followed by any sequence of letters, numerals (the digits 0 through 9), or the underscore symbol (_). (JavaScript permits slightly more general identifiers than suggested here, but throughout the book, tiny limitations to JS are implied to make it easier to learn and help avoid errors. There is no loss of expressiveness in programming.)

Identifiers are not allowed to contain spaces. The following are eight identifiers:

```
X
x
ru4it
nineteen_eighty_four
Time_O_Day
Identifiers_can_B_long_but_if_so_typing_them_can_be_a_pain
oO0O0o
elizaBETH
```

Notice two features of identifiers: The underscore symbol can be used as a word separator to make identifiers more readable, and identifiers in most programming languages, including JavaScript, are case sensitive, meaning that the uppercase and lowercase letters are different.

FITBYTE

Form Rules. User IDs, our login and email names, follow similar rules, but with a few important differences. For example, login or email names often allow a dash (-), but variable names do not, because the dash could be confused with the minus sign.

A VARIABLE DECLARATION STATEMENT

Programs are usually written "starting from scratch." That is, when beginning to program, you can think of the computer as if it were newly manufactured; it knows nothing but how to understand the programming language. So the first thing to do when writing any program is to state what variables will be used. Saying what variables will be used is called **declaring variables**, and we do it using a command called a **declaration**. In JavaScript, the **declaration command** is the word `var`, short for *variable*, followed by a list of the identifiers to be declared separated by commas. For example, to write a computation that computes the area of a circle given its radius, we would need variables `area` and `radius`. So we declare,

```
var radius, area;
```

This command *declares* that in the program we will use these two identifiers as variables. Notice that the first command in the espresso computation in Figure 18.1

```
var price;
```

is a variable declaration of this type. (The program uses other variables that will be explained momentarily.)

The declaration was just called a *command*, because it is commanding the computer to record which identifiers will be used as variables. But everything we tell a computer to do is a command, so we should call the declaration by its proper term, declaration **statement**.

The Statement Terminator

A program is simply a list of statements. Because we can't always write one statement per line as in a normal list, the statements are often run together, which means that each statement must be terminated by some punctuation symbol. The **statement terminator** in JavaScript is the semicolon (;). It's the same idea as terminating sentences in English with periods, question marks, or exclamation marks. The main difference is this If I forget to terminate an English sentence, like I just did, you still understand—both from the meaning and from the capital letter on the next sentence—that the sentence is over, that is, terminated. The computer isn't that clever. It needs the semicolon. So, the rule is: Terminate every statement (including the statements introduced below) with a semicolon.

FITTIP

First Mistake. *Everyone* makes mistakes when programming. One of the most common mistakes for beginners is to forget the semicolon. When the semicolon is missing the computer becomes confused. Debugging is necessary. Training ourselves to remember semicolons makes programming easier.

Rules for Declaring Variables

Every variable used in a program must be declared. JavaScript allows declaration statements anywhere in the list of program statements. But because variable declarations announce what variables *will* be used in the program, programmers like to place them first in the program. It's like saying, "Here's the list of variables I'll be using in the program that follows." We will declare variables first.

Undefined Values. The declaration states that the identifier is the name of a variable. But what is the name's value? It has no value yet! The value of a declared variable is not defined at first. It's a name that doesn't yet name anything. Similarly, when a group of people forms an intramural basketball team, say, Crunch, the intramural sports office can refer to the Crunch captain, even if the person who will be captain hasn't been chosen. The name is declared—it will be meaningful when the season is under way—but there is no value assigned yet. The value is **undefined**.

Initializing a Declaration. Often we know an **initial value** for the identifiers we declare. So JavaScript allows us to set the initial value as part of the declaration, that is, to **initialize** the variable. To declare that `taxRate` and `balanceDue` are to be variables in the program, and that their initial values are .087 and 0, respectively, we write

```
var taxRate = .087;
var balanceDue = 0;
```

We don't have to declare and initialize just one variable at a time in the `var` statement. We can declare and initialize any number of variables by separating them with commas:

```
var taxRate = .087, balanceDue = 0;
```

The computer doesn't care which style is used. They're equivalent. Typically programmers include several variables in a single declaration statement when the variables are logically related. The only purpose is to remind the programmer that the variables are related. For example, variables describing a person's features might be declared

```
var height, weight, hairColor, eyeColor, astrological_sign;
```

If the variables are not related, they are usually specified in separate statements. All approaches are equivalent and there is no "proper" way.

TRY IT

The *Alphabetize* CDs program used two variables, *Alpha* and *Beta*. Give a JavaScript declaration statement to declare them.

Answer: `var Alpha, Beta;`

TRY IT

What is the important difference between the preceding declaration and

```
var beta, alpha;
```

Answer: The important difference is the use of upper- and lowercase letters. Because JavaScript is case sensitive, the two statements declare different variables. (The order of the variables in a declaration is unimportant.)

THREE BASIC DATA TYPES OF JAVASCRIPT

The three types of data we will use in our JavaScript programs are numbers, strings, and Booleans.

Rules for Writing Numbers

The values assigned to the variables `taxRate` and `balanceDue` are **numbers**. Like everything in programming, there are rules for writing numbers, but basically numbers are written in the "usual way." (Details are provided in Appendix B.)

One "unusual" aspect of numbers in programming is that there are no "units." We can't write `33%` or `$10.89`; we must write `0.33` and `10.89`. This explains why there are no dollar signs in the program in Figure 18.1 even though it is a computation to figure the price of a coffee drink in dollars. In addition to normal numbers, JavaScript understands scientific notation, as in `6.022 e+23`, where `e` means "times 10 to the power of." `e` can also be `E`. Standard computer numbers can have about ten significant digits and range from as small as 10^{-324} to as large as 10^{308}. (Numbers and computer arithmetic are unexpectedly subtle. Our uses of numbers will be trivial and avoid any difficulties. As a general rule, the "safe zone" is the range from –2 billionths to –2 billion. Outside that range, learn more about computer arithmetic.)

Though computers frequently compute on numbers, they compute on other kinds of data as well.

Strings

For us, strings will be the most common kind of data. **Strings** are sequences of keyboard characters. For example, here are nine strings:

```
"abcdefghijklmnopqrstuvwxyz"         "May"  '!@#$%^&*()_+|}{:]['
"strings are surrounded by quotes"   " "    "M&M's"
'strings can contain blanks'         ""     '"No," she said.'
```

Notice that a string is always surrounded by single (`'`) or double (`"`) quotes.

Strings Can Initialize a Declaration. Like numbers, strings can be used to initialize variables in a declaration. For example,

```
var hairColor = "black", eyeColor = "brown",
     astrological_sign = "Leo";
```

We need strings when manipulating text, as when we're building Web pages, for example. The program in Figure 18.1 uses several string constants: `"espresso"`, `"latte"`, `"cappuccino"`, and `"Americano"`.

Rules for Writing Strings in JavaScript. The rules for writing strings in JavaScript, most of which can be seen in the examples above, are as follows:

1. Strings must be surrounded by quotes, either single (`'`) or double (`"`).
2. Most characters are allowed within quotes except the return character (Enter), backspace character, tab character, \, and two others (little used).
3. Double quoted strings can contain single quotes, and vice versa.
4. The apostrophe (`'`) is the same as the single quote.
5. Any number of characters is allowed in a string.
6. The minimum number of characters in a string is zero (`""`), which is called the **empty string**.

Rule (3) lets us include quotes in a string. To use double quotes in a string, for example, we enclose the string in single quotes, as in `'He said, "No!"'`. If we want a string containing single quotes, we enclose it in double quotes, as in `"Guide to B&B's"`. Because the apostrophe is common in English's possessives and contractions, it's a good idea to use double quotes as the default. Doing so allows free use of apostrophes. Change to single quotes only when the string contains double quotes. But both work, and the computer doesn't care.

Notice that by rule (6) the empty string is a legitimate value. That is, writing

```
var exValDef = "";
var exValUndef;
```

results in two quite different situations. After these two statements, asking the computer what kind of value `exValDef` has, the answer would be "a string," while the answer for `exValUndef` would be "an undefined value."

Literals. The numbers and strings discussed are known as either **string constants** or **string literals**. The term *literal* conveys the idea that the characters are typed literally in the program. So, the rules are about how to write these values explicitly in a computation. However, when literals become the values of variables and are stored in the computer, the representation changes slightly, especially for strings.

String Literals Stored in the Computer. First, because the surrounding quotes or double quotes are used only to delimit the string literal, they are removed when the literal is stored in the computer. That's why the empty string `""` has length of 0, rather than 2.

Second, any character can be stored in the computer memory. Specifically, although a prohibited character such as a tab character cannot be *typed* in a literal, it can be the value of a string in the computer. How do we do that? We use the "escape" mechanism, which we discussed in Chapters 4 and 8.

For JavaScript, the escape symbol is the backslash (\) and the escape sequences are shown in Table 18.1. Thus we can write declarations such as

```
var fourTabs = "\t\t\t\t", backUp = "\b",
    bothQuotesInOne = "'\"";
```

which give values to the variables that cannot be typed literally. The escape sequences are converted to the single characters they represent when they are stored in the computer's memory. So, the lengths of the values of these three string variables are 4, 1, and 2, respectively.

Table 18.1. *Escape sequences for characters prohibited from string literals*

Seq.	Character	Seq.	Character
\b	Backspace	\f	Form feed
\n	New-line	\r	Carriage return
\t	Tab	\'	Apostrophe or single quote
\"	Double quote	\\	Backslash

Boolean Values

Another kind of value is the **Boolean value** (**Booleans**). Unlike numbers and strings, there are only two Boolean values: `true` and `false`. Boolean values have their obvious logical meaning. It should be emphasized that although `true` and `false` are letter sequences, they are *values*, like 1 is a value, not identifiers or strings. Although Booleans are used implicitly throughout the programming process, as we'll see, they are used only occasionally for initializing variables. Examples might be

```
var foreignLanguageReq = false, mathReq = true, totalCredits = 0;
```

This last declaration illustrates that variables appearing in the same declaration can be initialized with different kinds of values.

FITBYTE

It's True. Boolean values get their name from George Boole. True. Boole was an English mathematician who invented true and false. False. True and false have been around since humans began to reason. Boole invented an algebra based on these two values that is basic to computer engineering and other fields.

The different kinds of values of a programming language are called its **data types** or its **value types** or simply its types. We have introduced three types for

JavaScript: numbers, strings, and Booleans. There are several other types, but these will be enough for most of what we will do in JavaScript. JavaScript is very kind to programmers with respect to types, as we will see later in this chapter.

TRY IT

Declare variables (of your choosing) to describe literary personalities, and initialize them to values appropriate for Mark Twain: his real name, the century in which he wrote, whether he was a humorist, and a famous quotation.

Answer:

```
var real_first_name = 'Samuel', real_last_name = "Clemens";
var humorist = true;
var century = 19;
var famous_quote = '"Nothing so needs reforming as other people\'s habits."'
```

Notice the use of escape apostrophe (`\'`) in `famous_quote`. It is required because the entire quotation is enclosed in single quotes to allow the text to include double quotes. In the computer's memory the value of `famous_quote` is the 54-character string:

```
"Nothing so needs reforming as other people's habits."
```

That is, the enclosing single quotes and the backslash are gone.

FITTIP

Meta-Brackets. In discussing programming languages, we often need to describe a syntactic structure, such as declaration statements. To separate the language being defined from the language doing the defining, we enclose terms of the defining language in "angle brackets," (< >), known as **meta-brackets**. Thus, the general form of the preceding JavaScript declaration would be `var` *<variable name>* = *<initial value>*, where the symbols not in meta-brackets are written literally and symbols or words in the meta-brackets stand for things of the sort indicated, as a kind of placeholder. Notice that these are *not* tags.

THE ASSIGNMENT STATEMENT

If variables are to change values in an algorithm or program, there should be a command to do so. The **assignment statement** changes a variable's value, and it is the workhorse of programming.

An assignment statement has three parts that always occur in this order:

<variable> *<assignment symbol>* *<expression>*`;`

Here *<variable>* is any declared variable in the program, *<assignment symbol>* is the language's notation for the assignment operation, discussed next, and *<expression>* is a kind of formula telling the computer how to compute the new value. Like any other statement, an assignment statement is terminated by a semicolon. JavaScript's *<assignment symbol>* is the equal sign (=), and we've already seen the assignment operation as the initializer for variable declarations.

Assignment Symbol

Different programming languages use different symbols for indicating assignment. The three most widely used symbols are the equal sign (=); the colon, equal sign pair (**:=**); and the left pointing arrow (←). There are others, but these three are the most common. The **:=** is considered a single symbol even though it is formed from two keyboard characters. Like JavaScript, most languages use =. Pascal uses **:=** and more mathematical languages like APL use ←. Regardless of which symbol the language uses, assignment is a standard and heavily used operation in every programming language.

An example assignment statement is

```
weeks = days/7;
```

variable — assignment symbol — expression — terminator

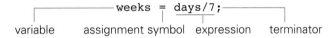

where **weeks** is the variable whose value is being changed, = is the assignment symbol, and **days/7** is the expression. Therefore, this assignment statement illustrates the standard form.

Interpreting an Assignment Statement

To understand how assignment works, you *must* think of a value flowing from the right side (expression side) of the assignment symbol to the left side (variable side). (This view makes the left arrow, ←, perhaps the most intuitive assignment symbol.) The **assignment symbol** should be read as "*is assigned*" or "*becomes*" or "*gets*." Therefore, our example can be read

> "the variable **weeks** *is assigned* the value resulting from dividing the value of the variable **days** by 7"

> "the value of **weeks** *becomes* the value resulting from dividing the value of the variable **days** by 7"

> "the variable **weeks** *gets* the value resulting from dividing the value of the variable **days** by 7"

FITBYTE

Get with the Program. Programmers mostly prefer *gets* when reading assignments. It conveys the idea of filling a container, as in a "mailbox *gets* a letter" or a "flour tin *gets* refilled." The variable is the container.

Terms like *is assigned*, *becomes*, and *gets* emphasize the role that the assignment symbol = plays, namely, to change the value of the variable named on the left side.

In an assignment statement, the expression (that is, everything to the right of the assignment symbol) is computed or evaluated first. If there are any variables used in the expression, their current values are used. This evaluation produces a value that then becomes the new value of the variable named on the left side. So, the effect of executing the example assignment statement

```
weeks = days/7;
```

is that the current value of the variable **days** is determined by looking in the memory (suppose it is 77), and that value is divided by 7, producing a new value, 11. This is a new value that then becomes the new value of the variable **weeks**, that is, **weeks** is assigned 11.

FITBYTE

Assignment to Memory. In the computer, an assignment statement causes the value in the memory location(s) corresponding to the variable to be replaced by the new value resulting from the expression.

Three Key Points about Assignment

There are three key points to remember about assignment statements. First, all three of the components must be given; if anything is missing, the statement is meaningless. Second, the flow of the value to the name is always right to left. Thus the two variable names in the assignment statement

```
variable_receiving_new_value = newly_computed_value;
```

correctly show the motion of information. Notice that the expression can simply be some other variable; it doesn't have to be a complicated formula. Third, the values of any variables used in the expression are their values before the start of execution of the assignment. This point is extremely important because the variable being changed in the assignment statement might also be used in the expression.

For example, a program simulating a basketball game would probably use the assignment statement

```
totalScore = totalScore + 3;
```

for a basket from outside the three-point circle. When the expression on the right side of the assignment statement, **totalScore + 3**, is evaluated, the value of **totalScore** used in the computation will be its value before starting this statement, that is, the score before the shot. When the assignment statement is completed, **totalScore** will have the updated value reflecting the three-point shot.

Similarly, the program might contain the code

```
shotClock = shotClock – 1;
```

to implement the "tick" of the shot clock. Again, when evaluating the right side expression, the values used for variables are those before the statement is executed.

Repeating, because this is the most important of all of the ideas of this chapter: The role of = is to *assign* the value computed on the right side to be the new value of the variable named on the left side.

FITBYTE

Programming Is Not Algebra. Like algebra, many programming languages use an equal sign in assignments. In programming "=" is read "becomes," which suggests the dynamic meaning of right-to-left value flow. In algebra "=" is read "equals," which emphasizes the static meaning that both sides are identical. In programming, the statement "$x = x + 1$" means the value of x becomes one larger; in algebra, the equation "$x = x + 1$" is meaningless because there is no number that is identical to itself plus 1. The unknowns in algebra are names whose values do not change.

AN EXPRESSION AND ITS SYNTAX

Although programming is not mathematics, it has its roots in higher math. So, it is not surprising that one of the concepts in programming is an algebra-like formula called an **expression**. Expressions describe the means of performing the actual computation. As we've already seen (**days/7** is an expression), expressions are built out of variables and **operators**, which are standard arithmetic operations as found on the keys of a calculator, such as addition or subtraction.

The symbols of basic arithmetic are called the **arithmetic operators**. The actual symbols used for some operators may be different, depending on the programming language, so we limit ourselves here to JavaScript operators. Examples of expressions include

```
a * (b + c)
height * width / 2
pi * diameter
(((days * 24) + hours) * 60 + minutes) * 60 + seconds
```

Arithmetic Operators

Expressions usually follow rules similar to algebraic formulas, but not quite. Multiplication must be given explicitly with the asterisk (*) multiply operator; so, we write `a * b` rather than `ab` or `a • b` or `a × b`. As with algebra, multiply and divide are performed before add and subtract—we say multiply and divide have *higher precedence* than add and subtract—unless parentheses group the operations differently. Therefore, `a*b + a*c` is equivalent to `(a*b) + (a*c)` because multiplication is automatically performed before addition. Also, because expressions must be typed on a single line, superscripts, as in x^2, are prohibited. Some languages have an operator for exponents or powers, but JavaScript does not. If we want to compute the area of a circle, we must multiply **R** times itself because we can't square it. So

```
pi * R * R
```

is the expression for computing the area of a circle (πr^2), assuming that the variable **pi** has the value 3.1415962.

Operators like `+` and `*` are called **binary operators** because they operate on two values. The values they operate on are called operands. There are also **unary operators**, like negate (`-`), which have only one operand. (Language parsers can easily figure out whether the minus means negate or subtract.)

One very useful operator in future chapters will be mod. The **modulus** (mod) **operation** (`%`) divides two integers and returns the remainder. So, the result of `a%b` for integers `a` and `b` is the remainder of the division `a/b`. In particular, the result of `4%2` is `0` because `2` evenly divides `4`, whereas `5%2` is `1` because `2` into `5` leaves a remainder of `1`.

Relational Operators

Expressions involving addition, subtraction, and so on are similar to algebra, but programmers use other kinds of expressions. **Relational operators** are used to make comparisons between numerical values—that is, to test the relationship between two numbers. The outcome of the comparison is a Boolean value, either `true` or `false`. The operators are illustrated here with sample operands `a` and `b` that should be replaced with variables or expressions:

`a <  b`	Is `a` less than `b`?
`a <= b`	Is `a` less than or equal to `b`?
`a == b`	Is `a` equal to `b`?
`a != b`	Is `a` not equal to `b`?
`a >= b`	Is `a` greater than or equal to `b`?
`a >  b`	Is `a` greater than `b`?

Notice that the "equal to" relational operator (`==`) is a double equal sign, making it different from assignment.

Examples of relational expressions include

```
bondRate > certificateDeposit
temperature <= 212
drink == "espresso"
```

Notice that relational tests can apply to string variables, as in the last example, which is taken from the program in Figure 18.1. Both equal (`==`) and not equal (`!=`) can be applied to string variables.

FITBYTE

One Character or Two? Several operators, such as `<=`, `>=`, and `!=`, are composed of two keyboard characters. They may not contain a space and are considered a single character. They were invented years ago to make up for the limited number of characters on a standard keyboard. If programming language research started today, compounds would not be necessary because it is now easy to introduce new symbols not on the keyboard, such as ≤, ≥, and ≠.

Logical Operators

The relational test results in a `true` or `false` outcome; that is, either the two operands are related to each other as the relational operator asks, making the test outcome `true`, or they are not, making the test outcome `false`. It is common to test two or more relationships together, requiring that relational expression results be combined. For example, teenagers are older than 12 and younger than 20. In programming, "teenagerness" is determined by establishing that the relational tests `age > 12` and `age < 20` are both true. In JavaScript the "teenage" expression is

```
age > 12 && age < 20
```

Logical And. The `&&` is the **logical and** operator, playing the same role AND plays in query expressions (Chapters 5 and 14). The outcome of *a* `&&` *b* is true if both *a* and *b* are true; otherwise, it is false. (The operands *a* and *b* can be variables, in which case they have Boolean values, or expressions, or a mixture.)

Thus, in the teenager expression, the current value of `age` is compared to 12, which yields a `true` or a `false` outcome. Then the current value of `age` is compared to 20, yielding another `true` or `false` outcome. Finally, these two outcomes, the operands of `&&,` are tested and if they are both `true`, the entire expression has a true outcome; otherwise, it is `false`. For example,

Value of `age`	`age > 12`	`age < 20`	`age > 12 && age < 20`
4	false	true	false
16	true	true	true
50	true	false	false

Notice that the operands for relational expressions must be numeric, but the operands for logical expressions must be Boolean (that is, `true` or `false`).

FITBYTE

Programming Is Still Not Algebra. In algebra, the notation *12 < age < 20* would be used to assert "teenagerness," the static condition of an age within the indicated limits. In programming, both tests must be specified and the two results "anded" (combined using `&&`) to produce the final answer. The difference, again, is that in algebra we are just stating a fact, whereas in programming we are *commanding* the computer to perform the operation of testing the two conditions.

Logical Or. Not surprisingly, there is also a **logical or** operator, `||`. The outcome of *a* `||` *b* is `true` if either *a* is `true` or *b* is `true`, and it is also true if they are both `true`; it is false only if both are `false`. A "preteen" test expression

```
age == 11 || age == 12
```

illustrates the use of the logical operator `||`. Because `&&` and `||` have lower precedence than the relational operators, the relations are always tested first. To include 10-year-olds as preteens, write an expression that states that either the person is age 10 or their age satisfies the previous preteen definition:

```
age == 10 || (age == 11 || age == 12)
```

Notice that the subexpression in parentheses produces a `true` or `false` value when evaluated, just like a relational test does. It doesn't matter how the operands of `||` are produced; it only matters that they are `true` or `false` values. Another way to achieve the same result is

```
(age == 10 || age == 11) || age == 12
```

Of course, it is also possible to test this definition of preteen with the expression

```
age >= 10 && age <= 12
```

which takes a bit less typing, and is like the teenager test. All of these expressions seem equally clear to a person, and the computer doesn't care which is used.

Logical Not. Another way the "teenagerness" expression can be written is by using `||` and the **logical not** operator, `!`. Logical not is a unary operator—it takes only a single operand—and its outcome is opposite of the value of its operand. Thus another teenager expression is

```
! (age <= 12 || age >= 20)
```

It works as follows. The subexpression in parentheses tests if a person is outside the range of being a teenager, that is, 12 or younger or 20 or older. If `true`, the person is not a teenager; if `false`, the person is a teenager. Then the logical not operator changes the outcome. Thus, the whole expression tests whether a person's age is not outside the range of being a teenager. If a person is not outside the range of being a teenager, the person is a teenager. The original formulation is probably clearer to a person, but they both produce the same result. And again, the computer doesn't care.

Operator Overload. Finally, we've reached **operator overload**. That might sound like the description of someone trying to learn too many new operators at a time—a state the reader has no doubt achieved!—but it is a technical term meaning the "use of an operator with different data types." The case of interest is `+`. Operators usually apply to a single data type, like numbers. So, we expect `4 + 5` to produce the numerical result of 9. And it does when the operands are numbers. But if the operands are the strings `"four" + "five"` the result is the string `"fourfive"`.

Concatenation. When we use + with strings, it joins the strings together by an operation called **concatenation**. In everyday writing, we simply place two strings together if we want them joined, but in programming, we are commanding the computer to do the work, so we need the operator concatenation to tell the computer to put two strings together. We have "overloaded" the meaning of + to mean addition when operands are numerical and concatenation when the operands are strings. Though overloading is common in some programming languages, + is the only example we'll see with our use of JavaScript.

FITTIP

Quote Note. When manipulating strings, as in the statement

```
fullName = firstName + " " + middleName + " " + lastName;
```

which creates a name from its parts using blanks as separators, it's easy to understand + as concatenation. But for a statement like

```
colt = "4" + "5";
```

the variable `colt` will be assigned the string `"45"`, not `9`, because the operands are (length 1) strings. Thus, we must be alert for quotes that tell us the operand is a string rather than a numerical value.

A CONDITIONAL STATEMENT

The *Alphabetize CDs* program in Chapter 10 required many tests. For example, there was a test to determine if the titles of two CDs were in alphabetic order. A specific statement type, called a **conditional statement** or a **conditional**, has been invented to make testing simpler. The conditional statement of JavaScript has the form

```
if (<Boolean expression>)
    <then-statement>;
```

Here the <*Boolean expression*> is any expression evaluating to a Boolean true or false outcome, such as relational expressions, and the <*then-statement*> is any JavaScript statement.

`if` Statements and Their Flow of Control

For example, an **`if`** statement that checks **`waterTemp`** in Fahrenheit

```
if (waterTemp < 32)
    waterState = "Frozen";
```

is a typical conditional statement. In a conditional the <*Boolean expression*>, called a **predicate**, is evaluated, producing a **`true`** or **`false`** outcome. If the outcome is **`true`**, the <*then-statement*> is performed. If the outcome is **`false`**, the <*then-statement*> is skipped. Therefore, in the example the value of the variable **`waterTemp`** is determined and compared to 32. If it is less than 32, the value of the variable **`waterState`** is changed to **`"Frozen"`**. Otherwise, the statement is passed over, and **`waterState`** remains unchanged. The following conditional

```
if (waterTemp >= 32 && waterTemp <= 212)
    waterState = "Liquid";
```

tests a range of values using relational operators and the and operator.

Some programming languages use the word *then* to separate the predicate from the <*then-statement*>, but JavaScript does not, because it is unnecessary. Writing the <*then-statement*> on the following line indented is actually only common practice, not a rule; the <*then-statement*> could be on the same line as the predicate,

```
if (waterTempC >= 0 && waterTempC <= 100) waterState = "Liquid";
```

It has the same meaning because white space is ignored in JavaScript. But programmers write the <*then-statement*> indented on the following line as a way of setting it off and emphasizing its conditional nature to anyone reading the program. By the way, when you read a conditional statement you *say* "then" after the predicate.

Sometimes we need to perform more than one statement on a `true` outcome of the predicate test. We could just repeat the test for each statement, as in

```
if (waterTemp < 32) waterState = "Frozen";
if (waterTemp < 32) description = "Ice";
```

Repeating statements can become tedious, however.

Compound Statements

Programming languages allow for a sequence of statements in the `then` clause. The problem is that if there are several statements, how will we know how many to skip in case the predicate has a `false` outcome? The solution is easy: We group the statements by surrounding them with "curly braces," `{}`, which collects them together to become a single statement known as a **compound statement**. Then they fulfill the requirements of the definition given above because now the <*then-statement*> refers to the (single) compound statement; it is skipped when the predicate outcome is `false`. For example,

```
if (waterTempC < 0) {
    waterState = "Frozen";
    description = "Ice";
}
```

Notice the location of the curly braces (`{}`). One immediately follows the predicate to signal that a compound statement is next, and the other is placed conspicuously on its own line below the *i* of `if`. Programmers do this so that compound statement grouping symbols—which are easily overlooked by a person if they are in an unexpected place in a program—are put where we will see them. As always, the computer doesn't care where the curly braces are placed.

The "exception proving the rule" that every statement must be terminated by a semicolon is the compound statement. The closing curly brace, `}`, should not be followed by a semicolon.

FITTIP

Show Your Braces. Since compound statement braces have a huge impact on program behavior, always put them in the standard place, where they will be noticed.

Another example of the use of the compound statement is from the espresso computation of Figure 18.1:

```
if (drink == "latte" || drink == "cappuccino") {
    if (ounce == 8)
        price = 1.55;
    if (ounce == 12)
        price = 1.95;
    if (ounce == 16)
        price = 2.35;
}
```

This code illustrates an `if` with a compound statement containing three simple `if` statements. If `drink` is neither a `"latte"` nor a `"cappuccino"`, the three statements will be skipped. Otherwise, if `drink` equals `"latte"` or drink equals `"cappuccino"`, the three statements will be performed. Notice that at most one predicate of the three statements of the compound statement can be true, because `ounce` can have only one value at a time: 8, 12, 16, or something else. So, `price` will be changed at most once.

if/else Statements

Of course, performing statements when a condition is true is handy, but how can statements be executed when the condition's outcome is false? There is another form of the `if` statement known as the **`if/else` statement**. It has the form

```
if (<Boolean expression>)
    <then-statement>;
else
    <else-statement>;
```

The *<Boolean expression>* is evaluated first. If the outcome is true, the *<then-statement>* is executed and the *<else-statement>* is skipped. If the *<Boolean expression>*'s outcome is false, the *<then-statement>* is skipped and the *<else-statement>* is executed. For example,

```
if (day == 'Friday' || day == 'Saturday')
    calendarEntry = "Party!";
else
    calendarEntry = "Study";
```

The *<then-statement>* and *<else-statement>* are single statements, but several statements can be grouped into a compound statement with curly braces when necessary. For example,

```
if ((year % 4)== 0) {
    leapYear = true;
    febDays = febDays + 1;
}
else
    leapYear = false;
```

This example uses the mod operator `%`, so the outcome of `(year%4)` is the remainder of `year / 4`; that is, the result is 0, 1, 2, or 3.

A typical example sets the same variables in both parts of the conditional. Consider a coin toss at the start of a soccer game, which can be expressed as

```
if (sideUp == sideCalled) {
     coinTossWinner = visitorTeam;
     firstHalfOffensive = visitorTeam;
     secondHalfOffensive = hostTeam;
}
else {
     coinTossWinner = hostTeam;
     firstHalfOffensive = hostTeam;
     secondHalfOffensive = visitorTeam;
}
```

Notice that the opening curly brace for the <*else-statement*> is placed right after the **else**, and the closing curly brace is placed conspicuously on its own line directly below the *e* of **else**.

Nested if/else Statements

The <*then-statement*> and the <*else-statement*> can contain an **if/else**, but you have to be careful, because it can be ambiguous which **if** an **else** goes with. The rule in JavaScript and most other programming languages is that the **else** associates with the (immediately) preceding **if**. For example, the code

```
if (Pooh == "bear")
   if (Eeyore == "bear")
      report = "Pooh and Eeyore are the same kind of animal";
else
   report = "Pooh is not a bear";       Caution: This code is deceptive!
```

has been *deceptively* indented so that it *appears* that the **else** associates with the first **if**. But white space is ignored. The JavaScript rule means that the **else** associates with the "inner" **if**, so that the following indentation matches the actual meaning:

```
if (Pooh == "bear")
   if (Eeyore == "bear")
      report = "Pooh and Eeyore are the same kind of animal";
   else
      report = "Pooh is not a bear"; Caution: This conclusion is wrong!
```

In fact, assuming Pooh is a bear and Eeyore is a donkey or any animal other than a bear, **report** gives the wrong answer. The best policy—the one successful programmers follow—is to enclose the <*then-statement*> or <*else-statement*> in compound curly braces whenever they contain an **if/else**. Thus the right way to express the statement would have been

```
if (Pooh == "bear") {
   if (Eeyore == "bear")
      report = "Pooh and Eeyore are the same kind of animal";
}
   else
      report = "Pooh is not a bear";
```

The braces ensure that the **else** matches with its **if**. This policy saves a lot of grief.

As one final example of **nested conditionals**, consider the four outcomes from flipping two coins expressed by nested conditionals:

```
if (flip1 == guess1) {
   if (flip2 == guess2)
      score = "win win";
   else                                  Inner if
      score = "win lose";
}                                                          Outer if
else {
   if (flip2 == guess2)
      score = "lose win";                Inner if
   else
      score = "lose lose";
}
```

This example shows clearly the logic of the true and false outcomes of the predicates.

THE ESPRESSO PROGRAM

We now return to the program in Figure 18.1. The program computes the price of four kinds of espresso drinks based on the type of drink, size of drink, and number of additional shots, plus tax. The input variables are listed at the start of the program, as is the output.

Input:

`drink`, a string with one of the values: `"espresso"`, `"latte"`, `"cappuccino"`, `"Americano"`
`ounce`, an integer, giving the size of the drink in ounces
`shots`, an integer, giving the number of shots

Output:

`price` in dollars of an order, including 8.7% sales tax

Program:

```
1.    var price;
2.    var taxRate = 0.087;
3.    if (drink == "espresso")
          price = 1.00;
4.    if (drink == "latte" || drink == "cappuccino") {
4a.       if (ounce == 8)
              price = 1.55;
4b.       if (ounce == 12)
              price = 1.95;
4c.       if (ounce == 16)
              price = 2.35;
      }
5.    if (drink == "Americano")
          price = 1.10 + .30 * (ounce/8);
6.    price = price + (shots - 1) * .70;
7.    price = price + price * taxRate;
```

The input variables are assumed to be given; see Chapter 19 for details on how this is done with a GUI. Because the program will create the output, we declare the output to be a variable as the first statement of the program.

Statements 3 through 5 determine the kind of drink and establish the base price. These statements have been written to show different programming techniques:

> **Line 3:** If the order is straight espresso, the first shot is priced at $1.00. This is an example of a basic conditional statement.

> **Lines 4–4c:** These statements establish the base prices for lattés and cappuccinos using an `if` statement with conditionals in the `then` statement compound statement.

> **Line 5:** This line uses a basic `if` statement to compute the base price for Americanos.

> **Lines 6, 7:** Finally, the total `price` is computed in Lines 6 and 7. In Line 6 the cost of additional shots is added to the base price. In Line 7 the tax is added in. This is accomplished by multiplying the total price by .087, then adding the result to the total price.

Notice that the if statements on Lines 3, 4, and 5 will always be executed, but because they apply to different drinks, the statement(s) of their `then` statements will be executed in only one of the cases.

Execution for a Double Tall Latté

To see the Espresso program in action, compute the price of a double tall latté, the second most common phrase used in Seattle after "it's still raining." A "double" means a total of two shots in the drink, that is, one extra shot. Thus the input variables to the program are

```
drink ⇔ "latte"
ounce ⇔ 12
shots ⇔ 2
```

where ⇔ means "has the value of" or "contains." This notation allows us to give the value of a variable without using the equal sign, which would look like an assignment statement.

The first statements are declarations, which are like definitions. In particular, we should treat `price` as not yet having any value. The following lines are executed:

> **Line 3** is executed first. The test `drink == "espresso"` fails, so its `then` statement is skipped.

> **Line 4** is executed next. The test `drink == "latte" || drink == "cappuccino"` has a true outcome because the subexpression `drink == "latte"` is true; the relational test `drink == "cappuccino"` is false, of course, but because one of the operands of the `||` is true, the whole expression is true. This means that the `then` statement containing the conditionals 4a–4c will be executed.

> **Line 4a** is executed next. The test `ounce == 8` has a false outcome, so its `then` statement is skipped.

> **Line 4b** is nexecuted. (I made up *nexecuted* for "next executed." Isn't it a great word?) The `ounce == 12` test is true, so the `then` statement is executed, giving `price` its initial value, `price ⇔ 1.95`.

> **Line 4c** is nexecuted. The `ounce == 16` test fails, so its `then` statement is skipped.

> **Line 5** is nexecuted. The `drink == "Americano"` test fails, so its `then` statement is skipped.

> **Line 6** is nexecuted. This causes the value of `shots` minus `1` to be multiplied by `.70`, resulting in the value `.70`, which is added to `price`, yielding `price ⇔ 2.65`.

> **Line 7** is nexecuted. The current value of `price` is multiplied by `taxRate`, whose value was initialized on line 2 (`taxRate ⇔ 0.087`), resulting in `0.23`, which is added to price to compute the final value of `2.88`, which is assigned to price.

Thus, `price ⇔ 2.88`, so a "double tall latté" costs $2.88.

SUMMARY

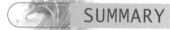

In this chapter, we introduced enough programming concepts—and their JavaScript syntax—to read and understand basic programs.

The chapter began by introducing the idea that a name can be separated from its value. Captain is a name for the team leader, but its value, that is, the person who is the captain, can change. In fact, the name exists, though with an undefined value, as soon as a team is formed. Names-with-changing-values is a familiar idea. File names work this way as we progressively update a file with, say, a word processor. Variables in programming languages have changing values, too. The reason is simple. A program is a fixed, finite specification for a computation written out in a few pages of code. Yet, when the computation is executed, many values may be created to produce the final answer. In the espresso computation, for example, the variable **`price`**, which is initially undefined, has three different values: the base price, the total price before tax, and the final price. At any point, the value of **`price`** is the price as computed so far, but the process of computing **`price`** continues until the program is finished. The separation is an important idea and is one of the ways that programming is different from algebra.

Next we introduced identifiers, the letter sequences that make up a variable's name. We explained how they work and how they must be declared. Variables can be initialized when they are declared. Then we introduced the idea of changing the value of a variable using assignment. An assignment statement has a variable on the left side of the assignment symbol, and an expression on the right side. The operation is to compute the value of the expression and make that result the new value of the variable. This makes information flow from right to left in an assignment statement. Statements like

```
x = x + 1;
```

make sense in programming, but not in algebra. This one is a command to the computer to find the current value of the variable **`x`**, add 1 to it, and make the result of the addition the new value of **`x`**.

Next we defined three JavaScript data types—numbers, strings, and Booleans—and explained how to build expressions to compute values of these types. We learned the standard arithmetic operators and relationals to compute on numbers, concatenation for combining strings, and logical operations for Booleans. (See the table in Appendix B for a full listing.) In defining concatenation, we introduced the idea of "operator overload." Expressions "do the computing" in our programs, and are generally a familiar idea.

As a rule, all of the statements of a program are executed one after another, starting at the beginning. The conditional statements are the exception. JavaScript's two conditional forms are **`if`** and **`if/else`**. These allow statements to be executed depending on the outcome of a Boolean expression called a predicate. Using conditionals, we can organize our computations so that operations are performed when "the conditions are right." We must be careful to group statements within a compound statement to make it plain which statements are skipped or executed. We also must be careful when we are using **`if/else`** in a conditional so that the **`if`** and **`else`** associate correctly.

Finally, we reviewed most of the ideas of the chapter by analyzing the Espresso program of Figure 18.1. The program uses both numeric and string data types, as well as the declaration, assignment, and conditional statement forms.

All that keeps us from running the program and demonstrating our knowledge is setting up the input to acquire the values for **`drink`**, **`ounce`**, and **`shots`**, and outputting the **`price`**. This will require a GUI written in HTML, and is the topic of Chapter 19.

EXERCISES

Multiple Choice

1. JavaScript is mainly used for:
   A. mainframe applications
   B. Web applications
   C. operating systems
   D. all of the above
2. On the computer, variables are:
   A. memory locations
   B. programs
   C. files
   D. all of the above
3. Which of the following can be used as part of a variable name?
   A. - hyphen
   B. b (space)
   C _ underscore
   D. ( ) parentheses
4. The symbol to terminate a statement in JavaScript is:
   A. : colon
   B. Enter
   C. ! exclamation
   D. ; semicolon
5. When declared, JavaScript variables are:
   A. automatically assigned a 0
   B. automatically assigned a blank
   C. undefined
   D. assigned a random number
6. Which of the following is not a term used to change the value of a variable?
   A. assign
   B. gets
   C. sets
   D. becomes
7. The right side of an assignment statement:
   A. must contain a formula
   B. must contain more than just a variable
   C. uses the values in the variables before the start of the execution of the statement
   D. all of the above

8. `grade = num_right * 2.5` is a(n):
   A. variable
   B. operator
   C. expression
   D. relational operator

9. Following the rules of precedence:
   A. addition is done before subtraction
   B. multiplication is done after division
   C. multiplication is done before subtraction
   D. everything is done left to right

10. In JavaScript, the relational test,
   `birth_year > 1944 && birth_year < 1965`, is:
   A. true if `birth_year` is 1952
   B. true if `birth_year` is less than 1965
   C. false if `birth_year` is greater than 1944
   D. none of the above

11. For a logical and operator to work:
   A. one of the conditions must be true
   B. neither condition can be false
   C. either one but not both conditions must be true
   D. none of the above

12. A typical computer program follows the pattern of:
   A. output, processing, input
   B. input, output, processing
   C. input, processing, output
   D. processing, input, output

Short Answer

1. A(n) ______ is a systematic way of solving a problem so that an agent can follow the instructions and get the correct result.
2. A(n) ______ is the letter sequence of a variable's name.
3. Variables are created using a(n) ______ statement.
4. A(n) ______ is a programming command to do something that's given to the computer.
5. To ______ a variable is to assign a value to a variable at the same time it is declared.
6. A(n) ______ is a sequence of alphanumeric and special characters.
7. `+`, `-`, `*`, and / are called ______.
8. ______ work on two values, such as `a * b`.
9. A(n) ______ operator has only one operand.

10. ______ are used to make comparisons.
11. The not logical operator is a(n) ______.
12. Joining two strings together using the + is called ______.
13. In programming, the if statement is called a ______.
14. When an if statement is false, the ______ statement(s) execute.
15. ______ are used to group several statements into a compound statement.

Exercises

1. For the following, fill in the math operator and the relational operator.

Name	**Math operator**	**Relational operator**
less than	______	______
less than or equal to	______	______
greater than	______	______
greater than or equal to	______	______
equal to	______	______
not equal to	______	______

2. Step through each line of the JavaScript program below. (This is the program from Figure 18.1.) Write down the value of each variable as you walk through it. Use an order of a 16 oz. latte.

```
var price;
var taxRate = 0.087;
if (drink == "espresso")
        price = 1.00;
if (drink == "latte" || drink == "cappuccino") {
        if (ounce == 8)
              price = 1.55;
        if (ounce == 12)
              price = 1.95;
        if (ounce == 16)
              price = 2.35;
}
if (drink == "Americano")
        price = 1.10 + .30 * (ounce/8);
price = price + (shots - 1) * .70;
price = price + price * taxRate;
```

3. Repeat the process using an 8 oz. Americano.
4. Modify the espresso program to include frappuccino. It comes in a 12 oz. size only and costs $2.50 plus tax.
5. Explain when you would use quotes and apostrophes for strings.
6. Give the JavaScript expression for determining overtime for a worker.

7. Explain why the following statements won't work.

```
wont_work = "five" * 5 + "5" - '5'
3 * 7 = wont_work
wont_work == a / b
"wont_work" = m * n
```

8. What are the answers for following?

   answer = (9 + 7) / 4 * 2 – 5
   answer = 6 * 3 / 9 – (17%5)
   answer = (4 + 5) – (2 + 3) * 4

9. Explain why the following statement works in programming but not math.

```
count = count + 1
```

10. Explain how the following statement works.

```
left = right
```

chapter

19

THE BEAN COUNTER

A JavaScript Program

learning objectives

> Use the Bean Counter application as a model to
  - Write input controls
  - Create a button table
  - Write an event handler in JavaScript
  - Write a GUI similar to that of the Bean Counter

> Trace the execution of the Bean Counter, saying what output is produced by a given input

> Explain event-based programming in JavaScript and the use of event handlers

Programming today is a race between software engineers striving to build bigger and better idiot-proofed programs, and the Universe trying to produce bigger and better idiots. So far the Universe is winning.

—RICH COOK

MUCH OF MODERN programming requires two activities. The first is creating the algorithm that directs the computer to solve a problem. The second is creating a user interface to assist in the human/computer interaction; specifically, a way to enter the input and a way to display the computed output. JavaScript is designed for Web applications, which means that JavaScript code is included in Web page source code written in HTML. The Web page is the graphical user interface; the JavaScript does the computing.

In Chapter 18, we wrote a program to charge for espresso drinks. That program is the logical component of our solution. In this chapter, we focus on creating a user interface and connecting it to the espresso program. So, one of our goals is to produce a user-friendly GUI for the program.

We will create the Bean Counter application. The first step is to make sure that the computation from Chapter 18 is correct. Then, after covering two preliminaries, we will follow these steps:

1. Review Web page programming, recalling some of the HTML basics, and introduce the idea of the HTML input controls.
2. Build the GUI for the Bean Counter program, so that the graphic looks right. Only the picture will be complete; the buttons will not work yet.
3. Introduce the idea of event programming and connect the buttons to the program logic.
4. Try out the Web page, evaluating it for its usefulness.
5. Revise the page and the logic so that it effectively solves the problem.

When the Web page is complete, we will have created our first complete JavaScript program.

The best way to learn both the ideas and the practical skills of this chapter is to build the program yourself as you read along.

PRELIMINARIES

Recall from Chapter 4 that HTML files are simple ASCII text. The fancy formatting of word processors like WordPerfect, MS Word, or ClarisWorks simply confuses Web browsers, and so must be avoided. Instead we'll use a basic text editor such as Notepad, SimpleText, WordPad, or BBText. The file format must be `text` or `txt`, and the filename's extension (the characters following the last dot) must be `.html`. So, `bean.html` would be a good name. In this way, the operating system knows that the file is to be processed by a Web browser, and the browser will be able to understand everything in the file without becoming confused.

To create your program, start by using the text editor to make a file whose first line is `<html>` and whose last line is `</html>`. To include JavaScript (JS) in an HTML file, enclose the JS text in `<script language="JavaScript">` `</script>` tags. The information that you include between these tags is the subject of this chapter, of course. When it's time to test your program, save it. Remember that the file format must be `text` and the file extension must be `.html`, though if you've specified the extension already, a simple **Save** should be enough. Then find the file on your computer, and double-click on it. Your standard Web browser should open the file and display the Web page you've constructed. It's that simple.

> **FITTIP**
>
> **"Modern" Software.** The JavaScript in this book requires a "contemporary" browser such as Internet Explorer 4 or higher, or Netscape 6 or higher. Because of browser inconsistencies, the figures shown in the text may differ slightly from what you see with your browser.

To work through the mechanics of running a JavaScript program, we will ignore the user interface for the moment and simply run the computational part of the program from Chapter 18. This is mostly an exercise, because we will not be able to interact with the result, and all that we will see is one number printed out. We begin this way to make sure the Bean Counter code is working. We'll use this code later in this chapter. The program structure needed to run just the computation is shown in Figure 19.1. You should *accurately* type it into a file, save it as `beanV0.html`, and run it.

Because we have not yet built the user interface, we have no way to give inputs. So we fake the input. We declare and initialize three new variables—**`drink`**, **`shots`**, and **`ounce`**—as the first three statements of the JavaScript code. We'll take these out later, when we add the buttons. These initializers are for a "double tall latté," that is, a 12-ounce café latté with two shots of espresso. After you type in and run the program, you should see the result shown in Figure 19.2.

```
<html>
  <head><title>Version 0</title></head>
  <body>
    <h1>Here's Version 0 of the Bean Counter</h1>
    <script language = "Javascript">
      var drink = "latte";   //Temporary Decl. for Version 0;
                             //to be removed
      var shots = 2;         //Temporary Decl. for Version 0;
                             //to be removed
      var ounce = 12;        //Temporary Decl. for Version 0;
                             //to be removed
      var price;
      var taxRate = 0.087;
      if (drink == "espresso")
          price = 1.00;
      if (drink == "latte" || drink == "cappuccino"){
        if (ounce == 8)
            price = 1.55;
        if (ounce == 12)
            price = 1.95;
        if (ounce == 16)
            price = 2.35;
      }
      if (drink == "Americano")
          price = 1.10 + .30 * (ounce/8);
      price = price + (shots - 1) * .70;
      price = price + price * taxRate;
      alert(price);     //Temporary statement to print result;
                        //to be changed
    </script>
  </body>
</html>
```

Figure 19.1. *Version 0 of the Bean Counter program without the user interface, and with fixed inputs:* `drink="latte", shots=2, ounce=12`.

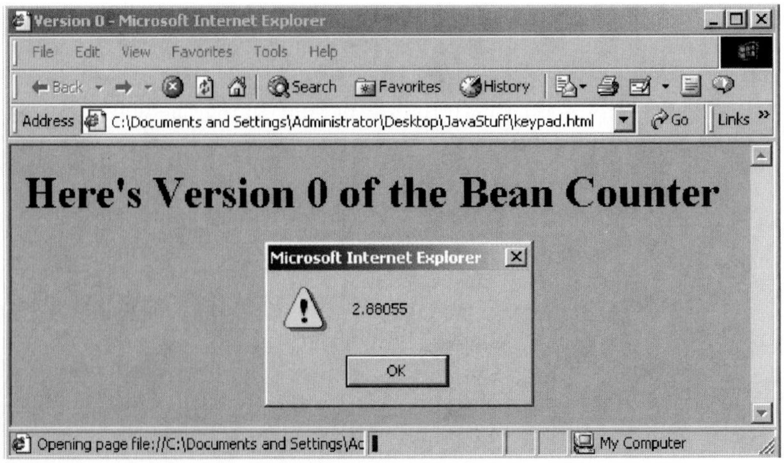

Figure 19.2. *Web page displayed by Version 0 of the Bean Counter program of Figure 19.1.*

The `alert(price)` command prints out the amount that the program computed for the `price`. We verify that the program did produce the same price for a "double tall latté" that we computed in Chapter 18. (The answer isn't rounded to a whole penny, but we'll solve that problem later.) Our next step is to construct the graphical user interface.

BACKGROUND FOR THE GUI

This section covers two introductory topics that we need to understand to create the JavaScript graphical user interface. First we present a quick review of HTML. If you need more information, reread Chapter 4. Next we explain a new HTML tag, the `<input...>` tag. This allows us to create buttons and print output.

The Bean Counter GUI (Figure 19.3) offers the user rows and columns of buttons, and a window in the right corner to display the total price of the espresso drink. The first column of buttons specifies the number of shots. The second column specifies the size of the drink, where S, T, and G stand for short, tall, and grande. The next column specifies the type of espresso drink. The meanings of the last two buttons in the rightmost column are obvious.

Figure 19.3. *Initial Web interface for the Bean Counter program.*

Review HTML Basics

Recall from Chapter 4 that HTML is a markup language that describes how a Web page should appear on a computer monitor, by using tags that surround the relevant text, images, and so on.

HTML Tags. An HTML file is enclosed in `<html> </html>` tags. It requires a head, which has the form

```
<head>
  <title>The Bean Counter</title>
</head>
```

and its body is surrounded by `<body> </body>` tags. All of the programming of this chapter is concentrated in the body of the document.

HTML has several levels of headings, such as the `<h1> </h1>` tags. Paragraphs are surrounded by `<p> </p>` tags, and text can be forced to a new line by the `<br>` tag. Text can be made italic using `<i> </i>` tags, or bold with `<b> </b>` tags. A horizontal line can be drawn with the horizontal rule tag, `<hr>`. The `<a href="`*fn*`"> </a>` tags place a link to another Web page with file name *fn*. The tag `<img src="`*fn*`">` places an image contained in the file *fn* into the document.

Most tags have attributes that customize the document to the situation. For example, the background color for a page can be specified, as can its font color and typeface. Thus

```
<body bgcolor="#804000" text="#FF9900" align="center">
   <font face="Helvetica", "Arial">
   <h1 align="center">
      <font color="#FFFFFF">the bean counter</font></h1>
   <hr width=50%>
   <p align="center"><b>figuring the price of espresso drinks<br>
      so barristas can have time to chat</b></p>
```

gives us a coffee-brown background color (`#804000`), a terracotta text color (`#FF9900`), and a sans serif font (`Helvetica`). All of the HTML just presented is to be part of our Bean Counter program in the file `bean.html`.

Tables in HTML. Often when we create interfaces for JavaScript programs, we organize the design as a table. We do this because tables give us some control over where information is displayed on a page. Recall that table definitions are enclosed by `<table></table>` tags and are a sequence of rows. Each row is surrounded by table row tags, `<tr></tr>`. Within each row, a sequence of table data items is given, each surrounded by `<td></td>` tags. There are several ways to make a fancier table, but our use of tables requires only these basics. Check Appendix A for more information.

Interacting with a GUI

Curiously, the input facilities like **buttons** and **checkboxes** are known as **controls**. When controls were introduced into HTML, they were designed to assist with activities like ordering products or answering survey questions. This is the view of a person filling out a form by clicking on buttons and filling in boxes. When the form was complete, it was sent to the computer for processing.

`Forms.` The designers of the input commands introduced the concept of a **form**, which must surround all of the input controls. Though the form tags `<form></form>` have several attributes, we will use only the `name` attribute, which gives a name to the form. Thus, to allow us to use input buttons, the next item in our HTML program is the pair

```
<form name = "Bean">
</form>
```

The rest of our GUI programming will be placed between these two tags. The file ends with

```
  </body>
</html>
```

By the way, the name, like everything in JavaScript, is case sensitive. Figure 19.4 shows the code for the page as it looks so far.

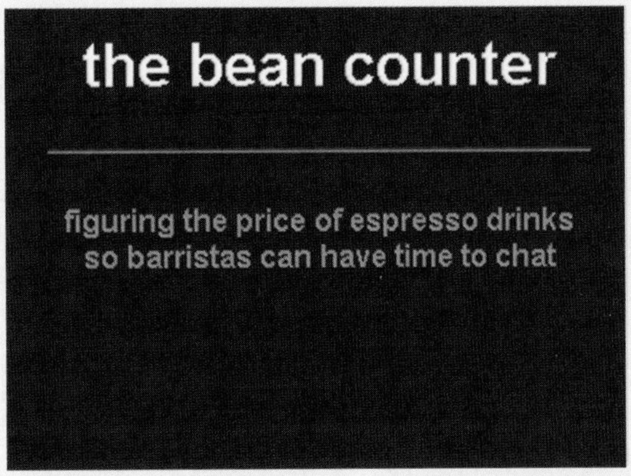

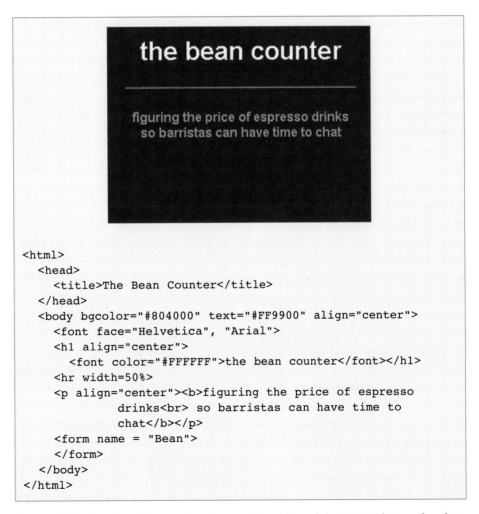

```
<html>
  <head>
    <title>The Bean Counter</title>
  </head>
  <body bgcolor="#804000" text="#FF9900" align="center">
    <font face="Helvetica", "Arial">
    <h1 align="center">
      <font color="#FFFFFF">the bean counter</font></h1>
    <hr width=50%>
    <p align="center"><b>figuring the price of espresso
            drinks<br> so barristas can have time to
            chat</b></p>
    <form name = "Bean">
    </form>
  </body>
</html>
```

Figure 19.4. *The Bean Counter interface to this point, and the HTML that produced it.*

Events and Event Handlers. GUI inputs such as controls cause an event when they are used. For example, when the user clicks on a command button, he or she causes a "click" event to occur. An **event** is an indication from the computer (operating system) that something just happened (mouse click).

We want our JavaScript program to respond to that click—for example, perform the operation corresponding to the button. The way this happens is that when JavaScript finds out about the event, it runs a piece of program called the event handler for that event. An **event handler** is the program that does the task to respond to an event. We will explain this concept further in a moment.

Three Input Controls

The <input . . . > tag specifies all of the input types, buttons, text boxes, checkboxes, and so on. The easiest way to learn the types is simply to study an example of each. The three input controls used in this book are the button, text, and radio controls.

Button. The form of the button control is

```
<input type=button value="label" onClick="JS text">
```

where **value** gives the text to be printed on the button, and **onClick** is an event handler composed of JavaScript instructions. When the user clicks on the button, the JavaScript code of the event handler is executed. Event handling will be discussed momentarily. The image for the button control is placed in the next position in the text of the HTML program.

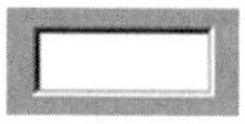

Text Box. The text box can be used to input or output numbers or words. Its general form is

```
<input type=text name="identifier" size=6
onChange="JS text">
```

where *identifier* is the name of the control, and **onChange** is the event handler. After the user has changed the contents of the text window, the JavaScript program instructions in *JS text* are performed. The image for the text control is placed in the next position in the text of the HTML program.

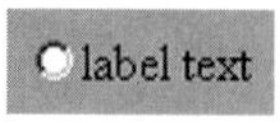

Radio. Radio buttons give a selection of preprogrammed settings. Their general form is

```
<input type=radio name="identifier"
onClick="JS text">label text
```

where *identifier* is the name of the control, *label text* is shown beside the control, and **onClick** is an event handler. When the user clicks on a radio button, the center darkens to indicate that it is set, and the JavaScript instructions in *JS text* are performed. If there are other radio buttons with the same name, they are also cleared. The image is placed in the next position in the text of the HTML program.

For the Bean Counter application, we need only the text and button controls. We will use radio buttons later.

CREATE THE GRAPHICAL USER INTERFACE

We are well on the way to creating our Bean Counter interface shown in Figure 19.3. The HTML in Figure 19.4 has the heading information, the horizontal line, and the slogan. "All" we have to do is create a table and fill in the entries. We should place the table between the form tags to ensure that the browser understands the input controls.

> FITTIP
>
> **Focus Point.** When faced with a task, it is a good idea to "think it through" before starting. List the steps required in the order you will do them. Then you can focus your attention on only one step at a time. This process, which is a main topic of Chapter 22, is illustrated here by writing down our plans before starting.

Notice that the table in Figure 19.3 is a four-row, four-column table with two empty cells. (The columns are not all the same size, but the browser will take care of making them the right size.) Buttons appear in all of the occupied cells but one, so our table will mostly be a table of buttons. This suggests the following strategy for building the table:

1. **Create a button table.** Program the HTML for a four-row, four-column table with a generic button in each cell. This is a good strategy because we can build such a table quickly using copy and paste.
2. **Delete two buttons.** Two of the cells of the table should be empty. Delete the buttons, but not the cells.
3. **Insert text control.** Replace the button control for the last cell, making it a text control.
4. **Label the buttons.** Pass through the table and set the value attribute of each button so that the label on the button is correct.
5. **Primp the interface.** Check the interface and adjust the specification where it is necessary.

Once these five steps are complete, the picture of the Bean Counter interface will be finished. Consider each step in detail.

1. Create a Button Table

The easiest way to build a copy-and-paste table is from the inside out. That is, we start with the cell. Then we copy the cell and surround it with `<tr></tr>` tags to make a row. Then we copy that and surround it with `<table></table>` tags to create the table. Of course, using this strategy means that the cell we start with must be generic.

Given the information about the button input control, we decide that the generic cell can have the form

```
<td>
  <input type=button value="b" onClick =' '>
</td>
```

Here `"b"` is a placeholder for the button label that we'll fix in Step 4, and `' '` is a placeholder for the *JS text* of the event handler that we'll write later.

We make four copies of the cell and surround them by row tags. We make four copies of the row copy and surround them with table tags. We save the page and look at it, and immediately notice that the buttons are left-justified. Wanting them centered, we surround our table tags with `<center> </center>` tags. The result is shown in Figure 19.5(a).

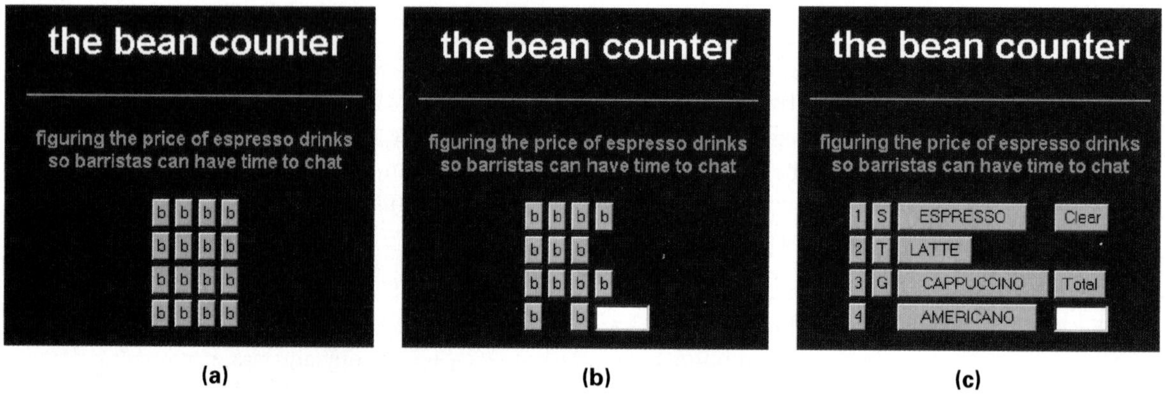

Figure 19.5. *Intermediate stages in the construction of the Bean Counter interface: (a) after Step 1, (b) after Step 3, (c) after Step 4.*

2. Delete Two Buttons

In row 2, cell 4, and row 4, cell 2, we remove the `<input...>` control because these cells are to be empty. In HTML, you can leave a cell empty, but you still need to surround it with the `<td> </td>` tags for it to be a cell.

3. Insert Text Control

From the last section, we decide to name the text control `"price"` because that is the information that will be printed. The window should be five characters wide because no combination of drink inputs will result in a price of more than four digits plus the decimal point. What's more, `onChange` needs a placeholder. So the button control in row 4, cell 4 should be replaced by

```
<input type=text name="price" value="0.00" size=4 onChange=' '>
```

which produces the result shown in Figure 19.5(b). This looks a little lopsided, but we haven't labeled the buttons yet.

4. Label the Buttons

The next task is to pass through the table cells and change the **value** attribute of each button from "b" to its proper button label. The first column is the number of shots (1, 2, 3, 4), the second column is the sizes (S, T, G), and the third column is the drinks (espresso, latté, cappuccino, Americano), which will be given in all uppercase letters.

Because of the row formulation of HTML tables, it is easiest to work row-wise through the table rather than column-wise. The result is shown in Figure 19.5(c). The results are close to being correct but we need to fix them up some.

5. Primp the Interface

Our guess that the form of the form wouldn't be quite right was right. Looking at the design in Figure 19.5(c), we notice that the number buttons are a little wimpy. If the **value="1"** text were to include a space before and after the numeral, **value="ƀ1ƀ"**, the button would be larger. A similar change for the sizes will make the column 2 buttons heftier as well. Spaces will have to be added to the drink buttons to make them all similar in size, but this will require a little experimentation. When the drink buttons are approximately the same size, they will look nicer if they are centered in the column. We can do this by adding the **align** attribute to each cell in column 3. For example,

```
<td align="center">
  <input type = button value = " ESPRESSO " onClick=' '>
</td>
```

These changes will arrange the buttons so that they match the organization in Figure 19.3.

The only remaining difference is that the table in Figure 19.3 is bordered. Adding the **border** attribute to the **<table>** tag would place a border around all of the cells of the table. But we want the border around the table as a whole. So, we use a handy trick: We make a table with only one cell and make the existing table be the table data for that cell; that is, we put the table we've just developed into a one-cell table:

```
<table border=2>
  <tr><td>
    existing table goes here
  </td></tr>
</table>
```

Now our interface matches Figure 19.3.

EVENT-BASED PROGRAMMING

How should the Bean Counter program work? Like a calculator, something should happen as each button is clicked, that is, in response to user-caused events. The rest of the time nothing should be happening. Programming the Bean Counter application amounts to defining in JavaScript the actions that should be performed when each button is clicked. This is called event-based programming. In this section we'll write that event-handling code.

The onClick() Event Handler

The greatest part of the programming task is already done, because the action for the `Total` button is to compute the final price, and that computation, shown between the `<script>` and `</script>` tags in Figure 19.2, has already been programmed. Because this code defines the action we want the computer to perform when the `Total` button is clicked, we make it the `onClick` event handler for the `Total` button. The input control for the `Total` button is now

```
<td>
  <input type = button value = "Total" onClick =' '>
</td>
```

where `onClick` is the **event-handling attribute** for the `Total` button. We insert the price computation code inside the quotes for the `onClick` attribute, as shown in Figure 19.6, and it becomes the `onClick` event handler.

Click Event

Here's what happens. When the barrista clicks on the `Total` button, it causes a **click event** in the browser. The browser, designed to perform an action in response to the click-event, looks for the `onClick` event handler in the `Total` button input control. What the browser should find there is JavaScript instructions to perform the action associated with the button. The browser runs those instructions, implementing the action, and then it waits for the next event. That's why we move the price computation instructions—the JavaScript text of Figure 19.1 with the temporary assignments removed—to go between the quotes of the `onClick` attribute. In this way we have specified what action the browser is to perform on the click-event and how it is to be performed. The browser can now *handle* the click-event. (One more instruction is required, as explained at the end of this section.)

Shots Button

Handling the click-events for the other buttons is even easier. In each case, we ask what action should be performed when this button is clicked. For the first column of buttons—the shots buttons—the answer is to specify the number of shots the customer requests. For example, clicking on the `1` button should cause the `shots` variable to have the value 1. So, to handle the click-event for the `1` button input control, we need to assign `shots` as follows:

```
<td>
<input type = button value = "Total" onClick =
' var price;
  var taxRate = 0.087;
  if (drink == "espresso")
       price = 1.00;
  if (drink == "latte" || drink == "cappuccino"){
       if (ounce == 8)
            price = 1.55;
       if (ounce == 12)
            price = 1.95;
       if (ounce == 16)
            price = 2.35;
  }
  if (drink == "Americano")
       price = 1.10 + .30 * (ounce/8);
  price = price + (shots - 1) * .70;
  price = price + price * taxRate;
//one more assignment is required here
'>
</td>
```

Figure 19.6. *The Total input control with the price computation inserted as the event handler. (Notice that the three temporary declarations of Figure 19.1 have been removed, as has the temporary "alert" command.)*

```
<td>
   <input type = button value = " 1 " onClick = 'shots = 1'>
</td>
```

Notice that the 2 button assigns **shots** the value 2, and so on. Thus the event handlers for the shots buttons require only one JavaScript command each: an assignment of the right number to **shots**.

Size and Drink Buttons

The buttons in the size and drink columns are similar. The action to be performed on a click-event for the size buttons is to assign the **ounce** variable the appropriate value, 8, 12, or 16, as in

```
<td>
   <input type = button value = " S " onClick = 'ounce = 8'>
</td>
```

For the drink column, the **drink** variable gets the name of the drink quoted:

```
<td align="center">
   <input type = button value = " ESPRESSO "
   onClick = 'drink = "espresso"'>
</td>
```

Notice that the single quote surrounds the assignment statement, which uses double quotes. To plan for the use of double-quoted string literals, we chose the single quote for the event handler placeholder in the generic button of the last section.

> FITTIP
>
> **Match Point.** You need to be careful when typing string literals like `"espresso"` because when the computer compares this value with the string literal in the `Total` button's event handler (Figure 19.6, line 3), they must match *exactly*. Misspellings (`"expresso"`), case differences (`"Espresso"`), or even unintentional blanks (`"  espresso"`) will fail to match.

Clear Button and Initializations

Clicking on the **`Clear`** button should reset all of the variables (**`drink`**, **`ounce`**, and **`shots`**) to their initial values. When we think about what those initial values are, we realize that we haven't initialized them yet. In fact, we haven't even declared the variables yet. As is common in programming, working on the solution to one task—setting up the **`Clear`** event handler—reminds us that we have another task to do—declare the variables. So, we first handle the declaration with initialization, and then return to the **`Clear`** event handler.

The declarations should be placed at the beginning of the program, but we don't really have a single program. Rather, we have many little program pieces in the form of event handlers. So, referring to Figure 19.2, we place the declarations for the three variables at the start of the body just after the **`<body>`** tag. As usual, the declarations must be enclosed in **`<script>`** tags. (Notice that **`<script>`** tags were not needed for the event handlers, because the controls *expect* JavaScript.) The declarations are

```
<script language = 'JavaScript'>
  var shots = 1;
  var drink = "none";
  var ounce = 0;
</script>
```

The initial value for **`shots`** is 1 because every espresso drink will have at least one shot. The initial values for **`drink`** and **`ounce`** are chosen to be illegal values, so that if the barrista forgets to specify either one, an erroneous result will be produced, indicating that an input has been forgotten. Finally, the **`Clear`** button should make these same assignments, resulting in its **`onClick`** event handler being

```
<td>
  <input type = button value = "Clear" onClick =
    'shots = 1;
     drink = "none";
     ounce = 0;
     document.Bean.price.value = "0.00"'>
</td>
```

completing both the initialization and **`Clear`** event handler specifications.

The last assignment statement of the **Clear** event handler

```
document.Bean.price.value = "0.00"
```

is important. It places **0.00** in the **price** window, reinitializing it. The next section explains how the assignment statement works.

Referencing Data across Controls

The document that is displayed by the browser can contain one or more forms. Our document has a form named **Bean**. Forms can contain one or more elements, such as **input controls**. Our **Bean** form has an input control named **price**. Input controls can have several attributes. The **price** input control has a value attribute, which was initially assigned **"0.00"**. (See 3. Insert Text Control above.) It is the **value** attribute of the **price** control of the **Bean** form of the document that is displayed by the window.

When we program in JavaScript and want a statement in one control (e.g., the **Clear** button) to change a value in another control (e.g., the value attribute of the **price** text window), we must tell the browser how to navigate among the controls. For that we need the dot operator.

Dot Operator.

The dot operator provides a means of navigation to the proper object. So, the reference

```
object.property
```

selects the **property of the object**. We usually read this reference *right to left*, saying the dot as "of," as in "*property of object*." So, the assignment in the **Clear** button event handler reinitializing the window

```
document.Bean.price.value = "0.00"
```

can be read "the **value** attribute *of* the **price** control *of* the **Bean** form *of* the **document** is assigned **0.00**." Said another way, when the **Clear** button control wants to change the window in the **price** control, it tells the browser to find the **Bean** form in the document, and then within it, find the **price** control, and then within it, find the **value** attribute, and change it.

Changing the Window.

Because the **value** attribute is the content displayed in the **price** window, when the assignment changes the value back to **0.00**, the browser displays the assigned value. In this way, the event handler of one control can refer to an attribute of another input control.

Notice that when the **value** is reassigned, the window displays the **0.00** and thus acts as an output. The idea that something called an *input* control is used to output information may seem strange. But the window can be seen from both the user's and the computer's point of view. If one side gets information (input) from it, the other must have put (output) the information. And vice versa. Input controls are for both input and output.

Displaying the Total. There is one other case where the event handler of one control must refer to the **value** attribute of **price**. The **Total** event handler, the one we built first, must output the price. It does this the same way the **Clear** button event handler clears the **price** window—by assigning to the **value** attribute of **price**. Thus the final line of the **Total** event handler—the one that is a comment in Figure 19.6 promising a revised statement—should be replaced by

```
document.Bean.price.value = price;
```

in order to display the final price. That change completes the **Total** event handler, which means we've finished the Bean Counter application. Run it!

CRITIQUING THE BEAN COUNTER

Every design must be critiqued to ensure that it meets the requirements of the problem and to determine if it can be improved. Therefore, the next task is to experiment with the Bean Counter application, trying a dozen or more sample values to see how well it works.

> FITTIP
>
> **Be a Reviewer.** This critique is most valuable if you have taken a moment to try out the application. Find it at: `www.aw.com/snyder/`

Does our design fulfill the barrista's needs? We'll organize our analysis by topic.

Numbers versus Money

The most obvious and annoying problem with the Bean Counter application is that the final price is shown as a decimal number with several digits of precision rather than as currency with only two digits to the right of the decimal point. This problem can be almost completely fixed by changing the last line of the **Total** button event handler to be

```
document.Bean.price.value = Math.round(price*100)/100;
```

The computation works as follows: The **price** is first multiplied by 100. This changes the price from a "dollars amount" to a "cents amount," that is, the price is expressed as the total number of pennies. That result is then rounded by using the built-in JavaScript function **Math.round()** to eliminate any digits to the right of the decimal point that now represent less than a penny. Finally, that result is divided by 100 again to convert back to a "dollars amount." The computation is a standard way to remove unwanted digits.

The solution doesn't quite solve the problem, because trailing zeros are dropped; that is, $3.00 would print as 3. But this is a small problem that does not arise with the values we have chosen and thus we will ignore it. (The full solution requires some advanced concepts, resulting in the assignment statement:

```
document.Bean.price.value =
      (Math.round(price*100)/100).toString().match(/[\.\d]{4}/);)
```

Organization

The organization of the buttons is generally consistent with how the application will be used. Because espresso drinks are typically named with syntax of the form

<shots> <size> <kind>

as in "double tall latté," the buttons are in a good order for the left-to-right cursor flow. It might make sense to put the **Clear** button on the left side to start the process off, but because there is no obvious place for it and because the cursor will generally be positioned on the **Total** button at the end of the previous purchase—that is, on the right side of the table below the **Clear** button—the design is not inconvenient. We will leave the page organized as it is.

Feedback

One problem with the design is that it doesn't give the barrista any feedback about the current settings of the variables. One principle of user interfaces from Chapter 2 is that there should always be feedback for every operation. There is *some* feedback because buttons are automatically highlighted when they are clicked. But once another button is clicked, the automatic highlighting moves to that button. Adding feedback—for example, a window above each column of buttons that gives the current setting—would be better.

Completeness

Does the Bean Counter fulfill the barrista's needs? Clearly there could be a much more extensive list of products, requiring that we add more buttons, but the application approximates the needs of a barrista with an espresso cart. As an example of extending the design, however, assume that the espresso business sells flavorings for the drinks such as vanilla, hazelnut, and raspberry. Customers would then order a "double tall vanilla latté," and get a shot of vanilla syrup in their drink as well as steamed milk and espresso. Adding a Flavor button to add in the charge for the flavoring might improve the design.

RECAP OF THE BEAN COUNTER APPLICATION

The sample program of Chapter 18 is now a useful application. In the process, we learned the basics of event-based programming using JavaScript. Because this chapter focused on building the application, we didn't spend much time discussing the ideas more generally. So let's review the major ideas now.

We created a graphical user interface for the Bean Counter application by first creating the HTML text to produce the picture of the interface, and then adding

JavaScript—mostly in event handlers for input controls—to make the application work. Though we discussed programs in Chapter 18 as if they were single, monolithic sequences of statements, the Bean Counter application is actually many tiny code segments that are mostly one or two statements long. This is typical of event-based programming. Other, less interactive forms of computing are more monolithic.

Referencing Variables

The only problem that the many-tiny-code-segments property caused is that we didn't immediately know where to place the declarations for the variables, **shots**, **ounce**, and **drink**. Declarations are usually placed at the start of the program. With many event handlers, however, it's as though we have many program "starts." We placed the declarations right after the **<body>** tag, which is not the start of a JavaScript program, just the start of the body of the HTML program. That's why the declarations had to go inside **<script> </script>** tags.

Though any event handler can reference the globally declared variables, the same was not true for the values of the text controls, such as the **price**. The **value** property of this window is local to the control. So, if an event handler of one control needs to place a value in the window of another control, it must describe how to navigate to the item it wants to change. That was the purpose of this code:

```
document.Bean.price.value = "0.00";
```

It uses the dot operator to navigate from the enclosing document to the target control value, by naming the appropriate item at each step along the path. The dot operator is best read right to left and can then be pronounced "of." So the statement reads, "assign **0.00** to the **value** attribute *of* the **price** control *of* the **Bean** form *of* the **document**."

The Bean Counter application illustrates three different ways to reference data values in an event handling program: as variables local to a routine (**taxRate**), as variables global to the routines (**drink**), and as a variable in another control (**document.Bean.price.value**). In the first two cases reference simply requires the variable name because they are defined in the routine (in the case of locals) or in an "enclosing" routine (in the case of globals). Only cross-control references require the dot operator.

Program and Test

The programming process for the Bean Counter application was incremental. We began by producing a minimal 14-line HTML program (Figure 19.4), and then we tested it. We added a skeleton table and tested it. We improved the table one feature at a time, testing as we went. We wrote JavaScript to solve one event handler at a time. And, recognizing similarities among the various events, we developed their event handlers together. Finally, we critiqued the result, improved it, and tested it some more. The result is a 109-line program of nearly 3000 characters. Compared to other first programs, that's huge! This strategy—the result of breaking the task into tiny pieces and testing after each small milestone—had two advantages: At no point did we have to solve any complex tasks that would tax our brains, and the continual testing meant that we immediately knew where any errors were located, namely, in the part we just added. Though the program in Appendix C looks impressive, it is not hard to produce by the program-and-test method. Obviously the approach works generally, as we'll see again in Chapter 22.

Assess the Program Design

When the initial design was completed, we critiqued the result. We were not critiquing the programming. Rather, we were critiquing how well our solution fulfilled the barrista's needs. This is an important part of any design effort, but it is especially critical for software. Since software can do anything, it should perfectly match the requirements. We found that our design did not give the barrista feedback, and so violated one of the principles listed in Chapter 2. This shortcoming could be remedied by adding feedback windows.

SUMMARY

The Bean Counter application has been created using the price computation of Chapter 18 and a GUI developed in this chapter. The result is a substantial program that performs a useful computation, at least if you are a barrista. The application is analogous to the calculator applications provided by operating systems: the user uses the application by clicking or typing. The requested computation is performed immediately in response to the input events.

Part of the activity of the chapter was to write HTML to set up a context in which event handlers perform the actual work. The setup involved placing buttons and other input controls on a Web page, so users could enter the data and receive the results. This is the input/output part of the application and it is principally written in HTML. The other activity was to write JavaScript code for the event handlers. This is the processing part of the application. We used the event-based programming style and the basic instructions we learned in Chapter 18. The style, which is ideal for interactive applications, will be used throughout the rest of this book. Though HTML and JavaScript are separate languages, that won't matter much. Generally, HTML will simply be the input/output part of a program written in JavaScript.

EXERCISES

Multiple Choice

1. HTML pages are made from:
   A. JavaScript
   B. ASCII text
   C. word processing files
   D. any of the above
2. The first tag of a Web page is:
   A. `<script>`
   B. `<head>`
   C. `<top>`
   D. `<html>`
3. Most of the content of a Web page goes inside the:
   A. `<head>` tag
   B. `<body>` tag
   C. `<content>` tag
   D. `<page>` tag
4. The `<bgcolor>` tag sets the:
   A. text color
   B. background color
   C. border color
   D. link color
5. The `<p>` tag is used to:
   A. insert a picture
   B. print a page
   C. insert a paragraph
   D. load a page
6. All of the following are input controls except:
   A. print
   B. radio button
   C. text box
   D. checkbox
7. In JavaScript, **onClick** is a(n):
   A. variable
   B. event
   C. event handler
   D. button

8. The operating system signals that a mouse click has occurred. This is called a(n):
   A. handler
   B. event
   C. trigger
   D. action

9. When a button is clicked, the browser:
   A looks for an `onClick` event handler
   B. looks for the JavaScript program to download
   C. creates the button for the program
   D. none of the above

10. The GUI for a Web-based application is built with:
    A. HTML
    B. JavaScript
    C. both of the above
    D. none of the above

Short Answer

1. The interface for a JavaScript program is a(n) ______.
2. The extension for an HTML page must be ______
3. The ______ tag is used to place a line horizontally across a Web page.
4. The ______ tag is used to place text in italic.
5. A(n) ______ is an indication from the computer that something just happened.
6. A(n) ______ is programming code that responds to an event.
7. A(n) ______ is used to change a value in another control.
8. In the line, **`document.bean.price.value = "0.00"`** the input control is ______, the attribute is ______, and ______ is the form.
9. ______ controls are used for both input and output.
10. ______ is a function used in JavaScript to round numbers.
11. The ______ principle of user interfaces states that an action by the user should get a response from the computer.
12. Java Script is used mainly for ______.
13. In HTML, ______ are used to place and display content.
14. A(n) ______ approach to programming breaks a task into small pieces and tests each piece along the way.

Exercises

1. How many inputs are needed for the Bean Counter program (Figure 19.1) to run correctly?
2. How many outputs does the Bean Counter program have?
3. Explain how variables are initialized. Why do variables need to be initialized?
4. Could radio buttons be used for this application? What would they be like?
5. What would the variable for storing a person's age be called? Create an input control that asks for a person's age.
6. The tax rate for the Bean Counter program is 8.7 percent. What needs to be changed if the tax rate drops to 7 percent?
7. What events are coded into the Bean Counter program?
8. Why won't you know how much your coffee costs until you click on the Total button?
9. Explain why none of these strings match:

   `'Espresso'`, `'espresso'`, `'ESPRESSO'`, `'Expresso'`, `' espresso '`
10. In layman's terms, explain what happens when the user clicks on the Tall button.
11. Why is a dot operator needed when referencing some variables and not others?
12. Can the user make this program crash?

chapter

20

THINKING BIG

Abstraction and Functions

learning objectives

- Discuss two advantages of using abstraction in computing
- Apply JavaScript rules for functions, declarations, return values, function calls, scope of reference, and local/global variable reference
- Write JavaScript functions with the proper structure
- Build a GUI that contains functions, analogous to the Memory Bank Web page
- Explain how computers generate random numbers

Civilization advances by extending the number of important operations which we can perform without thinking about them.

—ALFRED NORTH WHITEHEAD, 1911

THIS CHAPTER explains and demonstrates the concept of functions, the most fundamental idea in software. But as important as functions are to programmers, they are simply the computational form of a more general thinking process known as abstraction. So we will study abstraction as a way of understanding functions and to broaden our understanding of programming. You will notice abstraction in other situations and in other classes—architecture, geology, business, and so on. A clearer understanding of abstraction may make you a better observer and thinker beyond your Fluency class—a terrific bonus to learning the useful idea of functions.

The chapter begins by reviewing the idea of abstraction and its key features: naming, encapsulation, and parameterization. The two main advantages of using abstraction—managing complexity and promoting reuse—are explained. Next we walk through the steps of creating a function, relying heavily on intuition to take us through to the end of the whole process. We then show how to apply a function definition in several Web applications. Our intuitive introduction to functions skipped over many of the nitty-gritty details that we need to know, but once we have the whole picture in mind, we easily describe those details and give more examples. Next we create the Memory Bank, a Web page of useful computations, including the Body Mass Index, which helps us monitor our weight. Adding to this page, we write more functions and gain more experience. We explain random numbers and show how to flip an "electronic coin." Finally, we summarize the deep ideas of the chapter.

ABSTRACTION

As we programmed the Bean Counter in Chapter 19, we steadily changed from thinking about it as a long sequence of HTML and JavaScript commands to thinking about it more abstractly. What do we mean by "more abstractly"?

Names, Encapsulation, and Parameterization

Parts of the Bean Counter program—such as the features of the graphic image or groups of HTML commands—began to have a coherent identity in our minds, and so we *named* them. Thus, rather than just being an amorphous table with unconnected data entries, the program had

> *Button input controls*, a group of HTML commands

> `Total` *button event handler*, a sequence of JavaScript statements

> `shots` *click-events*, a set of actions

These things made sense to us because their shared features associated them in our minds, and we named them accordingly. HTML and JavaScript do not require these abstractions, nor did these abstractions emerge for mystical or magical reasons. They are simply a result of our thinking and reasoning processes. Abstraction is what humans do when they understand and recognize something significant.

Abstraction has two other aspects besides identifying a coherent form or behavior and giving it a name:

> **Encapsulation.** To communicate an abstraction to others (including computers), we must be specific about what the name names; that is, we must define the name. We say that the abstraction **encapsulates** (defines) the phenomenon when we specify the exact meaning for the name.

> **Parameterization.** When the instances share most but not all features (i.e., they are not exactly alike), we must be specific about how they are different. We do this with **parameters**. The parameters are the inputs to the abstraction that allow us to adjust its details.

Thus, when we abstract the common features of similar situations, we give them an identity by naming, encapsulation, and parameterization.

The Advantages of Abstraction in Computing

Though abstraction has a general importance, it is especially important to computing for two reasons.

First, it allows people to manage complexity. By abstracting a computation and giving it a name, we no longer need to think about it as the sequence of operations. For example, in Chapter 10 we named the program *Alphabetize CDs*, which allowed us to stop thinking about it as a sequence of statements for arranging

CDs, and instead summarize them with the *name* for the action. The name "stands" for the operations. We replace thinking about how it works with a name for what it does, making it easier to remember and understand. The complexity of the operation is no longer a concern.

The second reason abstraction is so important in computing is that it allows us to reuse our work and build on it. Programming languages allow us to "package" the operations that the abstraction names into **functions**, also known as **procedures**. The function's name is the name of the abstraction. Then, to perform the operations, we give the name, and the computer performs the operations of the package. In this way, we can build very sophisticated and complex software: First we build functions for simple abstractions; then we use those functions to implement more complex abstractions, which we also package into functions and give names, so they become the building blocks for the next layer of sophistication, and so on.

Because abstraction helps us handle complexity and promotes the reuse of our thinking, it is a fundamental tool of computing. It's a deep idea, but not a difficult one.

CREATING A JS FUNCTION: convertC2F()

When we exchange email with friends in other countries, they often mention their weather, knowing that it's a topic Americans talk about. But they always give the temperature in Celsius. Is 38°C cold or hot? The United States should join the rest of the world in using Celsius, of course, but because that is unlikely, we must convert Celsius to Fahrenheit. The conversion process is a coherent, well-defined process (an abstraction). It is ideal for packaging into a function. Recall from school that the formula for the relationship between the Fahrenheit and Celsius temperature scales is

$$Fahrenheit = \tfrac{9}{5}\ Celsius + 32$$

This is an equation, of course, not an assignment statement. With the equation, we can "solve for Celsius":

$$\tfrac{5}{9}\ (Fahrenheit - 32) = Celsius$$

To command the computer to convert Celsius to Fahrenheit, we must encode the first of these two equations into a JavaScript function. (We will encode the second equation in JavaScript later so we can convert back.)

Function Syntax

A function "packages" computation. JavaScript defines the packaging syntax as

```
function <name> ( <parameter list> ) {
   <function definition>
}
```

As usual, the text not in meta-brackets must be given literally. The <*name*>, given immediately after the keyword **function**, is followed by a pair of parentheses containing the <*parameter list*>. The parameters name the inputs to the computation; they are separated by commas. Finally, enclosed in a pair of curly braces, is the **function definition**, which is the sequence of JavaScript statements that define the computation. Notice that the closing curly brace is located conspicuously on its own line so that we notice it when reading the program.

Defining convertC2F()

To write the Celsius-to-Fahrenheit conversion as a function, we first decide on a name. We choose the name **convertC2F** because it briefly summarizes what's to be done. We need only one parameter, the temperature in Celsius; we'll name it **tempInC**. We'll call the answer **tempInF**, which makes it a variable and implies that it must be declared. Writing the statements for the function definition is straightforward given the preceding equation. Except for one detail, the entire function specification—it is called a **function declaration**—becomes

```
function convertC2F ( tempInC ) {
  var tempInF;
  tempInF = (9 / 5) * tempInC + 32;       //Incomplete
}
```

Notice that the **convertC2F** function matches the function syntax given earlier. Also, notice that the input parameter isn't declared. That's because the variables of the <*parameter list*> are automatically declared to be variables in JavaScript, which saves us some typing.

Returning the Answer

The purpose of functions is to package the computation so that when we provide the value(s) for the input parameter(s), for example, 38, the computation is performed for us and the result is returned. Thus, when we write **convertC2F(38)**, we expect to get the Fahrenheit temperature back because the computer will follow the instructions packaged in the function, thereby computing the answer. Because our conversion function computes only one value, it's pretty obvious what value to return as the answer, **tempInF**. But in general, function definitions compute many values, and the computer must be told which one is the answer. Thus, there is a statement in JavaScript,

```
return <answer>;
```

that says "the computation is now finished, and this is the answer." The <*answer*> can be either a variable or an expression, so we can complete our conversion function declaration with one additional line and, for good measure, a comment:

```
function convertC2F ( tempInC ) {
// Converts its parameter, assumed to be a Celsius
// temperature, into the equivalent Fahrenheit
   var tempInF;
   tempInF = (9 / 5) * tempInC + 32;
   return tempInF;
}
```

The function, which will be used by giving the name with a value for the parameter in parentheses, for example, **convertC2F(38)**, is defined and ready to use.

The equation given earlier describes the relationship between Celsius and Fahrenheit; the function just completed tells the computer (or anyone else) how to find the Fahrenheit temperature from the Celsius temperature. The equation states a relationship; the function describes a process.

APPLYING FUNCTIONS

We can use JavaScript to write a simple Web page that performs the **convertC2F()** function. (It is customary to write functions with their parentheses for the parameter list, even when the parameters are not given.)

An HTML Page to Host JavaScript

Figure 20.1 shows the text for running the **convertC2F()** function within an HTML document, and the resulting output. Notice that the JavaScript code in Figure 20.1 is surrounded by **<script> </script>** tags. The function is given and there is a special function, **document.write()**. We will explain **document.write()** momentarily.

How the convertC2F() Function Runs

Here's what happens when the program in Figure 20.1 runs. The browser begins by reading the HTML, but it doesn't create the page yet. Think of it as looking over the HTML to see what has to be done. When it reaches any **<script>** tag, the browser removes it and all the text up to and including the next **</script>** tag. It then turns over the text between the tags to the JavaScript Interpreter to process, before continuing to read the file.

The JS Interpreter works like a sophisticated Fetch/Execute Cycle (Chapter 9), fetching JavaScript statements and executing them. In the present case, the JS Interpreter records the fact that a function by the name of **convertC2F** is being declared, that it has a single parameter, and that its definition is the JavaScript code given. The function doesn't run at this point; the JS Interpreter just makes a note of its definition.

Once the JS Interpreter is past the closing curly brace, it comes to the **document.write()** function. Recognizing this as a built-in JavaScript function—that is, provided by the system—the JS Interpreter does what the function commands.

```
<html>
  <head><title>Converter Usage Example</title></head>
  <body><font face='Helvetica'><b><center>
    <script language = 'JavaScript'>
      function convertC2F ( tempInC ) {
      // Converts its parameter, assumed to be a Celsius
      // temperature, into the equivalent Fahrenheit
        var tempInF;
        tempInF = (9 / 5) * tempInC + 32;
        return tempInF;
      }
      document.write('<h2>38 degrees C is ' + convertC2F(38)
                              + ' degrees F</h2>');
  </script>
</body>
</html>
```

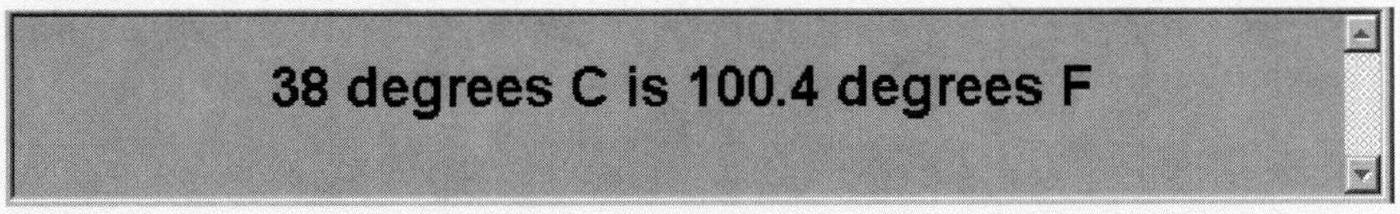
38 degrees C is 100.4 degrees F

Figure 20.1. *An HTML page showing the use of the* **convertC2F()** *JavaScript function to find the Fahrenheit equivalent of 38°C.*

The document.write() Function

The **document.write(<*text*>)** function is a special JavaScript function that outputs <*text*> directly into the HTML document. Most important, like all JavaScript statements, **document.write()** is performed before the page is created, allowing us to create HTML commands on-the-fly with JavaScript. This ability to create HTML commands with JavaScript and write them into the HTML file before the page is created means that we can create customized-to-the-situation Web pages.

Where does **document.write()** put the text in the HTML source? At the browser's current position. That is, the browser has just removed all of the text between **<script>** and **</script>**, so that's its current position. It is as if the JavaScript were replaced by the text from the **document.write()**. See Figure 20.2.

In the present case the **document.write()** will add a second-level header (**<h2>**) line to the HTML file.

The argument to the **document.write()** function is composed of three pieces joined together with the concatenate (+) operator. The three pieces are the string literal **'<h2>38 degrees C is '**, the value resulting from running the function **convertC2F(38)** with its input value of 38, and the string literal **' degrees F</h2>'**. The JS Interpreter cannot assemble these three pieces until it knows the value of the **convertC2F(38)** function.

HTML Source File

```
<html>
  <head><title>Explain</title></head>
  <body><p> The browser reads the
     HTML before it creates the page.
     When it comes to a script tag it
     processes it immediately. There
     may be document.write()s and
     if so, it writes the argument
     <script language="JavaScript">
        document.write("into the file");
     </script>
     at the point of the script tags.
   </body>
</html>
```

HTML Used for Page

```
<html>
  <head><title>Explain</title></head>
  <body><p> The browser reads the
     HTML before it creates the page.
     When it comes to a script tag it
     processes it immediately. There
     may be document.write()s and
     if so it writes the argument

     into the file

     at the point of the script tags.
   </body>
</html>
```

Figure 20.2. *An HTML source file containing a JavaScript* `document.write()`*, and the HTML text used by the browser to create the page.*

Applying `convertC2F()`

To find the value of `convertC2F(38)`, the JavaScript Interpreter performs the following operations (refer to the code in Figure 20.1):

1. Finds the declaration that it saved for the function
2. Assigns the value 38 to `tempInC`, the function's parameter
3. Declares `tempInF`; that is, notes that it will be used as a variable
4. Computes the value of the expression `(9 / 5) * tempInC + 32`, which is 100.4
5. Assigns the value 100.4 to `tempInF`
6. Returns the value of `tempInF`, that is, 100.4, as the value of the function

On completion of these steps, the JS Interpreter returns to working on the `document.write()`.

Having converted 38°C to 100.4°F, the JS Interpreter joins the three pieces to make the second-level header text. Then it inserts the header line text,

```
<h2>38 degrees C is 100.4 degrees F</h2>
```

which has been color coded to show its parts, into the HTML file. That completes the operation of the `document.write()` function.

At this point, the JS Interpreter has finished its work and quits, causing the browser to begin processing HTML again. But, now there is a new line in the HTML to process, namely the `<h2>` header line that has just been inserted. When the browser finishes reading the file, it composes the page and displays it.

Applying convertC2F() Again

Now that we know that 38°C is hot—at least as weather goes—we might consider other ways to use our new **`convertC2F()`** function.

A List of Temperature Equivalents. One possible use for our new **`convertC2F()`** function is to create a list of Celsius-to-Fahrenheit equivalents. Then, we could try to learn the pairs as an aid to estimating the temperature equivalents when there is no computer handy. Figure 20.3 shows the HTML and JavaScript for creating the list and the Web page they produce. The behavior is completely analogous to the description of the last paragraph; take a minute to work through it now.

A Table of Temperature Equivalents. The page in Figure 20.3 is not very pretty. The list should have been a two-column table. Revising the HTML and JavaScript to produce such a table is straightforward. The new code is shown in Figure 20.4. (Take another minute to work through it now.)

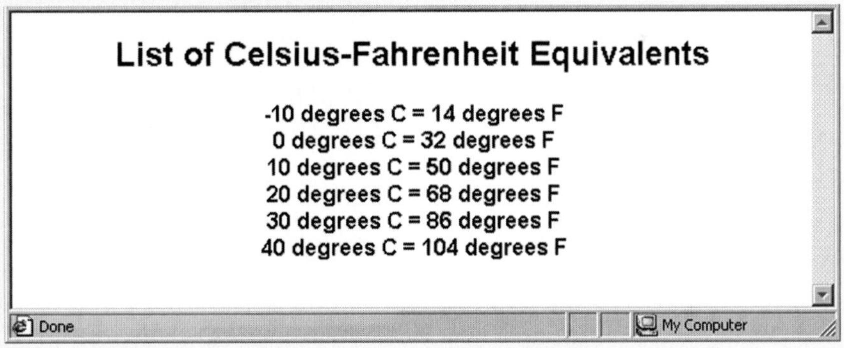


```
<html>
  <head><title>Conversion List</title></head>
  <body><font face='Helvetica'><b><center>
    <script language = 'JavaScript'>
      function convertC2F ( tempInC ) {
      // Converts its parameter, assumed to be a Celsius
      // temperature, into the equivalent Fahrenheit
        var tempInF;
        tempInF = (9 / 5) * tempInC + 32;
        return tempInF;
      }
      document.write('<h2> List of Celsius-Fahrenheit
                Equivalents </h2>');
      document.write('-10 degrees C = ' + convertC2F(-10)
                      + ' degrees F<br>');
```

```
      document.write('  0 degrees C = ' + convertC2F(0)
                          + ' degrees F<br>');
      document.write(' 10 degrees C = ' + convertC2F(10)
                          + ' degrees F<br>');
      document.write(' 20 degrees C = ' + convertC2F(20)
                          + ' degrees F<br>');
      document.write(' 30 degrees C = ' + convertC2F(30)
                          + ' degrees F<br>');
      document.write(' 40 degrees C = ' + convertC2F(40)
                          + ' degrees F<br>');
    </script>
  </body>
</html>
```

Figure 20.3. *The HTML and JavaScript to display a list of equivalent temperatures.*

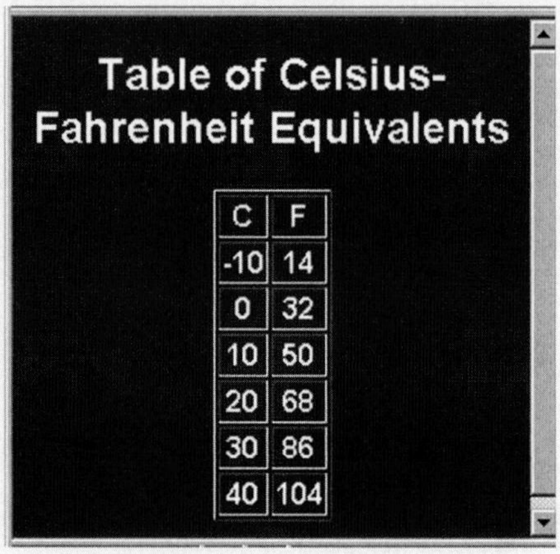

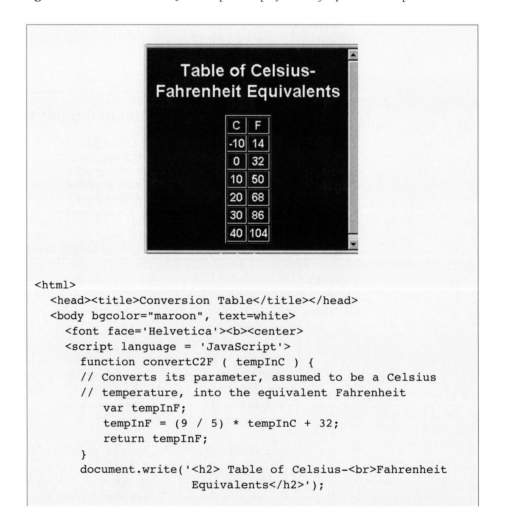

```
<html>
  <head><title>Conversion Table</title></head>
  <body bgcolor="maroon", text=white>
    <font face='Helvetica'><b><center>
    <script language = 'JavaScript'>
      function convertC2F ( tempInC ) {
      // Converts its parameter, assumed to be a Celsius
      // temperature, into the equivalent Fahrenheit
         var tempInF;
         tempInF = (9 / 5) * tempInC + 32;
         return tempInF;
      }
      document.write('<h2> Table of Celsius-<br>Fahrenheit
                     Equivalents</h2>');
```

```
        document.write('<table border=1><th> C </th><th> F
                        </th>');
        document.write('<tr align=center><td>-10</td><td>'
                        + convertC2F(-10) + '</td></tr>');
        document.write('<tr align=center><td> 0 </td><td>'
                          + convertC2F(0)    + '</td></tr>');
        document.write('<tr align=center><td> 10</td><td>'
                          + convertC2F(10)   + '</td></tr>');
        document.write('<tr align=center><td> 20</td><td>'
                          + convertC2F(20)   + '</td></tr>');
        document.write('<tr align=center><td> 30</td><td>'
                          + convertC2F(30)   + '</td></tr>');
        document.write('<tr align=center><td> 40</td><td>'
                          + convertC2F(40)   + '</td></tr>');
        document.write('</table>');
    </script>
  </body>
</html>
```

Figure 20.4. *HTML and JavaScript to produce a table of equivalents.*

Reusing Functions

All three of these Web pages have different HTML, but they all use the *same* **convertC2F()** function. This is the main point of all of the examples: Once we take the trouble to work out a function, we can use it over and over again. We've already thought through the logic and packaged it. Now, any time we need a conversion, we run the function by giving its name and its parameter(s)—that is, the number we want converted. The computer does the rest. In this way, we can focus on other things—how pretty the page looks, for example—rather than programming operations like conversion. The write-once-use-repeatedly property of procedures is one reason why functions are so important to us.

FITTIP

Hot Tip. Notice that it's not hard to estimate Celsius temperatures in Fahrenheit. Remember a couple of pairs, such as 20°C is 68°F or 30°C is 86°F, and for each 10° in Celsius up or down, add or subtract 18° in Fahrenheit. So, 10°C is 50°F.

JAVASCRIPT RULES FOR FUNCTIONS

We have shown how functions package computation, and the idea is reasonably intuitive. But like everything about computers, the details of functions must be exactly right. In this section, we explain the details of JavaScript functions carefully so you can meet the computer's exacting standards when you write your own functions. Though the rules are for JavaScript, most programming languages have a similar set of rules. The topics to be covered are the following:

- Function declarations
- Selecting names
- Parameter variables
- Return value
- Scope of reference
- Local variables
- Global variables
- Multiple parameters
- Calling functions
- Arguments
- Parameter reference

Along the way we give examples of functions.

Function Declarations

As mentioned earlier, the function declaration has the following syntax:

```
function <name> ( <parameter list> ) {
  <function definition>
}
```

The function declaration embodies the abstraction, specifying how the function works. For example, in the function declaration

```
function febDays ( year ) {
//A function giving the days in February
  if ((year % 4)== 0)          //Test for leap year
      return 29;               //Yes, incl. leap day
  else
      return 28;               //No, regular year
}
```

the *<name>* is **febDays**, the *<parameter list>* is the single parameter, **year**, and the *<function definition>* is everything between the curly braces (that is, the **if/else** statement). As a rule, programmers group their function declarations together so that they're easy to find.

Selecting Function Names

The function *<name>* is an identifier, just like variable names are identifiers. This means *<name>* follows the same rules as variable names: The function *<name>* must start with a letter and can contain any combination of letters, numerals, or underscore; it is case sensitive. Don't use JavaScript's reserved words, listed in Appendix B, or you will get *name conflicts*. It is smart to select a name that describes what the function does.

Parameters

Generally, the <*parameter list*> is a sequence of identifiers, separated by commas. A function doesn't have to have parameters, but it must still have the parentheses in its function declaration, as in

```
function cheshireCat () {
  return "Smile";
}
```

Parameters are the input to the computation, so most functions have them. (There are other ways to give input, as explained later, which is why parameters are not necessary.) Parameters can be thought of as *implicitly declared variables*. So, like function names and explicitly declared variable names, parameter names must follow the usual rules for identifiers.

Return Value

A JavaScript function can have any number of **return** statements, but when the JS Interpreter reaches one, it will treat the function as complete. (Also, functions need not have any **return** statements, as explained later.) Because the return value can be either a variable or a expression, it is common to make the last computation of a function part of the **return** statement. The Fahrenheit-to-Celsius conversion function, that is, the opposite conversion, shows this technique:

```
function convertF2C ( fTemp ) {
// Convert temps from Fahrenheit to Celsius
  return (5 / 9) * (fTemp – 32);
}
```

The technique saves a declaration, compared to the **convertC2F()** function, which needed the explicitly declared variable **tempInF**. (See the declaration for **convertC2F()**.) The approaches do the same thing, and it doesn't matter to the computer which you use.

Scope of Reference

As we saw with the Bean Counter program (Chapters 18 and 19), we usually assign a value to a variable at one place in a program and use the value at another place. When there are no functions, it's generally possible to assign a value to a variable at any place in the program and use the value anywhere else. However, with functions there are limits on where in the program this is possible. The **scope** of a variable describes where and when it can be referenced—that is, assigned and used. The two scopes of interest are local and global scopes corresponding to the two roles of variables, local and global.

Local Variables

If a variable is declared in a function, it is known only within that function (that is, only *inside* the curly braces). Thus **tempInF** can be used within `convertC2F()`, but not outside. This kind of variable is called a **local variable**. It is local to the function; it has local scope. This means that if two or more functions each use the same name for a variable, there is no conflict. Both variables are known only inside their respective functions. So, for example, in the functions

```
function convert2Frac (time) {
// Convert time in minutes to a fraction of an hour
  return time/60;
}
function convert2Min (time) {
// Convert time a fraction of an hour into minutes
  return time * 60;
}
```

that convert back and forth between time expressed in minutes and time expressed as a fraction of an hour, the two uses of the parameter `time` will not conflict should they both be used in the same Web page. (Recall that parameters are implicitly declared variables.)

Global Variables

Variables declared outside of a function declaration are called **global variables**. They are global to the function. We saw an example of global variable declarations in Chapter 19, when `shots`, `ounce`, and `drink` were declared in the Bean Counter example. Although we didn't explicitly use functions in that program, the JS Interpreter treats event handlers as functions, so the effect is the same. Variables like `shots` had to be declared outside of the event handlers so they could be known and used by several event handlers. Global variables are another way to get input into a function.

FITTIP

Very Global. An HTML file can have several blocks of JavaScript `<script> </script>` tags. All global variables declared within each pair are known in all of the other pairs.

Multiple Parameters

The parameter list of a function can have any number of items, separated by commas.

Two-Parameter Functions. Suppose we want to calculate our Body Mass Index (BMI)—an index of a person's weight in proportion to their height. ("Normal" is generally accepted as a BMI in the range 18.5 to 25.) We will need two parameters, weight and height. The formula for BMI when weight and height are given in metric units is simply

$Index = weight / height^2$

leading to the simple two-parameter function

```
function bmiM ( weightKg, heightM ) {
  // Figure Body Mass Index in metric units
    return weightKg / (heightM * heightM);
}
```

There is no "square" in JavaScript, so we must multiply **`heightM`** times itself.

For weight and height given in English units, BMI is defined as

$Index = 4.89\ weight / height^2$

where *weight* is in pounds and *height* is in feet. Because a height given in feet and inches is a little messy to work with, we take height in inches and convert it to feet. Therefore, the function declaration for the English BMI is

```
function bmiE ( weightLBS, heightIn ) {
  // Figure Body Mass Index in English units
    var heightFt = heightIn / 12;        // Change to feet
    return 4.89 * weightLBS / (heightFt * heightFt);
}
```

The **`heightFt`** variable is a decimal number of feet. For example, 66 inches, which is 5 feet, 6 inches, results in **`heightFt ⇔ 5.5`**.

Combining Functions. If we want a single function that takes **`"metric"`** or **`"English"`** as its first parameter, describing the units of the measurements, and the height and weight as the next two parameters, we can solve the problem generally with a three-parameter function:

```
function BMI (units, height, weight ) {
  // Compute BMI in either metric or English
    if (units == "English")
      return bmiE(weight, height);
    else
      return bmiM(weight, height);
}
```

Calling Functions

Notice that the **`BMI()`** function uses the earlier **`bmiE()`** and **`bmiM()`** functions when it needs the BMI calculated. Using a function—that is, asking for its computation to be performed—is known as **calling** or **invoking** the function. We might say, "The **`BMI()`** function invokes the **`bmiE()`** function when the units are English." There is only one function declaration because it is necessary to specify how the function works only once. But the whole point of writing functions is to use them, so they are usually called many times.

Arguments

When we call a function, we must supply values for the parameters. These input values are known as **arguments**. The key points about arguments are that there is the same number of them as there are parameters, and for each parameter there is a corresponding argument. So, to use the **BMI()** function to compute the index for a person standing 5 feet, 6 inches (66 in. or 1.65 m) and weighing 125 lbs. (55 kg), we must supply three arguments corresponding to the three parameters of type of units, height, and weight:

```
BMI("English", 66, 125)
```

And, because the arguments correspond to the parameters, we must give them in the same order as the parameters. So, the 66-inch height is the second argument because **height** is the second parameter of **BMI()**. If we list the arguments in the wrong order, we'll get the wrong result because the computer has no way of determining when arguments are mismatched with parameters. The function's definition determines how the arguments must be given. Period. So, for example, **weight** is the third parameter of **BMI()**, making 125 the third argument to the call. For **bmiE()**, the first parameter is **weightLBS**, so the arguments of its call have been customized to the situation, making

```
bmiE(125, 66)
```

the proper call. The answer is 20.2, by the way.

FITCAUTION

Wrong Arguments. Calling a function with the arguments given in the wrong order is an extremely difficult bug to find in a program because it goes unnoticed so easily. So take care when listing arguments in the first place.

Parameter Reference

When we call a function, the arguments are assigned to the parameters just as if they were assignment statements. Thus, calling the **BMI()** function

```
BMI("English", 66, 125)
```

is the same as if we had written in its place the code

```
var units = "English";              //Assign value to 1st param
var height = 66;                    //Assign value to 2nd param
var weight = 125;                   //Assign value to 3rd param
if (units == "English")             //Code of function def
    return bmiE(weight, height);
else
    return bmiM(weight, height);
```

As we said before, the parameters are like implicitly declared local variables, and they can be used as such. In each case, the initial assignment is the corresponding argument value. The best part about this view is that we can, if we wish, assign values to the parameters. So, we could have written the **bmiE()** function as follows:

```
function bmiE ( weightLBS, height ) {
  // Figure Body Mass Index in English units
  height = height / 12;    // height is inches;
                           // change to feet
  return 4.89 * weightLBS / (height * height);
}
```

That is, we do not have to declare a separate **heightFt** variable, the way we did before; we can simply change the **height** parameter from inches to feet.

> FITTIP
>
> **Easy Test.** JavaScript must run in an HTML Web page definition. Thus to test JS functions, it is smart to keep a text file handy with all the necessary HTML already in it, called, say, eztest.html. Then you can copy the JavaScript into it, making function testing easy. One such template is
>
> ```
> <html><head><title>EZ</title></head><body><script>
>   function definition goes here
>   alert(function call with arguments goes here);
> </script></body></html>
> ```
>
> where the italicized text must be replaced with the function to be tested.

THE MEMORY BANK WEB PAGE

Remembering useless trivia is easy, probably because it's fun to know. For example,

Q: Who was the fifth Beatle?
A: Stuart Sutcliffe was a founding member of the Beatles with Lennon, McCartney, and Harrison.

Remembering useful stuff seems to be more difficult for some reason. So, in this section, we create a Memory Bank Web page of useful computations as a memory aid. The Web page will give us a chance to practice programming with functions. We can also save the page in our Web space and perhaps add to it later.

Figure 20.5 shows the HTML image for the initial Memory Bank Web page. Here is how it is supposed to work. Each table row is a computation. Each window in the row except the last is an input to the computation; the last window is the output. The user types inputs into the window(s), and when they are all entered, gets the answer back in the output window by clicking. Looking at the HTML image, we notice that each row has two or more input controls that need event handlers. All we need to do is program the JavaScript to implement the computations and define the event handlers.

> FITTIP
>
> **Memory Aid.** The best way to learn both the ideas and the practical skills of the Memory Bank is to build the program yourself as you read along.

Plan the Memory Bank Interface

Before starting, notice the two new features in this page. All of the rows take text input, and the Body Mass Index row uses radio buttons.

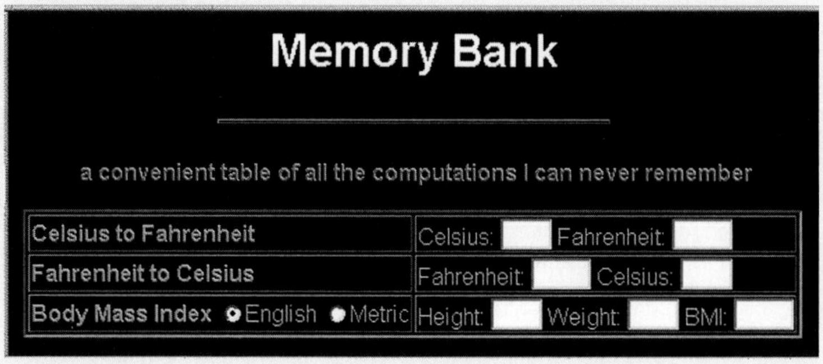


```
<html>
  <head><title>Memory Bank of Computations</title></head>
  <body bgcolor="#000000" text="#FF9900" >
    <font face="Helvetica", "Arial">
    <h1 align="center"><font color="#FFFFFF">
      Memory Bank</font></h1>
    <hr width=50%>
    <b><p align="center">
      <font color="#FF0000"> a convenient table of all
        the computations I can never remember </font></p>
      <form name="memory">
        <table align="center" border=2>
          <tr>
            <td><b>Celsius to Fahrenheit</b></td>
            <td> Celsius:
              <input type = text name = "cTemp" size = 4
               onChange=' C-to-F Event Handler '> Fahrenheit:
              <input type = text name = tempInF
               size = 5></td></tr>
          <tr>
            <td><b>Fahrenheit to Celsius</b></td>
            <td> Fahrenheit:
              <input type = text name = "fTemp" size = 5
               onChange=' F-to-C Event Handler '> Celsius:
              <input type = text name = tempInC
               size = 4></td></tr>
          <tr>
            <td><b>Body Mass Index </b>
              <input type = radio name = "pick1" checked =
                    true
               onClick=' The English Event Handler '>English
              <input type = radio name= "pick1"
               onClick=' The Metric Event Handler '>Metric</td>
            <td>Height:
              <input type = text name = "howtall" size = 4
               onChange = ' The Tall Event Handler '> Weight:
              <input type = text name = "howwide" size = 4
               onChange = ' The Wide Event Handler '> BMI:
```

```
                <input type = text name = "shape"
                 size = 5></td></tr>
            </table></b>
          </form>
        <script language = "JavaScript">
          Function declarations go here
        </script>
    </body>
</html>
```

Figure 20.5. *The initial Memory Bank interface and its image. This program can be downloaded from* `www.aw.com/snyder/`.

Using Text Windows for Input. We already know how to use the `input` control for output. Using it for input is different in only two ways. First, we don't need to mention the `value` attribute explicitly. The `value` property is still part of the control, and as before we will refer to the contents of the window using `value`. But if we are satisfied to have the window blank when the page loads, we don't need to initialize `value` explicitly. Second, we need an event handler to perform whatever action is to happen when the user enters information into the window. Typing into the window is analogous to clicking on a button, but it's called a *change-event* rather than a *click-event*. So the event handler is called `onChange`.

Using Radio Buttons. As introduced in Chapter 19, radio buttons are like regular button controls with a name attribute and an `onClick` event handler. Instead of having a label, however, a radio button has text following the input control. Radio buttons are different from standard buttons in two ways. First, several radio button controls are usually used together, and only one of them should be set at any time. This means, among other things, that all of the radio controls have to have the same name. Then, when one button is clicked, any other set radio button with the same name is cleared automatically. Second, it is often handy to preset one of the buttons. This is done with the `checked = true` attribute.

The Computations: Reuse Five Functions. Turning now to programming the Memory Bank Web page, notice that most of the work is already done for us. The functions we developed in the earlier sections, `convertC2F()`, `convertF2C()`, `bmiE()`, `bmiM()`, and `BMI()`, do most of the computation. So, our first step is to insert the declarations for these five functions between the `<script> </script>` tags of the Memory Bank page. The rest of the programming involves specifying event handlers.

Specify the Event Handlers

The Memory Bank page requires six event handlers, one each for the two temperature conversions and four for the Body Mass Index calculation. They are shown in italic text in Figure 20.5.

The C-to-F Event Handler. The Celsius to Fahrenheit table row of Figure 20.5 refers to the *C-to-F Event Handler* as follows:

```
<td><b>Celsius to Fahrenheit</b></td>
<td> Celsius:
  <input type = text name = "cTemp" size = 4
   onChange=' C-to-F Event Handler '> Fahrenheit:
  <input type = text name = tempInF size = 5></td>
```

What should happen when the user enters a Celsius temperature? Obviously, we must call the `convertC2F()` function with the entered temperature as the argument and place the result in the output window. The function is already defined, so the only questions are how to get the input out of the `cTemp` window and how to place the answer in the `tempInF` window. The answer to both questions is that the event handler will use the **dot notation**, as described in Chapter 19. For example,

```
document.memory.tempInF.value =
       convertC2F(document.memory.cTemp.value)
```

does the job. So, the event handler specification can be written as

```
onChange = 'document.memory.tempInF.value =
       convertC2F(document.memory.cTemp.value)'
```

However, because both windows are part of the same document, and they are part of the same form, we can drop the first two specifiers. So, the *C-to-F Event Handler* is

```
onChange = 'tempInF.value = convertC2F(cTemp.value)'
```

This can be read in English as "when there's a change to the `cTemp` window, use its `value` as the argument to the `convertC2F()` function, compute the result, and assign the result as the `value` of the `tempInF` window."

The F-to-C Event Handler. The *F-to-C Event Handler* is only slightly different from the *C-to-F* case. Only the three names are different—the name of the input window (`fTemp`), the name of the conversion function (`convertF2C()`), and the name of the output window (`tempInC`). Thus the event handler is

```
onChange = 'tempInC.value = convertF2C(fTemp.value)'
```

which completes the first two rows of the Memory Bank page.

The BMI Event Handlers. The Body Mass Index row requires four event handlers. The first two will handle clicking of the radio buttons. As with all event handlers, we ask, what should be done when the event happens? Clearly, we need to remember which unit is set, `English` or `metric`. We will use a variable to record this information, and because the variable will be used in all of the event handlers of this row, it should be a *global* variable—that is, defined outside of any function or handler. We'll call the variable `measure`, and declare it

```
var measure = "English";
```

just after the `<script>` tag. Giving **measure** the initial value of **English** makes it the default measurement, which is like having "preclicked" the English radio button. For this reason, we preset it using **checked = true**. (The **English** default is correct for the United States, of course, but elsewhere we would initialize it to **metric** and preset that radio button.)

Now we can define the event handlers for the **pick1** radio buttons:

```
<td>Body Mass Index
  <input type = radio name = "pick1" checked = true
   onClick=' The English Event Handler '>English
  <input type = radio name= "pick1"
   onClick=' The Metric Event Handler '>Metric</td>
```

They assign the correct value to **measure** in a single JavaScript assignment statement. Thus

```
onClick = 'measure = "English"'
```

is the *English Event Handler*, and

```
onClick = 'measure = "metric"'
```

is the *Metric Event Handler*. Notice that although **English** is the initial value for **measure**, we still need an *English Event Handler*, because the user might click on the **Metric** button, and then click on the **English** button. The *English Event Handler* resets **measure** back to **English**.

The last two event handlers, the *Tall Event Handler* and the *Wide Event Handler*, are simple now that everything has been set up:

```
<td>Height:
  <input type = text name = "howtall" size = 4
   onChange = ' The Tall Event Handler '> Weight:
  <input type = text name = "howwide" size = 4
   onChange = ' The Wide Event Handler '> BMI:
  <input type = text name = "shape" size = 5></td>
```

(The **shape input** control doesn't need an event handler because its window is used as an output.)

What should happen on a change to the **howtall** window (height specification)? It might seem that nothing should happen because the weight hasn't been specified yet. But maybe it has. There is no requirement that the windows be filled in left-to-right order. There are two ways to solve the problem. The easiest is to run the **BMI()** function in response to a change in either window. In this case

```
onChange =
     'shape.value=BMI(measure,howtall.value,howwide.value)'
```

is *both* the *Tall Event Handler* and the *Wide Event Handler*. Notice that the global variable **measure**, known to all functions and event handlers, is the argument for the first parameter position, the value from the **howtall** window is the argument for the second parameter position, and the value from the **howwide** window is the argument for the last parameter position.

Handling Input Given in Any Order

What happens if the **BMI()** runs when the user has entered only the height, that is, the **howwide** window is blank, which would be interpreted as 0? The two functions **bmiE()** and **bmiM()** both run and produce 0, so that's the value that will be set in the **shape** window. What happens if **BMI()** runs when the user has entered only the weight? The two functions **bmiE()** and **bmiM()** both run, but there is a divide by 0. This is an illegal operation in arithmetic, so **INFINITY** will be displayed in the **shape** window. Either way, there is an indication that the result is invalid, and in any event the user knows that one window hasn't been filled yet. So, it is a solution, but it is not a very elegant solution.

If only one of the inputs to a multiparameter function is set, it seems that nothing should happen. So the best solution is for the *Tall* and *Wide Event Handlers* to test to see if the **value** from the other window has been set. If it hasn't, do nothing. If it has, call **BMI()**. So, the *Tall Event Handler* is

```
onChange = 'if (howwide.value != 0)
      shape.value = BMI(measure,howtall.value,howwide.value)'
```

which tests to see whether the weight has also been changed—that is, whether its **value** is different from 0. If it has changed, the *Tall Event Handler* calls **BMI()**. Otherwise, nothing happens. The *Wide Event Handler*

```
onChange = 'if (howtall.value != 0)
      shape.value = BMI(measure,howtall.value,howwide.value)'
```

is the opposite, checking the **value** in the **howtall** window to see if it is different from 0. Including these two event handlers ensures that nothing happens until nonzero data is entered in each window.

Notice that the "test for 0 input" conditional statement in the event handlers could have been placed in the **BMI()** function. This would not have been a good choice, however. The reason is that the problem of not-yet-specified arguments is not caused by the way we are using the **BMI()** function and is not a property of the computation itself. Rather, the problem of not-yet-specified arguents is caused by the user giving the values one at a time in an unknown order. So, we must protect the **BMI()** function from computing with only partial data. It is a problem for the event handler, not the Body Mass Index computation. So that's where it should be handled.

Having completed the initial development, we consider next how to make the Memory Bank page more useful.

IMPROVING THE MEMORY BANK PAGE

The Memory Bank helps us convert temperatures and find our Body Mass Index, but there are many other features that we might like to have. Flipping coins—essential for deciding who buys coffee after class—would be handy. If we're using electronic money, we need electronic "coins" to make these decisions. So, we will add a row to our Memory Bank page to flip an electronic "coin." We'll also add a "think of a number between 1 and *n*" process. Both additions will allow us to discuss random numbers, an important IT topic, and will give us more experience with functions.

Random Numbers and Flipping Electronic Coins

The question of what is a random number is interesting philosophically. Is 2 a random number? If it comes from a process that produces numbers—say 1 and 2—and whether the next number produced will be 2 is completely unpredictable, then it is random. For example, 1 could correspond to heads and 2 to tails of a flipped coin. But is coin flipping unpredictable? Suppose we know the mass of the coin, the force with which it is flipped, the distance to the floor, etc. Perhaps, then, we could predict when 2 would be produced. Would it be random then? We avoid such philosophical problems by saying a **random number** is a measurement of an unpredictable natural phenomenon, like the particle emissions from the decay of a radioactive substance, say U_{238}, over a fixed time period.

Computers are deterministic (see Chapter 9). That is, if a computer performs a task with the known input, it is possible to predict perfectly what answer it computes and how it computes it. Determinacy makes it impossible to generate random numbers with a computer, because any program to produce random numbers will have a completely predictable output.

FITBYTE

Flipping Out. The mathematician John von Neumann, one of the pioneers of computing, once said, "Anyone who attempts to generate random numbers by deterministic means is, of course, living in a state of sin."

So, instead, computers generate something called **pseudo-random numbers**. Computer scientists have developed sophisticated algorithms to generate pseudo-random numbers, which for all practical purposes are as good as flipping fair coins. Therefore, from here on we will drop the "pseudo" part and just call them random numbers.

`Math.random()`. Because random numbers are important, programming languages provide a built-in random number generator. JavaScript is no exception with its **`Math.random()`** function. Every time **`Math.random()`** is called, it returns a new random number. To simplify their use, all random number generators produce a random decimal number strictly between 0 and 1. That is, the number is a fraction like 0.541507552309933 that will never be exactly equal to 0 or 1. So, to "flip an electronic coin," we can generate a random number and then round to the nearest integer,

```
Math.round(Math.random())
```

which produces either 0 if the fraction is less than 0.500000000000000, or 1 otherwise. By treating 0 as tails and 1 as heads, we have flipped an "electronic coin."

`Math.floor()`. There is another way to choose between two whole numbers, 0 and 1, and we are interested in it because it is more general. Here is the idea: Suppose we want to choose among four outcomes. Thinking about it, we notice that a decimal number from **`Math.random()`**, say, 0.3333 . . . , is just a fraction of the interval from 0 to 1, and that by multiplying by an integer *n*, we get the same fraction of the larger interval from 0 to *n*. (See Figure 20.6.) So, 4 × 0.3333 . . . = 1.333 . . . , means that 0.3333 is one-third of the way from 0 to 1, and 1.333 is one-third of the way from 0 to 4. Thus if **`Math.random()`** produces a random number between 0 and 1, *n* * **`Math.random()`** produces a random number between 0 and n, and the two numbers are in the same proportional position.

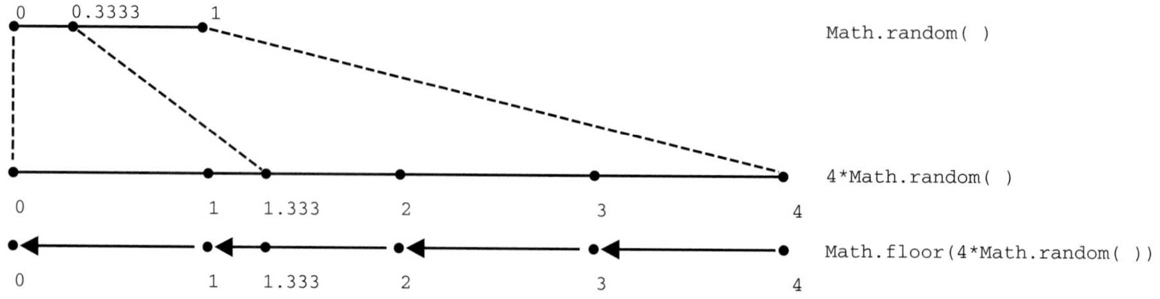

Figure 20.6. *Schematic diagram of the output* **`Math.random()`** *multiplied by 4 to expand to a larger interval, followed by the application of* **`Math.floor()`** *to convert to integer values.*

We cannot use **`Math.round()`** to convert the resulting fraction to an integer, however, because **`Math.round()`** changes a decimal number to the *closest* integer, which is not what we want. This can be seen by the relationships

```
0.0 < Math.round(4 * Math.random()) < 0.5 become 0
0.5 ≤ Math.round(4 * Math.random()) < 1.5 become 1
1.5 ≤ Math.round(4 * Math.random()) < 2.0 become 2
2.5 ≤ Math.round(4 * Math.random()) < 3.5 become 3
3.5 ≤ Math.round(4 * Math.random()) < 4.0 become 4
```

The rounding not only produces "too many" numbers (we're only choosing among four things), but it also assigns only a "half unit to the highest and lowest integers." The right solution is just to drop the digits to the right of the decimal point. This "rounding down" operation is called *floor*, and has exactly the right outcome, as these relationships show:

```
0.0 < Math.floor(4 * Math.random()) < 1.0 become 0
1.0 ≤ Math.floor(4 * Math.random()) < 2.0 become 1
2.0 ≤ Math.floor(4 * Math.random()) < 3.0 become 2
3.0 ≤ Math.floor(4 * Math.random()) < 4.0 become 3
```

Of course, a 4.0 will not be created, because `Math.random()` never produces a 1.0. Notice that `Math.floor(2 * Math.random())` is another way to produce the "electronic coin flip." Also, notice that we can change 0 to 4 to another interval, say, 1 to 5, by adjusting the output, for example, by adding 1.

`randNum().` Having worked out how a random number chosen within the interval 0 to 1 can be converted into an integer from a range 0 through *n*–1, we write a JavaScript function to implement the idea. The function will be called `randNum()` and will have one parameter, called `range`, which is the upper end of the interval. The code is

```
function randNum ( range ) {
  // Produces a random integer from 0 to range-1
    return Math.floor (range * Math.random());
}
```

Clearly, `randNum(4)` gives us a random choice from among four items, though they will be numbered 0 to 3. We can use this function in our Memory Bank page by adding a line of the form

The user can choose an interval size, which is preset to 10. Then, when the user clicks on the **Pick** button, the `randNum()` function runs. The HTML for the controls is by now familiar:

```
<tr>
  <td><b>Pick A Random Number From 1 To </b>
    <input type = text name = "topEnd"
      size = 2 value = "10"> </td>
    <td>
      <input type = button value = "Pick"
       onClick = "choice.value = 1 + randNum(topEnd.value)">
       Outcome from the range:
      <input type = text name = "choice" size = 2></td></tr>
```

The `value` field is used in the `topEnd` control to preset the range. Also, 1 is added to the result of the `randNum()` function because the interval it returns is 0 to `range-1`, but the user wants 1 to `range`.

Though this Memory Bank row can be used as a coin flip, by making range 2, we can create a more user-friendly Memory Bank application for coin flips. First, it will print **Heads** or **Tails** for the outcome, which is better than 1 or 2. Also, it will keep track of how many heads and tails are generated, because we assume that anyone who loses a flip may want to see the e-coin flipped a few times to make sure that it is producing an approximately equal number of heads and tails. The window we have in mind has the form

The HTML controls for this row of the Memory Bank page are

```
<tr>
  <td><b>Electronic Coin Flip </b></td>
  <td align="center">
    <input type = button value = "Flip"
     onClick = "runTrial()"> Outcome:
    <input type = text name = coin size = 5> Totals: H
    <input type = text name = heads size = 3 value = 0> T
    <input type = text name = tails size = 3 value = 0></td></tr>
```

We could have put all of the JavaScript programming for the **Flip** button click-event handler inside the **input** control, but it is better if we package it all into a function and simply call it. We will name the function **runTrial()**.

runTrial(). The **runTrial()** function handles click-events, so we ask, "What action should happen on a **Flip** click?" Clearly, **randNum(2)** must be run, the outcome window must be assigned **Heads** or **Tails**, and either the H or T count must increase by 1. The function is straightforward:

```
function runTrial() {
    if (randNum(2) == 1) {
        document.memory.coin.value = "Heads";
        headCount = headCount + 1;
        document.memory.heads.value = headCount;
    }
    else {
        document.memory.coin.value = "Tails";
        tailCount = tailCount + 1;
        document.memory.tails.value = tailCount;
    }
}
```

We must declare two global variables (right after the earlier **measure** declaration) to keep the counts,

```
var headCount = 0, tailCount = 0;
```

We don't need any local variables, and therefore no declarations. We call **randNum(2)** in the predicate of a conditional statement. Then, depending on which outcome results, three parallel statements are executed in either the **then** compound or the **else** compound. The first statement sets the **coin** window; the second statement increments the appropriate global variable, keeping track of the total count; and the third statement updates the appropriate **heads** or **tails** window. Notice that, unlike the earlier abbreviated uses of the dot operator, the full path **document.memory.heads.value** is needed because the reference within a function is a nonlocal reference relative to the form.

Finally, **runTrial()** is different from our earlier functions because it has no **return** statement. The function just finishes when it reaches the end of the definition. That is, it does not report the outputs from the call. The function does have three outputs: It changes the **coin** window, updates one of the two counts, and changes either the **heads** or **tails** window. But it does these operations by making direct references to the variables involved. What makes it different is not the missing **return** statements, but that it is customized to a very specific situation, rather than being a general solution.

Recap: Two Reasons to Write Functions

All of our previous functions—**convertC2F()**, **BMI()**, **randNum()**, and so on—are general. We wrote them for our application, but we hope that we will have a chance to use them again. Think of them as building blocks for programs that we may write in the future. But **runTrial()** is not a building block.

Because **runTrial()** contains explicit references like **document.memory.heads.value**, it must run within a document that has a memory form, and that form must have within it input controls named **coin**, **heads**, and **tails**. We do not expect this ever to happen again. Instead, we wrote the function to encapsulate the complexity of handling the **Flip** click-event, removing it from the HTML form. Giving the event-handling operation a name allowed us to write a function for it and get it out of the way.

Now we've seen two reasons to write functions: name a computation that may be useful, package it, and hope to use it again; and name a computation that is bulky, package it, and move it to somewhere out of the way. These are both good reasons for abstraction.

ADD FINAL TOUCHES TO MEMORY BANK

To wrap up our discussion of functions and the Memory Bank page development, we add two finishing touches: a date and Web links. Both features are simple, but they make the page more useful. Also, we add one bonus feature.

Add a Date

The date can be added at the top after the red motto text, centered. JavaScript gives us many ways to manipulate dates, but here we use only the **Date()** function. We could write a function to insert the date into the HTML document, but it is only a single line, so we write the code

```
<script language = 'JavaScript'>
  document.write('<center>' + (Date().toString()) +
                 '</center>');
</script>
```

placing it just after the motto line. Because the **document.write()** operation is a JavaScript statement, **<script>** tags must surround it, as usual. Like all JavaScript commands, **document.write()** will be performed while the browser is inputting the HTML file (that is, before the page is created). The JS Interpreter creates the string—remember that + is the concatenate operator for strings—and inserts the result at the right position in the HTML file, that is, just after the motto.

The expression in the center of the string (`Date().toString()`) references the date object, which contains the current date and time in numeric form. The numeric form can be converted to a printable form using `toString()`. So the expression says, "Get the current date and time converted to a printable string."

Add Web Links

Our Memory Bank page has concentrated on programming computations, but it's a Web page, so we can include useful links, too. These links are probably bookmarked in your browser, but by placing them on the Memory Bank page, they are available even when you're using a different computer or browser. What should those links be? Anything that is useful—an online dictionary and thesaurus for writing term papers, a link to the Fluency class's home page, a periodic chart for chemistry class, and maybe the CIA's fact book of country information for geography class.

Where should the links be located? We could add another column to the table, placing one link per row. Because the links are highlighted with a different color, they would appear to be in their own column. But, why should the number of links match the number of rows of the table? And furthermore, it's cumbersome to add columns to HTML tables.

An alternative is to add another row at the bottom of the table, spanning both columns, and fill it with the links. We choose this solution for two reasons. First, it gives us a free-form region in which to list the links and organize them by topic. Second, we can set it up so that adding more links is easy, encouraging us to include new ones. The HTML is shown in Figure 20.7.

Assess the Web Page Design

Notice first that to get the table data to span two columns, HTML's `colspan = 2` attribute is included with the `<td>` tag. Second, the links are grouped by topic, which uses the standard text color to stand out from the differently colored links. Third, a red bullet—a `.gif` image—is used to separate the entries because some of them are two or three words. (Of course, a file named `bullet.gif` must be in the same directory as this page, as explained in Chapter 4.) Finally, and most important, the link area has a very neat structure that makes adding new links almost trivial. The headings and entries all have a standard structure, and a schema has been developed and placed in a comment, so setting up for a new link is a simple copy-and-paste operation. This should encourage us to keep the content current.

We'll add one more feature to the web page.

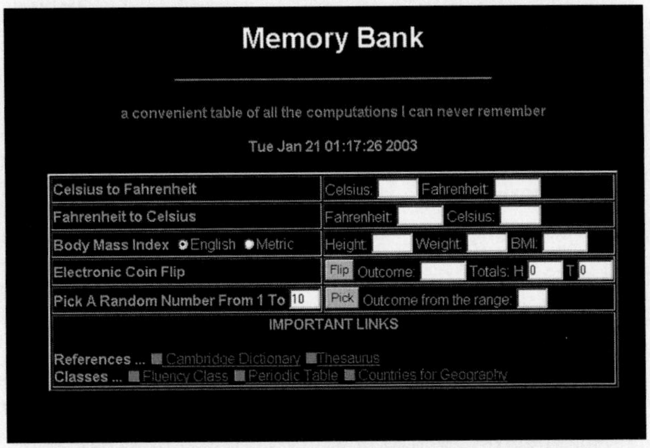


```
<tr>
<!— The standard form for the links is...

  <br><b>topic name ...</b>
    <img src='bullet.gif'>
    <a href='http:// url goes here'>
        anchor term(s) here</a>

  So, just copy/paste/edit it.—>

<td colspan = 2> <center>IMPORTANT LINKS</center>
  <br>Resource Links ...
    <img src='bullet.gif'>
    <a href='http://dictionary.cambridge.org'>
      Cambridge Dictionary</a>
    <img src='bullet.gif'>
    <a href='http://www.wordsmyth.net'>
      Thesaurus</a>
  <br>Classes...
    <img src='bullet.gif'>
    <a href='http://www.cs.washington.edu/100/'>
      Fluency Class</a>
    <img src='bullet.gif'>
    <a href='http://www.chemsoc.org/viselements/pages/
      pertable_j.htm'>
      Periodic Table</a>
    <img src='bullet.gif'>
    <a href='http://www.cia.gov/cia/publications/factbook/'>
      Countries for Geography</a>
  </td>
</tr>
```

Figure 20.7. HTML for the link area of the Memory Bank Web page.

FITLINK

Time of Your Life > >

One feature of computers that makes it easy for them to work with dates is that they mostly keep track of dates and time with "UNIX dates." (Recall that UNIX dates are used in cookies, as explained in Chapter 16.) The UNIX operating system began recording dates as the number of milliseconds since 1 January 1970 at 00:00:00 Universal Time, that is, New Year 1970 in Greenwich, England. Thus the number of milliseconds between any two dates after New Years 1970 can be found by subtracting the two UNIX dates, making it much easier to compute than if time were recorded in years, days and hours.

JavaScript uses UNIX dates. It also provides functions to refer to time as if it were recorded in days and hours, when that is convenient for us. We use these features to compute your age in seconds. (Of course, your age in milliseconds is just 1000 times more.) See Figure 20.8.

The JavaScript code, to be placed just before the `</script>` tag at the end of the Memory Bank program, is

```
var today = new Date();    // Get today's date
var myBdate = new Date(); // Get a date object to modify
var difference;            // Declare a temporary variable

myBdate.setFullYear(1984);// Set my birth year to 1984
myBdate.setMonth(6);       // Set my birth mo to July (mo.s start at 0)
myBdate.setDate(4);        // Set my birth day to 4th
myBdate.setHours(12);      // Set my hour of birth to noon
myBdate.setMinutes(0);     // Set my minute of birth to o'clock
myBdate.setSeconds(0);     // Set my second of birth on the hour

difference = today.getTime() - myBdate.getTime();
difference = Math.floor(difference/1000);
document.write("<center><font color=yellow> I'm " + difference
              + " seconds old. What <i>am</i> I doing with my
              life?</font></center>");
```

The code creates two date objects, one for today and one for your birthday. (Objects are a complex subject and will not be covered.) In the six statements after the declarations, we set your birthday as if it were exactly noon, July 4, 1984. To do this, we use JavaScript functions that allow us to refer to the time using months and hours. Once your birthday has been set, we compute `difference`, the difference between the present time and that date. This computation uses UNIX dates. We then divide the result by 1000 to convert it to seconds and print it out at the bottom of the Memory Bank page

With these additions, the Memory Bank page is complete for the moment. (An HTML and JavaScript listing is given in Appendix D.) More functions can be added in the future.

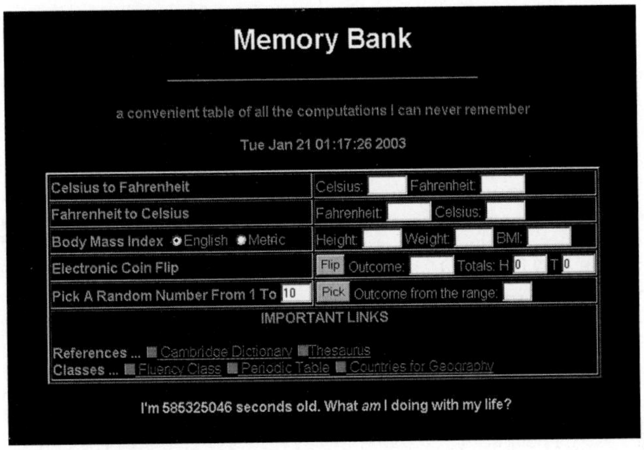

Figure 20.8. *Final version of the Memory Bank page.*

SUMMARY

This chapter began by introducing the concept of abstraction. Abstraction identifies significant components of a process, design, or other phenomenon based on form or behavior. To benefit computationally from abstraction, we name the abstraction, define it (*encapsulate*), and create *parameters* for the input. Abstractions are important to computing because they help us *manage complexity*: we can refer to the name of the abstraction rather than to its definition. And abstractions are important because they *promote reuse* when they are packaged into functions, which can be building blocks to more complex computations.

We next described the JavaScript syntax for function declarations and practiced by writing a function for converting Celsius into Farhenheit. The declaration contains the definition of a function. The use of the function is known as the function call. Using several small HTML programs, we explored calling the function for different purposes: to find a single Celsius temperature in Fahrenheit, to make a list of Celsius and Fahrenheit temperatures, and to make a table of equivalents. This write-once-use-many-times characteristic demonstrates the reusability feature of functions. We then worked on getting the details right, learning about local and global variables, parameters and arguments, and definitions and calls.

Using what we had learned, we developed the Memory Bank Web page, a combination of programming in JavaScript—mostly event handlers, because the functions were already written—and HTML. The Memory Bank showed how we could add useful content to a Web page through programming in JavaScript. After discussing random numbers, we wrote code to flip an electronic "coin" and to choose among a sequence of integers. Finally, we added a few more routine features—links and the date—to the Memory Bank to make it more useful.

Most of the functions of this chapter, like **`convertC2F()`** and **`randNum()`**, are general, so we can use them again in the future. These functions illustrate how abstraction promotes reuse of our work. One of the functions of the chapter, **`runTrial()`**, was written for a situation that is so specialized it will probably never arise again. We made it a function simply to encapsulate it so as not to think about it anymore—that is, to "get it out of the way." This function illustrates how abstraction helps us manage complexity and make our thinking easier. When we package abstractions into functions, we significantly improve our ability to understand the world.

EXERCISES

Multiple Choice

1. The building blocks of programming are:
   A. programming languages
   B. functions
   C. HTML and JavaScript
   D. variables and events
2. A curly brace, `}`, in a piece of JavaScript code:
   A. must be placed on its own line to work
   B. indicates the end of the code
   C. should be on its own line for clarity
   D. all of the above
3. In JavaScript, a line beginning with `//` is a(n)::
   A. assignment
   B. comparison
   C. comment
   D. function
4. In a function:
   A. each argument must be supplied with a parameter
   B. each parameter must have an argument
   C. parameters are input values
   D. parameters are output values
5. The event associated with the input control is:
   A. `onClick`
   B. `textChange`
   C. `onChange`
   D. `spareChange`
6. Radio buttons will work together when:
   A. the `checked` attribute is set to `TRUE`
   B. they are on the same form
   C. when all of them are selected
   D. when all of them have the same name
7. Random numbers are generated by using:
   A. `Math.random()`
   B. `Rnd`
   C. `Math.rnd`
   D. `Random.Math()`
8. The JavaScript `Date()` function:
   A. returns the date as a string
   B. returns the current date and time as a number
   C. is displayed as a decimal
   D. none of the above

9. In HTML, **`href:`**
   A. creates an image
   B. displays the answer to a JavaScript function
   C. creates a Web link
   D. is the extension for a Web page
10. UNIX is:
    A. an international date standard
    B. a program
    C. an operating system
    D. a cookie

Short Answer

1. ______ is a process where simple steps are grouped together and given a name that describes the process.
2. ______ are used to spell out the differences between related items.
3. In programming, packaged operations with reusable code are called either ______ or ______.
4. A(n) ______ is all the code needed to create a function.
5. ______ are variables in a function that do not need to be declared with a **`var`** statement.
6. The ______ of a variable describes where and when it can be referenced.
7. Input values for a function are called ______.
8. When you divide by zero in JavaScript, ______ is returned as the answer.
9. Computer-generated numbers for a coin toss are technically called ______.
10. A random number generated in JavaScript is always between ______ and ______.
11. In JavaScript, time is tracked in ______, each of which is one one-thousandth of a second.
12. JavaScript keeps track of dates using ______ dates, which are expressed as the number of milliseconds since January 1, 1970 at 00:00:00 Universal Time.

Exercises

1. Describe abstraction. How is nearly every idea an abstraction?
2. Describe how random numbers could be used to simulate the roll of a die. How could two dice be simulated using this function?
3. Identify the three parts of a function.
4. Describe how dates are tracked in JavaScript.
5. Calculate your age as a UNIX date.
6. How would the banking industry make use of the computer's ability to calculate the difference between two dates?
7. What are five words that cannot be used to name a function or a variable? What are five more?
8. Describe a function in terms of input, processing, and output.
9. Write a function to calculate your wages for a part-time job. (Don't worry about calculating overtime.)

chapter

21 ONCE IS NOT ENOUGH

Iteration Principles

learning objectives

- Trace the execution of a given `for` loop
- Write a World-Famous Iteration `for` loop
- Discuss the structure of nested loops
- Explain the use of indexes
- List the rules for arrays; describe the syntax of an array reference
- Explain the main programming tasks for online animations

There are three kinds of programmers: those who make off-by-one errors, and those who don't.

—ANONYMOUS

THE TOPIC of this chapter is iteration—the process of repetition. We are familiar with the English word *reiterate*, which means to repeat something, as in "The attorney reiterated her client's position." Because *iterate* already means to repeat, *reiterate* sounds redundant. But repetition is redundant; that's what it's about. So, English has both words, and maybe it needs a third, *rereiterate*, an even more redundant form meaning, perhaps, "repeated endlessly," as in "Beer commercials are rereiterated." Though repetition is usually tiresome, learning about it is not. And, iteration is the source of considerable computational power, making it a very important topic. By learning how to use iteration, we can make the computer do the tiresome parts of computing.

In this chapter, we complete our study of programming concepts by learning about iteration and applying it to computational problems. We begin by explaining the `for` statement, one of JavaScript's iteration statements and the key to iterative computation. Then we explore iteration more deeply by discussing how its components can vary. The key to understanding iteration is to focus on how the iteration variable changes values. We mention the Fundamental Principle of Iteration and then we return to the topic of random numbers. After that, we consider the companion topics of indexing and arrays. Together, indexing and arrays can be used with iteration to perform almost unlimited amounts of computation, making them a major source of computing power. Finally, to bring all of these topics together, we study online animation, which allows us to add action to our Web pages. We work through the animation of the familiar waiting icon to prepare us for more interesting animations.

ITERATION: *PLAY IT AGAIN, SAM*

The first fact to learn is the slight difference between *iterate* and *repeat*. When your mother said, "I've repeated myself four times," she meant, strictly speaking, she'd said the same thing five times. Usually, the first time isn't considered a "repeat." Only the second through last are "repeats." If she'd actually said the sentence exactly four times, she should have used *iterate*. (Pointing this out to her would *not* have been smart.) We often ignore this difference in terminology in common speech. For example, "reps" (for *repetitions*) in weight training count the total number. In this book, we follow common usage and use *repeat* and *iterate* interchangeably, except where precision is essential, in which case we use *iterate*. When something is iterated five times, there are five instances; you can't be off by one.

The for Loop Basic Syntax

Iteration—probably the fourth most important programming idea after assignment, conditionals, and functions—means looping through a series of statements to repeat them. In JavaScript, the main **iteration statement** is the **`for` loop**, which has the following syntax:

```
for ( <initialization>; <continuation>; <next iteration> ) {
      <statement list>
}
```

Here the text not in meta-brackets must be given literally. (Notice the prominent position of the closed curly brace.) The statement sequence to be repeated is in the <*statement list*>, and the constructs in parentheses—which we'll explain in a minute—control how many times the <*statement list*> is iterated. The whole statement sequence is performed in each iteration. So, if the `for` loop

```
for ( <initialization>; <continuation>; <next iteration> ) {
      document.write('A');
      document.write('AB');
      document.write('ABC');
}
```

iterates three times, it will produce

```
A
AB
ABC
A
AB
ABC
A
AB
ABC
```

That is, the computer completes the whole statement sequence of the <*statement list*> *before* beginning the next iteration.

The Iteration Variable. The three operations in the parentheses of the **`for`** loop, <*initialization*>, <*continuation*>, and <*next iteration*>, control the number of times the loop iterates and are called the **control specification**. They control the loop by using an **iteration variable**. Iteration variables are just normal variables, so they must be declared. They are called iteration variables only while they are serving to control the loop. Here's a typical example in which the iteration variable is `j`:

```
for ( j = 1 ; j <= 3 ; j = j + 1 ) {
      <statement list>
}
```

To see how these statements work, imagine that the **`for`** loop has been replaced with the schematic form

General Form

```
<initialization>;
if (<continuation>) {
       <statement list>;
       <next iteration>;
}
```

Specific Example with `j`

```
j = 1;
if ( j <= 3 ) {
       <statement list>
       j = j + 1;
}
```

The arrow means to go back to do the **`if`** statement again.

Here's what happens. The first operation of a **`for`** loop is the <*initialization*>. The **initialization** sets the iteration variable's value for the first (if any) iterations through the loop. Next, the **continuation** has the same form as the predicate in a conditional statement. If the <*continuation*> test has a **`false`** outcome, the loop terminates, the <*statement list*> is skipped, and it is as if nothing happened except that the iteration variable got assigned its initial value.

However, if the <*continuation*> test has a **`true`** outcome, the <*statement list*> is performed. The statement list can be any sequence of statements, including other **`for`** statements. When the statements are completed, the <*next iteration*> operation is performed. The next iteration expression will change the iteration variable. That completes the first iteration. The **next iteration** starts with the <*continuation*> test, performing the same sequence of operations. All following iterations proceed as the first one until the <*continuation*> test has a **`false`** outcome, terminating the loop. In this way, the statement sequence can be performed many times without having to write each of the statements that is to be performed.

FITTIP

Terminator, Too. The second item among the control operations is called the <*continuation*> test here, because if its outcome is **`true`**, the iteration continues, and if its outcome is **`false`**, it ends. But the proper programming term for this test is **termination test** because it is checking to see if the loop should terminate. However, as a termination test, the outcomes are backward—**`true`** means continue, **`false`** means terminate! Both terms are useful, but to remember the meanings of the outcomes, think of the test as asking "Continue?"

Following the Iteration Variable. In the **for** loop with iteration variable `j`, and in all **for** loops, the story is fully embodied in the operations involving the iteration variable. Consider the sequence of operations on `j` shown in Table 21.1.

Table 21.1. *The sequence of operations on* `j` *from the* **for** *loop with Control Specification* (*j=1; j <= 3; j=j+1*)

Operation	Operation Result	Role
`j = 1`	`j`'s value is 1	Initialize iteration variable
`j <= 3`	`true`, `j` *is less than* 3	First <*continuation*> test, continue
`j = j + 1`	`j`'s value is 2	First <*next iteration*> operation
`j <= 3`	`true`, j *is less than* 3	Second <*continuation*> test, continue
`j = j + 1`	`j`'s value is 3	Second <*next iteration*> operation
`j <= 3`	`true`, `j` *is equal to* 3	Third <*continuation*> test, continue
`j = j + 1`	`j`'s value is 4	Third <*next iteration*> operation
`j <= 3`	`false`, `j` *is greater than* 3	Fourth <*continuation*> test, terminate

The loop iterates three times by beginning at 1 and, after assigning a new value to `j`, testing to see if it should continue. The statements of the <*statement list*> are executed between the <*continuation*> test and the <*next iteration*> operation. Notice that `j` counts from 1 to 4, but at 4, the test finds out that `j` has counted too far, so it quits before performing the <*statement list*> again. Thus the <*statement list*> is performed the right number of times.

FITBYTE

No Planning. The for loop *might have been* designed to figure the number of iterations to perform before starting out, and then doing them. But iteration doesn't work that way. Instead, the computer just plods along, testing to see if it should continue before starting an iteration, doing the statement sequence, changing the iteration variable, and repeating. Plodding is more powerful, because it's not always possible to predict the number of iterations.

How a for Loop Works

To exercise our understanding of how **for** loops work, consider a computation on declared variables `j` and **text**,

```
text = "She said ";                    //Set text to a string
for (j = 1; j <= 3; j = j + 1) {       //Define a 3 cycle loop
    text = text + "Never! ";           //Concatenate on a string
}                                      // ... end of loop
alert(text);                           // Show result
```

which produces the alert box shown below.

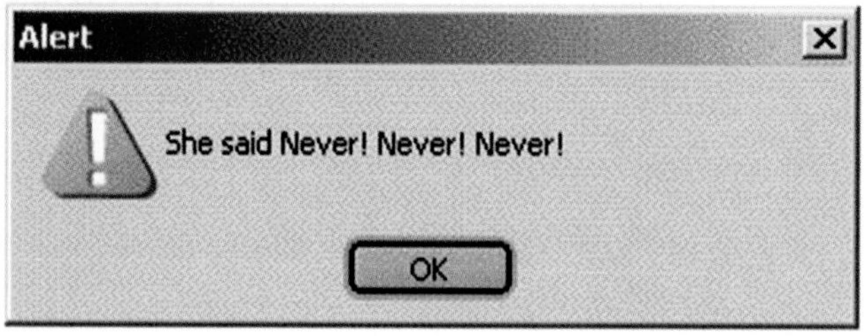

This `for` loop, which iterates three times, was used with two assignment statements to produce the value of `text` by appending three copies of the string `"Never! "`. To check the code's operation, notice that before the four continuation tests, the values of the variable `text` are the following strings:

`"She said "`	*Before the loop is entered*
`"She said Never! "`	*After one iteration*
`"She said Never! Never! "`	*After two iterations*
`"She said Never! Never! Never! "`	*After three iterations*

So the `for` loop allowed us to build the phrase one word at a time. Of course, this phrase could have been typed out, `"She said Never! Never! Never! "`. But the more emphatic phrase in which she says `"Never! "` 1000 times would be much harder to type. Using a `for` loop, we can simply change the 3 to 1000. It's easy to be emphatic with `for` loops.

JAVASCRIPT RULES FOR FOR LOOPS

A programmer would say that our "emphatic" `for` loop "iterates from 1 to 3 by 1." This is different from saying the `for` loop iterates three times. The programmer's description focuses on the most relevant feature of a `for` loop—its control. The key parts of the control are the starting point (1), the ending point (3), and the step size (1).

In this section, we consider some of the possibilities:

> The iteration variable

> A starting point

> Continuation/termination test

> Step size

> Reference to the iteration variable

> A World-Famous Iteration

The Iteration Variable

Iteration variables are normal variables that help with an iteration. They must be declared, and they follow the usual rules for identifiers. Programmers tend to choose short or even single-letter identifiers for iteration variables because they tend to be typed frequently, as we'll see. By far, `i`, `j`, and `k` are the most common.

A Starting Point

An iteration can begin anywhere, including with negative numbers. So, for example, in

```
for (j = -10; j <= 10; j = j + 1) { ... }
```

the iteration variable `j` assumes each of the 21 values from `-10` to `10`, that is, including 0. And, similarly, in

```
for (j = 990; j <= 1010; j = j + 1) { ... }
```

`j` assumes each of the 21 values around 1000. Finally, it's possible to start at a fractional number. So, in the loop

```
for (j = 2.5; j <= 6; j = j + 1) { ... }
```

`j` assumes the values `2.5`, `3.5`, `4.5`, and `5.5` because the continuation test will finally fail at `6.5`.

Continuation/Termination Test

If it is possible to begin an iteration anywhere, it must be possible to end it anywhere. The <*continuation*> test follows the rules for predicates—the tests in `if` statements. That is, the test is any expression resulting in a Boolean value.

The key point to remember about the continuation test is that to avoid an infinite loop (explained later in the section "Avoiding Infinite Loops"), it must involve the iteration variable. Other variables can be used as well as the logical operations and (`&&`), or (`||`), and not (`!`). For example, a loop that is supposed to stop at `j <= 6` could also be terminated by `((j < 6) || (j == 6))` or `j < 7`.

Step Size

The <*next iteration*> also allows considerable freedom. It allows us to specify an amount of change, known as the **step** or **step size**. For example, it is possible to step by units of 2, say, to iterate through the even numbers from 0 to 20:

```
for (j = 0; j < 20; j = j + 2) { ... }
```

In this case `j` takes the values of ten numbers because 20 is not included. The <*next iteration*> computation is often called the **increment** computation by programmers because, as we've seen, it is almost always *increasing* the value of the iteration variable. But it doesn't have to. The step can be negative, resulting in a **decrement**, and so we call it the <*next iteration*> computation to cover both the increasing and decreasing cases. For example, to count the 21 integers around 0, from *positive* to *negative* this time, we use the following:

```
for (j = 10; j >= -10; j = j - 1) { ... }
```

The successive values of `j` are `10`, `9`, `8`, . . . , `-9`, `-10`. Notice that reversing the direction of the enumeration of the values means the <*continuation*> test has to be adjusted, too.

FITTIP

Pluses and Minuses. Because incrementing and decrementing by 1 are so common, JavaScript has a special "post increment/decrement" notation. Thus `i++` means `i = i + 1`, and `i--` means `i = i - 1`. (The variable can be anything, of course.) This notation is handy for the <*next iteration*> component of a `for` loop.

Reference to the Iteration Variable

As we will soon see, the iteration variable is often used in the computations of the <*statement list*>, which is why we focus on the values of the iteration variable during the looping. We care what these values are because we compute with them. So, for example, the iteration variable `j` is used in the statement that computes 5 factorial (5!):

```
fact = 1;
for (j = 1; j <= 5; j = j + 1) {
      fact = fact * j;
}
```

That is, it computes `((((1 * 1) * 2) * 3) * 4) * 5 ⇔ 120`. Using the iteration variable in the computation is necessary and useful.

The World-Famous Iteration

Because JavaScript has the same **`for`** loop statement structure as the most popular programming languages (e.g., C, C++, and Java), thousands of **`for`** loops with the form just described are written every day—millions in the past decade. With so many loops, programmers have gotten in the habit of using one standard form most of the time:

```
for (j=0; j<n; j++) { ... }
```

Without a doubt this is the most frequently written **`for`** loop of all time, so we will call it the **World-Famous Iteration** (**WFI**). Of course, `j` and `n` can be replaced with other declared variables. It is worth taking a moment to study this form because you will see it again and again.

Notice first that the iteration variable starts at 0. You will see shortly why starting at 0 is better than starting at 1. The iteration counts up from 0 in steps of 1 because the post-increment `j++` is used. And the iteration ends when the iteration variable is no longer strictly less than `n`—that is, the loop's last iteration is for `j = n-1`. Thus the **`for`** loop <*statement list*> is performed `n` times: 0, 1, 2, ..., n–1. When used in this stylized form, the variable or expression following the < symbol—the `n` in this case—is exactly the number of times through the loop, so we can see the iteration count in an instant without thinking hard about it. And this form saves on typing, which is important if you consider how difficult it is to type programming symbols. When you see JavaScript in the **Source** listing of the Web pages you download, chances are you will see this World-Famous Iteration. Nearly every iteration in the rest of this book has this WFI form.

FITTIP

> **Off Again.** An extremely common error in computing—you've probably made it several times in *this* section—is to miscount by one. It's so common it has a name, *Off By One Error*. "Exam week is from the 3rd to the 10th," so how many days is it? We tend to subtract to get seven, but it's eight because it includes the end points. Figuring the number of iterations is similarly error prone. Happily, the World-Famous Iteration helps. The `n` following < in the WFI form is the *exact* iteration count.

THE FUNDAMENTAL PRINCIPLE OF ITERATION

Because looping is so fundamental to computing—we get a lot of computation for a little writing—iteration statements have many variations. Some kinds of loops test at the end rather than the beginning, as the `for` loop does. Others leave the <*initialization*> and <*next iteration*> computations to the programmer to do explicitly in the <*statement list*>, and so on. Learning all the variations is for professional programmers. We are only interested in the fundamental ideas about iteration. The most basic is the

> **Fundamental Principle of Iteration:** All iterations have a test to determine whether the iteration continues or terminates.

The principle's obvious truth is based on the fact that if there is no test, the iteration runs forever. That is, it is an **infinite loop**, and we would have to wait infinitely long for the computation to yield an answer. Our interest is only in finite algorithms—see the fifth property of algorithms, Chapter 10—so every iteration must end. Thus, all `for` loops should include the <*continuation*> test.

Making Iteration Variables Change

The Fundamental Principle of Iteration has an important *corollary*:

> **Corollary:** Some variable on which the iteration's test depends must change value during each iteration.

Suppose there are two consecutive iterations during which no variable on which the <*continuation*> test depends changes. How will the second iteration be different from the first? It may be different in many ways, but by hypothesis, the <*continuation*> test will have the same outcome as after the first iteration. But that outcome caused the second iteration. So, the loop will execute a third time. Because there is no difference in the outcome of the third test, the outcome will again be the same, causing a fourth iteration. And so on. The iteration will continue forever.

Thus, some variable on which the test depends must change, or we have an infinite loop. The corollary explains why the <*next iteration*> is a standard part of the **for** loop statement.

Avoiding Infinite Loops

The reason the corollary is so important is that, when programming **for** loops, it's not too difficult to make a mistake and create an infinite loop. For example,

```
for ( j = 1 ; j <= 3; i = i + 1) { ... }
```

looks almost like our earlier "emphatic" **for** loop, but it is broken and will loop forever. (Very emphatic, indeed!) The problem is that the variable being compared in the <*continuation*> test (`j`) is not the one incremented in the <*next iteration*> operation (`i`). Unless the iteration variable is changed in the loop—iteration variables should never be changed by statements in the <*statement list*>—the iteration will loop forever. Anyone carefully analyzing this **for** statement will spot the problem, but it's easy to miss. It's also easy enough to create, say, by making incomplete edits. (Imagine that the statement had previously used i as an iteration variable and was incompletely revised.)

> FITBYTE
>
> **Infinite Loops.** Infinite loops happen. It's a fact of programming. Luckily, JavaScript is kind to programmers making this mistake. Microsoft's Internet Explorer tells you that the script is running slowly and asks if you want to terminate it. Netscape and other browsers can simply be forced to close. In the past, you had to turn off the computer to stop an infinite loop.

Try writing an infinite loop, then run it and force the browser to terminate so that you recognize the behavior.

EXPERIMENTS WITH FLIPPING ELECTRONIC COINS

To practice **for** loops, we experiment with flipping electronic coins. Recall that in Chapter 20 we wrote a function **randNum()** taking an argument that is the range of integers from which to select. So, **randNum(2)**, which returns either `0` (tails) or `1` (heads), can be used for our experiments.

The first experiment is to find out how many heads and tails we get in 100 flips. We expect the numbers to be roughly equal. To run the experiment, we must set up an iteration in which our **randNum()** function is performed 100 times and statistics are gathered along the way. The code is

```
<html><head><title>Coin Flips</title></head>
<body><script language='JavaScript'>
var heads=0, tails=0;                         //Counters
var i;                                        //Iteration variable
```

```
for (i=0; i<100; i++ ){
     if (randNum(2) == 1)
          heads++;
     else
          tails++;
}
alert("Heads: " + heads + " and Tails: " + tails);
function randNum(range) {
   return Math.floor(range*Math.random());
}
</script></body></html>
```

(Because the output will be reported using **`alert()`**, the page doesn't matter, so we can compress the HTML.)

The **`for`** loop, which uses the WFI form, loops 100 times—**`i`** ranges from 0 through 99—and uses a conditional statement to check and record the outcomes of the random number generation. The post-increment (++) notation has been used three times, allowing us to replace statements like **`heads = heads + 1`** with the briefer **`heads++`**. Running the program gave me the results shown in the Alert below the first time I tried it on my computer. But you should experiment on your computer; expect to get different results.

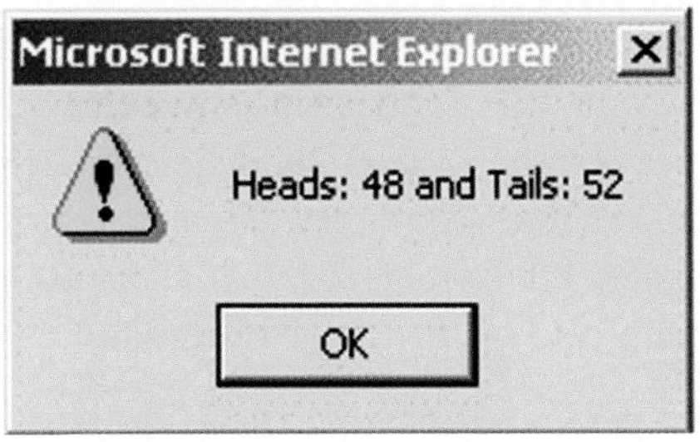

Running the program several times gives us different answers. My five runs ranged from a 50–50 outcome to a 57–43 outcome. This motivates us to run several trials.

A *trial* will be the 100-sample iteration just described. To run several trials, we want to iterate them. That is, we will iterate an iteration. Think of the earlier iteration

```
for (i=0; i<100; i++ ){                                    //Trial line 1
     if (randNum(2) == 1)                                  //Trial line 2
          heads++;                                         //Trial line 3
     else                                                  //Trial line 4
          tails++;                                         //Trial line 5
}                                                          //Trial line 6
alert("Heads: " + heads + " and Tails: " + tails);//Trial line 7
```

as a unit. (Notice that thinking of the loop as a unit is an *abstraction*, as discussed in Chapter 20.)

A Nested Loop

To iterate these statements, we create another **for** loop with the <*statement list*> containing this trial unit and a couple of additional statements needed to make the whole process work out. The additional statements must reinitialize the counters, because they should begin at 0 for each new trial. The result is

```
var heads = 0, tails = 0;
var i, j;                                        //Iteration vars
for (j = 0; j < 5; j++){                         //Outer loop start
    for (i=0; i<100; i++){                       //Trial line 1
        if (randNum(2) == 1)                     //Trial line 2
            heads++;                             //Trial line 3
        else                                     //Trial line 4
            tails++;                             //Trial line 5
    }                                            //Trial line 6
    alert("Heads: "+heads+" and Tails: "+tails); //Trial line 7
    heads = 0; tails = 0;                        //Additional
}                                                //Outer loop end
```

This structure—a loop within a loop—is called a **nested loop**. Notice that another iteration variable, `j`, had to be declared because the outer loop cannot use the same iteration variable as the inner loop.

The behavior of the nested loop should be clear: The outer loop on `j`, which also uses the WFI form, iterates five times; that is, `j` assumes the values 0 to 4. *For each of these* `j` *values*, the whole <*statement list*> is executed; that is, the inner loop on `i` iterates 100 times, the alert is printed out, and the counters are reinitialized. That will be a total of five trials of 100 flips each, or 500 total flips. Run the program, and see the range of results.

A Diagram of Results

Suppose we are interested in how far off from a perfect 50–50 score a trial is. Such information is easily displayed with a diagram. We compute the difference of the coin flip from 50–50 and show that number using asterisks. For example, the first trial, 49–51, would be represented by a single asterisk because it differs from perfect by one coin flip. Either of the quantities **heads–50** or **tails–50** gives us the right number of asterisks, but one expression will be positive and the other one will be negative. JavaScript has a function **Math.abs()** for the absolute value; that is, it makes all numbers—positive or negative—positive, implying that **Math.abs(heads-50)** is the number of asterisks to display.

As with the raw data, the line of asterisks will be added to **text** at the end of the inner loop. (Declare **text** and initialize it to `'  '`.) But how do we include a variable number of asterisks? With another iteration, of course. We replace the previous **alert** assignment statement with the statement sequence

```
text = text + 'Trial ' + j + ': ';
for (i = 0; i < (Math.abs(heads-50)); i++) {
    text = text + '*';
}
text = text + '\n';
```

The line for the jth trial result begins with the text `"Trial j: "`. Then, an iteration is performed in which asterisks are added one at a time, up to a total of `Math.abs(heads-50)`. We can reuse the iteration variable `i` because its previous use as an iteration variable is complete. It is also fine to put the math function in the <*continuation*> test. (Notice that the WFI form tells us immediately that we have the right number of iterations.) Finally, after the iteration, the new-line character is added. Add `alert(text)` as the last line. My program generated the output shown below.

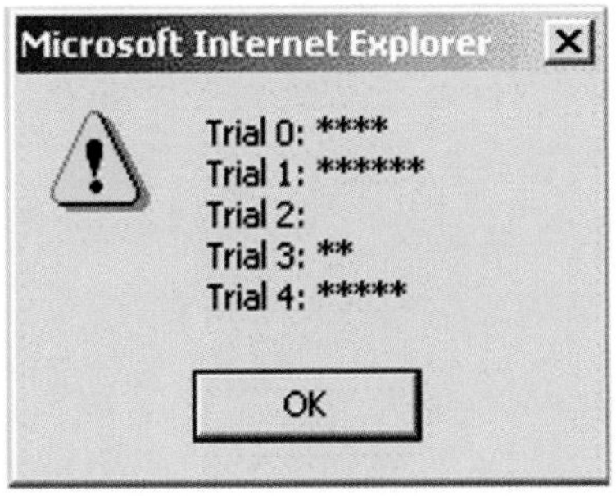

In the sample output, we notice that the successive values of `j` are, indeed, 0 through 4, that Trial 2 evidently resulted in a 50–50 outcome, and that Trial 1 had the widest variation, being 6 away from perfect, that is, either 44–56 or 56–44.

We can revise the program to print the trials 1 through 5 by changing the `text` assignment to

```
text = text + 'Trial ' + (j + 1) + ': ';
```

This is a very unusual statement because the + has two different meanings. The third + is addition, while the other three are concatenation. How does the computer know which one we mean? It looks to see if we are combining numbers (in which case, it adds) or strings (in which case, it concatenates). The special rule is that if there is one number and one string, it concatenates. So, we need the parentheses to cause the addition.

The final version of the coin-flipping program (Figure 21.1) uses three iterations, all in the WFI form.

Though it is only 21 lines long, the program performs hundreds of statements' worth of computation. We could easily change to 1000 sample trials, for no additional lines of program. And that's the value of iteration: it allows very few lines of code to command the computer to do a lot of work.

INDEXING

If you're familiar with Elizabeth II, Super Bowl XXV, *Rocky* 3, and Apollo 13, you are acquainted with indexing. **Indexing** is the process of creating a sequence of names by associating a base name ("Apollo") with a number ("13"). When a new name is needed, the next number in sequence is used ("Apollo 14"). Each indexed item is called an **element** of the base named object.

```
var heads = 0, tails = 0;                   //Counters
var i, j;                                   //Iteration variables
var text = '';                              //Output accumulator
for (j=0; j<5; j++){                        //"Trials" iteration
    for (i=0; i<100; i++){                  //"Flips" iteration
        if (randNum(2))
            heads++;
        else
            tails++;
    }
    text = text + 'Trial ' + (j + 1) + ': ';
    for (i = 0; i < (Math.abs(heads-50)); i++) {//"Stars"
        text = text + '*';
    }
text = text + '\n';
heads = 0; tails = 0;
}
alert(text);
function randNum(range) {
   return Math.floor(range*Math.random());
}
```

Figure 21.1. *The final version of the coin-flip trials program.*

Index Syntax

Naturally, in programming, indexing has a special syntax. An index is enclosed in square brackets in JavaScript, for example, `Apollo[13]`. The index can be a constant, variable, or expression. It must evaluate to a non-negative integer, the index value. (See the section "Array Reference Syntax" for more information.) Indexing is important in computing because of its close link to iteration: Iterations can be used to refer to all elements of a name; that is, a notation like `A[j]` can, on successive iterations over `j`, refer to different elements of `A`.

FITBYTE

Index Terms. The terms *indexes* and *indices* are both in common use to refer to more than one index.

Index Origin

When indexing queens, Super Bowls, popes, and so on, we usually start counting at 1, though often the first item doesn't initially get an index; for example, Queen Elizabeth I was just called Queen Elizabeth until Elizabeth II came along. Yard lines in football begin indexing with 0 (goal = 0). Movie sequels start at 2 because there can't be a *sequel* to nothing. The point at which indexing begins, that is, the least index, is known as the **index origin**.

ARRAYS

An indexed base name is called an **array** in programming; arrays must be declared. In JavaScript, arrays are declared with the syntax

`var` <*variable*> `= new Array(`<*number of elements*>`)`

Notice that unlike queens—Elizabeth I became an array element when Elizabeth II came along—variables either are or are not arrays; they don't change. In the example declaration

```
var week = new Array(7);
```

`week` is the identifier being declared, and `new Array(7)` specifies that the identifier will be an array variable. The number in parentheses gives the number of array elements. *JavaScript uses index origin 0*, meaning that the least index of any array is 0, and the greatest index will be the number of elements minus 1. Thus the array just declared has elements `week[0]`, `week[1]`, . . . , `week[6]`, that is, seven elements. The **array length** refers to the number of elements in an array. To refer to an array's length, use <*variable*>`.length`. For example, `week.length` ⇔ 7.

Rules for Arrays

To summarize, here are the rules for arrays in JavaScript:

- Arrays are normal variables initialized by `new Array(`<*number of elements*>`)`.
- <*number of elements*> in the declaration is just that—the number of array elements.
- Array indexing begins at 0.
- The number of elements in an array is its *length*.
- The greatest index of an array is <*number of elements*> – 1 because of the 0 origin.

Array Reference Syntax

An **array reference** consists of the array name together with an index—a constant, variable, or expression—enclosed in brackets and evaluating to a nonnegative integer, the **index value**. The value to which the index evaluates must be less than the array's length. Thus, the statements

```
var dwarf = new Array(7);          //Declarations use parentheses
var deux = 2;                      //Create value for examples
dwarf[0] = "Happy";                //References use brackets
dwarf[1] = "Sleepy";               //Index by a constant
dwarf[deux] = "Dopey";             //Index by a variable
dwarf[deux+1] = "Sneezy";          //Index by an expression
dwarf[2*deux] = "Bashful";
dwarf[3*deux-1] = "Grumpy";
dwarf[10-(2*deux)] = "Doc";
```

assign values to the array elements using a variety of index alternatives.

> FITBYTE
>
> **Sub Standard.** The index is also known as a *subscript*. In mathematics, indices, written below the line as in x_1 and y_1, are called subscripts. Programming inherits the same term but writes them in brackets.

When introducing the World-Famous Iteration, we said that the reason for indexing from `0` to `n-1` would soon be evident. Now we can see that 0-origin iteration is perfect for 0-origin indexing. Study the following version of the WFI:

```
for (j = 0; j < week.length ; j++) {
    week[j] = dwarf[j] + " & " + dwarf[(j+1)%7] + " do dishes";
}
```

The variable `j` ranges over all of the elements of the array **`week`**. By using <*array name*>`.length` in the <*continuation*> clause of the control, we set up to enumerate all of the array's elements. This iteration creates entries of the form

```
week[0] ⇔ "Happy & Sleepy do dishes"
week[1] ⇔ "Sleepy and Dopey do dishes"
...
week[6] ⇔ "Doc & Happy do dishes"
```

by referring to a consecutive pair of elements from **`dwarf`**. The final pair—Doc & Happy—which must "wraparound," use (*j*+1) *mod* 7 to index the **`dwarf`** array in the second reference. That is, `(j+1)%7` results in an index value of 0 because (6+1) divided by 7 has a 0 remainder, which is Happy.

> FITBYTE
>
> **Why So Famous?** Our focus on computing the index with an expression explains why the WFI is so popular. Because it's common to have to program *some* expression for the index values, it doesn't matter much whether the iteration variable counts starting at 0 or at 1 or at 14. The index expression can adjust the value as long as the *total* number of values is correct. The WFI does this, and does it better than other iterations.

THE BUSY ANIMATION

As we know, movies, cartoons, and flipbooks animate by the rapid display of many still pictures known as *frames*. Human visual perception is relatively slow—presumably because of the amazingly complicated tasks it performs—so it is fooled into observing smooth motion when the *display rate* is about 30 frames per second, that is, 30 Hz. In this section, we learn the principles of online animation—like the Dymaxion Map of Chapter 6—and practice using iteration, arrays, and indexing.

The animation we plan to construct is the familiar "busy" indicator, as shown in Figure 21.2. The eight frames contributing to the animation are shown with their indices. The rapid cyclic display of the frames makes the circle appear to revolve. Creating this Busy Animation is the goal of this section.

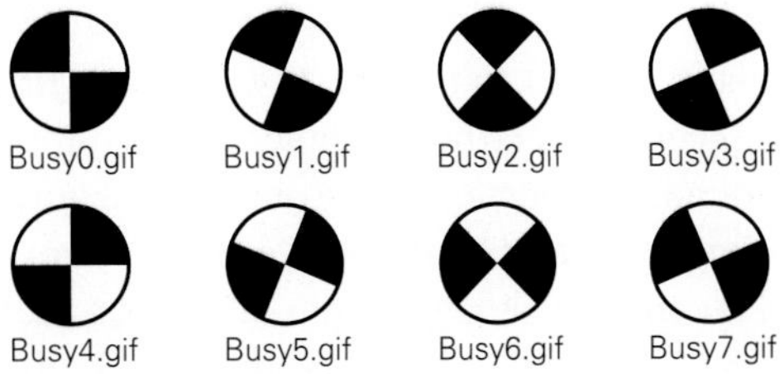

Figure 21.2. *The* `.gif` *images for the Busy Animation. These files are available at* `www.aw.com/snyder/`.

FITTIP **Fast Motion.** The quickest way to learn both the ideas and the practical skills of animation is to build the program yourself as you read along.

Before you can successfully program an animation in JavaScript, you must understand three concepts:

> Using a timer to initiate animation events

> Prefetching the frames of the animation

> Redrawing a Web page image

As the ideas are introduced, we program the Busy Animation.

Using a Timer to Initiate Animation

The animation we produce will be displayed by a Web browser. As we know, Web browsers are *event driven*. That is, they are told to perform some task, they do it, and then they sit idle waiting for some event to tell them to do the next task. If browsers are idle when they are not working on a task, how could they animate anything? Animations require action every 30 milliseconds. The obvious solution is to turn the activity of drawing the next frame into an event. The event will be the regular "ticking" of a clock. Use a timer analogy. We set a timer to wake up the browser to tell it to display the next frame, and then set it again for 30 milliseconds into the future. In 30 milliseconds, we repeat the process. In this way, we draw the frames at regular intervals, creating an animation. Such a scheme is for *online animations*. Animations like *Toy Story* apply these ideas differently. Not surprisingly, JavaScript comes equipped with all of the features, for example, timers, needed to implement online animation.

Setting a Timer. Computers have extremely fast internal clocks, but they're too fast for most programming purposes. Instead, programmers' timers typically "tick" once per millisecond. Timers are pretty intuitive. In JavaScript, the command to set a timer is

```
setTimeout("<event handler>", <duration>)
```

where *<event handler>* is a string giving the JavaScript computation that will run when the timer goes off, and *<duration>* is any positive number of milliseconds.

For example, to display a frame in 30 ms using the function **animate()** as an event handler to display it, write **setTimeout("animate()", 30)**. Thirty milliseconds later, the computer will run the **animate()** function, displaying the frame. Of course, the last step for the **animate()** function must be to set the timer so that it "wakes up" again. Otherwise, the animation stops. ("Every 30 milliseconds" is different from 30 times a second, of course, because 1000/30 = 33.333 ms. We can set the timer to 33 ms, but animation is not an exact science and 30 is close enough.)

Using a Handle to Refer to a Timer. Unlike mechanical timers, computer timers can keep track of many different times at once. How does the computer keep the settings straight? When we perform **setTimeout()**, we get back a special code—it's called a **handle**—that the computer uses to identify our timer. We can use the handle to refer to our timer, say, to cancel it. For example, if we declare a variable, **timerID**, with which to save the handle, and write

```
timerID = setTimeout("animate()", 30);
```

we can cancel the timer by writing

```
clearTimeout(timerID);
```

and the computer will know which of the timers it's keeping track of should be canceled.

Using Buttons to Start/Stop the Animation. Because timers can be set and canceled, we will include two buttons to start and stop our animation. Their definitions will be

```
<input type=button value=Start onClick=
   'setTimeout("animate()",30);'>
<input type=button value=Stop onClick='clearTimeout(timerID);'>
```

The **Start** button will set the timer for the first time. The animation keeps going on its own thereafter. Each time **animate()** sets the timer, the handle is stored in **timerID**. Then, when the **Stop** button is clicked, its event handler clears the timer, stopping the animation.

Prefetching Images

The next topic to consider is displaying images. Recall from Chapter 4 that to keep our Web pages tidy, we like to keep the **.gif** and **.jpg** images in a separate directory or folder. So, assume that the graphics files shown in Figure 21.2 are in a folder **gifpix**. Then, the first of the images would be displayed on a Web page with the HTML

```
<img src="gifpix/Busy0.gif">
```

We begin with the skeleton HTML page that includes the **<form>** tags and the two buttons:

```
<html><head><title>Busy Animation</title></head>
  <body><center>
  <img src=gifpix/Busy0.gif>       <!-- Intial Frame -->
  <form>
    <input type=button value=Start
        onClick='setTimeout("animate()",30);'>
    <input type=button value=Stop
        onClick='clearTimeout(timerID);'>
  </form>
  </center></body>
</html>
```

We would like to overwrite that single image with all of the other **`.gif`** files in **`gifpix`** in sequence, one every 30 ms. But we cannot do so directly. The problem is that loading the images will generally be too slow to allow us to show a new image so quickly. Web images must be transferred from the Web server across the Internet, where they encounter all sorts of delays. (We don't notice this while we're developing a Web application on our computers because all of the files are already stored locally.) Consequently, the strategy is to get the images first, store them locally so they will all be available in the computer's memory, and then display them. The process of loading the images ahead of time is called **prefetching**.

Where will the eight images (**`Busy0.gif`** through **`Busy7.gif`**) of the **`gifpix`** folder be put? Because they are indexed already, it's logical to use an array. We'll name the array **`pics`**, and declare it

```
var pics = new Array (8);
```

indicating that it will have eight elements.

Initializing to an Image Object. In order for the elements of the array to store an image, they must be initialized to an **image object**. An image object is a blank instance of an image (Chapter 2). Think of an image object as a skeleton that provides places for all of the information needed to store an image, such as its name, size of its two dimensions, and its actual pixels. To initialize the eight array elements to image objects requires an iteration and the new **`Image()`** operation,

```
for (i = 0; i < pics.length; i++) {
    pics[i] = new Image();
}
```

Using the src Component. Among the places in the image object is a field called **`src`** where the image's source is stored—that is, the file name of the file containing the image. This is the string that we give in the **`<img src="...">`** tag. When we assign to the **`src`** field using dot notation, the browser saves the name and gets the file, storing it in memory, just as we require. Thus,

```
pics[0].src = "gifpix/Busy0.gif"
```

parallels our earlier explicit fetch of the initial frame. Because there are eight images in total, we use a loop,

```
for (i = 0; i < pics.length; i++) {
    pics[i].src = "gifpix/Busy" + i + ".gif";
}
```

which constructs the file names on-the-fly. That is, we build up file name **Busy*i*.gif** using the iteration variable and concatenation.

There is an important difference between the prefetching by assigning to the **.src** field of an image variable, and using **<img src="...">** in HTML. The former is not visible on the screen, whereas the latter is. This works to our advantage both ways. The image variable, which is just a part of our JavaScript program, is not visible because it hasn't been placed on the page. But that's fine, because we don't want the user to see the prefetch happening anyway. The **<img src="...">** tag places an image on the page, and so is visible. We need both.

Redrawing an Image

To animate the initial frame that we placed earlier with **<img src="...">**, we need to overwrite it with the images that we just prefetched at a rate of one every 30 ms. How do we refer to the initial frame so as to overwrite it? Interestingly, Web browsers keep in the HTML document an array of the images that is just like our **pics** array. As the **<img src="...">** commands are encountered, the browser fills its images array just like we filled **pics**. So, **document.images[0]** is the name of the first image—that is, our initial frame **Busy0.gif**. Any additional **<img src="...">** images are indexed with higher numbers in sequence. The browser's images array elements have the **src** property too, and assigning to it overwrites the image. Thus, to change the initial frame, we write the assignment

```
document.images[0].src = pics[i].src;
```

which replaces the initial frame with the ith element of the **pics** array, causing it to be displayed. All that needs to happen to animate the Busy icon is to sweep through all of the **i** values, cyclically, one every 30 ms.

Defining the animate() Event Handler.

The **animate()** event handler overwrites the image, sets up for the next frame, and sets the timer to call itself again:

```
function animate () {
  document.images[0].src = pics[frame].src;
  frame = (frame + 1)%8;
  timerID = setTimeout ("animate()", 30);
}
```

With the concepts explained, the whole Busy Animation, including the familiar **Start** and **Stop** buttons, is shown in Figure 21.3.

As a postscript to Busy Animation, the reader is encouraged to click **Start** several times, followed by an equal number of **Stop** clicks. Can you explain the behavior?

```
<html><head><title>Bars</title></head><body bgcolor=white><center>
<img src=gifpix/Busy0.gif>
<script>
var i, frame = 0;                                       //Iteration vars
var timerID;                                            //Timer handle
var pics = new Array (8);                               //Array to prefetch into
for (i=0;i<pics.length ;i++) {                          //Init. array for images
    pics[i] = new Image();
}
for (i=0;i<pics.length;i++) {                           //Prefetch images
    pics[i].src = "gifpix/Busy" + i + ".gif";
}
function animate () {                                   //Draw pic, call self
  document.images[0].src = pics[frame].src;             //Change pic
  frame = (1+frame)%8;                                  //Move to next frame
  timerID = setTimeout("animate()", 30);                //Schedule next tick
}
</script>
<form>
<input type=button value=Start onClick='setTimeout("animate()",30)'>
<input type=button value=Stop onClick='clearTimeout(timerID)'>
</form>
</center></body></html>
```

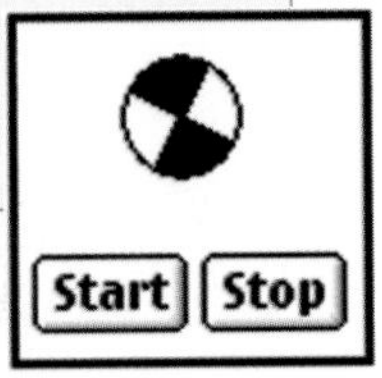

Figure 21.3. *The Busy Animation, assuming that the eight* **`.gif`** *files are stored in a directory* **`gifpix`**

SUMMARY

Our interest in studying the fundamentals of programming has been to understand the sources of power in computation. The concepts of this chapter—iteration, indexing, and arrays—account for much of it. There is much more to say about programming, but we leave the rest of it to the experts.

The basics of **`for`** loop iteration have been covered in detail. The control part of a **`for`** statement is written in parentheses, and the <*statement list*> is enclosed in curly braces. With each iteration, the entire statement list is performed. The number of iterations is determined by assignments to and tests of the iteration variable as specified in the control part. In the JavaScript **`for`** statement, the <*initialization*> component is executed first. Then, prior to each iteration, including the first, the <*continuation*> predicate is tested. If it is **`true`**, the <*statement list*> is performed; otherwise, it is skipped, and the **`for`** statement terminates. After each iteration, the <*next iteration*> operation is performed. The principles of iteration ensure that every iteration contains a test, and that the test is dependent on variables that change in the loop.

The **`for`** statement is very flexible. The <*initialization*> can begin anywhere, the <*continuation*> test can stop the loop anywhere, and the <*next iteration*> operation can step by various amounts as well as count upward or downward. Though **`for`** loops of many forms can be written, programmers have gotten into the habit of using the World-Famous Iteration (WFI)—a stylized iteration that begins at 0, tests that the iteration variable is strictly less than some limit, and increments by 1. There is no obligation to use the WFI, but doing so has the advantage that you can quickly determine the number of times around the loop—it's the limit to the right of `<`. Because it is common to make errors figuring out the number of iterations, programmers get in the habit of using the WFI to have a fast way to recognize the number of iterations.

In indexing we create a series of names by associating a number with a base name. Need more names? Count out more numbers. Indexed variables are known as **arrays** in programming. Like ordinary variables, arrays must be declared, but they use the **`new Array(`**<*length*>**`)`** syntax, in which <*length*> is the number of elements of the array. Array elements—referenced by giving the name and a nonnegative index in brackets—can be used like ordinary variables. Using many examples, we showed how arrays and iteration could be effectively used together.

We returned to random numbers and used **`for`** loops in experiments with flipping an electronic coin. And we introduced some basic concepts of online animation. All animations achieve the appearance of motion by rapidly displaying a series of still frames. For animating information displayed by a Web browser, it is advisable to prefetch the images so that they are readily accessible for rapid display. The key idea is to use a timer to create events, and then use the timer-event handler to redraw an image that has been placed on the Web page by the **`<img src="...">`** tag. These are referenced as the elements of the document's images array.

EXERCISES

Multiple Choice

1. In JavaScript the `for` statement is used for:
   A. assignment
   B. increment
   C. iteration
   D. selection
2. If your mother told you four times to clean up your room (or in the computer age, to clean up your Desktop), there were:
   A. four repetitions
   B. four iterations
   C. three iterations
   D. five iterations
3. In a `for` loop, the iteration value is changed by:
   A. the <*continuation*> test
   B. the <*next iteration*>
   C. a false <*continuation*> test
   D. the end of the statement sequence
4. A `false` outcome for a termination test means:
   A. terminate the loop
   B. terminate the program
   C. continue the loop
   D. do not enter the loop
5. The command to display an alert box in JavaScript is:
   A. `write.alert`
   B. `display.alert`
   C. `alert()`
   D. `alert = "text"`
6. The maximum number of times a loop can iterate is:
   A. 1024
   B. 65,536
   C. 1,048,576
   D. infinite
7. `i++` means:
   A. add the value of `i` to itself and store the result in `i`
   B. add 1 to `i`
   C. multiply `i` by itself
   D. check to see if `i` is positive

8. For the statement below, which of the following is true?

```
for (j = 0; j < n; j++) {...}
```

   A. the loop starts at 0
   B. the loop increments by 1
   C. the loop steps after *n* iterations
   D. all of the above

9. Array elements cannot be numbered with:
   A. negative numbers
   B. decimals
   C. numbers greater or equal to their number of elements
   D. all of the above

10. The timer in JavaScript is called:
   A. `setTimeout`
   B. `Math.Timer`
   C. `Timer`
   D. `setTick`

11. Given the line below, which of the following is a valid array reference?

```
var cols = New Array(9)
```

   A. `cols[0]`
   B. `cols[4.5]`
   C. `cols[9]`
   D. `cols[10]`

12. Loading an image ahead of time is known as:
   A. buffering
   B. prefetching
   C. caching
   D. backlogging

Short Answer

1. ______ means to loop through a series of statements to repeat them.
2. The ______ statement is used to start a loop in JavaScript.
3. A `for` loop is controlled by a ______.
4. ______ is the first operation of a `for` loop.
5. The first step of the second iteration of a loop is the ______ test.
6. The shortcut to subtract 1 from `i` is ______.
7. A loop that never ends is known as a(n) ______.
8. A loop inside a loop is called a(n) ______.
9. In JavaScript, the command to force a new line is ______.
10. `Math.abs()` is used in JavaScript to find ______.

11. ______ is the creation of a sequence of names by associating a base name with a number.
12. An indexed item is called a(n) ______.
13. The number of elements in an array is its ______.
14. A(n) ______ is an array name with its index.
15. The ______ is the number of frames per second that is displayed in an animation.

Exercises

1. You're making cookies (the real ones) and the directions say to stir until thoroughly mixed. Explain how a loop like this works.
2. Describe the Fundamental Principles of Iteration.
3. Write the code for a loop that starts at 0 and iterates seven times.
4. Write the code for a loop that starts at your birth year and iterates for each year of your age.
5. Young lovers often use a daisy to determine the true feelings of the other. With each petal they count, they alternate "She loves me" and "She loves me, not." Generate a random number up to 25 and then use that to determine if your girlfriend (or boyfriend) loves you. Even numbers mean love. Other numbers mean not. Display the process.
6. Use nested loops to "count" from 1 to 100. Use the inner loop for the ones digit and the outer loop for the tens digit. Concatenate them to display the "number."
7. What would it take to "count" to 1000 in exercise 6?
8. Create a loop to display a set of asterisks to create a set of "stairs."

```
      *
     **
    ***
   ****
  *****
 ******
*******
```

9. Create a loop to display a set of "stairs" that go down instead of up.
10. Compile a list of everyday items that make up an array.
11. Explain why loops can use negative numbers and decimals but an array cannot.
12. Explain how an animation uses still images and loops to create the illusion of motion.

chapter

22 THE SMOOTH MOTION

Case Study Algorithmic Problem Solving

learning objectives

- State and apply the Decomposition Principle
- Explain the problem-solving strategy used in creating the Smooth Motion application
- Explain the use in Smooth Motion of the JavaScript operations for iteration, indexing, arrays, functions, animation controls, and event handlers
- Explain how mouse events are handled in Smooth Motion

All parts should go together without forcing. You must remember that the parts you are reassembling were disassembled by you. Therefore, if you can't get them together again, there must be a reason. By all means, do not use a hammer.

—IBM MAINTENANCE MANUAL (1925)

THE PROGRAMMING that we've learned indicates how computers solve problems and what the source of their speed and versatility is. Further, we've learned enough programming to be able to embellish our Web pages, making them more adaptive and dynamic. But the great value of the knowledge we've acquired is neither insight nor embellishments. Rather, we can apply the programming ideas to general problem-solving situations. Processes, procedures, instructions and directions, decision-making, and so forth are phenomena we meet in daily life beyond the sphere of computers. Our knowledge applies in all of those cases, making us more effective at learning, performing, and planning tasks. Applying this knowledge by solving a more substantial task is the topic of this chapter.

Though the ideas have broad application, our interest and preparation are still with IT. Accordingly, the task we will solve is a Web application we'll call Smooth Motion, for testing a user's coordination at manipulating the mouse. How smooth are you? The application will use event programming, including "mouse events," animation, controls, more sophisticated HTML, functions, iteration, indexing, and arrays. Smooth Motion is a generic application that allows us to focus on the problem-solving activity. By patiently following this fully worked case study, we will have opportunities to discuss when and how to apply the ideas we have learned.

THE SMOOTH MOTION APPLICATION

Step 0 in solving any problem is to understand what must be accomplished. (Almost everything in this chapter is 0-origin!) The Smooth Motion application is a coordination test. (Try out Smooth Motion at `www.aw.com/snyder/`.) The graphical user interface is shown in Figure 22.1. Naming the components from top to bottom as an aid to discussing them, we have these parts:

> **Heading:** The text "Smooth Motion"

> **Grid:** The 7 × 20 grid of squares

> **Keys:** The row of seven brown/orange boxes

> **Controls:** The buttons and radio settings

> **Instructions:** The text at the bottom

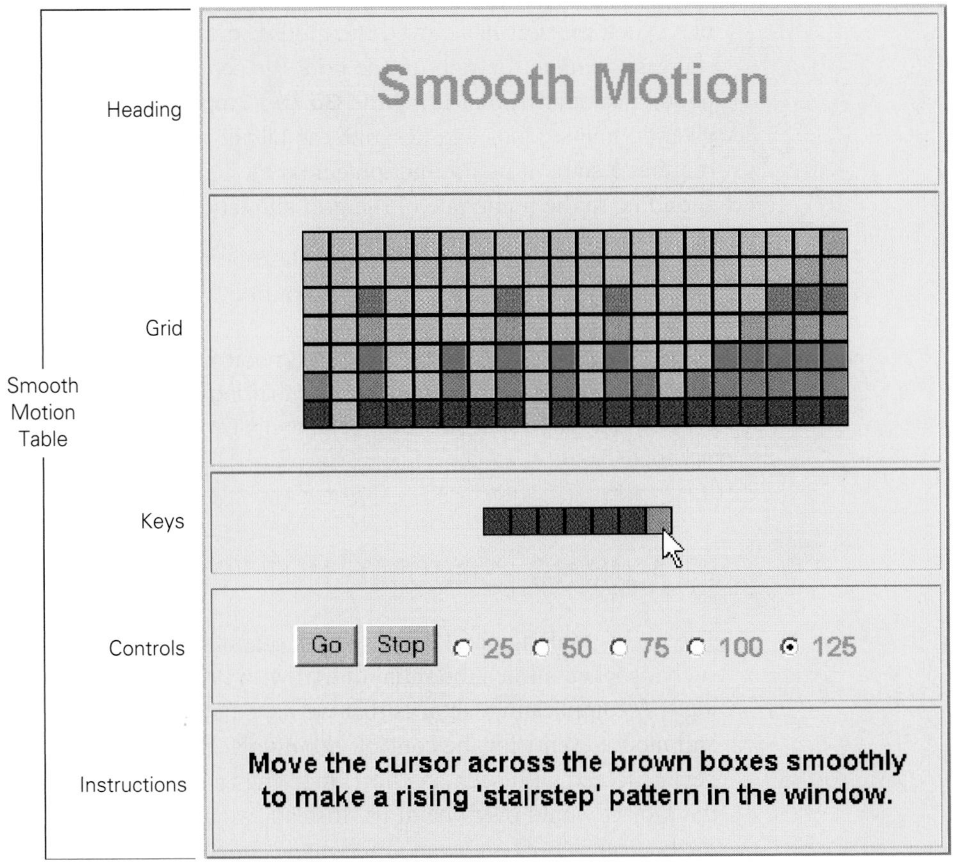

Figure 22.1. *The Smooth Motion application user interface. Try it* `www.aw.com/snyder`.

Further, the components are enclosed in a one-column table with a border and a colored background.

How the Smooth Motion Application Should Work

Smooth Motion works as follows. The application starts up automatically five seconds after it is loaded. It begins filling the grid from the right with random height stacks of blocks. The blocks move steadily to the left at a rate determined by the controls. Examples of the random stacks of blocks are shown in the left half of the grid in Figure 22.1.

The random stack generation continues until the user places the mouse cursor over one of the keys. At that point, the user is in control of the stacks of blocks displayed in the grid. The leftmost key = 1, the rightmost key = 7. Figure 22.1 shows the seven-block stack being selected by the cursor on key 7. If the mouse is over key *n*, a stack of *n* blocks appears in the grid.

The user's goal is to move the mouse across the brown keys as smoothly as possible. When the user has moved the mouse smoothly enough to create a perfect staircase rising to the right in the grid, the action stops. The process can be started or stopped at any point using the **Go** and **Stop** buttons. The speed selections are given in milliseconds and describe the rate at which the blocks move left. The test requires a smooth mouse motion across the keys from left to right at a rate corresponding to the frame rate of the grid animation.

Programming the Smooth Motion application is a substantial project, though surprisingly it requires only a modest amount of HTML and JavaScript.

> FITTIP
>
> **Smooth Move.** How would you program Smooth Motion? Before reading about problem solving in this chapter, spend five minutes thinking about how you would solve this problem. Truly, thinking about your own solution first will help you to understand the chapter quicker.

PLANNING SMOOTH MOTION

The goal is to design and construct the Smooth Motion application. Achieving such a goal entails a substantial design with several functions and some intricate logic. A complicating factor is that we have both timer events for the animation and mouse events for the controls taking place simultaneously. Most of us would never succeed with such an effort by trying to "brain it out." The complications of the project would overwhelm us. Instead, we will succeed by approaching it in a methodical step-by-step way, applying an important divide-and-conquer technique to simplify our work. By breaking the project into convenient, manageable pieces, we will succeed.

Apply the Decomposition Principle

A fundamental strategy for solving complex problems is the following principle:

> **Decomposition Principle:** Divide a large task into smaller subtasks that can be solved separately and then combined to produce the overall solution.

Of course, the subtasks may not be small enough to be worked out easily, so the Decomposition Principle can be applied again to each of the subtasks, producing even smaller subtasks, and so on. Eventually the components become small enough that it is possible to figure out how to solve them directly. When the subtasks are all solved, we begin the assembly process, combining the most primitive components to produce the more complex components, and so on until the overall problem is solved. The Decomposition Principle is little more than common sense, but when applied judiciously, it is a powerful technique for achieving large results.

List the Tasks

The Smooth Motion application has several parts that provide an obvious beginning point for applying the Decomposition Principle:

Task	Description
Build GUI	Create a Web page with the table and its constituent parts: title, grid, keys, controls, and instructions
Animate Grid	Move the block stacks to the left
Sense Keys	Handle the mouse events and transfer the control information to the grid animator
Detect Staircase	Recognize when among a stream of events the user has "met the test"
Build Controls	Implement the actions to control the application
Assemble Overall Design	Build the automatic random start-up, handle the starting and stopping, set the speeds, and interconnect the other components
Primp the Design	Make the page attractive and work smoothly

Only the Build GUI task is simple enough to be solved directly, and even it is fancier than the other Web pages we've constructed so far. All of the other tasks will require further decomposition when we start to solve them.

Decide on a Problem-Solving Strategy

Decomposing the problem into tasks is step number one in solving it. Step number two is to strategize how to solve each of the parts. The strategy concerns mostly in what order to solve the parts.

Build a Basic Web Page First. First, because JavaScript programming usually needs a Web page to host the computation, it makes sense to begin with the Build GUI task rather than any of the others. Such an approach gives us a place to test and save the solutions to the other tasks. The page becomes an organizing structure, a location where we record our progress by adding our JavaScript code to it.

FITCAUTION

Total Waste. One pitfall to avoid in any JavaScript design is spending hours constructing a splashy Web page only to discover that it doesn't fit well with the solutions to the other tasks. Such a mistake won't happen here—this is a "textbook example" after all—but it is an error to avoid on your other projects.

So, we begin by building the host page, but to avoid wasting time on a splashy-but-inappropriate page, we will build only the basic primitive page, and wait to embellish the design until after the parts are all working. Thus we're splitting the GUI construction into two parts.

Though our problem is too small to illustrate it, there is a problem solving strategy that creates a working prototype first before completing the whole design. This strategy is smart because it is easier to add to an already-working primitive design. Our plan to focus on the basic Web page and leave the cosmetic features to the end is in the spirit of this approach.

Solve Independent Tasks before Dependent Tasks. Deciding the order in which to solve the other tasks requires us to consider the **task dependencies**. That is, some tasks—for example, Detect Staircase—*rely on* or *depend on* the solution of other tasks, such as Sense Keys. Tasks that do not rely on the solution of any other tasks are *independent*. Independent tasks should be done first. Tasks that depend on the independent tasks can be done next, tasks that depend on them can follow, and so on. All of the tasks could be mutually dependent, though this is rare. In that case the dependent tasks are started, pushed as far as possible until they absolutely need the results of another task, and then are interrupted to work on the other task. For us, GUI construction is the independent task, and the Animate Grid task is dependent only on it. So, we'll schedule it second. Sense Keys is also dependent only on the GUI, but it is easier to test with the Animate Grid task complete. It will be our third task.

PERT Chart. Keeping track of many dependencies can be confusing, so systems engineers and managers draw a **task dependency graph**, or **PERT chart**. Standing for Program Evaluation and Review Technique, PERT charts were developed by the U.S. Navy in the 1950s.

There are several ways to draw them; we place tasks in circles and use arrows to show dependencies. In Figure 22.2 we have placed an arrow between two circles so that the task at the head of the arrow depends on the task at the tail of the arrow. In this (very common) form of a PERT chart, we begin with circles that have no incoming arrows. From any circle, the arrows show which tasks can be done next when the task in the circle is completed.

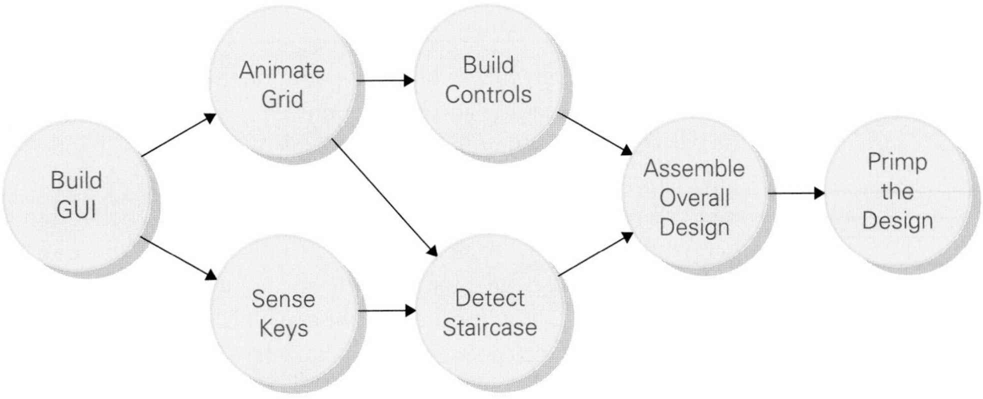

Figure 22.2. *A task dependency diagram, also known as a PERT chart, drawn so that tasks are in circles and arrows can be read as "task at head of arrow depends on task at tail of arrow."*

Summarizing Our Strategy

CHECKLIST>>

Our strategy is to solve the tasks in this order:

- *Build GUI, to give us the basic Web page.*
- *Animate Grid, which is dependent only on the Build GUI task.*
- *Sense Keys, which is dependent only on the Build GUI task.*
- *Detect Staircase, which is dependent on Animate Grid and Sense Keys.*
- *Build Controls, which is dependent on Animate Grid.*
- *Assemble Overall Design, wrapping up those parts not yet complete.*
- *Primp the Design, embellishing the Web page.*

Usually each of these tasks would be further simplified using the Decomposition Principle until all of its subtasks were simple enough to solve directly. Doing so ensures that the decomposition has produced a practical solution. For our purposes, we will use a slightly different strategy, choosing instead to assign a section to each task and apply the Decomposition Principle at the start of the section.

BUILD THE BASIC WEB PAGE GUI

The full graphical user interface for Smooth Motion will have a table with constituent parts: heading, grid, keys, controls, and instructions. For now, we'll create the basic structure. We'll call this the structural page. The "basic" features include the table, heading, and instructions as well as the background color, font style and color, and the centering of the application on the page. We'll improve it later when the application is completely working.

The Structural Page

The structural page will contain a five-row, one-column table; the text for the Smooth Motion heading and instructions are placed in the first and last rows. As we learned from making the Memory Bank Web page in Chapter 20, it is easiest to build tables "inside out," using copy and paste. That is, we construct a generic table cell with `<td>` tags, replicate that to make a row enclosed in `<tr>` tags, and then replicate the row to make the whole table enclosed in `<table>` tags. Then we fill it in. Because the table has only one column, it's not necessary to replicate the cells to make a row for the present situation. For us, the "generic" table cell is centered and contains a single blank character. The "basic" table has a border.

The Structural Page Heading

For the heading text, we use an `<h1>` heading, and for the instructions, we use a paragraph tag. Because the instructions text has a different text color than the other text on the page, we must set its font color.

The graphic and the HTML for the structural page definition are shown in Figure 22.3. Notice that the middle three rows of Figure 22.1 do not appear in Figure 22.3 because they are only white space, and so do not show. However, they are defined in the HTML, providing a site for our next programming, the Animate Grid task.

ANIMATE THE GRID

The Animate Grid task must animate the 7 × 20 = 140 grid of blocks moving from right to left. This task is much too complicated to solve directly, so we apply the Decomposition Principle again.

First Analysis

Luckily, the Busy Animation of Chapter 21 illustrated the basic steps of animation:

> Define and place the initial image.

> Prefetch the frames for updating the image.

> Set a timer and build a timer event handler, which updates the image.

These then are our starting decomposition for the Grid Animation. But these three steps don't fully solve the problem. We need to think and strategize further.

Frames for the Columns of Blocks. How will we organize the rapid redrawing of 140 images, keeping track of each block's trajectory? Reviewing how the application is supposed to work, we notice first that it only discusses "stacks" of blocks. This implies that there is no "motion" of images vertically, only horizontally. (This is obvious by the color scheme, too.) And, the horizontal

```
<html>
  <head><title>Smooth Motion Application</title></head>
  <body bgcolor="white" text="#FF6600">
      <font face='Helvetica'><center>
    <table border=2>
      <tr> <td align="center">
             <h1>Smooth Motion</h1>
             </td></tr>
      <tr> <td align="center">
             </td></tr>
      <tr> <td align="center">
             </td></tr>
      <tr> <td align="center">
             </td></tr>
      <tr> <td align="center">
             <p><font color='black'><b>
             Move the cursor across the brown boxes smoothly <br>
             to make a rising 'staircase' pattern in the
             window.</b></font></p></td></tr>
    </table></center>
  </body>
</html>
```

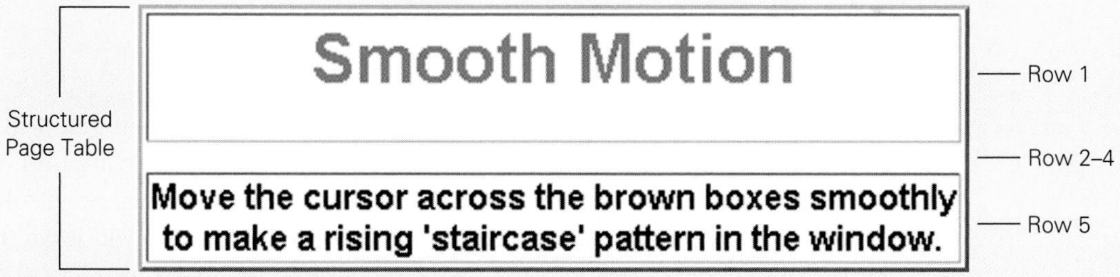

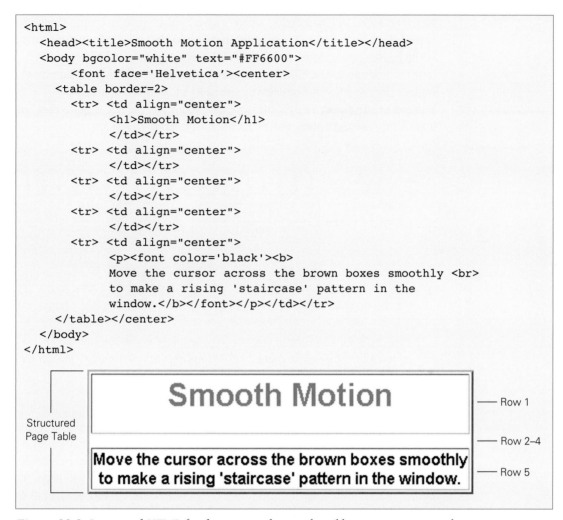

Figure 22.3. *Image and HTML for the structural page; the table appears compressed because rows 2–4 contain nothing and so are not displayed.*

motion is limited only to moving from right to left. From these observations we can conclude that we don't have to animate individual squares at all. The images can be whole columns. That simplification reduces the total number of images in the grid to 20, that is, the number of columns. Of course, we will need a frame image for each stack of blocks: a 0-stack, a 1-stack, . . . , and a 7-stack, resulting in a total of eight frames. So, one new subtask is to define and organize the column frames.

`Indexing Columns Left to Right.` Next consider the "motion of an image." On each time step a given column is replaced by the column to its right. If the 20 columns are indexed left to right, then the image in column i of the grid at a given time step is replaced on the next time step by the image in column $i+1$. See Figure 22.4. (The columns will be indexed from 0, left to right, because, as was mentioned in Chapter 21, when browsers place images on the page, they record them in the array **`document.images`** in the order encountered; that order is the construction sequence of an HTML page, top to bottom, left to right. So, the leftmost column of the Grid is **`document.images[0]`**.) Thus the action is to replace the contents of **`document.images[i]`** with the contents of **`document.images[i+1]`**. Shifting each column to the left is quite easy, and it leaves only the last column to be handled differently.

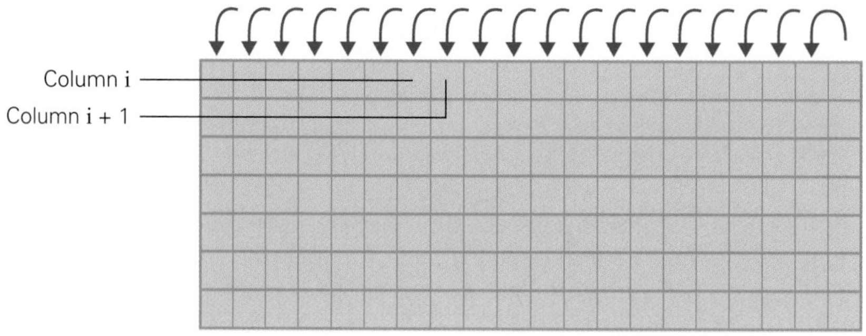

Figure 22.4. *With column 0 at the left, the image in column i should be replaced by the image in column i+1 to implement the left-moving motion for the Grid Animation event handler.*

Handling column 19 (last) is easy because we only need to assign a new image—that is, one of the eight frames. Which frame do we assign? If we are in the random start-up phase, it should be a random frame. If we are in user-controlled phase, it should be whichever frame the user has specified. We will leave this choice of the frame open for the time being because the Assemble Overall Design task will set the frame selection properly.

Second Analysis

From our first analysis it seems that we should add subtasks for defining an image-shifting process and for defining a column-19 fill process, but it's not necessary. Both activities will be part of the timer event handler, which is already on our list. So, our subtask list for the Animate Grid task is as follows:

1. Define and organize the eight columnar frames.
2. Define and place the initial images, 0 through 19.
3. Prefetch the eight frames for updating the image.
4. Set a timer with an event handler that shifts the images in columns 1 through 19 to columns 0 through 18, respectively, and introduces a new frame into column 19.

We'll assign a subsection to each subtask.

Subtask: Define and Organize the Frames. The eight frames for the Smooth Motion application are shown in Figure 22.5. The files are available online (`www.aw.com/snyder/`) and need not be created. Notice that they have names indexed in accordance with the block height. Also, the images have the necessary colors and lines to be placed densely side by side to construct the grid.

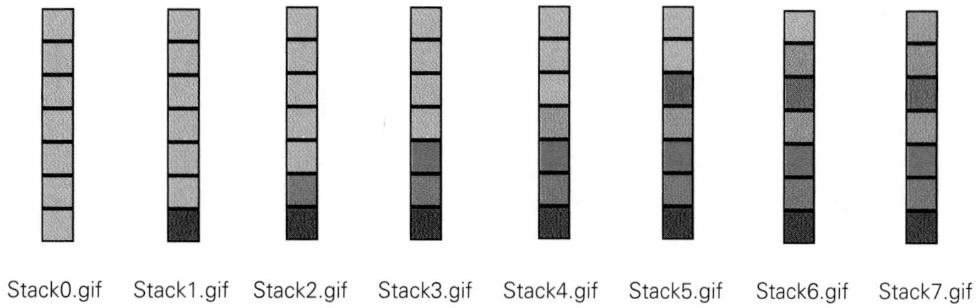

Figure 22.5. *The eight frames required for the Smooth Motion application.*

If the `gif` frames had not been available, we would have had to create them. Numerous tools are available for this purpose, from simple paint programs to sophisticated image editing facilities. Though the tools vary in capabilities, convenience, and sophistication, there are only two guidelines to follow when creating frame images for animations with any of these tools:

> Ensure that all images overwriting one another have the same dimensions in pixels; an easy way to meet this constraint is to create an initial "blank" frame, save it, and use it as the base for creating all of the other frames.

> Ensure that all files are saved using either the `.gif` or `.jpg` formats, and that they are used consistently; that is, only overwrite `.gif`s with `.gif`s.

To use images in HTML, it is recommended that they be placed in a separate directory, simply as an organizing technique. Following that advice, the stack `gifs` of Figure 22.5 will be saved in a directory called `gifpix`, meaning that their names relative to the HTML file are `gifpix/Stack0.gif`, `gifpix/Stack1.gif`, etc.

Subtask: Define and Place Initial Images. This subtask constructs the grid in the second row of the structural page (Figure 22.3). The initial state of the grid is created from 20 copies of `Stack0.gif`. As usual, to place an image on a page, the `<img src="...">` tag is used. But the 20 images will require 20 such tags. This calls for a loop. To use JavaScript's `for` statement, we place the `<script>` tags inside of the second row's `<td>` tags, and within them we write the necessary JavaScript. To have the images appear on the structural page, we must place them using the `document.write()` function.

The iteration can use the World-Famous Iteration form and must declare an iteration variable. The necessary code to implement these objectives is

```
<script language='JavaScript'>
var j;                                  //Declare iteration var
for (j = 0; j < 20; j++) {              //Initialize grid images
    document.write('<img src="gifpix/Stack0.gif">');
}
</script>
```

which completes the image initialization.

Subtask: Prefetch the Frame Images. As explained in Chapter 21, animating with images fetched from across the Internet is not likely to work because of delays that the `.gif` files might encounter during transfer. So, prefetching is necessary, and it is the goal of this subtask. (Review prefetching from the Busy Animation, if necessary.)

Relative to the creation of the Web page, the prefetching activity can be performed at any time prior to the start of the animation. Because the prefetching also requires JavaScript code, we decide to place it with the code from the initialization subtask just completed, say, after the declaration. This is a good location because to prefetch the frames, we need an eight-element image array to prefetch into, and so we will need another declaration for that array.

The three steps of prefetching are as follows:

1. Declare the array into which the images will be fetched.
2. Initialize the array elements to be image objects; that is, define the image structure for each array element using the `new Image()` specification.
3. Assign the names of the files to the `src` fields of the image objects, causing the browser to record the names and get the files, thus implementing the prefetch.

The file names are those given in Figure 22.5. We will call the array `pics`, and use a separate iteration for the second and third tasks, though combining the two operations into a single iteration is equivalent. The resulting code

```
var pics = new Array(8);            //Declare array for gifs
for (j = 0; j < 8; j++) {           //Make the elements images
    pics[j] = new Image();
}
for (j = 0; j < 8; j++) {           //Name source file & prefetch
    pics[j].src = "gifpix/Stack" + j + ".gif";
}
```

is inserted within the previous `<script>` tags, after the declaration. Notice that the file names are constructed on-the-fly to save us from typing separate statements.

Subtask: Set Timer and Build Timer Event Handler. The subtask is mostly concerned with writing the event handler to move each of the grid's images left one position, obliterating the 0 image and assigning a new image to position 19 . So we begin by constructing that event handler, called `animate()`. As we work on it, several additional details will arise that will require our attention.

The timer event handler `animate()` has three operations:

1. To move all images but the first left one position.
2. To assign a new frame to image 19.
3. To schedule itself for sometime in the future.

The mechanism for choosing the new frame is not yet worked out, but the Assemble Overall Design task will resolve it. For the moment, we simply assign a random frame as an easy way to have something different happening on each tick. And, assigning random frames is the way the application is to begin anyway.

Recall that browsers store the details of the images they display in an array called `images`, that the array is referenced as `document.images`, and that the source field, `src`, is the relevant one to change if we want a new image displayed. We use `document.images` and we program the three steps of the `animate()` function as

```
function animate() {
  for (j = 0; j < 19; j++) {                    //Shift left 1
    document.images[j].src = document.images[j+1].src;
  }
  document.images[19].src = pics[randNum(8)].src; //New image
  timerId = setTimeout("animate()", duration);   //Set timer
}
```

We have used the `randNum()` function developed in Chapter 20,

```
function randNum (range) {
  return Math.floor(range * Math.random());
}
```

and so we must include its declaration in order to reuse it. Also, we add a variable `duration` to the accumulating list of declarations:

```
var duration = 125;
```

To get the process started automatically after five seconds, we include before the function definitions the additional statement

```
timerId = setTimeout("animate()", 5000);
```

which sets the `animate()` function to be run 5000 ms after the browser starts. As with the Busy Animation, we save the handle received from the `setTimeout` function in a variable `timerId` (it must be declared!) so that the animation can be stopped. And, with that code, the Set Timer subtask is completed, completing the Animate Grid task. Figure 22.6 shows the state of the structural page at this point.

```
<html>
  <head><title>Smooth Motion Application</title></head>
    <body bgcolor="white" text="#FF6600"><font face='Helvetica'><center>
      <table border=2>
        <tr> <td align="center">
             <h1>Smooth Motion</h1>
             </td></tr>
        <tr> <td align="center">
             <script>
             var j;                                           //Declare iter var
             var duration = 125, timerId;                     // & other vars
             var pics = new Array(8);                         // & prefetch array
             for (j = 0; j < 8; j++) {                        //Initial img array
               pics[j] = new Image();
             }
             for (j = 0; j < 8; j++) {                        //Prefetch images
               pics[j].src = "gifpix/Stack" + j + ".gif";
             }
             for (j = 0; j < 20; j++) {                       //Place grid imgs
               document.write('<img src="gifpix/Stack0.gif">');
             }
             </script>
             </td></tr>
        <tr> <td align="center">
             </td></tr>
        <tr> <td align="center">
             </td></tr>
        <tr> <td align="center">
             <p><font color='black'><b>
               Move the cursor across the brown boxes smoothly <br>
               to make a rising 'staircase' pattern in the window.</b>
               </font></p>
             </td></tr>
      </table></center>
      <script language='JavaScript'>
        timerId = setTimeout("animate()", 5000);              //Initial timer
        function animate() {                                  //Animate event-h
          for (j = 0; j < 19; j++) {                          //Shift images L
            document.images[j].src = document.images[j+1].src;
          }
          document.images[19].src = pics[randNum(8)].src;     //Place random img
          timerId = setTimeout("animate()", duration);        //Set timer for next
        }
        function randNum (range) {                            //Rand No. fcn from
          return Math.floor(range * Math.random());           //  Chapter 20
        }
      </script>
    </body>
</html>
```

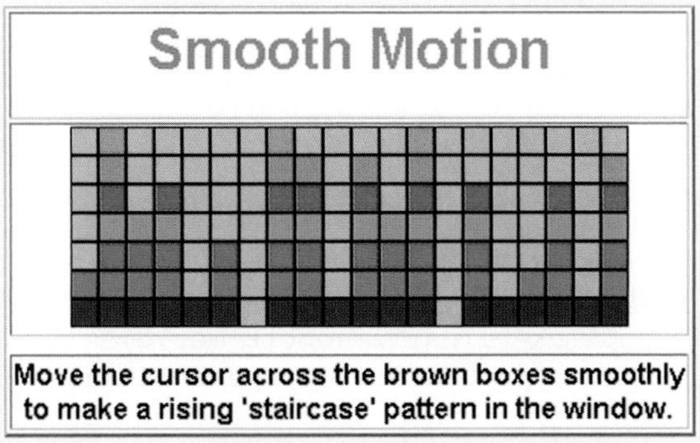

Figure 22.6. *Image, HTML, and JavaScript for the Smooth Motion implementation after the completion of the Animate Grid task.*

THE BEST LAID PLANS...

The third and next step in our task decomposition strategy is to solve key sensing. However, now that we have the grid animation worked out, we find it very cumbersome not to be able to start and stop the animation on demand. It would be very helpful to have the controls available to stop the animation so that we don't have to kill the browser application each time we run it. But the Build Controls task is planned for later. Perhaps it makes more sense to solve it now to simplify our subsequent development. As Robert Burns noted, our plans don't always work out, no matter how thoughtfully we developed them. (Burns put it more poetically, of course, *The best laid schemes o' mice and men gang aft agley*.) Adjusting the order of tasks is very typical of large projects because it isn't always possible to figure out all of the relevant interactions ahead of time. So, we proceed to the Build Controls task next.

BUILD CONTROLS

Inspecting the GUI in Figure 22.1, we see that the controls entry of the table contains seven input controls. Thus the fourth element of the table must contain `<form>` tags so that we can specify the controls. (Chapters 20 and 21 covered `<form>` tags.) The only challenge is in how to handle the click-events. As always, we ask, "What should happen when the control is clicked?" There are three cases:

> **`Go` button click-event.** Start the animation with `setTimeout()`, keeping track of the handle.

> **`Stop` button click-event.** End the animation by clearing the timer using the handle.

> **Radio button click-event.** Set the timer interval by assigning to `duration`.

None of these activities is more than a single statement, so rather than creating functions for the event handlers, we simply place the code in an input control:

```
<form>
  <input type=button value=Go
    onClick='timerId=setTimeout("animate()",duration)'>
  <input type=button value=Stop
    onClick="clearTimeout(timerId)">
  <input type=radio name=speed onClick="duration=25"> 25
  <input type=radio name=speed onClick="duration=50"> 50
  <input type=radio name=speed onClick="duration=75"> 75
  <input type=radio name=speed onClick="duration=100"> 100
  <input type=radio name=speed
    onClick="duration=125" checked=true> 125
</form>
```

We place the code in the fourth row of the structural page table (Figure 22.6). Notice that the last button is `checked` to indicate that `duration⇔125` is the default.

FITTIP

Easily Repeated. We could have used a `for` loop to place the radio buttons, though only the first four have the consistent structure suitable for a loop. Looping would require `<script>` tags, `document.write`, and so on. With so few repetitions, it's simpler to use Copy-Paste-Edit rather than a loop.

Having completed the Build Controls task, we can start and stop the animation. "We now return to our originally scheduled program."

SENSE THE KEYS

The Sense Keys task implements the ability to recognize when the mouse is over a given key. The task requires us to understand how mouse motions are sensed, a topic that has not yet been introduced. But, it's typical when solving a large problem not to know all of the constituent ideas and to have to learn about a new idea, system, or operation to solve the task. That's our situation with respect to sensing mouse motions. So, before attempting the task decomposition, we find out about mouse motions.

Actually, sensing mouse motions is very easy. Browsers recognize events on the objects of a Web page, such as images, just as they recognize events caused by controls. For example, if we click on an image, we cause a click-event, which we can process with an event handler. We specify the event handler by using the `onClick` attribute of the image tag, as in `<img src="..." onClick="doSomething()">`. This enables a mouse click on an image of a Web page to be recognized.

The browser, with the help of the operating system, is keeping track of where the mouse pointer is at any moment. (After all, it's the operating system that is drawing the mouse pointer in the first place.) When the mouse pointer moves over an image or other Web page object, a *MouseOver*-event is recognized. When the mouse pointer moves off of the object, a *MouseOut*-event is recognized. These are the two events that we need to follow the mouse cursor across the Smooth Motion keys. The keys are images, so all we do is write an event handler for each of the two mouse events. We specify them to the browser by the **onMouseOver** and **onMouseOut** event handler specifications in the <img src="..."> tag defining the key's image.

With that information, we can decompose the Sense Keys task by asking, "How should key sensing work?" First, we notice that there are no keys yet (see Figure 22.6), so we'll have to define them. Second, after thinking about their operation—they change their color from brown to orange on MouseOver and then change back to brown on MouseOut—it's clear that the keys are effectively another animation. The difference between the other animations we've written and the keys' animation is that the others are updated by a timer, whereas the keys are updated by mouse motions. This observation is a tremendous help to our planning, because we have solved animation problems before. So, we begin our problem decomposition with the standard animation decomposition used for the Animate Grid task:

1. Define and organize the necessary frames.
2. Place the initial images, creating the keys.
3. Prefetch the frames.
4. Build the event handlers.

This is a sufficient strategy to solve the problem.

Subtask: Define and Organize the Frames

The first subtask involves only two images,  and , available on the Web with the **Stack** images. They are known as **BrownBox.gif** and **OrangeBox.gif** and will be stored in the **gifpix** directory with the **Stack** images. Moving the files to that directory completes the first subtask.

Subtask: Place the Initial Images

Placing the images creates the keys. Seven images will be placed in the center of the third row of the structural page's table. They are all the **BrownBox.gif**. As before, we write a JavaScript loop to iterate the **document.write** of the <img src="..."> tags. The resulting code, which is still incomplete—but will be fixed momentarily—is

```
for (j = 0; j < 7; j++) {                          //Incomplete
    document.write('<img src="gifpix/BrownBox.gif">');
}
```

This completes the placement subtask for the time being.

Subtask: Prefetch the Frames

Prefetching the frames is also completely analogous to our earlier animations, and by now its three-subtask sequence is becoming familiar. There are only two frames to prefetch, leading to the declaration of a small array:

```
var keypix = new Array(2);
```

We add simple code for image initialization,

```
keypix[0] = new Image();
keypix[1] = new Image();
```

and prefetching,

```
keypix[0].src = "gifpix/BrownBox.gif";
keypix[1].src = "gifpix/OrangeBox.gif";
```

because it isn't worth writing loops. These lines complete the prefetch subtask.

Subtask: Build the Event Handlers

Finally, we build the two event handlers, **here()** for MouseOver and **gone()** for MouseOut. They're not difficult to build.

As with any event handler, we ask, "What should happen when the mouse moves over a key?" First, the key must change color to give feedback to the user that the mouse is on or off the key. This is simply updating the key's image with the **OrangeBox.gif** or the **BrownBox.gif** image. But how do we refer to the key's image? We know that it will be listed in the **images** array that the browser keeps of the images on the page. Because the keys come after the grid, the key images will obviously be stored in the array after the grid images. The grid images are **images[0], . . . , images[19]**, so by the preceding loop, the keys must be **images[20], . . . , images[26]**. Of course, if we know the position of the key, say, **pos**, we can refer to the image as **images[20+pos]**. We conclude that we need to record the position of each key in the sequence.

Next, the mouse sensing event handlers must tell the Grid Animation event handler which new **Stack** image to draw in the last position of the grid. All that that event handler needs is the key's position, so if we assign it to a global variable, say, **frame**, we've done the job. These observations lead us to declare a variable **frame** and to define the two mouse event handlers:

```
function here (pos) {
  document.images[20+pos].src = "gifpix/OrangeBox.gif";
  frame = pos + 1;
}
function gone (pos) {
  document.images[20+pos].src = "gifpix/BrownBox.gif";
  frame = 0;
}
```

We have made the key's position a parameter.

Notice how **here()** solves a problem of mismatched indices. The keys are 0-origin indexed (i.e., 0, 1, …, 6); **pos** will have one of these values. The stacks of blocks are 1-origin indexed (i.e., **Stack1.gif**, **Stack2.gif**, . . . , **Stack7.gif**); frame should have one of these values. That is, the mouse over **key[0]** means draw **Stack1.gif**. The **here()** function makes up for this mismatch with the assignment

```
frame = pos + 1;
```

Also, notice that for **gone()**, we don't know where the mouse is moving to. It could be moving to another key, or it could be moving off the keys entirely, which should draw the **Stack0.gif**. The safe thing is to set **frame = 0**. If the mouse moves to another key, its **MouseOver** event handler will be called immediately, setting **frame** to the right number.

Combine the Subtasks

With the two mouse event handlers defined, we return to the image initialization subtask to add the event handler specifications to the **<img src="...">** tags. The revised and final form of the initialization is

```
for (j = 0; j < 7; j++) {
    document.write('<img src="gifpix/BrownBox.gif" ' +
    'onMouseOver = "here(' + j + ')" ' +
    'onMouseOut = "gone(' + j + ')">');
}
```

The two mouse event handler functions have their position parameter specified by the **for** loop's iteration variable **j**. To test the Sense Keys task solution, we make one tiny change in the Grid Animation event handler, **animate()**, namely, to change the **frame** assigned to the last column from the random choice to the frame variable. The new line has the form

```
document.images[19].src = pics[frame].src;
```

allowing us to test the code.

Having thus completed the Sense Keys task, Figure 22.7 shows the code entered into the structural page in the third row. (The two declarations—**keypix** and **frame**—are included with the earlier declarations, and the event handling functions are included with the previously defined functions.)

STAIRCASE DETECTION

When the user has manipulated the mouse in such a way as to create a rising "staircase" of blocks in the grid, the animation should stop. How do we recognize the "staircase"? It's not possible to look at the grid, of course, so we must identify it by other characteristics. Observe that the user will have created a staircase when

```
<script language = 'JavaScript'>
  var keypix = new Array(2);                          //Array declaration
  for (j = 0; j < 7; j++) {                           //Image Placement
     document.write('<img src="gifpix/BrownBox.gif" ' +
     'onMouseOver = "here(' + j + ')" ' +
     'onMouseOut = "gone(' + j + ')">');
  }
  keypix[0] = new Image();                            //Image initialize
  keypix[1] = new Image();                            //
  keypix[0].src = "gifpix/BrownBox.gif";              //Prefetch images
  keypix[1].src = "gifpix/OrangeBox.gif";             //
</script>
```

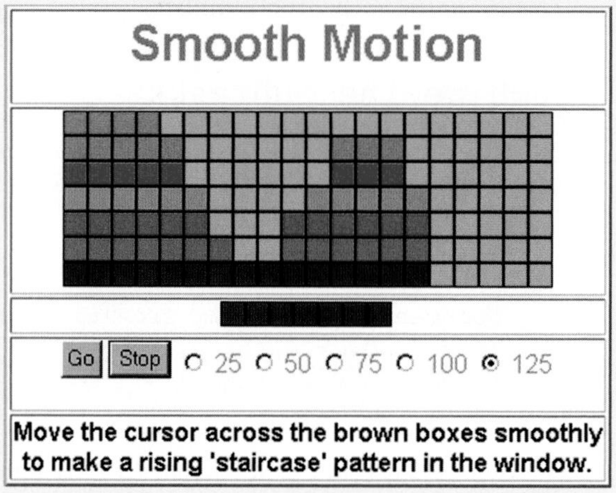

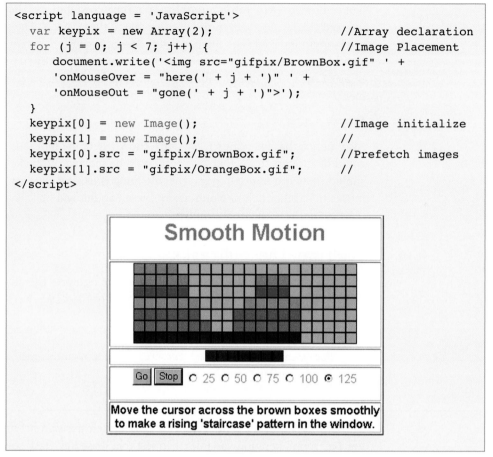

Figure 22.7. *JavaScript for the Sense Keys task; two declarations and the two event handlers, not shown.*

the **`frame`** values for seven consecutive **`animate()`** calls are 1, 2, 3, 4, 5, 6, 7. This is true because the value of **`frame`** tells the **`animate()`** event handler which **`Stack`** frame to display, and if it is directed to display the seven frames in order on seven consecutive ticks, there will be a staircase in the grid.

Subtask: Recognizing the Staircase

How do we recognize the seven consecutive **`frame`** values? There are many techniques. Some involve keeping an array of the seven most recent frame values and checking each time to see if the desired sequence occurs. Another involves looking at the **`src`** fields in the last seven images of the grid—it's almost like looking at the picture—to see if they have the right sequence of file names. But the one we will program requires slightly less programming and seems cleverer. The idea is to keep predicting the next **`frame`** value.

Subtask: Recognizing Continuity

Notice that we are trying to recognize continuity across a sequence of events, that is, seven events in which the value for **frame** is 1, 2, 3, 4, 5, 6, 7. By analogy, imagine you are sitting at the bus stop trying to determine if seven consecutive buses ever come by with the last digit of their license numbers making the sequence 1 through 7. But you have no paper to write down the data and your memory isn't so good. You do have exactly seven coins—your bus fare—and you put one coin in your left pocket. That's a prediction that the next bus has a license ending in 1.

Whenever any bus arrives, you check to see if the last digit of its license plate is equal to the number of coins in your left pocket. If so, and you still have coins, you add another coin to your left pocket. If not, you put all the coins, but one, back in your right pocket. If you ever try to add a coin, but have run out, it happened! What you are doing with the coins in your left pocket is predicting the number on the next bus's license plate. If it's right, you make the next prediction by adding another coin; but if not, you start back with 1. It's an easy idea for keeping the continuity of a series of events.

Implementing the bus analogy, we modify the **animate()** function at the point where it is about to set the timer for the next tick, because if the staircase is found, there should be no next tick. Additionally, we'll declare another variable, **next1**, that corresponds to the coins in your left pocket, that is, as if predicting an event. Implementing the steps of the process

```
if (frame == next1)                 //Is the prediction correct?
    next1 = next1 + 1;              //Yes, make next prediction
else                                //No
    next1 = 1;                      //Go back to the start
if (next1 != 8)                     //Are we still looking?
    timerId = setTimeout("animate()",duration); //Yes, set timer
```

Notice that the test in the last **if** statement compares to 8 rather than 7 because **next1** was already incremented previously, and so the condition of "no more coins left" is equivalent to **next1 ⇔ 8**. With that addition to **animate()** we have completed the Detect Staircase task.

ASSEMBLE OVERALL DESIGN

With the Build Controls task performed out of order and parts of the Assemble Overall Design task performed ahead of time, there is not much left to do to complete the programming of the Smooth Motion application. Nevertheless, this is the point at which we make sure that the whole application works as planned.

Reviewing the description at the start of the chapter, we notice that the display of randomly selected stacks of blocks isn't presently working. Originally we generated random stacks when we solved the Animate Grid task. But we took that feature out to test the keys. Now we want to put it back in. Basically we should set image 19 to **frame** or **randNum(8)**, depending on whether or not the user has ever passed the mouse over a key. How will we know? The MouseOver event handlers will recognize the situation, but at the moment, they are programmed only to return a **frame** value from 1 through 7. So, if we started out with frame initialized to some erroneous number, say, –1, and test it in the **animate()** event handler before using the **frame** value, we could recognize the two situations: –1 means the mouse has not yet passed over the keys for the first time; anything else means the mouse has passed over the keys the first time. Thus we must change the initialization of **frame** in its declaration to

```
var frame = -1;              //Set for initial random generation
```

and rewrite the assignment to the last column of the Grid one more time:

```
if (frame == -1)
    document.images[19].src = pics[randNum(8)].src;
else
    document.images[19].src = pics[frame].src;
```

This last change to **animate()** makes it quite cluttered with **if** statements, as can be seen in Figure 22.8. The clutter obscures the simple two-part logic of shifting the grid and checking for the staircase. So, we relegate both operations to functions. The resulting solution is no shorter—in fact, it is longer by four lines—but it makes the important **animate()** event handler clearer, making the exercise worthwhile.

After checking the operation of the Smooth Motion application, it seems that we've taken care of all of the design elements, except the fancy GUI, which is the last remaining task.

PRIMP THE DESIGN

The structural page we've built our application around can be made more attractive. In fact, the task of improving the aesthetics of Web pages is probably an unending task. We recognize the following changes that produce the page shown in Figure 22.1:

> Table background color

> Cell padding

These are considered advanced features of HTML and will not be taught here, because at the stage when a page is being enhanced, we usually have to familiarize ourselves with the advanced features again, having forgotten them since the last time a page was enhanced. For the record, the two enhancements can be programmed using attributes of the **<table>** tag:

```
<table border=2 cellspacing="3" cellpadding="20%"
   bgcolor="#FFFF99">
```

An explanation of how **cellpadding** and **cellspacing** work is found at **www.w3c.org/TR/REC-html40/struct/tables.html#h-11.3.3** and nearby pages. We leave it to the interested reader to explore alternative styles.

Assessment and Retrospective

When we are asked to design a solution to someone else's problem, we are usually finished when we've verified that we've done what we've been asked to do. If the design is to achieve a goal of our own choice, however, an assessment step remains. When we pick the goal, we usually do not have a fixed target like Figure 22.1 to work toward. Rather, we will have designed a solution to our original "best guess" and should now consider whether the result is the best possible. (We have used such assessments in Chapters 15 and 19.) Generally, having a working solution suggests many worthwhile improvements.

In this chapter, the first case applies, and so we are finished. Instead of an assessment, consider the ideas from earlier chapters applied in this chapter. There are three primary topics:

- Loops
- Parameterizing functions for reuse
- Managing complexity with functions

Applying these ideas has produced a better program. Consider how.

Loops. The Smooth Motion application used several **for** loops. These saved us from tedious activities like writing 20 **<img src="...">** statements in a row. Such loops simplified the programming. But at times, when we might have used loops, we chose not to. For example, we explicitly wrote the instructions for defining the radio buttons and for prefetching the key images. We used Copy/Paste/Edit rather than a loop, because it was easier programming. Had there been more iterations, or had the specification been slightly simpler, we might have used a loop. The computer does the same work either way.

Parameterized Functions for Reuse. The **here()** and **gone()** functions each use a single parameter that is the position of the key in sequence. The actual value is passed to the functions in the event handler specifications. For example, the third key from the left is defined by a **document.write** that produces

```
<img src="gifpix/BrownBox.gif"
     onMouseOver = "here(2)" onMouseOut = "gone(2)">
```

where the "**2**" indicates the key's 0-origin number. The parameter customizes the event handler for each key. We could have written separate functions in which the key's position is used explicitly everywhere **pos** occurs, but this would create a proliferation of almost-identical functions. The parameter says where and how the event handlers differ from each other, and their use produces a more abstract—and easier to understand—solution.

Managing Complexity with Functions. The functions **`shiftGrid()`** and **`checkStairAndContinue()`** shown in Figure 22.8 are examples of creating functions to manage complexity. Both functions "package" program logic allowing us to *name them* and *move them* out of the way, revealing the simple two-part logic of the **`animate()`** function.

```
function animate() {
  shiftGrid ();
  checkStairAndContinue ();
}
```

```
function animate() {
  for (j = 0; j < 19; j++) {
      document.images[j].src = document.images[j+1].src;
  }
  if (frame == -1)
      document.images[19].src = pics[randNum(8)].src;
  else
      document.images[19].src = pics[frame].src;
  if (frame == next1)
      next1 = next1 + 1;
  else
      next1 = 1;
  if (next1 != 8)
      timerId = setTimeout("animate()",duration);
}
```

becomes

```
function animate() {
  shiftGrid ();
  checkStairAndContinue ();
}
function shiftGrid() {
  for (j = 0; j < 19; j++) {
      document.images[j].src = document.images[j+1].src;
  }
  if (frame == -1)
      document.images[19].src = pics[randNum(8)].src;
  else
      document.images[19].src = pics[frame].src;
}
function checkStairAndContinue() {
  if (frame == next1)
      next1 = next1 + 1;
  else
      next1 = 1;
  if (next1 != 8)
      timerId = setTimeout("animate()",duration);
}
```

Figure 22.8. *Revision of the function* `animate()` *to encapsulate portions of the computation into functions.*

As with loops and parameters, this use of functions is intended to clarify to humans how the animation function works; it's all the same to the computer. Humans will see our choice of function names—for example **`shiftGrid()`**—and correctly interpret them as describing what the function does. If people need to know how the program shifts the grid, they can check the function; otherwise, it is out of the way, replaced by a succinct statement of what it does (its name). This role of shifting the grid might have been expressed as a comment at the start of the code sequence, but comments are often ignored. The abstraction—naming the function and giving its definition—creates a new concept in our minds, raising our level of understanding of Smooth Motion's animation process. Though these two functions will never be used again, the goal of simplifying the program justifies our effort of defining them. See Appendix E for a complete listing of Smooth Motion.

Thus we see that programming is as much about teaching viewers of our program how we solved the problem as it is about instructing the computer. Even for programs that are not part of textbooks, helping humans understand the program is essential. It helps with debugging—an important concern for us—and by organizing the solution in an understandable way, we instill in others confidence about the correctness of our solution.

SUMMARY

We have programmed a substantial application that would have been too complicated had we tried simply to solve it directly. To be successful, we applied the Decomposition Principle, first to create the high-level tasks that guided our overall solution, and then, when it came time to solve those tasks, we applied Decomposition again when a task was still too complicated to solve. Though it is mostly just common sense, the Decomposition Principle gives us a strategy that will work to solve hard problems.

Once the tasks were defined, we strategized about the order in which to solve them. Because there usually are dependencies among the tasks, we must find a feasible plan for solving them. A dependency diagram shows visually which tasks depend on others and can assist us in strategizing. Any order that is consistent with the diagram—that is, no task is scheduled ahead of the tasks it depends on—produces a workable plan. But it is also wise to consider features such as ease of testing, and try to adjust the schedule to address these other aspects as well.

The actual solution of the Smooth Motion program was direct. Each task was decomposed further into four to five subtasks. There was similarity among these subtasks for similar tasks. For example, the timer-driven animation and the key-driven animation used a similar set of subtasks. Unexpectedly, we decided to solve the tasks out of order from our original schedule, to give ourselves the ability to start and stop the animation. It was convenience that motivated us to depart from our original schedule, but originally it would not have been possible to predict the benefits of the alternative plan. Finally, we had to learn about mouse events, a topic that had not been encountered previously. Mouse events are not a difficult concept, and they illustrate a common feature of any large task—that it is often necessary to learn new information to solve a complex problem.

In our retrospective look at our solution, we noted how programming ideas from previous chapters were illustrated in the Smooth Motion application. Consistently, we used the programming facilities—loops, functions, parameters, and so on—as tools to instruct both the computer and anyone looking at the program. Those facilities clarified the program, making it plain how the problem was being solved.

Though this chapter has presented an IT application, the techniques have wide application. Expect to use decomposition in other problem solving, to abstract the components of your solution by giving them names and precise definitions, and to reduce the complexity of your solution to an understandable level. They are powerful problem-solving techniques.

EXERCISES

Multiple Choice

1. The first step in problem-solving is:
   A. develop an algorithm
   B. understand the problem
   C. create the interface
   D. determine the functions needed
2. The second step in problem-solving is:
   A. break the problem into smaller tasks
   B. plan how to solve the problems
   C. design the interface
   D. build the functions
3. The Build Controls task is dependent on:
   A. Overall Design
   B. Detect Staircase
   C. Sense Keys
   D. Animate Grid
4. Before the Animate Grid task can be completed, the:
   A. Build Controls task must be completed
   B. Detect Staircase task must be completed
   C. Build GUI task must be completed
   D. Sense Keys task must be completed
5. The Detect Staircase task is not dependent on:
   A. Build Controls
   B. Sense Keys
   C. Animate Grid
   D. Build GUI
6. Which of the following is an example of the World Famous Iteration form?
   A. `for (j = 0; j < 10; j++)`
   B. `for (i = 1; I <=5; i = i +1)`
   C. `for (k = 10; k > 1; k--)`
   D. `for (j = 1; j++; j<=5)`
7. To use a graphic that has been prefetched:
   A. the **`href`** command must be used
   B. the **`src`** command must be used
   C. a specific image must be placed in a specific location
   D. none of the above

8. To get the browser to delay 3 seconds, you need to set the `setTimeout` function to:
   A. 5
   B. 500
   C. 5000
   D. .5
9. It is worthwhile to write a loop to do a repetitive task when there are:
   A. 2 or more tasks
   B more than 3–5 tasks
   C. more than 8-10 tasks
   D. 20 or more tasks
10. A meaningful name for a function:
    A. makes the code easier to read
    B. raises the level of understanding for those that read the code
    C. means as much to the computer as a meaningless name
    D. all of the above

Short Answer

1. The ______ is used to break a task into smaller, easy-to-solve tasks.
2. ______ is the second step in problem-solving.
3. ______ are the relationships between tasks that determines the order in which the tasks in a program are solved.
4. When solving a problem, the ______ should be solved first.
5. PERT stands for ______.
6. A(n) ______ can be used to visually keep track of which tasks depend on another.
7. The ______ task must be completed before the Sense Keys task can be completed.
8. The Animate Grid task and the Sense Keys task both must be completed before the ______ task can be completed.
9. An array called ______ is where a browser stores information about the images on a page.
10. Clicking on a button on a Web page will trigger a(n) ______.
11. ______ are objects that, when placed in a group, work together to allow the user to select one item from the group.
12. The unit used for timing JavaScript events on the computer is called a ______.

Exercises

1. Describe the Decomposition Principle.
2. Apply the Decomposition Principle to cooking a meal.
3. Create a PERT chart for the preceding exercise.
4. List the dependent tasks and the independent tasks for cooking a meal.
5. On the Smooth Motion Web page, what objects are used for user input?
6. Explain why it's a good idea to create the GUI early in the process, but not finalize it until the end of the process.
7. What is the advantage of prefetching images for an animation?
8. How would you modify the Smooth Motion code to keep track of how long the user can keep the animation running and display it at the end?
9. Explain how the `onMouseOver` and `onMouseOut` events work.

chapter 23

COMPUTERS CAN DO ALMOST {❑ EVERYTHING, ❑ NOTHING}

Limits to Computation

learning objectives

- Explain what the Turing test was designed to show
- Discuss the issue of a computer being intelligent and able to think; refer to Deep Blue
- Discuss the issue of computer creativity; refer to the computer-generated Mondrian-like art
- State the meaning of the Universality Principle
- State the way in which the amount of work in a program is related to the speed of the program

The real danger is not that computers will begin to think like men, but that men will begin to think like computers.

—SYDNEY J. HARRIS

Artificial Intelligence is no match for natural stupidity.

—ANONYMOUS

COMPUTERS have achieved sustained speeds of over ten trillion additions per second. At one operation per second on a pocket calculator, it takes 1000 lifetimes (assuming 60 years of daily calculating for 14 hours each day) to perform a trillion operations. But so what? Everyone knows computers are amazingly fast at arithmetic. Shouldn't we be more impressed if a computer ever had an original thought, no matter how trivial? Absolutely! But it probably won't happen. As we have learned, for a computer to do anything, it must be programmed to do it, and so far "thought" in the sense we usually mean the term has eluded researchers. So, we have a curious situation. Computers can be truly awesome at some tasks and completely hopeless at others. Because they're so different from humans, it's reasonable to wonder what computers can and cannot do.

This chapter addresses philosophical issues that arise in computing. The first issue considered is whether a computer can think. Thinking about thinking leads us to the famed Turing test. Using that test to orient ourselves, we distinguish between the appearance of intelligence and the fact of intelligence. Playing chess requires intelligence, intuition, imagination, and analysis. Chess became a de facto goal of artificial intelligence research during the last half of the twentieth century. We explore how computers play chess, summarize the advancements, and report the victory of Deep Blue. After intelligence, we turn our attention to creativity and ask whether a computer can be creative. The discussion further serves to clarify the capabilities of humans and computers. Next, we consider the easy-to-understand but significant idea—the Universality Principle—that asks how different computers can be from each other. The Universality Principle explains why computers are so useful now, but it also implies they won't become more capable in the future. Any "new and improved" computer will be faster or larger, but not more capable. How important is more speed? We explore the question of how fast computers can solve various problems by revisiting the Alphabetize CDs algorithm from Chapter 10. The discussion characterizes the problems computers solve easily and for which a faster computer will deliver noticeable improvements. There are, however, many important problems that we would like to solve but that are too complex: a computer could solve them in principle, but not in practice. We'll give examples. Finally, there are problems that cannot be solved by a computer even in principle, not because they are too nebulous to specify for a computer, but because to do so would be a contradiction.

CAN COMPUTERS THINK?

The inventors of electronic computers thought that they were discovering how to "think with electricity." And to the extent that operations like addition and multiplication require humans to think, it's easy to see their point. Previously, electricity had been used directly as an energy source for driving motors and powering light bulbs. With the digital computer, electricity switched complex circuits implementing logical operations. The power was applied to manipulate information. The phenomenon was truly new.

Today electronic devices manipulating information are so common we have a less awestruck view of them. It is difficult to regard a pocket calculator as "thinking." But our view of what constitutes thinking has changed over time, too. In the Middle Ages, when very few people could read or reckon, as performing arithmetic was called, anyone who could add and multiply was thought to have special powers, divinely or perhaps mystically conferred. Reckoning was a uniquely human activity. It took centuries for addition and multiplication to be codified into the algorithms that we all learn in elementary school. Is a capability, once classified as thinking and believed to be a divine gift, no longer thinking when it turns out to be algorithmic? It required thinking when we learned it. Maybe all thought is algorithmic. Maybe it's thinking only as long as no one understands how it's accomplished.

FITBYTE

Sub Text. Computer scientist Edsger Dijkstra is quoted as saying, "The question of whether a computer can think is no more interesting than the question of whether a submarine can swim." But he seems to be in the minority.

The Turing Test

The problem of defining thinking for the purposes of deciding whether a computer thinks concerned Alan M. Turing, one of the pioneers of computation.

Turing was aware of definitions like "thinking is what people do," and the tendency for people to call an activity "thinking" until it turns out to be algorithmic. So, he decided to forget trying to define what thinking is and simply proposed an experiment that would demonstrate intelligence. Turing designed the following experimental setting, which has since become known as the **Turing test**.

> **Turing test:** Two identical rooms labeled A and B are connected electronically to a judge who can type questions directed to the occupant of either room. A human being occupies one room, and the other contains a computer. The judge's goal is to decide, based on the questions asked and the answers received, which room contains the computer. If after a reasonable period of time the judge cannot decide for certain, the computer can be said to be intelligent.

Thus, the computer is intelligent if it acts enough like a human to deceive the judge.

Passing the Test

Turing's experiment not only sidestepped the problem of defining thinking or intelligence, but it also got away from focusing on any specific ability such as performing arithmetic. The judge can ask any questions, so as to explore the entire range of thought processes. Apparent stumpers for the computer like

In Hamlet's famous soliloquy, what metaphors does Shakespeare use for 'death'?

might not be so hard if the computer has access to online sources of Shakespearean criticism. Apparent "gimmes" for the computer like

What are the prime factors of 72,914,426?

might be answered in more human-like ways such as being slow or refusing to answer such questions at all. When Turing proposed the test in 1950, there was little prospect that a computer could deceive the judge. Nevertheless, it emphasized the important point that thinking is a process, and how it is accomplished—with synapses or transistors—shouldn't matter.

Advances in the last half-century have definitely improved the computer's chances of "passing" the Turing test, though perhaps they are still not very good. Researchers reading Turing's paper in 1950 might have conceded that computers could be better than people at arithmetic, but probably all of them would have believed that "natural language"—a true human invention—was beyond the abilities of computers. For example, when Turing thought up the test, no algorithmic process was known for parsing (analyzing) English into its grammatical structure, as word processors' grammar checkers do today. Nor was "machine translation"—converting text from one language into its semantic equivalent in another language—anything more than science fiction. Nor was recognizing semantically meaningful information something a computer could perform, as Google does today.

{GREAT FIT MINDS}

Grand Turing >>

Englishman Alan Mathison Turing (1912–1954) was probably the most brilliant of all of the computer pioneers. In addition to the Turing test, he invented the first theoretical computer, now known as the Turing Machine, and discovered the Universality Principle (explained below). During World War II he worked at the British Government's Code and Cipher School at Bletchley Park breaking Germany's Enigma Code. The Cambridge educated mathematician and marathon runner received the OBE and was a member of the Royal Society. He died in 1954 of potassium cyanide poisoning under suspicious circumstances.

Admittedly, computers are still a long way from being perfect at any of these tasks, but they are pretty good at all three—at least good enough to be the basis for useful applications. More important, they are good enough at these language tasks that we can imagine a day when computers are better than most humans. And then, like reckoning, the tasks of parsing, translation, and semantic searching in natural language will have been reduced to algorithmic form. Does it add to our admiration of computers that they are closer to passing the Turing test? Or does it detract from our opinion of ourselves, suggesting that instead of computers being more like people, perhaps people are just computers. The questions are truly profound.

FITBYTE

Motto. IBM, the dominant computer manufacturer of the 1950s–1970s, used "Think" as its corporate motto. It was common to see the command in computer rooms and on programmers' desks. Perhaps one of the best signs employed "negative space" to get the reader's brain going.

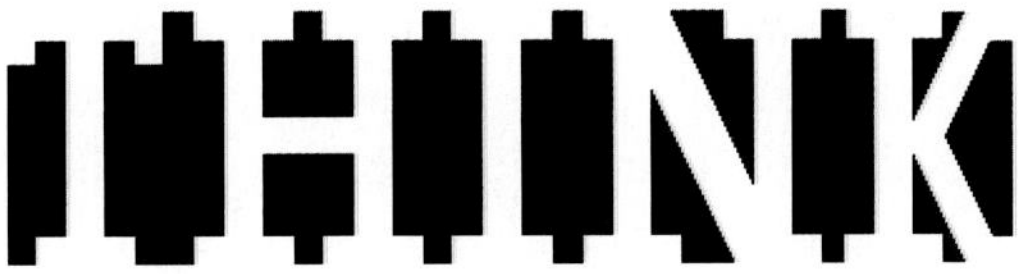

ACTING INTELLIGENTLY?

Anyone with even passing experience with grammar or spell checkers knows that they don't "understand" the sentences. They know the parts of speech such as prepositions and verbs, concepts like subject/object agreement, passive voice, and so on, but they don't understand complete sentences. Such concepts are not trivialities. It takes tremendously complex software and substantial dictionary resources to implement grammar and spell checking, and they're occasionally good enough to be helpful. But they definitely do not "understand" English.

The distinction between being intelligent and being programmed to seem intelligent concerned researchers in the 1950s and 1960s. The Doctor program (also known as Eliza) developed by MIT researcher Joel Weisenbaum demonstrated this difference clearly. Doctor was programmed to ask questions in a dialog like a psychotherapist:

User:	`I'm depressed.`
Doctor:	`Why are you depressed?`
User:	`My mother is not speaking to me.`
Doctor:	`Tell me about your mother.`
User:	`She doesn't want me to major in engineering.`
Doctor:	`No?`
User:	`No, she wants me to go into medicine.`

Doctor was programmed to keep the dialog going by asking questions and requesting more information. It would take cues from words like mother, including a reference to them in its next response. It would also notice uses of negative sentences, but the dialog was essentially preplanned. It may have appeared to be intelligent, but definitely was not. What would a computer have to do to be intelligent or to demonstrate that it "understands" something?

As the research field of artificial intelligence (AI) came into existence, a consensus grew that to exhibit intelligence, a computer would have to "understand" a complex situation and reason well enough to act on its "understanding." Moreover, the actions could not be scripted or predetermined in any way. Most complex situations require the ability to understand natural language and/or require much real-world knowledge. Both properties badly handicapped computers of the day.

Playing Chess

Playing chess, however, was much cleaner. It offered a challenging task that humans were both good at and interested in. The rules were clear, and success could be easily defined: beat a grandmaster in a tournament. Indeed, in the initial exuberance over computing, it was predicted as early as 1952 that a computer would beat a grand master "sometime in the next decade." Though it took more than a decade before computers could do much more than know the legal moves of chess, the problem was well established as a litmus test for AI.

The Board Configuration. How does a computer play chess? First, like all computational problems, the information must be represented in bits. The chess "world" is especially easy to represent because it is completely defined by an 8 × 8 checkered board, 32 pieces of two colors and six different types, and a single bit indicating whose turn it is to move. Because details are unimportant, think of the graphic of a chessboard as printed in game books or newspapers, and call it a **board configuration**, or simply a **board**.

The Game Tree. Next the computer must decide on a move. It does this in roughly the same way we do, by exploring moves to determine,

> *"Will a move of this piece to that position make me better off or worse off?"*

"Better off or worse off" are determined with respect to winning, of course, but it is very difficult to "compute" such information. Humans use intuition and experience. A computer uses an **evaluation function**, a procedure that assigns a numerical value to each piece and, taking into account things like captures and board position, computes a score for the board. If the score is positive, it's better; if it's negative, it's worse. Then, starting from the current board configuration, the computer checks the evaluation function on the result of every possible single legal move, as shown in the **game tree** of Figure 23.1. One of these moves—suppose there are 28 legal moves—will give the highest score, which might be the one that the computer should pick.

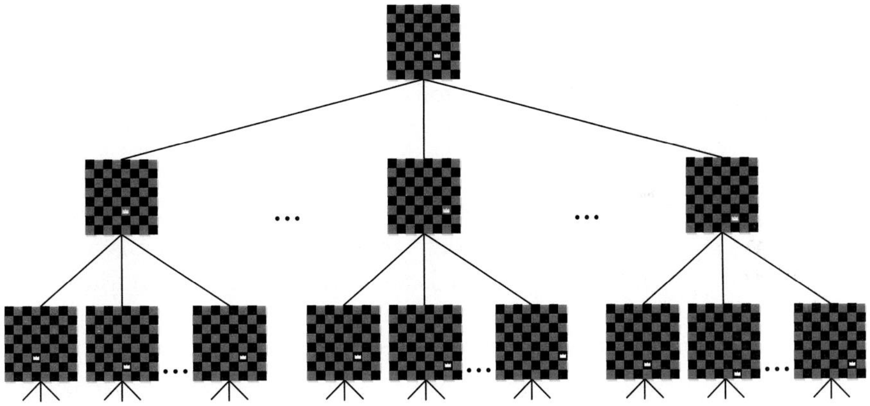

Figure 23.1. *A schematic diagram of a game tree for chess. The current board position is at the top (root). The boards produced in a single move are on the layer below, those reachable in two moves are on the layer below that, and so forth.*

Using the Game Tree Tactically. Before picking a move, the computer should consider what the opponent will do. So for each of these "1-move" board configurations considered so far, the computer considers every possible next move from each and evaluates them. These boards are two moves away from the current board configuration. Furthermore, because the opponent makes the second move, the interpretation of the evaluation function is reversed. That is, the best move for the opponent is presumably the worst move for the computer, so the computer assumes the opponent will choose the move with the most negative score in the computer's evaluation function. This process is known as "look ahead." Clearly, the further ahead the computer looks—it's described as *deeper* in chess because of the tree formulation—the more complete is the computer's knowledge about possible outcomes of the game.

It would seem that the computer, being very fast, could look all the way to the end of the game, find a winning path, and follow that. But checking the whole game tree is generally impossible because of the geometric increase in the number of boards that must be considered. For example, if there are 28 moves possible from the current position, and an average of 28 from each of those, and each of their descendents, and so on, then considering only six moves deep (i.e., three for each side) generates

$$28 + 28^2 + 28^3 + 28^4 + 28^5 + 28^6 = 499{,}738{,}092$$

which is a half billion boards. It's infeasible for a computer to look 50 moves into the future.

Which move should the computer select? Picking the best move at the first level is not the best strategy, because the evaluation function is generally a static assessment of the board configuration. If in that one move the computer could reach a checkmate, the evaluation function would be very positive and the computer should pick it. But if not, the situation needs more strategy, because the most positive evaluation might come from a capture that would give the computer a piece advantage, whereas another choice, though less desirable at the moment, might lead in a few moves to a win. To play an intelligent game—that is, to strategize, to sacrifice pieces, to force the opponent into specific behaviors—requires the computer to analyze the game tree much more carefully.

Using a Database of Knowledge. Finally, in addition to representing the game and making moves, the computer needs some knowledge. In chess, this takes the form of a database of openings and endgames. Because chess is interesting and has been studied for so long, much is known about how to start and finish chess games. Providing this database is like giving the computer chess experience. Because learning is probably even harder than being intelligent, loading the database saves the computer the need to "learn from experience." It's analogous to aspiring chess players reading books by grandmasters.

Using Parallel Computation

Slowly, as the basic logic just discussed got worked out, chess programs got better and better. Eventually they were beating duffers, then serious players, and then masters. Progress came as a combination of faster computers, more complete databases, and better evaluation and "strategizing" functions. In time, **parallel computation**—the application of several computers to the task—and custom hardware allowed computer researchers to entertain the possibility of beating a grandmaster under tournament conditions.

The Deep Blue Matches. In 1996, reigning grandmaster Garry Kasparov trounced an IBM computer dubbed Deep Blue. Deep Blue was a parallel computer composed of 32 general-purpose computers (IBM RS/6000 SP) and 256 custom chess processors, enabling it to consider on average 200 million board positions per second.

In one of the six games of the match, the computer played very well and won. Kasparov saw himself as victorious in defending the human race, but AI researchers were also ecstatic. At last a computer had played world-class chess in tournament conditions. A rematch was inevitable. On May 11, 1997, Kasparov lost 3.5–2.5 to an improved Deep Blue, achieving the "in the next decade" goal in a mere 45 years.

Interpreting the Outcome of the Matches

Did Deep Blue settle the question of whether computers can be intelligent? Not to everyone's satisfaction. To its credit, it answered one of the greatest technical challenges of the century. To do so required a large database of prior knowledge on openings and endgames, but that's analogous to reading books and playing chess. It also required special-purpose hardware that allowed rapid evaluation of board positions, but that's probably analogous to synaptic development in the brains of chess experts, giving them the ability over time to encapsulate whole board configurations as single mental units. But disappointingly—at least to some observers, and probably the AI pioneers who made the predictions in the first place—the problem was basically solved by speed. Deep Blue simply looked deeper. It did so *intelligently*, of course, because the geometric explosion of boards prevents success based simply on raw power. And that may be the strongest message from the Deep Blue/Kasparov matches. Intelligence may be the ability to consider many alternatives in an informed and directed way. Deep Blue surely demonstrated that.

The Deep Blue experience may have demonstrated that computers can be intelligent, or it may have demonstrated that IBM's team of chess experts and computer programmers is very intelligent. In the final analysis, the hardware was simply following the instructions that the programmers and engineers gave it. Such an objection has been raised in the "intelligence" debate since the beginning. It is a weak criticism because we can imagine intelligence, or creativity, or any other intellectual process being encoded in a general form, so that once started on a body of information, the program operates autonomously, responding to new inputs and realizing states not planned by its designers. Deep Blue operates autonomously in this sense and thus transcends its designers.

The main cautionary note regarding Deep Blue is that it is completely specialized to chess. That is, the 256 chess processors only evaluate board positions and are not useful for any other purpose. The 32 general-purpose processors can run other programs, of course, but none of Deep Blue's "intelligence" would be transferable to another computation unless a programmer abstracted the ideas from Deep Blue and incorporated them into that computation. The "intelligence" isn't formulated in any general-purpose way. Thus Deep Blue speaks only indirectly to the subject of general-purpose intelligence.

FITBYTE

Another View. John Searle, an outspoken critic of AI, offers a widely quoted criticism, The Chinese Room Argument. A monolingual English speaker is locked in a room and given rules in English for correlating symbols in three batches of Chinese text to produce translations. Ignorant of Chinese, the occupant follows the rules. The format is designed to mirror AI programs. The occupant is amazingly good, but unaware of his role. Amazed Chinese believe he's a native speaker. Is he intelligent? Or only following rules like a computer? Much has been said on both sides.

ACTING CREATIVELY

An alternative approach to understanding the limitations and potentialities of computers is to consider whether they can be "creative." For example, could a computer create art? It's not a question of whether they can be the art medium—artists have manipulated computers to produce art for decades. Rather the question is whether a computer could prevail in, perhaps, a "graphic version" of the Turing test: A judge visits an art gallery and decides whether a person or a computer produced the art. Could a computer be successful at fooling the judge? The task may be more daunting even than the original Turing test because creativity is by definition a process of breaking the rules, and computers only follow rules. How could they ever succeed at being creative? Perhaps there are rules—**metarules**—that describe how to break the rules or, perhaps, transcend existing rules. A computer could follow those. To see how this might be, let's first look at a program to create fine art.

There has been something of a fad recently in writing Java applets to create graphic designs after the famed cubist Piet Mondrian (1872–1944), whose paintings are exhibited in the great art collections of the world. See Figure 23.2.

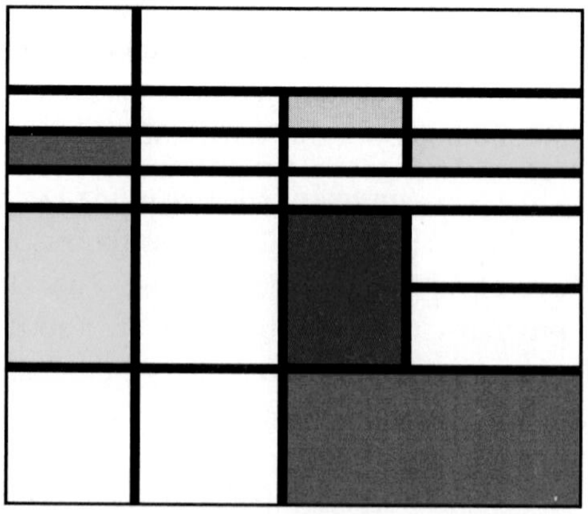

Figure 23.2. *Example of a computer-generated graphic in the style of Piet Mondrian. (Finding current examples only requires a Web search on terms like mondrian AND java; other geometrically regular graphics, for example, Moorish designs, can also be found.)*

The programs display a new Mondrian-like picture with each mouse click. Inspecting the code, we find that the programs use random numbers to steer a deterministic process for placing lines and filling regions with color. That is, the program encodes a set of rules for creating graphics in the style of Mondrian, using what looks to the casual observer to be the same design elements, same colors, and so on. The graphics are new in the sense that they have never before existed, but as art critics love to say, "The work is derivative."

But Mondrian is famous not because he created pleasing pictures with strong lines and bold primary colors, but because he had something to say about his world that he expressed through paintings. That is, he's famous for a body of work from which the program's rules have been (reasonably faithfully) abstracted. The program only produces variations on the application of the rules using random numbers. But to many, creativity means inventing the rules in the first place.

Creativity as a Spectrum

Computer scientist Bruce Jacob distinguishes between the form of creativity that comes from inspiration—"a flash out of the blue"—and the form that comes from hard work—"incremental revision." Inspiration remains a mystery; the hard work is algorithmic in Jacob's view. (This is remeniscent of Thomas Edison's famous description of genius: 1 percent inspiration, 99 percent perspiration.)

To organize our discussion, think of creativity as a spectrum ranging from "flash out of the blue" to "Mondrian in a click." To be creative in fine art at the "flash out of the blue" end, the computer would have to step outside of the "established order," inventing its own rules, whereas at the applet end of the spectrum, the computer just randomly assembles parts by the rules some programmer gave it, never extending or modifying them. Between those two extremes, there are still alternatives.

The Hard Work forms. Jacob illustrates the hard work form of creativity using canons, musical compositions that have the incremental-variation-on-a-theme property.

Jacob has developed a music composition system, **variations**, which attempts to create canons by extending a repertoire of base themes by (randomly) generating new themes, assessing them as "good" or "bad," and discarding the "bad" ones. Interestingly, Jacob points out that because the program must work within the underlying characteristics of the base themes, getting a random variation to "fit" within those constraints "sometimes requires creativity!" That is, forcing a random variation on the constraints imposed by a set of rules produces new techniques.

Calling Jacob's work **computer creativity** may seem difficult, because the program appears to embody much of the designer—the test for "bad" for instance—and there is a certain "stumbling onto a solution" quality from the randomness. Nevertheless, this and similar efforts, which span creative pursuits from inventing typefaces to making analogies, focus on the rule-making aspect of creativity and demonstrate that incremental revision is algorithmic. So, the conclusion seems to be that creativity is a spectrum, ranging from the "flash out of the blue" end to the Mondrian-in-a-click end.

FITBYTE

Classical Question. At a recent University of Oregon demonstration, three pianists played three different pieces of music in the style of Bach, one composed by Bach, one composed by Steven Larson (a UO professor), and one composed by EMI, a computer program. The audience voted on who they thought wrote which piece. Larson's composition was thought to be the program's, Bach's composition was thought to be Larson's, and EMI's composition was thought to be Bach's.

What Part of Creativity Is Algorithmic?

When the Turing test was invented, "Draw a picture in the style of Mondrian" would have been a request that a computer would have utterly failed at. Today it is a three-page Java program.

AI researchers have demonstrated in various contexts that the "hard work" form of creativity is algorithmic. If the matter of whether a computer can be creative is not taken to be a yes/no question, but rather is seen as an expedition into the process of creativity, we find our answer. The more deeply we understand creativity, the more we find ways in which it is algorithmic. Will it be found to be entirely algorithmic at some point in the future? Will there be rules for breaking the rules? Will it become like reckoning? Or will there necessarily be a non-algorithmic part at the inspirational end? No matter how it turns out, aspects of creativity are algorithmic. To the extent that creativity is algorithmic, a computer can be creative. But who needs a computer? If creativity is algorithmic, we can all be creative by following the rules. Progress in understanding creativity can benefit us, too. And how it is accomplished—with synapses or transistors—shouldn't matter.

FITBYTE

Fill in the Blank. In an essay in *Science* on creativity, Goldenberg, Mazursky, and Solomon report that, in one study, 89 percent of award-winning advertisements contain a use of one of six "creativity templates," that is, follow-the-rules techniques, and that one simple template, *Replacement*, accounted for 25 percent of all award-winning ads.

THE UNIVERSALITY PRINCIPLE

Another problem that concerned Turing and other computer pioneers was to determine what makes one computer more powerful than another. Their amazing discovery was that any computer using only very simple instructions could simulate any other computer. This fact—known as the Universality Principle—means, for example, that all computers have the same power!

FITBYTE

All Computers Are Created Equal. Though computer scientists have found different fundamental instruction sets, the six instructions `Add` (as described in Chapter 9), `Subtract`, `Test_For_Zero`, `Load`, `Store`, and `Branch_On_Zero` are sufficient to program any computation.

It goes without saying that every computer has these primitive instructions and much more. From the commercial point of view, the Universality Principle means that Intel and Motorola cannot compete with each other to build a computer that can compute more computations. Every computer the two companies have ever made is equivalent to all other computers in terms of what they can compute. The Universality Principle says that all computers compute the same set of computations. It's surprising.

The Universality Principle has deep theoretical implications, but there are important practical consequences, too.

FITBYTE

Getting Down to Basics. Another startling consequence of the Universality Principle is that *any* computation can be programmed using only the six basic instructions types. Any computation—playing chess or checking grammar or figuring income tax—has been simplified by programmers to the point where it could be expressed with only a half dozen different kinds operations.

Universal Information Processor

Perhaps the most important aspect of universality is that if we want to do some new information-processing task, we don't need to buy a new computer. The computer we already have is sufficient if we can write or buy the software for the task.

This is quite different, say, from wanting to perform a new task in the kitchen or the shop, where we will have to buy a new gadget. Machines that transform material must be specialized to each activity, requiring us—or enabling us, if you like to get new gadgets!—to buy a specialized device. By contrast, there is only one information-processing machine, the computer.

Because computers are general purpose, people play a greater role in setting them up and configuring them for a specific task—installing software, for example—than they do for single-purpose machines like food processors or table saws. This greater role in customizing the general-purpose device to our needs is one reason why it is important to become Fluent with IT.

Practical Consequences of the Universality Principle

The Universality Principle says computers compute the same way, and their speed is the only difference. Unfortunately, the Universality Principle's claim that any computer can simulate any other computer has the disadvantage that simulation does the work much more slowly.

{FITLINK}

Competing Machines and the Universality Principle > >

To understand why all computers are equivalent, imagine two computers, the ZAP^2 and the BXLE, and suppose they have the same hardwired instructions, except that ZAP^2 has one additional instruction. Its manufacturer claims, contrary to the Universality Principle, that the new instruction enables new computations on the ZAP^2 that are not possible on the BXLE. "Baloney," says BXLE's CEO. "Using the instructions already in BXLE, we will program a function that performs the operation of ZAP^2's special hardwired instruction. Then, in any program, we will replace every use of their special instruction with a call to our function. Anything ZAP^2 can do, BXLE can do, too." For a schematic diagram, see Figure 23.3.

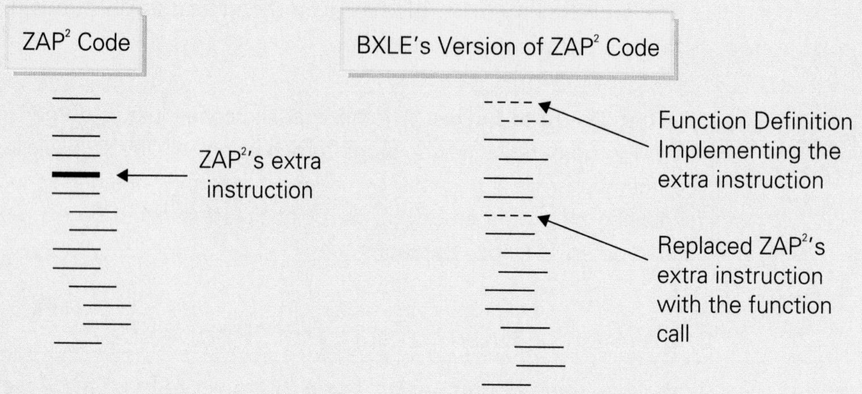

Figure 23.3. *Schematic diagram showing a revision of ZAP^2's program to run on the BXLE, in which the special instruction has been replaced by a function call.*

In effect, ZAP^2 performs the instruction in hardware while the BXLE performs the instruction in software, that is, by using a function. The argument holds up as long as the special instruction can be programmed with the basic instructions of the BXLE, which we can be confident will be possible. But the skeptic needn't accept that on faith. Rather, it's possible to write a program for the BXLE to simulate circuits and to simulate the entire circuitry of ZAP^2. Simulating ZAP^2 by the BXLE is possible because ZAP^2 is built from (zillions of) two-input logic gates. There are only 16 different gates, and they can be trivially simulated with the six basic instructions, which the BXLE surely has. Because BXLE can duplicate exactly the ZAP^2 operation in the simulator, it is possible to do all of the same computations, too. Notice that this solution also solves the problem in software.

Because all computers do the same computations, the main basis for technical competition among manufacturers is speed.

In the first solution of the ZAP^2/BXLE example, BXLE was only slower on the special instruction, which presumably takes several basic instructions to implement. The second case was much slower because each instruction of the ZAP^2 might take thousands of logical operations, and the BXLE must simulate each of these. So, although both computers can realize the same computations, they do them at different rates. For that reason, manufacturers *do* include special instructions for tasks such as digital signal processing, graphics, and encryption, hoping that their frequent use will speed up their computer.

The Universality Principle seems to conflict with our everyday experience, however. Three obvious difficulties arise:

> Macintosh software doesn't run on the PC and vice versa; if Macs and PCs are the same, why not?

> People say old machines become outmoded; how so, if they're all the same?

> Is it really true that the computer in my laptop is the same as the one in my microwave oven?

Despite these apparent problems, the Universality Principle is a practical fact. Consider each objection in turn.

Macintosh versus PC. PC and Mac processors are different—Intel's Pentium and Motorola's PowerPC—implying each has a different **combination** of instructions, though they include the six most basic mentioned earlier. These instruction sets are encoded differently, they operate slightly differently, each has instructions the other doesn't have, and so on. None of these differences is fundamental. It is possible to write a program for each machine to perform the instructions of the other machine, just as was argued earlier. It is not only possible in principle, computer scientists write such programs frequently.

But consumer software relies heavily on operating system facilities, too. So, to run a user application, the operating system (OS) would also need to be available. Running two operating systems—known as **dual booting**—is also possible, but it is not something most users want to worry about. Add to this the fact that the software will run more slowly than on the original platform, and the result doesn't justify the effort of applying the Universality Principle directly.

The alternative solution, which software companies like Adobe, Microsoft, and Oracle use, is to translate their programs to each computer family, as explained in Chapter 9. The software is written in a programming language like Basic, C, or Java, and then it is compiled—that is, translated—into the machine language of each processor type, Pentium or PowerPC. Special care is taken to ensure that operating system incompatibilities have been removed. The result is that rather than simulating the software of one computer on another computer, there is a separate custom version of the software for each vendor's computer. (And, of course, it won't run on another vendor's computer.) In that way, any application software can run on any computer and not be slowed by simulating another machine. So, the Universality Principle is used, but not in the way originally discussed.

Outmoded Computers. As noted, speed is the main difference between computers. Often, the reason why someone buys a new computer is that they own new software, doubtless loaded with slick new features, that runs slowly on their old machine. With the new software doing more, it is not surprising that a faster computer would help. But, for those who are patient, there is no need to change.

People usually give two reasons in support of their claim that older computers become "outmoded." The first reason is that hardware and/or software products are often not compatible with older machines. For example, input/output devices, such as modems and printers, are often not compatible with older computers because of other internal parts, such as the system bus. (See the computer anatomy diagram, Figure 9.2, in Chapter 9.) As a result, it is not possible to connect the new devices. However, these parts are not closely connected with instruction execution.

The second reason is that software vendors simply don't support old machines. As just explained, software vendors compile their programs to each platform—usually a processor/OS combination—to sell to customers. But, if there are too few customers running an old processor/OS combination, the vendor may decide it is not profitable to sell and maintain a version for that machine. Thus new software is often not available for old computers. This is a business decision; there is no technical impediment.

The Laptop and the Microwave. The computers embedded in consumer products like microwave ovens, brakes, and other devices are there not because the task of running a microwave is so complex that it needs a computer. Rather, it's cheaper to implement the system with a computer and a read-only memory (ROM) chip containing a fixed program than it is to implement it with custom electronics. It's a matter of economics, not a technical requirement.

Embedded computers have a rich enough instruction set to run any other computer application. Their main handicap as computers is usually neither their instruction repertoire nor their speed. Rather, embedded computers are, well, embedded. The program is fixed—giving you only options like popping popcorn or defrosting dinner—and it is connected to a very limited set of input/output devices, usually only the sensors and actuators of the system they control. If the embedded computer were connected to a keyboard and a monitor, as is the personal computer we're accustomed to, it could run the software just fine.

So, the Universality Principle is not only a theoretical fact, it is a practical fact, too.

MORE WORK, SLOWER SPEED

When we use computers, they are simply idling most of the time, waiting for us to give them something to do. For tasks like word processing, even including continuous grammar and spell checking doesn't keep them busy. So we listen to MP3 tunes, too, which is still not stressing them. Eventually, perhaps when we are manipulating digital images, we notice that certain activities, like making the image brighter, are computed very fast, but others, like turning the image on its side, are noticeably slower. This is curious when we think about it, because the image has the same number of pixels in both cases. What causes some tasks to take longer to compute?

Comparing *Alphabetize CDs* with *Face Forward*

The obvious and correct answer is that it takes more time to do more work. Recall the *Alphabetize CDs* example from Chapter 10. If the CD rack were smaller, the algorithm would complete sooner because fewer CDs would have to be considered. The point is even easier to see for a task like making sure the CDs all face forward.

The *Face Forward* algorithm requires only that we start at the beginning, inspect each CD to see which way it is facing, and, if it is not facing forward, reorient it and return it; in either case, we then move on to the next CD. If the rack holds 24 CDs, the algorithm takes 24 iterations of the inspect-and-reorient sequence because only one pass through the rack is sufficient. If the rack contains 48 CDs, 48 iterations will be required. The amount of work is proportional to the amount of data.

Cases of this type, where the amount of work is directly proportional to the amount of data, are said to be **work-proportional-to-*n*** algorithms. That is, the running time is at most the number of basic steps devoted to each item times the number n of data items. We say "at most" because not all of the steps may be needed on each data item. If some CDs are already facing forward, there will be no need for a reorient step. In the worst case, all CDs are facing backward, and it takes the maximum predicted time.

Orienting the CDs to face forward is an easier task than alphabetizing them. Recall that the *Alphabetize CDs* algorithm did not solve the problem in "one pass" through the rack. In fact, for each CD referenced by *Alpha*, all of the CDs after it had to be considered; this was called a *Beta* sweep. So, if there are 24 CDs in the rack, 23 CDs must be considered to get the first CD into position in the front because *Alpha's* reference doesn't change, but *Beta* references the 23 other CDs. Thus the "In Order?" test must be made 23 times to locate the alphabetically first CD. Then *Alpha* moves to the second position, referencing the next slot, and *Beta* must visit the 22 CDs after it. This continues until the last step, when *Alpha* references the next-to-last CD and *Beta* references only the last slot—that is, only one interchange of CDs is considered at the very end. Adding these numbers up yields

$$23 + 22 + \ldots + 1 = 276$$

That is, we test 276 times to see if a pair of CDs is possibly out of order in a 24-slot rack. In the same way, if the CD rack contains 48 CDs, locating the alphabetically first CD would require 47 CD references in the first *Beta* sweep, finding the second would require 46, and so on. Adding these numbers up we get

$$47 + 46 + \ldots + 1 = 1128$$

which is surprising because the rack is only twice as large, but the number of tests is more than four times larger. Clearly the repeated *Beta* sweeps of *Alphabetize CDs* require more work than the single sweep of the *Face Forward* algorithm.

{GREATFITMINDS}

Brainy Kid > >

At seven Johann Karl Friedrich Gauss (1777–1855), the mathematician whose face graces the Ten Deutsche Mark note, was asked by his teacher to add the numbers 1 to 100. He found the answer 5050 immediately by noting that adding the first plus last numbers (1 + 100) equals 101, adding the next-to-first and next-to-last numbers (2 + 99) also equals 101, etc., and that there are 50 pairs summing to 101. Young Gauss's idea always works, so adding numbers from 1 to n is $(n + 1)\ n/2$.

Work Proportional to *n*

Thus, although the *Face Forward* computation took only one pass through the rack, *Alphabetize CDs* took many passes. In the former case, the number of repetitions is proportional to n for an n-slot rack, and in the latter case, the number of repetitions is proportional to $(n + 1)n/2 = (n2 + n)/2$. Whereas *Face Forward* is said to be a **work-proportional-to-*n* algorithm**, *Alphabetize CDs* is said to be a **work-proportional-to-n^2 algorithm**. (Computer people don't worry about the other terms of the equation, only the most significant term, the n^2 here.)

Thus, if there are $n = 1000$ pieces of data, and a problem can be solved by a work-proportional-to-n algorithm, it will take about a thousand times the amount of work needed to do the task on one data item. But, if the problem is solved by a work-proportional-to-n^2 algorithm, the amount of work will be about a *million* = 1000×1000 times the amount of work needed to solve the problem on one data item. So, when we observe that one computation is taking more time than another despite requiring the same amount of data, it is generally because the algorithm does more work to solve the problem.

Notice that the explanation is that "the algorithm does more work to solve the problem," not that the problem *requires* more work to be solved. That is, the algorithm the programmer chose to solve the problem may not be the fastest. The fastest known algorithm is rarely the solution of choice. For example, there are faster ways to alphabetize CDs than the solution presented, though none with work proportional to n. And the alternatives are somewhat more complicated. Complexity and other factors contribute to a programmer's decision, and besides the computer is idle most of the time anyway.

HOW HARD CAN A PROBLEM BE?

With algorithms requiring work proportional to n, and proportional to n^2, it is a good guess that there are algorithms requiring work proportional to n^3, and n^4, and so on. There are, and they are all considered practical for computers to solve, though as the example of the last section made clear, the exponent does matter a lot to the user sitting there waiting for the answer.

NP-Complete Problems

There are much more difficult computations, many of which are important to business, science, and engineering. In fact, one of the most significant discoveries of the 1970s was that many problems of interest—for example, finding the cheapest set of plane tickets for touring n cities—don't have any known "practical" algorithmic solutions. Such problems are known by the rather curious name of **NP-complete** problems. In essence, the best-known algorithms do little more than try all possible solutions, and then pick the best. It seems that there should be cleverer algorithms than that. If there are, the person who discovers one will be extremely famous. In the meantime, such problems are said to be **intractable**—the best way to solve them is so difficult that large data sets cannot be solved with a realistic amount of computer time on any computer. Computers can solve them in principle, but not in practice.

FITBYTE

Hard Problems. Steve Cook of the University of Toronto and Dick Karp of UC Berkeley discovered NP-completeness. They also discovered the amazing fact that if anyone finds a better algorithm for just one NP-complete problem, their algorithm will improve every NP-complete problem.

Unsolvable Problems

Perhaps surprisingly, there are problems computers cannot solve at all. It's not that the algorithms take too long, but that there are no algorithms, period! These are not problems like being intelligent or creative, but precisely definable problems with a clear quantifiable objective. For example, it's impossible for an algorithm to determine if a program has a bug in it, like looping forever. Such an algorithm would have been quite useful in Chapter 21 in our study of looping, when we messed up the <*next iteration*> step, causing infinite loops. We'd simply give our program to this imagined Loop-Checker algorithm, and it would tell us whether or not our program loops forever. Notice that the Loop-Checker would be especially handy for computations having, say, work proportional to n^4 because we have to wait a long time for the results. While we're waiting, we'd like to be sure we're going to get a result eventually, rather than have the program caught in an infinite loop, forcing us to wait forever.

`The Nonexistent Loop Checker.` But the Loop-Checker can't exist. Suppose it did. That is, suppose there is a program **`LC(P, x)`** that takes as its input any program **`P`** and input data **`x`**, analyzes **`P`**, and answers back "Yes" or "No" as to whether **`P`** will loop forever on input **`x`**. This actually seems plausible, because **`LC`** could look through **`P`**, checking every loop to see if the *<next iteration>* and *<continuation>* tests are set right. And then it could follow the execution of **`P`** on **`x`**, looking to see if anything could go wrong. It seems plausible, but it's not. Here's why.

Create another program, **`CD(P)`**, that also takes as input a program **`P`**. **`CD`** is an abbreviation for "contradiction," and the program works according to the flowchart in Figure 23.4. What does **`CD(CD)`** compute? We're not sure what the assumed **`LC(CD,CD)`** will answer back, but suppose it says "No," **`CD`** does not loop forever when the **`CD`** program is its input. In that case, the left arrow out of the diamond is taken and **`CD`** loops forever. So, **`LC`** would have been wrong. Perhaps **`LC`** answers, "Yes," that **`CD`** will loop forever when **`CD`** is its input. In that case, the right arrow out of the diamond is taken, and the program doesn't loop forever, but just stops. Wrong again. The Loop-Checker cannot answer correctly—neither "Yes" nor "No" is the right answer. This problem cannot be algorithmically solved.

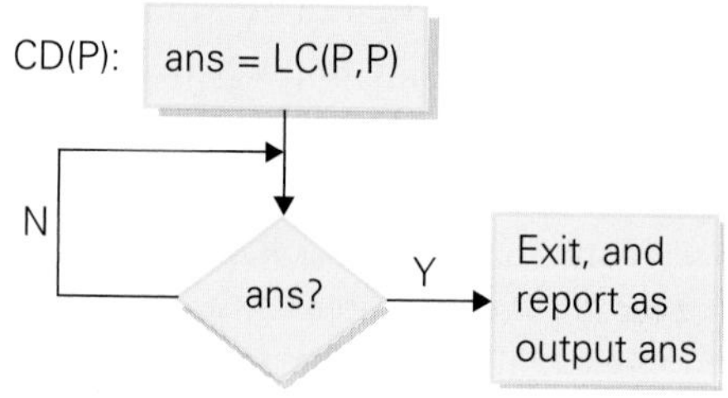

Figure 23.4. *The logic of the CD program, given the assumed program LC.*

`The Halting Problem.` The Loop-Checker is trying to solve a famous computation known as the **Halting Problem**. Alan M. Turing was the first to recognize the impossibility of creating the perfect debugger, like the theoretical Loop-Checker. It's too bad it can't be created, because having such a debugger would be handy. Interestingly, debugging—the topic of Chapter 7—is something that humans can do, admittedly with great difficulty sometimes. In fact, it requires considerable intelligence to figure out what has gone wrong when an IT task doesn't work out. It's something that computers won't ever be able to do in any general way. So, maybe we were looking in the wrong place for capabilities that are uniquely human. Making computers do our bidding *properly* is something only humans can do!

SUMMARY

We have explored the limits of computation. We began by asking a question that has puzzled people since computers were invented—can they think? The question challenged us to define what thinking is. We identified a tendency for people to decide that an intellectual activity isn't considered thinking if it is algorithmic. Thinking is probably best defined as what humans do, and therefore something computers can't do. The Turing test is an experimental setting in which we can compare the capabilities of humans with those of computers. We studied the question of computer chess and learned that computers use a game tree formulation, an evaluation function to assess board positions, and a database of openings and endgames. Deep Blue became the chess champion of the world in 1997, a monumental achievement, but not one that closed the book on the algorithmic nature of intelligence.

Next we studied creativity, deciding it occurs on a spectrum: from algorithmic variation (Mondrian-in-a-click) through incremental revision to a flash of inspiration. The degree to which the activities along the spectrum are algorithmic has advanced over the years. We presume that there will be further advancement, and we do not know where the "algorithmic frontier" will be drawn. Is creativity like reckoning—entirely algorithmic? It's too early to tell. But however it turns out, computers will be creative insofar as creativity is algorithmic. And so will we all.

Next we considered the Universality Principle, which implies that computers are equal in terms of what they can compute. This is not only a theoretical statement. We benefit from its practical consequences every day. For example, software companies can write a single application program and translate it into the machine language of any computer, making it available to everyone regardless of the kind of computer they own. This implied that computer vendors could only compete on speed, which led us to consider how fast computers can solve problems. The many proportional-to-n computations require less work than the proportional-to-n^2 computations even though both require n data values. Such computations are practical and form the large part of computing. But there are important problems—the so-called NP-complete problems—that require much more computational work. Many of the problems we would like to solve are NP-complete problems, but unfortunately the NP-complete problems are intractable—large instances are solvable by computer only in principle, not in practice. Finally, we learned the amazing fact that some computations—general-purpose debugging—cannot be solved by computer even in principle. If it were possible, we could solve the Halting Problem, and that's not logically possible. They're good computations to keep in mind for those times when it seems computers can do anything.

EXERCISES

Multiple Choice

1. Computers can:
   A. think
   B. manipulate information
   C. be creative
   D. all of the above
2. For the computer, chess is a series of:
   A. algorithms
   B. computations
   C. possible moves reduced to a an evaluation of the "best" move
   D. all of the above
3. Creativity can be:
   A. "a flash out of the blue"
   B. incremental revision of existing work
   C. hard work
   D. perhaps some of each, depending on the definition
4. The ability of any computer to imitate another computer is known as:
   A. mimicry
   B. the Imitation Principle
   C. the Universality Principle
   D. the Turing Test
5. All computers have the same:
   A. instruction set
   B. six computing instructions
   C. basic operating system
   D. processing power
6. Work-proportional-to-*n* algorithms:
   A. increase processing time proportionally to the data
   B. process data in roughly the same amount of time regardless of the amount of data
   C. work so fast that modern computers spend most of their time idling
   D. geometrically increase in processing time as the amount of data increases
7. The *Alphabetize CDs* algorithm is a:
   A. work-proportional-to-*n* algorithm
   B. work-proportional-to-n^2 algorithm
   C. either A or B, depending on the initial order of the CDs
   D. A XOR B

8. NP-complete problems:
   A. have no known solution
   B. have too many possibilities to solve
   C. must consider every possible solution to find the best one
   D. can be solved with a work-proportional-to-*n* algorithm

9. The only things humans can do that computers can't is:
   A. play games of chance
   B. sorting algorithms
   C. make computers work properly
   D. solve the Halting Problem

10. Putting together a puzzle by trying every possible combination and selecting the best result is an example of a(n):
    A. work-proportional-to-*n* algorithm
    B. work-proportional-to-n^2 algorithm
    C. NP-complete problem
    D. intractable problem

11. To play checkers with a computer:
    A. would be too complicated for Deep Blue to compute
    B. the algorithm for Deep Blue would work
    C. the possible "deep" moves would be much simpler than in chess
    D. all of the above

12. Calculating every possible move in a chess game is known as a:
    A. game tree
    B. Turing Test
    C. work-proportional-to-n algorithm
    D. none of the above

13. In a game, looking ahead for potential moves is called:
    A. deeper
    B. drill down
    C. variations
    D. none of the above

14. Putting several computers to work on the same problems is called:
    A. algorithmic thinking
    B. parallel computation
    C. Universality
    D. none of the above

15. All computer computations can be completed with just:
    A. 4 instructions
    B. 6 instructions
    C. 9 instructions
    D. 11 instructions

16. The simplest of the listed algorithmic solutions is the:
    A. work-proportional-to-*n* algorithm
    B. work-proportional-to-n^2 algorithm
    C. NP-complete problem
    D. intractable problem
17. A program debugger:
    A. works only on syntax errors
    B. works on logic errors
    C. works on both types of errors
    D. doesn't exist
18. The fastest computers can calculate up to:
    A. ten billion instructions per second
    B. a trillion instructions per second
    C. a million instructions per minute
    D. ten trillion instructions per second

Short Answer

1. ______ is the name of the IBM computer designed for chess.
2. The ______ is the test of computer intelligence.
3. AI is short for ______.
4. For computer chess, a(n) ______ shows the result of every possible legal move for the computer along with a numeric evaluation of each move.
5. Deep Blue is a good example of computer intelligence that is ______, not general purpose.
6. ______ are rules about rules.
7. The ______ maintains that any computer can be made to imitate any other computer.
8. All computer programming can be done with only ______ basic instructions.
9. The ______ is the only information-processing machine.
10. Any hardwired computer instructions can be simulated in ______.
11. ______ is the ability of a computer to run two operating systems on the same computer.
12. ______ is the process of translating a computer program into the machine language of the computer.
13. Lack of ______ and ______ are the two major claims put forth for computers becoming outdated.
14. ______ computers are computers built into other devices to implement it them with custom electronics.
15. ______ are problems with no practical algorithmic solutions.

Exercises

1. How many 0's in a trillion?
2. How long would it take to do a billion calculations?
3. Explain how computer art is derivative and not creative.
4. Where on the list does a chess algorithm fall for solving computer problems?
5. What type of algorithm is needed to solve a problem of finding the best route to take for a cross country trip?
6. Explain how a game tree could be used for card games.
7. Describe why the argument on whether computers can think has little impact on our daily lives. Use your word processor to answer this.
8. What does a computer have to do to pass the Turing Test?

chapter

24 COMMENCEMENT

A Fluency Summary

learning objectives

- Discuss the differences in remembering IT details and ideas when you are Fluent
- Discuss lifelong learning of IT through finding new uses, asking for help, and noticing new technology
- Discuss the benefits of achieving Fluency now and in the future

Commencement speakers have a good deal in common with grandfather clocks: Standing usually some six feet tall, typically ponderous in construction, more traditional than functional, their distinction is largely their noisy communication of essentially commonplace information.

—W. WILLARD WIRTZ,
U.S. SECRETARY OF LABOR, 1968

WE HAVE COME to the final chapter. It has been a substantive and, at times, challenging tour. But the barrier of intimidation has collapsed, and our ability to apply IT has dramatically improved. We have studied a very broad spectrum of topics, none thoroughly enough for us to be considered an expert, but all thoroughly enough to indicate in which areas we need to learn more. So, the study of IT topics is not finished, it has only just started. Achieving Fluency is a process of lifelong learning. We have reached a point where greater knowledge converts to greater effectiveness. We have not reached completion, but commencement.

In this chapter, we look at two of the "big ideas" that have recurred during our introduction to computation and information. Then, we discuss how our ideas-based study of information technology—though treating many topics—allows us to remember less rather than more. Next we consider what we must do to keep up with the changes in IT and to continue to improve our uses of IT. Three processes can promote lifelong learning. Finally, we evaluate our new knowledge of IT in the context of driving a car and discover that we can extract the full power today while others must wait.

TWO BIG IDEAS OF IT

Thinking back over the summaries of each chapter, several ideas have recurred in our study of IT. Two examples are structuring of information and strategies for nonalgorithmic tasks. We consider each in turn.

Structuring of Information

In Chapter 5 we learned that collections of information are structured hierarchically—that is, organized by descriptive metadata into groupings and subgroupings—in order to assist us in locating specific items. In Chapter 8 we found that the *Oxford English Dictionary's* digitization includes metadata structural tags enclosing the constituents of each definition. Knowing the purpose of each part of the *OED's* content (headword, citation, etc.) allows the computer to help with complex searches and analysis. In Chapter 13, specifying the structure of the information gave the same powerful advantage when we built databases. Specifying the characteristics of the data stored in a table—its type, whether it is key, etc.—allowed for sophisticated queries and prevented against erroneous uses that would produce garbage. XML gave a further structuring example in Chapter 16.

The idea is that *specifying structure is as essential as specifying content*. This idea comes up again and again because the value of information depends on how effectively we can use it, and all of the powerful applications rely on the computer's knowing the structure. The truth of this observation is clear from our studies. But can we learn anything more from it? Yes!

As we become increasingly more effective users, we will acquire a growing collection of personally important digital information. Years of old email correspondence, digital photographs, collections of MP3 tunes, etc., will fill our hard disks. As the collections grow, we may eventually decide to move certain information into databases or other structured archives in order to manipulate it efficiently. But along the way, while we accumulate the information as independent files, it is smart to keep it structured simply by the way we arrange it in directories and subdirectories. We should assign our MP3s and JPEGs to their own directories—substructured perhaps into folders based on content—just to be able to find files when we want them. This simple directory structure organization is not as effective as the examples above because the computer does not know the structure. But we know it and it will assist us in our manual navigation of our collections.

Strategies for Nonalgorithmic Tasks

Algorithms have been an important topic in our Fluency study. We learned the placeholder technique for reformatting text (Chapter 2), insertion sort for alphabetizing CDs (Chapter 10), effective query construction (Chapter 14)—build a supertable with joins and then trim it down using `Select` and `Project`—and many others.

But perhaps the most significant content of our study concerned the capabilities, which are not algorithmic. Finding accurate information (Chapter 5), satisfying our curiosity through research (Chapter 6), debugging (Chapter 7), formulating a password (Chapter 12), designing a database (Chapter 15), testing and assessing a user interface (Chapter 19), and programming a complex Web application (Chapter 22) are all examples in which there are no deterministic, guaranteed-to-yield-a-solution rules. In each case we could only give guidelines. For example, debugging is facilitated by these guidelines:

CHECKLIST>>

Debugging Guidelines

- *Make sure that you can reproduce the error.*
- *Determine exactly what the problem is.*
- *Eliminate the "obvious" causes.*
- *Divide the process, separating out the parts that work from the part that does not.*
- *When you reach a dead end, reassess your information, asking where you may be making wrong assumptions or conclusions; then step through the process again.*
- *As you work through the process from start to finish, make predictions about what should happen and verify that the predictions are fulfilled.*

The steps prescribe a rational approach to the task, but they don't form an algorithm.

The capabilities, which are nonalgorithmic, have been presented as though they form a separate knowledge base, and they do, in the sense that they each entail a separate list of guidelines. But generally the capabilities are all applications of logical reasoning in service of achieving some higher goal—true information, correct program, convenient application, etc. Reasoning is the key and was applied in small ways on nearly every page of this book. Indeed, an overarching theme of this text is that *precision and the directed application of logical reasoning can solve problems great and small, algorithmic and nonalgorithmic.* The more we apply such thinking, the better we get at it!

FLUENCY: LESS IS MORE

In reviewing the material covered in this book, it is sobering to realize the enormous amount of detailed information that we've covered. We've learned about anchor tags in HTML, the **`if/else`** statement in JavaScript, the Vacation Message, the Nyquist Rule, SQL SELECT commands, and on and on. How can we ever remember it all?

Recall that the Fluency knowledge is compartmentalized into three components:

- Skills—competency with contemporary IT applications like word processing.
- Concepts—understanding the foundations on which IT is built, like the Fetch/Execute Cycle.
- Capabilities—facility with higher-level thinking processes like reasoning.

These three kinds of knowledge are co-equal and interdependent. But when we analyze the three types of knowledge from the point of view of the amount of detail they involve, we realize that they are very much *unequal*.

- The skills all require much detailed knowledge. For example, are field names in SQL expressed as <*table name*>**.**<*field name*> or <*field name*>**.**<*table name*>? It is impossible to write SQL without knowing which is correct. Further, an annoying property of this detail is that the computer demands it be *exactly right*; it is unforgiving. We can't use computers without knowing such facts.
- The concepts might be quite detailed, but the "basic ideas" are not. We know a computer's Fetch/Execute Cycle is an infinite process for interpreting instructions, but now that we understand the core idea, we don't really need to know that the third of the five steps is called Data Fetch. It's the concept of an instruction execution engine that is important. IT concepts are like other scientific information. The idea must be explained in full detail for it to be understood, but after it's learned, only the idea, not the particulars, is important for the non-specialist.
- The capabilities are the least detailed of all. Capabilities are mostly approaches to thinking. Problem decomposition, for example, in which a complex task is broken into smaller tasks that either are solved directly or are themselves broken into smaller pieces still, is simply a rational way to tackle complex problems. Debugging—thinking objectively about a faulty IT application—is mostly a matter of being a good detective. Yes, there are guidelines on how to proceed, but mostly debugging comes down to forcing yourself to look at a situation the way it *is* rather than the way you've been seeing it so far and to apply logical reasoning. The capabilities require you to remember almost no detail whatsoever.

So there is a spectrum of detail from skills through concepts to capabilities.

Curiously, our Fluency study allows us to remember less, rather than requiring us to remember more. How could this be? We remember less *detail* because we remember instead the *basic ideas*.

The clearest example—but much of our study of Fluency works this way—was our discussion of what the digerati know (Chapter 2). The chapter seemed to be covering skill-level information about how to use a GUI, what's behind the **File** and **Edit** menus, how to use shift-select, and so on. Everyone needs to know this information to use IT. But what the chapter was really about was the capability of *thinking abstractly about technology*, and how we learn to think abstractly. We asked sweeping questions like,

> How do we learn technology?

> How do software designers, indeed any tool designers, expect users to learn to use their creations?

> When we're confronted with a task requiring technology, how do we figure out what to do?

The answers to these questions turned out not to be "Memorize thick, boring manuals." Rather, we pointed out that thinking abstractly about technology implies an adaptive approach to learning. Tool creators exploit consistent interfaces—every tape and CD player uses the same icons—so look for the consistency. Look for metaphors. When presented with a tool, explore it by "clicking around" to see what the inventor provided. Ask, what am I expected to do? And finally, simply "blaze away," trying things out and watching what happens, knowing that the garbage created when making mistakes must be thrown away (at no cost) before starting over. In other words, we don't memorize the tool's details. Rather, we learn the details as we need them. If we frequently use the software, we will become adept at the specifics, memorizing the details through use. If we rarely use the software, we will forget them. But even that's fine. We know abstractly what to do and how to figure them out again.

Thus the higher-level capabilities make us rational people, approaching IT tasks thoughtfully, enabling us to proceed in a directed and disciplined way toward the goal, solving problems as they arise, figuring out what to do as required, logically thinking out what's wrong when a bug has us blocked. We've learned how to learn IT. Fluency doesn't require that we use our heads to memorize details. It only requires that we use our heads.

LIFELONG LEARNING IN IT

Learning in information technology is a process of lifelong learning, but that doesn't mean you have to read 20 pages of *Programming in XML* every night before bed. In fact, it doesn't mean that you have to do much at all. To learn throughout life requires only that you engage in three activities:

> Pursue new uses of IT that fulfill your personal needs.

> Be rational about asking for help.

> Notice new ideas and technology as they arise.

There's no course of study to attend.

Finding New Uses

While studying Fluency, you have had to learn many new and unfamiliar applications. Though learning new skills may initially have been daunting, the process should have become steadily easier as your experience broadened and your facility with "clicking around" and "blazing away" developed. This success, and the fact that learning becomes easier the more you know, should give you confidence that you can learn IT on your own. And that's the best way to advance your knowledge. When you are engaged in information processing tasks—addressing envelopes, paying your bills, looking up Manila's time zone in the almanac—determine whether you should be using information technology to help with them. If so, be confident that you can learn the new application, and take the time to do so. Pushing out your uses of IT is the best way to continue to learn.

If you think objectively when you ask the question, "Can IT help in this situation?" the answer will not always be "yes." If the occasions when you address envelopes are limited to Mother's Day and Father's Day, IT will not help. Besides, do you want address labels on their greeting cards? If the envelope addressing is once a year for holiday greeting cards and you have only a modest list, again it may not pay. For the monthly reminders for the members of your book club—even if there are only five of them—it might pay to set up a postcard printing application. You'll send 60 reminders during a year, and once you've set up the announcement document and the address list, running the cards through the printer twice (two sides) might pay. When you're in charge of publicity for your club or other organization, the technology definitely pays. In summary, apply IT only if it helps, but if it can help, don't hesitate to apply it.

Asking for Help

A goal of studying Fluency is to convert you into a self-reliant computer and information user. Does that mean that you should solve all of your problems yourself? Of course not. In fact, it is certain that there are problems that are beyond your knowledge now, and there always will be. We always need experts. So, eventually we need to get assistance from someone more knowledgeable than we are.

But acknowledging that we need to get help doesn't mean that the moment things go awry we throw up our hands in desperation. Fluency has taught us how to troubleshoot our problems, and our experience has given us some perspective. We should assess whether the problem is probably one of our own stupidity—which we would eagerly fix on our own to save the embarrassment of revealing that stupidity to someone else—or something more fundamental that requires greater expertise. Only after we've applied reasonable efforts to solving our own problem will we need to ask for help. But when we do need it, we should ask. Of course, one factor in limiting our use of professionals is that it usually takes a while, and we'd rather solve our problem ourselves than wait.

As a contributor to lifelong learning, both trying to solve our own problems and asking for help when we're truly stuck can contribute to a greater understanding of IT. If we figure it out ourselves, we're at least more experienced at troubleshooting. If someone else helps us, we may learn some facts we didn't know. Either way, we come out ahead.

Noticing New Technology

If the technological changes of the last half-century are any guide to the changes to come, IT will be quite different at the end of the next half-century. To learn about and apply the coming advances will require some attention. Is the "advance" being touted in the press a fundamental leap forward that's potentially beneficial to me, or is it just hype about an old product in a different package? The latter is far more common than the former. We must be attentive and skeptical.

When there is a fundamental advancement—it happens more like once a decade than once a month—we need to be willing to learn about it. The media often covers the "science" of new technologies, and following these technologies should be easy given the concepts taught in this book. Using the technology might require taking a class, but more than likely it won't. After all, thinking about technology abstractly, we know that those eager to deploy a new technology will have prepared a "migration path" for those of us who are competent, daily users of the current technology. The new advance will likely be much harder to use than the mature technologies with which we are familiar, of course. But if as Fluent users we don't have the background and experience to overcome those difficulties—that is, if we can't be successful with the new technology—it isn't ready.

It often happens that technologies—small advances as well as large ones—are rushed to market before they're ready, so there is considerable risk in being an early adopter. But waiting has its risks, too. One of technology's defining characteristics is that it steadily improves. Inventing technology is a difficult creative activity, and engineering it to be perfect the first time never happens. So, there are steady improvements—automobiles improved throughout the entire twentieth century. Thus there will always be a next-generation technology that is more convenient, more functional, more versatile with better price performance, and so on. Waiting for perfection might require a hundred-year wait, and all that time you're not benefiting from the technology. The lesson: Adopt a technology as soon as there's a high probability that it will be beneficial to you, but expect it to continue to improve.

SHIFTING FOR YOURSELF

Ted Nelson, the inventor of hypertext, tells a story of his first meeting with a software development team for a project he was to direct. He tells how depressed he was to find that everyone on the team drove a car with a standard transmission (a car requiring the driver to shift gears manually). Nelson's point in telling the story is that software should be as easy for people to use as automatic transmissions are, and that programmers who enjoy shifting their own gears may not produce such software. Whether his point is correct or not, his story gives us a valuable—if different—perspective.

Fluency enables *us*, the users, to shift gears. It doesn't give us the ability to build a car, to repair it, or to modify it. But, we can control IT to extract its full power, to be in command, and to get to our goal. Nelson may be right regarding builders, but shifting is not an ability to be deplored for a user.

Whatever the IT equivalent of the automatic transmission is, it is still on the drawing board. It took 60 years for cars to come with automatic transmissions. With IT's sixtieth birthday still years away, we can't wait. We'll shift for ourselves.

EXERCISES

Multiple Choice

1. Specifying structure is:
   A. more important than specifying content
   B. less important than specifying content
   C. just as important as specifying content
   D. the same as specifying content
2. Examples of nonalgorithmic tasks include all of the following except:
   A. finding information
   B. using placeholders to reformat text
   C. database design
   D. creating a password
3. The first step in debugging is to:
   A. determine what the problem is
   B. reproduce the error
   C. eliminate obvious causes
   D. divide the problem into smaller parts
4. Debugging is:
   A. algorithmic
   B. procedural
   C. ordinal
   D. none of the above
5. Problems can be solved by approaching them:
   A. through the use of algorithms
   B. by applying more and faster computers to the problem
   C. by using logical reasoning
   D. through trial and error
6. Which of the following is not a component of Fluency knowledge?
   A. Skills
   B. Capabilities
   C. Content
   D. Concepts
7. Put the three Fluency components in order from the least detailed to the most detailed.
   A. Capabilities, Concepts, Skills
   B. Concepts, Capabilities, Skills
   C. Skills, Concepts, Capabilities
   D. Skills, Capabilities, Concepts

8. Thinking Fluently involves the use of:
   A. memorization
   B. repetition and practice
   C. abstract thinking
   D. attention to detail

9. You should adopt technology when:
   A. the price/performance ratio is in your favor
   B. as soon as you can get your hands on it
   C. only after most of the rest of the public has adopted it
   D. when there is a high probability that it will prove beneficial to you

10. Fundamental advances in IT come along:
    A. daily
    B. monthly
    C. yearly
    D. less often than that

Short Answer

1. ______ is involved when there is no deterministic, unfailing method to solve a problem.
2. ______ is a series of steps that, when taken, guarantees the successful completion of a task.
3. Debugging is not algorithmic, but, rather, it is ______.
4. Of the three Fluency components, the ability to use email is considered a ______.
5. Of the three Fluency components, the understanding of networking principles is considered a ______.
6. Of the three Fluency components, the understanding of algorithmic thinking is considered a ______.
7. ______ is the process of asking questions, pursuing ideas and interests, and being curious.
8. A list of files provides ______ for storing them, but it gives no indication of their ______.
9. Examples of ______ include, the Smooth Motion program, the insertion sort, and query construction.
10. With Fluency, ______ are to details what ______ are to the "big picture."

Exercises

1. Explain how knowledge of program debugging can be used to solve other problems.
2. Describe the debugging process as a loop. What condition allows you to end the loop?
3. Describe how the development of the GUI is like the shift (pardon the pun) from manual to automatic transmissions.
4. Why are computers very good at structure but very poor on content?
5. Why is the best technology often the most overlooked?
6. Why is structure as important as content?
7. At what point should you be satisfied with your knowledge of IT?
8. How are skills tied to details while capabilities are tied to the "big picture?"

TIM BERNERS-LEE is the Director of the World Wide Web Consortium (W3C) and Principal Research Scientist at MIT's Laboratory for Computer Science. In 1989, while working at the European Particle Physics Laboratory CERN, Tim invented an Internet-based hypermedia initiative for global information sharing, commonly known as the World Wide Web. A year later, he wrote the first Web client and server. Tim received his degree in physics from Oxford University in England in 1976.

You earned your first degree in physics. Why did you later pursue your PhD in Computer Science?

After my physics degree, the telecommunications research companies seemed to be the most interesting places to be. The microprocessor had just come out, and telecommunications was switching very fast from hardwired logic to microprocessor-based systems. It was very exciting.

How did your foundation in physics influence your design of the Web?

When you study physics, you imagine what rules of behavior on the very small scale could possibly give rise to the large-scale world as we see it. When you design a global system like the Web, you try to invent rules of behavior of Web pages and links and things that could create a large-scale world as we would like it. One is analysis and the other synthesis, but they are very similar.

You've often said that the Web is simply "not done yet." What do you envision it to be like when it is done?

As I say in my book, *Weaving the Web*, I have a dream for the Web . . . and it has two parts.

In the first part, the Web becomes a much more powerful means for collaboration between people. I have always imagined the information space as something to which everyone has immediate and intuitive access, and not just to browse, but to create. Furthermore, the dream of people-to-people communication through shared knowledge must be possible for groups of all sizes, interacting electronically with as much ease as they do now in person.

In the second part of the dream, collaborations extend to computers. Machines become capable of analyzing all the data on the Web—the content, links, and transactions between people and computers. A "Semantic Web," which should make this possible, has yet to emerge, but when it does, the day-to-day mechanisms of trade, bureaucracy, and our daily lives will be handled by machines talking to machines, leaving humans to provide inspiration and intuition . . . This machine-understandable Web will come about through the implementation of a series of technical advances and social agreements that are now beginning.

Once the two-part dream is reached, the Web will be a place where the whim of a human being and the reasoning of a machine coexist in an ideal, powerful mixture.

And what does that mixture look like?

There is just one Web, whatever your browser, it's always available, and anyone can access it no matter what hardware device, software vendor, geographical position, disability, language, or culture.

What do you find most challenging about your work?

When two groups disagree strongly about something, but want in the end to achieve a common goal, finding exactly what they each mean and where the misunderstandings are can be very demanding. The chair of any working group knows that. However, this is what it takes to make progress toward consensus on a large scale.

What challenges are you facing in trying to achieve the Semantic Web?

Technically, there are many standards to make in the area of rules of query languages and web services, and at the same time there is the job of working out how these will all fit together as logical systems.

Commercially, it is difficult to find a short-term business model for anything web-like, because its value depends on the extent to which others are also using it.

Legally, the threat of patents hangs over any standards area until everyone involved has agreed to make the common infrastructure royalty-free.

These are three of the larger challenges we are facing, but overcoming them is the excitement, creativity, and business wisdom of many people who are working together in different ways.

What do you think students should be aware of as Web technology advances?

Be aware that what you can make with communications and computing technology is limited only by your imagination. Be aware also that while technology gives us more choices as to what we do, it does not change the essential nature, limitations and strengths of a human being.

interview

TIM BERNERS-LEE

appendix

A HTML REFERENCE

The following brief descriptions form an alphabetical list of the HTML tags used in this book. Check Chapter 4 for further explanation or consult **`www.w3.org/hypertext/WWW/MarkUp/MarkUp.html`**.

> **FIT CAUTION**
>
> **Text Only!** Remember, HTML source files must contain only standard keyboard text (ASCII). Word processors include fancy formatting that confuses browsers. Use simple text editors only, such as Simple Text, BBtext, or Notepad. Also, the file name extension—the characters after the last dot in the file name—must be html.

HTML Document Structure

Every HTML source file must contain the following tags in the given order:

```
<html>
  <head>
      All header content goes here
  </head>
  <body>
      All body content goes here
  </body>
</html>
```

HTML Tags

Anchor (`<a> </a>`): Defines a hyperlink using the **`href="`*fn*`"`** attribute, where fn is a file name. The text between the two tags is known as the link and is highlighted.

```
<a href="nextPage.html">Click here for next page</a>
```

Body (`<body> </body>`): Specifies the extent of the body of the HTML document (refer to the preceding section to see the HTML document structure). Useful attributes include

> `background="`*fn*`"` fills the page background with the image (possibly tiled) from the file fn

> `bgcolor="`*color*`"` paints the background the specified *color*

> `text="`*color*`"` displays text the specified *color*

> `link="`*color*`"` displays links the specified *color*

Bold (`<b> </b>`): Specifies that the style of the enclosed text is to be bold font.

```
<b>This text prints as bold</b>
```

Caption (`<caption> </caption>`): Specifies the caption of a table, and must be enclosed by Table tags. See “Table” in this list for an example.

Comment (`<!--`*comment goes here*`-->`): The comment text is enclosed within the angle brackets; avoid using angle brackets in the comments, which can confuse browsers.

```
<!-- This text will not be displayed -->
```

Definitional List (`<dl> </dl>`): Defines a definitional list, which is composed of two-part entries, called the definitional-list term (`<dt> </dt>`) and the definitional-list definition (`<dd> </dd>`). Terms are on separate lines and the definitions are on the line following. A useful attribute is `compact`, which displays terms and definitions on the same line.

```
<dl>
  <dt>First term</dt>
  <dd>First definition goes here</dd>
  <dt>Second term </dt>
  <dd>Second definition goes here</dd>
</dl>
```

Font (`<font> </font>`): Defines a range of text in which the style of the font is to be adjusted from the prevailing style. Useful attributes include

> `color="`*color*`"` displays the text the specified *color*

> `face="`*type*`"` displays text the specified *type* face

```
<font face="Helvetica"> This text is san serif </font>
```

Header (`<head> </head>`): Defines the extent of the header of the HTML document, which must include a Title. Refer to the first section, “HTML Document Structure,” for an example.

Headings (<hi> </hi>): Specifies that the enclosed text is to be one of eight levels of headings. The smaller the number the larger and more prominent the text will be.

```
<h1> Heading level 1 </h1> Most prominent
<h2> Heading level 2 </h2>
     ...
<h7> Heading level 7 </h7>
<h8> Heading level 8 </h8> Least prominent
```

Horizontal Rule (`<hr>`): Defines a line that spans the window, though it can be reduced in size using the `width="`*p*`%"` attribute. The attribute `size="`*n*`"` specifies the (point) thickness of the line.

```
<hr width="75%">
```

HTML (`<html> </html>`): Defines the beginning and end of the document. Refer to the first section, "HTML Document Structure," for an example.

Image (`<img> </img>`): Causes an image—specified by the `src="`*fn*`"` attribute—to be placed in the document at the current position. Positioning information uses the `align` attribute to specify the position on the line—`top`, `middle`, `bottom`—and the position in the window—`left`, `center`, `right`. Also, `height` and `width` attributes specify the displayed image's size in pixels.

```
<img src="prettyPic.html" align='left' height='200' width='140'>
```

Italics (`<i> </i>`): Specifies that the syle of the enclosed text is to be italic.

```
<i>This text is emphasized by italics</i>
```

Line Break (`<br>`): Ends the current line and continues the text on the next line.

```
This text is on one line.<br> This text is on the next line.
```

List Item (`<li> </li>`): Specifies an entry in either an ordered or an unordered list. See examples in the "Ordered List" and "Unordered List" definitions.

Ordered List (`<ol> </ol>`): Specifies the extent of an ordered list, whose entries are list items. The list items are prefixed with a number.

```
<ol>
  <li>First list item</li>
  <li>Second list item</li>
</ol>
```

Paragraph (`<p> </p>`): Specifies the extent of a paragraph. Paragraphs begin on a new line.

```
<p> This text forms a small paragraph</p>
```

Title (`<title> </title>`): Defines the title for the page, and must be given in the Header section of the HTML source.

```
<title> Titles display at the top of the browser window
</title>
```

Table (`<table> </table>`): Defines a table of Table Rows; the rows contain Table Data. The first row of the definition can optionally be formed of Table Heading tags. A useful attribute is border, giving the table a border.

```
<table border>
  <caption>Description</caption>
  <tr>
     <th>Head Col 1</th>
     <th>Head Col 2</th>
     <th>Head Col 3</th>
  </tr>
  <tr>
     <td>Row 1, Cell 1</td>
     <td>Row 1, Cell 2</td>
     <td>Row 1, Cell 3</td>
  </tr>
  <tr>
     <td>Row 2, Cell 1</td>
     <td>Row 2, Cell 2</td>
     <td>Row 2, Cell 3</td>
  </tr>
  <tr>
     <td>Row 3, Cell 1</td>
     <td>Row 3, Cell 2</td>
     <td>Row 3, Cell 3</td>
  </tr>
</table>
```

Table Data (`<td> </td>`): Specifies a cell in a table, and must be enclosed by Table Row tags. A useful attribute is `bgcolor="`*color*`"`. See “Table” for an example.

Table Heading (`<th> </th>`): Specifies a cell in the heading row of a table, and must be enclosed by Table Row tags. A useful attribute is `bgcolor="`*color*`"`. See “Table” for an example.

Table Row (`<tr> </tr>`): Specifies a row in a table, and must be enclosed by table tags. A useful attribute is `bgcolor="`*color*`"`. See “Table” for an example.

Unordered List (`<ul> </ul>`): Specifies the extent of an unordered list, whose entries are list items. The list items are prefixed with a bullet. A list item can enclose another list.

```
<ol>
  <li>First list item</li>
  <li>Second list item</li>
</ol>
```

RGB Colors

Table A.1 shows the hexadecimal coding for commonly used colors. The numbers, when used in attribute specifications, should have the form "#dddddd".

***Table A.1** Web-Safe Colors for Web Page Design*

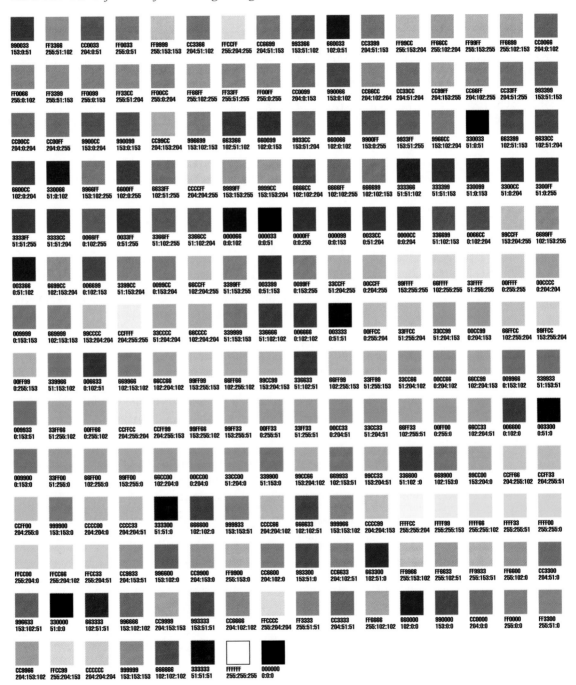

990033 153:0:51	FF3366 255:51:102	CC0033 204:0:51	FF0033 255:0:51	FF9999 255:153:153	CC3366 204:51:102	FFCCFF 255:204:255	CC6699 204:51:153	993366 153:51:102	660033 102:0:51	CC3399 204:51:153	FF99CC 255:153:204	FF66CC 255:102:204	FF99FF 255:153:255	FF6699 255:102:153	CC0066 204:0:102
FF0066 255:0:102	FF3399 255:51:153	FF0099 255:0:153	FF33CC 255:51:204	FF00CC 255:0:204	FF66FF 255:102:255	FF33FF 255:51:255	FF00FF 255:0:255	CC0099 204:0:153	990066 153:0:102	CC66CC 204:102:204	CC33CC 204:51:204	CC99FF 204:153:255	CC66FF 204:102:255	CC33FF 204:51:255	993399 153:51:153
CC00CC 204:0:204	CC00FF 204:0:255	9900CC 153:0:204	990099 153:0:153	CC99CC 204:153:204	996699 153:102:153	663366 102:51:102	660099 102:0:153	9933CC 153:51:204	660066 102:0:102	9900FF 153:0:255	9933FF 153:51:255	9966CC 153:102:204	330033 51:0:51	663399 102:51:153	6633CC 102:51:204
6600CC 102:0:204	330066 51:0:102	9966FF 153:102:255	6600FF 102:0:255	6633FF 102:51:255	CCCCFF 204:204:255	9999FF 153:153:255	9999CC 153:153:204	6666CC 102:102:204	6666FF 102:102:255	666699 102:102:153	333366 51:51:102	333399 51:51:153	330099 51:0:153	3300CC 51:0:204	3300FF 51:0:255
3333FF 51:51:255	3333CC 51:51:204	0066FF 0:102:255	0033FF 0:51:255	3366FF 51:102:255	3366CC 51:102:204	000066 0:0:102	000033 0:0:51	0000FF 0:0:255	000099 0:0:153	0033CC 0:51:204	0000CC 0:0:204	336699 51:102:153	0066CC 0:102:204	99CCFF 153:204:255	6699FF 102:153:255
003366 0:51:102	6699CC 102:153:204	006699 0:102:153	3399CC 51:153:204	0099CC 0:153:204	66CCFF 102:204:255	3399FF 51:153:255	003399 0:51:153	0099FF 0:153:255	33CCFF 51:204:255	00CCFF 0:204:255	99FFFF 153:255:255	66FFFF 102:255:255	33FFFF 51:255:255	00FFFF 0:255:255	00CCCC 0:204:204
009999 0:153:153	669999 102:153:153	99CCCC 153:204:204	CCFFFF 204:255:255	33CCCC 51:204:204	66CCCC 102:204:204	339999 51:153:153	336666 51:102:102	006666 0:102:102	003333 0:51:51	00FFCC 0:255:204	33FFCC 51:255:204	33CC99 51:204:153	00CC99 0:204:153	66FFCC 102:255:204	99FFCC 153:255:204
00FF99 0:255:153	339966 51:153:102	006633 0:102:51	669966 102:153:102	66CC66 102:204:102	99FF99 153:255:153	66FF66 102:255:102	99CC99 153:204:153	336633 51:102:51	66FF99 102:255:153	33FF99 51:255:153	33CC66 51:204:102	00CC66 0:204:102	66CC99 102:204:153	009966 0:153:102	339933 51:153:51
009933 0:153:51	33FF66 51:255:102	00FF66 0:255:102	CCFFCC 204:255:204	CCFF99 204:255:153	99FF66 153:255:102	99FF33 153:255:51	00FF33 0:255:51	33FF33 51:255:51	00CC33 0:204:51	33CC33 51:204:51	66FF33 102:255:51	00FF00 0:255:0	66CC33 102:204:51	006600 0:102:0	003300 0:51:0
009900 0:153:0	33FF00 51:255:0	66FF00 102:255:0	99FF00 153:255:0	66CC00 102:204:0	00CC00 0:204:0	33CC00 51:204:0	339900 51:153:0	99CC66 153:204:102	669933 102:153:51	99CC33 153:204:51	336600 51:102 :0	669900 102:153:0	99CC00 153:204:0	CCFF66 204:255:102	CCFF33 204:255:51
CCFF00 204:255:0	999900 153:153:0	CCCC00 204:204:0	CCCC33 204:204:51	333300 51:51:0	666600 102:102:0	999933 153:153:51	CCCC66 204:204:102	666633 102:102:51	999966 153:153:102	CCCC99 204:204:153	FFFFCC 255:255:204	FFFF99 255:255:153	FFFF66 255:255:102	FFFF33 255:255:51	FFFF00 255:255:0
FFCC00 255:204:0	FFCC66 255:204:102	FFCC33 255:204:51	CC9933 204:153:51	996600 153:102:0	CC9900 204:153:0	FF9900 255:153:0	CC6600 204:102:0	993300 153:51:0	CC6633 204:102:51	663300 102:51:0	FF9966 255:153:102	FF6633 255:102:51	FF9933 255:153:51	FF6600 255:102:0	CC3300 204:51:0
996633 153:102:51	330000 51:0:0	663333 102:51:51	996666 153:102:102	CC9999 204:153:153	993333 153:51:51	CC6666 204:102:102	FFCCCC 255:204:204	FF3333 255:51:51	CC3333 204:51:51	FF6666 255:102:102	660000 102:0:0	990000 153:0:0	CC0000 204:0:0	FF0000 255:0:0	FF3300 255:51:0
CC9966 204:153:102	FFCC99 255:204:153	CCCCCC 204:204:204	999999 153:153:153	666666 102:102:102	333333 51:51:51	FFFFFF 255:255:255	000000 0:0:0								

appendix

B JAVASCRIPT PROGRAMMING RULES

This appendix summarizes in brief statements the 'rules' for writing JavaScript and the rules that JavaScript follows when executing programs. The chapter in which each rule was introduced is given in brackets. Notice the Tables B.1–B.2.

Program Structure

White space is ignored [18]. Any number of spaces, tabs, or new-line characters can generally separate the components of a program. Avoid breaking up identifiers and literals such as numbers and strings.

Place declarations first [18]. Declarations should appear before other statements. If there are multiple blocks of JavaScript code, place global declarations at the beginning of the first block.

First-to-last execution [18]. Program statements are all executed from first to last, unless specifically commanded to skip using conditional statements or told to repeat using for statements.

Terminate statements with semicolons [18]. Every statement, including those on their own line, must be terminated with a semicolon (`;`), except the compound statement (i.e., the } is *not* followed by a semicolon).

Slash slash comment [18]. Text from `//` to the end of the line is treated as a comment. For example,

```
x = 3.1;    //Set rate
```

Slash star-star slash comment [18]. All text enclosed by the symbols `/*` and `*/` is treated as a comment, and so can span several lines. For example,

```
/* The text in a Slash Star-Star Slash comment can spill across
lines of program, but the Slash Slash comment is limited to the
end of one line.  */
```

Data Types

Four rules for numbers [18]. Numerical constants:

1. Keep the digits together without spaces, so `3.141 596` is wrong, whereas `3.141596` is right.
2. Don't use digit grouping symbols of any type, so 1,000,000 is wrong, whereas `1000000` is right.
3. Use a period as the decimal point so `0,221` is wrong, whereas `0.221` is right
4. Use no units, so `33%` and `$10.89` are wrong, whereas `0.33` and `10.89` are right.

Six rules for strings [18]. When typing string literals

1. The characters must be surrounded by quotes, either single (`'`) or double (`"`).
2. Most characters are allowed within quotes except new-line, backspace, tab, \, formfeed, and return.
3. Double-quoted strings can contain single quotes, and vice versa.
4. The apostrophe (`'`) is the same as the single quote.
5. Any number of characters is allowed in a string.
6. The minimum number of characters in a string is zero (`""`), which is called the empty string.

String literal escape characters [18]. Table B.1 gives the escape sequences for the special characters of string literals that cannot be typed directly. For example, `"\b\b"` is a string of two backspaces.

Boolean data type [18]. There are two Boolean values: true, false.

Table B.1. *Escape sequences for characters prohibited from string literals*

Seq.	Character	Seq.	Character
`\b`	Backspace	`\f`	Form feed
`\n`	New-line	`\r`	Carriage return
`\t`	Tab	`\'`	Apostrophe or single quote
`\"`	Double quote	`\\`	Backslash

Variables and Declarations

Identifier structure [18]. Identifiers must begin with a letter and may contain any combination of letters, numerals, or underscore (_). Identifiers cannot contain white space. For example, `green`, `eGGs`, `ham_and_2_eggs` are three identifiers.

Case sensitivity [18]. JavaScript identifiers are case sensitive, so `y` and `Y` are different.

Reserved words [18]. Some words, such as `var` and `true`, are reserved by JavaScript and cannot be identifiers. Table B.2 lists these words. To use a word in the list as an identifier, prefix it with an underscore (for example, `_Date`), but it's safer (and smarter) to think up a different identifier.

Declare variables [18]. All variables must be declared using `var`. Do not declare any variable more than once.

Variable declaration list separated by commas [18]. For example,

```
var prices, hemlines, interestRates;
```

Variable declaration initializers can be expressions [18]. For example,

```
var minutesInDay = 60 * 24;
```

Expressions

Operators [18]. A selection of JavaScript operators is given in Table B.3.

Use parentheses [18]. Though JavaScript uses precedence to determine the order in which to perform operators when no parentheses are given, that feature is for professionals. Parenthesize all complex expressions to be safe.

Operator overloading [18]. Plus (+) means addition for numerical operands; it means concatenation for string operands. If + has an operand of each type (e.g., `4 + "5"`), the number converts to a string and returns a string (e.g., `"45"`).

Arrays and Indexes

Array declarations [21]. Arrays are declared using the var statement using the new Array (<*elements*>) designation, where <*elements*> is the number of array elements. For example,

```
var zodiacSigns = new Array (12);
```

Arrays are 0-origin, meaning the least index value is 0, and the largest index is <*elements*> `- 1`.

Array references [21]. Array elements can be referenced by the syntax

```
<array_name>[<index>]
```

where <*array_name*> is a declared array and <*index*> is any integer value from 0 to <*elements*> `- 1`. An array reference, e.g., `A[i]`, is a variable and can be used wherever variables can be used.

Index values [21]. An index value can be any expression, including a constant (e.g., `3`), a variable (e.g., `i`), or an expression involving operators (e.g., `(i+12)%5`) that evaluates to an integer in the range from 0 to the highest index of the array, <*elements*> `- 1`.

Table B.2. Reserved words and property terms in JavaScript

`abstract`	`export`	`name`	`self`
`alert`	`extends`	`NaN`	`setInterval`
`arguments`	`false`	`native`	`setTimeout`
`Array`	`final`	`netscape`	`short`
`blur`	`finally`	`new`	`static`
`boolean`	`find`	`null`	`status`
`Boolean`	`float`	`number`	`statusbar`
`break`	`for`	`Object`	`stop`
`byte`	`focus`	`open`	`String`
`callee`	`frames`	`opener`	`super`
`caller`	`function`	`outerHeight`	`switch`
`captureEvents`	`Function`	`outerWidth`	`synchronized`
`case`	`goto`	`package`	`this`
`catch`	`history`	`Packages`	`throw`
`char`	`home`	`pageXOffset`	`throws`
`class`	`if`	`pageYOffset`	`toolbar`
`clearInterval`	`import`	`parent`	`top`
`clearTimeout`	`implements`	`parseFloat`	`toString`
`close`	`in`	`parseInt`	`transient`
`closed`	`infinity`	`personalbar`	`true`
`confirm`	`innerHeight`	`print`	`try`
`const`	`innerWidth`	`private`	`typeof`
`constructor`	`instanceof`	`prompt`	`unescape`
`continue`	`int`	`protected`	`unwatch`
`Date`	`interface`	`prototype`	`valueOf`
`debugger`	`isFinite`	`public`	`var`
`default`	`isNaN`	`RegExp`	`void`
`defaultStatus`	`java`	`releaseEvents`	`watch`
`delete`	`length`	`resizeBy`	`while`
`do`	`location`	`resizeTo`	`window`
`document`	`locationbar`	`return`	`with`
`double`	`long`	`routeEvent`	
`else`	`Math`	`scroll`	
`enum`	`menubar`	`scrollbars`	
`escape`	`moveBy`	`scrollBy`	
`eval`	`moveTo`	`scrollTo`	

Note: These words cannot be or should not be used as identifiers.

Statements

Assignment statement [18]. The assignment statement (e.g., `lap = lap + 1`) updates the value of a variable on the left side of the = (e.g., `lap`) by computing the value of the expression on the right side of = (e.g., `lap + 1`) and making it the new value of the variable. The value flow is from the right side to the left side.

Compound statements [18]. A sequence of statements enclosed by `{ }` is a compound statement and is treated as one statement, say, for purposes of the <*statement list*> in **`if`**, **`if/else`**, iteration statements, and function declarations. The compound statement is not terminated by a semicolon, though statements it contains must be.

`if` statement [18]. The `if` statement, or conditional statement, has the form

```
if (<Boolean expression>)
      <then-statement>;
```

If the value of the Boolean expression is `true`, the *<then-statement>* is performed; if the Boolean expression is `false`, the *<then-statement>* is skipped.

`if/else` statement [18]. The if statement, or conditional statement, has the form

```
if (<Boolean expression>)
      <then-statement>;
else
      <else-statement>;
```

If the result of the Boolean expression is true, the *<then-statement>* is performed and the *<else-statement>* is skipped. If the Boolean expression is false, the *<then-statement>* is skipped and the <else-statement> is performed.

Conditional within a conditional [18]. If a conditional's *<then-statement>* or *<else-statement>* contains another conditional, make it a compound statement (enclose it in `{}`) to avoid ambiguity as to which `if` statement the `else` associates with.

`for` loops [21]. The `for` statement has the syntax

```
for ( <initialization>; <continuation>; <next iteration> ) {
      <statement list>
}
```

The *<initialization>* is an assignment to the iteration variable, the *<continuation>* is a Boolean expression like those used in if statements, and the *<next iteration>* is an assignment to the iteration variable.

`for` loop operation [21]. A `for` loop works as follows: The initialization assignment is performed first, followed by the continuation test. If the test result is `false`, the *<statement list>* is skipped and the `for` loop ends. If the test result is `true`, the *<statement list>* is performed followed by the next iteration assignment. That completes one iteration. At the completion of an iteration, the process repeats with the continuation test.

`World-Famous Iteration` [21]. The World-Famous Iteration (WFI) is a `for` statement that has the following standard form:

```
for ( <iteration var> = 0; <iteration var> < <limit> ; <iteration var>++ ) {
      <statement list>
}
```

The *<iteration var>* is any declared variable, and the *<limit>* is any expression or variable. An example is

```
for ( j = 0; j < n ; j++ ) {
      <statement list>
}
```

The number of iterations—the number of times the loop loops—is `n`.

Functions

Function declaration [20]. Functions are declared using the following syntax:

```
function <name>  ( <parameter list> ) {
     <statement list>
}
```

Notice the conspicuous position of the closed brace on its own line, below the *f* in function. An example is

```
function prefixTitle ( familyName, mORf ) {
  if (mORf = "M")
      return "Mr. " + familyName;
  else
      return "Ms " + familyName;
}
```

Function names are identifier [20]. Function names, e.g., **`prefixTitle`**, follow the rules for identifiers. It is best if the chosen name says what the function does.

Parameters are identifier [20]. Function parameters, e.g., **`familyName`**, follow the rules for identifiers.

Parameters are not declared [20]. Function parameters should not be declared because the JavaScript interpreter automatically declares them.

Return statement [20]. A function completes when it reaches a return statement,

```
return <expression>
```

The result of the function is the result of <*expression*>, which could simply be a variable.

Guidelines

Programmer's rules: Professional programmers have a set of good programming practices, including:

> Choose meaningful identifiers for variables. For example, **`interestRate`** is better than, say, **`p`**.

> Insert white space liberally to improve readability of code. For example,

```
if(input!="")name=first+last;
```

is poor, while

```
if ( input != "" )
 name = first + last;
```

is preferred.

> Comment programs liberally, saying what the variables mean and what the logic is doing.

> Align code—especially when the statements are logically related—and be consistent; it helps locate errors.

Wrong:

```
 able="a;
baker = 'b';
   charlie   =   "c";
```

Right:

```
able    = "a";
baker   = "b";
charlie = "c";
```

Table B.3. *JavaScript operators used in this text*

Name	Symbol	Operands and Data Types	Example	Comment	Result of Example
Addition	+	2 Numerical	4 + 5		9
Concatenation	+	2 String 6 + " pack"	"four"+"five"	1 numeric operand implies concatenate	"fourfive" "6 pack"
Subtraction	-	2 Numerical	9 – 5		4
Multiplication	*	2 Numerical	-2 * 4		-8
Division	/	2 Numerical	10/3		0.33333…
Modulus	%	2 Numerical	10%3	Remainder	1
Increment	++	1 Numerical	3++	See Chapter 20	4
Decrement	—	1 Numerical	3—	See Chapter 20	2
Less Than	<	2 Numerical	4 < 4		false
Less Than or Equal	<=	2 Numerical	4 <= 4		true
Equal	==	2 Numerical 2 String	4 == 4 "a" == "A"		true false
Not Equal	!=	2 Numerical 2 String	4 != 4 "a" != " a"		false true
Greater Than or Equal	>=	2 Numerical	4 >= 4		true
Greater Than	>	2 Numerical	4 > 4		false
Negation	-	1 Numerical	– 4		-4
Logical Not	!	1 Boolean	! true		false
Logical Add	&&	2 Boolean	true && true		true
Logical Or	||	2 Boolean	false || true		true

Note: The examples use literal data (actual numbers) to show the operation; generally the operands will be variables.

appendix

C BEAN COUNTER PROGRAM

The final HTML and JavaScript code for the Bean Counter application in Chapter 19 is as follows. Notice that variations in Web browsers will affect how closely it matches the sample output in the figure.

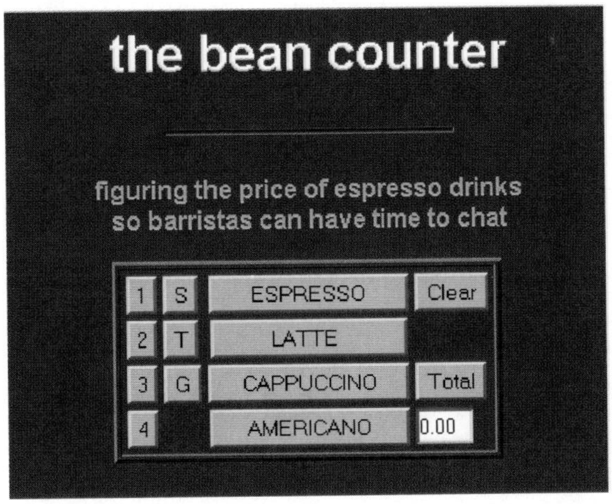


```
<html>
 <head>
    <title>The Bean Counter</title>
 </head>
  <body bgcolor="#804000" text="#FF9900" align="center">
   <script language = 'JavaScript'>
    var shots = 1;
    var drink = "none";
    var ounce = 0;
   </script>
   <font face="Helvetica", "Arial">
   <h1 align="center">
      <font color="#FFFFFF">the bean counter</font></h1>
```

```
<hr width=50%>
<p align="center"><b>figuring the price of espresso drinks<br>
   so barristas can have time to chat</b></p>
<form name = "Bean" >
 <center>
 <table border=2>
 <tr><td>
  <table>
   <tr>
     <td>
       <input type=button value="  1  " onClick = 'shots = 1'>
     </td>
     <td>
       <input type=button value="  S  " onClick = 'ounce = 8 '>
     </td>
     <td align="center">
       <input type=button value="  ESPRESSO  "
              onClick = 'drink = "espresso"'>
     </td>
     <td>
       <input type = button value = " Clear "
              onClick = 'shots = 1;
              drink = "none";
              ounce = 0;
              document.Bean.price.value = "0.00"'>
     </td>
  </tr>
  <tr>
     <td>
       <input type=button value="  2  " onClick = 'shots = 2'>
     </td>
     <td>
       <input type=button value="  T  " onClick = 'ounce = 12'>
     </td>
     <td align="center">
       <input type=button value="      LATTE      "
              onClick = 'drink = "latte"'>
     </td>
     <td>
     </td>
  </tr>
  <tr>
     <td>
       <input type=button value="  3  " onClick = 'shots = 3'>
     </td>
     <td>
       <input type=button value="  G  " onClick = 'ounce = 16'>
     </td>
     <td align="center">
       <input type=button value="CAPPUCCINO"
              onClick = 'drink = "cappuccino"'>
     </td>
```

```
        <td>
          <input type = button value = " Total " onClick =
         'var price;
          var taxRate = 0.087;
          if (drink == "espresso")
               price = 1.00;
          if (drink == "latte" || drink == "cappuccino"){
               if (ounce == 8)
                    price = 1.55;
               if (ounce == 12)
                    price = 1.95;
               if (ounce == 16)
                    price = 2.35;
          }
          if (drink == "Americano")
               price = 1.10 + .30 * (ounce/8);
          price = price + (shots - 1) * .70;
          price = price + price * taxRate;
          document.Bean.price.value = Math.round(price*100)/100;
          '>
        </td>
     </tr>
     <tr>
        <td>
          <input type=button value="  4  " onClick = 'shots = 4'>
        </td>
        <td>
        </td>
        <td align="center">
          <input type=button value=" AMERICANO "
                 onClick = 'drink = "Americano"'>
        </td>
          <td bgcolor="red" align="center">
          <input type=text name=price value="0.00" size=5>
        </td>
     </tr>
    </table>
    </td></tr>
    </table>
    </center>
  </form>
 </body>
</html>
```

appendix D

MEMORY BANK CODE

The following HTML and JavaScript code produces the Memory Bank page in Chapter 20 (Figure 20.8).

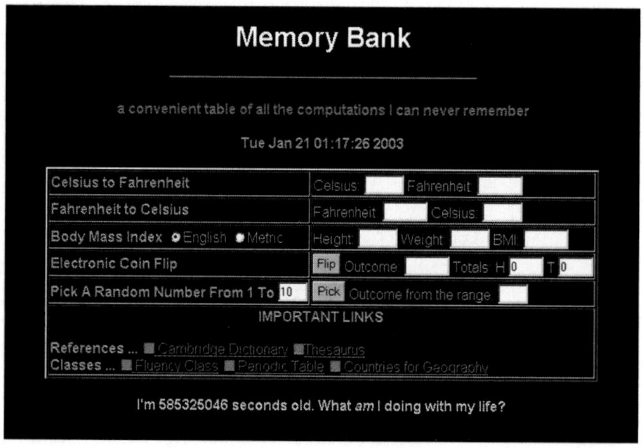


```
<html>
<head><title>Memory Bank of Computations</title></head>
<body bgcolor="#000000" text="#FF9900" >
  <font face="Helvetica", "Arial">
  <h1 align="center"><font color="#FFFFFF">Memory Bank</font></h1>
  <hr width=50%>
  <b><p align="center"> <font color="#FF0000"> a convenient table
      of all the computations I can never remember </font></p>
  <script language = 'JavaScript'>
     document.write('<center>' + (Date().toString()) + '</center>');
  </script>
  <form name="memory">
  <table align="center" border=2>
  <tr>
    <td><b>Celsius to Fahrenheit</b></td>
```

```
  <td>
   Celsius: <input type = text name = cTemp size = 4
      onChange="tempInF.value=convertC2F(cTemp.value)">
   Fahrenheit: <input type = text name = tempInF size = 5></td></tr>
<tr>
  <td><b>Fahrenheit to Celsius</b></td>
  <td>
   Fahrenheit: <input type = text name = fTemp size = 5
      onChange="tempInC.value = convertF2C(fTemp.value)">
   Celsius: <input type = text name = tempInC size = 4></td></tr>
<tr>
  <td><b>Body Mass Index</b>
    <input type = radio name = pick1 checked = true
      onClick='measure="English"'>English
    <input type = radio name= pick1
      onClick='measure="metric"'>Metric</td>
  <td>Height:
    <input type = text name = howtall size = 4
      onChange = 'if (howwide.value != 0)
              shape.value = BMI(measure, howtall.value, howwide.value)'> Weight:
    <input type = text name = howwide size = 4
      onChange = 'if (howtall.value != 0)
              shape.value = BMI(measure, howtall.value, howwide.value)'> BMI:
    <input type = text name = shape size = 5></td></tr>
<tr>
  <td><b>Electronic Coin Flip </b></td>
  <td>           <input type = button value = "Flip" onClick="runTrial()">
      Outcome:   <input type = text name = coin size = 5>
      Totals:  H <input type = text name = heads size = 3 value = 0>
           T <input type = text name = tails size = 3 value = 0></td></tr>
<tr>
  <td><b>Pick A Random Number From 1 To </b>
   <input type = text name = topEnd size = 2 value = 10> </td>
  <td>
    <input type = button value = "Pick"
        onClick="choice.value=1+randNum(topEnd.value)"> Outcome from the range:
    <input type = text name = choice size = 2></td></tr>
<tr>
  <td colspan = 2> <center><b>IMPORTANT LINKS </b></center>

  <!--  The standard form for the links is ...
      <br><b> ___topic name___...</b>
       <img src='bullet.gif'><a href='http://____url goes here_______'>
              _____anchor term(s)_here_____</a>
  -->

   <br><b>References ... </b>
      <img src='bullet.gif'><a href='http://dictionary.cambridge.org'>
        Cambridge Dictionary</a>
      <img src='bullet.gif'><a href='http://www.wordsmyth.net'>Thesaurus</a>

   <br><b>Classes ... </b>
```

```
        <img src='bullet.gif'><a href='http://www.cs.washington.edu/100/'>
          Fluency Class</a>
          <img src='bullet.gif'><a
            href='http://www.chemsoc.org/viselements/pages/pertable_j.htm'>
          Periodic Table</a>
        <img src='bullet.gif'><a href='http://www.cia.gov/cia/publications/factbook/'>
          Countries for Geography</a>
      </td></tr>
</table></b>
</form>
<script language = "JavaScript">
  // Declare a global variable
  var measure = "English";  // The default measure;
  var headCount = 0, tailCount = 0; // Keep score

  function convertC2F( cTemp ) {
     // Figures Fahrenheit equivalent of cTemp
     return Math.round( 9 * cTemp / 5 + 32);
  }

  function convertF2C( fTemp ) {
     // Figures Celsius equivalent of fTemp
     return Math.round(5 / 9 *(fTemp - 32));
  }

  function bmiE ( weightLBS, heightIn ) {
     // Figure Body Mass Index in English units
     var heightFt = heightIn / 12;  // Change to feet
     return 4.89 * weightLBS / (heightFt * heightFt);
  }

  function bmiM ( weightKg, heightM ) {
     // Figure Body Mass Index in Metric units
     return weightKg / (heightM * heightM);
  }

  function BMI( units, height, weight ) {
     // Calculate Body Mass Index in English or Metric
     if (units == "English")
         return Math.round(bmiE(weight, height)*10)/10;
     else
         return Math.round(bmiM(weight, height)*10)/10;
  }

  function randNum(range) {
     return Math.floor(Math.random()* range);
  }

  function runTrial() {
     if (randNum(2) == 1) {
         document.memory.coin.value = "Heads";
         headCount = headCount + 1;
```

```
            document.memory.heads.value = headCount;
        }
        else {
            document.memory.coin.value = "Tails";
            tailCount = tailCount + 1;
            document.memory.tails.value = tailCount;
        }
    }
        var today = new Date();     // Get today's date
        var myBdate = new Date();   // Get a date object to modify
        var difference;              //
        myBdate.setFullYear(1984); // Set my birth year to 1984
        myBdate.setMonth(6);        // Set my birth month to July (mo.s start at 0)
        myBdate.setDate(4);         // Set my birth day to 4th
        myBdate.setHours(11);       // Set my hour of birth to noon
        myBdate.setMinutes(0);      // Set my minute of birth to o'clock
        myBdate.setSeconds(0);      // Set my second of birth to smack on the hour
        difference = today.getTime() - myBdate.getTime();
        difference = Math.floor(difference/1000);
        document.write("<center><b><font color=yellow> I'm " + difference +
            " seconds old.  What <i>am</i> I doing with my life?</font></b></center>");
    </script>
  </body>
</html>
```

appendix

E SMOOTH MOTION PROGRAM

The following HTML and JavaScript code produces the Smooth Motion program of Chapter 22 (Figure 22.1).

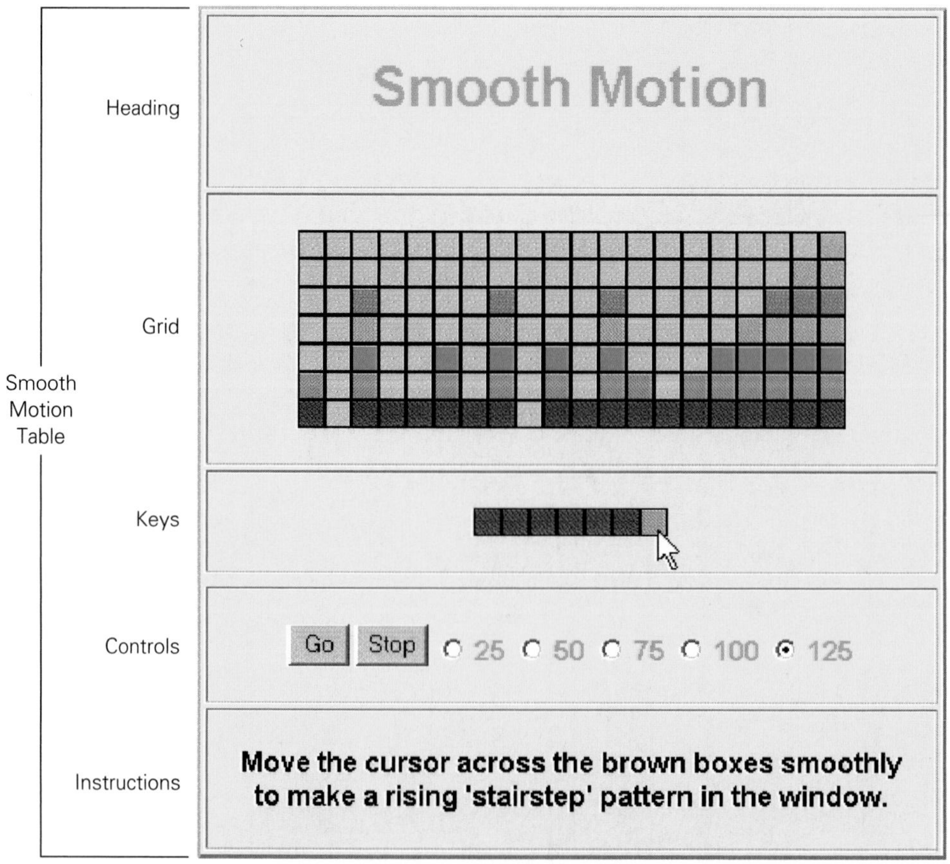

```
<html>
<head><title>Smooth Motion Application</title></head>
 <body bgcolor="white" text="#FF6600"> <font face='Helvetica'>
   <center>
   <table border=2 cellspacing="3" cellpadding="20%"
          bgcolor="#FFFF99">
     <tr> <td align="center">
          <h1>Smooth Motion</h1>
          </td></tr>
     <tr> <td align="center">
          <script>
           var j;                               //Declare iter var
           var duration = 125, timerId;         // & other vars
           var pics = new Array(8);             // & prefetch array
           var keypix = new Array(2);
           var next1 = 0, frame = -1;
           for (j = 0; j < 8; j++) {            //Initial img array
               pics[j] = new Image();
           }
           for (j = 0; j < 8; j++) {            //Prefetch images
               pics[j].src = "gifpix/Stack" + j + ".gif";
           }
           for (j = 0; j < 20; j++) {        //Place grid imgs
               document.write('<img src="gifpix/Stack0.gif">');
           }
          </script>
          </td></tr>
     <tr> <td align="center">
          <script>
           keypix[0] = new Image();
           keypix[1] = new Image();
           keypix[0].src = "gifpix/BrownBox.gif";
           keypix[1].src = "gifpix/OrangeBox.gif";
           for (j = 0; j < 7; j++) {
               document.write('<img src="gifpix/BrownBox.gif" ' +
               'onMouseOver = "here(' + j + ')" ' +
               'onMouseOut = "gone(' + j + ')">');
           }
          </script>
          </td></tr>
     <tr> <td align="center">
          <form>
           <input type=button value=Go
            onClick='timerId=setTimeout("animate()",duration)'>
           <input type=button value=Stop
            onClick="clearTimeout(timerId)">
           <input type=radio name=speed onClick="duration=25"> 25
           <input type=radio name=speed onClick="duration=50"> 50
           <input type=radio name=speed onClick="duration=75"> 75
           <input type=radio name=speed onClick="duration=100"> 100
           <input type=radio name=speed
            onClick="duration=125" checked=true> 125
```

```
            </form>
            </td></tr>
        <tr> <td align="center">
            <p><font color='black'><b>
              Move the cursor across the brown boxes smoothly <br>
              to make a rising 'staircase' pattern in the
              window.</b></font></p>
            </td></tr>
      </table></center>
      <script language='JavaScript'>
        timerId = setTimeout("animate()", 5000);              //Initial timer
        function animate() {
          shiftGrid ()
          checkStairAndContinue ();
        }
        function shiftGrid() {
          for (j = 0; j < 19; j++) {
              document.images[j].src = document.images[j+1].src;
          }
          if (frame == -1)
              document.images[19].src = pics[randNum(8)].src;
          else
              document.images[19].src = pics[frame].src;
        }
        function checkStairAndContinue() {
          if (frame == next1)
             next1 = next1 + 1;
          else
             next1 = 1;
          if (next1 != 8)
             timerId = setTimeout("animate()",duration);
        }
        function here (pos) {
          document.images[20+pos].src = "gifpix/OrangeBox.gif";
          frame = pos + 1;
        }
        function gone (pos) {
          document.images[20+pos].src = "gifpix/BrownBox.gif";
          frame = 0;
        }
        function randNum (range) {                            //Rand No. fcn from
          return Math.floor(range * Math.random());           //  Chapter 20
        }
    </script>
  </body>
</html>
```

GLOSSARY

This glossary contains a partial listing of the bold key terms in the book. For a complete list, visit `www.aw.com/snyder`.

Acronyms have their letters spoken, as in H-T-M-L, unless pronunciation is indicated, as in *JAY·peg*.

1-way cipher, see one-way cipher

2-tier, see two-tier

3-tier, see three-tier

A

absolute pathname, navigation information for locating files in HTML using complete URLs

abstract, to remove an idea, concept, or process from a specific situation

administrative authority, see superuser

algorithm, a precise and systematic method for producing a specified result

alphanumeric, describing characters or text as being composed solely of letters, numbers, and possibly a few special characters like spaces and tabs, but not punctuation

ALU, acronym for arithmetic/logic unit

analog signal, a continuously varying representation of a phenomenon, e.g., a sound wave

anchor, the HTML tag that specifies a link, or the text associated with the reference that is highlighted in the document

applet, a small application program, often written in Java, that is executed on a client

argument, a value provided for a parameter in a function call

arithmetic/logic unit (ALU), a subsystem of a computer that performs the operations of an instruction

array, in programming, a variable having multiple elements named by the composition of an identifier and an index

assembly language, a symbolic form of a binary machine language

assignment statement, a programming command expressed with a variable on the left and a variable or expression on the right of an assignment symbol, usually =

asynchronous communication, indicates that the actions of senders and receivers occur at separate times, as in the exchange of email

attribute, in HTML, a parameter used within HTML tags to specify additional information; in databases, a property of an entity; also called a field

B

b, abbreviation for bit, e.g., Kb is kilobits

B, abbreviation for byte, e.g., KB is kilobytes

bandwidth, the bit-transmission capacity of a channel, usually measured in bits per second

binary, having two related components

binary number, a quantity expressed in radix 2 number representation

binary operator, an operator such as addition (+) having two operands

binary representation, any information encoding using symbols formed from two patterns; also called PandA representation in this book

bit, basic unit of information representation having two states, usually denoted 0 and 1

bit-mapped, as in bit-mapped display, indicates that the display's video image is stored pixel-by-pixel in the computer's memory

bookmark, to record a URL locally to simplify referencing it again

Boolean, having the property of being either true or false

boot, to start a computer and load its operating system

broadcast, a type of transmission of information from one sender to all receivers

bug, an error in a computer, program, or process

byte, a sequence of eight bits treated as a unit

C

cable, a bundle of wires carrying power and signals between computer components; also called cord or wires

cancel, a command button that stops a dialog or series of operations without penalty or effect

card, a small printed circuit board usually plugged into a socket on a motherboard to provide additional functionality; also called a daughter board

CGI, acronym for Common Gateway Interface

character, an upper- or lowercase Latin letter, Arabic numeral, or English punctuation; can be used more generally to include the alphabet and punctuation for other natural languages

classifier, a component of an optical character recognition system that ranks characters by the probability that they match a given set of features

cleartext, information before encryption or after decryption

click, to press and release a mouse button

click-with-shift, in selection, to maintain the selected status of all items except the clicked item, which is either selected if it is not selected or vice versa; also called shift-select

client, a computer that receives the services in a client/server structure

client/server structure, a relationship between two computers in which the client computer requests services from the server computer

close, to terminate a GUI window and, if the window is the primary or only window, to terminate the application

collating sequence, an ordering for a set of symbols used to sort them; for example, alphabetical ordering

command button, a synthesized image of a GUI appearing to be a 3D button used to cause some operation to be performed; the HTML button input control

Common Gateway Interface (CGI), an extension to HTML allowing browsers to cause a Web server to run programs on their behalf with specific data

compile, to translate a programming language into a language the computer can interpret (machine language)

compression, encoding information with fewer bits than a given representation by exploiting properties of regularity or unimportance

compression ratio, the factor by which compression reduces an encoding from its uncompressed size

computable, a task that can be performed by computer, algorithmic

computer, a device that deterministically follows instructions to process information

conditional, a programming statement, usually identified by `if`, that optionally executes statements depending on the outcome of a Boolean test

continuation test, a Boolean expression to determine whether an iteration statement will execute its statement sequence again; also called a termination test

control, a subsystem of a computer that is the hardware implementation of the Fetch/Execute Cycle

cookie, information stored on a Web client computer by an http server computer

copyright, the legal protection of many forms of intellectual property

cracker, a person attempting to break a code

crawler, a program that navigates the Internet, cataloging and indexing the Web pages by the words they contain for use by a query processor

CRT, acronym for cathode ray tube, a video display technology

cryptography, the study of encryption and decryption methods

cycle power, to turn a computer off, wait a moment, and then turn it back on

D

daemon, a program that periodically "wakes up" to perform some system management task

data controller, in Fair Information Practices, the person who sets policies, responds to individuals regarding their information, if any, and is accountable for those policies and actions

Data Fetch, third step in the Fetch/Execute Cycle, the action of retrieving the instruction's operands from memory

data type, a set of values for which operations are defined, e.g., number

database scheme or **schema**, the declaration of entities and relationships of a database

debugging, the act of discovering why a system is not working properly

decrypt, to recover the original information from a digitally encrypted representation

definiteness, a property of algorithms that requires a specific sequence of steps be defined

DF, in processor design, an acronym for Data Fetch

digital signal, a discrete or "step levels" representation of a phenomenon, varying "instantaneously"

digitally decrypt, see decrypt

digitally encrypt, see encrypt

digitize, originally to encode with decimal numerals, now to encode in bits

directory, a named collection of files or other directories; also called a folder on Mac and Windows operating systems

discrete, distinct or separable, not able to be changed by continuous variation

display rate, in animation, the frequency with which the images are changed

domain, in networking, a related set of networked computers, e.g., `edu` is the set of education-related computers

Domain Name System (DNS), the collection of Internet-connected computers that translate domain addresses into IP addresses

dual booting, loading two operating systems at once

E

eCommerce, electronic commerce, the use of electronic data communication to conduct business

effectiveness, a property of algorithms requiring that all instructions be performed mechanically within the capabilities of the executing agent

element, an indexed item; also called array element

empty string, a character sequence of zero length

emoticon, a character sequence written to express by its physical form an emotion, common in email; for example, the "smiley face" `:)` to express happiness or humor

encrypt, to transform a digital representation so the information cannot be readily discerned

ER diagram, Entity-Relationship diagram, a visual presentation of some or all of a database schema

escape symbol, a character, often `&` or \, prefixing another character or word to enlarge a character encoding, e.g., `&infinity` to encode ∞

EX, in processor design, the abbreviation for Instruction Execution

execute, to perform the instructions of a program, usually by a computer; to run a program

Extensible Markup Language (XML), a W3C standard for structured information encoding

F

factor of improvement, the amount by which a first measurement must be multiplied to be equivalent to the second measurement when computing scale of change

fair use, a concept in copyright law in which copyright limitations are waived for explicitly listed, socially valuable purposes

feature, a component of a character in a optical character recognition system

Fetch/Execute Cycle, the basic instruction execution process of a computer

field inputs, character input such as telephone numbers with a specific structure

finiteness, a property of algorithms requiring that they terminate with the intended result or an indication that no solution is possible

firmware, instructions incorporated into the hardware, usually changeable by external means with difficulty

flame-a-thon, email battle; also called flame war

floppy disk, a storage device providing persistent memory using (removable) diskettes; also called floppy drive

for statement, a common programming structure for iterating a sequence of instruction over a regular range of index values

formal language, synthetic notation designed for expressing algorithms and programs

frame, in animation, one of many images rapidly redrawn to create the illusion of motion

freeware, software available on the Web at no cost

full backup, a complete copy of a body of information usually as of a specific point in time

function, a programming structure with a name, optional parameter list, and a definition that encapsulates an algorithm

function body, the definition of a function's computation

function declaration, the specification of a function, including its name, parameters, and body

G

game tree, a conceptualization of the possible future configurations of a multiperson game

generalize, to formulate an idea, concept, or process so that it abstracts multiple situations

GIF, file extension, e.g., `picture.gif`, specifying a graphic image format, pronounced with either soft or hard *g*

giga-, prefix for billion; pronounced with a hard g

global variable, a variable declared outside the scope of a function, usually at the start of the program

graphical user interface (GUI), the synthesized visual medium of interaction between a user and a computer

GUI, acronym for graphic user interface, pronounced *gooey*

H

Halting Problem, the problem of determining if a computation halts for a given input, a problem that cannot be solved by computer

handle, in programming, a binary value returned by a function or server to be used for subsequent references

haptic device, an input/output technology interfacing with the sense of touch

hard disk, a storage device providing persistent memory; also called a disk or hard drive

hardware, the physical implementation of a computer, usually electronic, including the processor, memory, and usually its peripheral devices

heuristic, a guideline to help solve a problem but one that does guarantee a solution; for example, "when looking for a lost article check the last place you used it"

hex digit, one of the sixteen numerals of hexadecimal, 0, 1, 2, 3, 4, 5, 6, 7, 8, 9, A, B, C, D, E, F

hexadecimal, radix 16 number representation

hierarchical index, a structure for organizing information using descriptive terms that partition the information

hierarchy, an organizing structure composed of a sequence of levels that partition all items so that those of one level are partitioned into smaller groups at the next level

hit, for a Web search, a match to a query; for a Web site, a visit

hop, in networking, the transfer of a packet or message to an adjacent router

Hypertext Markup Language (HTML), a common notation for specifying the form of a Web page to a browser

hypertext transfer protocol (HTTP), the rules governing interaction between client and server on the World Wide Web

Hz, abbreviation for Hertz, cycles, or repetitions per second

I

ID, in processor design, an acronym for Instruction Decode

identifier, a legal sequence of letters, numerals, or punctuation marks forming the name of variable, file, directory, etc.

IF, in processor design, an acronym for Instruction Fetch

`if` statement, a programming a structure allowing the conditional execution of statements based on the outcome of a Boolean test

index, in information structures, a organizing mechanism used to find information in a large collection; in programming, the number that together with an identifier forms an array reference

index origin, the number at which indexing begins; the least index

index value, the result of evaluating an index expression; the number of an array element

indexing, in programming, the mechanism of associating a number and an identifier to locate an element

infix operator, a binary operator, e.g., +, whose syntax requires that it be written between its operands, as in 4 + 3

Input Unit, a subsystem of a computer transferring information from the physical world via an input device to the computer's memory

instance, the current values of an entity, table, or database

Instruction Decode, second step in the Fetch/Execute Cycle, the action of determining which operation is to be performed and computing the addresses of the operands

Instruction Execution, the fourth step in the Fetch/Execute Cycle, the action of performing a machine instruction

Instruction Fetch, first step in the Fetch/Execute Cycle, the action of retrieving a machine instruction from the memory address given by the program counter

integer, a whole number; in programming, a data type for a whole number, either positive or negative

integration, in silicon technology, the ability to fabricate both active and connective parts of a circuit using a family of compatible materials in a single complexity-independent process

intellectual property, creations of the human mind that have value to others

Internet, the totality of all wires, fibers, switches, routers, satellite links, and other hardware used to transport information between named computers

Internet Service Provider (ISP), a utility that connects private and business computers to the Internet

interpolation, the smooth movement from one discrete value to another.

intractable, a description for computations solvable by computer in principle, but not in practice

invocation (of a function), to call the function

IP, acronym for Internet Protocol

IP address, the address of an Internet-networked computer composed of four numbers in the range 0–255

IP packet, a fixed quantum of information packaged together with an IP address and other data for sending information over the Internet

ISO, acronym for the International Standards Organization

ISP, acronym for Internet Service Provider

iterate, in programming, to repeatedly execute a sequence of statements

iteration variable, any variable controlling an iteration statement such as a `for` statement

J

JPEG, acronym for the nickname Joint Photographic Experts Group, a committee of the ISO; pronounced *JAY·peg*

JPG, file extension, e.g., `picture.jpg`, for JPEG encoding

K

key, in databases, field(s) that make the rows of an entity (table) unique; in cryptography, selectable code used to encrypt and subsequently decrypt information

kilo-, prefix for thousand; if prefixing a quantity counted in binary, e.g., memory, prefix for 1,024

L

LAN, acronym for local area network, usually pronounced

latency, the time required to deliver or generate information

LCD, acronym for liquid crystal display, a video display technology

length (of an array), the number of elements in an array

lexical structure, a specification of the form of character input; for example, telephone numbers in North America are formed of ten Arabic numerals with a space following the third and a hyphen following the sixth

local area network (LAN), a network connecting computers within a small physical space such as a building

local variable, a variable declared within a function

logical operators, any of the connectives *and*, *or*, or *not*

lossless compression, the process of reducing the number of bits required to represent information in which the original form can be exactly reconstructed

lossy compression, the process of reducing the number of bits required to represent information in which the original cannot be exactly reconstructed

M

machine language, computer instructions expressed in binary, respecting the form required for a specific machine

mask, in fabrication technology, a material similar to a photographic negative containing the pattern to be transferred to the silicon surface in the process of constructing a chip

mega-, prefix for million; if prefixing a quantity counted in binary, e.g., memory, prefix for 1,048,576

memory, device capable of storing information, usually in fixed size, addressable units; a subsystem of a computer used to store programs and their data while they execute

memory address, a whole number designating a specific location in a computer's memory

menu, a list of available operations from which a user can select by clicking on one item

metadata, information describing the properties of other information

microprocessor, see processor

middleware, software intermediating between Web clients and databases or other systems for producing online services

mnemonic, any aid to remembering

moderator, a person responsible for deciding what is to be sent out to a mailing list

monitor, a computer's video output device or display; also called a *screen*

motherboard, a printed circuit board containing the processor chip, memory, and other electronics of a computer

MPEG, acronym for the nickname Motion Picture Experts Group, a committee of the ISO, pronounced *EM·peg*

MPG, file extension, e.g., `flick.mpg`, for MPEG encoding

multicast, a type of transmission of information from one sender to many receivers

N

***n*-tier**, a multilayer system design, usually for providing Web services

name conflict, the attempt to give a different definition, e.g., variable declaration, to an identifier with an existing meaning

navigation, in searching, to follow a series of links to locate specific information often in a hierarchy

nested loop, the condition of a loop (inner loop) appearing in the statement sequence of another loop (outer loop)

netiquette, etiquette on the Internet

NP-complete, a measure of difficulty of problems believed to be intractable for computers

Nyquist Rule, a digitization guideline stating that the sampling frequency should exceed the signal frequency by at least two times

O

OCR, acronym for optical character recognition

one-way cipher, a form of encryption that cannot easily be reversed, i.e., decrypted, often used for passwords

operand, the data used in computer instructions; the value(s) on which operators compute

operating system (OS), software that performs tasks for the computer; it controls input and output, keeps track of files and directories, and controls peripheral devices such as disk drives and printers.

operator overloading, a property of some programming languages in which operators like + have different meanings depending on their operand data types, e.g., + used for both addition or concatenation in JavaScript

optical character recognition (OCR), a computer application in which printed text is converted to the ASCII letters that it represents

Output Unit, a subsystem of a computer that transfers information from the computer's memory to the physical world via an output device

overflow exception, an error condition for operations such as addition in which a result is too large to be represented in the available number of bits

P

PandA, in this book, a mnemonic for "present and absent encoding," the fundamental physical representation of information; also called binary representation

parallel computation, the use of multiple computers to solve a single problem

parameter, an input to a function

partial backup, the new information copied to another medium that has been added to a system since the last full or partial backup

PC, acronym for program counter, for printed circuit (board), and for personal computer

photolithography, a process of transferring a pattern by means of light shown through a mask or negative

photoresist, a material used in a silicon chip fabrication process that is chemically changed by light, allowing it to be patterned by a mask

picture element or **pixel**, the smallest displayable unit of a video monitor

pins, stiff wires in a cable's plug that insert into sockets to make the connection

pixel, contraction for picture element

placeholder technique, a searching algorithm in which strings are temporarily replaced with a special character to protect them from change by other substitution commands

plaintext, synonym for cleartext

point-to-point communication, a type of transmission of information from one sender to one receiver

pop-up menu, a menu that is displayed at the cursor position when the mouse is clicked

precedence, the relationship among operators describing which is to be performed first

prefetching, in online animation the process of loading the images prior to beginning an animation

primary source, a person who provides information based on direct knowledge or experience

privacy, the right of people to choose freely the circumstances under which and the extent to which they will reveal themselves, their attitudes, and their behaviors to others

procedural abstraction, the encapsulation of a sequence of instructions (algorithm) into a function or procedure

processor, the component of a computer that computes, that is, performs the instructions

program, an algorithm encoded for a specific situation

program counter, a register in a computer that stores the address of the next instruction to be executed

public domain, the status of a work in which the copyright owner has explicitly given up the rights

public key, a key published by the receiver and used by the sender to encrypt messages

pull-down menu, a menu positioned at the top of a GUI window, also called a drop-down menu

Q

QBE, acronym for Query by Example

query, database command defining a table expressed using the five database operators

Query by Example, a method for defining queries in a database

query processor, the part of a search engine that uses the crawler's index to report Web pages associated with keywords provided by a user

quotient-remainder form of division, a means of expressing the division of a/b as the solution to the equation $a = b \cdot c + d$, where c is the quotient and d is the remainder

R

radix, the "base" of a numbering system; equivalently, the number of digits in each place

RAM, acronym for random access memory

random access, to reference an item directly; contrast with sequential access

random access memory, memory; a subsystem of a computer used for storing programs and data while they execute

reboot, to restart a computer by clearing its memory and reloading its operating system

reckon, archaic term for performing arithmetic calculations

reference, in HTML, the displayed and highlighted portion of an anchor tag

refresh rate, the frequency with which a video display is redisplayed

relational operator, one of six operators ($< \leq = \neq \geq >$) that compare two values; in JavaScript programming, one of the six operators (`<  <=  ==  !=  >=  >`)

relationship, a correspondence between two tables of a database

relative pathname, local navigation information for locating a file in HTML

replacement string, in editing, the letter sequence that substitutes for the search string

Result Return, the fifth and final step of the Fetch/Execute Cycle, the action of storing to memory the value produced by executing a machine instruction

RGB, acronym for red, green, blue, a color encoding method

ROM, acronym for "read only memory," permanently set memory, pronounced

row, a set of values for the fields of a table, also called a *tuple*

RR, in processor design, an acronym for Result Return

RSA, a public key encryption method invented by Rivest, Shamir, and Adelman

run-length encoding, a representation in which numbers are used to give the lengths of consecutive sequences of 0s or 1s.

S

sample, to take measurements at a regular intervals as in sound digitization

sampling rate, the number of samples per second

scope, in programming, the range of statements over which a variable or other defined object is known

screen saver, a changing image or animation that displays on a computer's monitor while the computer is idle

scroll bar, a slider control appearing at the side and/or bottom of a window when the information cannot be fully displayed

SCSI, acronym for "small computer system interface," pronounced *scuzzy*

search engine, a software system composed of a crawler and a query processor that helps users locate specific information on the World Wide Web or specific Web site

search string, the information being sought in a text search

seat, to firmly insert a plug into a socket after an initial alignment

secondary source, a person providing information without direct knowledge or experience of the topic; contrast primary source

self-describing encoding, a representation using meta-data tags that embeds its own structure, as in XML

sequential access, a memory reference pattern in which no item can be referenced without passing (skipping or referencing) the items that precede it; contrast random access

serialized behavior, a property of transactions that execute simultaneously stating that only a single result is produced no matter in what order their constituent operations are performed

server, a computer providing the services in a client/server structure

shareware, software available on the Web, paid for on the honor system

shift-select, a GUI command in which the shift key is pressed while the mouse selects an item, to avoid deselecting the items already selected; also called click-with-shift

slider control, a synthesized slot in which a bar can be moved to select a position in a continuous range

software, a collective term for programs

source, in context of the World Wide Web, the HTML or other text description of how a Web page should be displayed

SQL, acronym for Structured Query Language

string, in searching, a sequence of characters; in programming, a data type for a sequence of characters

Structured Query Language, a standard notation for defining tables from tables in a database

subscript, a synonym for index

substitution, in searching, the result of replacing a substring of a character sequence with another string

superuser authority, the capability to access all functions of a computer or software system, including overriding passwords, also called administrative authority

symbol, an information code formed from a specific sequence of base patterns; for example, 01000001 is the ASCII symbol for *A* formed from patterns 0 and 1

synchronous communication, indicates that the actions of senders and receivers occur at the same time, as in a telephone call

T

table, an organizing mechanism for database entities

tag, a word or abbreviation enclosed in angle brackets, usually paired with a companion starting with a slash, that describes a property of data or expresses a command to be performed; e.g., `<italic>You're It!</italic>`

TCP/IP, acronym for Transmission Control Protocol, Internet Protocol

template, the structural information of a document with placeholders for content that is filled in to produce a complete document

tera-, prefix for trillion; in prefixing, a quantity counted in binary, e.g., memory, prefix for 1,099,511,627,776

termination test, synonym for continuation test

text, a sequence of characters; in searching, the material being searched

text editor, basic software to create and modify text files; contrast with word processor

three-tier, a three-layer system design, often the client/server structure extended with a backend database

toggling, reversing the state of an item, as in to toggle between selected and deselected

token, a symbol sequence treated as a single unit in searching or languages

transducer, device converting waves of one form into waves of another, usually electrical

translate, as an image, to move an image to a new position unchanged; in programming, to convert a program from one formal language to another, usually a simpler one; a synonym for *compile*

triangle pointers, small triangles indicating hidden information; clicking on the triangle pointer displays the information

Trojan horse, a useful and apparently innocuous program containing hidden code that allows the unauthorized collection, exploitation, or destruction of data

tuple, a set of values for the attributes of an entity, also called a *row*

Turing Test, an experimental setting to determine if a computer and a person can be distinguished by their answers to a judge's questions

two-tier, a two-layer system design, usually the client/server structure

U

unary operator, an operator such as negation (-) with a single operand

Universal Resource Locator (URL), a two-part name for a Web page composed of an IP address followed by the filename, which can default to `index.html`

universality, a property of computation that all computers with a minimal set of instructions can compute the same set of computations

V

vacation message, an automated reply to email when there is a planned delay in reading it

variable, a named quantity in a programming language

virtual, a modifier meaning not actually, but as if

virus, a program that "infects" another program by embedding a (possibly evolved) copy of itself

volatile, the property of integrated circuit memory in which the stored information is lost when the power is removed

W

W3C, acronym for World Wide Web Consortium

WAN, acronym for wide area network

Web, short form for World Wide Web

Web browser, a software application that locates and reads HTML pages. Modern browsers can display sound and video, as well as text and graphics (although plug-ins may be required for multimedia).

Web client, a computer requesting services from a Web server; a computer running a Web browser

Web server, a computer providing pages to Web clients; a computer hosting a Web page

wide area network, a network connecting computers over a wider area than a few kilometers

word processor, software to create and modify text files that include formatting tags; contrast text editor

work-proportional-to-*n*, a description of the time required to solve a problem with input of size *n*

World Wide Web (WWW), the collection of all HTML servers connected by the Internet and their information resources

World Wide Web Consortium, a standards body composed mainly of companies that produce Web software

worm, an independent program that replicates itself from machine to machine across network connections

WYSIWYG, acronym for "what you see is what you get," pronounced *WHIZ·ee·wig*

X

XML, acronym for extensible markup language

ANSWERS TO SELECTED QUESTIONS

Chapter One

Multiple Choice

1. A. Monitors use bit-mapped technology generated by the computer whereas TVs use recorded images.
3. C. A laptop has an LCD display and uses RGB color.
5. D. Follow the acronym, PILPOF, plug in last, pull out first.
7. B. A display has over 750,000 pixels that are generated and controlled in memory.
9. D.

Short Answer

1. digerati
3. screen saver
5. 786,432 or 1024 × 768
7. tip of the arrow
9. Execute
11. abstraction
13. word processor
15. generalization

Chapter 2

Multiple Choice

1. A. Those with computer skills are sometimes called digerati.
3. D. Both A and B are correct. Ease of use is one of the driving forces behind software development and one of the reasons for the popularity of some software.
5. B. You'll find all except door handles in a typical GUI.
7. B. In Windows, you can close a subwindow, such as a spreadsheet or word processing file, and the application will keep running.
9. A. Open and Print will bring up a dialog box. The Open dialog lets the user select the file to open and the Print dialog lets the user select printing options.

Short Answer

1. digerati
3. analogies
5. Triangle pointers
7. menus

9. Help
11. drop-down menu
13. gray
15. command

Chapter 3

Multiple choice

1. D. The Internet is a great medium for asynchronous communication.
3. B. The ability to create and publish Web pages has made it easier for people to express their opinions and creativity.
5. C. For every *n* computers attached to the Internet, an additional computer adds *n* connections.
7. B. The right side shows the domain. That will get the message to the correct location. From there, the mail server will have to get it to the correct address. This is very similar to the postal service.
9. C. The government, educational institutions, and big business put together the first system in the late 1960s.

Short answer

1. electronic commerce
3. multicast
5. peers
7. channel
9. gateways
11. Web servers
13. FTP
15. Hypertext Markup Language

Chapter 4

Multiple choice

1. C. The commands used in HTML are called tags. They are enclosed in **< >**.
3. A. The first one has the tags properly paired.
5. C. These are paragraph tags and put a double space around the text to set it off from the rest of the page.
7. B. As you move left or right in an address across the slash marks, you move up or down a directory.
9. A. **img src = "filename.ext"** will get the image. Then use **align** = and enclose the proper alignment in quotes.

Short answer

1. Web authoring software
3. `<pre>`
5. attributes
7. relative
9. Graphics Interchange Format
11. 000000

Chapter 5

Multiple choice

1. A. Some use the Web for their own gains and slant their content accordingly.
3. C. ERIC has citations covering over 750 professional journals.
5. B. The query processor looks at the search information and performs the search.
7. C. Google was the first search engine to get its keywords from the anchor tags of Web pages to identify content on a page and to find pages to crawl.
9. C. Use the minus sign (–) in front of the word to exclude pages that have that word.

Short answer

1. library
3. Single links
5. Google
7. logical (or Boolean) operators
9. hierarchy
11. hits
13. AND
15. InterNIC

Chapter 6

True/False and Multiple Choice

1. F. A tertiary source is removed from the source by time or space. A tertiary source reports what happened but isn't an eyewitness.
3. D. In addition, mistakes in print tend to stay mistakes.
5. B. An eyewitness and a participant are examples of primary sources.

Short Answer

1. Curiosity-driven research
3. History
5. primary source

Chapter 7

Multiple Choice/Short Answer

1. B. The computer doesn't understand the information it was given. This usually means the user didn't understand what the computer wanted or the user simply entered the wrong information.
3. B. See if the error repeats itself. If it doesn't, then you're in the clear. If it does, then you need to work through the debugging process.
5. A. Look again for the error. See if you can duplicate the problem.

Short Answer

1. Field inputs
3. ~~b~~
5. bug
7. workaround

Chapter 8

Multiple Choice

1. C. 6 times 6 is 36 and 6 times 6 times 6 is 216.
3. D. The Tab key can work alone. The other keys are used in conjunction with another key.
5. A. A clock with hands is analog. If the clock displays digits, it is digital.
7. D. It's called a syllogism. From the two statements, I can deduce the third statement.
9. A. The coating on floppies and hard disks is an iron compound that can store a magnetic charge.

Short Answer

1. molecules
3. Present and Absent
5. collating sequence
7. escape character
9. Bit
11. Hex
13. ASCII code

Chapter 9

Multiple Choice

1. A. The computer executes its instructions literally. There is no allowance for free will, creativity, or intuition.
3. D. The fastest personal computers can sustain speeds even higher than that, and each generation of computers is faster.
5. A. The ALU gets instructions and .returns their results.

7. B. Branch and jump make the computer switch tasks so it doesn't always grab the next instruction.
9. B. The correct order is thousands, millions, billions, trillions.

Short Answer

1. Computers
3. RAM
5. deterministically
7. information processing
9. keyboard
11. Programming
13. Instruction interpretation
15. gate

Chapter 10

Multiple Choice

1. C. There are five basic requirements: inputs specified, outputs specified, definiteness, effectiveness, and finiteness.
3. A. A natural language lacks the rigorous structure and precise meaning of the others.
5. C. These steps must be repeated in order to put the whole set of CDs in order.
7. A. You took a specific example and generated an idea from it.
9. D. The *Alpha* sweep organizes the first item. The Beta sweep organizes the rest, one at a time.

Short Answer

1. algorithm
3. algorithm, program
5. *Beta* sweep
7. nonredundant
9. loop

Chapter 11

Multiple Choice

1. B. Each intensity has a range from 0–255. That gives you 256 possible settings for each color or 16,777,216 possible colors.
3. B. Analog information is not discrete. It can always be divided into a smaller sampling.
5. B. The larger each sampling is, the closer it can be to the true sound. The size of each sample is the bit rate.
7. A. MP3 is the audio layer of MPEG movies.
9. C. A supermarket uses UPC codes, the little sets of numbers and black and white lines on packages.

Short Answer

1. black
3. Interpolation
5. transducer
7. ISO
9. optical character recognition (OCR)
11. virtual reality
13. Haptic devices
15. Bias-free Universal Medium Principle

Chapter 12

Multiple Choice

1. B. Multicasting means you can send the same email message to more than one person at a time. Each of the other options is a limitation of email.
3. B. Take some time to cool down before you reply. Or take the high road and don't reply at all.
5. B. Although it can happen, messages for a list-serve are seldom edited or censored.
7. C. The first was accidentally released in 1988.
9. D. Under the "fair use" policy, educational and scholarly use of small parts of a copyrighted piece is allowed.

Short Answer

1. Netiquette
3. asynchronous, chat sessions
5. moderator
7. virus
9. Intellectual property
11. public domain
13. fail-soft

Chapter 13

Multiple Choice

1. D. A set of entities is information. It can be almost anything.
3. A. A tuple is a row in a database and contains information defined by the other three.
5. A. Customary naming of a field name consists of the table name and the field name, so this field is named with both the name of the table and the name of the field.
7. C. Often a phone number is shared. Students in a dorm or those sharing an apartment often share a phone number.

9. B. The `Project` operation takes selected fields from a table and creates a new table from them.
11. B. The `Product` operation adds the fields together and multiplies the rows to create a new table.

Short Answer

1. database
3. picture, structure
5. Attributes
7. primary key
9. Test
11. concatenation
13. common field
15. relational database

Chapter 14

Multiple Choice

1. C. SQL, sometimes pronounced "sequel," is a popular commercial database system.
3. B. Relationships define the connection between entities in a database.
5. C. A row in one table should have a row in the other table that corresponds to it.
7. B. Tables can be physical tables that actually store information or logical tables that are created each time they're needed.
9. B. SQL is a language designed to let users extract information from databases.

Short Answer

1. view
3. redundancy
5. garbage in, garbage out
7. logical database
9. `FROM`
11. ON
13. one-to-one

Chapter 15

Multiple Choice

1. D. The needs analysis is the first step. The physical design is the next step.
3. B. The `Clients` table stores information on each individual.
5. C. Social Security numbers are not suitable for a key field.
7. D. `CustomerID` maintains the relationship between the two tables.
9. B. Each rental requires gear. The relationship between the two is one-to-one.
11. C. The `Union` operation joins two tables together.

Short Answer

1. needs analysis
3. one-to-one
5. infinity sign
7. database administrator
9. form
11. Trimming
13. relationship
15. `SELECT`

Chapter 16

Multiple Choice

1. B. The business transactions include all except database design and development. Although, an eCommerce site will need databases.
3. D. All of the above are limits of static HTML pages and client/server structures.
5. C. Most cookies have an expiration date. Some last days or months. Most expire after a year or so.
7. A. The URL stores data for the request. The server processes this information and uses it to fulfill requests.
9. C. XML is concerned with the content of the data and lets HTML handle the presentation.

Short Answer

1. eCommerce
3. two-tiered
5. discrete event problem
7. CGI (Common Gateway Interface)
9. Serialized behavior
11. Extensible Markup Language
13. partial backup

Chapter 17

Multiple Choice

1. D. There are few limits on how businesses can use the information.
3. D. Gathering information in a business transaction is permitted although there is some disagreement as to just what information is allowable.
5. B. According to the Quality principle, your personal information should be accurate.
7. B. The EC requires others to follow its guidelines when information on EC citizens is used outside their countries.
9. B. The principle of Safe Harbor allows them to use the information, provided they follow the OECD principles of the EC.
11. C. XOR means you can have x or y, but not both.

Short Answer

1. Privacy
3. Cash
5. due diligence test
7. European Data Protection Directive
9. cryptosystem
11. one-way cipher

Chapter 18

Multiple Choice

1. B. JavaScript is used mainly for the Web.
3. C. An underscore can be used to separate words in a variable name. That makes the variable name easier to read.
5. C. When declared, the value of a variable is undefined. Be sure to assign a value to it before you use it.
7. C. The values of the variables before the start of the statement are used in a calculation.
9. C. Multiplication and division are done before addition and subtraction.
11. B. Both must be true for the operator to work.

Short Answer

1. program
3. declaration
5. initialize
7. operators
9. unary
11. `!`
13. conditional statement
15. `{}` or curly braces

Chapter 19

Multiple Choice

1. B. HTML pages are saved as ASCII code.
3. B. The `<body>` tag holds the body of the page, what the viewer will see.
5. C. The `<p>` tag starts a new paragraph.
7. C. When there is an event, it is handled by an event handler.
9. A. A click triggers an onClick event handler.

Short Answer

1. Web page
3. `<hr>`
5. event

7. dot operator
9. Input
11. feedback
13. tags

Chapter 20

Multiple Choice

1. B. Functions are used to solve simple tasks. When put together, they solve complicated tasks.
3. C. Two slashes are used to start a comment.
5. C. `onChange` is used. When the input is changed, the event is triggered.
7. A. `Math.random()` returns a number greater than 0 and less than 1.
9. C. Links are created using `href`, short for hypertext reference.

Short Answer

1. Abstraction
3. functions, procedures
5. Implicitly declared variables
7. arguments
9. pseudo-random numbers
11. milliseconds

Chapter 21

Multiple Choice

1. C. The for statement is used for iteration.
3. B. The <*next iteration*> changes the value of the iteration value.
5. C. The `alert()` command is used.
7. B. It means to add 1 to i.
9. D. All of the above are elements with invalid numbers.
11. C. The array starts at 0, ends at 8, has nine elements, and does not have any with decimals.

Short Answer

1. Iteration
3. variable
5. continuation or termination
7. infinite loop
9. `"\n"`
11. Indexing
13. length
15. display rate

Chapter 22

Multiple choice

1. B. You must understand the problem before you can do anything else.
3. D. The Animate Grid task must be completed before the Build Controls task can be completed.
5. A. Build Controls is not dependent on the Detect Staircase task.
7. B. Graphics are placed using the src command.
9. B. Usually, when there are 3 to 5 tasks or more, it becomes useful to use a loop.

Short Answer

1. Decomposition Principle
3. Task dependencies
5. Program Evaluation and Review Technique
7. Build GUI
9. images
11. Radio buttons

Chapter 23

Multiple Choice

1. B. Computers are great at manipulating information, but that's about it.
3. D. Creativity is hard to define and hard to explain.
5. B. All have the same six basic instructions.
7. B. Regardless of the order the CDs are in, the computer must make a pass to check it.
9. C. Getting computers to work properly is the only thing humans can do better than computers.
11. C. Checkers is a much simpler game than chess so the algorithm is much simpler.
13. A. The process is called deeper.
15. B. There are just six basic instructions.
17. A. A program debugger can detect syntax errors, but it cannot find logical errors.

Short Answer

1. Deep Blue
3. artificial intelligence
5. specialized.
7. Universality Principle
9. computer
11. Dual booting
13. Compatibility and support
15. NP-complete problems
17. NP-complete problems
19. natural language

21. deeper
23. work-proportional-to-n^2 algorithm
25. ten trillion

Chapter 24

Multiple choice

1. C. The value of information depends on how we use it.
3. B. The first step is to make sure the error happens again. If you cannot duplicate the error, then there probably isn't a bug.
5. C. Logical reasoning can be applied to most problems with successful results.
7. A. The Capabilities component has the broadest range. Skills has the most detail.
9. D. There are risks to being too early or too late with new developments.

Short Answer

1. Nonalgorithmic thinking
3. rational
5. Concept
7. Lifelong learning
9. algorithms

INDEX